Instant Pot® Bible
the Next Generation

ALSO BY BRUCE WEINSTEIN
AND MARK SCARBROUGH

The Essential Air Fryer Cookbook • From Freezer to Instant Pot: The Cookbook •
The Instant Pot Bible • The Kitchen Shortcut Bible • The Ultimate Ice Cream Book •
The Ultimate Party Drink Book • The Ultimate Candy Book • The Ultimate Shrimp Book •
The Ultimate Brownie Book • The Ultimate Potato Book • Great Grilling •
The Ultimate Muffin Book • The Ultimate Chocolate Cookie Book • Cooking for Two •
The Ultimate Frozen Dessert Book • The Ultimate Peanut Butter Book •
The Ultimate Cook Book • Pizza: Grill It! Bake It! Love It! • Cooking Know-How •
Ham: The Obsession with the Hindquarter • Real Food Has Curves • Goat: Meat, Milk, Cheese •
Lobsters Scream When You Boil Them • The Complete Quick Cook • Grain Mains •
The Great American Slow Cooker Book • Vegetarian Dinner Parties •
The Great Big Pressure Cooker Book • The Boozy Blender • A La Mode •
The Turbo Blender Dessert Revolution •
All-Time Favorite Sheet Cakes and Slab Pies

Instant Pot® Bible
the Next Generation

---

350 TOTALLY NEW RECIPES
FOR EVERY SIZE AND MODEL

BRUCE WEINSTEIN and MARK SCARBROUGH

Photographs by Eric Medsker

VORACIOUS
LITTLE, BROWN AND COMPANY
NEW YORK BOSTON LONDON

Voracious / Little, Brown and Company
Hachette Book Group
1290 Avenue of the Americas, New York, NY 10104
littlebrown.com

First Edition: November 2020

Voracious is an imprint of Little, Brown and Company, a division of
Hachette Book Group, Inc. The Voracious name and logo are trademarks
of Hachette Book Group, Inc.

The publisher is not responsible for websites (or their content) that are
not owned by the publisher.

The Hachette Speakers Bureau provides a wide range of authors for
speaking events. To find out more, go to hachettespeakersbureau.com or
call (866) 376-6591.

ISBN 978-0-316-54109-1
Library of Congress Control Number: 2020945770

10 9 8 7 6 5 4 3 2 1

LSC-C

Printed in the United States of America

Printing 1, 2020

Contents

CHAPTER 3: Pasta and Noodles

CHAPTER 4: Chicken and Turkey

Chicken Negimaki 193
Tikka-Spiced Chicken Kebabs 194
Bacony Barbecue Chicken Breasts 196
Fiery Coconut Curry Chicken Breasts 197
Bistro Chicken Thighs 198
Buttery Chicken Thighs with Leeks and Vinegar 200
Pesto Chicken and Balsamic Potato Dinner 202
Ginger and Garlic Chicken Dinner with Couscous 203
Sweet & Spicy Chicken Thighs 204
Lemon-Ginger Chicken Thighs 205
Sesame Chicken Wings 206
Spicy Beer-Glazed Wings 207
Not-Really-P.F.-Chang's Chicken Lettuce Wraps 208
Jerk Chicken and Mango Lettuce Wraps 209
Curried Chicken Meatballs 210
Chicken Picadillo 212
Cider-Brined Turkey Breast 213
Bacony Turkey Thigh and Potato Dinner 214
Turkey Tacos with Red Cabbage–Lime Slaw 215
Cheesy-Spicy Turkey Casserole 216
Super-Easy Italian Turkey Meatballs in Cream Sauce 217
Real-Deal Turkey Meatballs in Tomatoes and Cream 218
Thanksgiving Turkey Meat Loaf 220
World's Easiest Shepherd's Pie 221

CHAPTER 5: **Beef, Pork, and Lamb**

Not-Really-Taco-Bell's Taco Meat 224
Sloppy Joe Subs 226
Chimichurri Ground Beef Sandwiches 227
Meatball and Spaghetti Squash Dinner 228
Meatball Steak 229
One-Pot Cheese-Stuffed Meatballs 230
The Cutest Ever Mini Meat Loaves 231
Beef Kofta with Tzatziki 232
Miso and Scallion Meatballs and Sushi Rice Dinner 234
Not-Really-Wendy's Chili 236
Real-Deal Texas Chili 237
French-Onion-Soup Meat Loaf 238
Barbecue Meat Loaf and Sour-Cream Mashed Potato Dinner 240
Ballpark Meat Loaf and Buttery Potato Dinner 241
Stuffed Cabbage 242
Un-Stuffed-Pepper Stew 244
Gingery Beef, Rice, and Scallion Casserole 245
Ground Beef and Eggplant Stew 246
Ground Beef, Dried Fig, and Jalapeño Picadillo 248
Good-for-What-Ails-You Beef and Stout Stew 250
Kalimotxo Beef Stew 252
Beef Enchilada Stew 254
Throwback Takeout Pepper Steak 255
Not-Really-Chipotle's Barbacoa Beef 256
Balsamic Beef Stew 258
Make-Your-Own-Curry Beef Stew 260
Braised Brisket 262
Dinner-Party-Worthy Corned Beef & Cabbage 264
Not-Really-P.F.-Chang's Mongolian Beef 266
Braised Beef Bottom Round with Tomatoes and Cinnamon 267
No-Brainer Orange Beef with Broccoli 268
Jalapeño-Braised Beef Bottom Round 270
Spicy-Sweet Beef Short Ribs 272
Sauerbraten-Style Tri Tip Roast 274
Tri Tip Stew with Mushrooms and Sour Cream 276
Tri Tip Kebabs with Easy Garlic Aioli 278
Tomatoey Sausage and Polenta Dinner 279
Osso Buco with Red Cabbage and Dill 280
Osso Buco with Fennel and Green Olives 282
Smoked Sausage and Lentil Stew 284
No-Brainer Pierogi and Sausage Salad 285
Pork Spiedies 286
Falling-off-the-Bone Pork Ribs 288
Sticky-Sweet Soy Pork Ribs 290
Honey-Orange Pork Ribs 292
Barbecue Country-Style Pork Ribs 294
Pork Tenderloins with Herbs and Garlic 296
Pork Tenderloins with Mushrooms and Cream 298
Pork Tenderloins with Spiced Cherry Sauce 300
Teriyaki Pork Tenderloin and Rice Dinner 302
Bone-In Pork Chop and Buttery Cauliflower Rice Dinner 303
Mini Lion's Head Meatballs with Steamed Bok Choy 304
Boneless Pork Loin Chops in a Creamy Mustard Sauce 306

CHAPTER 6: Sides, Grains, and Vegetable Mains

CHAPTER 7: Desserts

CHAPTER 8: The 10-Quart Bonanza: Meals and Desserts for the Biggest Instant Pot

Introduction

Since we all know the Instant Pot revolution is here to stay, it's high time for the next generation of Instant Pot cookbooks. You may know us from our international bestseller, *The Instant Pot Bible*. Its 350 recipes can help you get started with our favorite multicooker. Now we're back with an *all-new, great-big* collection of recipes that show you how to make the most of the appliance that has changed the way millions of us cook.

Things are so different than they were in the early days of the Instant Pot. There are many more ways to up your game, whether you're a newbie or a pro. So we're offering 350 new recipes...and not just more of the same.

Don't worry: We have plenty of new braises, stews, porridges, cakes, and side dishes in this book. But those are now just a starting point because we've set out to take advantage of the widely available IP accessories that can upgrade your cooking. In addition to the equipment used in *The Instant Pot Bible*—that is, the rack that comes with the pot, a 7-inch (or 6-cup) Bundt cake pan, and a 7-inch springform pan—we now show you how to harness the power of pot-in-pot cooking. We go all out for steaming, as well as braising. And we use egg-bite molds for way more than egg bites.

Why? Because we want pancakes! And tamales. And delicate cream sauces. We even use stackable containers to create whole dinners in an Instant Pot: meat and potatoes under one lid. We've long thought that the best thing about an Instant Pot is that you can open the machine and look at your main course.

Now, you can look at your *whole* meal, main and sides all at once.

Our cardinal rule for these recipes remains what it's always been: If we can't find an ingredient in our rural New England supermarket, we can't use it in a recipe (except maybe in the **Beyond** section, where we show you how to take a dish over the top).

Does that limit us too much? Just wait until you see this next generation of recipes: insanely easy turkey meatballs in the simplest cream sauce (page 217), a huge range of one-pot pasta suppers with the dried pasta cooked right in the sauce, and the best rice, quinoa, and polenta ever.

We also have a few copycat recipes, inspired by favorites from popular, North American restaurants. Since these are not the exact recipes but are our own creations, the recipes are called "Not Really" plus the chain's name. Mostly, we upgraded these copycats a bit: using cream cheese instead of cottage cheese in Starbucks' egg bites (page 32), upping the vegetables and spices for more flavor in every spoonful of Wendy's chili (page 236), and using steel-cut oats (what?!) to achieve the characteristic texture of Taco Bell's taco meat (page 224), We should note that the mention of restaurants, restaurant groups, or the companies that own them does not imply our (or the publisher's) endorsement of any of them, nor does it imply that these corporations or their subsidiaries have endorsed us, our publisher, or these recipes.

But our work hasn't *only* been about upping the game. We simplified things, too. We felt free to use boxed cake mixes and pancake mixes to make breakfasts and desserts. In fact, we might be most excited about the ways we doctored these mixes to create tasty treats.

Since we're going down the list of what's in this book, we should let you know that we include some outright crazy recipes, ones that require a little extra oomph on your part. These may not be for weeknights. And there's not more than a dozen of them. But it was all part of the luxurious thought that we could be as free as we wanted to be in this next-generation tome.

Here's another genius shift in our strategy: We now use *low* pressure a lot more. Low means 1) we don't have to swamp a dish with too much liquid, and 2) we can use cream without fear of its curdling. In most cases, low adds a minute or two to the time under pressure. We felt the trade-off was worth it, but we'll explain more in the recipes' headnotes.

Because we want to give *you* a lot of freedom, too, almost every recipe is adjusted for every size of Instant Pot: 3-, 5-, 6-, 8-, and 10-quart. Yes, there are a few recipes that can't be made in a 3- or 5-quart pot because of their smaller sizes. And a handful can't be made in the giant 10-quart because the ingredient ratios are too complex to scale up with ease. But for the vast majority of dishes here, we let you know how to get a recipe made in whatever pot you have, even the Max pots that can (but don't have to) cook at a higher pressure.

And in response to popular demand, we include some recipes that use the new Instant Pot Air Fryer Lid, if, for example, you want to hoist a casserole or chicken wings to crunchy bliss. Because that lid only fits the 6- or 8-quart pot as of this writing, we often give you ways to get that crunch under your oven's broiler as well. And to be honest, this crunchification mostly takes place in the **Beyond** sections of recipes, not in the numbered steps.

Even with everything we just told you, one chapter stands out: the last one, in which all thirty-three recipes can *only* be made in a 10-quart pot. We've grown to love this monster-size cooker because we can make two whole chickens, two big pork loins, or (for heaven's sake) half a ham. (We *love* feeding our friends and family.) We can even make full-size desserts: 9-inch cheesecakes and 10-inch Bundts.

But no matter which pot you've got, welcome to the next generation of Instant Pot recipes!

Notes on the Recipes

Here's a guide to how they lie on the page.

The recipe header tags

Next to the recipe title, you'll find a shorthand list of what the recipe involves:

- The number of ingredients (we count water, salt, and pepper—no cheating!)

- The number of servings (you may be hungrier than we are—doubt it, but maybe)

- The cooking technique used (more on that in a bit)

- Any special equipment you need (egg-bite molds, for example—more below, too)

- The pressure setting (pay close attention because it varies widely)

- How long the ingredients undergo pressure (this includes the **combined** timing if the pot goes under pressure twice)

- What sort of (pressure) release is required

- Our best estimate as to the total time with pressure

- Our best estimate as to the total time with slow cooking

- And a rudimentary set of dietary guides: vegetarian, can be vegetarian (with simple substitutions), vegan, can be vegan (again, with simple subs), gluten-free, or can be gluten-free (usually with gluten-free condiments like mayonnaise, rather than the more standard versions).

The cooking charts

Because almost every recipe is designed for every pot, we have to list some of the cooking information in chart form. If you own *The Instant Pot Bible,* you may be familiar with this feature. Even so, here's a quick run-down of how the charts work.

The first chart you're likely to encounter covers the SAUTÉ function. We've charted it because of the varying ways the models register the desired temperature in the pot: MEDIUM, NORMAL, or CUSTOM 300°F, for example. But note that this SAUTÉ chart may not be in a recipe because, well, often you don't have to do much more than dump in the ingredients and lock on the lid. But it *will* be in every recipe in which you must warm a fat, heat a liquid, brown a protein, or reduce a sauce.

Then there's the pressure and slow-cooking chart. After its header, it *can* have up to three lines:

- **A line for Max pots.** This line can *only* be used with the Max models, which can cook at a higher pressure than any other IP. Whether you open or close the pressure valve is moot because the max machine does it for you (thus, the simple line in that spot on the chart).

- **A line for all other pots, whether at HIGH or LOW pressure.** If you've got any other IP model besides a Max, this is your line. *And* if there's no line for MAX pressure, you *must* use the more standard HIGH pressure even in your Max machine. (Check your owner's manual for the details.)

Why? Because the ingredients are too fragile to work at the higher MAX setting. If you use MAX when the recipe calls for only HIGH, or if you use MAX or HIGH when the recipe calls for LOW, you'll get the BURN notice, period.

- **A line for slow-cooking timings.** All slow-cooker settings in this book are *only* for HIGH because all Instant Pot models slow-cook at the same temperature on HIGH but not at the same temperature on LOW.

The release

That is, the pressure release. Both in the header tags and in the recipe itself, there will be an indication of how to do it. As you may know, the two standard ways are **quick** and **natural** with two variations.

- **Quick release.** You must manually turn the lid's pressure valve to open it and release a forceful jet of steam; *or* if you have a Max, you must press the necessary key on its touchpad to make the pot open the valve for you. It bears repeating: You *must* read your owner's manual to know how to work a quick release in your pot because there are variations among the models.

- **Natural release.** You must turn the pot off and wait—patiently!—for the pressure inside to dissipate of its own accord (that is, as the temperature drops). This step can take up to 40 minutes, depending on the bulk of the proteins and vegetables as well as the liquid levels. Make sure the KEEP WARM setting is turned off. Otherwise, the pot will take a *very* long time to come back to normal pressure because it will be holding itself at a slightly higher temperature to, well, keep things warm.

- **Modified natural release.** For this variation, turn off the pot (as if you were doing a natural release); then after the stated number of minutes, use the quick-release method to get rid of the pot's residual pressure (since it hasn't fully come back to normal yet). A modified natural release is a great way to get a piece of meat tender without its turning spongy. After all, the cut is still "cooking" even if the pot is turned off, so long as the pressure is elevated inside. The modified natural release is also a great way to protect fragile ingredients. A quick release is violent *inside* the pot (not just outside as the steam jets up). Some delicate ingredients can blow apart. A modified natural release gives them a moment to set before they have to undergo the stress.

- **Modified quick release.** Here, use the quick-release method to drop the pressure instantly, but do not open the pot. Rather, leave the lid latched, even though there's no residual pressure inside, because there's still quite a lot of steam in there. A modified quick release is best for cooked grains, which can then be "steam-fluffed" for a few minutes before you serve them.

Other pots

Pay attention to the size of Instant Pots that can be used in the main portion of a recipe: 5-, 6-, and 8-quart, for example. If your pot is *not* one of these, check the **Other Pots** section in the sidebar for ways to adapt the recipe to, say, a 3-quart or a 10-quart pot. There may be instructions for changing the amount of broth or water in the insert to get the necessary steam. Often, there's a note for how to alter a recipe to make even *more* servings in an 8- or 10-quart pot.

Beyond

Here, you'll find simple ways to take a recipe over the top, usually with additional spices or suggested garnishes. We've felt free to call for more unusual ingredients here, like Korean spice pastes. Or we've offered you a way to skip a bottled seasoning blend and make your own. Sometimes, we tell you how to use the Instant Pot Air Fryer Lid to crisp a dish. Nothing in the **Beyond** section is necessary to the recipe's success.

Notes on Specialty Equipment

Here are a few common pieces of additional equipment used in these recipes as well as a note about something we *never* use. Check out the next section of the introduction, "Notes On Cooking Techniques," for more information about egg-bite molds and stacks.

The two basic baking dishes

Throughout this book, we call for either a *1-quart, 6-inch-round, high-sided, pressure-safe baking or soufflé dish* or a *2-quart, 7-inch-round, high-sided, pressure-safe baking or soufflé dish*. By "high-sided," we mean at least 2¾ inches for the 6-inch dish or 3¼ inches for the 7-inch one. By the way, 6 and 7 inches refers to the dish's *diameter,* not its circumference. A baking dish usually sits on a pressure-safe rack or trivet in the insert (more on that below), unless (rarely) it sits directly on top of some food item, like a layer of small potatoes.

Don't use the baking dishes interchangeably. The smaller baking dish is most often used in 3-quart adaptations (because the 7-inch-round baking dish won't fit in the 3-quart insert while allowing steam to move around). However, the smaller baking dish is also used for smaller amounts of sauce or side dishes, often made on top of or underneath the main course in a larger pot.

The larger, 7-inch-round baking dish is the gold standard for most pots in this book. We even use it in 10-quart pots. But there is one substitution. The *insert* for a 3-quart Instant Pot works as a stand-in for the larger, 7-inch baking dish in all *8- or 10-quart* pot-in-pot (PIP) soup and pasta casserole recipes, as well as in delicate braises that are cooked PIP. But note that the 3-quart insert will *not* work as a substitute for the 2-quart dish in recipes for "baked" goods (cakes, for example) or for custard desserts. The insert's sides are too high and will disrupt the heat patterns. Keep in mind that if you use the 3-quart insert in a larger pot, the insert must be set up on a pressure-safe rack or trivet, just like any baking dish.

A pressure-safe rack or trivet

Over and over, we ask you to first put a rack in the pot's insert. In recipe-testing, we *always* used the rack that came with its pot. Each rack is perfectly sized to fit its pot's insert.

That said, we do love the newly available silicone racks with silicone handles that make lifting things out of the insert a breeze. However, many of these silicone racks have flexible slats or compartments, like a honeycomb. Unfortunately, you can't put some foods right on them. Small meatballs and little red potatoes will fall through.

If you've lost your pot's rack or if you've an older model that's missing a rack, we *strongly* urge you to buy a replacement for your pot. Yes, you can use other wire racks or even trivets. But they *must* be pressure-safe. They *must not* have rubber feet (which can melt against the insert's hot surface). And as you'll see when we get to the steaming technique, they often must be food-safe, too.

A steamer basket

Use a steamer basket specifically made for an Instant Pot. In fact, the brand itself makes a silicone steamer basket that looks like a flexible version of a Chinese bamboo steamer. It even comes with a footed stand and handles. Other models have flexible sides; some are mesh and made for specific pots. Yes, you can use the old-fashioned metal basket with sides that open out like lotus petals, but it's more precarious and hot ingredients tend to fall out as you lift it. Most steamer baskets have feet. If yours does not, you'll need to put a pressure-safe rack or trivet under it. And one warning: We don't recommend using a bamboo steamer basket in the IP because the bamboo warps and bubbles after repeated rounds of pressure.

A foil sling (maybe)

Although we called for aluminum foil slings in our other Instant Pot books, we *never* call for one in this book. Most racks now have handles; egg-bite molds often have handles. There are myriad new ways to get things out of the pot's insert.

But if you want to go old-school and make a foil sling to put under a baking dish or other equipment so you can lift it out of the insert, take a 15-inch-long piece of aluminum foil and fold it in thirds lengthwise. Set the baking dish or egg-bite mold at its center, then lift up the ends to pick up the dish or mold. Set the whole thing down in the pot (usually on a rack) and fold the ends down so you can easily close the lid. After cooking, unfurl these ends to lift the dish or mold out of the pot.

Notes on Cooking Techniques

Once again, we cannot cover every operation for your pot. You must consult your owner's manual. If you've lost your copy, it's available online. Familiarize yourself with the basics, like how to lock on the lid and how to reduce the pressure after cooking. The cooking techniques and methods in this book are the results of our experience in working with various models of the Instant Pot, tools, and ingredients. When you work with any of these recipes, take care to use the pots, tools, and materials properly. Read those instruction manuals, because we and our publisher cannot take responsibility for any injury and/or damage to person or property that results of the use or misuse of the instructions and techniques in this book. Having said all that, here are some further considerations before you dive into the recipes.

First, let's define some terms in the recipe titles.

Two need more explanation:

- **No-Brainer.** If a recipe title includes these words, they mean, in cookbook parlance, that the recipe is a "dump-and-stir." In other words, you dump everything in the insert, stir it up, and lock on the lid: no sweating the onions, no browning the meat—zip.

- **Dinner.** If a recipe includes this word in its title, it means you're about to make a full meal, main course and sides. This usually happens via the PIP technique or stacks.

Next, let's talk about that *sauté* function.

What we're about to say about our recipes is very different from many other IP recipes you'll find: In our book, there's no need to wait until the pot reads HOT. For every recipe in this book, turn the pot to SAUTÉ at the heat level requested, count slowly to ten, and start cooking, letting the pot continue to heat as you work. In almost all recipes, we say to "warm the oil" or "melt the butter" before you start adding other ingredients. If you do so, the pot *is* heating as you're getting ready to put in the onions or what have you. In some fast recipes, the pot may never switch to its HOT reading before you must turn off the SAUTÉ function, lock on the lid, and cook under pressure.

Now let's get to the specific techniques called for in this book.

There are six:

- **Standard.** This is the tried-and-true method: often (but not always) sautéing something in the insert, adding the other ingredients, locking on the lid, and cooking under pressure. There's nothing fancy here, just the basics of operating an electric pressure cooker.

- **Fast/slow.** A recipe with this marker can either be made with a pressure-cook setting (MAX, HIGH, and/or LOW) *or* with the slow-cook setting (always HIGH). Remember: You *must* leave the pressure valve in place but open for slow cooking.

- **Pot-in-pot.** Or PIP in IP lingo. This technique involves putting a separate cooking vessel inside the pot's insert to mitigate the heat coming off the insert's bottom. Things that could burn against that surface (cream soups, plain white rice) can now cook more gently. Cakes can rise without burning. In almost all cases, the PIP method requires you to use a pressure-safe rack or trivet to hold a baking dish, springform pan, or Bundt pan. However, there are a few PIP recipes in which you set the baking dish on top of another *ingredient,* like small potatoes or chicken thighs.

- **Egg bites.** This technique uses a silicone egg-bite mold with seven conical indentations (or with four of them for 3-quart pots), each holding a scant ½ cup. The indentations are set in a circle, usually six around a center one. Most molds come with lids. If you've lost yours, you can seal the mold with aluminum foil. Pay close attention to whether we tell you to cover the mold (thereby sealing the lid onto it) or just lay the cover or a piece of aluminum foil loosely over the mold. (The difference has to do with how much foods inside will expand under pressure.) Some egg-bite molds are footed; many are not. We always call for a rack or trivet under the mold, a step you can skip if your mold has feet. And one more note: Silicone does *not* mean nonstick. In many cases, we advise you to grease the indentations because the pancake or brownie bites are too fragile or because the meatballs are too sticky to come out intact.

- **Stacks.** Often called "stackable steamer insert pans" (although there are no holes for steaming, so go figure), or sometimes called "tiffins," these are layered, stackable, circular pans, the top one with a lid. In them, you can cook a whole meal, the main course in one layer and the side dish in the other. We *only* call for *two-layer* stacks. There are three-layer stacks on the market but the individual pans are smaller and will not fit the ingredient ratios in our recipes. Most stacks have feet; some do not. If your set doesn't have a built-in rack or some footed design, you *must* use a pressure-safe rack or trivet under it. And pay close attention to which foods we put in which layer. The difference in cooking can be dramatic. If the polenta is to be put in the top layer and you put it in the bottom, it can end up burned. Or if the pork chops are to go in the bottom layer and you put them in the top, they will not be done in the stated time. Many stacks come with two lids: one with holes and one without (that is, a solid lid). We *never* call for the lid with holes. If you only have such a lid, you'll need to cover it with aluminum foil for these recipes.

- **Steam.** Here, you'll lift an ingredient—say, a pork shoulder—off the bottom of the cooker on a rack, thereby letting it steam in the pot, rather than braise in the liquid. You can use the STEAM button, if your pot has it. It will bring the pot to high pressure, just like the MANUAL or standard PRESSURE setting. However, you *must* manually adjust the timing to fit the recipe in hand. And one important note: Whenever you're steaming in the pot, you *must* use a pressure- *and food-safe* rack or trivet, since you're cooking directly on it. Once again, the stainless-steel rack that came with your pot fits the bill.

Finally . . .

Here are two notes on specialty matters.

- **More about the *total* time with pressure and slow cooking.** We hate the lie that a recipe "takes 5 minutes" just because it cooks for 5 minutes under pressure. It takes longer. You have to chop the onion, you have to brown the meat, the pot has to come to pressure (anywhere from 5 to 25 minutes, depending on the liquid levels and the temperature of the various ingredients), the pot has to cook at pressure, and a natural release can take up to 40 minutes. We want to be honest and give you the actual time a recipe takes, so you don't walk in after work at seven o'clock and think you're going to get through a big chuck roast braise before you pass out. That said, this total timing marker is a bit dodgy because we don't know how quickly you work. (We don't cook with a five-year-old in the kitchen. You might.) What's more, a 10-quart pot takes longer to come to high pressure than a 5-quart does. Still, the overall timing is our best estimate.

- **More about taking out the pot's insert.** An electric pressure cooker is something like an electric stove: It doesn't cool down the moment you shut it off. It stays hot because 1) the heating element is slowly cooling, and 2) the pot itself offers some insulation around the insert. We often advise that you transfer the insert to a wire rack after cooking—to keep thickeners (like flour, potato starch, or cornstarch) from burning, or to let a sauce cool so you can skim the surface fat, or to keep cheese from breaking in a sauce. Remember: The insert is super hot! Use hot pads or silicone baking mitts to grasp its edge and get it to a wire rack. And put that rack right next to the pot. Don't walk across your kitchen carrying a hot insert.

Notes on Specific Ingredients

Throughout, we use some ingredients that might not be self-evident if you're a new cook or if you're expanding your range. In a few cases, we've made assumptions about ingredients (butter, onions, and garlic, for example) that need clarification.

Butter

We assume you use *salted* butter because less than a quarter of the butter sold in North America in unsalted. Yes, it is a cookbook cliché to call for *un*salted butter. But we've gone with the flow and adjusted the salt in buttery recipes to reflect the additional salt in the butter. If you *are* using unsalted butter, you might want more salt in a dish. Rather than adding it up front, pass more at the table.

Buttermilk

In North America, there are two types: cultured and uncultured (or "natural"). The cultured product is thickened like kefir or even yogurt. *Uncultured* buttermilk is not nearly so thick and more like the liquid left over from butter-churning back in the day. Every recipe in this book was tested with *uncultured* buttermilk (such as Kate's). The cultured is often too thick to make a sauce without the BURN notice. It's also often too thick to make a successful batter, particularly if it's added to a cake mix (which already has thickeners in it).

Canned chipotle chiles in adobo sauce

Common in Mexican, Latin American, Caribbean, and Filipinx cooking, this ingredient is easy to spot at the supermarket, usually with other canned chiles or sometimes in the international aisle. A chipotle is a smoked, dried jalapeño; adobo sauce is an aromatic and vinegary blend, often thickened. Unfortunately, there are many pale imitations on North American shelves. Search out online suppliers for smokier chiles in a more fragrant sauce. *No* recipe in this book calls for *a can of* chipotles in adobo sauce. They all call for *1 or more canned chiles,* often with some of the sauce from the can. Just a note: That sauce may not be gluten-free but thickened with wheat derivatives. Read the can's ingredient list to be sure.

Chili powder and *chile* powder

Standard, North American *chili powder* is a blend of ground dried chiles, ground cumin, dried oregano, sometimes salt, and even other herbs or spices in some bottlings. We call for it frequently, even when we up its game by adding *more* ground cumin or dried oregano to the dish. However, in rare instances we call for *pure chile powder,* which is simply ground dried chiles, like ancho chile powder or chipotle chile powder. Here, we want a brighter, spicy bite.

Cream

In the United States, there are essentially two types: heavy cream and light cream. As to "heavy cream," use what's called *either* "whipping cream" (with 30 to 36 percent fat) or "heavy whipping cream" (with at least 36 percent fat). The alternative, so-called "light cream," is a somewhat lower-fat version of heavy cream (with 18 to 30 percent fat). We sometimes say you can even substitute half-and-half (with 10.5 to 18 percent fat). *Do not* substitute so-called "fat-free half-and-half," which is loaded with thickeners and stabilizers. And (gads!) be careful of heavy whipping cream these days: Even it can contain thickeners! Search for the pure dairy product.

Dried rice noodles

We call for them in some Asian-style noodle dishes. In almost all cases, we do not mean dried rice pasta used as a gluten-free substitute for *Italian* spaghetti. Rather, we mean pale-white, opaque rice stick or rice vermicelli pasta, for pad Thai and some Vietnamese dishes. Even so, there are notable exceptions, including the type of *gluten-free* noodles we prefer in the pot if you're substituting them for standard pasta (see the chapter introduction for Pasta and Noodles on page 103). And once in this book, we *do* call for brown-rice spaghetti (Gluten-Free Spaghetti & Meatballs, page 115). Otherwise, when we mention dried rice noodles, we're talking about the Asian standard. Look for them in the Asian aisle, at an Asian grocery store, or online.

Eggs

We only call for large eggs, the North American cookbook standard. Don't substitute any other size. But there's another bit of almost clichéd culinary advice that we reject in about half of the recipes that use eggs. We call for *refrigerator-cold* eggs in casseroles, egg bites, and even bread puddings. We figure most people don't even want to think about dragging eggs out to the counter and letting them come to room temperature before making dinner. So we adjusted the timings in many a savory dish to work with cold eggs. *However,* in almost all of the recipes that require you to make a batter (that is, in almost all "baking" recipes), we still stand by the cookbook cliché: *room-temperature* eggs. If you want to know the specifics for why tepid eggs work better in the pot, check out the introduction to the dessert chapter on page 385.

Gluten-free condiments

Many recipes are marked "can be gluten-free." In other words, they *can* be with no change in the ingredients other than substituting a gluten-free version of a more standard condiment like mayonnaise, mustard, or barbecue sauce. If you have celiac disease or are severely gluten-intolerant, you'll want to take extra precautions beyond ours, given the amount of cross-contamination in the modern food supply chain.

Hoisin sauce

This Chinese condiment is available in almost every grocery store in North America, usually in the Asian aisle. Although "hoisin" means "seafood" in Chinese, there's no fish or shellfish in the sauce, nor is it used exclusively for seafood. It's a sweet-salty, dark-colored blend of aromatic spices, vinegar, fermented soybean paste, often with fennel, sometimes with sweet potatoes, and sometimes with chiles. Better versions are more than just a salt bomb. Most bottlings contain gluten, although there are now gluten-free versions, mostly available online or at large Asian supermarkets. A sealed bottle can stay in the fridge for up to 1 year.

Lean ground proteins

We *love* fatty burgers, but lean ground meats are your best bet in the IP. There is no evaporation in a sealed cooker. The fat has nowhere to go. It won't condense or run off, the way it would in the oven or on the grill. It gets trapped in the stew and makes an oily mess. Lean proteins make successful dishes, *not* for health reasons, but for culinary ones.

Low-sodium canned goods

And now to reverse ourselves on the salt issue, given what we said about using salted butter. (Hey, inconsistency is the mark of great minds. Some philosopher said that.) Although we have not marked the ingredients this way, mostly because tastes vary, we *strongly* suggest that you use low-sodium canned tomatoes, broth, beans, diced green chiles, and just about any condiment. Just like excess fat in ground meat, added salt in canned goods has nowhere to go in the pot and ends up turning many a meal into a drink from the Dead Sea. You can always pass more salt at the table.

Nonstick spray and baking spray

There are two types of cooking spray on the North American market: 1) nonstick spray, such as Pam, which is just oil (sometimes vegetable oil, sometimes even olive oil) with a propellant; and baking spray, such as Baker's Joy or Pam *baking* spray, which is a combination of oil and flour. We call for both sorts in this book. Please don't mix them up. There's no sense in putting a coating of flour around meatballs! If you don't want to use these sprays, you can go old school: If the recipe calls for nonstick spray, simply grease a pan with some oil on a paper towel or brush the food with oil. If the recipe calls for baking spray, grease or butter the inside of the pan and then dust it with a light coating of flour. We'll confess to you that after thirty-six cookbooks and some fancy awards, we often reach for the spray. Again, just don't mix the two types up.

Onions, shallots, and garlic cloves

We assume they're *peeled*, unless otherwise stated. We always give the volume amount for these and many other ingredients because we also assume many of you are buying them already chopped from the produce section. However, volumes do vary between minced and chopped items. Consider minced to mean "cut into ⅛-inch squares," diced as ¼ inch, and chopped as ½ inch unless otherwise stated.

Parmigiano-Reggiano

In other words, what most US citizens call "parmesan cheese." In all cases, we encourage you to buy a chunk and grate it yourself. In fact, we encourage you to pay a little more and buy a chunk of the real thing, a super-crumbly, beige, hard cheese with its name stamped over and over on its tan rind. Domestic versions can be stuffed with non-dairy additives and fillers. And as for the grated stuff in the cans, it's sometimes not even 100 percent cheese.

Unseasoned rice vinegar

An Asian pantry staple, this low-acid vinegar gives a muted spark to many dishes. There are two types: seasoned (with sugar and salt) and unseasoned (sometimes not so labeled, just not labeled as "seasoned"). We *only* call for *unseasoned* rice vinegar. There's no substitute, given its mild, gentle flavors. But it will keep in a sealed bottle in a cool pantry for up to 1 year. Look for it in the Asian aisle.

Let's Get Cooking!

Wow, did we eat well while we tested these recipes! By the time this book gets into your hands, there will still be containers of stews and braises in our basement freezer. We hope you eat just as well and have just as much fun as we did. We'd love to connect with you. You can find us under our own names on Facebook, Instagram, and Twitter (Bruce is *Bruce A. Weinstein* on Instagram). You can email us through our website, bruceandmark.com. And you can find out more about specific recipes if you look up the video collection on our YouTube channel, Cooking with Bruce and Mark. And you can listen to us cut up and be nuts and talk endlessly about food on our podcast, Cooking with Bruce and Mark (found on lots of platforms like iTunes, Spotify, and Deezer). We'd love to hear more about your Instant Pot stories. Join us!

Breakfast

You probably think it's not worth the effort to drag out big kitchen equipment first thing in the morning. You're wrong. The Instant Pot makes some fine porridges, as well as breakfast treats that can perk up a Monday morning. Sometimes, you might want to pull out all the stops. For those days, check out our recipes for Shakshuka (page 36) and a New England favorite, Red Flannel Hash (page 38).

Don't worry: Not every recipe in this chapter is grandiose. Lots are for a simple hot cereal. In the original *Instant Pot Bible,* we have plenty of those, too, almost all using steel-cut oats. Those can be prepared right in the pot's insert.

The recipes in this book, by contrast, call for *standard* rolled oats. As you'll see, these require the pot-in-pot (PIP) method to 1) prevent scorching, and 2) get the best results.

Speaking of the PIP method (and for more information, see page 15 in the introduction), pay special attention to the size of the required baking dish in this chapter. Some recipes call for a *1-quart, 6-inch-round,* high-sided, pressure-safe baking or soufflé dish; others, for a *2-quart, 7-inch-round* one. The two are not interchangeable.

The same advice goes for our three breakfast cakes that get "baked" in a 7-inch-round springform pan. Don't be tempted to swap it out for a different size.

Since we sound a bit like culinary scolds, we might as well press on. You *must* pay attention to whether we ask you to cover the baking dish, springform pan, or egg-bite mold. Our timings are based on that added insulation (when it's needed). What's more, this whole covering bit is a little more complicated than at first glance: Some recipes ask you to *seal* the cover to the dish, pan, or mold; others, to *loosely cover* it so that things inside are protected but can expand; and some others don't ask you to cover the pan at all. What's more, a few recipes ask you to lay a paper towel over the top of a baking dish to protect a coffee cake or breakfast treat from drips off the underside of the lid. It's a little extra effort up front to save a lot of disappointment later.

But breakfast is not just about baked goods: We also have a list of egg dishes using egg-bite molds, as well as pancake bites using those same molds—and made with purchased pancake mix, to boot! (For more information on these molds, check out the fuller description on page 15 of the introduction. Or watch our videos on our YouTube channel, Cooking with Bruce and Mark, for up-close visuals.)

Finally, an admission: We've included no yogurt recipe in this chapter. Why? Not every model of the IP has a yogurt function. Sure, people make yogurt in the pot without the special button. Out in the Wild West of the internet, you can find a wide variety of suggestions on how to get the job done. Truth be told, many of those solutions do not meet USDA safety requirements, which we must follow. Heating a pot with only the KEEP WARM function, turning the pot off, and wrapping it in a big bath towel for eight hours does *not* result in a constant temperature inside. Your safety is at risk. There are too many variables, such as how tightly you wrap the pot and how hot or cold your house gets. Just be safe. Make yogurt if your model can. Follow the manufacturer's instructions. Don't play Russian roulette with your digestive tract.

Instead, pick a morning to drag out a big piece of cooking equipment and make some fine egg bites, oatmeals, pancake bites, or even breakfast cakes. You might not have expected it, but these are some of the best reasons to own an Instant Pot.

The Basic Oatmeal Recipe You've Waited For

3 ingredients	**SPECIAL EQUIPMENT:** a 1-quart, 6-inch-round, high-sided, pressure-safe baking or soufflé dish and a pressure-safe rack or trivet
2–3 SERVINGS	
METHOD: pot-in-pot	

PRESSURE: high	**TOTAL TIME WITH PRESSURE:** about 30 minutes
TIME UNDER PRESSURE: 10 minutes	**VEGAN**
RELEASE: natural	**CAN BE GLUTEN-FREE**

2½ cups water

1 cup standard rolled oats (certified gluten-free, if necessary—do *not* use steel-cut or quick-cooking oats)

½ teaspoon table salt

In the original *Instant Pot Bible,* we have plenty of porridges that use *steel-cut* oats, made right in the pot's insert. We avoided *standard* rolled oats because they stick (and burn) to the hot bottom of the insert unless they're so swamped with liquid they turn into a thin gruel, no one's idea of a mouthwatering breakfast. We've solved that problem by using the PIP method to protect standard rolled oats while softening them under pressure, all to create a perfectly creamy oatmeal. A little more effort for better results: Consider this a marital strategy, too.

1. Pour 1½ cups water into the insert set in a **5-, 6-, or 8-quart Instant Pot.** Set a pressure-safe rack or trivet in the insert.

2. Stir the oats, salt, and 1 cup water in a 1-quart, 6-inch-round, high-sided, pressure-safe baking or soufflé dish. Do not cover the dish. Set it on the rack and lock the lid on the pot.

3.

	Set pot for	Set level to	Valve must be	Set time for	If needed, press
For *all* pots	PRESSURE COOK or MANUAL	HIGH	Closed	10 minutes with the KEEP WARM setting off	START

4. When the pot has finished cooking, turn it off and let the pressure **return to normal naturally,** about 12 minutes. Unlatch the lid and open the cooker.

5. Stir the oatmeal in the baking dish for 1 minute to make it super creamy. Use hot pads or silicone baking mitts to transfer the (hot!) dish to a nearby wire rack. Cool for a couple of minutes before dishing up the cereal.

Other Pots

- For a 3-quart Instant Pot, you *must* use only 1 cup water in the insert while otherwise completing the recipe as stated.

- For 5-, 6-, or 8-quart Instant Pots, you *can* double the servings if you keep the amount of water in the insert the same but double all of the other ingredients (including the water in the cereal) and use a 2-quart, 7-inch-round, high-sided, pressure-safe baking or soufflé dish for the smaller baking dish. If you do so, you *must* increase the cooking time to 15 minutes.

- For a 10-quart Instant Pot, you *must* increase the amount of water in the insert to 2½ cups for either of the two, following options: 1) You *can* otherwise complete the recipe as stated; or 2) you *can* double the remaining ingredient amounts (including the water in the cereal) and use a 2-quart, 7-inch-round, high-sided, pressure-safe baking or soufflé dish—*in which case,* you *must* increase the cooking time to 13 minutes.

Beyond

- Substitute dairy milk of any sort, almond milk, or oat milk for the water in the oatmeal (not in the insert).

- Stir up to ½ cup raisins, dried currants, or chopped dried fruit into the oatmeal *after* cooking.

- Stir up to 3 tablespoons light or dark brown sugar, honey, maple syrup, or agave nectar into the oatmeal *after* cooking.

No, Wait, the Cinnamon-Banana Oatmeal Recipe You've Waited For

7 ingredients

2–3 SERVINGS

METHOD:
pot-in-pot

SPECIAL EQUIPMENT:
a 2-quart, 7-inch-round, high-sided, pressure-safe baking or soufflé dish and a pressure-safe rack or trivet

PRESSURE:
high

TIME UNDER PRESSURE:
10 minutes

RELEASE:
natural

TOTAL TIME WITH PRESSURE:
about 30 minutes

VEGETARIAN

CAN BE GLUTEN-FREE

1½ cups water

1¾ cups whole, low-fat, or fat-free milk

1 cup standard rolled oats (certified gluten-free, if necessary—do not use steel-cut or quick-cooking oats)

¼ cup purchased caramel sauce (gluten-free, if necessary)

½ teaspoon vanilla extract

¼ teaspoon ground cinnamon

1 ripe banana, peeled and sliced into thin rounds

Other Pots

- For a 3-quart Instant Pot, you *must* halve almost all of the ingredient amounts *except* you *must* use 1 cup water in the insert. You *must* also use a 1-quart, 6-inch-round, high-sided, baking or soufflé dish.

- For a 10-quart Instant Pot, you *must* increase the amount of water in the insert to 2½ cups while otherwise completing the recipe as stated.

Beyond

- Substitute dulce de leche for the caramel sauce.

- Substitute ¼ teaspoon grated nutmeg for the cinnamon.

- Or omit the cinnamon and use up to ½ teaspoon dried pumpkin pie or apple pie spice blend.

- Stir up to ½ cup chopped pecans or almonds into the oatmeal *after* cooking. (They have a milder flavor against the banana if they're added afterwards.)

Caramel sauce in oatmeal? Why not, when the ice-cream topping makes oatmeal so delicious? We couldn't pull off this trick in the pot without the PIP method because the caramel sauce would burn on the insert's surface (as would the oats). Within the protective walls of a baking dish, the sauce melts to give this decadent breakfast an incredibly smooth texture.

1. Pour the water into the insert set in a **5-, 6-, or 8-quart Instant Pot.** Set a pressure-safe rack or trivet in the insert.

2. Stir the milk, oats, caramel sauce, vanilla extract, and cinnamon in a 2-quart, 7-inch-round, high-sided, pressure-safe baking or soufflé dish until the sauce dissolves. Stir in the banana. Do not cover the dish. Set it on the rack and lock the lid on the pot.

3.

	Set pot for	Set level to	Valve must be	Set time for	If needed, press
For *all* pots	PRESSURE COOK or MANUAL	HIGH	Closed	10 minutes with the KEEP WARM setting off	START

4. When the pot has finished cooking, turn it off and let the pressure **return to normal naturally,** about 12 minutes.

5. Unlatch the lid and open the pot. Stir the oatmeal in the baking dish for 1 minute to make it super creamy. Use hot pads or silicone baking mitts to transfer the (hot!) dish to a nearby wire rack. Cool for a couple of minutes before dishing up the cereal.

The Oatmeal for Almond Lovers

7 ingredients

2–3 SERVINGS

METHOD:
pot-in-pot

SPECIAL EQUIPMENT:
a 1-quart, 6-inch-round, high-sided, pressure-safe baking or soufflé dish and a pressure-safe rack or trivet

PRESSURE:
high

TIME UNDER PRESSURE:
10 minutes

RELEASE:
natural

TOTAL TIME WITH PRESSURE:
about 30 minutes

VEGAN

CAN BE GLUTEN-FREE

1½ cups water

1¾ cups plain unsweetened (sometimes called "original") almond milk

1 cup standard rolled oats (certified gluten-free, if necessary—do not use steel-cut or quick-cooking oats)

¼ cup sliced almonds

2 tablespoons honey (see the headnote for more information)

¼ teaspoon almond extract

¼ teaspoon table salt

By loading this oatmeal with almond milk, sliced almonds, and almond extract, we can ensure that it's got enough almond flavor to satisfy all the nut nuts. The flavors in the oatmeal will be even more enhanced by a strongly flavored honey—use something beyond "mere" wildflower honey, perhaps a tree honey (like eucalyptus), buckwheat honey, or even gallberry honey, a Southern favorite.

1. Pour the water into the insert set in a **5-, 6-, or 8-quart Instant Pot.** Set a pressure-safe rack or trivet in the insert.

2. Stir the almond milk, oats, almonds, honey, almond extract, and salt in a 1-quart, 6-inch-round, high-sided, pressure-safe baking or soufflé dish until the honey dissolves. Do not cover the dish. Set it on the rack and lock the lid on the pot.

3.

	Set pot for	Set level to	Valve must be	Set time for	If needed, press
For *all* pots	PRESSURE COOK or MANUAL	HIGH	Closed	10 minutes with the KEEP WARM setting off	START

4. When the pot has finished cooking, turn it off and let the pressure **return to normal naturally,** about 12 minutes.

5. Unlatch the lid and open the pot. Stir the oatmeal in the baking dish for 1 minute to make it creamy and smooth. Use hot pads or silicone baking mitts to transfer the (hot!) dish to a nearby wire rack. Cool for a couple of minutes before dishing up the cereal.

Other Pots

- For a 3-quart Instant Pot, you *must* use only 1 cup water in the insert while otherwise completing the recipe as stated.

- For 5-, 6-, or 8-quart Instant Pots, you *can* double the servings if you keep the amount of water in the insert the same but double all of the other ingredients and use a 2-quart, 7-inch-round, high-sided, pressure-safe baking or soufflé dish. If you do so, you *must* increase the cooking time to 15 minutes.

- For a 10-quart Instant Pot, you *must* increase the amount of water in the insert to 2½ cups for either of the two, following options: 1) You *can* otherwise complete the recipe as stated; or 2) you *can* double the remaining ingredient amounts and use a 2-quart, 7-inch-round, high-sided, pressure-safe baking or soufflé dish—*in which case,* you *must* increase the cooking time to 13 minutes.

Beyond

- For a sweeter oatmeal, substitute vanilla almond milk for the plain almond milk.

- For a sophisticated flavor, first toast the almonds in a dry skillet set over medium-low heat, stirring often, until lightly browned, about 5 minutes. Cool for 10 minutes before using.

Maple-Pecan Oatmeal

6 ingredients

2–3 SERVINGS

METHOD:
pot-in-pot

SPECIAL EQUIPMENT:
a 2-quart, 7-inch-round, high-sided, pressure-safe baking or soufflé dish and a pressure-safe rack or trivet

PRESSURE:
high

TIME UNDER PRESSURE:
10 minutes

RELEASE:
natural

TOTAL TIME WITH PRESSURE:
about 30 minutes

VEGAN

CAN BE GLUTEN-FREE

1½ cups water

1¾ cups plain unsweetened oat milk (certified gluten-free, if necessary)

1 cup standard rolled oats (certified gluten-free, if necessary—do not use steel-cut or quick-cooking oats)

¼ cup maple syrup

½ cup chopped pecans

¼ teaspoon table salt

Other Pots

- For a 3-quart Instant Pot, you *must* halve almost all of the ingredient amounts *except* you *must* use 1 cup water in the insert. You *must* also use a 1-quart, 6-inch-round, high-sided, baking or soufflé dish.

- For a 10-quart Instant Pot, you *must* increase the amount of water in the insert to 2½ cups while otherwise completing the recipe as stated.

Beyond

- Stir up to 1 teaspoon vanilla extract, ½ teaspoon ground cinnamon, and/or ¼ teaspoon ground ginger into the oat mixture before cooking.

- For a more sophisticated flavor, toast the pecans in a dry skillet set over medium-low heat, stirring often, until lightly browned, about 4 minutes. Cool for 10 minutes before using.

In our New England, people barely understand the concept of breakfast without maple syrup. (By the way, it's not a condiment. It's a beverage.) We prefer a light or medium amber maple syrup for this oatmeal because the flavor is more mellow, less assertive. No matter what, you'd better have the real stuff, not fake-flavored pancake syrup. Don't make an old Yankee farmer come to your house and yell at you.

1. Pour the water into the insert set in a **5-, 6-, or 8-quart Instant Pot.** Set a pressure-safe rack or trivet in the insert.

2. Stir the oat milk, oats, maple syrup, pecans, and salt in a 2-quart, 7-inch-round, high-sided, pressure-safe baking or soufflé dish until the syrup dissolves. Do not cover the dish. Set it on the rack and lock the lid on the pot.

3.

	Set pot for	Set level to	Valve must be	Set time for	If needed, press
For *all* pots	PRESSURE COOK or MANUAL	HIGH	Closed	10 minutes with the KEEP WARM setting off	START

4. When the pot has finished cooking, turn it off and let the pressure **return to normal naturally,** about 12 minutes.

5. Unlatch the lid and open the pot. Stir the oatmeal in the baking dish for 1 minute to make it super creamy and smooth. Use hot pads or silicone baking mitts to transfer the (hot!) dish to a nearby wire rack. Cool for a couple of minutes before dishing up.

Creamy and Sweet *Breakfast* Risotto

7 ingredients	**SPECIAL EQUIPMENT:** none
4–6 SERVINGS	
METHOD: standard	**PRESSURE:** max or high

TIME UNDER PRESSURE: 7 or 10 minutes	**TOTAL TIME WITH PRESSURE:** about 20 minutes
RELEASE: quick	**VEGETARIAN**
	GLUTEN-FREE

---

3 cups water

3 tablespoons butter, cut into small bits, plus additional for garnishing

½ teaspoon table salt

1 cup raw white Arborio rice

½ cup heavy or light cream, or half-and-half

¼ cup packed light brown sugar

½ teaspoon ground cinnamon

Other Pots

- For a 3-quart Instant Pot, you *must* halve all of the ingredient amounts.

- For an 8-quart Instant Pot, you *can* increase all of the ingredient amounts by 50 percent.

- For a 10-quart Instant Pot, you *must* increase all of the ingredient amounts by 50 percent. Or you *can* even double almost all of the amounts, *except* you *must* use *only* ¾ teaspoon ground cinnamon.

Beyond

- Stir in up to ½ cup chopped dried fruit (raisins, cranberries, stemmed figs, mango, pitted prunes, or nectarines) with the cream.

- Omit the cinnamon and substitute your favorite *flavored* dairy or non-dairy coffee creamer (like hazelnut or salted caramel—but gluten-free, if necessary) for the cream or half-and-half.

Italian grandmothers may be outraged by the idea, but don't let them stop you from giving this breakfast version of risotto a shot! Consider this: The pot makes super-creamy cereals *and* it makes risotto super fast. This recipe gives you a warm, sweet rice casserole that cries out for a slice of buttered, whole-wheat toast.

1.

	Press	Set it for	Set time for	If needed, press
In all models	SAUTÉ	MEDIUM, NORMAL, or CUSTOM 300°F	10 minutes	START

2. As the pot heats, pour the water into the insert set in a **5-, 6-, or 8-quart Instant Pot.** Add the butter and salt. Heat the water until it is quite hot, not boiling, but definitely steaming, about 5 minutes. Stir in the rice—seriously stir; don't just dump. Turn off the heat and lock the lid on the pot.

3.

	Set pot for	Set level to	Valve must be	Set time for	If needed, press
For Max pots only	PRESSURE COOK	MAX	—	7 minutes with the KEEP WARM setting off	START
For all other pots	PRESSURE COOK or MANUAL	HIGH	Closed	10 minutes with the KEEP WARM setting off	START

4. When the pot has finished cooking, use the **quick-release method** to bring the pressure back to normal. Unlatch the lid and open the cooker.

5.

	Press	Set it for	Set time for	If needed, press
In all models	SAUTÉ	MEDIUM, NORMAL, or CUSTOM 300°F	5 minutes	START

6. Stir in the cream, brown sugar, and cinnamon. Continue cooking, stirring quite often, until the porridge is bubbling and thickened a bit, about 2 minutes. Turn off the heat, transfer the (hot!) insert from the pot to a nearby wire rack (to stop the cooking), and set aside for a couple of minutes to let the rice set up, although the porridge should still be a bit soupy when you serve it. Serve with bowlfuls garnished with extra butter.

Quinoa Porridge

6 ingredients	SPECIAL EQUIPMENT: none	TIME UNDER PRESSURE: 1 minute	TOTAL TIME WITH PRESSURE: about 17 minutes
2–3 SERVINGS			
METHOD: standard	PRESSURE: high	RELEASE: natural	CAN BE VEGAN
			GLUTEN-FREE

2 cups almond milk

1 cup raw white (or blond) quinoa, rinsed as necessary in a fine-mesh sieve

2 tablespoons honey, maple syrup, agave nectar, or rice syrup

1 teaspoon vanilla extract

¼ teaspoon ground cinnamon

¼ teaspoon table salt

This healthy porridge is made with almond milk, which has a sweet nutty flavor that balances quinoa's earthy flavor better than cow's milk. Commercially packaged quinoa is often rinsed because the grains have a natural but bitter chemical that protects them from, well, mammals' molars. However, bulk-bin quinoa and some organic varieties are *not* rinsed. And even if a package claims the grains are rinsed, you still might want to repeat the process, just to be sure. Use a fine-mesh strainer to rinse the tiny grains with cool tap water, stirring them to make sure they get a dousing. Drain them well. If you don't have a fine-mesh strainer, line a standard colander with cheesecloth or a double layer of paper towels. The grains will need to drain a bit longer because the cheesecloth or paper towels are less porous than the strainer.

1. Stir the almond milk, quinoa, honey or syrup, vanilla, cinnamon, and salt in the insert set in a **3-, 5-, or 6-quart Instant Pot** until the honey dissolves. Lock the lid on the pot.

2.

	Set pot for	Set level to	Valve must be	Set time for	If needed, press
For *all* pots	PRESSURE COOK or MANUAL	HIGH	Closed	1 minute with the KEEP WARM setting off	START

3. When the pot has finished cooking, turn it off and let the pressure **return to normal naturally,** about 12 minutes. Unlatch the lid and open the cooker. Stir well, then set aside for a minute or two so the quinoa continues to absorb some of the liquid. Serve warm.

Other Pots

- For an 8-quart Instant Pot, you *must* increase all of the ingredient amounts by 50 percent.

- For a 10-quart Instant Pot, you *must* double all of the ingredient amounts.

Beyond

- Garnish the servings with a spoonful of yogurt (particularly vanilla yogurt), fresh blackberries, toasted sliced almonds, sliced bananas, and/or a dab of brown sugar.

Superfood Porridge

9 ingredients

3–4 SERVINGS

METHOD:
pot-in-pot

SPECIAL EQUIPMENT:
a 2-quart, 7-inch-round, high-sided, pressure-safe baking or soufflé dish and a pressure-safe rack or trivet

PRESSURE:
high

TIME UNDER PRESSURE:
12 minutes

RELEASE:
natural

TOTAL TIME WITH PRESSURE:
about 30 minutes

VEGETARIAN

CAN BE GLUTEN-FREE

1½ cups water

2½ cups whole, low-fat, or fat-free milk

¾ cup standard rolled oats (certified gluten-free, if necessary)

⅓ cup raw white (or blond) quinoa, rinsed well in a fine-mesh sieve (see the headnote for Quinoa Porridge on page 27 for more information)

¼ cup sliced almonds

¼ cup dried blueberries

2 tablespoons ground flaxseeds

¼ teaspoon ground cinnamon

¼ teaspoon table salt

Other Pots

- For a 3-quart Instant Pot, you *must* use 1 cup water in the insert while halving the remaining ingredient amounts. You *must* also use a 1-quart, 6-inch-round, high-sided, pressure-safe baking or soufflé dish.

- For a 10-quart Instant Pot, you *must* increase the amount of water in the insert to 2½ cups while otherwise completing the recipe as stated.

Beyond

- Other than the dried fruit, there's no sweetening in this porridge. If desired, top the servings with muscovado sugar, coconut sugar, agave nectar, honey, or maple syrup.

- Add ¼ teaspoon ground dried ginger and/or ¼ teaspoon ground dried turmeric with the cinnamon.

- Garnish the servings with goji berries (aka wolfberries).

Because there are standard rolled oats in this *super*-healthy hot cereal, the PIP method is the only way to ensure the creamiest results. Since dried blueberries are expensive, you can substitute dried cranberries; but first chop them into smaller pieces so they don't puff up into searing sugar bombs.

1. Pour the water into the insert for a **5-, 6-, or 8-quart Instant Pot.** Put a pressure-safe rack or trivet in the insert.

2. Stir the milk, oats, quinoa, almonds, dried blueberries, ground flaxseeds, cinnamon, and salt in a 2-quart, 7-inch-round, high-sided, pressure-safe baking or soufflé dish. Do not cover the dish. Set it on the rack and lock the lid on the pot.

3.

	Set pot for	Set level to	Valve must be	Set time for	If needed, press
For *all* pots	PRESSURE COOK or MANUAL	HIGH	Closed	12 minutes with the KEEP WARM setting off	START

4. When the pot has finished cooking, turn it off and let the pressure **return to normal naturally,** about 12 minutes. Unlatch the lid and open the cooker. Stir the porridge, then use hot pads or silicone baking mitts to transfer the (hot!) dish to a nearby wire rack. Cool for a couple of minutes so the grains continue to absorb the liquid. Serve warm.

Shirred Eggs

7 ingredients	**SPECIAL EQUIPMENT:** 6-ounce (or ¾-cup) pressure safe custard cups or ramekins and a pressure-safe rack or trivet	**PRESSURE:** high	**RELEASE:** quick	VEGETARIAN
UP TO 6 SERVINGS (MORE IN LARGER POTS)		**TIME UNDER PRESSURE:** 2 minutes	**TOTAL TIME WITH PRESSURE:** about 7 minutes	GLUTEN-FREE
METHOD: pot-in-pot				

1½ cups water

FOR EACH SHIRRED EGG:

Butter, for greasing

1 tablespoon heavy or light cream

1 refrigerator-cold large egg

1 teaspoon minced chives, fresh or dried, or minced bits from the green part of a scallion

⅛ teaspoon table salt, or to taste

⅛ teaspoon ground black pepper, or to taste

Shirred eggs (pronounced "shurred") are usually eggs baked in ramekins. They have firmer whites than poached eggs and no watery mess. These, of course, are pressure-cooked (still in ramekins) for a quicker breakfast. Our timing yields soft, runny egg yolks. If you like firmer yolks, add 1 minute under pressure. Make sure you have the right-size custard cups or ramekins. Smaller ones will overflow; larger won't fit in the insert.

1. Pour the water into the insert set in a **6- or 8-quart Instant Pot.** Set a pressure-safe rack or trivet in the insert.

2. Butter the inside of *up to* six 6-ounce (or ¾-cup) pressure-safe custard cups or ramekins. Put 1 tablespoon cream in each cup, then crack an egg into each. Top the eggs with chives, salt, and pepper. Do not cover the cups. Place them on the rack, stacking them so that any on a second layer sit stable on the edges of at least two of the three cups below. Lock the lid on the pot.

3.

	Set pot for	Set level to	Valve must be	Set time for	If needed, press
For *all* pots	PRESSURE COOK or MANUAL	HIGH	Closed	2 minutes with the KEEP WARM setting off	START

4. When the pot has finished cooking, use the **quick-release method** to bring the pressure back to normal. Unlatch the lid and open the cooker. Use hot pads or silicone baking mitts to transfer the cups or ramekins to a wire rack. Cool for 1 minute before serving warm.

Other Pots

- For a **3-quart Instant Pot,** you'll only be able to fit three 6-ounce (or ¾-cup) cups or ramekins. Also, you *must* reduce the water in the insert to 1 cup.

- For a **5-quart Instant Pot,** you'll only be able to fit four 6-ounce (or ¾-cup) cups or ramekins. You *must* use 1½ cups water in the insert (as stated).

- For an **8-quart Instant Pot,** you *can* actually fit up to eight 6-ounce (or ¾-cup) cups or ramekins in the insert. You *must* maintain the stated amount of water (1½ cups).

- For a **10-quart Instant Pot,** you *can* fit up to ten 6-ounce cups or ramekins in the pot if you use a large rack or trivet. No matter how many cups you use, you *must* increase the amount of water in the insert to 2½ cups.

Beyond

- For a heartier non-vegetarian breakfast, after buttering the insides of the cups or ramekins, line them with a thin strip of prosciutto before adding the eggs and other ingredients.

- For a dairy-free alternative, use vegetable oil instead of butter and use full-fat coconut milk instead of the cream.

Basic Egg Bites

5 ingredients	
7 EGG BITES	
METHOD: egg bites	

SPECIAL EQUIPMENT: one seven-indentation egg-bite mold and a pressure-safe rack or trivet

PRESSURE: high

TIME UNDER PRESSURE: 8 minutes

RELEASE: modified natural

TOTAL TIME WITH PRESSURE: about 18 minutes

VEGETARIAN

GLUTEN-FREE

1½ cups water

5 refrigerator-cold large eggs

⅓ cup heavy or light cream, or half-and-half

1 teaspoon table salt

Butter, vegetable oil, olive oil, or nonstick spray

Other Pots

- For a **3-quart Instant Pot,** you *must* decrease the amount of water in the insert to 1 cup and you *must* use two, four-indentation egg-bite molds specifically made for this smaller model, leaving one of the indentations empty. You *must* stack the molds on top of each other in the insert.

- For a **6- or 8-quart Instant Pot,** you *can* double almost all of the ingredient amounts *except* you *must* use the stated 1½ cups water in the insert. You *must* then use *two* seven-indentation egg-bite molds, one stacked on top of the other in the pot so that the indentations of the top mold sit on the walls of the bottom mold, not into the bottom indentations themselves (except for the center indentation of the top mold which will now hover above the center indentation below).

- For a **10-quart Instant Pot,** you *must* increase the amount of water in the insert to 2½ cups. You *can* either complete the recipe as stated or you *can* double the other ingredient amounts, in which case you *must* use two seven-indentation egg-bite molds, stacking them on top of each other in the insert.

These egg bites come out like omelet puffs. They must be kept plain and simple because additional ingredients (cheese, bacon, what have you) change the timings. Don't worry: There are other, more complicated variations on egg bites in this chapter. But the simplicity of these means they travel really well (in a sealed container, of course) for an on-the-go breakfast or a mid-morning snack. The recipe calls for cream or half-and-half. Don't use a less-fat dairy product. You need the extra oomph to protect the eggs.

1. Pour the water into the insert set in a **5-, 6-, or 8-quart Instant Pot.** Set a pressure-safe rack or trivet in the insert.

2. Whisk the eggs, cream or half-and-half, and salt in a medium bowl until smooth and uniform. Seriously. Uniform. One bit of egg white in the mix will compromise the bites.

3. Lightly butter, oil, or spray the seven indentations of a standard egg-bite mold. (See page 15 for more information on these molds.) Divide the egg mixture evenly among the indentations. Lay the silicone lid or a piece of aluminum foil loosely over the mold, covering it without sealing the lid or the foil to the mold. Set the mold on the rack and lock the lid on the pot.

4.

	Set pot for	Set level to	Valve must be	Set time for	If needed, press
For *all* pots	PRESSURE COOK or MANUAL	HIGH	Closed	8 minutes with the KEEP WARM setting off	START

5. When the pot has finished cooking, turn it off and let the pressure **return to normal naturally for 5 minutes.** Then use the **quick-release method** to remove any residual pressure before unlatching the lid and opening the pot.

6. Use hot pads or silicone baking mitts to transfer the (hot!) egg-bite mold to a nearby wire rack. Cool the still-covered mold for 2 minutes before uncovering and unmolding the egg bites.

Beyond

- For egg salad, cool these egg bites to room temperature, chop them up, and mix them with mayonnaise (gluten-free, if necessary), yellow mustard (gluten-free, if necessary), pickle relish, a little minced celery, a very little minced red onion, salt, and pepper.

Herbed Goat Cheese Egg Bites

8 ingredients

7 EGG BITES

METHOD:
egg bites

SPECIAL
EQUIPMENT:
one seven-
indentation
egg-bite mold, a
pressure-safe rack
or trivet, and a
standard blender

PRESSURE:
high

TIME UNDER
PRESSURE:
8 minutes

RELEASE:
modified natural

TOTAL TIME WITH
PRESSURE:
about 25 minutes

VEGETARIAN

GLUTEN-FREE

1½ cups water

5 refrigerator-cold large eggs

3 tablespoons heavy or light cream

2 ounces soft goat cheese (¼ cup)

½ teaspoon table salt

½ teaspoon ground black pepper

1½ tablespoons minced fresh green herbs (such as dill, oregano, thyme, tarragon, marjoram, and/or chervil)

Olive oil or olive oil nonstick spray

Tangy, tender, full-flavored: This is an egg bite's best life. As with the Not-Really-Starbucks' Cheesy Egg-White Bites (page 32), you'll need a blender for this egg-bite recipe, since the goat cheese needs to be emulsified for the smoothest texture. Blend only on LOW to avoid a foamy mess and air pockets. Once you add the herbs, only *pulse* the blender one or two times to keep the herbs in discreet bits, rather than turning the egg-bite mixture green. (Mincing the herbs before pulsing also keeps the mixture from quickly becoming a puree.)

1. Pour the water into the Insert set in a **5-, 6-, or 8-quart Instant Pot.** Set a pressure-safe rack or trivet in the insert.

2. Put the eggs, cream, goat cheese, salt, and pepper in a blender. Cover and blend on LOW for a couple of minutes, until smooth and thick. Add the herbs, cover, and pulse once or twice to combine.

3. Oil the inside of the seven indentations of an egg-bite mold with olive oil or olive oil spray. (See page 15 for more information on these molds.) Divide the egg mixture evenly among the indentations. Lay the silicone lid or a piece of aluminum foil loosely over the mold, covering it without sealing the lid or the foil to the mold. Set the mold on the rack and lock the pot.

4.

	Set pot for	Set level to	Valve must be	Set time for	If needed, press
For *all* pots	PRESSURE COOK or MANUAL	HIGH	Closed	8 minutes with the KEEP WARM setting off	START

5. When the pot has finished cooking, turn it off and let the pressure **return to normal naturally for 5 minutes.** Then use the **quick-release method** to remove any residual pressure before unlatching the lid and opening the pot.

6. Use hot pads or silicone baking mitts to transfer the (hot!) egg-bite mold to a nearby wire rack. Cool the still-covered mold for 2 minutes before uncovering and unmolding the egg bites onto plates or a serving platter.

Other Pots

- For a 3-quart Instant Pot, you *must* decrease the amount of water in the insert to 1 cup and you *must* use two, four-indentation egg-bite molds specifically made for this smaller model, leaving one of the indentations empty. You *must* stack the molds on top of each other in the insert.

- For a 6- or 8-quart Instant Pot, you *can* double almost all of the ingredient amounts *except* you *must* use the stated 1½ cups water in the insert. You *must* then use *two* seven-indentation egg-bite molds, stacking them on top of each other in the insert.

- For a 10-quart Instant Pot, you *must* increase the amount of water in the insert to 2½ cups. You *can* either complete the recipe as stated or you *can* double the other ingredient amounts, in which case you *must* use two seven-indentation egg-bite molds, stacking them on top of each other in the insert.

Not-Really-Starbucks' Cheesy Egg-White Bites

8 ingredients

7 EGG-WHITE BITES

METHOD: egg bites

SPECIAL EQUIPMENT: one seven-indentation egg-bite mold, a pressure-safe rack or trivet, and a standard blender

PRESSURE: high

TIME UNDER PRESSURE: 10 minutes

RELEASE: modified natural

TOTAL TIME WITH PRESSURE: about 25 minutes

CAN BE VEGETARIAN

CAN BE GLUTEN-FREE

1½ cups water

6 refrigerator-cold large egg whites

2 ounces (¼ cup) regular or low-fat cream cheese (vegetarian and/or gluten-free, if necessary—do not use fat-free cream cheese)

3 tablespoons heavy or light cream

2 tablespoons drained jarred minced pimientos

½ teaspoon table salt

½ teaspoon ground black pepper

Olive oil or olive oil nonstick spray

No, these aren't egg-white bites for health. They're made to mimic a certain coffee chain's popular sous-vide egg bites—but where theirs are made with cottage cheese (blech!), ours have cream cheese (yeah!) to protect the egg whites and create a richer (and better!) breakfast.

You'll need a blender to get the egg-white mixture smooth enough with these ratios, but *do not* blend the ingredients on high. The mixture will turn foamy and the egg bites will end up with slimy air pockets (back to blech).

1. Pour the water into the insert set in a **5-, 6-, or 8-quart Instant Pot.** Set a rack or a pressure-safe rack or trivet in the insert.

2. Put the egg whites, cream cheese, and cream in a blender. Cover and blend on LOW for a couple of minutes, until smooth and thick. Add the pimientos, salt, and pepper. Pulse just to combine.

3. Grease the inside of the seven indentations of an egg-bite mold with olive oil or olive oil nonstick spray. (See page 15 for more information on these molds.) Divide the egg-white mixture evenly among the indentations. Lay the silicone lid or a piece of aluminum foil loosely over the mold, covering it without sealing the lid or the foil to the mold. Set the mold on the rack and lock the lid on the pot.

4.

	Set pot for	Set level to	Valve must be	Set time for	If needed, press
For *all* pots	PRESSURE COOK or MANUAL	HIGH	Closed	10 minutes with the KEEP WARM setting off	START

5. When the pot has finished cooking, turn it off and let the pressure **return to normal naturally for 5 minutes.** Then use the **quick-release method** to remove any residual pressure before unlatching the lid and opening the pot.

6. Use hot pads or silicone baking mitts to transfer the (hot!) egg-bite mold to a nearby wire rack. Cool the still-covered mold for 2 minutes before uncovering and unmolding the egg bites onto plates or a serving platter.

Other Pots

- For a 3-quart Instant Pot, you *must* decrease the amount of water in the insert to 1 cup and you *must* use two, four-indentation egg-bite molds specifically made for this smaller model, leaving one of the indentations empty. You *must* stack the molds on top of each other in the insert.

- For a 6- or 8-quart Instant Pot, you *can* double almost all of the ingredient amounts *except* you *must* use the stated 1½ cups water in the insert. You *must* then use *two* seven-indentation egg-bite molds, stacking them on top of each other in the insert.

- For a 10-quart Instant Pot, you *must* increase the amount of water in the insert to 2½ cups. You *can* either complete the recipe as stated or you *can* double the other ingredient amounts, in which case you *must* use two seven-indentation egg-bite molds, stacking them on top of each other in the insert.

Beyond

- Add up to ¼ teaspoon garlic and/ or onion powder to the egg whites before blending.

- Garnish the bites with Sriracha.

- Make sandwiches by slicing these egg bites and layering them with thinly sliced tomatoes on toasted whole wheat bread spread with deli mustard and/or mayonnaise (both gluten-free, if necessary).

Bacon & Cheese Egg Bites

9 ingredients

7 EGG BITES

METHOD:
egg bites

SPECIAL EQUIPMENT:
one seven-indentation egg-bite mold and a pressure-safe rack or trivet

PRESSURE:
high

TIME UNDER PRESSURE:
8 minutes

RELEASE:
modified natural

TOTAL TIME WITH PRESSURE:
about 25 minutes

CAN BE GLUTEN-FREE

1½ cups water

Butter, softened

4 thin strips of bacon (gluten-free, if necessary), cooked crisp and crumbled

7 tablespoons shredded Swiss or Gruyère cheese

3 tablespoons finely minced chives or the green part of a scallion

4 refrigerator-cold large eggs

¼ cup heavy or light cream, or half-and-half

½ teaspoon table salt

½ teaspoon ground black pepper

Get your 1970s groove on because these egg bites are like crustless quiches lorraines. You'll get the most authentic flavor with Gruyère cheese, but Swiss is a fine substitute (or even Monterey Jack). If you want to go really simple, use purchased, already-cooked bacon, often available near the eggs at the supermarket. (Avoid the bacon bits in bottles for salads.)

The cheese in the molds stays at the bottom and melts to become a topping for the egg bites when they're unmolded. These egg bites need to cool a little longer than some others to give the cheese a chance to set.

1. Pour the water into the insert set in a **5-, 6-, or 8-quart Instant Pot.** Set a pressure-safe rack or trivet in the insert.

2. Lightly butter the inside of the seven indentations of an egg-bite mold. (For more information on egg-bite molds, see page 15.) Divide the bacon bits, cheese, and chives or scallion among the indentations.

3. Whisk the eggs, cream, salt, and pepper in a medium bowl until smooth and uniform. There must be no bits of translucent egg white floating in the mix.

4. Divide this mixture evenly among the seven egg-bite indentations. Pour gently and slowly so as not to dislodge the ingredients already inside. Lay the silicone lid or a piece of aluminum foil loosely over the mold, covering it without sealing the lid or the foil to the mold. Set the mold on the rack and lock the lid on the pot.

5.

	Set pot for	Set level to	Valve must be	Set time for	If needed, press
For *all* pots	PRESSURE COOK or MANUAL	HIGH	Closed	8 minutes with the KEEP WARM setting off	START

6. When the pot has finished cooking, turn it off and let the pressure **return to normal naturally for 5 minutes.** Then use the **quick-release method** to remove any residual pressure before unlatching the lid and opening the pot.

7. Use hot pads or silicone baking mitts to transfer the (hot!) egg-bite mold to a nearby wire rack. Cool the still-covered mold for 5 minutes before uncovering unmolding the egg bites onto plates or a serving platter.

Other Pots

- For a 3-quart Instant Pot, you *must* decrease the amount of water in the insert to 1 cup and you *must* use two, four-indentation egg-bite molds specifically made for this smaller model, leaving one of the indentations empty. You *must* stack the molds on top of each other in the insert.

- For a 6- or 8-quart Instant Pot, you *can* double almost all of the ingredient amounts *except* you *must* use the stated 1½ cups water in the insert. You *must* then use *two* seven-indentation egg-bite molds, stacking them on top of each other in the insert.

- For a 10-quart Instant Pot, you *must* increase the amount of water in the insert to 2½ cups. You *can* either complete the recipe as stated or you *can* double the other ingredient amounts, in which case you *must* use two seven-indentation egg-bite molds, stacking them on top of each other in the insert.

Beyond

- Serve with flaky, buttery croissants for the true quiche experience!

- If you don't want pork, substitute turkey bacon for the standard bacon.

Shakshuka

14 ingredients
4 SERVINGS

METHOD:
fast/slow

SPECIAL EQUIPMENT:
none

PRESSURE:
low twice

TIME UNDER PRESSURE:
11 minutes

RELEASE:
quick twice

TOTAL TIME WITH PRESSURE:
about 30 minutes

TOTAL TIME WITH SLOW COOKING:
about 4½ hours

VEGETARIAN

GLUTEN-FREE

2 tablespoons olive oil

1 medium yellow or white onion, chopped (1 cup)

2 medium red or yellow bell peppers, stemmed, cored, and cut into ½-inch strips

1 medium fresh jalapeño chile, stemmed, cored (seeded, if desired), and cut into narrow strips

2 medium garlic cloves, minced (2 teaspoons)

1 teaspoon ground coriander

1 teaspoon ground cumin

1 teaspoon mild smoked paprika

1 teaspoon granulated white sugar

½ teaspoon table salt

½ teaspoon ground black pepper

½ cup vegetable broth

One 14-ounce diced tomatoes *packed in juice* (1¾ cups)

4 refrigerator-cold large eggs

A traditional Middle Eastern dish, shakshuka is a spicy tomato sauce that often (as here) holds poached eggs. It's a great weekend brunch, particularly if you've got houseguests. (It's often dinner at our house after a busy day.) Our timing results in soft-set eggs, the better to break and run into the sauce. If you open the cooker and want firmer eggs, set the lid askew over the pot and wait for a few minutes—or just increase the cooking time in step 7 to 2 minutes.

1.

	Press	Set it for	Set time for	If needed, press
In all models	SAUTÉ	MEDIUM, NORMAL, or CUSTOM 300°F	10 minutes	START

2. As the pot heats, warm the oil in the insert set in a **5- or 6-quart Instant Pot.** Add the onion, bell pepper, and jalapeño; cook, stirring often, until the onion just begins to soften, about 2 minutes. Stir in the garlic, coriander, cumin, smoked paprika, sugar, salt, and pepper until aromatic, just a few seconds.

3. Pour in the broth and scrape up any browned bits on the pot's bottom. (There will be almost none.) Turn off the heat and stir in the tomatoes with their juice. Lock the lid on the pot.

4.

	Set pot for	Set level to	Valve must be	Set time for	If needed, press
For *all* pots	PRESSURE COOK or MANUAL	LOW	Closed	10 minutes with the KEEP WARM setting off	START
For the slow-cook function	SLOW COOK	HIGH	Open	4 hours with the KEEP WARM setting off	START

5. When the pot has finished cooking under pressure, use the **quick-release method** to bring the pressure back to normal. Whichever cooking method you've used, unlatch the lid and open the cooker.

6. Stir the tomato mixture in the pot, then use the back of a large cooking spoon or a wooden spoon to make four indentations in the sauce. Crack an egg into each indentation and lock the lid back on the cooker.

7.

	Set pot for	Set level to	Valve must be	Set time for	If needed, press
For *all* pots	PRESSURE COOK or MANUAL	LOW	Closed	1 minute with the KEEP WARM setting off	START

8. When the pot has finished cooking, use the **quick-release method** to bring the pressure back to normal. Unlatch the lid and open the cooker. Serve in bowls by scooping up an egg into each, along with plenty of the tomato sauce.

Other Pots

- For a **3-quart Instant Pot**, you *must* halve all of the ingredient amounts.

- For an **8-quart Instant Pot**, you *must* increase all of the ingredient amounts by 50 percent.

- For a **10-quart Instant Pot**, you *must* double almost all of the ingredient amounts *except* you *must* increase the broth to 1½ cups.

Beyond

- For a more authentic flavor, stir in up to 1 tablespoon hot or mild harissa with the tomatoes and their juice.

- Garnish the servings with a drizzle of olive oil and finely chopped fresh basil leaves.

- Serve with warmed pita rounds.

See photo in insert.

Red Flannel Hash

11 or 12 ingredients

4–5 SERVINGS

METHOD:
standard

SPECIAL EQUIPMENT:
none

PRESSURE:
max or high

TIME UNDER PRESSURE:
7 or 10 minutes

RELEASE:
quick

TOTAL TIME WITH PRESSURE:
about 25 minutes

CAN BE GLUTEN-FREE

1½ cups water

¾ pound small red-skinned potatoes (do not peel), cut into 1-inch pieces

¾ pound red beets, trimmed, peeled, and cut into 1-inch pieces

¾ pound sweet potatoes, peeled and cut into 1-inch pieces

½ stick (4 tablespoons or ¼ cup) butter

8 ounces thin strips of bacon, chopped (gluten-free, if necessary)

1 small red onion, chopped (½ cup)

1 teaspoon rubbed or ground sage

1 teaspoon dried thyme

½ teaspoon celery seed

½ teaspoon table salt (optional)

½ teaspoon ground black pepper

If you aren't in the New-England know, red flannel hash is made with beets, sweet potatoes, *and* regular potatoes. It's also made (better!) with bacon instead of corned beef. Dig in, then go milk a cow.

This recipe works in the reverse order of many IP hash recipes. Here, the vegetables are cooked under pressure, then the dish is finished with the SAUTÉ setting. If we fried the bacon and spices, then cooked it all together under pressure (as in most recipes), the whole thing would end up a too-soft, unappetizing mess. We prefer a crust on those vegetables!

1. Pour the water into the insert set in a **5-, 6-, or 8-quart Instant Pot.** Dump in the potatoes, beets, and sweet potatoes. Lock the lid on the pot.

2.

	Set pot for	Set level to	Valve must be	Set time for	If needed, press
For Max pots only	PRESSURE COOK	MAX	—	7 minutes with the KEEP WARM setting off	START
For all other pots	PRESSURE COOK or MANUAL	HIGH	Closed	10 minutes with the KEEP WARM setting off	START

3. When the pot has finished cooking, use the **quick-release method** to bring the pressure back to normal. Unlatch the lid and open the cooker.

4. Use hot pads or silicone baking mitts to remove the (hot!) insert from the machine; drain the vegetables in a colander set in the sink. Wipe out the (still hot!) insert, then set it back in the pot.

5.

	Press	Set it for	Set time for	If needed, press
In all models	SAUTÉ	MEDIUM, NORMAL, or CUSTOM 300°F	15 minutes	START

6. Melt the butter in the insert, then add the bacon. Cook, stirring often, until the bacon starts to brown at the edges, about 4 minutes.

7. Add the onion and cook, stirring often, until softened, about 3 minutes. Stir in the sage, thyme, celery seeds, salt (if using), and pepper; cook until fragrant, just a few seconds.

8. Pour the cooked vegetables into the pot, stir well, and press down gently to make a loosely compact, fairly even layer. Cook until the bottom of the mixture is really sizzling, maybe even sticking a bit. A good crust makes a great hash. Don't let it burn but cook it a little further than you might imagine, about 5 minutes.

9. Turn off the heat and immediately use hot pads or silicone baking mitts to transfer the (hot!) insert to a nearby wire rack (to stop the cooking). Use a metal spatula to scrape the hash out of the pot and serve it.

Other Pots

- For a **3-quart Instant Pot**, you *must* halve almost all of the ingredient amounts *except* you *must* use 1 cup water in the insert.

- For an **8-quart Instant Pot**, you *can* increase almost all of the ingredient amounts by 50 percent while *maintaining* 1½ cups water in the insert.

- For a **10-quart Instant Pot**, you *must* increase the amount of water in the insert to 2½ cups while otherwise completing the recipe as stated. Or you *can* increase the other ingredient amounts by 50 percent or even double them (while maintaining the increased 2½ cups water).

Beyond

- Top with poached or fried eggs.

- Substitute turkey or even vegan bacon for the standard bacon.

- Offer well-toasted whole-wheat English muffins on the side.

Apple-Cinnamon Breakfast Bread Pudding

11 ingredients

4–6 SERVINGS

METHOD:
pot-in-pot

SPECIAL EQUIPMENT:
a 2-quart, 7-inch-round, high-sided, pressure-safe baking or soufflé dish and a pressure-safe rack or trivet

PRESSURE:
max or high

TIME UNDER PRESSURE:
10 or 12 minutes

RELEASE:
quick

TOTAL TIME WITH PRESSURE:
about 20 minutes

VEGETARIAN

1½ cups water

Baking spray

2 refrigerator-cold large eggs

¾ cup canned apple pie filling

¾ cup whole, low-fat, or fat-free milk

¼ cup chopped walnuts

¼ cup light brown sugar

½ teaspoon ground cinnamon

½ teaspoon vanilla extract

½ teaspoon table salt

8 ounces (½ pound) sliced country-style white bread, cut into 1-inch squares (do not remove the crusts)

Other Pots

- For a 3-quart Instant Pot, you *must* halve almost all of the ingredients *except* you *must* use 1 cup water in the insert. You also *must* use a 1-quart, 6-inch-round, high-sided, pressure-safe baking or soufflé dish.

- For a 10-quart Instant Pot, you *must* increase the amount of water in the insert to 2½ cups while otherwise completing the recipe as stated.

Beyond

- For the easiest way to cook bacon, lay the strips in a single layer on a lipped baking sheet. (They can be snug against each other.) Bake at 375°F without turning for 15 minutes for softer bacon, or as much as 25 minutes for bacon that breaks into shards.

- Add up to ¼ cup raisins with the bread.

- Or substitute canned peach pie filling for the apple pie filling. (Avoid cherry or blueberry pie filling.)

Here's a sweet and easy weekend surprise: a bread pudding that's plenty rich (thanks to the eggs) but also easy (thanks to the canned apple pie filling). When you serve it, you'll need something to cut the sweet. If you're not opposed to meat, how about bacon on the side? (See the **Beyond** section for a great cooking tip.)

1. Pour the water into the insert set in a **5-, 6-, or 8-quart Instant Pot**. Set a pressure-safe rack or trivet in the insert. Evenly coat the inside of a 2-quart, 7-inch-round, high-sided, pressure-safe baking or soufflé dish with baking spray.

2. In a large bowl, whisk the eggs until uniform, with no bits of egg white floating in the batch. Stir in the apple pie filling, milk, walnuts, brown sugar, cinnamon, vanilla, and salt until uniform.

3. Add the bread and toss well until most of the liquid ends up in the bread. Dump and spread this mixture into the prepared baking dish, making sure you get every drop of liquid. Gently compact the mixture to create a fairly flat top. Cover the baking dish tightly with aluminum foil, set it on the rack, and lock the lid on the pot.

4.

	Set pot for	Set level to	Valve must be	Set time for	If needed, press
For Max pots only	PRESSURE COOK	MAX	—	10 minutes with the KEEP WARM setting off	START
For all other pots	PRESSURE COOK or MANUAL	HIGH	Closed	12 minutes with the KEEP WARM setting off	START

5. When the pot has finished cooking, use the **quick-release method** to bring the pressure back to normal. Unlatch the lid and open the cooker. Use hot pads or silicone baking mitts to transfer the (hot!) baking dish to a wire rack. Uncover it and cool for 5 minutes. Use a large cooking spoon to dish the warm bread pudding into serving bowls.

Bacon and Croissant Breakfast Bread Pudding

8 ingredients

4 SERVINGS

METHOD:
pot-in-pot

SPECIAL EQUIPMENT:
a 2-quart, 7-inch-round, high-sided, pressure-safe baking or soufflé dish and a pressure-safe rack or trivet

PRESSURE:
max or high

TIME UNDER PRESSURE:
10 or 12 minutes

RELEASE:
quick

TOTAL TIME WITH PRESSURE:
about 30 minutes

1½ cups water

Baking spray

3 refrigerator-cold large eggs

1 cup whole or low-fat milk (do not use fat-free)

½ cup heavy or light cream

4 purchased croissants (about 2½ ounces each), torn into ½-inch pieces

2 ounces Swiss cheese, shredded (½ cup)

4 thin slices of bacon, cooked, drained, and crumbled

Other Pots

- For a 3-quart Instant Pot, you *must* halve almost all of the ingredients *except* you *must* use 1 cup water in the insert. You *must* also use a 1-quart, 6-inch-round, high-sided, pressure-safe baking or soufflé dish.

- For a 10-quart Instant Pot, you *must* increase the amount of water in the insert to 2½ cups while otherwise completing the recipe as stated.

Beyond

- Although this dish is warm and rich out of the pot, you can crisp it up to make it even better if you use a 6- or 8-quart Instant Pot and a broiler-safe baking dish. Once the recipe is completed, clean and wipe out the (hot!) insert. Set the air-frying basket in the insert and set the casserole in it. Put the Instant Pot Air Fryer Lid on top and cook on HIGH for 6 minutes at 400°F to crisp the top.

Let's go way over the top (as often as possible). So get this: If you like croissant sandwiches, you'll love this breakfast bread pudding! The croissant bits almost melt into the casserole, making it incredibly soft and decadent. For the best flavor, use croissants made with butter, not shortening.

1. Pour the water into the insert set in a **5-, 6-, or 8-quart Instant Pot.** Put a pressure-safe rack or trivet in the insert. Evenly coat the inside of a 2-quart, 7-inch-round, high-sided, pressure-safe baking or soufflé dish with baking spray.

2. In a large bowl, whisk the eggs, milk, and cream until very smooth and fully uniform. Add the croissant pieces and stir well to coat thoroughly. Set aside for 5 minutes so the croissant bits absorb most of the milk mixture.

3. Stir in the cheese and bacon until uniform. Dump and spread this mixture into the prepared baking dish, getting every drop of liquid into the pan and compacting the mixture gently to form a fairly even top. Cover the baking dish tightly with aluminum foil, set it on the rack, and lock the lid on the pot.

4.

	Set pot for	Set level to	Valve must be	Set time for	If needed, press
For Max pots only	PRESSURE COOK	MAX	—	10 minutes with the KEEP WARM setting off	START
For all other pots	PRESSURE COOK or MANUAL	HIGH	Closed	12 minutes with the KEEP WARM setting off	START

5. When the pot has finished cooking, use the **quick-release method** to bring the pressure back to normal. Unlatch the lid and open the cooker. Use hot pads or silicone baking mitts to transfer the (hot!) baking dish to a wire rack. Uncover it and cool for 5 minutes. Use a large cooking spoon to dish the warm bread pudding into serving bowls.

Overnight French Toast

10 ingredients	SPECIAL EQUIPMENT:	PRESSURE: high	TOTAL TIME WITH PRESSURE:
4 SERVINGS	a 2-quart, 7-inch-round, high-sided, pressure-safe baking or soufflé dish and a pressure-safe rack or trivet	TIME UNDER PRESSURE: 18 minutes	about 8 hours 45 minutes (includes refrigerating overnight)
METHOD: pot-in-pot		RELEASE: modified natural	VEGETARIAN

Butter, for greasing

3 refrigerator-cold large eggs

⅔ cup heavy or light cream

½ cup whole or low-fat milk (do not use fat-free milk)

¼ cup packed light brown sugar

½ teaspoon vanilla extract

¼ teaspoon ground cinnamon

¼ teaspoon table salt

7 slices country-style white bread

1½ cups water

Other Pots

- Because of complicated ratios with smaller pan sizes, this recipe is not easily adaptable for a 3-quart Instant Pot.

- For a 10-quart Instant Pot, you *must* increase the amount of water to 2½ cups while otherwise completing the recipe as stated.

Beyond

- Garnish the servings with fresh blackberries, fresh blueberries, some softened butter, and/or maple syrup.

This old-school, North American breakfast casserole can be a great weekend brunch...*provided* you remember to start the thing the night before. To save a few minutes in the morning, the cooking time here is a tad longer than you might expect because we skipped letting the casserole come to room temperature when it comes out of the fridge. We had the option to either leave it on the counter for 30 minutes or simply increase the cooking time by a few minutes. Didn't seem like a real choice to us.

1. Generously butter the inside of a 2-quart, 7-inch-round, high-sided, pressure-safe baking or soufflé dish. Whisk the eggs, cream, milk, brown sugar, vanilla, cinnamon, and salt in a large bowl until creamy and smooth.

2. Dip a slice of bread in the egg mixture, turning it to soak both sides. Place it in the casserole dish. Continue dipping slices of bread, tearing them as necessary to fill in nooks and crannies, to make a (fairly) evenly layered casserole in the dish. Pour any remaining egg mixture over the top of the bread slices. Cover the dish tightly with aluminum foil and refrigerate overnight, for at least 8 hours or up to 12 hours.

3. Pour the water into the insert set in a **5-, 6-, or 8-quart Instant Pot.** Place a pressure-safe rack or trivet in the insert. Set the covered baking dish on the rack and lock the lid on the pot.

4.

	Set pot for	Set level to	Valve must be	Set time for	If needed, press
For *all* pots	PRESSURE COOK or MANUAL	HIGH	Closed	18 minutes with the KEEP WARM setting off	START

5. When the pot has finished cooking, turn it off and let the pressure **return to normal naturally for 10 minutes.** Then use the **quick-release method** to get rid of any residual pressure in the pot. Unlatch the lid and open the cooker. Use hot pads or silicone baking mitts to transfer the (hot!) baking dish to a nearby wire rack. Uncover the baking dish and cool for about 5 minutes to let the casserole set up. Serve warm by big spoonfuls.

Breakfast Fruit Cobbler

7 ingredients	**SPECIAL EQUIPMENT:** a 2-quart, 7-inch-round, high-sided, pressure-safe baking or soufflé dish and a pressure-safe rack or trivet	**PRESSURE:** high	**TOTAL TIME WITH PRESSURE:** about 35 minutes
4 SERVINGS		**TIME UNDER PRESSURE:** 12 minutes	**VEGETARIAN**
METHOD: pot-in-pot		**RELEASE:** modified natural	

1½ cups water

6 cups mixed fresh fruit or berries: peeled, seeded, and chopped apples; pitted and chopped peaches, nectarines, or plums; hulled and sliced strawberries; pitted cherries; and/ or blackberries, blueberries, and/or raspberries

½ cup granulated white sugar

2 tablespoons cornstarch

¼ teaspoon ground cinnamon

¼ teaspoon table salt

2 cups purchased granola

This recipe makes an easy fruit filling for a breakfast version of cobbler. All you have to do is top with purchased granola for serving. Use any sort of granola you like, although we think the crunchier, the better. And use any combination of fruit you like, just so long as "drier" fruits like apples and plums includes some "wetter" fruit like peaches, blackberries, or raspberries.

1. Pour the water into the insert set in a **5-, 6-, or 8-quart Instant Pot.** Put a pressure-safe rack or trivet in the insert.

2. Stir the fruit, sugar, cornstarch, cinnamon, and salt in a 2-quart, 7-inch-round, high-sided, pressure-safe baking or soufflé dish until the fruit is evenly coated in the sugar and cornstarch. Cover the dish tightly with aluminum foil, set the dish on the rack, and lock the lid on the pot.

3.

	Set pot for	Set level to	Valve must be	Set time for	If needed, press
For all pots	PRESSURE COOK or MANUAL	HIGH	Closed	12 minutes with the KEEP WARM setting off	START

4. When the pot has finished cooking, turn it off and let the pressure **return to normal naturally for 10 minutes.** Then use the **quick-release method** to get rid of any residual pressure in the pot. Unlatch the lid and open the cooker. Use hot pads or silicone baking mitts to transfer the (hot!) baking dish to a nearby wire rack. Cool for 5 minutes, then divide the fruit mixture among four serving bowls and top each with ½ cup granola.

Other Pots

- For a 3-quart Instant Pot, you *must* halve almost all of the ingredients *except* you *must* use 1 cup water in the insert. You *must* also use a 1-quart, 6-inch-round, high-sided, pressure-safe baking or soufflé dish.

- For a 10-quart Instant Pot, you *must* increase the amount of water in the insert to 2½ cups while otherwise completing the recipe as stated.

Beyond

- For a sophisticated flavor, stir 2 tablespoons butter (cut into tiny bits), toasted walnut oil, or hazelnut oil into the fruit mixture before it goes under pressure.

- Toast the purchased granola on a lipped baking sheet in a 300°F oven for 5 to 10 minutes, stirring often, until warm and even a little browned at the edges.

See photo in insert.

Cinnamon-Sugar Pancake-Mix Bites

8 ingredients

7 pancake bites

METHOD:
egg bites

SPECIAL EQUIPMENT:
one seven-indentation egg-bite mold and a pressure-safe rack or trivet

PRESSURE:
high

TIME UNDER PRESSURE:
15 minutes

RELEASE:
quick

TOTAL TIME WITH PRESSURE:
about 30 minutes

CAN BE VEGETARIAN

1½ cups water

Baking spray

¼ cup granulated white sugar

1 tablespoon ground cinnamon

1 cup regular pancake mix (vegetarian, if necessary)

⅔ cup whole, low-fat, or fat-free milk

2 tablespoons vegetable, canola, or other neutral-flavored oil

1 teaspoon vanilla extract

These pancake bites come out of the egg-bite mold like cake donut holes—all without any frying! The bites are best while warm since all steamed cakes turn gummy as they cool to room temperature.

This recipe calls for a purchased pancake mix. For this recipe (and any recipe in this book that does so), use a *standard* pancake mix, such as Bisquick Pancake and Waffle Mix or even a store brand. Do *not* use a biscuit mix. And do not use a buttermilk, sugar-free, or gluten-free mix. (Gluten-free pancake bites can be found on page 52.) Some pancake mixes do include animal fats. Read the label carefully, if this is a concern.

1. Pour the water into the insert set in a **5-, 6-, or 8-quart Instant Pot.** Set a pressure-safe rack or trivet in the insert. Lightly coat the seven indentations of an egg-bite mold with baking spray. (For more information about these molds, see page 15.)

2. Stir the sugar and cinnamon together in a small bowl, then divide this mixture evenly among the indentations, sprinkling it to get on the sides of each and shaking the mold so that the sugar coats each interior surface evenly. Turn the mold over and gently tap out any excess sugar mixture.

3. Whisk the pancake mix, milk, oil, and vanilla in a medium bowl until smooth. Divide this mixture among the prepared indentations, taking care to spoon it in gently so as not to dislodge the sugar mixture.

4. Lay the silicone lid or a piece of aluminum foil loosely over the mold, covering it without sealing the lid or the foil to the mold. Set the mold on the rack and lock the lid on the pot.

5.

	Set pot for	Set level to	Valve must be	Set time for	If needed, press
For *all* pots	PRESSURE COOK or MANUAL	HIGH	Closed	15 minutes with the KEEP WARM setting off	START

6. When the pot has finished cooking, use the **quick-release method** to bring the pressure back to normal. Unlatch the lid and open the pot. Use hot pads or silicone baking mitts to transfer the (hot!) egg-bite mold to a nearby wire rack. Uncover and cool for 5 minutes before unmolding the pancake bites onto plates or a serving platter.

Other Pots

- For a 3-quart Instant Pot, you *must* decrease the amount of water in the insert to 1 cup and you *must* use two, four-indentation egg-bite molds specifically made for this smaller model. You *must* then stack the molds on top of each other in the insert. If you fill all eight indentations, the individual bites will be slightly smaller than those made in a seven-indentation mold.

- For a 6- or 8-quart Instant Pot, you *can* double almost all of the ingredient amounts *except* you *must* use the stated 1½ cups water in the insert. You *must* then use *two* egg-bite molds, one stacked on top of the other in the insert so that the indentations of the top mold sit on the walls of the bottom mold, not into the bottom indentations themselves (except for the center indentation of the top mold which will now hover above the center indentation below).

- For a 10-quart Instant Pot, you *must* increase the amount of water in the insert to 2½ cups. You *can* either complete the recipe as stated or you *can* double the other ingredient amounts, in which case you *must* use two egg-bite molds, stacking them as directed above for the 6- or 8-quart pots.

Beyond

- Substitute plain oat milk, unsweetened plain almond milk, or unsweetened plain soy milk for the dairy milk.

- Split these pancake bites in half lengthwise and serve them with butter and maple syrup—or even butter and honey.

See photo in insert.

Apple Fritter Pancake-Mix Bites

7 ingredients

7 pancake bites

METHOD:
egg bites

SPECIAL EQUIPMENT:
one seven-indentation egg-bite mold and a pressure-safe rack or trivet

TIME UNDER PRESSURE:
15 minutes

PRESSURE:
high

RELEASE:
modified natural

TOTAL TIME WITH PRESSURE:
about 25 minutes

CAN BE VEGETARIAN

1½ cups water

Baking spray

1 cup regular pancake mix (vegetarian, if necessary—for more information, see the headnote to Cinnamon-Sugar Pancake-Mix Bites on page 44)

½ cup canned apple pie filling with the apple slices cut into smaller bits

⅓ cup whole, low-fat, or fat-free milk

1 large egg, *at room temperature*

1 tablespoon vegetable, canola, or other neutral-flavored oil

These pancake bites are made with canned apple pie filling, a super-fast way to make a (sort of) apple fritter. There's only one problem: Canned apple slices can be too big and will poke up out of the egg-bite molds. To remedy this, open the can and use kitchen shears or a paring knife to cut the slices into smaller bits right in the can (watch out for any sharp edges!) so you can get bits of apple evenly distributed in the batter.

Since these pancake bites have egg in the mix and are thus a little denser than some of the other pancake bites in this chapter, we let them sit in the machine for a few minutes before releasing the pressure, giving them a little time to firm up.

1. Pour the water into the insert set in a **5-, 6-, or 8-quart Instant Pot.** Set a pressure-safe rack or trivet in the insert. Lightly coat the seven indentations of an egg-bite mold with baking spray. (For more information on these molds, see page 15.)

2. Stir the pancake mix, apple pie filling, milk, egg, and oil in a large bowl until smooth. Divide this mixture among the prepared indentations. Lay the silicone lid or a piece of aluminum foil loosely over the mold, covering it without sealing the lid or the foil to the mold. Set the mold on the rack and lock the lid on the pot.

Beyond

- Substitute plain oat milk, unsweetened plain almond milk, or unsweetened plain soy milk for the dairy milk.

- Serve these little bites with maple syrup for dipping.

- Or slice them in half lengthwise and top with sweetened cream cheese or sweetened mascarpone cheese.

3.

	Set pot for	Set level to	Valve must be	Set time for	If needed, press
For *all* pots	PRESSURE COOK or MANUAL	HIGH	Closed	15 minutes with the KEEP WARM setting off	START

4. When the pot has finished cooking, turn it off and let the pressure **return to normal naturally for 3 minutes**. Then use the **quick-release method** to remove any residual pressure before unlatching the lid and opening the pot. Use hot pads or silicone baking mitts to transfer the (hot!) egg-bite mold to a nearby wire rack. Uncover and cool for 5 minutes before unmolding the pancake bites onto plates or a serving platter.

Other Pots

- For a 3-quart Instant Pot, you *must* decrease the amount of water in the insert to 1 cup and you *must* use two, four-indentation egg-bite molds specifically made for this smaller model. You *must* then stack the molds on top of each other in the insert. If you fill all eight indentations, the individual bites will be slightly smaller than those made in a seven-indentation mold.

- For a 6- or 8-quart Instant Pot, you *can* double almost all of the ingredient amounts *except* you *must* use the stated 1½ cups water in the insert. You *must* then use *two* egg-bite molds, one stacked on top of the other in the insert so that the indentations of the top mold sit on walls of the bottom mold, not into the bottom indentations themselves (except for the center indentation of the top mold which will now hover above the center indentation below).

- For a 10-quart Instant Pot, you *must* increase the amount of water in the insert to 2½ cups. You *can* either complete the recipe as stated or you *can* double the other ingredient amounts, in which case you *must* use two egg-bite molds, stacking them as directed above for the 6- or 8-quart pots.

Cinnamon-Roll Pull-Apart Bread

6 ingredients

6 SERVINGS

METHOD:
pot-in-pot

SPECIAL
EQUIPMENT:
a 7-inch-round
springform pan
and a pressure-safe
rack or trivet

PRESSURE:
max or high

TIME UNDER
PRESSURE:
16 or 20 minutes

RELEASE:
modified natural

TOTAL TIME WITH
PRESSURE:
about 45 minutes

CAN BE
VEGETARIAN

1½ cups water

Baking spray

One 17½-ounce can cinnamon rolls that includes a small container of icing (vegetarian, if necessary)

2 tablespoons butter, melted (no need to cool)

½ cup chopped pecans

2 tablespoons honey

Breakfast? Brunch? Okay, if you insist. But we'll confess this decadent, sweet, pull-apart bread has been a midnight splurge in our house more than once. Better yet, because time is of the essence in the small hours, the recipe is super fast, thanks to canned cinnamon rolls and a trusty Instant Pot. But one warning: The cake is quite hot out of the cooker. It will need to cool for at least 10 minutes before you chow down.

Some canned cinnamon rolls are made with animal fats. Read the label, if this is a concern.

1. Pour the water into the insert set in a **5-, 6-, or 8-quart Instant Pot.** Set a pressure-safe rack or trivet in the insert. Coat the inside of a 7-inch-round springform pan with baking spray.

2. Open the can of cinnamon rolls and set the icing container aside. Cut the cinnamon rolls into quarters. Toss these in a medium bowl with the butter and about half of the chopped pecans. (Eyeball it.) Pile this mixture loosely into the prepared pan. Top with the remaining nuts and drizzle evenly with the honey.

3. Set the springform pan on the rack. Lay a paper towel loosely over the top of the pan and lock the lid on the pot.

4.

	Set pot for	Set level to	Valve must be	Set time for	If needed, press
For Max pots only	PRESSURE COOK	MAX	—	16 minutes with the KEEP WARM setting off	START
For all other pots	PRESSURE COOK or MANUAL	HIGH	Closed	20 minutes with the KEEP WARM setting off	START

5. When the pot has finished cooking, turn it off and let the pressure **return to normal naturally for 10 minutes.** Then use the **quick-release method** to get rid of any residual pressure in the pot. Unlatch the lid and open the cooker. Use hot pads or silicone baking mitts to transfer the (hot!) pan to a wire rack. Remove the paper towel and cool for 10 minutes.

6. If the icing in the container has solidified, uncover it (removing any metal rims, too) and microwave on high for 5 seconds to loosen it up. Unlatch the springform pan and remove its ring side. Drizzle the icing over the cake before serving.

Other Pots

- Because of the size of the pan and the number of cinnamon rolls in a can, this recipe cannot be efficiently sized for a 3-quart Instant Pot.

- For a 10-quart Instant Pot, you *must* increase the amount of water in the insert to 2½ cups while otherwise completing the recipe as stated.

Beyond

- Substitute any nut you like: walnuts, hazelnuts, almonds, or even peanuts (which, yes, are not technically nuts).

- If you want to make your own icing, mix about 2 teaspoons fresh lemon juice into 1 cup confectioners' sugar, then add more juice in dribs and drabs until you have an icing that can be drizzled from the tines of a fork but still holds its shape.

- There's a how-to video for this recipe on our YouTube channel, Cooking with Bruce and Mark.

Banana-Walnut Pancake-Mix Bites

7 ingredients

7 pancake bites

METHOD:
egg bites

SPECIAL EQUIPMENT:
one seven-indentation egg-bite mold and a pressure-safe rack or trivet

PRESSURE:
high

TIME UNDER PRESSURE:
12 minutes

RELEASE:
quick

TOTAL TIME WITH PRESSURE:
about 25 minutes

CAN BE VEGETARIAN

1½ cups water

Baking spray

¾ cup regular pancake mix (vegetarian, if necessary—for more information, see the headnote to Cinnamon-Sugar Pancake-Mix Bites on page 44)

7 tablespoons whole, low-fat, or fat-free milk

¼ teaspoon ground cinnamon

½ cup diced peeled banana (about half a medium banana)

¼ cup chopped walnuts

Other Pots

- For a 3-quart Instant Pot, you *must* decrease the amount of water in the insert to 1 cup and you *must* use two, four-indentation egg-bite molds specifically made for this smaller model. You *must* then stack the molds on top of each other in the insert. If you fill all eight indentations, the individual bites will be slightly smaller than those made in a seven-indentation mold.

- For a 6- or 8-quart Instant Pot, you can double almost all of the ingredient amounts *except* you *must* use the stated 1½ cups water in the insert. You *must* then use *two* egg-bite molds, one stacked on top of the other in the insert so that the indentations of the top mold sit on walls of the bottom mold, not into the bottom indentations themselves.

- For a 10-quart Instant Pot, you *must* increase the amount of water in the insert to 2½ cups. You *can* either complete the recipe as stated or you *can* double the other ingredient amounts, in which case you *must* use two egg-bite molds, stacking them as directed above.

If, like us, you love banana bread but are ready to branch out beyond the classic loaf, you've come to the right recipe! Don't be tempted to overstock the batter with banana. The bites won't cook evenly.

Here's a hack we discovered while we were testing recipes for all of these pancake bites: The easiest way to get batter into an egg-bite mold is with an ice-cream scoop.

1. Pour the water into the insert set in a **5-, 6-, or 8-quart Instant Pot.** Set a pressure-safe rack or trivet in the insert. Lightly coat the seven indentations of an egg-bite mold with baking spray. (For more information on these molds, see page 15.)

2. Whisk the pancake mix, milk, and cinnamon in a large bowl until smooth. Stir in the banana and walnut bits. Divide this mixture evenly among the prepared indentations. Lay the silicone lid or a piece of aluminum foil loosely over the mold, covering it without sealing the lid or the foil to the mold. Set the mold on the rack and lock the lid on the pot.

3.

	Set pot for	Set level to	Valve must be	Set time for	If needed, press
For *all* pots	PRESSURE COOK or MANUAL	HIGH	Closed	12 minutes with the KEEP WARM setting off	START

4. When the pot has finished cooking, use the **quick-release method** to bring the pressure back to normal. Unlatch the lid and open the pot. Use hot pads or silicone baking mitts to transfer the (hot!) egg-bite mold to a nearby wire rack. Uncover and cool for 5 minutes before unmolding the pancake bites onto plates or a serving platter.

Beyond

- Substitute plain oat milk, unsweetened plain almond milk, or unsweetened plain soy milk for the dairy milk.

- These *need* to be sliced open and smeared with a little peanut butter and jelly.

Hasty Pudding Pancake Bites

11 ingredients

7 pancake bites

METHOD:
egg bites

SPECIAL
EQUIPMENT:
one seven-
indentation egg-
bite mold and a
pressure-safe rack
or trivet

PRESSURE:
high

TIME UNDER
PRESSURE:
12 minutes

RELEASE:
quick

TOTAL TIME WITH
PRESSURE:
about 25 minutes

VEGETARIAN

1½ cups water

Baking spray

⅔ cup cornflake crumbs

¼ cup almond *meal* or finely ground almonds (do not use almond flour)

¼ cup packed light brown sugar

1 teaspoon baking powder

¼ teaspoon ground cinnamon

¼ teaspoon table salt

2 large eggs, *at room temperature*

3 tablespoons whole, low-fat, or fat-free milk

1 teaspoon vanilla extract

These pancake bites have the flavor and consistency of corn pudding, not the Thanksgiving side dish, but the old-fashioned American dessert. Our recipe calls for purchased cornflake crumbs and almond meal (that is, ground almonds that are not as fine as flour—look for it in the health-food section of your supermarket). However, you can make both yourself by grinding first 1¼ cups cornflakes and then ⅓ cup slivered almonds in a food processor, each until the mixture is like fine sand, not powdery. Unfortunately, this recipe does not work with gluten-free cornflakes.

1. Pour the water into the insert set in a **5-, 6-, or 8-quart Instant Pot.** Set a pressure-safe rack or trivet in the insert. Lightly coat the seven indentations of an egg-bite mold with baking spray. (For more information on these molds, see page 15.)

2. Stir the cornflake crumbs, almond meal, brown sugar, baking powder, cinnamon, and salt in a large bowl until uniform. Whisk in the eggs, milk, and vanilla until very smooth.

3. Divide this mixture evenly among the prepared indentations. Lay the silicone lid or a piece of aluminum foil loosely over the mold, covering it without sealing the lid or the foil to the mold. Set the mold on the rack and lock the lid on the pot.

4.

	Set pot for	Set level to	Valve must be	Set time for	If needed, press
For *all* pots	PRESSURE COOK or MANUAL	HIGH	Closed	12 minutes with the KEEP WARM setting off	START

5. When the pot has finished cooking, use the **quick-release method** to bring the pressure back to normal. Unlatch the lid and open the pot.

6. Use hot pads or silicone baking mitts to transfer the (hot!) egg-bite mold to a nearby wire rack. Uncover and cool for 5 minutes before unmolding the pancake bites onto plates or a serving platter.

Other Pots

- For a 3-quart Instant Pot, you *must* decrease the amount of water in the insert to 1 cup and you *must* use two, four-indentation egg-bite molds specifically made for this smaller model. You *must* then stack the molds on top of each other in the insert. If you fill all eight indentations, the individual bites will be slightly smaller than those made in a seven-indentation mold.

- For a 6- or 8-quart Instant Pot, you *can* double almost all of the ingredient amounts *except* you *must* use the stated 1½ cups water in the insert. You *must* then use *two* egg-bite molds, one stacked on top of the other in the insert so that the indentations of the top mold sit on walls of the bottom mold, not into the bottom indentations themselves (except for the center indentation of the top mold which will now hover above the center indentation below).

- For a 10-quart Instant Pot, you *must* increase the amount of water in the insert to 2½ cups. You *can* either complete the recipe as stated or you *can* double the other ingredient amounts, in which case you *must* use two egg-bite molds, stacking them as directed above for the 6- or 8-quart pots.

Beyond

- Serve the pancake bites with sweetened vanilla yogurt.

- Or slice them up and use them to top a bowl of maple yogurt and fresh blueberries.

Gluten-Free Buttermilk Pancake-Mix Bites

7 ingredients

7 pancake bites

METHOD:
egg bites

SPECIAL EQUIPMENT:
one seven-indentation egg-bite mold and a pressure-safe rack or trivet

PRESSURE:
high

TIME UNDER PRESSURE:
10 minutes

RELEASE:
quick

TOTAL TIME WITH PRESSURE:
about 20 minutes

VEGETARIAN

GLUTEN-FREE

1½ cups water

Nonstick spray

1 cup gluten-free pancake mix (see the headnote for more information)

1 cup uncultured buttermilk (see page 17 for more information)

1 large egg, *at room temperature*

2 tablespoons butter, melted and cooled

½ teaspoon certified gluten-free vanilla extract

By using buttermilk with a gluten-free pancake mix, you can make some incredibly light, delicate pancake bites. For the best success, the gluten-free pancake mix should have rice flour as its base, not just one of its ingredients. In other words, make sure rice flour is at the top of the ingredient list. All the gluten-free pancake mixes we've found do not contain animal fats. However, if this is a concern, read the labels carefully.

Because these bites puff up so much, you cannot double the recipe in larger pots because you cannot stack the egg-bite molds on top of each other.

1. Pour the water into the insert set in a **5-, 6-, or 8-quart Instant Pot.** Set a pressure-safe rack or trivet in the insert. Generously coat the seven indentations of an egg-bite mold with nonstick spray. (For more information on these molds, see page 15.)

2. Whisk the pancake mix, buttermilk, egg, butter, and vanilla in a large bowl until smooth. Divide this mixture evenly among the egg-bite indentations. Do not cover. Set the mold on the rack and lock the lid on the pot.

3.

	Set pot for	Set level to	Valve must be	Set time for	If needed, press
For *all* pots	PRESSURE COOK or MANUAL	HIGH	Closed	10 minutes with the KEEP WARM setting off	START

4. When the pot has finished cooking, use the **quick-release method** to bring the pressure back to normal. Unlatch the lid and open the cooker. Use hot pads or silicone baking mitts to transfer the (hot!) mold to a wire rack. Cool for 2 to 3 minutes, then turn the bites out of the mold and serve hot.

Other Pots

- For a 3-quart Instant Pot, you must decrease the amount of water in the insert to 1 cup and you must work in two batches with a four-indentation egg-bite mold made for this smaller pot (thereby making seven bites in two batches). You cannot stack the molds in the pot because of the way the bites puff up.

- For a 10-quart Instant Pot, you *must* increase the amount of water in the insert to 2½ cups while otherwise completing the recipe as stated.

Beyond

- Although these bites get a little hard as they cool, you can soften them up by microwaving them on high for 10 or 15 seconds.

Gluten-Free Oatmeal–French Toast Bites

11 ingredients

7 French toast bites

METHOD:
egg bites

SPECIAL EQUIPMENT:
one seven-indentation egg-bite mold, a pressure-safe rack or trivet, and a standard blender

PRESSURE:
high

TIME UNDER PRESSURE:
10 minutes

RELEASE:
quick

TOTAL TIME WITH PRESSURE:
about 20 minutes

VEGETARIAN

GLUTEN-FREE

1½ cups water

Nonstick spray

3 large eggs, *at room temperature*

1 cup certified gluten-free plain *quick-cooking* oats

⅓ cup gluten-free pancake mix (see the headnote for Gluten-Free Buttermilk Pancake-Mix Bites on page 52 for more information)

⅓ cup maple syrup

2 tablespoons canola, vegetable, or other neutral-flavored oil

2 tablespoons whole, low-fat, or fat-free milk

2 tablespoons light brown sugar

½ teaspoon ground cinnamon

½ teaspoon table salt

These egg-rich pancake bites taste like French toast, especially if they're dipped in (or slathered with) maple syrup. Because the bites puff up under pressure, you cannot cover the molds—which means you can't double the recipe by stacking molds on top of each other. If you want to make a second batch, you can double the ingredients, then have a second egg-bite mold ready to go when the first one comes out of the pot.

1. Set a rack or pressure-safe trivet in the insert in a **5-, 6-, or 8-quart Instant Pot.** Pour the water into the insert. Generously coat the seven indentations of an egg-bite mold with nonstick spray. (For more information about these molds, see page 15.)

2. Put the eggs, oats, pancake mix, maple syrup, oil, milk, brown sugar, cinnamon, and salt in a blender. Cover and blend until the consistency is like a smoothie with bits of oats in it.

3. Divide this mixture among the indentations in the egg-bite mold. Do not cover. Set the mold on the rack and lock the lid on the pot.

4.

	Set pot for	Set level to	Valve must be	Set time for	If needed, press
For *all* pots	PRESSURE COOK or MANUAL	HIGH	Closed	10 minutes with the KEEP WARM setting off	START

5. When the pot has finished cooking, use the **quick-release method** to bring the pressure back to normal. Unlatch the lid and open the cooker. Use hot pads or silicone baking mitts to transfer the (hot!) mold to a wire rack. Cool for 2 to 3 minutes, then turn the bites out of the mold and serve hot.

Other Pots

- For a **3-quart Instant Pot**, you *must* decrease the amount of water in the insert to 1 cup and you *must* work in two batches with a four-indentation egg-bite mold made for this smaller pot (thereby making seven bites in two batches).

- For a **10-quart Instant Pot**, you *must* increase the amount of water in the insert to 2½ cups while otherwise completing the recipe as stated.

Beyond

- Serve the bites with more maple syrup. Either split them open, butter the cut sides, and drizzle them with syrup, or dip the larger bites right in a bowl of maple syrup.

- The bites will harden if they sit for more than 10 minutes at room temperature. To soften, microwave on HIGH for 10 or 15 seconds.

Gluten-Free Date-Nut Bread Bites

12 ingredients

7 quick-bread bites

METHOD:
egg bites

SPECIAL EQUIPMENT:
one seven-indentation egg-bite mold, a pressure-safe rack or trivet, and a standard blender

PRESSURE:
high

TIME UNDER PRESSURE:
10 minutes

RELEASE:
quick

TOTAL TIME WITH PRESSURE:
about 20 minutes

VEGETARIAN

GLUTEN-FREE

1½ cups water

Nonstick spray

¾ cup whole, low-fat, or fat-free milk

1 large egg, *at room temperature*

4 large soft pitted dates, preferably Medjool dates

2 tablespoons canola, vegetable, or other neutral-flavored oil

1 tablespoon granulated white sugar

½ teaspoon certified gluten-free vanilla extract

½ teaspoon table salt

¼ teaspoon ground cinnamon

3 tablespoons chopped walnuts

¾ cup gluten-free pancake mix (see the headnote for Gluten-Free Buttermilk Pancake-Mix Bites on page 52 for more information)

Other Pots

- For a **3-quart Instant Pot, you** *must* decrease the amount of water in the insert to 1 cup and you *must* work in two batches with a four-indentation egg-bite mold made for this smaller pot (thereby making seven bites in two batches).

- For a **10-quart Instant Pot, you** *must* increase the amount of water in the insert to 2½ cups while otherwise completing the recipe as stated.

Beyond

- Go beyond retro! Enjoy gluten-free date-nut bread with gluten-free cream cheese.

These pancake bites are reminiscent of date-nut bread, a 1970s favorite that *needs* a comeback. For this recipe, we prefer Medjool dates, which should be soft, large, and luxurious. Make sure the ones you have aren't dried out and hard. If so, soak them in a bowl of very hot water for 3 minutes to soften. By the way, you can store Medjools in a sealed bag in the freezer for up to 1 year (thaw before using here).

1. Pour the water into the insert set in a **5-, 6-, or 8-quart Instant Pot.** Put a pressure-safe rack or trivet in the insert. Generously coat the seven indentations of an egg-bite mold with nonstick spray. (For more information on these molds, see page 15.)

2. Put the milk, egg, dates, oil, sugar, vanilla, salt, and cinnamon in a blender. Cover and blend until the dates are smashed into a fairly smooth slurry. Add the nuts and pulse until chopped.

3. Pour the pancake mix into a large bowl. Pour the contents of the blender canister over the mix. Stir until well blended. Divide this mixture among the prepared indentations in the egg-bite mold. Do not cover. Set the molds on the rack and lock the lid on the pot.

4.

	Set pot for	Set level to	Valve must be	Set time for	If needed, press
For *all* pots	PRESSURE COOK or MANUAL	HIGH	Closed	10 minutes with the KEEP WARM setting off	START

5. When the pot has finished cooking, use the **quick-release method** to bring the pressure back to normal. Unlatch the lid and open the cooker. Use hot pads or silicone baking mitts to transfer the (hot!) mold to a wire rack. Cool for 2 to 3 minutes, then turn the bites out of the mold and serve hot.

Blueberry Pancake-Mix Cake

7 ingredients	SPECIAL EQUIPMENT: a 7-inch-round springform pan and a pressure-safe rack or trivet	TIME UNDER PRESSURE: 40 minutes	TOTAL TIME WITH PRESSURE: about 1 hour 10 minutes
4–6 SERVINGS			
METHOD: pot-in-pot		RELEASE: natural	CAN BE VEGAN
	PRESSURE: high		

3 cups water

Baking spray

2 cups regular pancake mix (vegan, if necessary—for more information on the best type of mix, see the headnote to Cinnamon-Sugar Pancake-Mix Bites on page 44)

¼ cup vegetable, canola, or other neutral-flavored oil

1 teaspoon vanilla extract

½ teaspoon ground cinnamon

1 cup *fresh* blueberries (do not use frozen, even if thawed)

Other Pots

- Because of the size of the pan and complicated baking ratios, this recipe is not easily adapted for a 3-quart Instant Pot.

- For a 10-quart Instant Pot, you *must* increase the amount of water in the insert to 2½ cups while otherwise completing the recipe as stated (including using the stated 1½ cups water in the batter).

Beyond

- For a richer cake, substitute 1½ cups whole milk for the water *in the batter.*

- Put canned blueberry pie filling in a microwave-safe bowl and warm in a microwave on HIGH in 10-second bursts, stirring after each. Spread the filling on a plate and set a slice of cake on top. Dust with confectioners' sugar to go all out.

Think of this breakfast cake as an Instant Pot coffee cake made with pancake mix. While it might be tempting to make the cake the night before and save it for breakfast, the consistency turns gummy once the cake cools. (All that steam in the pot has to go somewhere— unfortunately, right into the cake's crumb!)

We kept the cake from being cloying by letting the sugar in the pancake mix handle the sweetening. The cake slices can then handle a drizzle of maple syrup or a slather of strawberry jam.

1. Pour 1½ cups water into the insert set in a **5-, 6-, or 8-quart Instant Pot.** Set a pressure-safe rack or trivet in the insert. Lightly coat the inside of a 7-inch springform pan with baking spray, taking care to get the spray mixture along the seam between the sides and bottom of the pan.

2. Whisk the pancake mix, oil, vanilla, cinnamon, and the remaining 1½ cups water in a large bowl until very smooth. Add the blueberries. To avoid mashing them, fold them in with a rubber spatula.

3. Pour the batter into the prepared pan; smooth the top with the spatula. Do not cover the pan. Put it on the rack and lock the lid on the pot.

4.

	Set pot for	Set level to	Valve must be	Set time for	If needed, press
For *all* pots	PRESSURE COOK or MANUAL	HIGH	Closed	40 minutes with the KEEP WARM setting off	START

5. When the pot has finished cooking, turn it off and let the pressure **return to normal naturally,** about 12 minutes. Unlatch the lid and open the pot. Use hot pads or baking mitts to transfer the (hot!) springform pan to a nearby wire rack. Cool for 15 minutes, then unlatch the pan's ring side and remove it. Cut the cake into wedges to serve.

See photo in insert.

Pecan-Buttermilk Pancake-Mix Cake

7 ingredients

4–6 SERVINGS

METHOD:
pot-in-pot

SPECIAL
EQUIPMENT:
a 7-inch-round
springform pan
and a pressure-
safe rack or trivet

PRESSURE:
high

TIME UNDER
PRESSURE:
40 minutes

RELEASE:
natural

TOTAL TIME WITH
PRESSURE:
about 1 hour 10
minutes

CAN BE
VEGETARIAN

1½ cups water

Baking spray

2 cups regular pancake mix (vegetarian, if necessary—for more information on the best type of mix, see the headnote to Cinnamon-Sugar Pancake-Mix Bites on page 44)

1 cup finely chopped pecans

2 tablespoons light brown sugar

1½ cups uncultured buttermilk (see page 17 for more information)

2 tablespoons vegetable, canola, or other neutral-flavored oil

Although this flavorful if rather simple cake with a delicate crumb can be a breakfast treat, it would also be welcome with a cup of tea in the afternoon. Or you could serve it for dessert after a barbecue, topping the slices with ice cream and chocolate sauce. Pecans can go rancid. Smell yours to make sure they're sweet, not acrid or musty. Store pecans in a sealed plastic bag in the refrigerator for up to 2 months or in the freezer for up to 1 year.

1. Pour the water into the insert of a **5-, 6-, or 8-quart Instant Pot.** Set a pressure-safe rack or trivet in the insert. Lightly coat the inside of a 7-inch-round springform pan with baking spray, taking care to get the spray mixture along the seam between the sides and bottom of the pan.

2. Whisk the pancake mix, pecans, and brown sugar in a large bowl until uniform. Whisk in the buttermilk and oil until smooth.

3. Pour the batter into the prepared pan; smooth the top with a rubber spatula. Do not cover the pan. Put the pan on the rack and lock the lid on the pot.

4.

	Set pot for	Set level to	Valve must be	Set time for	If needed, press
For *all* pots	PRESSURE COOK or MANUAL	HIGH	Closed	40 minutes with the KEEP WARM setting off	START

5. When the pot has finished cooking, turn it off and let the pressure **return to normal naturally,** about 12 minutes. Unlatch the lid and open the pot. Use hot pads or baking mitts to transfer the springform pan to a wire rack. Cool for 15 minutes, then unlatch the pan's ring side and remove it. Cut the cake into wedges to serve.

Other Pots

- Because of the size of the pan and complicated baking ratios, this recipe is not easily adapted for a 3-quart Instant Pot.

- For a 10-quart Instant Pot, you *must* increase the amount of water in the insert to 2½ cups while otherwise completing the recipe as stated.

Beyond

- Slice the cake into wedges, then cut these into smaller pieces. Make a trifle by layering them in a glass serving bowl with sweetened whipped cream, sliced fresh strawberries, fresh raspberries, and perhaps caramel sauce. If you really want to go all out, add a layer of vanilla pudding to the trifle.

Cranberry-Orange Pancake-Mix Cake

8 ingredients	**SPECIAL EQUIPMENT:** a 7-inch-round springform pan and a pressure-safe rack or trivet	**PRESSURE:** high	**TOTAL TIME WITH PRESSURE:** about 1 hour 10 minutes
4–6 SERVINGS		**TIME UNDER PRESSURE:** 40 minutes	**CAN BE VEGAN**
METHOD: pot-in-pot		**RELEASE:** natural	

2½ cups water

Baking spray

2 cups regular pancake mix (vegan, if necessary—for more information on the best type of mix, see the headnote to Cinnamon-Sugar Pancake-Mix Bites on page 44)

½ cup orange juice (fresh, canned, or made-from-frozen-concentrate)

2 tablespoons vegetable, canola, or other neutral-flavored oil

1 teaspoon vanilla extract

¾ cup fresh cranberries, roughly chopped

½ cup sliced almonds

Cranberry and orange create a combination of sweet and tart that is nearly impossible to beat. However, cranberries can be hard to track down in the spring and summer. When you see packages in the fall or winter, buy several to squirrel away in your freezer. You'll then need to thaw them for this recipe because they're almost impossible to chop when frozen. Yep, we really have thought of everything.

1. Pour 1½ cups water into the insert set in a **5-, 6-, or 8-quart Instant Pot.** Set a pressure-safe rack or trivet in the insert. Lightly coat the inside of a 7-inch springform pan with baking spray, taking care to get the spray mixture along the seam between the sides and bottom of the pan.

2. Whisk the pancake mix, orange juice, oil, vanilla extract, and the remaining 1 cup water in a large bowl until smooth. Use a rubber spatula to fold in the cranberries and almonds. Pour the batter into the prepared pan; smooth the top. Do not cover the pan. Put it on the rack or trivet and lock the lid on the pot.

3.

	Set pot for	Set level to	Valve must be	Set time for	If needed, press
For *all* pots	PRESSURE COOK or MANUAL	HIGH	Closed	40 minutes with the KEEP WARM setting off	START

4. When the pot has finished cooking, turn it off and let the pressure **return to normal naturally,** about 12 minutes. Unlatch the lid and open the pot. Use hot pads or baking mitts to transfer the (hot!) springform pan to a nearby wire rack. Cool for 15 minutes, then unlatch the pan's ring side and remove it. Cut the cake into wedges to serve.

Other Pots

- Because of the size of the pan and ingredient ratios, this recipe is not easily adapted for a 3-quart Instant Pot.

- For a 10-quart Instant Pot, you *must* use 2½ cups water in the insert while otherwise completing the recipe as stated (including using 1 cup of water in the batter).

Beyond

- For a spiced cranberry cake, whisk in 1 teaspoon ground cinnamon, ½ teaspoon ground allspice, ½ teaspoon ground ginger, and ¼ teaspoon grated nutmeg with the dry ingredients. Or simply use 1½ teaspoons apple pie or pumpkin pie spice blend (your choice).

2

Soup

Kenny Bania once said the fateful words, "Soup is not a meal," denying Jerry Seinfeld's attempt to settle his debt and even the score. Problem is, Kenny didn't know about these soups. They're not prissy starters. We've filled the pot with dinner. Even our Cream of Asparagus Soup can be a meal (with crunchy bread on the side, of course).

We start with these basics, three "cream of" soups. They're made pot-in-pot so 1) we can use cream without its curdling, and 2) we don't have to resort to a late-stage thickening that can result in lumps and clumps. Frankly, these are some of the most luscious soups we've ever crafted for a pressure cooker.

Then we move through some simpler soups to a few copycat recipes (or if we can be so bold, some better-than-the-original recipes). After those, we end up with chowders and even an IP take on a regional classic, Frogmore Soup. All of these can be stand-out weeknight dinners, even when you're too tired to do much more than plug in the pot.

But before all that, a little advice: Soup is all about its broth. In fact, soup is *mostly* broth with added ingredients. Don't waste your efforts or your time with watery, overly salty varieties.

We wouldn't be professional food writers if we didn't encourage you to make stock from scratch. If you're interested, we have some great recipes in the original *Instant Pot Bible*. If you make a potful, you can freeze it in small containers. Even ½ cup of homemade stock, added with whatever canned or boxed broth you use, will improve these recipes' already-good results.

But you don't have to go all out. If you want to up your cooking game, spend a few dollars and buy several canned and boxed broths from the supermarket. Open and taste them, right at room temperature. You'll immediately figure out which one tastes like the ocean, which one smells like a bag of moldy onions, and which one has all the heft of air. More importantly, you'll figure out which is the best according to your taste.

Many of these recipes yield soups that freeze well. Make a batch of soup, then freeze the leftovers in sealed containers for that moment when you need a fast meal. However, soups with grains in the mix can tighten up when frozen and thawed (and sometimes, even when stored in the fridge). They'll need extra broth to even out the texture when reheated. And soups with thickeners (flour, cornstarch, potato starch, or masa harina) or those that include pasta suffer too much when frozen and thawed. If you're cooking for one or two, share some with your neighbor!

Several of these recipes call for dicing vegetables and proteins. No doubt about it, doing so increases the prep time. But smaller bits of ingredients are preferable in a pressure-cooker soup because...

1. The pressure extracts more flavor more quickly from these bits.
2. The smaller bits cook more evenly.
3. You'll be able to get more bits in every spoonful.

And more in every spoonful is just about the whole reason everyone but Kenny Bania *knows* that soup is indeed a meal.

Midwestern Fix-It

10 ingredients

3–4 SERVINGS

METHOD:
pot-in-pot

SPECIAL
EQUIPMENT:
a 2-quart, 7-inch-round, high-sided, pressure-safe baking or soufflé dish and a pressure-safe rack or trivet

PRESSURE:
high

TIME UNDER
PRESSURE:
30 minutes

RELEASE:
quick

TOTAL TIME WITH
PRESSURE:
about 45 minutes

CAN BE
VEGETARIAN

1½ cups water

10 ounces whole white mushrooms, brushed clean

1 cup chicken or vegetable broth

1 cup heavy cream

¼ cup all-purpose flour (dip and level—do not pack)

1 teaspoon dried thyme

½ teaspoon onion powder

½ teaspoon garlic powder

½ teaspoon table salt

½ teaspoon ground black pepper

Other Pots

- For a 3-quart Instant Pot, you *must* halve almost all of the ingredient amounts *except* you *must* use 1 cup water in the insert. You *must* also use a 1-quart, 6-inch-round, high-sided, pressure-safe baking or soufflé dish.

- For a 10-quart Instant Pot, you *must* use 2½ cups water in the insert while otherwise completing the recipe as stated.

Beyond

- For a fancier soup, add 2 tablespoons dry sherry and ¼ teaspoon grated nutmeg with the broth.

- Go all out with exotic mushrooms. Hen of the woods or shiitake caps would make a sophisticated soup (which will not be creamy beige but darker brown).

You may know it as cream of mushroom soup. We know it as Midwestern Fix-It. Either way, it's so much more than just a pantry staple for casseroles. It's an unbelievably delicious meal on its own.

Truth be told, there are lots of recipes out there for cream of mushroom soup from an Instant Pot. More truth be told, they're mostly misguided. They involve making a soup right in the insert, then thickening the soup *after* cooking—which results in a gloppy mess with an unpleasant, raw-cream flavor. Many use too much cornstarch or potato starch, giving the servings a gelatinous (aka ick) quality. To solve these problems, we use the pot-in-pot method so that these extra steps are unnecessary. Plus, we cook flour right in the soup from the get-go for the creamiest spoonfuls.

1. Pour the water into the insert set in a **5-, 6-, or 8-quart Instant Pot.** Set a pressure-safe rack or trivet in the insert.

2. Roughly chop about half of the mushrooms and set them aside. Finely chop the remainder and set them aside as well.

3. Whisk the broth, cream, flour, thyme, onion powder, garlic powder, salt, and pepper in a 2-quart, 7-inch-round, high-sided, pressure-safe baking or soufflé dish until the flour dissolves. Stir in both sets of mushrooms. Do not cover the dish. Set it on the rack and lock the lid on the pot.

4.

	Set pot for	Set level to	Valve must be	Set time for	If needed, press
For *all* pots	PRESSURE COOK or MANUAL	HIGH	Closed	30 minutes with the KEEP WARM setting off	START

5. When the pot has finished cooking, use the **quick-release method** to bring the pressure back to normal. Unlatch the lid and open the pot. Whisk the soup to blend until smooth. Use hot pads or silicone baking mitts to transfer the (hot!) baking dish to a nearby wire rack. Cool for a couple of minutes but serve hot.

Cream of Chicken Soup

12 ingredients

3–4 SERVINGS

METHOD:
pot-in-pot

SPECIAL EQUIPMENT:
a 2-quart, 7-inch-round, high-sided, pressure-safe baking or soufflé dish and a pressure-safe rack or trivet

PRESSURE:
high

TIME UNDER PRESSURE:
30 minutes

RELEASE:
quick

TOTAL TIME WITH PRESSURE:
about 45 minutes

1½ cups water

2½ cups chicken broth

1 cup heavy cream

2 tablespoons all-purpose flour

2 tablespoons cornstarch or potato starch

½ teaspoon ground or rubbed sage

½ teaspoon celery seeds

½ teaspoon onion powder

½ teaspoon garlic powder

½ teaspoon table salt

½ teaspoon ground black pepper

8 ounces boneless skinless chicken breasts or thighs, diced (¼- to ½-inch pieces)

Feeling under the weather? This super-creamy soup might not solve the problem, but it'll probably make you feel better. Use either dark- or white-meat chicken: Dark gives the soup a richer flavor; white, a (somewhat) lighter feel.

The pot-in-pot method ensures that the soup isn't gloppy from too much thickener. However, we do add a little extra starch here because the chicken gives off so much liquid and it's impossible to thicken the mixture with flour alone.

1. Pour the water into the insert set in a **5-, 6-, or 8-quart Instant Pot.** Set a pressure-safe rack or trivet in the insert.

2. Whisk the broth, cream, flour, cornstarch or potato starch, sage, celery seeds, onion powder, garlic powder, salt, and pepper in a 2-quart, 7-inch-round, high-sided, pressure-safe baking or soufflé dish until the flour dissolves. Stir in the chicken. Do not cover. Set the baking dish on the rack and lock the lid on the pot.

3.

	Set pot for	Set level to	Valve must be	Set time for	If needed, press
For *all* pots	PRESSURE COOK or MANUAL	HIGH	Closed	30 minutes with the KEEP WARM setting off	START

4. When the pot has finished cooking, use the **quick-release method** to bring the pressure back to normal. Unlatch the lid and open the pot. Whisk the soup to blend until smooth. Use hot pads or silicone baking mitts to transfer the (hot!) baking dish to a nearby wire rack. Cool for a couple of minutes but serve hot.

Other Pots

- For a 3-quart Instant Pot, you *must* halve almost all of the ingredient amounts *except* you *must* use 1 cup water in the insert. You *must* also use a 1-quart, 6-inch-round, high-sided, pressure-safe baking or soufflé dish.

- For a 10-quart Instant Pot, you *must* use 2½ cups water in the insert while otherwise completing the recipe as stated.

Beyond

- Ladle the soup over bowls of cooked, drained, and buttered noodles, then garnish with minced fresh dill fronds or even dried dill.

Cream of Asparagus Soup

11 ingredients

3–4 SERVINGS

METHOD:
pot-in-pot

SPECIAL EQUIPMENT:
a 2-quart, 7-inch-round, high-sided, pressure-safe baking or soufflé dish and a pressure-safe rack or trivet

PRESSURE:
high

TIME UNDER PRESSURE:
30 minutes

RELEASE:
quick

TOTAL TIME WITH PRESSURE:
about 45 minutes

CAN BE VEGETARIAN

1½ cups water

1 cup chicken or vegetable broth

1 cup heavy cream

1 cup whole milk (do not use low-fat or fat-free)

¼ cup all-purpose flour (dip and level—do not pack)

2 tablespoons minced chives or the green part of a scallion

½ teaspoon celery seeds

½ teaspoon garlic powder

½ teaspoon table salt

½ teaspoon ground black pepper

12 ounces pencil-thin asparagus spears, cut into ¼-inch segments

Asparagus used to be a spring treat. These days, it's available year-round—although not always of the best quality in the winter. This soup will fit the bill any time of year, giving you a creamy, light soup that can put you in a spring mood even in January.

For the best results, choose thin asparagus spears. If you can only find fat spears, discard the woody ends, then halve or even quarter the spears lengthwise before slicing them into ¼-inch segments. FYI, if you're cutting down larger spears, you'll need 12 ounces of *trimmed* spears.

1. Pour the water into the insert set in a **5-, 6-, or 8-quart Instant Pot.** Set a pressure-safe rack or trivet in the insert.

2. Whisk the broth, cream, milk, flour, chives, celery seeds, garlic powder, salt, and pepper in a 2-quart, 7-inch-round, high-sided, pressure-safe baking or soufflé dish until the flour dissolves. Stir in the asparagus bits. Do not cover the dish. Set it on the rack and lock the lid on the pot.

3.

	Set pot for	Set level to	Valve must be	Set time for	If needed, press
For *all* pots	PRESSURE COOK or MANUAL	HIGH	Closed	30 minutes with the KEEP WARM setting off	START

4. When the pot has finished cooking, use the **quick-release method** to bring the pressure back to normal. Unlatch the lid and open the pot. Whisk the soup to blend smoothly. Use hot pads or silicone baking mitts to transfer the (hot!) baking dish to a nearby wire rack. Cool for a couple of minutes but serve hot.

Other Pots

- For a 3-quart Instant Pot, you *must* halve almost all of the ingredient amounts *except* you *must* use 1 cup water in the insert. You *must* also use a 1-quart, 6-inch-round, high-sided, pressure-safe baking or soufflé dish.

- For a 10-quart Instant Pot, you *must* use 2½ cups water in the insert while otherwise completing the recipe as stated.

Beyond

- Garnish servings with stemmed, fresh thyme leaves.

- And/or crumbled crisp bacon.

- And/or crumbled blue cheese.

Buttery Carrot-Ginger Soup

6 ingredients

4–6 SERVINGS

METHOD:
standard

SPECIAL EQUIPMENT:
an immersion or standard blender

PRESSURE:
max or high

TIME UNDER PRESSURE:
12 or 15 minutes

RELEASE:
quick

TOTAL TIME WITH PRESSURE:
about 25 minutes

CAN BE VEGETARIAN

GLUTEN-FREE

1 stick (8 tablespoons or ½ cup) butter

½ teaspoon baking soda

1½ pounds carrots, peeled and cut into 2-inch pieces, any large bottom pieces halved lengthwise

¼ cup chopped candied or crystallized ginger

½ teaspoon table salt

3 cups chicken or vegetable broth

Other Pots

- For a 3-quart Instant Pot, you *must* halve all of the ingredient amounts but you *must* use ½ cup broth as stated in step 2 (thereby using 1 cup broth in step 5).

- For an 8-quart Instant Pot, you *must* increase all of the ingredient amounts by 50 percent.

- For a 10-quart Instant Pot, you *must* double all of the ingredient amounts.

Beyond

- If you want more ginger flavor, add up to ½ teaspoon ground ginger with the candied or crystallized ginger.

- Here's another great soup for bread bowls (see the Beyond with Not-Really-Panera-Bread's Summer Corn Chowder for more information, page 66).

- Garnish bowlfuls with pickled sushi ginger.

Get this: Carrots are braised in butter, then pureed into a soup with candied ginger for a delicately sweet-yet-spicy finish. We first learned about this braising-in-butter-and-baking-soda trick from culinary wizard Nathan Myrvhold's *Modernist Cuisine*. It's such an amazing bit of kitchen wizardry that we used it extensively in the original *Instant Pot Bible*. Here's how it works: The baking soda changes the pH of the mixture, which then keeps the milk solids in the butter from browning and burning as they normally would under pressure against the insert's hot surface. Voilà: butter as a braising medium. (But note: This trick only works with pressure cooking, not standard stovetop cooking.)

1.

	Press	Set it for	Set time for	If needed, press
In all models	SAUTÉ	MEDIUM, NORMAL, or CUSTOM 300°F	5 minutes	START

2. As the pot heats, melt the butter in the insert set in a **5- or 6-quart Instant Pot.** Add the baking soda and stir well. Add the carrots, ginger, and salt. Stir to coat the carrots in the butter. Stir in ½ cup of the broth and turn off the heat. Lock the lid on the pot.

3.

	Set pot for	Set level to	Valve must be	Set time for	If needed, press
For Max pots only	PRESSURE COOK	MAX	—	12 minutes with the KEEP WARM setting off	START
For all other pots	PRESSURE COOK or MANUAL	HIGH	Closed	15 minutes with the KEEP WARM setting off	START

4. When the pot has finished cooking under pressure, use the **quick-release method** to bring the pressure back to normal.

5. Unlatch the lid and open the pot. Pour in the remaining 2½ cups broth. Use an immersion blender right in the pot to puree the soup. Or transfer a third of it to a blender, cover, take the center knob out of the lid, cover the opening with a clean kitchen towel, and blend until smooth. If using a blender, transfer this pureed soup to a bowl and blend the rest of the soup in two batches, eventually stirring it all together in that bowl. In any case, serve warm.

See photo in insert

Not-Really-La-Madeleine's Tomato-Basil Soup

13 ingredients

4–6 SERVINGS

METHOD:
fast/slow

SPECIAL EQUIPMENT:
an immersion or standard blender

PRESSURE:
max or high

TIME UNDER PRESSURE:
7 or 10 minutes

RELEASE:
quick

TOTAL TIME WITH PRESSURE:
about 35 minutes

TOTAL TIME WITH SLOW COOKING:
about 4½ hours

CAN BE VEGETARIAN

---

3 tablespoons butter

1 medium yellow onion, chopped (1 cup)

2 medium carrots, chopped (1 cup)

3 medium celery stalks, chopped (1 cup)

4 cups (1 quart) chicken or vegetable broth

One 28-ounce can diced tomatoes *packed in juice* (3½ cups)

3 tablespoons tomato paste

¼ cup loosely packed, stemmed, fresh basil leaves

1 tablespoon loosely packed, stemmed, fresh oregano leaves

1 teaspoon table salt

¼ cup all-purpose flour (dip and level—do not pack)

2 ounces Parmigiano-Reggiano, finely grated (1 cup)

1 cup heavy or light cream

Believe it or not, this rich, buttery soup is a little bit *less* buttery than the version served at the popular bakery chain. Don't worry: There's still plenty of butter! But we wanted a slightly better balance among the flavors. Mostly, we added more vegetables, giving the soup a deeper all-around flavor. And because we cut down on the butter, we felt free to add some cheese for sheer over-the-top-ness. You could leave it out. But why?

1.

	Press	Set it for	Set time for	If needed, press
In all models	SAUTÉ	MEDIUM, NORMAL, or CUSTOM 300°F	10 minutes	START

2. As the pot heats, melt the butter in the insert set in a **5-, 6-, 8, or 10-quart Instant Pot.** Add the onion, carrots, and celery, stirring to coat the vegetables in the butter. Cook for 1 minute, stirring often, just to warm the vegetables.

3. Add the broth, the canned tomatoes with their juice, the tomato paste, basil, oregano, and salt, stirring until the tomato paste dissolves. Turn off the heat and lock the lid on the pot.

4.

	Set pot for	Set level to	Valve must be	Set time for	If needed, press
For Max pots only	PRESSURE COOK	MAX	—	7 minutes with the KEEP WARM setting off	START
For all other pots	PRESSURE COOK or MANUAL	HIGH	Closed	10 minutes with the KEEP WARM setting off	START
For the slow-cook function	SLOW COOK	HIGH	Open	4 hours with the KEEP WARM setting off	START

5. When the pot has finished cooking under pressure, use the **quick-release method** to bring the pressure back to normal. Whichever cooking method you've used, unlatch the lid and open the pot.

6. Use an immersion blender to puree the soup right in the pot, sprinkling in the flour as you blend until smooth. Or transfer about a third of the soup to a blender, add a third (or so) of the flour, cover, take the center knob out of the lid, cover the opening with a clean kitchen towel, and blend until smooth. If using a blender, transfer the soup to a bowl and continue on blending the rest of the soup in two more batches with more of the flour each time, before returning it all to the pot.

7.

	Press	Set it for	Set time for	If needed, press
In all models	SAUTÉ	MEDIUM, NORMAL, or CUSTOM 300°F	5 minutes	START

8. As the soup bubbles, stir quite often until the soup is somewhat thickened, about 2 minutes. Stir in the cheese and cream. Stir until smooth. Turn off the heat, use hot pads or silicone baking mitts to transfer the (hot!) insert to a nearby wire rack, and cool for a couple of minutes—but definitely serve warm.

Other Pots

- For a 3-quart Instant Pot, you *must* halve all of the ingredient amounts.

- For a 10-quart Instant Pot, you *can* increase almost all of the ingredient amounts by 50 percent *except* you *must* use only 5 tablespoons loosely packed basil leaves and only a couple of leaves more than the stated 1 tablespoon loosely packed oregano leaves.

Beyond

- If you really miss all the butter of the original, float pats on each serving.

- Serve this soup with herbed croutons. To make your own: Slice a baguette into ½-inch cubes, set on a baking sheet, drizzle with olive oil, and add some table salt as well as dried herbs like thyme or parsley (about 2 teaspoons). Toss well and bake in a 350°F oven until well browned and crunchy, stirring occasionally, about 10 minutes.

Not-Really-Panera-Bread's Summer Corn Chowder

15 ingredients

6 SERVINGS

METHOD:
fast/slow

SPECIAL EQUIPMENT:
none

PRESSURE:
high

TIME UNDER PRESSURE:
10 minutes

RELEASE:
quick

TOTAL TIME WITH PRESSURE:
about 25 minutes

TOTAL TIME WITH SLOW COOKING:
about 4 hours 15 minutes

VEGETARIAN

6 cups (1½ quarts) vegetable broth

4 cups fresh corn kernels, or thawed frozen kernels

One 12-ounce russet or baking potato, peeled and diced (1¼ cups)

1 medium green bell pepper, stemmed, cored, and chopped (1 cup)

1 large globe tomato, chopped (¾ cup)

2 medium celery stalks, thinly sliced (⅔ cup)

1 small yellow or white onion, chopped (½ cup)

Up to 1 small fresh jalapeño chile, stemmed, cored (seeded, if desired), and finely chopped

3 medium garlic cloves, minced (1 tablespoon)

1 teaspoon mild smoked paprika

1 teaspoon table salt

1 teaspoon ground black pepper

¼ cup all-purpose flour (dip and level—do not pack)

1½ cups heavy or light cream

Finely chopped, stemmed, fresh cilantro leaves, for garnishing

Although Panera Bread may only serve this chowder in the summer, you can have it all year long, thanks to the Instant Pot. A lot of copycat recipes for this favorite come out more like wallpaper paste because they're thickened up front—or are thin because the soup is not stocked with enough ingredients to make a rich broth. We solve those problems by thickening the soup at the end (a step we often try to avoid but that is needed here) and by stocking the pot with lots of vegetables to add body and deepen the flavors.

1. Stir 5 cups of the broth, the corn, potato, bell pepper, tomato, celery, onion, jalapeño, garlic, smoked paprika, salt, and pepper in the insert set in a **5-, 6-, 8-, or 10-quart Instant Pot**. Lock the lid onto the cooker.

2.

	Set pot for	Set level to	Valve must be	Set time for	If needed, press
For *all* pots	PRESSURE COOK or MANUAL	HIGH	Closed	10 minutes with the KEEP WARM setting off	START
For the slow-cook function	SLOW COOK	HIGH	Open	4 hours with the KEEP WARM setting off	START

3. When the pot has finished cooking under pressure, use the **quick-release method** to bring the pressure back to normal. Whichever cooking method you've used, unlatch the lid and open the cooker. Stir well. Whisk the flour into the remaining 1 cup broth until smooth.

4.

	Press	Set it for	Set time for	If needed, press
In all models	SAUTÉ	MEDIUM, NORMAL, or CUSTOM 300°F	5 minutes	START

5. As the soup begins to bubble, whisk occasionally. Once the soup is bubbling, whisk in the flour slurry in a slow, steady stream. Continue cooking, *whisking constantly,* until somewhat thickened, about 1 minute. Whisk in the cream and continue cooking, *whisking constantly,* for 1 minute to get rid of the cream's raw taste. Turn off the heat and use hot pads or silicone baking mitts to transfer the (hot!) insert to a nearby wire rack (so the flour doesn't fall out of suspension and burn on the still-hot surface). Set aside for a couple of minutes, then dish it up hot and garnish with the cilantro.

Other Pots

- For a 3-quart Instant Pot, you *must* halve all of the ingredient amounts.
- For a 10-quart Instant Pot, you *can* increase all of the ingredient amounts by 50 percent.

Beyond

- This soup is excellent in bread bowls. Buy small, round loaves (or "boules"), particularly those with a solid, thick crust. Slice off a little of the top, then scoop out the inner bits of bread while leaving enough of the "walls" to give the bowl structural security. Set the tops back on their loaves, then warm them on a baking sheet in a 300°F oven for 10 minutes before uncovering and ladling the soup inside. Always serve bread bowls in dinnerware bowls, never on a plate!

Spiced Carrot and Apple Soup

12 ingredients	
4–6 SERVINGS	
METHOD: fast/slow	

SPECIAL EQUIPMENT: an immersion or standard blender

PRESSURE: max or high

TIME UNDER PRESSURE: 12 or 15 minutes

RELEASE: quick

TOTAL TIME WITH PRESSURE: about 25 minutes

TOTAL TIME WITH SLOW COOKING: about 4 hours 20 minutes

VEGETARIAN

GLUTEN-FREE

---

2 tablespoons butter

2 teaspoons fennel seeds

½ teaspoon cumin seeds

5 cups (1 quart plus 1 cup) vegetable broth

1½ pounds "baby" carrots (see the headnote for more information)

1 large sweet apple, such as a Honey Crisp, peeled, cored, and chopped

1 teaspoon table salt

½ teaspoon ground black pepper

2 bay leaves

One 3-inch cinnamon stick

½ cup regular or low-fat plain Greek yogurt

1 tablespoon lemon juice

Although this is a warming, autumnal soup, fit for a chilly day when the apples are crisp and fresh, the real heroes of the recipe are the fennel and cumin seeds, toasted in butter. They add a savory richness underneath the carrots and apple.

FYI, so-called "baby" carrots are not immature carrots. They're larger carrots cut down so six-year-old hands can handle them. The pared-down carrots are also an easy ingredient for this soup, since you can just dump them into the insert from the bag.

1.

	Press	Set it for	Set time for	If needed, press
In all models	SAUTÉ	MEDIUM, NORMAL, or CUSTOM 300°F	5 minutes	START

2. As the pot heats, melt the butter in the insert set in a **5-, 6-, 8-, or 10-quart Instant Pot.** Add the fennel and cumin seeds. Stir until sizzling and fragrant, about 2 minutes.

3. Stir in the broth, carrots, apple, salt, pepper, bay leaves, and cinnamon stick. Turn off the heat and lock the lid on the pot.

4.

	Set pot for	Set level to	Valve must be	Set time for	If needed, press
For Max pots only	PRESSURE COOK	MAX	—	12 minutes with the KEEP WARM setting off	START
For all other pots	PRESSURE COOK or MANUAL	HIGH	Closed	15 minutes with the KEEP WARM setting off	START
For the slow-cook function	SLOW COOK	HIGH	Open	4 hours with the KEEP WARM setting off	START

5. When the pot has finished cooking under pressure, use the **quick-release method** to bring the pressure back to normal. Whichever cooking method you've used, unlatch the lid and open the cooker. Fish out and discard the bay leaves and cinnamon stick. Stir in the yogurt until smooth.

6. Use an immersion blender to puree the soup right in the insert. Or transfer about a third of the soup to a blender, cover, remove lid's center knob, drape a clean kitchen towel over the opening, and blend until smooth. If using a blender, transfer this puree to a bowl and blend the soup in two more batches before getting it all back into the pot.

7.

	Press	Set it for	Set time for	If needed, press
In all models	SAUTÉ	MEDIUM, NORMAL, or CUSTOM 300°F	5 minutes	START

8. As the soup comes to a simmer, stir it fairly often to keep it from sticking. Stir in the lemon juice, cook for a few seconds, turn off the heat, and cool for 1 or 2 minutes before serving hot.

Other Pots

- For a 3-quart Instant Pot, you *must* halve all of the ingredient amounts.

- For an 8-quart Instant Pot, you *can* increase all of the ingredient amounts by 50 percent.

- For a 10-quart Instant Pot, you *must* increase all of the ingredient amounts by 50 percent or you *can* even double the amounts.

Beyond

- For perfect aesthetics, substitute ground white pepper for the black pepper. They'll be no specks of black! (The flavor will also be muskier.)

- For more flavor, add 1 teaspoon coriander seeds with the fennel and cumin.

Vegan (Don't @ Us) Gumbo

15 ingredients

4–6 SERVINGS

METHOD:
standard

SPECIAL EQUIPMENT:
none

PRESSURE:
max or high

TIME UNDER PRESSURE:
12 or 15 minutes

RELEASE:
modified natural

TOTAL TIME WITH PRESSURE:
about 30 minutes

VEGAN

GLUTEN-FREE

3 cups vegetable broth

8 ounces capped and sliced fresh small okra spears (2 cups); or frozen "cut" okra (no need to thaw)

One 10-ounce can mild or hot diced tomatoes and green chiles, such as Rotel (1¼ cups)

1 large yellow or white onion, chopped (1½ cups)

1 large red bell pepper, stemmed, cored, and chopped (1½ cups)

3 medium celery stalks, thinly sliced (1 cup)

2 medium garlic cloves, minced (2 teaspoons)

1 cup brown lentils, picked over for small stones, then rinsed

2 tablespoons red wine vinegar

1 teaspoon dried oregano

1 teaspoon mild paprika

½ teaspoon celery seeds

Up to ½ teaspoon ground dried cayenne

½ teaspoon table salt

Riced cauliflower, for garnishing

Other Pots

- For a 3-quart Instant Pot, you *must* halve all of the ingredient amounts.

- For an 8-quart Instant Pot, you *can* increase almost all of the ingredient amounts by 50 percent *except* you *should* use the originally stated amount of cayenne (unless you want a *very* fiery soup).

- For a 10-quart Instant Pot, you *must* increase almost all of the ingredient amounts by 50 percent or you *can* even double almost all of the amounts, *except* you *should* use no more than ¾ teaspoon ground dried cayenne.

This recipe is essentially a no-brainer vegan (*and* lower carb) variation of the classic, with riced cauliflower as a substitute for cooked rice. Don't worry: It still packs all the flavor of the original. But note that if we were to ladle the soup over riced cauliflower when serving, the dish would turn watery as the cauliflower releases its internal moisture. Instead, we mound the riced cauliflower over the soup so that it can soften yet retain some of its crunch.

One warning: If you use hot diced tomatoes and green chiles, you might want to ease up on the cayenne. You can always pass a hot red pepper sauce, like Tabasco sauce, at the table.

1. Stir the broth, okra, canned tomatoes and chiles, the onion, bell pepper, celery, garlic, lentils, vinegar, oregano, paprika, celery seeds, cayenne, and salt in the insert set in a **5-, 6-, or 8-quart Instant Pot.** Lock the lid on the cooker.

2.

	Set pot for	Set level to	Valve must be	Set time for	If needed, press
For Max pots only	PRESSURE COOK	MAX	—	12 minutes with the KEEP WARM setting off	START
For all other pots	PRESSURE COOK or MANUAL	HIGH	Closed	15 minutes with the KEEP WARM setting off	START

3. When the pot has finished cooking, turn it off and let its pressure **return to normal naturally for 10 minutes.** Then use the **quick-release method** to get rid of any residual pressure in the pot. Unlatch the lid and open the cooker.

4. Stir well, then ladle the soup into bowls. Top each serving with a small mound of riced cauliflower as the garnish.

Beyond

- For extra garnishing, try jarred (hot or "tamed") pickled jalapeño rings or sliced spicy pickled okra.

Cheddar Ale Soup with Bacony Croutons

15 ingredients	SPECIAL EQUIPMENT: none	TIME UNDER PRESSURE: 3 or 5 minutes	TOTAL TIME WITH PRESSURE: about 20 minutes
6 SERVINGS			
METHOD: fast/slow	PRESSURE: max or high	RELEASE: quick	TOTAL TIME WITH SLOW COOKING: about 2 hours 45 minutes

4 thin strips of bacon

2 cups purchased plain dried croutons

2 tablespoons butter

1 small yellow or white onion, chopped (½ cup)

1 small carrot, peeled and chopped (⅓ cup)

1 celery stalk, chopped (⅓ cup)

½ teaspoon table salt

½ teaspoon ground black pepper

1 bay leaf

One 12-ounce bottle ale, such as a red ale; or a nonalcoholic beer

2 cups chicken broth

One 12-ounce can whole, low-fat, or fat-free evaporated milk (1½ cups)

1 teaspoon ground dried mustard

1 teaspoon dried thyme

1 pound American sharp cheddar cheese, shredded (4 cups)

Other Pots

- For a 3-quart Instant Pot, you *must* halve all of the ingredient amounts.
- For a 10-quart Instant Pot, you *must* double all of the ingredient amounts.

Beyond

- To complete your pub experience, serve this soup with air-fried onion ring nachos (seriously—check out the recipe in *The Essential Air-Fryer Cookbook*).

See photo in insert.

Here's an American pub favorite made super fast (and even more delicious). The bacon is fried for a garnish, then the croutons are toasted in the bacon fat. While the soup is under pressure, consider moving those croutons to a clean plate so they don't turn soggy.

1.

	Press	Set it for	Set time for	If needed, press
In all models	SAUTÉ	HIGH or MORE	15 minutes	START

2. As the pot heats, add the bacon to the insert set in a **5-, 6-, or 8-quart Instant Pot.** Fry, turning once or twice, until crisp, about 5 minutes. Use kitchen tongs to transfer the bacon to a nearby plate.

3. Dump the croutons into the bacon fat in the insert and cook, stirring often, until they are coated and extra crunchy, about 3 minutes. Line another plate with paper towels and transfer them to it.

4. Melt the butter in the insert; then add the onion, carrot, and celery. Cook, stirring occasionally, until the onion has softened, about 3 minutes. Stir in the salt, pepper, and bay leaf.

5. Pour in the ale and scrape up any browned bits on the pot's bottom. When the ale is boiling, stir in the broth, evaporated milk, ground mustard, and thyme. Turn off the heat and lock the lid on the pot.

6.

	Set pot for	Set level to	Valve must be	Set time for	If needed, press
For Max pots only	PRESSURE COOK	MAX	—	3 minutes with the KEEP WARM setting off	START
For all other pots	PRESSURE COOK or MANUAL	HIGH	Closed	5 minutes with the KEEP WARM setting off	START
For the slow-cook function	SLOW COOK	HIGH	Open	2½ hours with the KEEP WARM setting off	START

7. When the pot has finished cooking under pressure, use the **quick-release method** to bring the pressure back to normal. Whichever cooking method you've used, unlatch the lid and open the pot. Fish out and discard the bay leaf. Stir in the cheese. Set the lid askew over the pot and set it aside for 5 minutes as the cheese melts. Stir well, then ladle into bowls. Crumble the bacon over each serving and garnish with the bacony croutons.

Creamy Garlic and Cheese Soup

13 ingredients

6 SERVINGS

METHOD:
fast/slow

SPECIAL EQUIPMENT:
an immersion or standard blender

PRESSURE:
max or high

TIME UNDER PRESSURE:
12 or 15 minutes

RELEASE:
quick

TOTAL TIME WITH PRESSURE:
about 45 minutes

TOTAL TIME WITH SLOW COOKING:
about 4½ hours

CAN BE GLUTEN-FREE

¾ stick (6 tablespoons) butter

4 medium heads of garlic, the cloves separated and peeled (about 40 cloves)

1 large sweet white onion, such as a Vidalia onion, chopped (about 1½ cups)

2 teaspoons finely grated lemon zest

½ teaspoon baking soda

2 fresh thyme sprigs

¾ cup dry white wine, such as Chardonnay; or unsweetened apple juice

4 cups (1 quart) chicken broth

1 cup *fresh* plain bread crumbs (gluten-free, if necessary)

¼ cup heavy or light cream

2 tablespoons brandy or cream sherry, or more chicken broth

1 teaspoon table salt

4 ounces Gruyère or Emmentaler cheese, grated (1 cup)

This soup is stocked with garlic, about 40 cloves of it. A bowlful is super comforting when you're under the weather…and guaranteed to open your sinus cavities. You can use the peeled garlic cloves found in plastic jars at the supermarket, but they'll have less moisture than those still in a head. Take care these already-peeled ones don't burn darkly in step 2. The SAUTÉ setting on LOW will help, but you'll still need to stir quite a bit.

1.

	Press	Set it for	Set time for	If needed, press
In all models	SAUTÉ	LOW or LESS	20 minutes	START

2. As the pot heats, melt the butter in the insert set in a **5-, 6-, or 8-quart Instant Pot.** Add the garlic and cook, stirring often, until very lightly browned, about 10 minutes.

3. Add the onion and continue cooking, stirring *quite often,* until very soft, about 8 minutes. Stir in the zest, baking soda, and thyme sprigs. Pour in the wine or juice and scrape up any browned bits on the pot's bottom. Turn off the heat and lock the lid on the pot.

4.

	Set pot for	Set level to	Valve must be	Set time for	If needed, press
For Max pots only	PRESSURE COOK	MAX	—	12 minutes with the KEEP WARM setting off	START
For all other pots	PRESSURE COOK or MANUAL	HIGH	Closed	15 minutes with the KEEP WARM setting off	START
For the slow-cook function	SLOW COOK	HIGH	Open	4 hours with the KEEP WARM setting off	START

5. When the pot has finished cooking under pressure, use the **quick-release method** to bring the pressure back to normal. Whichever cooking method you've used, unlatch the lid and open the pot. Fish out and discard the thyme stems. Stir in the broth, bread crumbs, cream, brandy or its substitute, and the salt.

6. Use an immersion blender right in the pot to puree the soup. Or transfer about a third of the soup to a blender, cover, take the center knob out of the lid, drape a clean kitchen towel over the opening, and blend until smooth. If using a blender, transfer this puree to a bowl and blend the soup in two more batches before returning it all to the pot.

7.

	Press	Set it for	Set time for	If needed, press
In all models	SAUTÉ	LOW or LESS	5 minutes	START

8. Stir constantly as the soup comes to a simmer. Once it does, turn off the heat and stir in the cheese. Use hot pads or silicone baking mitts to transfer the (hot!) insert to a nearby wire rack (to keep the bread crumbs from falling out of suspension). Cool for 2 to 3 minutes, stirring at least twice; serve warm.

Other Pots

- For a 3-quart Instant Pot, you *must* halve all of the ingredient amounts.

- For a 10-quart Instant Pot, you *must* increase almost all of the ingredient amounts by 50 percent *except* you *must* use only 5 medium heads of garlic (or about 50 cloves).

Beyond

- For a deeper flavor (and slightly less thick soup), toast the *fresh* bread crumbs on a baking sheet in a 275°F oven until lightly browned, about 8 minutes, stirring quite often.

Cheesy Broccoli and Sausage Soup

11 ingredients	**SPECIAL EQUIPMENT:** none	**TIME UNDER PRESSURE:** 3 or 5 minutes	**TOTAL TIME WITH PRESSURE:** about 20 minutes
4–6 SERVINGS			
METHOD: standard	**PRESSURE:** max or high	**RELEASE:** quick	**CAN BE GLUTEN-FREE**

1½ quarts (6 cups) chicken broth

1 pound fresh, 1- to 1½-inch broccoli florets; or frozen broccoli florets (do not thaw)

6 ounces smoked sausage, such as kielbasa (gluten-free, if necessary), diced

1 small yellow or white onion, diced (about ½ cup)

1 teaspoon dried thyme

½ teaspoon rubbed or ground sage

¼ teaspoon grated nutmeg

¼ cup heavy or light cream

2 tablespoons cornstarch

4 ounces Monterey Jack cheese, shredded (1 cup)

2 ounces Parmigiano-Reggiano, finely grated (1 cup)

Other Pots

- For a 3-quart Instant Pot, you *must* halve all of the ingredient amounts.
- For a 10-quart Instant Pot, you *must* increase all of the ingredient amounts by 50 percent or you *can* even double the amounts.

Beyond

- If you don't like broccoli, substitute an equal amount of cauliflower.
- For more heat, use a spicy smoked sausage.
- And garnish the servings with Sriracha.

This is *not* a pureed broccoli soup with sausage added later. Instead, it's a chunky soup, almost a stew, with that sausage flavor infused from the start. The only real effort here involves *dicing* the sausage, so that you can get a little piece in every spoonful. Cut the sausage into ¼-inch-thick rounds, then cut each of these piece into ¼-inch "squares" (some with rounded sides, of course, because of the shape of the sausage).

1. Stir the broth, broccoli, sausage, onion, thyme, sage, and nutmeg in the insert set in a **5-, 6-, or 8-quart Instant Pot.** Lock the lid on the pot.

2.

	Set pot for	Set level to	Valve must be	Set time for	If needed, press
For Max pots only	PRESSURE COOK	MAX	—	3 minutes with the KEEP WARM setting off	START
For all other pots	PRESSURE COOK or MANUAL	HIGH	Closed	5 minutes with the KEEP WARM setting off	START

3. When the pot has finished cooking, use the **quick-release method** to bring the pressure back to normal. Unlatch the lid and open the pot. Whisk the cream and cornstarch in a small bowl until smooth.

4.

	Press	Set it for	Set time for	If needed, press
In all models	SAUTÉ	MEDIUM, NORMAL, or CUSTOM 300°F	5 minutes	START

5. Stir the soup as it comes to a full bubble. Stir in the cornstarch slurry. Continue cooking, stirring constantly, until somewhat thickened, less than 1 minute. Stir in both cheeses, then immediately turn off the heat. Use hot pads or silicone baking mitts to transfer the (hot!) insert to a nearby wire rack. Cool for 2 to 3 minutes to melt the cheese, then stir well and serve warm.

Not-Really-La-Madeleine's Country Potato Soup

12 ingredients	
6 SERVINGS	
METHOD: standard	

SPECIAL EQUIPMENT: none	TIME UNDER PRESSURE: 20 minutes	TOTAL TIME WITH PRESSURE: about 40 minutes
PRESSURE: low	RELEASE: quick	VEGETARIAN
		CAN BE GLUTEN-FREE

8 ounces thin strips of bacon (gluten-free, if necessary), chopped

3 tablespoons butter

1 large yellow or white onion, chopped (about 1½ cups)

1 large leek, white and pale green parts only, halved lengthwise, rinsed well for internal grit, and thinly sliced (¾ cup)

6 cups (1½ quarts) vegetable broth

3 pounds yellow potatoes, such as Yukon Golds, peeled and cut widthwise into ½-inch-thick slices

½ cup heavy or light cream

3 fresh multi-stemmed thyme sprigs

2 bay leaves

1 teaspoon table salt

½ teaspoon ground black pepper

Shredded American sharp cheddar cheese, for garnishing

Other Pots

- For a 3-quart Instant Pot, you *must* halve all of the ingredient amounts.
- For an 8-quart Instant Pot, you *can* increase all of the ingredient amounts by 50 percent.
- For a 10-quart Instant Pot, you *must* increase all of the ingredient amounts by 50 percent or you *can* even double the amounts.

Beyond

- For a richer (but not vegetarian) soup, substitute chicken broth for the vegetable broth.
- Add minced chives (or the green part of a scallion) to the garnishes.

This rib-sticker is all about the fresh thyme and (of course) the cream, as well as the two toppings: bacon and cheese.

In the chain's original, there are more leeks than what we've used. We swapped some out for onion because we think its sweetness better complements the creamy richness. The original also calls for peeled potatoes, but we don't mind a bit of peel poking through the soup and so felt the effort unwarranted. Feel free to peel, if you've got time on your hands.

1.

	Press	Set it for	Set time for	If needed, press
In all models	SAUTÉ	MEDIUM, NORMAL, or CUSTOM 300°F	15 minutes	START

2. As the pot heats, put the bacon in the insert set in a **5-, 6-, or 8-quart Instant Pot.** Cook, stirring often, until the bacon is quite crisp, about 8 minutes. Use a slotted spoon to transfer the bacon pieces out of the pot and onto a nearby plate lined with paper towels. Set aside. Use a big cooking spoon to discard most of the rendered bacon fat, leaving about 1 tablespoon in the insert.

3. Melt the butter in the insert. Add the onion and leek; cook, stirring frequently, until the onion softens, about 3 minutes. Pour in the broth and scrape up any browned bits on the pot's bottom.

4. Stir in the potatoes and cream, then turn off the heat. Stir in the thyme sprigs, bay leaves, salt, and pepper. Lock the lid on the pot.

5.

	Set pot for	Set level to	Valve must be	Set time for	If needed, press
For *all* pots	PRESSURE COOK or MANUAL	LOW	Closed	20 minutes with the KEEP WARM setting off	START

6. When the pot has finished cooking, use the **quick-release method** to bring the pressure back to normal. Unlatch the lid and open the cooker. Fish out and discard the thyme sprigs and bay leaves. Stir well, then serve the soup in big bowls, garnished with the bacon bits and lots of shredded cheese.

No-Brainer Wild Rice and Sweet Potato Soup

12 ingredients

4–6 SERVINGS

METHOD:
standard

SPECIAL
EQUIPMENT:
none

PRESSURE:
max or high

TIME UNDER
PRESSURE:
18 or 25 minutes

RELEASE:
modified natural

TOTAL TIME WITH
PRESSURE:
about 45 minutes

VEGAN

GLUTEN-FREE

6 cups (1½ quarts) vegetable broth

1½ pounds sweet potatoes, peeled and cut into 1-inch cubes (2½ cups)

12 ounces white or brown button mushrooms, cleaned and thinly sliced

4 ounces packed, chopped, stemmed kale (2 cups—do not use baby kale)

¾ cup raw wild rice (do not use a wild-rice blend that includes brown rice)

2 large carrots, peeled and thinly sliced (1 cup)

2 medium celery stalks, thinly sliced (⅔ cup)

1 tablespoon apple cider vinegar

1 teaspoon table salt

½ teaspoon rubbed or ground sage

½ teaspoon ground dried turmeric

½ teaspoon ground black pepper

Wild rice is *not* a grain. It's an aquatic grass. It's also quite tasty: grassy, herbaceous, and sweet. But since it's also fairly expensive, we've called for less of it than you might expect in a recipe like this one. We've used just enough to keep those characteristic flavors without breaking the bank in this light but satisfying soup, made with lots of vegetables and even mushrooms for a little earthy heft. And here's another little bit of culinary know-how you might not expect: There's no onion here. Its natural sweetness can mute the woodsy flavor of the wild rice.

1. Stir everything in the insert set in a **5-, 6-, 8-, or 10-quart Instant Pot.** Lock the lid on the pot.

2.

	Set pot for	Set level to	Valve must be	Set time for	If needed, press
For Max pots only	PRESSURE COOK	MAX	—	18 minutes with the KEEP WARM setting off	START
For all other pots	PRESSURE COOK or MANUAL	HIGH	Closed	25 minutes with the KEEP WARM setting off	START

3. When the pot has finished cooking, turn it off and let its pressure **return to normal naturally for 12 minutes.** Then use the **quick-release method** to get rid of any residual pressure in the pot. Unlatch the lid and open the cooker. Stir well before serving hot.

Other Pots

- For a 3-quart Instant Pot, you *must* halve all of the ingredient amounts.

- For a 10-quart Instant Pot, you *can* increase all of the ingredient amounts by 50 percent or you *can* even double the amounts.

Beyond

- For heat, add up to 1 teaspoon red pepper flakes with the sage and other spices.

Spicy Sweet Potato and Peanut Soup

12 ingredients

4 SERVINGS

METHOD:
fast/slow

SPECIAL EQUIPMENT:
none

PRESSURE:
max or high

TIME UNDER
PRESSURE:
7 or 10 minutes

RELEASE:
quick

TOTAL TIME WITH
PRESSURE:
about 30 minutes

TOTAL TIME WITH
SLOW COOKING:
about 3 hours 15
minutes

VEGAN

GLUTEN-FREE

---

2 tablespoons peanut or olive oil

1 small red onion, diced (about ½ cup)

1 or 2 canned chipotle chiles in adobo sauce, stemmed, cored, and chopped (seeded, if desired—and gluten-free, if necessary)

2 medium garlic cloves, minced (2 teaspoons)

2 cups vegetable broth

1½ pounds sweet potatoes, peeled and diced into ½-inch cubes (a rounded 2 cups)

One 14-ounce can stewed tomatoes *packed in juice* (1¾ cups)

One 14-ounce can *light* coconut milk (1¾ cups)

½ cup roasted unsalted peanuts

2 tablespoons smooth regular peanut butter

1 teaspoon table salt

2 cups loosely packed, chopped baby spinach leaves (2 ounces)

Other Pots

- For a 3-quart Instant Pot, you *must* halve all of the ingredient amounts.
- For a 10-quart Instant Pot, you *must* double almost all of the ingredient amounts *except* you *must* use no more than 3 canned chipotle chiles in adobo sauce, stemmed, cored, and minced.

Beyond

- For an easier soup (without sweet potatoes), substitute purchased cubed peeled butternut squash. Cut larger pieces into ½-inch cubes or bits.
- Serve the soup with warmed flat bread (or even flour tortillas) and plenty of butter.

The original recipes for this West African soup has become something of a North American staple in recent years. In keeping with most of those recipes, ours is fairly chunky soup, a good textural contrast to the rich base of coconut milk and peanut butter. But we *have* deviated from more standard offerings by calling for canned chipotle chiles in adobo sauce. We love that bit of smoky flavor highlighted against the sweet potatoes and peanut butter.

1.

	Press	Set it for	Set time for	If needed, press
In all models	SAUTÉ	MEDIUM, NORMAL, or CUSTOM 300°F	10 minutes	START

2. As the pot heats, warm the oil in the insert set in a **5-, 6-, or 8-quart Instant Pot.** Add the onion and cook, stirring often, until softened, about 3 minutes. Add the chipotle and garlic; cook, stirring all the while, until aromatic, about 15 seconds.

3. Pour in the broth and scrape up any browned bits on the pot's bottom. Stir in the sweet potatoes, tomatoes with their juice, coconut milk, peanuts, peanut butter, and salt until the peanut butter dissolves. Turn off the heat and lock the lid on the pot.

4.

	Set pot for	Set level to	Valve must be	Set time for	If needed, press
For Max pots only	PRESSURE COOK	MAX	—	7 minutes with the KEEP WARM setting off	START
For all other pots	PRESSURE COOK or MANUAL	HIGH	Closed	10 minutes with the KEEP WARM setting off	START
For the slow-cook function	SLOW COOK	HIGH	Open	3 hours with the KEEP WARM setting off	START

5. When the pot has finished cooking under pressure, use the **quick-release method** to bring the pressure back to normal. Whichever cooking method you've used, unlatch the lid and open the pot. Stir in the spinach, set the lid askew over the pot, and set aside to cool for 2 to 3 minutes to wilt the spinach and blend the flavors. Stir well and serve warm.

Meatless Hot & Sour Soup

13 ingredients	
4–6 SERVINGS	
METHOD: fast/slow	
SPECIAL EQUIPMENT: none	

PRESSURE: max or high	
TIME UNDER PRESSURE: 3 or 5 minutes	
RELEASE: quick	

PRESSURE: max or high
TIME UNDER PRESSURE: 3 or 5 minutes
RELEASE: quick

TOTAL TIME WITH PRESSURE: about 20 minutes
TOTAL TIME WITH SLOW COOKING: about 2 hours 15 minutes

VEGAN
CAN BE GLUTEN-FREE

---

6 cups (1½ quarts) vegetable broth

2 cups (8 ounces) purchased shredded coleslaw mix

1½ cups purchased julienned carrots (8 ounces)

6 medium scallions, trimmed and sliced into ¼-inch bits (2 cups)

6 ounces shiitake mushroom caps, thinly sliced

One 8-ounce can sliced bamboo shoots, drained and rinsed

One 2-inch piece of fresh ginger, peeled, cut lengthwise into ⅛-inch-thin strips, then these cut into matchsticks

3 tablespoons regular or low-sodium soy sauce, or gluten-free tamari sauce

2 tablespoons rice wine vinegar

Up to 2 tablespoons sambal oelek or other thick red chile sauce

3 tablespoons water

2 tablespoons cornstarch

1 pound firm silken tofu (gluten-free, if necessary), cut into 1-inch cubes

Other Pots

- For a 3-quart Instant Pot, you *must* halve all of the ingredient amounts.
- For a 10-quart Instant Pot, you *must* increase all of the ingredient amounts by 50 percent or you *can* even double the amounts.

Beyond

- Garnish servings with fresh bean sprouts or even a little nest of radish sprouts.
- And/or drizzle the servings with toasted sesame oil.

If we were going to be thoroughly authentic, hot and sour soup starts with a long-simmered broth made from pork bones. But we're going for a vegetarian alternative here. And few people buy an IP for recipes that take all day—or more than a day! To that end, we can get as much flavor with a lot less effort in this soup because of the way the pressure extracts body and even bulk out of the vegetables. We save the tofu for the end so that it doesn't break up under pressure.

1. Stir the broth, slaw mix, carrots, scallions, shiitakes, bamboo shoots, ginger, soy or tamari sauce, vinegar, and sambal oelek in the insert of a **5-, 6-, or 8-quart Instant Pot.** Lock the lid on the pot.

2.

	Set pot for	Set level to	Valve must be	Set time for	If needed, press
For Max pots only	PRESSURE COOK	MAX	—	3 minutes with the KEEP WARM setting off	START
For all other pots	PRESSURE COOK or MANUAL	HIGH	Closed	5 minutes with the KEEP WARM setting off	START
For the slow-cook function	SLOW COOK	HIGH	Open	2 hours with the KEEP WARM setting off	START

3. When the pot is finished cooking under pressure, use the **quick-release method** to bring the pressure back to normal. Whichever cooking method you've used, unlatch the lid and open the pot. Whisk the water and cornstarch in a small bowl until a smooth slurry.

4.

	Press	Set it for	Set time for	If needed, press
In all models	SAUTÉ	MEDIUM, NORMAL, or CUSTOM 300°F	5 minutes	START

5. Stir often as the soup starts bubbling. When it's simmering, stir in the slurry. Cook, stirring all the while, until somewhat thickened, less than 1 minute. Turn off the heat and use hot pads or silicone baking mitts to transfer the (hot!) insert to a nearby wire rack. Very gently stir in the tofu, then set the soup aside for a minute or two to warm the tofu. Serve hot.

Millennial-Friendly Pasta e Fagioli Soup (Because Kale)

12 ingredients	
6 SERVINGS	
METHOD: fast/slow	

SPECIAL EQUIPMENT: none

PRESSURE: max or high

TIME UNDER PRESSURE: 4 or 5 minutes

RELEASE: quick

TOTAL TIME WITH PRESSURE: about 20 minutes

TOTAL TIME WITH SLOW COOKING: about 3 hours 15 minutes

VEGAN

CAN BE GLUTEN-FREE

---

8 cups (2 quarts) vegetable broth

One 15-ounce can pink beans, drained and rinsed (1¾ cups)

One 14-ounce can diced tomatoes *packed in juice* (1¾ cups)

2 medium carrots, peeled and sliced into thin coins

4 ounces dried small shells or dried small elbow pasta (gluten-free, if necessary)

1 teaspoon dried oregano

1 teaspoon dried thyme

1 teaspoon onion powder

1 teaspoon table salt

½ teaspoon garlic powder

½ teaspoon red pepper flakes

2 cups loosely packed, chopped *baby kale* (2 ounces)

Other Pots

- For a 3-quart Instant Pot, you *must* halve all of the ingredient amounts.
- For a 10-quart Instant Pot, you *can* increase all of the ingredient amounts by 50 percent.

Beyond

- Garnish the servings with a drizzle of balsamic vinegar.
- If the servings don't need to be vegan, also garnish with finely grated Parmigiano-Reggiano.

We dumped the sausage that's popular in American versions of this classic soup and instead crafted a vegetarian version with kale for the kids…and to create some hearty meat-free fare that's easy to make on a busy night. Listen, the youngsters are onto something: Kale is brilliantly flavored. What's more, baby kale has fewer bitter notes for an all-around sweet finish in these simple but nicely sophisticated bowls of updated-if-still-old-school comfort.

Make sure you pick up a loaf of Italian bread. Warm it in the oven so it's irresistibly crunchy (mostly so the slices can stand up to being dunked in the soup).

1. Stir the broth, beans, tomatoes and their juice, carrots, pasta, oregano, thyme, onion powder, salt, garlic powder, and red pepper flakes in a **5-, 6-, 8-, or 10-quart Instant Pot.** Lock the lid on the pot.

2.

	Set pot for	Set level to	Valve must be	Set time for	If needed, press
For Max pots only	PRESSURE COOK	MAX	—	4 minutes with the KEEP WARM setting off	START
For all other pots	PRESSURE COOK or MANUAL	HIGH	Closed	5 minutes with the KEEP WARM setting off	START
For the slow-cook function	SLOW COOK	HIGH	Open	3 hours with the KEEP WARM setting off	START

3. When the pot is finished cooking under pressure, use the **quick-release method** to bring the pressure back to normal. Whichever cooking method you've used, unlatch the lid and open the pot. Stir in the chopped kale. Set the lid askew over the pot and set aside for 3 to 5 minutes to wilt the greens and blend the flavors before serving warm.

Grandmother-Friendly Potato Soup (Because Cabbage)

11 ingredients

6 SERVINGS

METHOD:
fast/slow

SPECIAL EQUIPMENT:
none

PRESSURE:
max or high

TIME UNDER PRESSURE:
16 or 20 minutes

RELEASE:
modified natural

TOTAL TIME WITH PRESSURE:
about 55 minutes

TOTAL TIME WITH SLOW COOKING:
about 4 hours 15 minutes

VEGAN

GLUTEN-FREE

---

4 cups (1 quart) vegetable broth

One 28-ounce can diced tomatoes *packed in juice* (3½ cups)

3 medium yellow potatoes (about 4 ounces each), such as Yukon Golds, *diced* (no need to peel)

2 small carrots, *diced*

¼ cup loosely packed fresh dill fronds, chopped

1 tablespoon apple cider vinegar

1 teaspoon caraway seeds

1 teaspoon onion powder

1 teaspoon granulated white sugar

1 teaspoon table salt, plus more to taste

6 cups chopped cored savoy or green cabbage (about 1½ pounds, half a large head)

Other Pots

- For a 3-quart Instant Pot, you *must* halve almost all of the ingredient amounts *except* you *must* use 3 tablespoons fresh dill fronds, chopped.

- For a 10-quart Instant Pot, you *can* increase almost all of the ingredient amounts by 50 percent *except* you *must* use only 5 tablespoons fresh dill fronds, chopped.

Beyond

- Add up to 1 teaspoon red pepper flakes and/or 1 teaspoon dried thyme with the other spices.

- If the servings don't need to be vegan, add ¾ pound diced, purchased deli corned beef (any coatings trimmed off) or diced (raw) boneless skinless chicken breasts with the broth and other ingredients in step 1.

Here's the sort of soup your Eastern European grandmother fed you to get you ready for threshing or harvest (even though she lived in a co-op in Manhattan). Our version is as filling as hers but lighter and not quite as thick. It's pretty simple, too, with just a few ingredients beyond the seasonings. We think it's best on a sunny winter day when no one works in the fields anyway.

One tip: Dice the potatoes and carrots into ¼-inch cubes. They'll cook evenly (and more quickly), and you'll get more variety in every bite, the way your grandmother would have wanted it.

1. Stir the broth, tomatoes and their juice, potatoes, carrots, dill, vinegar, caraway seeds, onion powder, sugar, and salt in the insert set in a **5-, 6-, 8-, or 10-quart Instant Pot.** Add the cabbage and gently press some of it down into the liquid without pushing the cabbage against the pot's bottom. Lock the lid on the cooker.

2.

	Set pot for	Set level to	Valve must be	Set time for	If needed, press
For Max pots only	PRESSURE COOK	MAX	—	16 minutes with the KEEP WARM setting off	START
For all other pots	PRESSURE COOK or MANUAL	HIGH	Closed	20 minutes with the KEEP WARM setting off	START
For the slow-cook function	SLOW COOK	HIGH	Open	4 hours with the KEEP WARM setting off	START

3. When the pot has finished cooking under pressure, turn it off and let the pressure **return to normal naturally for 10 minutes.** Then use the **quick-release method** to remove any remaining pressure from the pot. Whichever cooking method you've used, unlatch the lid and open the pot. Stir the soup and check if it needs additional salt. Serve hot.

Not-Really-Olive-Garden's Chicken Gnocchi Soup

12 ingredients

6 SERVINGS

METHOD:
standard

SPECIAL EQUIPMENT:
none

PRESSURE:
high

TIME UNDER PRESSURE:
0 minutes

RELEASE:
natural

TOTAL TIME WITH PRESSURE:
about 25 minutes

½ stick (4 tablespoons or ¼ cup) butter

1 medium yellow or white onion, chopped (about 1 cup)

3 medium celery stalks, chopped (about 1 cup)

¼ cup all-purpose flour (dip and level—do not pack)

4 cups (1 quart) chicken broth

1 pound boneless skinless chicken breasts, cut into ½-inch cubes

2 cups heavy or light cream

One 14½-ounce bag frozen potato gnocchi, thawed

½ teaspoon dried thyme

½ teaspoon grated nutmeg

½ teaspoon table salt

3 cups loosely packed, chopped baby spinach leaves (3 ounces)

Other Pots

- For a 3-quart Instant Pot, you *must* halve all of the ingredient amounts.

- For a 10-quart Instant Pot, you *must* increase all of the ingredient amounts by 50 percent.

Beyond

- Substitute baby kale or baby arugula for the baby spinach.

- To add heat to the soup, stir in up to 1 teaspoon red pepper flakes with the spices.

- Serve with a lot of breadsticks!

We've upped the game for this popular soup by increasing the spices and adding a bit more chicken than the standard. You can even up the game a bit more by substituting sweet potato gnocchi for the more standard potato gnocchi.

There are three tricks to success. First, whisk like mad in step 3 to make sure the flour has dissolved into the broth.

Second, cook the soup under pressure *just until* the pin locks the lid on the pot. Don't leave the kitchen. Don't even let the pot get to full pressure. The moment you see the pin pop, unplug the pot and wait until the pin drops down again. Doing so ensures that the flour won't fall out of suspension and burn on the pot's bottom.

Finally, make sure the chicken is in tiny cubes so that it will cook in the very short amount of time given.

1.

	Press	Set it for	Set time for	If needed, press
In all models	SAUTÉ	MEDIUM, NORMAL, or CUSTOM 300°F	10 minutes	START

2. As the pot heats, melt the butter in the insert set in a **5-, 6-, or 8-quart Instant Pot.** Add the onion and celery; cook, stirring often, until softened, about 3 minutes.

3. *Whisk* in the flour to combine with the butter and vegetables. Whisking all the while, pour in the broth in a slow, steady stream, continuing to whisk like a maniac until the flour has dissolved in the broth.

4. Put the whisk down and pick up a wooden spoon. Stir in the chicken until it's well coated in the floured vegetables. Continue cooking, stirring constantly, for 1 minute. Then stir in the cream, gnocchi, thyme, nutmeg, and salt. Cook, stirring almost constantly, until wisps of steam rise from the liquid. Turn off the heat, stir in the spinach, and lock the lid on the pot.

5.

	Set pot for	Set level to	Valve must be	Set time for	If needed, press
For *all* pots	PRESSURE COOK or MANUAL	HIGH	Closed	0 or 1 minute with the KEEP WARM setting off	START

6. *Do not* let the machine come to full pressure. Instead, **the moment the pin pops up** to lock the lid onto the pot, turn it off and set it aside until the pressure **returns to normal naturally,** about 10 minutes. Unlatch the lid and open the cooker. Stir well before serving hot.

Red Lentil and Couscous Soup

15 ingredients

4–6 SERVINGS

METHOD:
fast/slow

SPECIAL EQUIPMENT:
none

PRESSURE:
max or high

TIME UNDER PRESSURE:
7 or 10 minutes

RELEASE:
quick

TOTAL TIME WITH PRESSURE:
about 35 minutes

TOTAL TIME WITH SLOW COOKING:
about 3½ hours

VEGETARIAN

3 tablespoons butter

2 medium yellow or white onions, chopped (2 cups)

3 medium garlic cloves, minced (1 tablespoon)

1 teaspoon ground cumin

1 teaspoon mild paprika

½ teaspoon ground cinnamon

½ teaspoon ground coriander

½ teaspoon ground dried ginger

½ teaspoon table salt

6 cups (1½ quarts) vegetable broth

1½ cups dried red lentils

½ cup raw regular or whole-wheat couscous (discard any spice packet)

2 tablespoons tomato paste

2 tablespoons lemon juice

Up to ½ teaspoon ground dried cayenne

Both red lentils and couscous almost melt under pressure, yielding a soup that's more like a savory porridge. FYI, red lentils are yellow lentils that have been hulled and split, offering a subtly sweet, not-very-earthy flavor. They're especially popular in Middle Eastern and Indian cooking.

As to the couscous, this recipe (and every couscous recipe in this book) uses the North American and European standard—which is (despite not often being so-called) *instant* couscous, a parboiled and dried product made from durum wheat. It's the sort of couscous you'll most likely find on the grocery store shelf under brand names like Near East and Rice Select. It's the kind that you put in a bowl, cover with boiling water, and set aside for 5 to 10 minutes until it's ready. More traditional North African varieties of couscous (the sort you *don't* want for this book) take much longer to prepare, usually by steaming them in a *couscoussier*.

The soup will thicken as it sits. If you save some in a covered container in the fridge, you'll need to thin it out with plenty of broth when you reheat it.

1.

	Press	Set it for	Set time for	If needed, press
In all models	SAUTÉ	MEDIUM, NORMAL, or CUSTOM 300°F	20 minutes	START

2. As the pot heats, melt the butter in the insert set in a **5-, 6-, or 8-quart Instant Pot.** Add the onions and cook, stirring often, until softened and even lightly browned, about 12 minutes. Stir in the garlic, cumin, paprika, cinnamon, coriander, ginger, and salt until fragrant, just a few seconds.

3. Pour in the broth and scrape up all the browned bits on the pot's bottom. Stir in the lentils, couscous, and tomato paste until the tomato paste dissolves. Give the soup a couple more minutes to get hot, then turn off the heat and lock the lid on the pot.

4.

	Set pot for	Set level to	Valve must be	Set time for	If needed, press
For Max pots only	PRESSURE COOK	MAX	—	7 minutes with the KEEP WARM setting off	START
For all other pots	PRESSURE COOK or MANUAL	HIGH	Closed	10 minutes with the KEEP WARM setting off	START
For the slow-cook function	SLOW COOK	HIGH	Open	3 hours with the KEEP WARM setting off	START

5. When the pot has finished cooking under pressure, use the **quick-release method** to bring the pressure back to normal. Whichever cooking method you've used, unlatch the lid and open the pot. Stir in the lemon juice and cayenne (to taste). Use hot pads or silicone baking mitts to transfer the (hot!) insert to a nearby wire rack. Cool for 2 to 3 minutes, stirring several times; serve warm.

Other Pots

- For a 3-quart Instant Pot, you *must* halve all of the ingredient amounts.
- For a 10-quart Instant Pot, you *must* increase all of the ingredient amounts by 50 percent or you *can* even double almost all of the amounts *except* you *must* keep the lemon juice at 3 tablespoons (that is, only 50 percent more than the original amount).

Beyond

- Top each serving with a poached egg.
- Or dress some micro greens, sprouts, or even chopped baby arugula with a light vinaigrette and set a mound on top of each serving

Not-Really-Olive-Garden's Zuppa Toscana

10 ingredients	
6 SERVINGS	
METHOD: fast/slow	

SPECIAL EQUIPMENT: none

PRESSURE: max or high

TIME UNDER PRESSURE: 10 or 12 minutes

RELEASE: quick

TOTAL TIME WITH PRESSURE: about 40 minutes

TOTAL TIME WITH SLOW COOKING: 3½ hours

CAN BE GLUTEN-FREE

---

1 tablespoon olive oil

1 pound sweet or mild Italian *chicken* sausage, any casings removed; or bulk sweet Italian chicken sausage meat (gluten-free, if necessary)

1 large yellow or white onion, chopped (about 1½ cups)

6 cups (1½ quarts) chicken broth

3 large russet or baking potatoes (about 12 ounces each), peeled and cut into ½-inch cubes (3¾ cups)

2 teaspoons minced, stemmed, fresh oregano leaves

1 teaspoon table salt

Up to ½ teaspoon red pepper flakes

3 cups loosely packed, chopped baby kale leaves (3 ounces)

1 cup heavy cream

Ours, like the original recipe for this chain's favorite, is a sausage, potato, and kale soup. But we've made a couple of changes that make the soup, well, better. First, almost all copycat recipes for this soup call for pork sausage and then ask you to drain off the rendered fat. Doing so is a pain! And even if you drain off the fat, more comes out under pressure. So we substituted chicken sausage—which means you don't have to drain the pot and the soup doesn't get an oil slick. Even better, because we've used a lower-fat sausage, we can then use cream (rather than half-and-half, as called for in the original) to make more satisfying bowlfuls.

The original also calls for regular kale but we feel baby kale is easier (because it doesn't need to be stemmed) and sweeter (so it tastes better alongside the cream).

1.		Press	Set it for	Set time for	If needed, press
	In all models	SAUTÉ	MEDIUM, NORMAL, or CUSTOM 300°F	10 minutes	START

2. Warm the oil in the insert set in a **5-, 6-, or 8-quart Instant Pot.** Crumble in the sausage meat and cook, stirring often to break up any clumps, until lightly browned, about 3 minutes.

3. Add the onion and continue cooking, stirring more frequently, until the onion softens, about 3 minutes. Pour in the broth and scrape up any browned bits on the pot's bottom.

4. Stir in the potatoes, oregano, salt, and red pepper flakes. Turn off the heat and lock the lid on the pot.

5.

	Set pot for	Set level to	Valve must be	Set time for	If needed, press
For Max pots only	PRESSURE COOK	MAX	—	10 minutes with the KEEP WARM setting off	START
For all other pots	PRESSURE COOK or MANUAL	HIGH	Closed	12 minutes with the KEEP WARM setting off	START
For the slow-cook function	SLOW COOK	HIGH	Open	3 hours with the KEEP WARM setting off	START

6. When the pot has finished cooking under pressure, use the **quick-release method** to bring the pressure back to normal. Whichever cooking method you've used, unlatch the lid and open the cooker

7.

	Press	Set it for	Set time for	If needed, press
In all models	SAUTÉ	MEDIUM, NORMAL, or CUSTOM 300°F	5 minutes	START

8. As the soup comes to a simmer, stir in the baby kale and cream. Cook, stirring frequently, for 2 minutes to wilt the kale completely and nix the taste of raw cream. Turn off the heat and set the pot aside for 2 to 3 minutes before serving warm.

Other Pots

- For a **3-quart Instant Pot**, you *must* halve all of the ingredient amounts.

- For a **10-quart Instant Pot**, you *must* increase all of the ingredient amounts by 50 percent or you *can* even double them.

Beyond

- Use a half-and-half combo of sweet and spicy chicken sausage

- Drizzle servings with olive oil.

- And top them with finely grated Pecorino Romano.

See photo in insert.

Not-Really-Chili's Chicken Enchilada Soup

13 ingredients	
4 SERVINGS	
SPECIAL EQUIPMENT: none	
TIME UNDER PRESSURE: 3 or 4 minutes	
TOTAL TIME WITH PRESSURE: about 25 minutes	
METHOD: fast/slow	
PRESSURE: max or high	
RELEASE: quick	
TOTAL TIME WITH SLOW COOKING: about 2½ hours	
	GLUTEN-FREE

1 tablespoon butter

1 medium yellow or white onion, chopped (about 1 cup)

1½ pounds boneless skinless chicken breasts, diced

1 medium garlic clove, minced (1 teaspoon)

1 tablespoon standard chili powder

1 teaspoon ground coriander

1 teaspoon ground cumin

½ teaspoon table salt

Up to ¼ teaspoon ground dried cayenne

5 cups (1 quart plus 1 cup) chicken broth

¼ cup instant masa harina, such as the Maseca brand

4 ounces Velveeta, cut into small cubes

4 ounces Monterey Jack cheese, shredded (1 cup), plus more for garnish

Most copycat recipes of this popular soup use precooked chicken, but we feel that cooking the chicken *in* the soup results in more flavor in every bite.

One tip: It's crucial that you stir the soup constantly once you add the masa harina. Doing so will not only offer more "tortilla" flavor as the masa distributes evenly throughout the soup, but stirring continuously will also allow the soup to thicken while ensuring the masa doesn't fall out of suspension and glom onto the pot's bottom.

1.

	Press	Set it for	Set time for	If needed, press
In all models	SAUTÉ	MEDIUM, NORMAL, or CUSTOM 300°F	10 minutes	START

2. As the pot heats, melt the butter in the insert set in a **5-, 6-, or 8-quart Instant Pot.** Add the onion and cook, stirring often, until softened, about 3 minutes. Add the chicken and cook, stirring more often, until it loses its raw, pink color, about 3 minutes.

3. Stir in the garlic, chili powder, coriander, cumin, salt, and cayenne until fragrant, just a few seconds. Pour in the broth and scrape up any browned bits on the pot's bottom. Turn off the heat and lock the lid on the pot.

4.

	Set pot for	Set level to	Valve must be	Set time for	If needed, press
For Max pots only	PRESSURE COOK	MAX	—	3 minutes with the KEEP WARM setting off	START
For all other pots	PRESSURE COOK or MANUAL	HIGH	Closed	4 minutes with the KEEP WARM setting off	START
For the slow-cook function	SLOW COOK	HIGH	Open	2 hours with the KEEP WARM setting off	START

5. When the pot has finished cooking under pressure, use the **quick-release method** to bring the pressure back to normal. Whichever cooking method you've used, unlatch the lid and open the cooker. Stir in the masa harina.

6.

	Press	Set it for	Set time for	If needed, press
In all models	SAUTÉ	MEDIUM, NORMAL, or CUSTOM 300°F	5 minutes	START

7. As the soup comes to a simmer, stir constantly until bubbling and slightly thickened, about 1 minute. Turn off the heat and stir in the Velveeta and Monterey Jack until melted. Use hot pods or silicone baking mitts to *immediately* transfer the (hot!) insert to a nearby wire rack to keep the masa from falling out of suspension. Continue stirring for 1 minute, then serve hot, garnishing each bowlful with more shredded Jack cheese.

Other Pots

- For a **3-quart Instant Pot**, you *must* halve all of the ingredient amounts.
- For a **10-quart Instant Pot**, you *must* increase almost all of the ingredient amounts by 50 percent *except* you *must* double the amount of standard chili powder.

Beyond

- At Chili's, this soup gets some pico de gallo on top. You can buy a batch at most supermarkets. To make your own, stir together 4 chopped large Roma or plum tomatoes, 1 minced small single-lobed shallot, up to 1 stemmed and minced (seeded, if desired) fresh jalapeño chile, the juice of 1 or 2 small limes (to taste), and 1 teaspoon table salt in a small bowl. Set aside at room temperature for 10 minutes to blend the flavors before serving.

No-Brainer Chicken Barley Soup

11 ingredients

4–6 SERVINGS

METHOD:
fast/slow

SPECIAL EQUIPMENT:
none

PRESSURE:
max or high

TIME UNDER PRESSURE:
35 or 45 minutes

RELEASE:
natural

TOTAL TIME WITH PRESSURE:
about 1½ hours

TOTAL TIME WITH SLOW COOKING:
about 5½ hours

GLUTEN-FREE

6 cups (1½ quarts) chicken broth

1 pound boneless skinless chicken breasts, diced

1 cup raw pearl barley

1 medium yellow or white onion, chopped (1 cup)

2 medium carrots, peeled and chopped (1 cup)

2 medium celery stalks, thinly sliced (⅔ cup)

¼ cup loosely packed, stemmed, fresh dill fronds, minced

½ teaspoon ground allspice

½ teaspoon garlic powder

½ teaspoon table salt

½ teaspoon ground black pepper

Beef barley soup is undoubtedly one of the famous classics of the soup world, but our favorite—chicken barley—is more like a J-level celebrity. What a shame! Ours is hearty but lighter, a perfect dish for a spring evening. The dill really perks up the flavors, turning the dish into something like the traditional chicken soup served for Passover. But with all that barley, hold the matzoh balls!

1. Stir everything in the insert set in a **5-, 6-, 8-, or 10-quart Instant Pot.** Lock the lid onto the cooker.

2.

	Set pot for	Set level to	Valve must be	Set time for	If needed, press
For Max pots only	PRESSURE COOK	MAX	—	35 minutes with the KEEP WARM setting off	START
For all other pots	PRESSURE COOK or MANUAL	HIGH	Closed	45 minutes with the KEEP WARM setting off	START
For the slow-cook function	SLOW COOK	HIGH	Open	5 hours with the KEEP WARM setting off	START

3. When the pot has finished cooking under pressure, turn it off and let the pressure **return to normal naturally,** about 25 minutes. Whichever cooking method you've used, unlatch the lid and open the cooker. Stir well before serving hot.

Other Pots

- For a **3-quart Instant Pot,** you *must* halve all of the ingredient amounts.

- For an **8- or 10-quart Instant Pot,** you *can* increase all of the ingredient amounts by 50 percent.

- For a **10-quart Instant Pot,** you *can* even double almost all of the ingredient amounts *except* you *must* use only 6 tablespoons loosely packed stemmed fresh dill fronds, chopped.

Beyond

- For more heft, open the pot after cooking, then set the SAUTÉ setting on MEDIUM, NORMAL, or CUSTOM 300°F. Bring the soup to a simmer, then stir in 3 cups (about 8 ounces) packed baby spinach leaves, chopped. Cook for 1 minute, stirring often, until the spinach wilts. Turn off the heat and set aside for a couple of minutes to blend the flavors.

- For a brighter soup, stir in 1 tablespoon white balsamic vinegar after opening the pot.

No-Brainer Smoked Turkey and Split Pea Soup

11 ingredients	SPECIAL EQUIPMENT: none
6 SERVINGS	
METHOD: fast/slow	PRESSURE: max or high

TIME UNDER PRESSURE: 7 or 10 minutes

RELEASE: natural

TOTAL TIME WITH PRESSURE: about 1 hour

TOTAL TIME WITH SLOW COOKING: about 4 hours 15 minutes

CAN BE GLUTEN-FREE

7 cups (1 quart plus 3 cups) chicken broth

1 pound smoked boneless deli turkey (gluten-free, if necessary), diced

2 cups raw green or yellow split peas

1 large yellow or white onion, chopped (1½ cups)

1 large carrot, peeled and chopped (¾ cup)

2 medium celery stalks, thinly sliced (⅔ cup)

1 teaspoon rubbed or ground sage

½ teaspoon ground dried turmeric

½ teaspoon garlic powder

½ teaspoon table salt, plus more to taste

½ teaspoon ground black pepper

Split pea soup couldn't be easier in the pot, but we have to warn you: Our version is nothing like your grandmother's wallpaper paste. We use a lot more broth so 1) the split peas don't congeal into a porridge and 2) the soup stays, well, a true soup. The results are lighter because of all that broth and because we've used smoked turkey, rather than the more traditional smoked ham (which releases a great deal of fat under pressure).

1. Stir everything in the insert set in a **5-, 6-, 8-, or 10-quart Instant Pot.** Lock the lid on the pot.

2.

	Set pot for	Set level to	Valve must be	Set time for	If needed, press
For Max pots only	PRESSURE COOK	MAX	—	7 minutes with the KEEP WARM setting off	START
For all other pots	PRESSURE COOK or MANUAL	HIGH	Closed	10 minutes with the KEEP WARM setting off	START
For the slow-cook function	SLOW COOK	HIGH	Open	4 hours with the KEEP WARM setting off	START

3. When the pot has finished cooking under pressure, turn it off and let the pressure **return to normal naturally,** about 25 minutes. Whichever cooking method you've used, unlatch the lid and open the pot. Stir the soup, taste it to see if it needs any additional salt, and serve warm.

Other Pots

- For a 3-quart Instant Pot, you *must* halve all of the ingredient amounts.

- For an 8- or 10-quart Instant Pot, you *can* increase all of the ingredients by 50 percent.

- For a 10-quart Instant Pot, you *can* even double almost all of the ingredient amounts *except* you *must* use only ¾ teaspoon ground dried turmeric and ¾ teaspoon garlic powder (only 50 percent more than the original amounts).

Beyond

- For a smokier flavor, put a smoked turkey neck or turkey wing in the insert with the broth (but no other ingredients). Lock on the lid and cook at MAX pressure (for Max models only) for 40 minutes or at HIGH pressure (for all other pots) for 45 minutes, then turn the machine off and let the pressure return to normal naturally, about 25 minutes. Remove the neck or wing; take off any meat you can and stir it into the smoky broth. Add the remaining ingredients and continue with the recipe as stated.

- Serve the soup with dollops of sour cream and spoonfuls of chutney.

Chunky Black Bean and Chorizo Soup

13 ingredients	SPECIAL EQUIPMENT: none	TIME UNDER PRESSURE: 3 or 5 minutes
4 SERVINGS		TOTAL TIME WITH PRESSURE: about 25 minutes
METHOD: fast/slow	PRESSURE: max or high	RELEASE: quick

TOTAL TIME WITH SLOW COOKING: about 2 hours 15 minutes

CAN BE GLUTEN-FREE

---

1 tablespoon olive oil

4 ounces dried Spanish chorizo (gluten-free, if necessary), diced

1 medium yellow or white onion, chopped (1 cup)

3 cups chicken broth

Two 15-ounce cans black beans, drained and rinsed (3½ cups)

One 10-ounce can mild or hot diced tomatoes and green chiles, such as Rotel (1¼ cups)

1 jarred whole roasted red pepper, chopped

2 medium garlic cloves, minced (2 teaspoons)

1 teaspoon ground cumin

1 teaspoon dried oregano

½ teaspoon table salt

1 tablespoon lime juice

Up to 1 tablespoon hot red pepper sauce (gluten-free, if necessary), such as Tabasco sauce

Other Pots

- For a 3-quart Instant Pot, you *must* halve all of the ingredient amounts.

- For a 10-quart Instant Pot, you *must* increase all of the ingredient amounts by 50 percent or you *can* even double almost all of the ingredient amounts *except* you *must* use ¾ teaspoon table salt (only 50 percent more than the original amount).

A soup like this one is often pureed—which means the whole thing ends up as some weird version of culinary glue. We leave the soup chunky, so we can 1) omit the extra step of blending it, and 2) add the chorizo right up front to let its flavor infuse the soup under pressure.

We call for Spanish chorizo (a dried sausage), not Mexican (a fresh one). The flavor of the dried sausage is more intense.

1.

	Press	Set it for	Set time for	If needed, press
In all models	SAUTÉ	MEDIUM, NORMAL, or CUSTOM 300°F	10 minutes	START

2. As the pot heats, warm the oil in the insert set in a **5-, 6-, or 8-quart Instant Pot.** Add the chorizo and cook, stirring often, until the oil is red, about 3 minutes. Add the onion and continue cooking, stirring often, until softened, about 3 minutes.

3. Stir in the broth and scrape up any browned bits on the pot's bottom. Add the beans, canned tomatoes and green chiles, the roasted red pepper, garlic, cumin, oregano, and salt. Stir well, turn off the heat, and lock the lid on the pot.

4.

	Set pot for	Set level to	Valve must be	Set time for	If needed, press
For Max pots only	PRESSURE COOK	MAX	—	3 minutes with the KEEP WARM setting off	START
For all other pots	PRESSURE COOK or MANUAL	HIGH	Closed	5 minutes with the KEEP WARM setting off	START
For the slow-cook function	SLOW COOK	HIGH	Open	2 hours with the KEEP WARM setting off	START

5. When the pot has finished cooking under pressure, use the **quick-release method** to bring the pressure back to normal. Whichever cooking method you've used, unlatch the lid and open the pot. Stir in the lime juice and hot red pepper sauce (to taste). Cool for a couple of minutes and serve warm.

Beyond

- Garnish servings with sour cream and chopped, stemmed, fresh cilantro leaves. Have lots of corn tortillas on hand.

Steak & Potato Lover's Soup

16 ingredients

6 SERVINGS

METHOD:
fast/slow

SPECIAL EQUIPMENT:
none

PRESSURE:
max or high

TIME UNDER PRESSURE:
16 or 20 minutes

RELEASE:
quick

TOTAL TIME WITH PRESSURE:
about 55 minutes

TOTAL TIME WITH SLOW COOKING:
about 3½ hours

CAN BE GLUTEN-FREE

1 tablespoon butter

1 tablespoon olive oil

1¼ pounds boneless beef sirloin, cut into 1½-inch pieces

1 cup light but dry red wine, such as Pinot Noir; or unsweetened cranberry juice

6 cups (1½ quarts) beef broth

3 tablespoons tomato paste

3 tablespoons bottled steak sauce (gluten-free, if necessary)

2 medium garlic cloves, minced (2 teaspoons)

2 teaspoons dried oregano

2 teaspoons dried thyme

1 teaspoon table salt

1 teaspoon ground black pepper

2 bay leaves

1 pound yellow potatoes, such as Yukon Golds, cut into 1-inch cubes

3 tablespoons stemmed, fresh parsley leaves, chopped

1 tablespoon red wine vinegar

Other Pots

- For a 3-quart Instant Pot, you *must* halve all of the ingredient amounts.

- For a 10-quart Instant Pot, you *can* increase all of the ingredient amounts by 50 percent.

Beyond

- Garnish the servings with finely grated sharp American cheddar or Monterey Jack cheese.

- Or top with sour cream and minced chives.

When you prepare this hearty, delicious soup for the Fred Flintstones in your world, make sure to take your time when browning the meat. Get good, dark color on every piece, preferably even on the "sides" of each piece (not just the bigger, flat surfaces). Believe us: The extra time will pay off.

1.

	Press	Set it for	Set time for	If needed, press
In all models	SAUTÉ	MEDIUM, NORMAL, or CUSTOM 300°F	25 minutes	START

2. As the pot heats, melt the butter in the oil in the insert set in a **5-, 6 , 8, or 10-quart Instant Pot.** Add about a third of the sirloin pieces and brown them well on all sides, about 6 minutes, turning occasionally. Use a slotted spoon to transfer these pieces to a nearby bowl and continue browning the remaining pieces in two additional batches.

3. When all the beef is in the bowl, add the wine to the insert and scrape up *all* the browned bits on its bottom. Stir in the broth and tomato paste until the tomato paste dissolves. Stir in the steak sauce, garlic, oregano, thyme, salt, pepper, and bay leaves.

4. Turn off the heat and stir in the potatoes as well as the steak pieces plus any accumulated juice in their bowl. Lock the lid on the pot.

5.

	Set pot for	Set level to	Valve must be	Set time for	If needed, press
For Max pots only	PRESSURE COOK	MAX	—	16 minutes with the KEEP WARM setting off	START
For all other pots	PRESSURE COOK or MANUAL	HIGH	Closed	20 minutes with the KEEP WARM setting off	START
For the slow-cook function	SLOW COOK	HIGH	Open	3 hours with the KEEP WARM setting off	START

6. When the pot has finished cooking under pressure, use the **quick-release method** to bring the pressure back to normal. Whichever cooking method you've used, unlatch the lid and open the pot. Fish out and discard the bay leaves. Stir in the parsley and vinegar. Set aside for a couple of minutes, then serve warm.

Ginger-Garlic Beef and Noodle Soup

13 ingredients	
4–6 SERVINGS	
METHOD: fast/slow	
SPECIAL EQUIPMENT: none	
PRESSURE: max or high twice	
TIME UNDER PRESSURE: 13 or 17 minutes	
RELEASE: quick twice	
TOTAL TIME WITH PRESSURE: about 35 minutes	
TOTAL TIME WITH SLOW COOKING: about 2 hours 20 minutes	
GLUTEN-FREE	

7 cups (1 quart plus 3 cups) chicken broth

1½ pounds boneless beef sirloin, trimmed and cut into ¼-inch-thick slices as if for stir-fry

8 dried shiitake mushrooms, stems removed and discarded, the caps broken into small bits

6 medium scallions, trimmed and thinly sliced (2 cups)

3 medium garlic cloves, minced (1 tablespoon)

2 tablespoons minced peeled fresh ginger

2 tablespoons unseasoned rice vinegar

1 tablespoon granulated white sugar

1 teaspoon table salt

2 teaspoons ground black pepper

One 3-inch cinnamon stick

2 small heads of baby bok choy (about 5 ounces each), stemmed and roughly chopped (2 cups)

4 ounces raw dried wide flat rice noodles, broken as necessary to fit in the pot

Other Pots

- For a 3-quart Instant Pot, you *must* halve all of the ingredient amounts.

- For a 10-quart Instant Pot, you *can* increase almost all of the ingredient amounts by 50 percent *except* you *must* use 2½ tablespoons unseasoned rice vinegar.

Beyond

- Squeeze Sriracha or other hot red pepper sauce over each serving.

- And/or drizzle each serving with toasted sesame oil.

- And/or add drained canned or jarred baby corn as a garnish.

- And/or mound some bean sprouts in the middle of each serving.

Talk about a bowl of comfort! But the prep is a tad involved. Bear with us. You'll need to put the ingredients under pressure twice. The first time infuses the flavor of the dried mushrooms and cinnamon into the broth. The second time cooks the rice noodles and the bok choy quickly so they don't get squishy. Your efforts will pay off. Promise.

We call for chicken broth here, not beef, because it gives the soup a clearer color and a milder flavor, the better to see and taste all the vegetables and noodles.

1. Stir the broth, sirloin, broken shiitake caps, scallions, garlic, ginger, vinegar, sugar, salt, pepper, and cinnamon in the insert set in a **5-, 6-, 8-, or 10-quart Instant Pot.** Lock the lid on the pot.

2.

	Set pot for	Set level to	Valve must be	Set time for	If needed, press
For Max pots only	PRESSURE COOK	MAX	—	12 minutes with the KEEP WARM setting off	START
For all other pots	PRESSURE COOK or MANUAL	HIGH	Closed	15 minutes with the KEEP WARM setting off	START
For the slow-cook function	SLOW COOK	HIGH	Open	2 hours with the KEEP WARM setting off	START

3. When the pot has finished cooking under pressure, use the **quick-release method** to bring the pressure back to normal. Whichever cooking method you've used, unlatch the lid and open the pot. Fish out and discard the cinnamon stick. Stir in the bok choy and broken noodles. All the noodles may not be covered by the liquid in the pot. Lock the lid back onto the cooker.

4.

	Set pot for	Set level to	Valve must be	Set time for	If needed, press
For Max pots only	PRESSURE COOK	MAX	—	1 minute with the KEEP WARM setting off	START
For all other pots	PRESSURE COOK or MANUAL	HIGH	Closed	2 minutes with the KEEP WARM setting off	START

5. When the pot has finished cooking a second time, use the **quick-release method** to bring the pressure back to normal. Unlatch the lid and open the pot. Stir well before serving.

See photo in insert.

Ground Beef and Lentil Soup

15 ingredients

4–6 SERVINGS

METHOD: fast/slow

SPECIAL EQUIPMENT: none

PRESSURE: max or high

TIME UNDER PRESSURE: 15 or 20 minutes

RELEASE: quick

TOTAL TIME WITH PRESSURE: about 45 minutes

TOTAL TIME WITH SLOW COOKING: about 2 hours 45 minutes

GLUTEN-FREE

1 tablespoon butter

1 pound lean ground beef, preferably 90 percent lean or more

4 cups (1 quart) beef broth

One 14-ounce can crushed tomatoes *packed in juice* (1¾ cups)

8 ounces bagged shredded coleslaw mix (that is, undressed shredded cabbage and carrots—2 cups)

1 cup brown lentils, picked over for small stones and rinsed

1 medium yellow or white onion, chopped (1 cup)

2 medium celery stalks, thinly sliced (⅔ cup)

1 teaspoon table salt

½ teaspoon dried thyme

½ teaspoon mild paprika

½ teaspoon ground black pepper

¼ teaspoon garlic powder

1 bay leaf

2 cups loosely packed, chopped baby spinach leaves (2 ounces)

Other Pots

- For a 3-quart Instant Pot, you *must* halve all of the ingredient amounts.
- For an 8- or 10-quart Instant Pot, you *can* increase all of the ingredient amounts by 50 percent.
- For a 10-quart Instant Pot, you *can* even double all of the amounts.

Beyond

- For a spicier soup, substitute two 10-ounce cans of hot or mild canned diced tomatoes and green chiles (such as Rotel) for the single can of diced tomatoes.

We're not fans of ground beef soups…unless they're made under pressure, which extracts a great deal of flavor from the meat. All that flavor mixes perfectly with the earthy lentils, which will (mostly) hold their shape under pressure, offering a little starchy thickening to the soup.

1.

	Press	Set it for	Set time for	If needed, press
In all models	SAUTÉ	MEDIUM, NORMAL, or CUSTOM 300°F	5 minutes	START

2. As the pot heats, melt the butter in the insert set in a **5-, 6-, 8-, or 10-quart Instant Pot.** Crumble in the ground beef and cook, stirring often to break up any clumps, until the meat loses its raw, red color, about 3 minutes.

3. Pour in the broth and scrape up any browned bits on the pot's bottom. Turn off the heat. Stir in the crushed tomatoes with their juice, the slaw mix, lentils, onion, celery, salt, thyme, paprika, pepper, garlic powder, and bay leaf. Lock the lid on the pot.

4.

	Set pot for	Set level to	Valve must be	Set time for	If needed, press
For Max pots only	PRESSURE COOK	MAX	—	15 minutes with the KEEP WARM setting off	START
For all other pots	PRESSURE COOK or MANUAL	HIGH	Closed	20 minutes with the KEEP WARM setting off	START
For the slow-cook function	SLOW COOK	HIGH	Open	2½ hours with the KEEP WARM setting off	START

5. When the pot has finished cooking under pressure, use the **quick-release method** to bring the pressure back to normal. Whichever cooking method you've used, unlatch the lid and open the cooker. Fish out and discard the bay leaf. Stir in the baby spinach.

6.

	Press	Set it for	Set time for	If needed, press
In all models	SAUTÉ	MEDIUM, NORMAL, or CUSTOM 300°F	5 minutes	START

7. Stir the soup as it comes to a simmer. Continue cooking, stirring occasionally, until the spinach wilts, about 1 minute. Turn off the heat, use hot pads or silicone baking mitts to transfer the (hot!) insert to a nearby wire rack, and set the soup aside for a couple of minutes to blend the flavors before serving warm.

No-Brainer Corned Beef & Cabbage Soup

10 ingredients

6 SERVINGS

METHOD: fast/slow

SPECIAL EQUIPMENT: none

PRESSURE: max or high

TIME UNDER PRESSURE: 22 or 28 minutes

TOTAL TIME WITH PRESSURE: about 45 minutes

RELEASE: quick

TOTAL TIME WITH SLOW COOKING: about 3 hours 15 minutes

CAN BE GLUTEN-FREE

---

6 cups (1½ quarts) chicken broth

1 medium red cabbage (about 1½ pounds), quartered, cored, and chopped (6 cups)

1 pound packaged corned beef (not deli corned beef—but gluten-free, if necessary), any spice packet discarded, rinsed well, and *diced*

1 medium sweet red apple, such as a Gala, peeled, cored, and chopped (¾ cup)

1 small red onion, chopped (about ½ cup)

¼ cup loosely packed, stemmed, fresh dill fronds, chopped

2 tablespoons light brown sugar

2 tablespoons apple cider vinegar

½ teaspoon ground black pepper

2 bay leaves

We've got a fancy preparation for corned beef and cabbage coming up (page 264). But we so love the meaty, briny flavors of corned beef that we wanted to turn the classic into a bowl of comfort for when you're stressed out or under the weather. And frankly, there are few easier soups in this chapter! The corned beef has plenty of salt in it, which means the soup has plenty in it, too. If you want a less salty soup, look for a low-sodium corned beef.

Stock up on corned beefs when they go on sale after the March holiday and put them in your freezer. It's always good to be able to make a simple soup when life gets busy.

1. Stir all the ingredients in a **5-, 6-, 8-, or 10-quart Instant Pot.** Lock the lid onto the cooker.

2.

	Set pot for	Set level to	Valve must be	Set time for	If needed, press
For Max pots only	PRESSURE COOK	MAX	—	22 minutes with the KEEP WARM setting off	START
For all other pots	PRESSURE COOK or MANUAL	HIGH	Closed	28 minutes with the KEEP WARM setting off	START
For the slow-cook function	SLOW COOK	HIGH	Open	3 hours with the KEEP WARM setting off	START

3. When the pot has finished cooking under pressure, use the **quick-release method** to bring the pressure back to normal. Whichever cooking method you've used, unlatch the lid and open the cooker. Fish out and discard the bay leaves. Cool for a couple of minutes, then serve warm.

Other Pots

- For a **3-quart Instant Pot**, you *must* halve all of the ingredient amounts.

- For a **10-quart Instant Pot**, you can increase almost all of the ingredient amounts by 50 percent, but use 2 medium sweet red apples, peeled, cored, and chopped (1½ cups).

Beyond

- Have Irish soda bread on hand!

- Or try it with pretzel nuggets (even floated in the soup).

Manhattan-Style Clam Chowder

11 ingredients	**SPECIAL EQUIPMENT:** none	**TIME UNDER PRESSURE:** 5 or 7 minutes
4–6 SERVINGS	**PRESSURE:** max or high	
METHOD: fast/slow	**RELEASE:** modified natural	

TOTAL TIME WITH PRESSURE: about 40 minutes	**TOTAL TIME WITH SLOW COOKING:** about 2 hours 15 minutes
	CAN BE GLUTEN-FREE

6 ounces slab bacon (gluten-free, if necessary), diced

2 medium yellow or white onions, chopped (2 cups)

4 medium celery ribs, thinly sliced (1⅓ cups)

5 cups (1 quart + 1 cup) chicken broth

3 cups minced fresh shucked clams; or frozen chopped clams, thawed, with any accumulated juices retained

One 14-ounce can diced tomatoes *packed in juice* (1¾ cups)

½ pound red-skinned potatoes, diced (1¾ cups)

1½ teaspoons dried oregano

1½ teaspoons dried thyme

½ teaspoon red pepper flakes

Table salt, to taste

Other Pots

- For a **3-quart Instant Pot**, you *must* halve all of the ingredient amounts.

- For a **10-quart Instant Pot**, you *can* increase almost all of the ingredient amounts by 50 percent *except* you *must* use only 8 ounces slab bacon, diced.

Beyond

- For more flavor, stir in up to 2 teaspoons dried parsley, 1 teaspoon dried basil, and/or 1 teaspoon celery seeds with the dried herbs.

Manhattan chowder is traditionally made with tomatoes, not cream—and with bacon (of course) for a smoky, salty flavor. Rather than strips, we call for slab bacon because the diced meat offers a bit more "bite" (or textural balance) in the soup. Lay the slab bacon one large side down on your cutting board, then slice into ¼-inch-thick strips. Slice these into ¼-inch matchsticks that you then cut into ¼-inch pieces.

Large supermarkets now stock pasteurized cans of shucked clams in front of or near the fish counters. We can sometimes even find fresh, shucked clams up here in New England—a true luxury! Either of these will be better than the shelf-stable cans of chopped clams.

1.

	Press	Set it for	Set time for	If needed, press
In all models	SAUTÉ	MEDIUM, NORMAL, or CUSTOM 300°F	10 minutes	START

2. As the pot heats, put the bacon pieces in the insert set in a **5-, 6-, 8-, or 10-quart Instant Pot.** Cook, stirring occasionally, until the cubes are browned on all sides, about 7 minutes. Add the onions and celery; cook, stirring more often, until the onions have softened, about 3 minutes.

3. Stir in the broth and scrape up any browned bits on the pot's bottom. Turn off the heat; then stir in the clams, tomatoes and their juice, the potatoes, oregano, thyme, and red pepper flakes. Lock the lid on the pot.

4.

	Set pot for	Set level to	Valve must be	Set time for	If needed, press
For Max pots only	PRESSURE COOK	MAX	—	5 minutes with the KEEP WARM setting off	START
For all other pots	PRESSURE COOK or MANUAL	HIGH	Closed	7 minutes with the KEEP WARM setting off	START
For the slow-cook function	SLOW COOK	HIGH	Open	2 hours with the KEEP WARM setting off	START

5. When the pot has finished cooking under pressure, turn it off and let its pressure **return to normal naturally for 5 minutes.** Then use the **quick-release method** to get rid of the residual pressure in the pot. Whichever cooking method you've used, unlatch the lid and open the pot. Taste the soup to see if it needs any salt before serving.

New England–Style Clam Chowder

15 ingredients

4–6 SERVINGS

METHOD: fast/slow

SPECIAL EQUIPMENT: none

PRESSURE: max or high

TIME UNDER PRESSURE: 5 or 7 minutes

RELEASE: modified natural

TOTAL TIME WITH PRESSURE: about 30 minutes

TOTAL TIME WITH SLOW COOKING: about 2 hours 30 minutes

GLUTEN-FREE

2 tablespoons butter

4 thin slices of prosciutto, chopped

2 large single-lobe shallots, halved lengthwise and thinly sliced

2 medium celery stalks, thinly sliced (⅔ cup)

4 cups (1 quart) chicken broth

1 cup bottled clam juice

1 pound large white potatoes (do not use russet or baking potatoes), peeled and diced (3¾ cups)

2 cups minced fresh shucked clams; or frozen chopped clams, thawed, with any accumulated juices

One 12-ounce can whole, low-fat, or fat-free evaporated milk (1½ cups)

½ teaspoon rubbed or ground sage

½ teaspoon dried thyme

½ teaspoon ground black pepper

¼ cup heavy or light cream

2 tablespoons cornstarch

Table salt, to taste

Is there anything more typically New England than a big bowl of creamy clam chowder? Fair enough, but we've dared the culinary tyrants and switched things up a bit. Rather than a heavy hit of smoky flavor from bacon, we prefer prosciutto in ours, a milder and salty (but okay, porky) taste that pairs well with the sweet and briny clams. We didn't peel the potatoes in Manhattan-Style Clam Chowder (page 95), but we do so here to keep the soup a true blond with no distracting streaks. If you really want pitch-perfect aesthetics, follow the suggestion in the **Beyond** and substitute ground white pepper for the black pepper.

1.

	Press	Set it for	Set time for	If needed, press
In all models	SAUTÉ	MEDIUM, NORMAL, or CUSTOM 300°F	10 minutes	START

2. As the pot heats, melt the butter in the insert set in a **5-, 6-, 8-, or 10-quart Instant Pot.** Add the prosciutto and cook, stirring often, until lightly browned and frizzled at the edges, about 3 minutes. Add the shallots and celery; cook, stirring almost constantly, until the shallots soften, about 2 minutes.

3. Pour in the broth and clam juice, then scrape up any browned bits on the pot's bottom and turn off the heat. Stir in the potatoes, clams, evaporated milk, sage, thyme, and pepper. Lock the lid on the pot.

4.

	Set pot for	Set level to	Valve must be	Set time for	If needed, press
For Max pots only	PRESSURE COOK	MAX	—	5 minutes with the KEEP WARM setting off	START
For all other pots	PRESSURE COOK or MANUAL	HIGH	Closed	7 minutes with the KEEP WARM setting off	START
For the slow-cook function	SLOW COOK	HIGH	Open	2 hours with the KEEP WARM setting off	START

5. When the pot has finished cooking under pressure, turn it off and let the pressure **return to normal naturally for 5 minutes.** Then use the **quick-release method** to get rid of any residual pressure in the pot. Whichever cooking method you've used, unlatch the lid and open the pot. Whisk the cream and cornstarch in a small bowl until smooth.

6.

	Press	Set it for	Set time for	If needed, press
In all models	SAUTÉ	MEDIUM, NORMAL, or CUSTOM 300°F	10 minutes	START

7. Stir the soup as it comes to a simmer. Stir in the cornstarch slurry, then continue to cook, stirring constantly, until somewhat thickened, less than 1 minute. Turn off the heat and use hot pads or silicone baking mitts to transfer the (hot!) insert to a nearby wire rack. Check to see if the soup needs any salt before serving warm.

Other Pots

- For a 3-quart Instant Pot, you *must* halve all of the ingredient amounts.
- For a 10-quart Instant Pot, you *can* increase all of the ingredient amounts by 50 percent.

Beyond

- Substitute ground white pepper for the black pepper.
- Serve the soup over thick rounds of toasted sliced Italian bread.

Streamlined Frogmore Soup

14 ingredients

4 SERVINGS

METHOD:
fast/slow

SPECIAL
EQUIPMENT:
none

PRESSURE:
max or high

TIME UNDER
PRESSURE:
7 or 10
minutes

RELEASE:
modified
natural

TOTAL
TIME WITH
PRESSURE:
about 40
minutes

TOTAL TIME
WITH SLOW
COOKING:
about 2½
hours

CAN BE
GLUTEN-
FREE

3 cups chicken broth

1 cup tomato juice (do *not* use V8)

1 pound smoked andouille (gluten-free, if necessary), thinly sliced

1 pound very small red-skinned potatoes, each no more than the size of a large olive, scrubbed

4 medium Roma or plum tomatoes, chopped (1 cup)

2 cups fresh corn kernels; or canned kernels, drained; or frozen kernels, thawed

1 large leek, white and pale green part only, trimmed, split lengthwise, washed for internal grit, and thinly sliced (¾ cup)

1 medium celery stalk, thinly sliced (⅓ cup)

2 medium garlic cloves, minced (2 teaspoons)

1 tablespoon stemmed fresh thyme leaves

1 tablespoon Old Bay seasoning

1 teaspoon finely grated lemon zest

1½ pounds large shrimp (about 30 per pound), shelled and deveined

Table salt, to taste

There are no frogs in Frogmore Soup! It's named for an unincorporated low-country community on St. Helena Island, near Hilton Head, South Carolina, a storied recipe from the African-American heritage that is a significant part of the backbone of the United States' culinary scene.

Frogmore soup is traditionally a "boil"—that is, a combination of large ingredients (corn on the cob, head-on shrimp) in an aromatic brew of spices and broth. We've adapted all that for an Instant Pot soup with a smaller number of ingredients—and overall smaller size ingredients, too! Ours is a bit easier than the original, but it's still stocked with vegetables.

Although we call for smoked andouille, a Louisiana classic that offers a strong, meaty kick to the soup, feel free to substitute any smoked sausage (although we'd steer clear of dried, Spanish chorizo which will turn the soup a lurid red).

1. Stir the broth, tomato juice, andouille, potatoes, tomatoes, corn, leek, celery, garlic, thyme, Old Bay, and lemon zest in the insert set in a **5-, 6-, or 8-quart Instant Pot**. Lock the lid on the pot.

2.

		Set pot for	Set level to	Valve must be	Set time for	If needed, press
	For Max pots only	PRESSURE COOK	MAX	—	7 minutes with the KEEP WARM setting off	START
	For all other pots	PRESSURE COOK or MANUAL	HIGH	Closed	10 minutes with the KEEP WARM setting off	START
	For the slow-cook function	SLOW COOK	HIGH	Open	2 hours with the KEEP WARM setting off	START

3. When the pot has finished cooking under pressure, turn it off and let its pressure **return to normal naturally for 5 minutes.** Then use the **quick-release method** to get rid of the residual pressure in the pot. Whichever cooking method you've used, unlatch the lid and open the pot.

4.

	Press	Set it for	Set time for	If needed, press
In all models	SAUTÉ	MEDIUM, NORMAL, or CUSTOM 300°F	5 minutes	START

5. Stir the soup as it comes to a simmer. Add the shrimp and cook, stirring occasionally, until they are pink and firm, about 2 minutes. Turn off the heat and use hot pads or silicone baking mitts to transfer the (hot!) insert to a nearby wire rack. Cool for only 1 or 2 minutes, then taste the soup for salt before serving hot.

Other Pots

- For a 3-quart Instant Pot, you *must* halve all of the ingredient amounts.

- For a 10-quart Instant Pot, you *must* increase all of the ingredient amounts by 50 percent or you *can* even double the amounts.

Beyond

- Offer garlic bread as a side: First, make a paste of olive oil, butter, minced garlic, and finely grated Parmigiano-Reggiano in a 2-to-2-to-1-to-1 ratio (by volume). Spread this mixture on the cut side of halved ciabatta rolls or thick slices of Italian bread. Toast on a baking sheet under a heated broiler until sizzling and lightly browned, 1 to 2 minutes. Sprinkle with salt (preferably coarse salt) while hot.

- Garnish each serving with a nest of baby arugula that's been dressed with a little lemony vinaigrette.

Laksa Noodle Soup

15 ingredients	SPECIAL EQUIPMENT: food processor	TIME UNDER PRESSURE: 4 or 7 minutes	TOTAL TIME WITH PRESSURE: about 30 minutes	
4 SERVINGS				
METHOD: standard	PRESSURE: max or high twice	RELEASE: quick twice	GLUTEN-FREE	

1½ pounds medium shrimp (about 30 per pound), shelled but the shells reserved, the shrimp also deveined

1 large yellow or white onion, quartered

5 cups (1 quart plus 1 cup) chicken broth

2 large single-lobe shallots, quartered

¼ cup sliced almonds

¼ cup fish sauce

2 medium fresh jalapeño chiles, stemmed, quartered, and seeded

2 tablespoons minced peeled fresh ginger

1 teaspoon ground dried coriander

½ teaspoon ground dried turmeric

¼ cup canola, vegetable, or other neutral-flavored oil

One 14-ounce can unsweetened *light* coconut milk (1¾ cups)

2 tablespoons light brown sugar

8 ounces raw dried wide flat rice noodles (sometimes called "rice stick noodles" or "pad Thai noodles"), broken as necessary to fit in the pot

Lime wedges, for garnishing

We promised a few crazy recipes in this book because, well, it's the next generation. Here's one: Laksa is a Southeast Asian curried noodle soup, sometimes made *without* coconut milk, but sometimes with it, as here—for no better reason than the beautiful richness it imparts to the shrimp and chiles. You must use "lite" (or low-fat) coconut milk to prevent scorching.

You'll start by using shrimp shells (and a quartered onion) to turn plain old chicken broth into shrimp stock. From there, you'll make an aromatic paste, toast it, and use it with that stock for the base for the noodle soup. It's worth the work to see your friends gawp over your culinary creds.

1. Mix the reserved shrimp shells, onion quarters, and broth in the insert set in a **5-, 6-, or 8-quart Instant Pot.** Lock the lid on the pot.

2.

	Set pot for	Set level to	Valve must be	Set time for	If needed, press
For Max pots only	PRESSURE COOK	MAX	—	3 minutes with the KEEP WARM setting off	START
For all other pots	PRESSURE COOK or MANUAL	HIGH	Closed	5 minutes with the KEEP WARM setting off	START

3. When the pot has finished cooking, use the **quick-release method** to bring the pressure back to normal. Unlatch the lid and open the pot.

4. Use hot pads or silicone baking mitts to drain the stock from the (hot!) insert through a large colander or mesh strainer and into a bowl to catch the liquid. Reserve the stock and toss out all the solids. Wipe out the pot's insert and return it to the machine.

5. Place the shallots, almonds, fish sauce, jalapeños, ginger, coriander, and turmeric in a food processor fitted with the chopping blade. Cover and process into a paste, stopping the machine at least once to scrape down the inside of the canister.

6.

	Press	Set it for	Set time for	If needed, press
In all models	SAUTÉ	HIGH or MORE	5 minutes	START

7. After the pot has heated for 1 or 2 minutes, add the oil, then the shallot paste. Cook, stirring all the while, until very fragrant, about 1 minute. Stir in the coconut milk, sugar, and the reserved shrimp-shell stock. Turn off the heat; add the shrimp and broken rice noodles. Stir well, although all the noodles will not be submerged. Lock the lid on the pot.

8.

	Set pot for	Set level to	Valve must be	Set time for	If needed, press
For Max pots only	PRESSURE COOK	MAX	—	1 minute with the KEEP WARM setting off	START
For all other pots	PRESSURE COOK or MANUAL	HIGH	Closed	2 minutes with the KEEP WARM setting off	START

9. When the pot has finished cooking, use the **quick-release method** to bring the pressure back to normal. Unlatch the lid, open the pot, and stir the soup. Offer servings in big bowls with lime wedges for squeezing.

Other Pots

- For a 3-quart Instant Pot, you *must* halve all of the ingredient amounts.
- For a 10-quart Instant Pot, you *must* increase all of the ingredient amounts by 50 percent or you *can* even double the amounts.

Beyond

- For a spicier soup, substitute 1½ teaspoons Madras (or red) curry powder for the coriander and turmeric.

3

Pasta
& Noodles

Who wasn't skeptical the first time they made pasta in an Instant Pot? We were. But as if by some weird magic, the pot can cook noodles perfectly, neither too soft nor underdone…but *only* under *specific* guidelines. As you'll see, you shouldn't stir dried spaghetti or other noodles into a sauce, but rather lay the dried noodles on top, sometimes in a crosshatch (or crisscross) pattern. The steam from the sauce will soften and cook the noodles under pressure, then you stir it all together.

Other dried pastas like ziti or penne are sturdier and can be stirred into the sauce before cooking, with the proviso that they are *minimally* stirred into thicker sauces, just until some of the pieces are moistened, not until they touch the insert's bottom. Thicker sauces can cause pasta to glom onto the hot insert, bringing on the infamous BURN notice. Be gentle when you mix in that pasta!

We've got a few specifically gluten-free pasta dishes in this chapter, but we've also let you choose a gluten-free option in almost all of the recipes. After years of testing, we feel the best gluten-free pasta for the Instant Pot is made from a blend of starchy ingredients, with preferably corn, chickpeas, and/ or quinoa in the mix. In almost all cases, the least successful choice is made solely from brown- or white-rice flour (or a mix of the two but with so little of the other flours that they barely register in the ingredient list). There are two exceptions to this rule. The first is when we call for rice stick noodles, rice "fettuccine," and rice vermicelli. Although the noodles are made solely from white-rice flour, they work because they are set into much wetter sauces. And the second exception: our specifically Gluten-Free Spaghetti & Meatball recipe.

No recipe in this chapter calls for whole-wheat pasta. In the original *Instant Pot Bible,* we used a lot of whole-wheat pasta because the sauces had more moisture and tended to overcook standard dried pasta. Here, we are able to reduce the moisture

content in the sauces because we felt free to use the LOW pressure setting. That's why we can use the more familiar, standard dried pasta. A word to the wise: Pay close attention to the pressure levels in these recipes.

Many of these recipes ask you to break dried spaghetti into smaller bits so they fit in the insert. The noodles should lie flat on top of the sauce; they cannot if they're full length. That said, you never need to break dried spaghetti in a 10-quart pot because the insert is large enough to accommodate whole noodles. What's more, you can now buy pot-length dried pasta—noodles that are two-thirds to three-quarters the length of standard varieties—in most North American supermarkets. Just make sure you have the proper *weight* amount of dried spaghetti for a recipe.

We start with some fast pasta meals, maybe even after-school snacks. Then we work our way through a few pasta casseroles. We have a whole slew of one-pot pasta suppers, the dried pasta cooked right in decadent sauces and yummy ragùs. We move on to a set of dishes for dried orzo and Israeli couscous, then round out the chapter with a set of dishes that use rice noodles. Across this chapter, you'll find a few surprises, like a very fine Vegan Bolognese (page 128), made with nuts and riced cauliflower.

If you're new to this IP game, don't be skeptical of pasta in the pot. We've made hundreds of satisfying dishes. We have the cross-trainer to prove it.

Buttery Macaroni with Basil

8 ingredients

4–6 SERVINGS

METHOD:
standard

SPECIAL EQUIPMENT:
none

PRESSURE:
max or high

TIME UNDER PRESSURE:
3 or 4 minutes

RELEASE:
quick

TOTAL TIME WITH PRESSURE:
about 15 minutes

VEGETARIAN

CAN BE GLUTEN-FREE

---

4 cups (1 quart) chicken or vegetable broth

1 stick (8 tablespoons or ½ cup) butter

2 medium garlic cloves, minced (2 teaspoons)

½ teaspoon table salt

½ teaspoon ground black pepper

1 pound raw dried small elbow macaroni (gluten-free, if necessary—for more information, see the chapter introduction on page 103)

3 ounces Parmigiano-Reggiano, finely grated (1½ cups)

½ cup loosely packed, stemmed, fresh basil leaves, chopped

Other Pots

- For a 3-quart Instant Pot, you *must* halve all of the ingredients.

- For a 10-quart Instant Pot, you *must* increase all of the ingredient amounts by 50 percent or you *can* even double almost all of the amounts *except* you *must* use only ¾ cup loosely packed fresh basil leaves, chopped.

Beyond

- Add up to 1 teaspoon red pepper flakes with the garlic.

- For the basil, substitute ¼ cup loosely packed fresh sage leaves, chopped; or 3 tablespoons chopped fresh tarragon leaves.

- Add up to 2 ounces (½ cup) shredded semi-firm mozzarella with the Parmigiano-Reggiano.

Buttery pasta was a staple of most of our childhoods, but when did we stop enjoying this oh-so-simple dish? It's the ultimate comfort food. Or the best dorm food. Or the best late-night snack.

Please note: You *must* let the broth get steamy before you add the pasta. If you don't, the macaroni will fall to the bottom and stick to the insert, prompting that BURN notice. Otherwise, there's not much effort required for this simple dish. Look in the **Beyond** section for ways to gussy it up.

1.

	Press	Set it for	Set time for	If needed, press
In *all* models	SAUTÉ	HIGH or MORE	10 minutes	START

2. As the pot heats, put the broth, butter, garlic, salt, and pepper in the insert set in a **5-, 6-, or 8-quart Instant Pot.** Heat until the butter melts and wisps of steam rise off the liquid. Stir in the macaroni, turn off the heat, and lock the lid on the pot.

3.

	Set pot for	Set level to	Valve must be	Set time for	If needed, press
For Max pots only	PRESSURE COOK	MAX	—	3 minutes with the KEEP WARM setting off	START
For all other pots	PRESSURE COOK or MANUAL	HIGH	Closed	4 minutes with the KEEP WARM setting off	START

4. When the pot has finished cooking, use the **quick-release method** to bring the pressure back to normal. Unlatch the lid and open the cooker. Stir in the cheese and basil leaves. Use hot pads or silicone baking mitts to transfer the (hot!) insert to a nearby wire rack. Cool for 3 to 5 minutes so the pasta absorbs any remaining sauce and the cheese melts. Stir again before serving warm.

One-Pot Sesame Noodles

11 ingredients	
4 SERVINGS	
METHOD: standard	

SPECIAL EQUIPMENT: none

PRESSURE: max or high

TIME UNDER PRESSURE: 5 or 6 minutes

RELEASE: quick

TOTAL TIME WITH PRESSURE: about 20 minutes

VEGAN

CAN BE GLUTEN-FREE

---

2 cups vegetable broth

½ cup soy sauce, preferably low-sodium soy sauce; or gluten-free tamari sauce

¼ cup tahini (sesame seed paste), or natural-style smooth peanut butter, or a 50/50 combo of the two

2 tablespoons toasted sesame oil

2 tablespoons light brown sugar

2 tablespoons unseasoned rice vinegar

Up to 2 tablespoons thick red chile sauce, such as sambal oelek

1 tablespoon minced peeled fresh ginger

Up to 3 medium garlic cloves, minced (about 1 tablespoon)

8 ounces raw dried spaghetti (gluten-free, if necessary—for more information, see the chapter introduction on page 103), broken as needed to fit in the pot

Minced scallions, for garnishing

Other Pots

- For a 3-quart Instant Pot, you *must* halve all of the ingredient amounts and you *must* break the dried spaghetti into even smaller pieces to fit in the pot.

- For an 8-quart Instant Pot, you *can* increase all of the ingredient amounts by 50 percent.

- For a 10-quart Instant Pot, you *must* increase all of the ingredient amounts by 50 percent and you *can* even double the amounts. You do not need to break dried spaghetti for the large pot.

Sesame noodles are a perennial Chinese-American take-out favorite. We've whipped up this recipe so you can make the dish at home as a one-pot wonder. If you like cold sesame noodles (the *true* Chinese-American favorite), make the recipe ahead, then save the noodles (not yet garnished) in a container in the fridge for the next day (or a midnight food raid).

1.

	Press	Set it for	Set time for	If needed, press
In all models	SAUTÉ	MEDIUM, NORMAL, or CUSTOM 300°F	10 minutes	START

2. As the pot heats, stir the broth, soy sauce, tahini and/or peanut butter, the sesame oil, brown sugar, rice vinegar, chile sauce, ginger, and garlic in the insert set in a **5-, 6-, or 8-quart Instant Pot** until the tahini and/or peanut butter dissolves. Continue cooking, stirring frequently, until wisps of steam come off the broth mixture, about 5 minutes.

3. Lay the broken spaghetti in a crosshatch pattern on top of the sauce. Do not press down. Turn off the heat and lock the lid on the pot.

4.

	Set pot for	Set level to	Valve must be	Set time for	If needed, press
For Max pots only	PRESSURE COOK	MAX	—	5 minutes with the KEEP WARM setting off	START
For all other pots	PRESSURE COOK or MANUAL	HIGH	Closed	6 minutes with the KEEP WARM setting off	START

5. When the pot has finished cooking, use the **quick-release method** to bring the pressure back to normal. Unlatch the lid and open the cooker. Stir well, then use hot pads or silicone baking mitts to transfer the (hot!) insert to a nearby wire rack. Let sit for 3 to 5 minutes so the spaghetti can continue to absorb the sauce. Serve in bowls, garnished with minced scallions.

Beyond

- Finely chop or even julienne some cucumber as a garnish with the scallions.
- And/or add some chopped, salted peanuts as a garnish.
- And/or drizzle Sriracha over each serving.

No-Brainer Gnocchi in Cream Sauce

6 ingredients

4 SERVINGS

METHOD:
pot-in-pot

SPECIAL EQUIPMENT:
a 2-quart, 7-inch-round, high-sided, pressure-safe baking or soufflé dish and a pressure-safe rack or trivet

PRESSURE:
max or high

TIME UNDER PRESSURE:
10 or 12 minutes

RELEASE:
modified natural

TOTAL TIME WITH PRESSURE:
about 35 minutes

VEGETARIAN

CAN BE GLUTEN-FREE

1½ cups water

One 14-ounce package frozen potato, sweet potato, or cauliflower gnocchi (gluten-free, if necessary), thawed

1 cup jarred alfredo sauce (gluten-free, if necessary)

¼ cup vegetable broth

¼ cup purchased pesto

2 ounces semi-firm mozzarella, shredded (½ cup)

Not many recipes are easier than this gnocchi casserole, although (admittedly) it can only be made PIP (otherwise, the sauce will scorch against the hot insert). If you keep jarred alfredo sauce and frozen gnocchi on hand, you can make this satisfying dish for a quick weekend lunch or easy dinner—or a simple kids' favorite to squeeze in between practice and homework.

1. Pour the water into the insert set in a **5-, 6-, or 8-quart Instant Pot.** Set a pressure-safe rack or trivet in the insert.

2. Stir the gnocchi, alfredo sauce, and broth in a 2-quart, 7-inch-round, high-sided, pressure-safe baking or soufflé dish until uniform. Dollop the pesto on top. Cover the baking dish with aluminum foil, set the dish on the rack, and lock the lid on the pot.

3.

	Set pot for	Set level to	Valve must be	Set time for	If needed, press
For Max pots only	PRESSURE COOK	MAX	—	10 minutes with the KEEP WARM setting off	START
For all other pots	PRESSURE COOK or MANUAL	HIGH	Closed	12 minutes with the KEEP WARM setting off	START

4. When the pot has finished cooking, turn it off and let the pressure **return to normal naturally for 10 minutes.** Then use the **quick-release method** to get rid of the pot's residual pressure. Unlatch the lid and open the cooker.

5. Use hot pads or silicone baking mitts to transfer the (hot!) baking dish from the cooker to a nearby wire rack. Uncover the baking dish, then stir in the cheese. Let sit for 3 to 5 minutes so the cheese melts and gnocchi continue to absorb the sauce. Stir again and serve warm.

Other Pots

- For a 3-quart Instant Pot, you *must* halve almost all of the ingredient amounts *except* you *must* use 1 cup water in the insert. You *must* also use a 1-quart, 6-inch-round, high-sided, pressure-safe baking or soufflé dish.

- For a 10-quart Instant Pot, you *must* use 2½ cups water in the insert while otherwise completing the recipe as stated.

Beyond

- Rather than serving with the standard chopped salad, try this piquant variation: Chop sun-dried tomatoes packed in oil, reserving their oil and adding a little of it to a serving bowl with them; then add sliced pitted black olives, lots of thinly sliced celery, and lots of thinly sliced radishes. Add a splash of rice vinegar and toss well with table salt and ground black pepper to taste. You can also add drained and chopped jarred artichoke hearts packed in water, minced red onion, and/or minced fresh parsley leaves.

Creamy Spinach and Shells

12 ingredients	
4–6 SERVINGS	
METHOD: standard	

SPECIAL EQUIPMENT: none	
PRESSURE: max or high	

TIME UNDER PRESSURE: 5 or 6 minutes	
RELEASE: quick	

TOTAL TIME WITH PRESSURE: about 25 minutes	
VEGETARIAN	
CAN BE GLUTEN-FREE	

2 tablespoons butter

1 medium single-lobed shallot, chopped (¼ cup)

2 medium garlic cloves, minced (about 2 teaspoons)

1 teaspoon rubbed or ground sage

½ teaspoon table salt

½ teaspoon ground black pepper

¼ teaspoon grated nutmeg

3 cups loosely packed chopped baby spinach leaves (3 ounces)

2½ cups vegetable broth

12 ounces raw dried medium pasta shells (gluten-free, if necessary—for more information, see the chapter introduction on page 103)

½ cup heavy or light cream

8 ounces Swiss or *white* cheddar cheese, shredded (2 cups)

Other Pots

- Because of the more complicated ratios between spinach and pasta, this recipe does not work well in a 3-quart or 10-quart Instant Pot.

Beyond

- For heat, omit the black pepper and add up to 1 teaspoon red pepper flakes with the sage.

- Substitute chopped baby kale or baby arugula for the baby spinach.

Consider this dish a cross between a traditional pasta in cream sauce and that steak-house favorite, creamed spinach. Don't be tempted to cut corners and dump whole baby spinach leaves into the pot. They'll wad around the pasta, making a slimy mess. Chop them into smaller bits so that they don't get in the way of the creamy deliciousness.

1.

	Press	Set it for	Set time for	If needed, press
In all models	SAUTÉ	MEDIUM, NORMAL, or CUSTOM 300°F	5 minutes	START

2. As the pot heats, melt the butter in the insert set in a **5-, 6-, or 8-quart Instant Pot.** Add the shallot and garlic; cook, stirring often, until softened, about 2 minutes. *Do not brown.* Stir in the sage, salt, pepper, and nutmeg until aromatic, just a few seconds.

3. Add the spinach and stir well to combine. Pour in the broth and scrape up any browned bits on the pot's bottom. Warm for 1 minute, then turn off the heat. Stir in the shells until coated and lock the lid on the pot.

4.

	Set pot for	Set level to	Valve must be	Set time for	If needed, press
For Max pots only	PRESSURE COOK	MAX	—	5 minutes with the KEEP WARM setting off	START
For all other pots	PRESSURE COOK or MANUAL	HIGH	Closed	6 minutes with the KEEP WARM setting off	START

5. When the pot has finished cooking, use the **quick-release method** to bring the pressure back to normal. Unlatch the lid and open the cooker.

6.

	Press	Set it for	Set time for	If needed, press
In all models	SAUTÉ	MEDIUM, NORMAL, or CUSTOM 300°F	5 minutes	START

7. Bring the pasta mixture to a low simmer, stirring constantly. Add the cream and continue cooking, stirring almost constantly, to reduce the liquid and remove the cream's raw flavor, about 2 minutes. Turn off the heat and stir in the cheese. Use hot pads or silicone baking mitts to transfer the (hot!) insert to a nearby wire rack. Let sit for 3 to 5 minutes to melt the cheese. Stir again before serving warm.

Pasta with Easy Buttery Tomato Sauce

8 ingredients	
4 SERVINGS	
METHOD: standard	

| SPECIAL EQUIPMENT: none | |
| PRESSURE: max or high | |

| TIME UNDER PRESSURE: 4 or 6 minutes | |
| RELEASE: quick | |

TOTAL TIME WITH PRESSURE: about 25 minutes	
VEGETARIAN	
CAN BE GLUTEN-FREE	

One 28-ounce can whole tomatoes *packed in juice* (3½ cups)

3 cups vegetable broth

Up to 3 medium garlic cloves, minced (1 tablespoon)

1 teaspoon table salt

½ teaspoon grated nutmeg

¾ stick (6 tablespoons) butter

12 ounces raw dried spaghetti (gluten-free, if necessary—for more information, see the chapter introduction on page 103), broken as needed to fit in the pot

Finely grated Parmigiano-Reggiano, for garnishing

Other Pots

- For a 3-quart Instant Pot, you *must* halve all of the ingredient amounts and you *must* break the dried spaghetti into even smaller pieces to fit in the pot.

- For an 8-quart Instant Pot, you *can* increase all of the ingredient amounts by 50 percent.

- For a 10-quart Instant Pot, you *must* increase all of the ingredient amounts by 50 percent and you *can* even double the amounts. You do not need to break dried spaghetti for the large pot.

Beyond

- Garnish the servings with stemmed and finely chopped fresh basil leaves along with the cheese.

- And/or a sprinkling of red pepper flakes.

- And/or a little aromatic olive oil, particularly a fine "finishing" olive oil used as a condiment rather than a cooking fat.

Picture pure simplicity: a buttery, garlicky tomato sauce (without meat or herbs), coating tender spaghetti. An easy meal on its own, it would also be a great side dish to a grilled steak for a retro, steak-house meal. Use canned *whole* tomatoes, not diced. What's more, you *must* hand-crush them into the pot. Doing so keeps the somewhat larger pieces intact under pressure, giving the dish a better texture.

1. Pour the tomatoes and their juice into the insert set in a **5-, 6-, or 8-quart Instant Pot.** Use your clean hands to crush the tomatoes into smaller bits. Get in there! You know you want to!

2.

	Press	Set it for	Set time for	If needed, press
In all models	SAUTÉ	MEDIUM, NORMAL, or CUSTOM 300°F	10 minutes	START

3. As the pot heats, stir in the broth, garlic, salt, and nutmeg. Add the butter. Cook, stirring occasionally, until the butter melts and the entire mixture gets steamy, on the edge of simmering, about 5 minutes.

4. Turn off the heat and lay the broken spaghetti in a crosshatch pattern on the top of the sauce. Press down gently so some of the pasta is in the sauce but none of it touches the insert's bottom. Lock the lid on the pot.

5.

	Set pot for	Set level to	Valve must be	Set time for	If needed, press
For Max pots only	PRESSURE COOK	MAX	—	4 minutes with the KEEP WARM setting off	START
For all other pots	PRESSURE COOK or MANUAL	HIGH	Closed	6 minutes with the KEEP WARM setting off	START

6. When the pot has finished cooking, use the **quick-release method** to bring the pressure back to normal. Unlatch the lid and open the cooker. Stir well, then set the lid askew over the pot and set aside for 2 to 3 minutes so the pasta continues to absorb some of the excess sauce. Serve warm, garnished with finely grated Parmigiano-Reggiano.

See photo in insert.

Easy Pasta Puttanesca

12 ingredients

4 SERVINGS

METHOD:
standard

SPECIAL EQUIPMENT:
none

PRESSURE:
max or high

TIME UNDER PRESSURE:
4 or 6 minutes

RELEASE:
quick

TOTAL TIME WITH PRESSURE:
about 25 minutes

CAN BE GLUTEN-FREE

¼ cup olive oil

Up to 5 medium garlic cloves, minced (1 tablespoon plus 2 teaspoons)

Up to 3 tinned anchovy fillets, minced

Up to ½ teaspoon red pepper flakes

3 cups vegetable broth

One 28-ounce can diced tomatoes *packed in juice* (3½ cups)

½ cup pitted black olives, preferably Kalamata olives, halved lengthwise

1½ tablespoons drained and rinsed small capers

1 tablespoon packed, stemmed, fresh oregano leaves, minced

1 tablespoon packed, stemmed, fresh rosemary leaves, minced

½ teaspoon table salt

¾ pound raw dried penne (gluten-free, if necessary—for more information, see the chapter introduction on page 103)

Other Pots

- For a 3-quart Instant Pot, you *must* halve all of the ingredient amounts.
- For an 8-quart Instant Pot, you *can* increase all of the ingredient amounts by 50 percent.
- For a 10-quart Instant Pot, you *must* increase all of the ingredient amounts by 50 percent and you *can* even double the amounts.

Beyond

- Garnish the servings with lots of stemmed and finely chopped fresh parsley leaves.
- Offer garlic bread on the side (see page 99).

This pasta supper is for the adults in the room, not the kids—unless you've got kids who like garlic and anchovies. (If so, you can retire from your role as a superhero parent right now.) The sauce uses canned diced tomatoes, rather than whole tomatoes (as in Pasta with Easy Buttery Tomato Sauce, page 108), because we want those smaller tomato bits to break down into a smooth sauce. Fresh herbs work best with the bold flavors.

1.

	Press	Set it for	Set time for	If needed, press
In all models	SAUTÉ	MEDIUM, NORMAL, or CUSTOM 300°F	10 minutes	START

2. As the pot heats, warm the oil in the insert set in a **5-, 6-, or 8-quart Instant Pot.** Add the garlic, anchovy, and red pepper flakes. Stir until aromatic, about 1 minute.

3. Pour in the broth, then stir in the tomatoes and their juice, the olives, capers, oregano, rosemary, and salt. Warm for 1 minute, then turn off the heat. Add the penne and stir lightly to coat most of it in the sauce. Lock the lid on the pot.

4.

	Set pot for	Set level to	Valve must be	Set time for	If needed, press
For Max pots only	PRESSURE COOK	MAX	—	4 minutes with the KEEP WARM setting off	START
For all other pots	PRESSURE COOK or MANUAL	HIGH	Closed	6 minutes with the KEEP WARM setting off	START

5. When the pot has finished cooking, use the **quick-release method** to bring the pressure back to normal. Unlatch the lid and open the cooker. Stir well, then set the lid askew over the pot and set it aside for 2 to 3 minutes so the pasta continues to absorb some of the excess sauce. Serve warm.

Easy Spaghetti with Clam Sauce

14 ingredients	
4 SERVINGS	
METHOD: standard	

| SPECIAL EQUIPMENT: none | |
| PRESSURE: max or high | |

| TIME UNDER PRESSURE: 4 or 6 minutes | |
| RELEASE: quick | |

| TOTAL TIME WITH PRESSURE: about 25 minutes | |
| CAN BE GLUTEN-FREE | |

¾ stick (6 tablespoons) butter

6 tablespoons olive oil

1 medium yellow or white onion, chopped (1 cup)

Up to 5 medium garlic cloves, minced (1 tablespoon plus 2 teaspoons)

6 tablespoons dry white wine, such as Chardonnay; or dry vermouth; or unsweetened apple juice

2¼ cups chicken broth

Three 6½-ounce cans chopped clams, or 1 to 1¼ pounds shucked, pasteurized clams; in either case, the clams drained through a fine-mesh sieve *with their juices reserved*

1½ tablespoons lemon juice

1½ tablespoons dried parsley

1½ teaspoons dried oregano

1½ teaspoons dried thyme

½ teaspoon ground black pepper

12 ounces raw dried spaghetti (gluten-free, if necessary—for more information, see the chapter introduction on page 103), broken as needed to fit in the pot

1½ ounces Parmigiano-Reggiano, finely grated (¾ cup)

No, this dish is not the traditional one served in Italian-American restaurants—that is, clams still in their shells, set over garlicky pasta. Instead, this is a faster, weeknight version made with canned clams. The best flavor would be from pasteurized containers of clams, often sold in the refrigerator case at the fish counters of larger supermarkets.

1.

	Press	Set it for	Set time for	If needed, press
In all models	SAUTÉ	MEDIUM, NORMAL, or CUSTOM 300°F	10 minutes	START

2. As the pot heats, melt the butter in the oil in the insert set in a **5-, 6-, or 8-quart Instant Pot.** Add the onion and cook, stirring often, until softened, about 3 minutes. Add the garlic and cook, stirring almost constantly, for 1 minute.

3. Pour in the wine and scrape up any browned bits on the pot's bottom. Stir in the broth as well as *the juice from the clams.* (But not the clams themselves.) Cook, stirring frequently, until very hot, almost simmering, about 2 minutes. Stir in the lemon juice, parsley, oregano, thyme, and pepper. Turn off the heat.

4. Lay the broken spaghetti in a crosshatch pattern over the sauce. Press down gently so some of the pasta is in the sauce but none of it touches the insert's bottom. Lock the lid onto the cooker.

5.

	Set pot for	Set level to	Valve must be	Set time for	If needed, press
For Max pots only	PRESSURE COOK	MAX	—	4 minutes with the KEEP WARM setting off	START
For all other pots	PRESSURE COOK or MANUAL	HIGH	Closed	6 minutes with the KEEP WARM setting off	START

6. When the pot has finished cooking, use the **quick-release method** to bring the pressure back to normal. Unlatch the lid and open the cooker. Stir in the chopped clams and the cheese, then set the lid askew over the pot and set aside for 2 to 3 minutes so the pasta continues to absorb some of the excess sauce. Serve warm.

Other Pots

- For a 3-quart Instant Pot, you *must* halve all of the ingredient amounts and you *must* break the dried spaghetti into even smaller pieces to fit in the pot.

- For an 8-quart Instant Pot, you *can* increase all of the ingredient amounts by 50 percent.

- For a 10-quart Instant Pot, you *must* increase all of the ingredient amounts by 50 percent and you *can* even double the amounts. You do not need to break dried spaghetti for the large pot.

Beyond

- Garnish the pasta with unseasoned bread crumbs. Better yet, lightly brown those bread crumbs in some melted butter and/or olive oil in a skillet set over medium-low heat, stirring often, before using them to top the servings.

Not-Really-Panera-Bread's Mac & Cheese

9 ingredients

4–6 SERVINGS

METHOD:
pot-in-pot

SPECIAL EQUIPMENT:
a 2-quart, 7-inch-round, high-sided, pressure-safe baking or soufflé dish and a pressure-safe rack or trivet

PRESSURE:
high twice

TIME UNDER PRESSURE:
20 minutes

RELEASE:
quick twice

TOTAL TIME WITH PRESSURE:
about 40 minutes

VEGETARIAN

7½ cups water

2 tablespoons olive oil

1 teaspoon table salt

1 pound raw dried small elbow macaroni

2 cups whole milk (do not use low-fat or fat-free)

¼ cup all-purpose flour (dip and level—do not pack)

12 ounces shredded *sharp white* cheddar cheese, shredded (3 cups)

1 cup heavy or light cream

2 teaspoons Dijon mustard

Super creamy, super rich, super satisfying—it's no wonder this dish is a hit at this popular chain. To get the copycat version right, you have to work in stages. First, you cook the macaroni (only on HIGH), *then* you use the PIP method to create a thick, rich cheese sauce (again, only on HIGH). The sauce is tossed with the cooked pasta, now out of the pot. Some internet recipes cook the two together—which ends up with a broken, grainy sauce or overcooked pasta. We feel a little more work is worth the payoff of a perfect copycat.

1.

	Press	Set it for	Set time for	If needed, press
In all models	SAUTÉ	MEDIUM, NORMAL, or CUSTOM 300°F	10 minutes	START

2. As the pot heats, stir 6 cups water, the oil, and salt in the insert set in a **5-, 6-, or 8-quart Instant Pot.** Heat until wisps of steam rise off the water, about 5 minutes. Stir in the macaroni, turn off the heat, and lock the lid onto the cooker.

3.

	Set pot for	Set level to	Valve must be	Set time for	If needed, press
For *all* pots	PRESSURE COOK or MANUAL	HIGH	Closed	4 minutes with the KEEP WARM setting off	START

4. When the pot has finished cooking, use the **quick-release method** to bring the pressure back to normal. Unlatch the lid and open the cooker. Use hot pads or silicone baking mitts to lift the (hot!) insert out of the cooker and drain the macaroni into a large colander set in the sink. Wipe out and return the (still hot!) insert to the pot.

5. Pour the remaining 1½ cups water into the insert. Set a pressure-safe rack or trivet in the insert.

6. Whisk the milk and flour in a 2-quart, 7-inch-round, high-sided, pressure-safe baking or soufflé dish until smooth. Whisk in the cheese, cream, and mustard. Do not cover the dish. Set it on the rack and lock the lid on the pot.

7.

	Set pot for	Set level to	Valve must be	Set time for	If needed, press
For *all* pots	PRESSURE COOK or MANUAL	HIGH	Closed	16 minutes with the KEEP WARM setting off	START

8. When the pot has finished cooking, use the **quick-release method** to bring the pressure back to normal. Unlatch the lid and open the cooker.

9. Pour the cooked macaroni into a large bowl. Use hot pads or silicone baking mitts to lift the (hot!) baking dish out of the cooker. Pour and scrape its contents over the macaroni. Toss well, then set aside for a couple of minutes so the pasta absorbs some of the sauce. Serve warm.

Other Pots

- For a 3-quart Instant Pot, you *must* halve almost all of the ingredient amounts *except* you *must* use 4 cups (1 quart) of water in the insert in step 2 and you *must* use 1 cup water in the insert in step 5. You *must* also use a 1-quart, 6-inch-round, high-sided, pressure-safe baking or soufflé dish.

- For a 10-quart Instant Pot, you *must* use 2 quarts (8 cups) water in the insert in step 2 and you *must* use 2½ cups water in the insert in step 5 while otherwise completing the recipe as stated.

Beyond

- If you pour the macaroni and sauce into a broiler-safe baking dish, you can give it a crusty top by setting the baking dish on a lipped baking sheet, positioning the oven rack 6 inches from the broiler, heating the broiler, and broiling the casserole until browned and bubbling, 2 to 3 minutes. Or if you're working in a 6- or 8-quart Instant Pot, you can start out using a broiler-safe baking dish—once the pasta casserole has been assembled in step 9, wipe out the pot's insert, set the air-frying basket in the insert, set the baking dish inside, set the Instant Pot Air Fryer Lid on top, and cook at 400°F until browned, about 7 minutes.

Hamburger Mac & Cheese

12 ingredients	**SPECIAL EQUIPMENT:** none	**TIME UNDER PRESSURE:** 5 or 6 minutes
4 SERVINGS		
METHOD: standard	**PRESSURE:** max or high	**RELEASE:** quick

TOTAL TIME WITH PRESSURE: about 30 minutes

CAN BE GLUTEN-FREE

---

1 tablespoon butter

1 medium yellow or white onion, chopped (1 cup)

1 pound lean ground beef, at least 90 percent lean or more

1 teaspoon dried oregano

½ teaspoon mild paprika

½ teaspoon grated nutmeg

½ teaspoon table salt

½ teaspoon ground black pepper

2 cups chicken broth

8 ounces raw dried medium shell pasta (gluten-free, if necessary—for more information, see the chapter introduction on page 103)

¾ cup heavy or light cream

5 ounces American sharp cheddar cheese, shredded (1¼ cups)

Other Pots

- For a **3-quart Instant Pot**, you *must* halve all of the ingredient amounts.

- For an **8-quart Instant Pot**, you *must* increase all of the ingredient amounts by 50 percent.

- For a **10-quart Instant Pot**, you *must* double all of the ingredient amounts.

Beyond

- For heat, rather than adding some red pepper flakes with the other spices, drizzle the servings with Sriracha.

Ah, the old debate: Is mac-and-cheese a side dish or a meal? We solved the problem by adding ground beef to the casserole and turning the whole thing into a riff on a cheeseburger. (The pasta is like the bun, right?) Now it's dinner!

1.

	Press	Set it for	Set time for	If needed, press
In all models	SAUTÉ	MEDIUM, NORMAL, or CUSTOM 300°F	10 minutes	START

2. As the pot heats, melt the butter in the insert set in a **5- or 6-quart Instant Pot.** Add the onion and cook, stirring often, until softened, about 3 minutes. Crumble in the ground beef and cook, stirring often, until it loses its raw, red color, about 3 minutes.

3. Stir in the oregano, paprika, nutmeg, salt, and pepper until fragrant, just a few seconds. Pour in the broth and scrape up any browned bits on the pot's bottom. Stir in the pasta until it's coated. Turn off the heat and lock the lid on the pot.

4.

	Set pot for	Set level to	Valve must be	Set time for	If needed, press
For Max pots only	PRESSURE COOK	MAX	—	5 minutes with the KEEP WARM setting off	START
For all other pots	PRESSURE COOK or MANUAL	HIGH	Closed	6 minutes with the KEEP WARM setting off	START

5. When the pot has finished cooking, use the **quick-release method** to bring the pressure back to normal. Unlatch the lid and open the pot.

6.

	Press	Set it for	Set time for	If needed, press
In all models	SAUTÉ	MEDIUM, NORMAL, or CUSTOM 300°F	5 minutes	START

7. Add the cream and cheese. Stir until the cheese melts, just a minute or two. Turn off the heat and use hot pads or silicone baking mitts to transfer the (hot!) insert to a nearby wire rack to stop the cooking. Let sit for 3 to 5 minutes to let the pasta absorb any remaining liquid. Stir again before serving warm.

Gluten-Free Spaghetti & Meatballs

11 ingredients

4 SERVINGS

METHOD:
standard

SPECIAL
EQUIPMENT:
none

PRESSURE:
max or high, then
high

TIME UNDER
PRESSURE:
9 or 10 minutes

RELEASE:
quick twice

TOTAL TIME WITH
PRESSURE:
about 30 minutes

GLUTEN-FREE

---

1 pound lean ground beef, preferably 90 percent lean or more

¼ cup dried potato flakes (that is, instant mashed potatoes)

1 refrigerator-cold large egg, lightly beaten in a small bowl

1 teaspoon dried oregano

1 teaspoon dried thyme

½ teaspoon table salt

½ teaspoon ground black pepper

¼ teaspoon grated nutmeg

2 cups chicken or beef broth

2 cups gluten-free plain marinara or spaghetti sauce

8 ounces raw dried flat white or brown rice noodles or gluten-free "rice spaghetti," broken to fit in the pot as necessary

Other Pots

- For a 3-quart Instant Pot, you *must* halve all of the ingredient amounts and you *must* break the dried spaghetti into even smaller pieces to fit in the pot

- For an 8-quart Instant Pot, you *can* increase all of the ingredient amounts by 50 percent.

- For a 10-quart Instant Pot, you *must* increase all of the ingredient amounts by 50 percent and you *can* even double the amounts. The pasta does not need to be broken to fit in this larger pot.

Beyond

- Garnish the servings with chopped fresh parsley leaves.

- And/or with shredded gluten-free cheese, particularly provolone.

Here's a gluten-free pasta dish without any ingredient substitutes. The potato flakes make the meatballs light but *incredibly* fragile. When shaping the meatballs, take extra care to compact them.

With the meatballs on the bottom of the pot, the mixed-grain gluten-free pasta we've suggested as a substitute for standard dried pasta on page 103 won't work so well here. The noodles have to sit too far out of the sauce to get soft before the meatballs break apart. Instead, use dried, flat rice pasta for this recipe, such as rice fettuccine: not the pale white noodles favored in Southeast Asian dishes, but the yellow or golden dried spaghetti sold as a gluten-free alternative to standard spaghetti. Better yet, look for "brown rice spaghetti," like the stuff made by Lundberg Family Farms.

1. Mix the ground beef, potato flakes, egg, oregano, thyme, salt, pepper, and nutmeg in a medium bowl until uniform. Form this mixture into 8 even balls (about a rounded ¼ cup each).

2. Pour the broth into the insert set in a **5-, 6-, or 8-quart Instant Pot**. Set the meatballs into the broth. Lock the lid on the pot.

3.

	Set pot for	Set level to	Valve must be	Set time for	If needed, press
For Max pots only	PRESSURE COOK	MAX	—	5 minutes with the KEEP WARM setting off	START
For all other pots	PRESSURE COOK or MANUAL	HIGH	Closed	6 minutes with the KEEP WARM setting off	START

4. When the pot has finished cooking, use the **quick-release method** to bring the pressure back to normal. Unlatch the lid and open the cooker.

5. Lay the broken noodles on top of the meatballs. (Be careful: The meatballs are still fragile.) Pour the marinara sauce over the noodles. Lock the lid back onto the pot.

6.

	Set pot for	Set level to	Valve must be	Set time for	If needed, press
For all pots	PRESSURE COOK or MANUAL	HIGH	Closed	4 minutes with the KEEP WARM setting off	START

7. When the pot has finished cooking, again use the **quick-release method** to bring the pressure back to normal. Unlatch the lid and open the cooker. Stir very gently to keep the meatballs intact. Set the lid askew over the pot and set aside for 2 or 3 minutes.

Taco Spaghetti

15 ingredients

4–6 SERVINGS

METHOD:
standard

SPECIAL EQUIPMENT:
none

PRESSURE:
max or high

TIME UNDER PRESSURE:
4 or 6 minutes

RELEASE:
quick

TOTAL TIME WITH PRESSURE:
about 30 minutes

CAN BE GLUTEN-FREE

2 tablespoons canola, vegetable, or other neutral-flavored oil

1 medium yellow or white onion, chopped (about 1 cup)

1 medium green bell pepper, stemmed, seeded, and chopped (about 1 cup)

Up to 3 medium garlic cloves, minced (about 1 tablespoon)

1 pound lean ground beef, preferably 90 percent lean or more

1½ tablespoons standard chili powder

1½ tablespoons mild paprika

1 teaspoon ground cumin

1 teaspoon onion powder

½ teaspoon table salt

Two 10-ounce cans hot or mild diced tomatoes and green chiles, such as Rotel (or one of each type—2½ cups total volume)

2 cups chicken or beef broth

1 cup fresh corn kernels, drained canned corn kernels, or thawed frozen corn kernels

12 ounces raw dried spaghetti (gluten-free, if necessary—for more information, see the chapter introduction on page 103), broken as needed to fit in the pot

8 ounces shredded American sharp cheddar cheese, shredded (2 cups)

Two things right up front: One, taco spaghetti is an internet rage. If you're not in the know, it's essentially cooked spaghetti with a sauce that is a slightly wetter, spicy, ground-meat taco filling. And two, we're never ones to leave well enough alone. So we improved the standard by increasing the number of vegetables with the addition of bell pepper and corn for a better balance of flavors. We've also upped the spices for a tastier sauce.

Many bottlings of standard chili powder include salt, so we've lowered the amount of salt here to compensate. Read the label on your bottle. If it doesn't include salt, increase the table salt to 1 teaspoon.

1.

	Press	Set it for	Set time for	If needed, press
In all models	SAUTÉ	MEDIUM, NORMAL, or CUSTOM 300°F	10 minutes	START

2. As the pot heats, warm the oil in the insert set in a **5-, 6-, or 8-quart Instant Pot.** Add the onion and bell pepper; cook, stirring often, until the onion softens, about 3 minutes. Add the garlic and stir well until aromatic, just a few seconds.

3. Crumble in the ground beef. Continue cooking, stirring more often to break up the meat, until it loses its raw, red color, about 3 minutes. Stir in the chili powder, paprika, cumin, onion powder, and salt until fragrant, just a few seconds.

4. Pour in the canned tomatoes and chiles. Stir well to scrape up any browned bits on the pot's bottom. Stir in the broth and corn. Continue cooking, stirring occasionally, until steam rises off the liquid in the pot.

5. Lay the broken spaghetti in a crosshatch pattern on top of the sauce. Press down gently so some of the pasta is in the sauce but none of it touches the insert's bottom. Turn off the heat and lock the lid on the pot.

6.

	Set pot for	Set level to	Valve must be	Set time for	If needed, press
For Max pots only	PRESSURE COOK	MAX	—	4 minutes with the KEEP WARM setting off	START
For all other pots	PRESSURE COOK or MANUAL	HIGH	Closed	6 minutes with the KEEP WARM setting off	START

7. When the pot has finished cooking, use the **quick-release method** to bring the pressure back to normal. Unlatch the lid and open the cooker. Stir in the cheese, then set the lid askew over the pot and set it aside for a couple of minutes to melt the cheese. Stir again and serve warm.

Other Pots

- For a 3-quart Instant Pot, you *must* halve all of the ingredient amounts and you *must* break the dried spaghetti into even smaller pieces to fit in the pot.

- For an 8-quart Instant Pot, you *can* increase all of the ingredient amounts by 50 percent.

- For a 10-quart Instant Pot, you *must* increase all of the ingredient amounts by 50 percent and you *can* even double the amounts. You do not need to break dried spaghetti for the large pot.

Beyond

- Garnish servings with sour cream and either pico de gallo (see the Beyond for the Not-Really-Chili's Chicken Enchilada Soup, page 86) or jarred salsa.

One-Pot Beef and Udon Stir-Fry

11 ingredients	SPECIAL EQUIPMENT: none
4 SERVINGS	
METHOD: standard	

PRESSURE: low	RELEASE: quick
TIME UNDER PRESSURE: 1 minute	TOTAL TIME WITH PRESSURE: about 20 minutes

Two 14½-ounce packages cooked udon noodles

2 tablespoons toasted sesame oil

1 medium yellow or white onion, halved and sliced into thin half-moons

2 tablespoons minced peeled fresh ginger

1 pound cube steak, cut into ¼-inch-wide strips

1 cup chicken or beef broth

¼ cup regular or low-sodium soy sauce

¼ cup hoisin sauce (see page 18 for more information)

2 tablespoons light brown sugar

Up to 1 teaspoon red pepper flakes

10 ounces fresh small broccoli florets (2 cups)

Udon noodles are not ramen noodles, nor are they lo mein noodles. They're thicker than both, have more chew, and are more in keeping with this sweet and salty dish as it's sometimes served in Japanese and Korean restaurants in North America.

These days, you can find cooked udon noodles at most North American supermarkets. (Hey, if we can find them in rural New England, we know they're out there!) Look for them near the tofu and kimchi in the produce section. They usually come in two sleeves inside one 14½-ounce package. For this recipe, you want *four* sleeves from *two* packages. The noodles are super delicate and easily broken, so handle very gently when draining and once they're in the sauce.

1. Remove the noodles from any packaging, discard any seasoning packets, and set the noodles in a large bowl of warm tap water. Be gentle: They're fragile.

2.

	Press	Set it for	Set time for	If needed, press
In all models	SAUTÉ	MEDIUM, NORMAL, or CUSTOM 300°F	10 minutes	START

3. As the pot heats, warm the sesame oil in the insert set in a **5-, 6-, or 8-quart Instant Pot.** Add the onion and ginger; cook, stirring often, until the onion softens, about 3 minutes. Add the steak and cook, stirring more often, until it loses its raw, red color, about 2 minutes.

4. Pour in the broth and scrape up any browned bits on the pot's bottom. Stir in the soy sauce, hoisin, brown sugar, and red pepper flakes. Bring the sauce to a full simmer. Stir in the broccoli, turn off the heat, and lock the lid on the pot.

5.

	Set pot for	Set level to	Valve must be	Set time for	If needed, press
For *all* pots	PRESSURE COOK or MANUAL	LOW	Closed	1 minute with the KEEP WARM setting off	START

6. When the pot has finished cooking, use the **quick-release method** to bring the pressure back to normal. Unlatch the lid and open the cooker.

7. Drain the noodles in a colander set in the sink, then gently nestle them into the pot's sauce. Set the lid askew over the pot and set aside for 2 minutes before continuing with the next step.

8.

	Press	Set it for	Set time for	If needed, press
In all models	SAUTÉ	MEDIUM, NORMAL, or CUSTOM 300°F	5 minutes	START

9. Uncover the pot and bring the sauce to a very low bubble. Very gently stir the noodles into the sauce. Turn off the heat and serve hot.

Other Pots

- For a **3-quart Instant Pot**, you *must* halve all of the ingredient amounts.

- For an **8-quart Instant Pot**, you *can* increase all of the ingredient amounts by 50 percent.

- For a **10-quart Instant Pot**, you *must* increase all of the ingredient amounts by 50 percent or you *can* even double the ingredient amounts.

Beyond

- Garnish with shreds from a sheet of nori (dried seaweed).

- And/or top with chopped salted roasted cashews.

Tortellini Primavera

7 ingredients	
4 SERVINGS	
METHOD: pot-in-pot	

SPECIAL EQUIPMENT: a 2-quart, 7-inch-round, high-sided, pressure-safe baking or soufflé dish and a pressure-safe rack or trivet

PRESSURE: max or high

TIME UNDER PRESSURE: 12 or 15 minutes

RELEASE: modified natural

TOTAL TIME WITH PRESSURE: about 30 minutes

CAN BE VEGETARIAN

1½ cups water

2 cups purchased plain marinara or plain spaghetti sauce

½ cup chicken or vegetable broth

12 ounces fresh meat or cheese tortellini, or thawed frozen

4 ounces (½ cup) small fresh broccoli florets, or thawed frozen broccoli florets

½ cup shelled fresh peas, or thawed frozen peas

4 ounces semi-firm mozzarella, shredded (1 cup)

You walk in from the day. You're bushed. You just want dinner. No worries: We've got you covered with this super-easy and satisfying casserole, made with store-bought tortellini and marinara sauce, all cooked pot-in-pot so it can get as comforting and delicious as possible. The servings are a little heartier than just sauced tortellini on a plate, thanks to the fact that we can stock the baking dish with lots of added vegetables, a side benefit of the PIP technique.

1. Pour the water into the insert set in a **5-, 6-, or 8-quart Instant Pot.** Put a pressure-safe rack or trivet in the insert.

2. Stir the sauce and broth in a 2-quart, 7-inch-round, high-sided, pressure-safe baking or soufflé dish until uniform. Add the tortellini, broccoli florets, and peas; stir until coated. Top everything with an even layer of the shredded cheese. Seal the dish tightly with aluminum foil, set it on the rack, and lock the lid on the pot.

3.

	Set pot for	Set level to	Valve must be	Set time for	If needed, press
For Max pots only	PRESSURE COOK	MAX	—	12 minutes with the KEEP WARM setting off	START
For all other pots	PRESSURE COOK or MANUAL	HIGH	Closed	15 minutes with the KEEP WARM setting off	START

4. When the pot has finished cooking, turn it off and let its pressure **return to normal naturally for 10 minutes.** Then use the **quick-release method** to get rid of any residual pressure in the pot. Unlatch the lid and open the cooker. Use hot pads or silicone baking mitts to transfer the (hot!) dish to a nearby wire rack. Uncover and cool for 5 minutes before dishing up by the spoonful.

Other Pots

- For a 3-quart Instant Pot, you *must* halve almost all of the ingredient amounts *except* you *must* use 1 cup water in the insert. You *must* also use a 1-quart, 6-inch-round, high-sided, pressure-safe baking or soufflé dish.

- For a 10-quart Instant Pot, you *must* use 2½ cups water in the insert while otherwise completing the recipe as stated.

Beyond

- For an easy side salad, dress sliced cucumbers and very thinly sliced red onion rings with rice vinegar, a pinch of granulated white sugar, and table salt and ground black pepper to taste. Grate a little lemon zest over each serving.

Meat and Mushroom Manicotti

11 ingredients	SPECIAL EQUIPMENT: a food processor	PRESSURE: low
4 SERVINGS		
METHOD: standard		TIME UNDER PRESSURE: 12 minutes

RELEASE: natural

TOTAL TIME WITH PRESSURE: about 50 minutes

---

4 ounces white or brown button mushrooms, brushed clean

½ pound lean ground beef, preferably 90 percent lean or more

¼ cup Italian-style seasoned panko bread crumbs

1 refrigerator-cold large egg, lightly beaten in a small bowl

½ ounce Parmigiano-Reggiano, finely grated (¼ cup), plus *lots* more for garnishing

2 teaspoons dried oregano

1 teaspoon dried basil

½ teaspoon table salt

8 raw dried manicotti tubes (each about 5 inches long—*do not* use no-boil manicotti or cannelloni tubes)

1½ cups chicken or beef broth

1½ cups plain marinara sauce (do not use a chunky variety)

Surprise! You *can* make stuffed manicotti in an Instant Pot without the PIP method! Problem is, you can't stuff the tubes with a lot of cheese (or with *only* cheese, for that matter). The cheese leaks out under pressure and inevitably burns against the insert's surface. But by using a meat mixture with a little cheese, the filling stays compact. Admittedly, the filling is a bit drier than the classic oven-casserole version of this dish; but we fixed that by adding finely ground mushrooms to give it more moisture and keep it exceptionally toothsome, even after it cooks under pressure.

1. Put the mushrooms in a food processor fitted with the chopping blade, cover, and pulse until finely ground but not a paste.

2. Scrape the mushroom mixture into a large bowl. Stir in the ground beef, bread crumbs, egg, cheese, oregano, basil, and salt until uniform. Use your clean hands to stuff this mixture evenly into the manicotti tubes.

3. Stir the broth and marinara sauce in a **6- or 8-quart Instant Pot.** Place the filled tubes side by side in the sauce. Lock the lid on the pot.

4.

	Set pot for	Set level to	Valve must be	Set time for	If needed, press
For *all* pots	PRESSURE COOK or MANUAL	LOW	Closed	12 minutes with the KEEP WARM setting off	START

5. When the pot has finished cooking, turn it off and let the pressure **return to normal naturally,** about 15 minutes. Unlatch the lid and open the cooker. Serve the stuffed manicotti garnished with lots of finely grated Parmigiano-Reggiano.

Other Pots

- Because of the size of the manicotti tubes, this recipe will not work in a 3- or 5-quart Instant Pot.

- For a 10-quart Instant Pot, you *must* double the broth and marinara sauce amounts. You *can* increase the ingredients for the meat stuffing by 50 percent and use 12 dried manicotti tubes.

Beyond

- For a fancier preparation, melt 1 tablespoon butter in 2 tablespoons olive oil in a large skillet set over medium heat, then sauté up to ½ pound thinly sliced white or brown button mushrooms until softened, stirring often, about 5 minutes. Deglaze the skillet with ¼ cup dry white wine, dry vermouth, or unsweetened apple juice—then bring the sauce to a bubble and let it simmer to a glaze, about 1 minute. Add stemmed and chopped fresh oregano leaves and/or fresh parsley leaves to taste, as well as table salt. Spoon these mushrooms over the prepared manicotti, then garnish with lots of finely grated Parmigiano-Reggiano.

See photo in insert.

Cheese Ravioli and Meatball Casserole

6 ingredients

4 SERVINGS

METHOD:
pot-in-pot

SPECIAL EQUIPMENT:
a 2-quart, 7-inch-round high-sided, pressure-safe baking or soufflé dish and a pressure-safe rack or trivet

PRESSURE:
max or high

TIME UNDER PRESSURE:
12 or 15 minutes

RELEASE:
modified natural

TOTAL TIME WITH PRESSURE:
about 45 minutes

1½ cups water

1 pound fresh square cheese ravioli, or thawed frozen ravioli (do not use mini or jumbo ravioli)

Twelve ½- to 1-ounce frozen cooked Italian meatballs, thawed

1½ cups purchased plain marinara or tomato-based spaghetti sauce

¼ cup chicken or vegetable broth

4 ounces semi-firm mozzarella, shredded (1 cup)

Other Pots

- Unfortunately, this recipe will not work in a 3-quart Instant Pot. Because you must use a smaller baking dish, the ravioli will stick up too far to hold the sauce and meatballs under pressure.

- For a 10-quart Instant Pot, you *must* use 2½ cups water in the insert while otherwise completing the recipe as written.

Beyond

- This casserole needs a salad tossed with a lemon vinaigrette. Our favorite dressing is made with olive oil and lemon juice in a 2-to-1 ratio. Add a little minced fresh lemon zest, a touch of Dijon mustard, a generous sprinkle of dried oregano, a very small pinch of garlic powder, as well as table salt and ground black pepper to taste. Whisk all those ingredients in a salad bowl until uniform, then add greens and any other salad fixings you like before you toss well to coat.

Ravioli and meatballs, together in one tomatoey casserole! What could be more satisfying? And what could be easier, since this one is made with *purchased* ravioli, meatballs, and marinara sauce? After you arrange them in the baking dish, they cook into a tasty pasta main course that's ready in minutes. Voilà: dinner!

There's a wide variety of bottled marinara sauces on the market. Get one without corn syrup and with a list of ingredients similar to what you'd use if you were making it from scratch. (FYI, we have a 10-minute from-scratch version in *The Kitchen Shortcut Bible*.)

1. Pour the water into the insert set in a **5-, 6-, or 8-quart Instant Pot.** Put a pressure-safe rack or trivet in the insert.

2. Stand the ravioli on their edges to fill a 2-quart, 7-inch-round, high-sided, pressure-safe baking or soufflé dish, packing them in one layer, sort of like fins sticking up across the dish. Scatter the meatballs over the ravioli.

3. Whisk the sauce and broth in a medium bowl until uniform. Pour this sauce over the ravioli and meatballs. Shake the dish to make sure the sauce goes down between the ravioli. Sprinkle the cheese across the top and seal the baking dish tightly with aluminum foil. Set the dish on the rack and lock the lid on the pot.

4.

	Set pot for	Set level to	Valve must be	Set time for	If needed, press
For Max pots only	PRESSURE COOK	MAX	—	12 minutes with the KEEP WARM setting off	START
For all other pots	PRESSURE COOK or MANUAL	HIGH	Closed	15 minutes with the KEEP WARM setting off	START

5. When the pot has finished cooking, turn it off and let the pressure **return to normal naturally for 10 minutes.** Then use the **quick-release method** to get rid of the pot's residual pressure. Unlatch the lid and open the pot. Use hot pads or silicone baking mitts to transfer the (hot!) dish to a nearby wire rack. Uncover and cool for 5 minutes before dishing up by the spoonful.

Low-Carb Cauliflower Lasagna Casserole

5 ingredients	**SPECIAL EQUIPMENT:** a 2-quart, 7-inch-round, high-sided, pressure-safe baking or soufflé dish and a pressure-safe rack or trivet	**PRESSURE:** max or high	**TOTAL TIME WITH PRESSURE:** about 50 minutes
4 SERVINGS		**TIME UNDER PRESSURE:** 16 or 20 minutes	**CAN BE GLUTEN-FREE**
METHOD: pot-in-pot		**RELEASE:** modified natural	

8 ounces spicy or mild Italian sausages, any casings removed; or bulk spicy or mild Italian sausage meat (gluten-free, if necessary)

1½ cups water

4 cups riced cauliflower (1 pound)

2 cups jarred pasta sauce of any variety (red or white—gluten-free, if necessary)

6 ounces semi-firm mozzarella, shredded (1½ cups)

Other Pots

- For a 3-quart Instant Pot, you *must* halve almost all of the ingredient amounts *except* you *must* use 1 cup water in the insert. You *must* also use a 1-quart, 6-inch-round, high-sided, pressure-safe baking or soufflé dish.

- For a 10-quart Instant Pot, you *must* use 2½ cups water in the insert while otherwise completing the recipe as stated.

Beyond

- If you miss the tomatoes in this pasta casserole, add a layer of pliable, sun-dried tomatoes before the second layer of cauliflower.

- For a vegetarian casserole, use vegan soy meat crumbles. There's no need to cook these—just layer them right into the casserole.

By using riced cauliflower, we can create a "noodle effect" in this casserole without any pasta. Make sure you pack the cauliflower into the baking dish. Don't smoosh it into a paste but just create an even, uniform layer.

Although you can use any jarred pasta sauce, we prefer a white sauce for a super-creamy casserole.

1.

	Press	Set it for	Set time for	If needed, press
In all models	SAUTÉ	MEDIUM, NORMAL, or CUSTOM 300°F	5 minutes	START

2. As the pot heats, crumble the sausage meat into the insert set in a **5-, 6-, or 8-quart Instant Pot.** Cook, stirring often, until the meat no longer retains its raw, red color, about 3 minutes. Turn off the heat and use a slotted spoon to transfer the meat to a nearby bowl.

3. Pour out and discard any grease from the (hot!) insert and wipe out the (still hot!) insert. Set it back in the machine and pour the water into the insert. Set a pressure-safe rack or trivet in it.

4. Pack in 1 cup of the rice cauliflower in an even, compact layer in a 2-quart, 7-inch-round, high-sided, pressure-safe baking or soufflé dish. Top with a third of the cooked sausage, ½ cup of the sauce, and 6 tablespoons of the cheese, making even layers of each. Repeat this layering process twice. Then make a final layer with the remaining riced cauliflower, the remaining sauce, and the remaining cheese. Seal the dish tightly with aluminum foil, set the dish on the rack, and lock the lid on the pot.

5.

	Set pot for	Set level to	Valve must be	Set time for	If needed, press
For Max pots only	PRESSURE COOK	MAX	—	16 minutes with the KEEP WARM setting off	START
For all other pots	PRESSURE COOK or MANUAL	HIGH	Closed	20 minutes with the KEEP WARM setting off	START

6. When the pot has finished cooking, turn it off and let the pressure **return to normal naturally for 10 minutes.** Then use the **quick-release method** to get rid of any residual pressure in the pot. Unlatch the lid and open the cooker. Use hot pads or silicone baking mitts to transfer the (hot!) dish to a nearby wire rack. Uncover and cool for 5 minutes before dishing up by the spoonful.

Ravioli Lasagna

5 ingredients

4 SERVINGS

METHOD:
pot-in-pot

SPECIAL EQUIPMENT:
a 2-quart, 7-inch-round, high-sided, pressure-safe baking or soufflé dish and a pressure-safe rack or trivet

PRESSURE:
max or high

TIME UNDER PRESSURE:
12 or 15 minutes

RELEASE:
modified natural

TOTAL TIME WITH PRESSURE:
about 50 minutes

8 ounces fresh spicy or mild Italian sausages, any casings removed; or bulk spicy or mild Italian sausage meat

1½ cups water

1 pound fresh round or square cheese ravioli, or thawed frozen ravioli (do not use mini or jumbo ravioli)

8 ounces semi-firm mozzarella, shredded (2 cups)

2 cups jarred pasta sauce of any sort (red or white)

We've cracked the secret to a perfect lasagna that won't have you hunched over a baking dish as you painstakingly spread each layer of ingredients, all before having to wash a billion dishes that held all those ingredients. We saved you all that trouble simply by using store-bought ravioli as a substitute for the noodles and cheese. Even better, you can use any sort of pasta sauce you like, even a creamy one like an alfredo sauce, customizing this lasagna to your own taste. No matter which you use, the results are astoundingly simple and good.

1.

	Press	Set it for	Set time for	If needed, press
In all models	SAUTÉ	MEDIUM, NORMAL, or CUSTOM 300°F	5 minutes	START

2. As the pot heats, crumble the sausage meat into the insert set in a **5-, 6-, or 8-quart Instant Pot.** Cook, stirring often, until the meat no longer retains its raw, red color, about 3 minutes. Turn off the heat and use a slotted spoon to transfer the meat to a nearby bowl.

3. Pour out and discard any grease from the (hot!) insert (but not down your drain) and wipe out the (still hot!) insert. Set it back in the machine and pour the water into the insert. Set a pressure-safe rack or trivet in it.

4. Lay one-fourth of the ravioli in a fairly even layer in a 2-quart, 7-inch-round, high-sided, pressure-safe baking or soufflé dish. Top the ravioli with a third of the meat, one-fourth the cheese (½ cup), and one-fourth of the sauce (½ cup), again making fairly even layers. No need to get obsessive—you just don't want a mounded part in the center of the baking dish. Repeat this layering process *twice*, using the same amounts. For the fourth layer, use the remaining ravioli, *then* the remaining sauce followed by the remaining cheese. Seal the baking dish tightly with aluminum foil, set it on the rack, and lock the lid on the pot.

5.

	Set pot for	Set level to	Valve must be	Set time for	If needed, press
For Max pots only	PRESSURE COOK	MAX	—	12 minutes with the KEEP WARM setting off	START
For all other pots	PRESSURE COOK or MANUAL	HIGH	Closed	15 minutes with the KEEP WARM setting off	START

6. When the pot has finished cooking, turn it off and let the pressure **return to normal naturally for 10 minutes**. Then use the **quick-release method** to get rid of any residual pressure in the pot. Unlatch the lid and open the cooker. Use hot pads or silicone baking mitts to transfer the (hot!) dish to a nearby wire rack. Uncover and cool for 5 minutes before dishing it up by the spoonful.

Other Pots

- For a 3-quart Instant Pot, you *must* halve almost all of the ingredient amounts *except* you *must* use 1 cup water in the insert. You *must* also use a 1-quart, 6-inch-round, high-sided, pressure-safe baking or soufflé dish.

- For a 10-quart Instant Pot, you *must* use 2½ cups water in the insert while otherwise completing the recipe as stated.

Beyond

- Sure, you could dress a salad with a bottled Italian vinaigrette. But why? Mix olive oil and red wine vinegar in a 3-to-1 ratio, then add a little Dijon, some dried oregano, a pinch of granulated white sugar, as well as table salt and ground black pepper to taste. Whisk until uniform—or make a batch in a jar, cover it, shake well, and save the rest in the fridge for up to 2 weeks.

Salisbury Meatballs with Gravy Noodles

19 ingredients

4 SERVINGS

METHOD:
egg bites and PIP

SPECIAL EQUIPMENT:
one seven-indentation egg-bite mold, a 6- or 7-inch-round cake pan, and a pressure-safe rack or trivet

PRESSURE:
max or high, then high

TIME UNDER PRESSURE:
14 or 16 minutes

RELEASE:
quick twice

TOTAL TIME WITH PRESSURE:
about 40 minutes

1½ cups chicken broth

Olive oil or olive oil spray, as needed

1 pound ground beef, at least 90 percent lean

¼ cup plain panko bread crumbs

1 refrigerator-cold large egg

1 small single-lobe shallot, minced (2 tablespoons)

2 tablespoons ketchup

1 teaspoon dried oregano

½ teaspoon dried thyme

1 teaspoon table salt

1 teaspoon ground black pepper

1 cup beef broth

½ cup whole or low-fat milk (do not use fat-free)

2 tablespoons all-purpose flour

2 teaspoons Dijon mustard

½ teaspoon dried dill

4 ounces white or brown button mushrooms, cleaned and thinly sliced

2 teaspoons butter

6 ounces raw dried wide or no-yolk egg noodles

Everyone loves noodles in the Instant Pot. And everybody loves Salisbury steak. But nobody has combined them all into one dish. Yet. To do so, we have to bring out all the tools. First, you'll create a rich gravy in a cake pan with the PIP method while also cooking the meatballs in an egg-bite mold. Once those components are done, you'll cook the noodles under pressure in the pot's broth before (finally!) putting everything back together for some tried-and-true comfort food.

1. Pour the chicken broth into the insert set in a **5-, 6-, or 8-quart Instant Pot.** Set a pressure-safe rack or trivet in the insert. Use olive oil or olive oil spray to grease the insides of the seven indentations of an egg-bite mold.

2. Mix the ground beef, bread crumbs, egg, shallot, ketchup, oregano, thyme, ½ teaspoon salt, and ½ teaspoon pepper in a large bowl until uniform. (Clean hands work best!) Divide this mixture among the prepared egg-bite mold indentations. Cover the mold loosely with its silicone lid (without sealing it) or lay a piece of aluminum foil over the mold (again, without sealing it). Set the mold on the rack.

3. Whisk the beef broth, milk, and flour in a pressure-safe 6- or 7-inch-round cake pan until smooth. Whisk in the mustard, dill, the remaining ½ teaspoon salt, and the remaining ½ teaspoon pepper. Stir in the mushrooms and butter. Set this uncovered pan securely on top of the covered egg-bite mold. Lock the lid on the pot.

4.

	Set pot for	Set level to	Valve must be	Set time for	If needed, press
For Max pots only	PRESSURE COOK	MAX	—	10 minutes with the KEEP WARM setting off	START
For all other pots	PRESSURE COOK or MANUAL	HIGH	Closed	12 minutes with the KEEP WARM setting off	START

5. When the pot has finished cooking, use the **quick-release method** to bring the pressure back to normal. Unlatch the lid and open the cooker. Use hot pads or silicone baking mitts to transfer the (hot!) cake pan to a nearby wire rack. Whisk the mushroom gravy in that pan until smooth.

6. Use those same hot pads or mitts to uncover the egg-bite mold. Tip it a bit so the (hot!) juices in the indentations run into the pot. Transfer the (still hot!) egg-bite mold to that wire rack. Stir the noodles into the liquids in the pot. Lock the lid back onto the cooker.

7.

	Set pot for	Set level to	Valve must be	Set time for	If needed, press
For *all* pots	PRESSURE COOK or MANUAL	HIGH	Closed	4 minutes with the KEEP WARM setting off	START

8. When the pot has finished cooking, use the **quick-release method** to bring the pressure back to normal. Unlatch the lid and open the cooker. Pour the mushroom sauce from the cake pan into the pot. Add the meatballs from the egg-bite molds. Stir gently but well before serving to warm everything up.

Other Pots

- This recipe cannot be made in a 3-quart Instant Pot because the combination of a rack, a baking dish, and an egg-bite mold is too tall for the smaller pot.

- For a 10-quart Instant Pot, you *must* double all of the ingredient amounts—which means you *must* use two egg-bite molds, stacked on top of each other in the insert so that the indentations of the one above sit on the rims between the indentations of the one below. And you *must* increase the cooking time on HIGH in step 4 to 15 minutes (there is no max setting in a 10-quart machine as of this writing).

Beyond

- For a more elegant presentation, use kitchen tongs to transfer the noodles from the pot to a large, lipped serving platter. Pick out the meatballs and set them on top of the noodles, then pour the sauce over everything. Garnish with stemmed and minced fresh thyme leaves and red pepper flakes.

Vegan Bolognese

18 ingredients

6–8 SERVINGS

METHOD:
fast/slow

SPECIAL
EQUIPMENT:
none

PRESSURE:
max or high

TIME UNDER
PRESSURE:
4 or 5 minutes

RELEASE:
quick

TOTAL TIME
WITH PRESSURE:
about 30 minutes

TOTAL TIME
WITH SLOW
COOKING:
about 1½ hours

VEGAN

CAN BE GLUTEN-
FREE

2 tablespoons olive oil

8 ounces white or brown button mushrooms, cleaned and *very finely* chopped

1 medium yellow or white onion, very finely chopped (at little less than 1 cup)

1 large carrot, peeled and shredded through the large holes of a box grater

1 medium celery stalk, very finely chopped (a little less than ⅓ cup)

Up to 4 medium garlic cloves, minced (4 teaspoons)

2 tablespoons regular or low-sodium soy sauce, or gluten-free tamari sauce

1 teaspoon dried marjoram

1 teaspoon dried oregano

1 teaspoon dried thyme

¼ teaspoon grated nutmeg

¼ teaspoon red pepper flakes

1 cup dry white wine, such as Chardonnay; or unsweetened apple juice

1 cup almond milk or cashew milk

One 28-ounce can diced tomatoes *packed in juice* (3½ cups)

2 cups riced cauliflower (8 ounces)

½ cup finely chopped walnuts

3 tablespoons tomato sauce

We've got a delicious Bolognese sauce in the original *Instant Pot Bible,* as well as some mushroom and lentil ragùs. But this sauce is, well, *far* different. It's made from riced cauliflower and chopped nuts, thick and rich with every spoonful, like the meaty version but a bit earthier and quite satisfying. FYI, this recipe is not for a one-pot meal. You'll need cooked and drained spaghetti or other pasta noodles as a bed for the sauce.

The hardest part of this recipe is chopping the mushrooms. You can use a food processor, but you don't want to make mushroom paste. Only pulse it on and off. Also, open the machine once in a while to rearrange the mushrooms in the canister.

1.

	Press	Set it for	Set time for	If needed, press
In all models	SAUTÉ	MEDIUM, NORMAL, or CUSTOM 300°F	10 minutes	START

2. As the pot heats, warm the oil in the insert set in a **5- or 6-quart Instant Pot.** Add the mushrooms, onion, carrot, celery, and garlic. Cook, stirring frequently, until the liquid comes out of the mushrooms, about 5 minutes.

3. Stir in the soy sauce, marjoram, oregano, thyme, nutmeg, and red pepper flakes until fragrant, just a few seconds. Pour in the wine or juice and scrape up any browned bits on the pot's bottom. Turn off the heat. Stir in the almond or cashew milk; then stir in the tomatoes and their juice, the riced cauliflower, and walnuts. Lock the lid on the pot.

4.

	Set pot for	Set level to	Valve must be	Set time for	If needed, press
For Max pots only	PRESSURE COOK	MAX	—	4 minutes with the KEEP WARM setting off	START
For all other pots	PRESSURE COOK or MANUAL	HIGH	Closed	5 minutes with the KEEP WARM setting off	START
For the slow-cook function	SLOW COOK	HIGH	Open	1 hour with the KEEP WARM setting off	START

5. When the pot has finished cooking under pressure, use the **quick-release method** to bring the pressure back to normal. Whichever cooking method you've used, unlatch the lid and open the cooker

6.

	Press	Set it for	Set time for	If needed, press
In all models	SAUTÉ	MEDIUM, NORMAL, or CUSTOM 300°F	5 minutes	START

7. Stir the sauce constantly as it comes to a simmer while the pot is heating. Stir in the tomato paste until dissolved. Continue cooking, stirring constantly, until a bit thickened, about 2 minutes. Turn off the heat and use hot pads or silicone baking mitts to transfer the (hot!) insert to a nearby wire rack (to stop the cooking). Cool for 2 to 3 minutes before serving.

Other Pots

- For a 3-quart Instant Pot, you *must* halve all of the ingredient amounts.
- For an 8-quart Instant Pot, you *must* increase almost all of the ingredient amounts by 50 percent *except* you *must* use only 2¾ cups riced cauliflower.
- For a 10-quart Instant Pot, you *must* double almost all of the ingredient amounts *except* you *must* use only 3¼ cups riced cauliflower and 5 tablespoons tomato sauce.

Beyond

- Cooked and drained *fresh* pasta is best for this sauce, especially spinach fettuccine.
- Or serve the sauce over split-open baked potatoes.

One-Pot Eggplant Caponata Sauce with Penne

15 ingredients	
4 SERVINGS	
METHOD: standard	

SPECIAL EQUIPMENT: none	
PRESSURE: low	

TIME UNDER PRESSURE: 8 minutes	
RELEASE: quick	

TOTAL TIME WITH PRESSURE: about 30 minutes	
CAN BE GLUTEN-FREE	

2 tablespoons olive oil

1 or 2 tinned anchovy fillets, chopped

1 large yellow or white onion, chopped (1½ cups)

2 medium celery stalks, trimmed and cut into 1-inch pieces

2 medium garlic cloves, minced (2 teaspoons)

1 tablespoon packed, stemmed, fresh rosemary leaves, chopped

2 teaspoons drained and rinsed capers, chopped

1 teaspoon fennel seeds

½ teaspoon table salt

½ teaspoon red pepper flakes

3 cups chicken broth

One large 1-pound eggplant, stemmed, peeled, and cut into 1-inch cubes (4 cups)

12 ounces raw dried penne (gluten-free, if necessary—for more information, see the chapter introduction on page 103)

¼ cup tomato paste

1 tablespoon red wine vinegar

We love to adapt classic recipes for the Instant Pot, sometimes using fewer ingredients, usually making the dishes easier in their prep or technique. But a habit is made to be broken, right? So we didn't cut any corners with this one. It's modeled on caponata, a sweet-and-sour eggplant and tomato condiment or sauce. And our version is about as Sicilian as it gets, right down to the anchovies at the base of the sauce. You might be leery of those fishy bits, but they melt into the sauce, offering an umami richness.

1.

	Press	Set it for	Set time for	If needed, press
In all models	SAUTÉ	MEDIUM, NORMAL, or CUSTOM 300°F	10 minutes	START

2. As the pot heats, warm the oil in the insert set in a **5-, 6-, or 8-quart Instant Pot.** Add the anchovy and cook, stirring often, until frizzled and aromatic, about 2 minutes. Add the onion and celery; cook, stirring more frequently, until the onion softens, about 3 minutes.

3. Add the garlic and cook, stirring all the while, for about 20 seconds. Stir in the rosemary, capers, fennel seeds, salt, and red pepper flakes until aromatic, just a few seconds. Pour in the broth and scrape up any browned bits on the pot's bottom.

4. Add the eggplant and stir well. Turn off the heat, then add the penne and stir gently until just coated in the sauce. Lock the lid onto the pot.

5.

	Set pot for	Set level to	Valve must be	Set time for	If needed, press
For *all* pots	PRESSURE COOK or MANUAL	LOW	Closed	8 minutes with the KEEP WARM setting off	START

6. When the pot has finished cooking, use the **quick-release method** to bring the pressure back to normal. Unlatch the lid and open the cooker.

7.

	Press	Set it for	Set time for	If needed, press
In all models	SAUTÉ	MEDIUM, NORMAL, or CUSTOM 300°F	5 minutes	START

8. As the sauce comes to a bubble, stir in the tomato paste and vinegar. Continue cooking, stirring often, until the tomato paste has dissolved into the sauce and thickened it a bit, about 1 minute. Turn off the heat and use hot pads or silicone baking mitts to transfer the (hot!) insert to a nearby wire rack. Cool for 3 to 5 minutes to blend the flavors. Stir well and serve warm.

Other Pots

- For a 3-quart Instant Pot, you *must* halve all of the ingredient amounts.
- For a 10-quart Instant Pot, you *must* increase all of the ingredient amounts by 50 percent and you *can* even double the amounts.

Beyond

- For a fuller meal, top servings with grilled, peeled and deveined medium or large shrimp—or even with warmed purchased cooked cocktail shrimp.

One-Pot Chile-Spiced Meat Sauce and Spaghetti

11 ingredients	SPECIAL EQUIPMENT: none
4–6 SERVINGS	
METHOD: standard	PRESSURE: max or high

TIME UNDER PRESSURE: 5 or 6 minutes	TOTAL TIME WITH PRESSURE: about 25 minutes
RELEASE: quick	CAN BE GLUTEN-FREE

2 tablespoons peanut or toasted sesame oil

6 ounces lean ground beef, preferably 90 percent lean or more

1 small yellow or white onion, halved and sliced into thin half-moons

2 tablespoons minced peeled fresh ginger

2 medium garlic cloves, minced (2 teaspoons)

¼ cup regular or low-sodium soy sauce, or gluten-free tamari sauce

¼ cup mirin (a sweetened rice wine); or dry white wine plus 1½ teaspoons granulated white sugar; or unsweetened apple juice

Up to 2 tablespoons thick red chile sauce, such as sambal oelek

3½ cups chicken or beef broth

12 ounces raw dried spaghetti (gluten-free, if necessary—for more information, see the chapter introduction on page 103), broken as needed to fit in the pot

6 ounces packed stemmed chopped kale (3 cups—do not use baby kale)

Other Pots

- For a 3-quart Instant Pot, you *must* halve all of the ingredient amounts and you *must* break the dried noodles into even smaller pieces.

- For a 10-quart Instant Pot, you *must* double all of the ingredient amounts. You do not need to break dried noodles for the large pot.

Beyond

- Add more flavor by adding one cinnamon stick and/or one star anise pod with the onion. Discard these spices before serving.

This recipe makes a simplified and saucier variation of dan dan noodles, the fiery Sichuan take-out favorite of noodles and ground meat in an aromatic sauce. We strayed from a more "authentic" take by adding extra meat to the sauce, bringing together the best qualities of a hearty Italian-American spaghetti dish and cravings-worthy Chinese-American flavors.

1.

	Press	Set it for	Set time for	If needed, press
In all models	SAUTÉ	MEDIUM, NORMAL, or CUSTOM 300°F	10 minutes	START

2. As the pot heats, warm the oil in the insert set in a **5-, 6-, or 8-quart Instant Pot.** Crumble in the ground beef and cook, stirring often, until lightly browned, about 4 minutes.

3. Add the onion, ginger, and garlic. Cook, stirring more frequently, until the onion softens, about 3 minutes. Stir in the soy sauce, mirin, and chile sauce. Scrape up any browned bits on the pot's bottom. Stir in the broth and turn off the heat.

4. Lay the broken spaghetti noodles in a crisscross pattern across the top of the other ingredients without pressing the pasta down into the sauce. Spread the kale evenly over the spaghetti without pressing down. Lock the lid on the pot.

5.

	Set pot for	Set level to	Valve must be	Set time for	If needed, press
For Max pots only	PRESSURE COOK	MAX	—	5 minutes with the KEEP WARM setting off	START
For all other pots	PRESSURE COOK or MANUAL	HIGH	Closed	6 minutes with the KEEP WARM setting off	START

6. When the pot has finished cooking, use the **quick-release method** to bring the pressure back to normal. Unlatch the lid and open the cooker. Stir well, then set the lid askew over the pot and set it aside for 2 to 3 minutes so the spaghetti continues to absorb some of the liquid. Serve warm in bowls.

One-Pot Butter Chicken with Ziti

13 ingredients

4–6 SERVINGS

METHOD:
standard

SPECIAL EQUIPMENT:
none

PRESSURE:
max or high

TIME UNDER PRESSURE:
5 or 6 minutes

RELEASE:
quick

TOTAL TIME WITH PRESSURE:
about 30 minutes

CAN BE GLUTEN-FREE

1 stick (8 tablespoons or ½ cup) butter

1 medium yellow or white onion, chopped (1 cup)

3 medium garlic cloves, minced (1 tablespoon)

1 tablespoon minced peeled fresh ginger

1 tablespoon yellow curry powder

1 teaspoon ground cumin

½ teaspoon ground cinnamon

½ teaspoon table salt

Up to ½ teaspoon ground dried cayenne

2 pounds boneless skinless chicken breasts, diced

One 14-ounce can diced tomatoes *packed in juice* (1¾ cups)

3 cups chicken broth

1 pound raw dried ziti (gluten-free, if necessary—for more information, see the chapter introduction on page 103)

Other Pots

- For a 3-quart Instant Pot, you *must* halve all of the ingredient amounts.

- For a 10-quart Instant Pot, you *must* increase all of the ingredient amounts by 50 percent or you *can* even double the amounts.

Beyond

- Spice up the dish by using red or Madras curry powder.

- For a richer dish, stir ¼ cup heavy or light cream into the pasta after cooking and before you set it aside for a couple of minutes.

- Garnish with stemmed and minced fresh cilantro leaves.

Here, we've taken an Instant Pot favorite, butter chicken, and turned it into a one-pot pasta casserole. Don't shortchange the amount of butter! You need that richness to balance all the spices. Plus, the butter will give the dish an almost "Indian mac-and-cheese" feel. That makes no culinary sense, but who cares when it's so utterly warming and comforting?

1.

	Press	Set it for	Set time for	If needed, press
In all models	SAUTÉ	MEDIUM, NORMAL, or CUSTOM 300°F	10 minutes	START

2. As the pot heats, melt the butter in the insert set in a **5-, 6-, or 8-quart Instant Pot.** Add the onion—maybe before all the butter is melted, just so the butter doesn't brown. Cook, stirring often, until softened, about 3 minutes. Stir in the garlic, ginger, curry powder, cumin, cinnamon, salt, and cayenne until fragrant, just a few seconds.

3. Add the chicken and toss well to coat in the spices and onion. Pour in the tomatoes and their juice; scrape up any browned bits on the pot's bottom.

4. Pour in the broth. Turn off the heat, add the ziti, and use the back of a wooden spoon to press it gently into the liquid without stirring it in. The pasta must not sit on the insert's bottom. Lock the lid on the pot.

5.

	Set pot for	Set level to	Valve must be	Set time for	If needed, press
For Max pots only	PRESSURE COOK	MAX	—	5 minutes with the KEEP WARM setting off	START
For all other pots	PRESSURE COOK or MANUAL	HIGH	Closed	6 minutes with the KEEP WARM setting off	START

6. When the pot has finished cooking, use the **quick-release method** to bring the pressure back to normal. Unlatch the lid and open the cooker. Stir well, then set the lid askew over the pot and set aside for 2 to 3 minutes so the pasta absorbs some of the remaining sauce. Stir again before serving warm.

One-Pot Turkey Tetrazzini

12 ingredients	
4–6 SERVINGS	

SPECIAL EQUIPMENT:	none
METHOD:	standard
PRESSURE:	max or high

TIME UNDER PRESSURE:	4 or 6 minutes
RELEASE:	quick

TOTAL TIME WITH PRESSURE:	about 30 minutes
CAN BE GLUTEN-FREE	

2 tablespoons butter

2 medium single-lobe shallots, halved lengthwise and thinly sliced (½ cup)

Up to 3 medium garlic cloves, minced (1 tablespoon)

1 pound turkey breast cutlets, sliced into ¼-inch-wide strips

1 teaspoon dried oregano

½ teaspoon grated nutmeg

½ teaspoon table salt

½ teaspoon ground black pepper

2¾ cups chicken broth

12 ounces raw dried spaghetti (gluten-free, if necessary—for more information, see the chapter introduction on page 103), broken as necessary to fit the pot

½ cup heavy or light cream

2 ounces Parmigiano-Reggiano, finely grated (1 cup)

Other Pots

- For a 3-quart Instant Pot, you *must* halve all of the ingredient amounts and you *must* break the dried spaghetti into even smaller pieces to fit in the pot.

- For a 10-quart Instant Pot, you *must* increase all of the ingredient amounts by 50 percent and you *can* even double the amounts. You do not need to break dried spaghetti for the large pot.

Beyond

- Garnish each serving with a small dollop of purchased pesto.

Sure, you could first make a sauce for turkey tetrazzini, then pour that sauce over cooked pasta from a separate pan (or made in a second go in the Instant Pot). But here's a way to make this decadent favorite in one pot.

1.

	Press	Set it for	Set time for	If needed, press
In all models	SAUTÉ	MEDIUM, NORMAL, or CUSTOM 300°F	10 minutes	START

2. As the pot heats, melt the butter in the insert set in a **5-, 6-, or 8-quart Instant Pot.** Add the shallots and garlic; cook, stirring often, for just 1 minute. *Do not brown.*

3. Add the turkey and cook, stirring often, until it loses its raw, pink color, about 3 minutes. Stir in the oregano, nutmeg, salt, and pepper until fragrant, just a few seconds.

4. Stir in the broth and scrape up any browned bits on the pot's bottom. Turn off the heat and lay the broken spaghetti in a crosshatch pattern across the top of the sauce. Press down gently so some of the pasta is in the sauce but none of it touches the insert's bottom. Lock the lid onto the cooker.

5.

	Set pot for	Set level to	Valve must be	Set time for	If needed, press
For Max pots only	PRESSURE COOK	MAX	—	4 minutes with the KEEP WARM setting off	START
For all other pots	PRESSURE COOK or MANUAL	HIGH	Closed	6 minutes with the KEEP WARM setting off	START

6. When the pot has finished cooking, use the **quick-release method** to bring the pressure back to normal. Unlatch the lid and open the cooker.

7.

	Press	Set it for	Set time for	If needed, press
In all models	SAUTÉ	MEDIUM, NORMAL, or CUSTOM 300°F	5 minutes	START

8. Add the cream and stir well to get all the noodles into the sauce. Continue cooking, stirring all the while, until the sauce bubbles, about 1 minute. Stir in the cheese, turn off the heat, and use hot pads or silicone baking mitts to transfer the (hot!) insert to a nearby wire rack (to stop the cooking). Cool for 3 to 5 minutes so the pasta continues to absorb the sauce. Stir well and serve warm.

One-Pot Philly Cheesesteak and Noodles

14 ingredients

4–6 SERVINGS

METHOD:
standard

SPECIAL EQUIPMENT:
none

PRESSURE:
high

TIME UNDER PRESSURE:
4 minutes

RELEASE:
quick

TOTAL TIME WITH PRESSURE:
about 15 minutes

---

3 cups beef or chicken broth

2 tablespoons butter, cut into small bits

2 tablespoons Worcestershire sauce

1 teaspoon onion powder

½ teaspoon dried thyme

½ teaspoon ground allspice

½ teaspoon celery seeds

½ teaspoon garlic powder

½ teaspoon table salt

½ teaspoon ground black pepper

1¼ pounds shaved beef (do *not* use Steak-Umms)

12 ounces raw dried wide egg or no-yolk noodles

8 ounces American sharp or mild cheddar cheese, shredded (2 cups)

¼ cup heavy or light cream

This pasta casserole couldn't be simpler thanks to shaved beef, which is usually found at the meat counter or sometimes in the supermarket's freezer section (in which case it must be thawed before use). Butcher counters may even sell it by the pound (at least ours do in rural New England).

Because the noodles are thin and delicate and because the sauce is thick and stocked with beef, you must pour the pasta on top of everything *without* stirring it in. Unfortunately, gluten-free egg noodles are not recommended here because they turn to mush with these liquid levels and this technique.

1. Stir the broth, butter, Worcestershire sauce, onion powder, thyme, allspice, celery seeds, garlic powder, salt, and pepper in the insert set in a **5-, 6-, or 8-quart Instant Pot** until evenly combined.

2. Add the meat slice by slice; stir gently to combine. Dump the noodles on top without stirring them in. Lock the lid onto the cooker.

3.

	Set pot for	Set level to	Valve must be	Set time for	If needed, press
For *all* pots	PRESSURE COOK or MANUAL	HIGH	Closed	4 minutes with the KEEP WARM setting off	START

4. When the pot has finished cooking, use the **quick-release method** to bring the pressure back to normal. Unlatch the lid and open the cooker. Stir in the cheese and cream. Set the lid askew over the pot and set aside for 2 to 3 minutes to let the pasta absorb some of the liquid. Stir again and serve warm.

Other Pots

- For a **3-quart Instant Pot**, you *must* halve all of the ingredient amounts.

- For a **10-quart Instant Pot**, you *must* increase all of the ingredient amounts by 50 percent or you *can* double the ingredient amounts.

Beyond

- Garnish the servings with drained chopped pimientos from a jar.

- And/or pickled onions.

One-Pot Tomato-Free Mushroom Sauce with Ziti

11 ingredients	SPECIAL EQUIPMENT: none	TIME UNDER PRESSURE: 8 minutes	TOTAL TIME WITH PRESSURE: about 25 minutes
4 SERVINGS			
METHOD: standard	PRESSURE: low	RELEASE: quick	VEGETARIAN
			CAN BE GLUTEN-FREE

2 tablespoons olive oil

12 ounces white or brown button mushrooms, cleaned and thinly sliced

Up to 3 medium garlic cloves, minced (1 tablespoon)

1 teaspoon dried oregano

½ teaspoon table salt

½ teaspoon ground black pepper

¼ teaspoon ground cinnamon

2½ cups vegetable broth

One medium 12-ounce eggplant, stemmed, peeled, and cut into 1-inch cubes (3 cups)

12 ounces raw dried ziti (gluten-free, if necessary—for more information, see the chapter introduction on page 103)

Shredded semi-firm mozzarella, for garnishing

Other Pots

- For a 3-quart Instant Pot, you *must* halve all of the ingredient amounts.

- For an 8-quart Instant Pot, you *must* increase all of the ingredient amounts by 50 percent.

- For a 10-quart Instant Pot, you *must* increase all of the ingredient amounts by 50 percent and you *can* even double the amounts.

Beyond

- For a tastier garnish, omit the mozzarella and grate Manchego over the servings.

- Or garnish with a little minced preserved lemon: Halve a preserved lemon, then scrape out and discard the pulp and seeds. Mince the rind and sprinkle over the cheese garnish (maybe with some stemmed and minced fresh parsley leaves, too).

If you don't like tomato-based pasta sauces, you've come to the right place. And if you're looking for a hearty meatless meal, you're also in the right place. (*And* if you leave out the cheese garnish, you've got a vegan dinner on tap.) The results are a sophisticated but comforting mix of earthy mushrooms and sweet pasta, best for an autumn evening with a glass of white wine. (Smaller servings would also make a nice side dish to grilled lamb chops.)

1.

	Press	Set it for	Set time for	If needed, press
In all models	SAUTÉ	MEDIUM, NORMAL, or CUSTOM 300°F	10 minutes	START

2. As the pot heats, warm the oil in the insert set in a **5- or 6-quart Instant Pot.** Add the mushrooms and cook, stirring often, until they give off their liquid and it reduces to a glaze, about 5 minutes.

3. Stir in the garlic, oregano, salt, pepper, and cinnamon until fragrant, just a few seconds. Pour in the broth and scrape up any browned bits on the pot's bottom. Turn off the heat and stir in the eggplant. Add the ziti and stir gently, just until lightly coated. Do not let the ziti sink to the bottom of the insert. Lock the lid on the pot.

4.

	Set pot for	Set level to	Valve must be	Set time for	If needed, press
For *all* pots	PRESSURE COOK or MANUAL	LOW	Closed	8 minutes with the KEEP WARM setting off	START

5. When the pot has finished cooking, use the **quick-release method** to bring the pressure back to normal. Unlatch the lid and open the cooker. Stir well, then set the lid askew over the pot and set aside for 2 to 3 minutes so the pasta continues to absorb the sauce. Stir again and serve warm, garnished with shredded mozzarella.

One-Pot Kale and Farfalle

11 ingredients	**SPECIAL EQUIPMENT:** none
4 SERVINGS	**TIME UNDER PRESSURE:** 5 or 6 minutes
METHOD: standard	**PRESSURE:** max or high
	RELEASE: quick
	TOTAL TIME WITH PRESSURE: about 25 minutes
	CAN BE GLUTEN-FREE

2 tablespoons olive oil

2 medium garlic cloves, minced (2 teaspoons)

2 tinned anchovy fillets, minced

1 teaspoon fennel seeds

½ teaspoon table salt

½ teaspoon red pepper flakes

12 ounces kale leaves, stemmed and chopped (6 packed cups—do not use baby kale)

¼ cup dry white wine, such as Chardonnay; or dry vermouth; or unsweetened apple juice

3 cups chicken or vegetable broth

2 cups canned crushed tomatoes

12 ounces raw dried farfalle (or butterfly) pasta (gluten-free, if necessary—for more information, see the chapter introduction on page 103)

Other Pots

- For a 3-quart Instant Pot, you *must* halve all of the ingredient amounts.
- For an 8-quart Instant Pot, you *can* increase all of the ingredient amounts by 50 percent.
- For a 10-quart Instant Pot, you *must* increase all of the ingredient amounts by 50 percent and you *can* even double the amounts.

Beyond

- Stir in up to ½ cup slivered sun-dried tomatoes packed in oil and/or ½ cup chopped marinated artichoke hearts with the crushed tomatoes.
- Garnish the servings with finely grated Parmigiano-Reggiano or dry, aged Asiago.

Although not a vegetarian dish (because of the anchovies), this is a perfect meal for a (near) meatless Monday meal: aromatic, comforting, and fairly hearty. Don't fear those anchovies. They add a briny hit of umami, taking the dish from the ordinary to something much better. Store any remaining anchovies in their sealed jar or tin in the fridge for up to 4 months—or in the freezer for up to 1 year.

1.

	Press	Set it for	Set time for	If needed, press
In all models	SAUTÉ	MEDIUM, NORMAL, or CUSTOM 300°F	10 minutes	START

2. As the pot heats, warm the oil in the insert set in a **5-, 6-, or 8-quart Instant Pot.** Add the garlic, anchovy, fennel seeds, salt, and red pepper flakes. Cook, stirring constantly, until quite aromatic, about 1 minute.

3. Add the kale and cook, stirring often, until wilted, about 2 minutes. Pour in the wine and scrape up any browned bits on the pot's bottom. Turn off the heat.

4. Stir in the broth and crushed tomatoes until uniform. Add the pasta and stir gently, just to coat, not to submerge. Lock the lid on the pot.

5.

	Set pot for	Set level to	Valve must be	Set time for	If needed, press
For Max pots only	PRESSURE COOK	MAX	—	5 minutes with the KEEP WARM setting off	START
For all other pots	PRESSURE COOK or MANUAL	HIGH	Closed	6 minutes with the KEEP WARM setting off	START

6. When the pot has finished cooking, use the **quick-release method** to bring the pressure back to normal. Unlatch the lid and open the cooker. Stir well, then set the lid askew over the pot and set it aside for 2 to 3 minutes, so the pasta can continue to absorb some of the liquid. Stir again and serve warm.

One-Pot Barbecue Brisket Ragù with Noodles

13 ingredients

6 SERVINGS

METHOD:
fast/slow

SPECIAL EQUIPMENT:
a pressure- and food-safe rack or trivet

PRESSURE:
max or high, then high

TIME UNDER PRESSURE:
59 minutes or 1 hour 14 minutes

RELEASE:
natural, then quick

TOTAL TIME WITH PRESSURE:
about 2 hours 20 minutes

TOTAL TIME WITH SLOW COOKING:
about 6½ hours

1 tablespoon canola, vegetable, or other neutral-flavored oil

2½ pounds flat-cut (or first-cut) beef brisket, trimmed of any fat globs

One 14-ounce can diced tomatoes *packed in juice,* drained through a sieve or colander into a bowl, the juice reserved

2 cups beef broth

2 tablespoons apple cider vinegar

1½ tablespoons mild smoked paprika

1 tablespoon Worcestershire sauce

1 tablespoon jarred yellow mustard

1 teaspoon ground coriander

½ teaspoon ground cumin

Up to ½ teaspoon ground cloves

2 tablespoons dark brown sugar

12 ounces raw dried wide egg or no-yolk noodles

If your brain works at all as ours do, you've wondered what sort of magic you could create by using brisket as a pasta sauce. Ta da! This recipe gives you a one-pot wonder: brisket along with noodles cooked right in a homemade barbecue sauce, a meal that doesn't need much more than iced tea to complete it. Notice that because of the brown sugar in the sauce, the second cooking under pressure is only at HIGH (not MAX).

Use only a flat-cut (sometimes called a "first-cut") brisket because it's less fatty and won't weigh down the sauce.

1.

	Press	Set it for	Set time for	If needed, press
In all models	SAUTÉ	MEDIUM, NORMAL, or CUSTOM 300°F	20 minutes	START

2. As the pot heats, warm the oil in the insert set in a **5-, 6-, 8-, or 10-quart Instant Pot.** Add the brisket and brown it well on both sides, turning once, about 12 minutes total. Plenty of dark brown marks on the meat = plenty of flavor. When done, transfer the brisket to a nearby large plate or cutting board.

3. Pour the liquid from the drained tomatoes into the pot and scrape all the browned bits on the pot's bottom. Stir in the broth, vinegar, smoked paprika, Worcestershire sauce, mustard, coriander, cumin, and cloves. Turn off the heat.

4. Place a pressure- and food-safe rack or trivet in the insert. The liquid may come a bit above the rack itself. Set the brisket flat side down on the rack. Pour the tomatoes on top of the meat, then sprinkle the tomatoes and meat evenly with the brown sugar. Lock the lid on the pot.

5.

	Set pot for	Set level to	Valve must be	Set time for	If needed, press
For Max pots only	PRESSURE COOK	MAX	—	55 minutes with the KEEP WARM setting off	START
For all other pots	PRESSURE COOK or MANUAL	HIGH	Closed	1 hour 10 minutes with the KEEP WARM setting off	START
For the slow-cook function	SLOW COOK	HIGH	Open	6 hours with the KEEP WARM setting off	START

6. When the pot has finished cooking under pressure, turn it off and let the pressure **return to normal naturally,** about 35 minutes. Whichever cooking method you've used, unlatch the lid and open the cooker.

7. Use a meat fork or kitchen tongs to remove the rack from under the brisket, letting the meat fall into the sauce. Use two forks or perhaps a large spoon and a meat fork to shred the brisket into shards. Stir in the noodles and toss gently until they're coated in the sauce without touching the bottom of the insert. Lock the lid on the pot.

8.

	Set pot for	Set level to	Valve must be	Set time for	If needed, press
For all other pots	PRESSURE COOK or MANUAL	HIGH	Closed	4 minutes with the KEEP WARM setting off	START

9. When the pot has finished cooking, use the **quick-release method** to bring the pot's pressure back to normal. Unlatch the lid and open the pot. Stir well, then set aside for a minute or two so the noodles continue to absorb the sauce. Stir again and serve warm.

Other Pots

- For a 3-quart Instant Pot, you *must* halve all of the ingredient amounts.

- For a 10-quart Instant Pot, you *can* increase all of the ingredient amounts by 50 percent but you *must* then also increase the cooking time in step 5 to 1 hour 20 minutes on HIGH (there is no MAX setting in the larger pot as of this writing).

Beyond

- For more flavor, stir ¼ cup of your favorite barbecue sauce into the sauce in step 9 before you set the pot aside for a minute or two.

- For a spaghetti sandwich, serve on whole-wheat buns with sliced tomatoes and plenty of pickle relish—and maybe jarred (hot or "tamed") pickled jalapeño rings as well.

See photo in insert.

One-Pot Pork Ragù with Rigatoni

16 ingredients

4–6 SERVINGS

METHOD:
fast/slow

SPECIAL EQUIPMENT:
none

PRESSURE:
max or high

TIME UNDER PRESSURE:
31 or 38 minutes

RELEASE:
quick twice

TOTAL TIME WITH PRESSURE:
about 1 hour

TOTAL TIME WITH SLOW COOKING:
about 4 hours 45 minutes

CAN BE GLUTEN-FREE

---

2 tablespoons olive oil

1¾ pounds boneless country-style pork ribs

1 medium yellow or white onion, chopped (1 cup)

1 medium green bell pepper, cored, seeded, and chopped (1 cup)

Up to 3 medium garlic cloves, minced (1 tablespoon)

½ cup dry red wine, such as Cabernet Sauvignon; or extra chicken broth

One 28-ounce can whole tomatoes *packed in juice* (3½ cups)

3 cups chicken broth

1 tablespoon dried basil

1 tablespoon dried oregano

1 teaspoon dried thyme

1 teaspoon table salt

½ teaspoon grated nutmeg

Up to ½ teaspoon red pepper flakes

12 ounces raw dried rigatoni (gluten-free, if necessary—for more information, see the chapter introduction on page 103)

¼ cup tomato paste

We admit it: This recipe is complicated and might be a project better suited to a Sunday afternoon than a Wednesday evening. However, the results make for stand-out deliciousness! The country-style pork ribs are not too fatty for a still-rich sauce and the rigatoni is a thicker pasta that can stand up to the heartier sauce. (So it all needs a couple extra minutes under pressure.)

1.

	Press	Set it for	Set time for	If needed, press
In all models	SAUTÉ	MEDIUM, NORMAL, or CUSTOM 300°F	20 minutes	START

2. As the pot heats, warm the oil in the insert set in a **5-, 6-, or 8-quart Instant Pot.** Add the country-style ribs and brown well on all sides, even the ends, turning occasionally, about 12 minutes. Get lots of good color on the pork for better flavor. When you're done, transfer the meat to a nearby plate or cutting board.

3. Add the onion and bell pepper to the pot. Cook, stirring often, until the onion softens, about 3 minutes. Stir in the garlic, then pour in the wine and scrape up any browned bits on the pot's bottom.

4. Wash your hands and use them to crush the whole tomatoes one by one as you add them to the pot with their juice. Stir in the broth, basil, oregano, thyme, salt, nutmeg, and red pepper flakes. Turn off the heat.

5. Return the pork and any accumulated juices to the pot. Coat the ribs in the sauce before you lock the lid on the pot.

6.

	Set pot for	Set level to	Valve must be	Set time for	If needed, press
For Max pots only	PRESSURE COOK	MAX	—	24 minutes with the KEEP WARM setting off	START
For all other pots	PRESSURE COOK or MANUAL	HIGH	Closed	30 minutes with the KEEP WARM setting off	START
For the slow-cook function	SLOW COOK	HIGH	Open	4 hours with the KEEP WARM setting off	START

7. When the pot has finished cooking under pressure, use the **quick-release method** to bring the pressure back to normal. Whichever cooking method you've used, unlatch the lid and open the pot. Stir well to break up the pork into bits for a pasta sauce. Stir in the pasta and lock the lid back onto the pot.

8.

	Set pot for	Set level to	Valve must be	Set time for	If needed, press
For Max pots only	PRESSURE COOK	MAX	—	7 minutes with the KEEP WARM setting off	START
For all other pots	PRESSURE COOK or MANUAL	HIGH	Closed	8 minutes with the KEEP WARM setting off	START

9. When the pot has finished cooking, use the **quick-release method** to bring the pressure back to normal. Unlatch the lid and open the cooker. Stir in the tomato paste until melted and uniform. Set the lid askew over the pot and set it aside for 3 to 5 minutes so the pasta absorbs some of the excess liquid and the flavors meld a bit more. Stir again and serve warm.

Other Pots

- For a 3-quart Instant Pot, you *must* halve all of the ingredient amounts.

- For a 10-quart Instant Pot, you *must* increase all of the ingredient amounts by 50 percent or you *can* even double the amounts.

Beyond

- You'll want lots of grated cheese for the servings. Rather than the standard Parmigiano-Reggiano, try a hard Asiago or even crumbled Gorgonzola.

- Garnish the servings with stemmed and minced fresh oregano and/or thyme leaves.

One-Pot Turkey Pot-Roast Ragù with Penne

13 ingredients

4 SERVINGS

METHOD: fast/slow

SPECIAL EQUIPMENT: none

PRESSURE: max or high twice

TIME UNDER PRESSURE: 32 or 46 minutes

RELEASE: natural, then quick

TOTAL TIME WITH PRESSURE: about 1 hour 45 minutes

TOTAL TIME WITH SLOW COOKING: about 3½ hours

CAN BE GLUTEN-FREE

---

2 tablespoons butter

1 bone-in turkey thigh (about 1½ pounds), skin removed

1 large yellow or white onion, chopped (1½ cups)

Up to 3 medium garlic cloves, minced (1 tablespoon)

1 tablespoon stemmed, fresh thyme leaves, minced

1 tablespoon stemmed, fresh sage leaves, minced

½ teaspoon ground cinnamon

½ teaspoon table salt

½ teaspoon ground black pepper

3 cups chicken broth

2 tablespoons maple syrup (do not—ever!—use maple-flavored pancake syrup)

3 medium thin parsnips, peeled and sliced into thin rounds

8 ounces raw dried penne (gluten-free, if necessary—for more information, see the chapter introduction on page 103)

This recipe is the result of one of those moments when we thought, "Why can't we make Thanksgiving a weeknight pasta supper?" Sounds crazy, right? But listen, sometimes you need a little holiday flare to get through the week.

To skin a turkey thigh, grasp one "corner" of the skin with a paper towel. Pull the skin up and over the meat, taking it off with the paper towel still in hand.

1.

	Press	Set it for	Set time for	If needed, press
In all models	SAUTÉ	MEDIUM, NORMAL, or CUSTOM 300°F	15 minutes	START

2. As the pot heats, melt the butter in the insert set in a **5-, 6-, or 8-quart Instant Pot.** Add the turkey thigh and brown it well on both sides, about 8 minutes, turning once. Transfer the thigh to a nearby plate or cutting board.

3. Add the onion and cook, stirring often, until softened, about 3 minutes. Stir in the garlic, thyme, sage, cinnamon, salt, and pepper until fragrant, just a few seconds. Pour in the broth and scrape up any browned bits on the pot's bottom. Turn off the heat.

4. Stir in the maple syrup, then return the thigh and any accumulated juices to the pot, nestling the meat into the sauce. Lock the lid on the pot.

5.

	Set pot for	Set level to	Valve must be	Set time for	If needed, press
For Max pots only	PRESSURE COOK	MAX	—	27 minutes with the KEEP WARM setting off	START
For all other pots	PRESSURE COOK or MANUAL	HIGH	Closed	40 minutes with the KEEP WARM setting off	START
For the slow-cook function	SLOW COOK	HIGH	Open	3 hours with the KEEP WARM setting off	START

6. When the pot has finished cooking under pressure, turn it off and let the pressure **return to normal naturally,** about 35 minutes. Whichever cooking method you've used, unlatch the lid and open the cooker.

7. Use two forks to shred the turkey meat right in the pot while removing (and discarding) the bone and any attached cartilage that hasn't melted into the sauce. Stir in the parsnips, then the pasta, coating it in the sauce without pressing it down to the insert's bottom. Lock the lid back onto the pot.

8.

	Set pot for	Set level to	Valve must be	Set time for	If needed, press
For Max pots only	PRESSURE COOK	MAX	—	5 minutes with the KEEP WARM setting off	START
For all other pots	PRESSURE COOK or MANUAL	HIGH	Closed	6 minutes with the KEEP WARM setting off	START

9. When the pot has finished cooking, use the **quick-release method** to bring the pressure back to normal. Unlatch the lid and open the cooker. Stir well, then set the cooker aside for a couple of minutes so the pasta can absorb some of the remaining liquid. Stir again and serve warm.

Other Pots

- Because of the size of a turkey thigh, you cannot make this recipe in a 3-quart Instant Pot.

- For a 10-quart Instant Pot, you *must* double all of the ingredient amounts.

Beyond

- Garnish the servings with cranberry relish, chunky cranberry sauce, or even a cranberry or plum chutney.

- For a richer dish, spoon servings over mounds of ricotta.

One-Pot Lamb Ragù with Farfalle

13 ingredients	**SPECIAL EQUIPMENT:** none
4–6 SERVINGS	**PRESSURE:** max or high twice
METHOD: fast/slow	**TIME UNDER PRESSURE:** 40 or 51 minutes

RELEASE: natural, then quick	**TOTAL TIME WITH SLOW COOKING:** about 4½ hours
TOTAL TIME WITH PRESSURE: about 1 hour 40 minutes	**CAN BE GLUTEN-FREE**

2 tablespoons olive oil

One 1½-pound boneless leg of lamb (any netting removed)

1 large yellow or white onion, chopped (1½ cups)

2 medium carrots, peeled and chopped (1 cup)

2 tablespoons stemmed, fresh rosemary leaves, minced

2 tablespoons stemmed, fresh sage leaves, minced

½ teaspoon table salt

½ teaspoon ground black pepper

2½ cups beef broth

2 cups bold red wine, such as Zinfandel; or 1½ cups additional beef broth plus ½ cup unsweetened cranberry juice

2 tablespoons butter

12 ounces raw dried farfalle (or butterfly pasta—gluten-free, if necessary—for more information, see the chapter introduction on page 103)

¼ cup tomato paste

This one's a second option for those who love pasta but don't love tomato sauce (for the first, see One-Pot Tomato-Free Mushroom Sauce with Ziti on page 136). It's sort of like a lamb pot roast turned into a thick pasta sauce (with the pasta cooked right in the sauce for more flavor in every bite).

Leg of lamb offers the right ratio of meat to fatty richness (lamb shoulder produces a too-oily sauce). The butter and the tomato paste, added at different points toward the end of the cooking process, balance the flavors, creating a silky richness.

If you find the farfalle is still a little chewy for your taste in step 9, don't put the pot back under pressure. Instead, set it aside with the lid on top but askew for about 5 minutes.

1.

	Press	Set it for	Set time for	If needed, press
In all models	SAUTÉ	MEDIUM, NORMAL, or CUSTOM 300°F	20 minutes	START

2. As the pot heats, warm the oil in the insert set in a **5-, 6-, or 8-quart Instant Pot.** Add the leg of lamb and brown it on all sides, turning occasionally and getting good, dark color on the meat, about 12 minutes. Transfer the lamb to a nearby large plate or cutting board.

3. Add the onion and carrots to the pot; cook, stirring often, until the onion softens, about 4 minutes. Stir in the rosemary, sage, salt, and pepper until fragrant, just a few seconds. Pour in the broth and wine. Scrape up any browned bits on the pot's bottom.

4. Turn off the heat. Return the meat to the pot. Turn it once so it's coated in the sauce. Lock the lid on the pot.

5.

	Set pot for	Set level to	Valve must be	Set time for	If needed, press
For Max pots only	PRESSURE COOK	MAX	—	35 minutes with the KEEP WARM setting off	START
For all other pots	PRESSURE COOK or MANUAL	HIGH	Closed	45 minutes with the KEEP WARM setting off	START
For the slow-cook function	SLOW COOK	HIGH	Open	4 hours with the KEEP WARM setting off	START

6. When the pot has finished cooking under pressure, turn it off and let the pressure **return to normal naturally,** about 35 minutes. Whichever cooking method you've used, unlatch the lid and open the cooker.

7. Add the butter. Use two forks or a big spoon and a meat fork to break the lamb into shreds. Add the pasta and toss well to coat without pressing the pasta toward the insert's bottom. Lock the lid back onto the pot.

8.

	Set pot for	Set level to	Valve must be	Set time for	If needed, press
For Max pots only	PRESSURE COOK	MAX	—	5 minutes with the KEEP WARM setting off	START
For all other pots	PRESSURE COOK or MANUAL	HIGH	Closed	6 minutes with the KEEP WARM setting off	START

9. When the pot has finished cooking, use the **quick-release method** to bring the pressure back to normal. Unlatch the lid and open the cooker. Stir in the tomato paste until dissolved. Set the pot aside for a couple of minutes, so the pasta continues to absorb the sauce. Stir again and serve warm.

Other Pots

- For a 3-quart Instant Pot, you *must* halve all of the ingredient amounts.

- For a 10-quart Instant Pot, you *must* double all of the ingredient amounts but you *must* also increase the cooking time on HIGH in step 5 to 55 minutes (there is no MAX pressure setting in the larger pot at this writing).

Beyond

- Garnish servings with minced fresh parsley leaves.

- Or a crumble of soft goat cheese.

- Or shave a hard aged goat cheese over the servings.

- Or top with a little plain goat yogurt.

One-Pot Creamy Veal Ragù with Ziti

14 ingredients	PRESSURE: max or high twice
4–6 SERVINGS	TIME UNDER PRESSURE: 55 minutes or 1 hour 6 minutes
METHOD: fast/slow	
SPECIAL EQUIPMENT: none	

RELEASE: natural, then quick

TOTAL TIME WITH PRESSURE: about 2 hours 15 minutes

TOTAL TIME WITH SLOW COOKING: about 4½ hours

CAN BE GLUTEN-FREE

2 tablespoons butter

4 ounces pancetta (certified gluten-free, if necessary), chopped

One 1½-pound boneless veal shoulder roast, trimmed of any large fat globs and any netting removed

1 cup frozen pearl onions (no need to thaw)

8 ounces sliced white or brown button mushrooms, brushed clean

2 tablespoons stemmed, fresh sage leaves, minced

½ teaspoon ground allspice

½ teaspoon table salt, plus more for seasoning to taste

½ teaspoon ground black pepper

1 cup dry white wine, such as Chardonnay; or unsweetened apple juice

3 cups chicken broth

12 ounces raw dried ziti (gluten-free, if necessary—for more information, see the chapter introduction on page 103)

2 ounces Gruyère or swiss cheese, shredded (½ cup)

¼ cup heavy or light cream

This dish is by far the richest ragù in this book. The veal shoulder gets incredibly tender, creating a silky finish with the noodles, all bound in the flavors with the cream and allspice (a warming flavor that balances it all to perfection). Just to take this dish as far over the top as we can, we add cheese *and* cream before serving. Make sure you give the pot some time to sit after you stir in both. You want to melt the cheese evenly and get rid of the raw taste of cream with the pot's residual heat.

1.

	Press	Set it for	Set time for	If needed, press
In all models	SAUTÉ	MEDIUM, NORMAL, or CUSTOM 300°F	25 minutes	START

2. As the pot heats, melt the butter in the insert set in a **5-, 6-, or 8-quart Instant Pot.** Add the pancetta and cook, stirring often, until the pieces are browned and frizzled at the edges, about 7 minutes. Use a slotted spoon to transfer the pancetta to a nearby large plate or cutting board.

3. Add the veal shoulder and brown it on all sides, turning as little as possible, about 10 minutes. Make sure there are dark spots on the meat. Transfer the veal to that same plate or cutting board.

4. Add the pearl onions to the pot and cook, stirring often, until lightly browned, about 3 minutes. Add the mushrooms and continue cooking, stirring much more often so the onions don't burn, until the mushrooms give off some of their internal liquid and it reduces to a glaze, about 4 minutes.

5. Stir in the sage, allspice, salt, and pepper until fragrant, just a few seconds. Pour in the wine and scrape up any browned bits on the pot's bottom. Turn off the heat.

6. Stir in the broth, then return the pancetta pieces and the veal to the pot along with any accumulated juices. Turn the veal over once to coat it in the sauce. Lock the lid on the pot.

7.

	Set pot for	Set level to	Valve must be	Set time for	If needed, press
For Max pots only	PRESSURE COOK	MAX	—	50 minutes with the KEEP WARM setting off	START
For all other pots	PRESSURE COOK or MANUAL	HIGH	Closed	1 hour with the KEEP WARM setting off	START
For the slow-cook function	SLOW COOK	HIGH	Open	4 hours with the KEEP WARM setting off	START

8. When the pot has finished cooking under pressure, turn it off and let the pressure **return to normal naturally,** about 35 minutes. Whichever cooking method you've used, unlatch the lid and open the cooker.

9. Use two forks or a big spoon and a meat fork to break the veal into shreds and small bits fit for a pasta sauce. Stir in the ziti until it's coated in the sauce but don't press down so the pasta sits on the insert's bottom. Lock the lid back onto the pot.

10.

	Set pot for	Set level to	Valve must be	Set time for	If needed, press
For Max pots only	PRESSURE COOK	MAX	—	5 minutes with the KEEP WARM setting off	START
For all other pots	PRESSURE COOK or MANUAL	HIGH	Closed	6 minutes with the KEEP WARM setting off	START

11. When the pot has finished cooking, use the **quick-release method** to bring the pressure back to normal. Unlatch the lid and open the cooker. Stir in the cheese and cream until uniform. Turn off the heat and use hot pads or silicone baking mitts to transfer the (hot!) insert to a nearby wire rack. Let sit for 2 to 3 minutes to blend the flavors. Stir again and serve warm with more salt to taste.

Other Pots

- For a 3-quart Instant Pot, you must *halve* all of the ingredient amounts.

- For a 10-quart Instant Pot, you *must* increase all of the ingredient amounts by 50 percent or you *can* even double them. If you double them, you *must* increase the cooking time under pressure in step 7 to 1 hour 10 minutes on HIGH (there is no MAX pressure setting for the large pot at this writing).

Beyond

- Stir in up to 1 cup thawed frozen peas with the cream.

- To deepen the flavors even more, stir in ½ ounce dried porcini mushrooms, crumbled, with the spices.

- Garnish servings with minced fresh chives.

Orzo with Olives and Capers

8 ingredients	**SPECIAL EQUIPMENT:** none	**TIME UNDER PRESSURE:** 5 or 6 minutes
4 SERVINGS		
METHOD: standard	**PRESSURE:** max or high	**RELEASE:** quick

TOTAL TIME WITH PRESSURE: about 20 minutes

VEGAN

CAN BE GLUTEN-FREE

3½ cups vegetable broth

One 4-ounce jar diced pimientos (do not drain)

¼ cup chopped pitted green olives

2 teaspoons drained and rinsed capers, finely chopped

1 teaspoon dried oregano

1 teaspoon dried rosemary, crushed

1 pound raw dried orzo (gluten-free, if necessary—for more information, see the chapter introduction on page 103)

2 teaspoons balsamic vinegar

Other Pots

- For a 3-quart Instant Pot, you *must* halve all of the ingredient amounts.
- For a 10-quart Instant Pot, you *must* increase all of the ingredient amounts by 50 percent or you *can* even double the amounts.

Beyond

- For heat, add up to 1 teaspoon red pepper flakes with the dried herbs.
- For a richer (but not a vegan) dish, substitute chicken broth for the vegetable broth.
- For a vegetarian (but not a vegan) dish, garnish the servings with crumbled soft goat cheese.

Sure, this simple dish could be a side for a roast or a steak off the grill. However, it also makes a light vegan entrée, perfect for a warm evening. There's no added salt because the pressure leaches a great deal from the olives and jarred pimientos.

Take particular note of step 2: You *must* let the broth get hot enough that steam comes off it before you add the orzo. Otherwise, the pasta will fall to the insert's bottom and stick there as the liquid comes up to a boil in the sealed pot.

1.

	Press	Set it for	Set time for	If needed, press
In all models	SAUTÉ	HIGH or MORE	10 minutes	START

2. As the pot heats, stir the broth, pimientos, olives, capers, oregano, and rosemary in the insert set in a **5-, 6-, or 8-quart Instant Pot.** Heat until many wisps of steam come off the broth, until it's just on the verge of simmering, about 8 minutes. Stir in the orzo, turn off the heat, and lock the lid on the pot.

3.

	Set pot for	Set level to	Valve must be	Set time for	If needed, press
For Max pots only	PRESSURE COOK	MAX	—	5 minutes with the KEEP WARM setting off	START
For all other pots	PRESSURE COOK or MANUAL	HIGH	Closed	6 minutes with the KEEP WARM setting off	START

4. When the pot has finished cooking, use the **quick-release method** to bring the pressure back to normal. Unlatch the lid and open the cooker. Stir in the balsamic vinegar; then set the lid askew over the cooker and set it aside for 2 to 3 minutes so the pasta continues to absorb some of the sauce. Stir again and serve warm.

Creamy Orzo with Spinach

9 ingredients

4 SERVINGS

METHOD:
standard

SPECIAL EQUIPMENT:
none

PRESSURE:
max or high

TIME UNDER PRESSURE:
5 or 6 minutes

RELEASE:
quick

TOTAL TIME WITH PRESSURE:
about 20 minutes

VEGETARIAN

CAN BE GLUTEN-FREE

---

3 cups vegetable broth

2 tablespoons butter

2 medium garlic cloves, minced (2 teaspoons)

½ teaspoon table salt

½ teaspoon ground black pepper

1 pound raw dried orzo (gluten-free, if necessary—for more information, see the chapter introduction on page 103)

10-ounces packed chopped stemmed fresh spinach (4 cups)

1 ounce Parmigiano-Reggiano, finely grated (½ cup)

¼ cup heavy or light cream

Sometimes, life calls for cream—maybe just a touch to make things a little more decadent, or comforting, or just plain delicious. Whatever the case, here's the dish for that moment. A small amount of cream gives this pasta a silky, luxurious feel, sort of like an orzo version of risotto (if that makes sense). If you want to go over the top, double the butter, not the cream.

1.

	Press	Set it for	Set time for	If needed, press
In all models	SAUTÉ	HIGH or MORE	10 minutes	START

2. As the pot heats, stir the broth, butter, garlic, salt, and pepper in the insert set in **a 5-, 6-, or 8-quart Instant Pot.** Heat the mixture until many wisps of steam rise off the broth, until it's just on the verge of simmering, about 8 minutes. Stir in the orzo, then pile the spinach on top of the mixture without pressing it down or stirring it in. Lock the lid on the pot.

3.

	Set pot for	Set level to	Valve must be	Set time for	If needed, press
For Max pots only	PRESSURE COOK	MAX	—	5 minutes with the KEEP WARM setting off	START
For all other pots	PRESSURE COOK or MANUAL	HIGH	Closed	6 minutes with the KEEP WARM setting off	START

4. When the pot has finished cooking, use the **quick-release method** to bring the pressure back to normal. Unlatch the lid and open the cooker. Stir in the cheese and cream. Use hot pads or silicone baking mitts to transfer the (hot!) insert to a nearby wire rack. Cool for 2 to 3 minutes so the pasta continues to absorb the sauce. Stir again and serve warm.

Other Pots

- For a 3-quart Instant Pot, you *must* halve all of the ingredient amounts.

- For a 10-quart Instant Pot, you *must* increase all of the ingredient amounts by 50 percent or you *can* even double the amounts.

Beyond

- For more flavor, add up to 1 tablespoon stemmed and minced fresh herbs with the salt and pepper. Choose between thyme, parsley, oregano, sage, and/or tarragon leaves. Or add up to 2 teaspoons Italian dried spice blend.

Israeli Couscous with Peppers and Sausage

8 ingredients	**SPECIAL EQUIPMENT:** none
4 SERVINGS	
METHOD: standard	

PRESSURE: max or high	**RELEASE:** quick
TIME UNDER PRESSURE: 7 or 10 minutes	**TOTAL TIME WITH PRESSURE:** about 30 minutes

½ pound sweet or mild pork, turkey, or chicken Italian sausages (in their casings), cut into 1-inch-thick pieces

One 1-pound bag frozen bell pepper strips, thawed (2½ cups)

2½ cups chicken broth

¼ cup loosely packed chopped fresh basil leaves

½ teaspoon fennel seeds

½ teaspoon table salt

½ teaspoon red pepper flakes

2 cups raw dried Israeli couscous

So-called "Israeli couscous" isn't really couscous per se. Or it's not what most people think of when they think of "couscous." Instead, Israeli couscous is made from a semolina flour paste that's machine-formed into small spheres. It was created in Israel (where it's called "ptitim") as an easy way to feed so many immigrants arriving in the 1950s. Here, we mix it with sausage and peppers for a simple one-pot meal that only needs a tossed salad on the side.

We tried this dish with several gluten-free versions of Israeli couscous. None worked. The little spheres blew apart or became way too gummy.

1.

	Press	Set it for	Set time for	If needed, press
In all models	SAUTÉ	MEDIUM, NORMAL, or CUSTOM 300°F	15 minutes	START

2. As the pot heats, put the sausage pieces in the insert set in a **5-, 6-, or 8-quart Instant Pot.** Brown them well, turning occasionally, about 6 minutes. Add the bell pepper strips and toss well.

3. Pour in the broth and scrape up any browned bits on the pot's bottom. Stir in the basil, fennel seeds, salt, and red pepper flakes. Continue cooking, stirring once or twice, until many wisps of steam rise off the liquid, about 4 minutes. Turn off the heat, stir in the Israeli couscous, and lock the lid on the pot.

4.

	Set pot for	Set level to	Valve must be	Set time for	If needed, press
For Max pots only	PRESSURE COOK	MAX	—	7 minutes with the KEEP WARM setting off	START
For all other pots	PRESSURE COOK or MANUAL	HIGH	Closed	10 minutes with the KEEP WARM setting off	START

5. When the pot has finished cooking, use the **quick-release method** to bring the pressure back to normal. Unlatch the lid and open the cooker. Stir well, then set aside for a couple of minutes, until the couscous has absorbed some of the excess liquid. Stir again and serve warm.

Other Pots

- For a 3-quart Instant Pot, you *must* halve all of the ingredient amounts.
- For an 8-quart Instant Pot, you *can* increase all of the ingredient amounts by 50 percent.
- For a 10-quart Instant Pot, you *must* increase all of the ingredient amounts by 50 percent or you *can* even double the amounts.

Beyond

- Garnish the servings with grated Parmigiano-Reggiano, Swiss, provolone, or Asiago cheese.
- Or drizzle with Sriracha and top with crumbled blue cheese.

Israeli Couscous with Turkey and Pecans

11 ingredients

4 SERVINGS

METHOD:
standard

SPECIAL EQUIPMENT:
none

PRESSURE:
max or high

TIME UNDER PRESSURE:
7 or 10 minutes

RELEASE:
quick

TOTAL TIME WITH PRESSURE:
about 30 minutes

2 tablespoons butter

1 large yellow or white onion, chopped (1½ cups)

3 medium celery stalks, chopped (1 cup)

⅓ cup chopped pecans

1 pound boneless skinless turkey breast cutlets, diced

½ teaspoon rubbed or ground sage

½ teaspoon dried thyme

½ teaspoon table salt

½ teaspoon ground black pepper

3½ cups chicken broth

1⅔ cups raw dried Israeli couscous

Other Pots

- For a **3-quart Instant Pot**, you *must* halve all of the ingredient amounts.
- For an **8-quart Instant Pot**, you *can* increase all of the ingredient amounts by 50 percent.
- For a **10-quart Instant Pot**, you *must* increase all of the ingredient amounts by 50 percent and you *can* even double the amounts.

Beyond

- Garnish the servings with cranberry sauce or cranberry chutney.

Turkey, pecans, and butter are a perfect combo: Together they create a flavor profile that's not too sweet or nutty, savory but not bitter. Add tender Israeli couscous to that mix and this main course proves almost irresistible. Just one tip: Make sure the broth mixture is quite hot before you add the Israeli couscous.

1.

	Press	Set it for	Set time for	If needed, press
In all models	SAUTÉ	MEDIUM, NORMAL, or CUSTOM 300°F	10 minutes	START

2. As the pot heats, melt the butter in the insert set in a **5-, 6-, or 8-quart Instant Pot.** Add the onion, celery, and pecans; cook, stirring often, until the onion is softened, about 3 minutes.

3. Add the turkey and cook, stirring more often, until the meat loses its raw, pink color, about 2 minutes. Stir in the sage, thyme, salt, and pepper until fragrant, only a few seconds.

4. Pour in the broth and scrape up any browned bits on the pot's bottom. Continue cooking, stirring a couple of times, until the broth gets quite steamy (but not yet simmering), about 4 minutes. Stir in the Israeli couscous. Turn off the heat and lock the lid on the pot.

5.

	Set pot for	Set level to	Valve must be	Set time for	If needed, press
For Max pots only	PRESSURE COOK	MAX	—	7 minutes with the KEEP WARM setting off	START
For all other pots	PRESSURE COOK or MANUAL	HIGH	Closed	10 minutes with the KEEP WARM setting off	START

6. When the pot has finished cooking, use the **quick-release method** to bring the pressure back to normal. Unlatch the lid and open the cooker. Stir well, then set the lid askew over the pot and set it aside for 2 to 3 minutes to let the couscous absorb some of the liquid. Stir again and serve warm.

Israeli Couscous with Lamb and Nuts

15 ingredients	**SPECIAL EQUIPMENT:** none
4 SERVINGS	
METHOD: standard	

PRESSURE: max or high	**RELEASE:** quick
TIME UNDER PRESSURE: 7 or 10 minutes	**TOTAL TIME WITH PRESSURE:** about 30 minutes

¼ cup pine nuts

¼ cup shelled unsalted pistachios

1 tablespoon butter

1 tablespoon olive oil

¼ pound ground lamb

1 large yellow or white onion, halved, then sliced into thin half-moons

3¼ cups chicken broth

1 tablespoon finely grated lemon zest

1 teaspoon table salt

½ teaspoon ground black pepper

1⅔ cups raw dried Israeli couscous

One 3-inch cinnamon stick

½ cup loosely packed, stemmed, fresh Italian parsley leaves, chopped

¼ cup raisins

Balsamic vinegar, preferably an aged, syrupy balsamic, for garnishing

Other Pots

- For a 3-quart Instant Pot, you *must* halve all of the ingredient amounts.

- For an 8-quart Instant Pot, you *can* increase all of the ingredient amounts by 50 percent.

- For a 10-quart Instant Pot, you *must* increase all of the ingredient amounts by 50 percent and you *can* even double the amounts.

Beyond

- Skip the vinegar and dollop a little crème fraîche on each serving.

This Israeli couscous dish cannot sideline as a side dish. It's a meal in the pot, made with ground lamb and Mediterranean seasonings, all flavors reminiscent of moussaka.

Unfortunately, because of the way Israeli couscous continues to absorb liquid as it sits, any dish made with it doesn't store well. At the very least you'll need to thin out leftovers with a good amount of broth when reheating.

1.

	Press	Set it for	Set time for	If needed, press
In all models	SAUTÉ	MEDIUM, NORMAL, or CUSTOM 300°F	15 minutes	START

2. As the pot heats, put the pine nuts and pistachios in the insert set in a **5-, 6-, or 8-quart Instant Pot.** Cook, stirring occasionally, until fragrant and lightly browned, 2 or 3 minutes. Transfer to a bowl.

3. Melt the butter in the oil in the insert. Crumble in the lamb and cook, stirring often to break up any clumps, until lightly browned, about 3 minutes. Add the onion and continue cooking, stirring more frequently, until the onion begins to brown lightly along the edges of the pieces, about 5 minutes.

4. Stir in the broth, zest, salt, and pepper. Scrape up any browned bits on the pot's bottom. Continue cooking, stirring occasionally, until the broth mixture is quite steamy (but not yet simmering), about 4 minutes. Turn off the heat. Stir in the Israeli couscous and the cinnamon stick. Lock the lid on the pot.

5.

	Set pot for	Set level to	Valve must be	Set time for	If needed, press
For Max pots only	PRESSURE COOK	MAX	—	7 minutes with the KEEP WARM setting off	START
For all other pots	PRESSURE COOK or MANUAL	HIGH	Closed	10 minutes with the KEEP WARM setting off	START

6. When the pot has finished cooking, use the **quick-release method** to bring the pressure back to normal. Unlatch the lid and open the cooker. Fish out and discard the cinnamon stick.

7. Stir in the toasted nuts, parsley, and raisins. Set the lid askew over the pot and set it aside for 2 to 3 minutes so the pasta can continue to absorb the sauce. Stir again and serve warm, drizzled with balsamic vinegar.

One-Pot Chicken Pad Thai

12 ingredients	
4 SERVINGS	

SPECIAL EQUIPMENT: none	TIME UNDER PRESSURE: 4 minutes	TOTAL TIME WITH PRESSURE: about 25 minutes	
METHOD: standard	PRESSURE: high	RELEASE: quick	CAN BE GLUTEN-FREE

8 ounces boneless skinless chicken breast cut for stir-fry (discard any flavoring packets)

1½ cups chicken broth

3 medium scallions, trimmed and thinly sliced (1 cup)

¼ cup roasted unsalted peanuts

3 tablespoons fish sauce (gluten-free, if necessary)

3 tablespoons dark brown sugar

2 tablespoons unseasoned rice vinegar

Up to 6 medium garlic cloves, minced (2 tablespoons)

1 tablespoon regular or low-sodium soy sauce, or gluten-free tamari sauce

8 ounces raw dried wide flat rice noodles (sometimes called "rice stick noodles" or "pad Thai noodles"), broken as necessary to fit in the pot

1 yellow bell pepper, stemmed, cored, and cut into ¼-inch strips

Lime wedges, for garnishing

There's nothing fancy here, other than a fine rendition of sweet-and-salty pad Thai without much trouble and without any additional steps. So although it might not be a fancy meal, we might file it under a "treat-yourself" recipe, given that it's a fine way to create a beloved comfort-food meal with much less work.

1. Stir the chicken, broth, scallions, peanuts, fish sauce, brown sugar, rice vinegar, garlic, and soy sauce in a **5-, 6-, or 8-quart Instant Pot** until the brown sugar dissolves.

2. Lay the broken rice noodles on top of this sauce mixture and press down gently, just until some are submerged with none getting close to the pot's bottom. Gently pile the pepper strips on top of the noodles, then lock the lid on the pot.

3.

	Set pot for	Set level to	Valve must be	Set time for	If needed, press
For *all* pots	PRESSURE COOK or MANUAL	HIGH	Closed	4 minutes with the KEEP WARM setting off	START

4. When the pot has finished cooking, use the **quick-release method** to bring the pressure back to normal. Unlatch the lid and open the cooker. Stir gently until well combined. Serve warm with lime wedges to squeeze over each serving.

Other Pots

- For a **3-quart Instant Pot**, you *must* halve all of the ingredient amounts and you *must* break the dried noodles into even smaller pieces.

- For an **8-quart Instant Pot**, you *can* increase all of the ingredient amounts by 50 percent.

- For a **10-quart Instant Pot**, you *must* increase all of the ingredient amounts by 50 percent and you *can* even double the amounts. You do not need to break dried noodles for the large pot.

Beyond

- For a heftier meal, add up to 8 ounces firm tofu, diced, or up to 8 ounces peeled and deveined medium shrimp (about 30 per pound) with the bell pepper strips.

- Garnish the servings with Sriracha, chopped fresh mint leaves, chopped fresh cilantro leaves, and/or more peanuts.

See photo in insert.

Basil Chicken with Rice Noodles

12 ingredients	SPECIAL EQUIPMENT: none	TIME UNDER PRESSURE: 5 minutes	TOTAL TIME WITH PRESSURE: about 20 minutes
4 SERVINGS			
METHOD: standard	PRESSURE: high	RELEASE: quick	CAN BE GLUTEN-FREE

1½ pounds boneless skinless chicken thighs, cut into 1-inch pieces

1½ cups chicken broth

4 medium scallions, trimmed and thinly sliced (1⅓ cups)

3 tablespoons fish sauce (gluten-free, if necessary)

2 tablespoons orange or ginger marmalade

2 tablespoons regular or low-sodium soy sauce, or gluten-free tamari sauce

2 tablespoons unseasoned rice vinegar

Up to 2 tablespoons thick red chile sauce, such as sambal oelek

2 teaspoons minced peeled fresh ginger

8 ounces raw dried wide flat rice noodles (sometimes called "rice stick noodles" or "pad Thai noodles"), broken as necessary to fit in the pot

¼ cup packed, stemmed, fresh basil leaves, chopped

Lime wedges, for garnishing

Other Pots

- For a 3-quart Instant Pot, you *must* halve all of the ingredient amounts and you *must* break the dried noodles into even smaller pieces.

- For an 8-quart Instant Pot, you *can* increase all of the ingredient amounts by 50 percent.

- For a 10-quart Instant Pot, you *must* double all of the ingredient amounts. You do not need to break dried noodles for the large pot.

Beyond

- Garnish the servings with bean sprouts.
- And/or stemmed and minced fresh mint leaves.

Here's a sweet-and-sour, highly aromatic dish—not really a Thai dish at all (although it's sometimes presented as that on North American menus), but really something of a nouveau diner favorite across the United States. It's made with slippery rice noodles, lots of scallions, some fish sauce, and plenty of ginger. Rather than the more traditional brown sugar (or palm sugar) in the mix, we've here opted for marmalade—maybe orange, but preferably ginger, a British favorite—and a great hit of bright flavors that take the dish over the top.

Adjust the amount of chile sauce, depending on how hot you want the final dish. Remember: The pressure cooker kills off a lot of the chile heat. You might be able to tolerate more than you imagine (but be safe the first time you make the dish, if you have any concerns).

1. Stir the chicken, broth, scallions, fish sauce, marmalade, soy sauce, vinegar, chile sauce, and ginger in the insert set in a **5-, 6-, or 8-quart Instant Pot** until the marmalade dissolves and everything is evenly mixed.

2. Lay the broken rice noodles on top of this sauce mixture and press down gently, just until some are submerged with none getting close to the pot's bottom. Lock the lid on the pot.

3.

	Set pot for	Set level to	Valve must be	Set time for	If needed, press
For *all* pots	PRESSURE COOK or MANUAL	HIGH	Closed	5 minutes with the KEEP WARM setting off	START

4. When the pot has finished cooking, use the **quick-release method** to bring the pressure back to normal. Unlatch the lid and open the cooker. Add the basil and stir well. Set the lid askew over the pot and set it aside for 2 to 3 minutes so the noodles absorb some more of the sauce. Stir well and serve warm with lime wedges to squeeze over each bowlful.

Spicy Rice Noodles with Chicken and Kimchi

7 ingredients	SPECIAL EQUIPMENT: none	TIME UNDER PRESSURE: 4 minutes	TOTAL TIME WITH PRESSURE: about 20 minutes
4 SERVINGS			
METHOD: standard	PRESSURE: high	RELEASE: quick	CAN BE GLUTEN-FREE

2¼ cups chicken broth

1 pound boneless skinless chicken breasts cut for stir-fry (discard any flavoring packets)

1 cup drained, loosely packed, mild or spicy kimchi, chopped

1 tablespoon toasted sesame oil

1 tablespoon dark brown sugar

Up to 1 teaspoon ground dried cayenne

8 ounces raw dried wide flat rice noodles (sometimes called "rice stick noodles" or "pad Thai noodles"), broken as necessary to fit in the pot

Other Pots

- For a 3-quart Instant Pot, you *must* halve all of the ingredient amounts and you *must* break the dried noodles into even smaller pieces.
- For an 8-quart Instant Pot, you *can* increase all of the ingredient amounts by 50 percent.
- For a 10-quart Instant Pot, you *must* double all of the ingredient amounts. You do not need to break dried noodles for the large pot.

Beyond

- For more salty/umami flavor, add 2 tablespoons white miso paste with the broth.
- For more authentic flavor, substitute gochugaru (ground dried Korean chiles) for the ground cayenne.
- Garnish the servings with thinly sliced scallions and/or chopped fresh cilantro leaves.

We love cooking with kimchi! It adds a bright, sour flavor to stews and noodle dishes. We've even been known to slip a tablespoon or two of chopped kimchi into a standard pot of chicken noodle soup, just to give the servings a little added oomph. In this recipe, we've crafted a rice-noodle dish that relies on kimchi's characteristic flavors to give the chicken more flavor and soothe whatever aches you've got, particularly since kimchi mellows so well under pressure.

If you haven't cooked with it, kimchi is made from fermented, chile-spiced vegetables, usually cabbage, although sometimes with other leafy vegetables or radishes. You can find a giant selection of kimchi at Korean supermarkets like H Mart. Feel free to try any kind. In more standard North American supermarkets, look for kimchi in the produce section, usually near the tofu. You'll mostly find mild varieties. Because of that, we add quite a bit of ground cayenne here. If you have spicy kimchi (or you just don't want so much burn), reduce the cayenne by half, if not by three-quarters.

1. Stir the broth, chicken, kimchi, sesame oil, brown sugar, and cayenne in the insert set in a **5-, 6-, or 8-quart Instant Pot** until the brown sugar dissolves.

2. Place the broken noodles in the insert on top of the sauce. Gently press down so some of the noodles are submerged without any coming near the pot's bottom. Lock the lid on the pot.

3.

	Set pot for	Set level to	Valve must be	Set time for	If needed, press
For *all* pots	PRESSURE COOK or MANUAL	HIGH	Closed	4 minutes with the KEEP WARM setting off	START

4. When the pot has finished cooking, use the **quick-release method** to bring the pressure back to normal. Unlatch the lid and open the cooker. Stir gently but well before serving hot.

Pork in Peanut Sauce with Rice Vermicelli

12 ingredients	**SPECIAL EQUIPMENT:** none
4 SERVINGS	**PRESSURE:** high
METHOD: standard	**RELEASE:** modified natural

TIME UNDER PRESSURE: 0 minutes	**TOTAL TIME WITH PRESSURE:** about 25 minutes
	CAN BE GLUTEN-FREE

---

1 tablespoon canola, vegetable, or other neutral-flavored oil

6 medium scallions, trimmed and thinly sliced (2 cups)

1 tablespoon minced peeled fresh ginger

2 medium garlic cloves, minced (2 teaspoons)

1 pound lean ground pork

¼ cup natural-style peanut butter, preferably chunky peanut butter

2 tablespoons Worcestershire sauce (gluten-free, if necessary)

2 tablespoons regular or low-sodium soy sauce, or gluten-free tamari sauce

1 tablespoon honey

1 tablespoon unseasoned rice vinegar

2¾ cups chicken broth

8 ounces raw dried rice vermicelli (do *not* use angel-hair rice pasta, a gluten-free alternative for Italian dishes)

Other Pots

- For a 3-quart Instant Pot, you *must* halve all of the ingredient amounts.

- For an 8-quart Instant Pot, you *can* increase all of the ingredient amounts by 50 percent.

- For a 10-quart Instant Pot, you *must* increase all of the ingredient amounts by 50 percent or you *can* even double the ingredient amounts.

Beyond

- Garnish the servings with julienned carrots or red bell pepper strips. You can often find these already prepped in the produce section of most large North American supermarkets.

This simple but highly flavored classic is best made with lean ground pork because the noodles can get too oily with standard ground pork. If you can't find any lean ground pork, buy 1 pound of boneless center-cut pork loin chops, cut them into 1-inch pieces, then pulse them in two batches in a food processor until finely ground, stopping the machine at least once to scrape down the inside of the canister.

Only let the pot cook under pressure until the pin pops up in the lid, when the pot is near but not yet at full pressure. Immediately turn off the pot for a modified natural release.

1.

	Press	Set it for	Set time for	If needed, press
In all models	SAUTÉ	MEDIUM, NORMAL, or CUSTOM 300°F	5 minutes	START

2. As the pot heats, warm the oil in the insert set in a **5-, 6-, or 8-quart Instant Pot.** Add the scallions, ginger, and garlic. Cook, stirring quite often, until fragrant, about 1 minute. Crumble in the pork and continue cooking, stirring more often, until it loses its raw, red color, about 2 minutes.

3. Stir in the peanut butter, Worcestershire sauce, soy or tamari sauce, honey, and vinegar until the peanut butter dissolves. Pour in the broth and scrape up any browned bits on the pot's bottom. Turn off the heat. Set the wad of vermicelli into the sauce, gently pressing down just so some of it is submerged but none touches the pot's bottom. Lock the lid on the pot.

4.

	Set pot for	Set level to	Valve must be	Set time for	If needed, press
For *all* pots	PRESSURE COOK or MANUAL	HIGH	Closed	0 or 1 minute with the KEEP WARM setting off	START

5. *The moment the pin pops up to lock the lid in place,* turn off (or unplug) the pot and let the pressure **return to normal naturally for 3 minutes.** Use the **quick-release method** to get rid of any remaining pressure in the pot. Unlatch the lid and open the pot.

6. Use two forks to break up the softened vermicelli, stirring it into the meat sauce to coat it evenly and thoroughly. Set the pot aside for 1 or 2 minutes so the vermicelli can absorb some of the sauce.

Gingery Beef with Rice Vermicelli

9 ingredients

4 SERVINGS

METHOD: standard

SPECIAL EQUIPMENT: none

PRESSURE: high

TIME UNDER PRESSURE: 0 minutes

RELEASE: modified natural

TOTAL TIME WITH PRESSURE: about 25 minutes

CAN BE GLUTEN-FREE

---

1 tablespoon canola, vegetable, or other neutral-flavored oil

3 tablespoons minced peeled fresh ginger

1 pound lean ground beef, preferably 90 percent lean or more

2 tablespoons regular or low-sodium soy sauce, or gluten-free tamari sauce

2 tablespoons mirin; or dry white wine plus ½ teaspoon granulated white sugar; or unsweetened apple juice

½ teaspoon ground dried ginger

2 cups chicken or beef broth

8 ounces raw dried rice vermicelli (do *not* use angel-hair rice pasta, a gluten-free alternative for Italian dishes)

Toasted sesame oil, for garnishing

Other Pots

- For a 3-quart Instant Pot, you *must* halve all of the ingredient amounts.
- For an 8-quart Instant Pot, you *can* increase all of the ingredient amounts by 50 percent.
- For a 10-quart Instant Pot, you *must* increase all of the ingredient amounts by 50 percent or you *can* even double the ingredient amounts.

Beyond

- To garnish, lightly dress pea shoots with unseasoned rice vinegar and set a small nest on top of each bowlful.

This recipe calls for two types of ginger: fresh ginger (although, yes, you can use the minced jarred stuff you can find in the produce section—but it still counts as *fresh*) as well as ground dried ginger. The fresh gives the flavors a characteristic "bite;" the dried contributes a bit of musky sophistication to bring the flavors into better balance.

As with Pork in Peanut Sauce with Rice Vermicelli (page 156), the dish is cooked under pressure *only* until the pin pops up in the lid to lock it on.

1.

	Press	Set it for	Set time for	If needed, press
In all models	SAUTÉ	MEDIUM, NORMAL, or CUSTOM 300°F	10 minutes	START

2. As the pot heats, warm the oil in the insert set in a **5-, 6-, or 8-quart Instant Pot.** Add the fresh ginger and cook, stirring all the while, until very fragrant, about 1 minute. Crumble in the ground beef and cook, stirring frequently, until lightly browned, about 3 minutes.

3. Stir in the soy sauce, mirin, and ground ginger. Then pour in the broth and scrape up any browned bits on the pot's bottom. Turn off the heat.

4. Set the wad of dried vermicelli into the sauce, gently pressing down just so some of it is submerged but none touches the pot's bottom. Lock the lid on the pot.

5.

	Set pot for	Set level to	Valve must be	Set time for	If needed, press
For *all* pots	PRESSURE COOK or MANUAL	HIGH	Closed	0 to 1 minute with the KEEP WARM setting off	START

6. *The moment the pin pops up to lock the lid in place,* turn off (or unplug) the pot and let the pressure **return to normal naturally for 3 minutes.** Use the **quick-release method** to get rid of the pot's residual pressure. Unlatch the lid and open the cooker.

7. Use two forks to break up the softened vermicelli, stirring it into the meat sauce to coat it evenly and thoroughly. Set the pot aside for 1 or 2 minutes so the vermicelli can absorb some of the sauce. Stir well and serve warm, garnishing the servings with toasted sesame oil.

Chicken & Turkey

This chapter is *big*: fifty-two recipes! Even so, you probably already know why it's almost a whole cookbook in itself. Chicken cooks quickly in an Instant Pot. It's easy to make it tasty. And chicken is mostly good for your waistline, when compared to beef or lamb.

All true except for one thing: Chicken is temperamental, too. Who hasn't had to choke down the unappetizing shards of overcooked boneless skinless chicken breasts? Most of us know that one solution is to leave the skin on the meat to protect it. But doing so in an IP yields notoriously squishy results.

We have lots of ways around these problems. For example, boneless skinless chicken breasts can be cooked on LOW pressure for *much* better results. They can also be pressure-steamed on a rack to produce the best boneless skinless meat we've ever had out of an IP.

If the skin is left on, nothing beats a good browning to keep it appetizing after it endures the hot, humid environment inside the cooker. Don't skimp: Brown is good. Dark brown blotches, better. The compensation for your work is a better meal.

Throughout this chapter, pay close attention to the recipe's timing under pressure. Some recipes call for longer cooking plus either a modified natural or a standard natural release. These recipes are all about shredding the chicken for salads or pulled dishes. Shorter times under pressure and quick releases are all about keeping the cut whole, better for a knife and a fork.

And while we're at this sort of culinary advice, pay *very close* attention to the size of the chicken cuts in these recipes, particularly when it comes to chicken breasts, bone-in or boneless. The sizes vary widely. We use giant, 1-pound boneless skinless breasts in some and much smaller breasts in others. We vary the sizes based on the overall time other ingredients in a recipe need to undergo pressure to get done. A 6-ounce potato in a pot with a 4-ounce breast means that either the potato will be a rock when the chicken is perfect or the chicken will be porridge when the potato is tender. Use the sizes called for and you'll be right every time.

Eight recipes for turkey dishes fall at the end of this chapter. If that leaves you wishing for more, remember that you can substitute *lean* ground turkey for ground chicken in any recipe in this chapter, thereby extending the turkey dishes to recipes like a copycat version of P. F. Chang's lettuce wraps (page 208).

However, you can't substitute ground chicken for ground turkey. Ground chicken is both stickier and drier than ground turkey (because of more cartilage and less fat). Ground chicken just won't work in a ground turkey recipe here.

So what *is* here? A lot of one-pot chicken salads and even chicken pasta salads. Some cheesy chicken casseroles, a handful of knock-off recipes from popular eateries, and complete chicken dinners right out of the pot (sides and all). Plus, sets of recipes for specific poultry cuts, more ideas for ground chicken than we've ever included in a book, and even a few surprises, like our Instant Pot take on negimaki (page 193). No wonder this chapter is so big.

Warm Chicken and Potato Salad

12 ingredients	**SPECIAL EQUIPMENT:** steamer basket	**TIME UNDER PRESSURE:** 8 or 10 minutes	**TOTAL TIME WITH PRESSURE:** about 40 minutes
6 SERVINGS			
METHOD: steam	**PRESSURE:** max or high	**RELEASE:** quick	**CAN BE GLUTEN-FREE**

1½ cups water

1 pound russet or baking potatoes, peeled and cut into 2- to 3-inch pieces

Three 8-ounce boneless skinless chicken breasts

3 tablespoons olive oil

4 thin strips of bacon (gluten-free, if necessary), chopped

1 small yellow or white onion, chopped (½ cup)

1 tablespoon Dijon mustard (gluten-free, if necessary)

1 tablespoon Worcestershire sauce (gluten-free, if necessary)

¼ cup apple cider vinegar or *white balsamic vinegar*

3 medium celery stalks, thinly sliced (1 cup)

1 teaspoon table salt

Up to 1 teaspoon ground black pepper

People say you shouldn't mess with a good thing. And surely there's nothing better than a warm potato salad with bacon. But we decided to take a risk and add chicken to the recipe to turn your favorite side dish into a meal. The gamble paid off.

You might be surprised by our use of russets (or baking) potatoes for a potato salad, rather than yellow- or red-skinned potatoes. We feel russets add a lot of creaminess and so make for a good match to the crunchy celery.

Note: These boneless skinless chicken breasts are large, not the 4-ounce ones that come frozen in bags at big-box stores. These larger cuts can better stand up to the longer cooking time the potatoes require.

1. Pour the water into the insert set in a **5-, 6-, or 8-quart Instant Pot.** Place an IP-safe steamer basket in the insert (see page 14 in the introduction for more information).

2. Put the potato pieces in the basket in as close to one layer as possible. Set the chicken breasts in one layer over the potatoes. (Stacking the breasts will result in uneven cooking.) Lock the lid on the pot.

3.

	Set pot for	Set level to	Valve must be	Set time for	If needed, press
For Max pots only	PRESSURE COOK	MAX	—	8 minutes with the KEEP WARM setting off	START
For all other pots	PRESSURE COOK or MANUAL	HIGH	Closed	10 minutes with the KEEP WARM setting off	START

4. When the pot has finished cooking, use the **quick-release method** to bring the pressure back to normal. Unlatch the lid and open the cooker. Use hot pads or silicone baking mitts to transfer the (hot!) steamer basket with the chicken breasts and potatoes to a nearby cutting board. Cool for 5 minutes. Empty the water from the pot's (hot!) insert and wipe it out. Return it to the pot.

5.

	Press	Set it for	Set time for	If needed, press
In all models	SAUTÉ	MEDIUM, NORMAL, or CUSTOM 300°F	10 minutes	START

6. Warm 1 tablespoon oil in the insert. Add the bacon and cook, stirring occasionally, until crisp, about 4 minutes. Use a slotted spoon to transfer the bacon to a nearby plate.

7. Add the remaining 2 tablespoons oil to the pot, then the onion. Cook, stirring often, until the onion begins to soften, about 2 minutes. Stir in the mustard, Worcestershire sauce, and vinegar; then scrape up any browned bits on the pot's bottom. Turn off the heat and use hot pads or silicone baking mitts to transfer the (hot!) insert to a nearby wire rack.

8. Chop the chicken and potatoes into bite-size bits. Put them in the pot's insert; add the bacon bits, celery, salt, and pepper. Stir gently to combine, coating the chicken and potatoes in the "sauce." Serve warm out of the insert or transfer to a nicer but heat-safe serving bowl.

Other Pots

- For a 3-quart Instant Pot, you *must* halve all of the ingredient amounts.

- For a 10-quart Instant Pot, you *must* increase the amount of water in the insert to 2½ cups. You *can* complete the recipe as otherwise stated or you *can* increase the other ingredient amounts by 50 percent provided you use a very large steaming basket.

Beyond

- Substitute diced pancetta for the bacon for a clearer (that is, not-smoky) flavor.

- Add up to 1 teaspoon celery seeds, 1 teaspoon caraway seeds, and/or 1 teaspoon red pepper flakes with the salt and pepper.

Easy Southwestern Chicken Pasta Salad

8 ingredients	
4–6 SERVINGS	
METHOD: standard	

SPECIAL EQUIPMENT: none	
PRESSURE: max or high	

TIME UNDER PRESSURE: 5 or 7 minutes	
RELEASE: quick	

TOTAL TIME WITH PRESSURE: about 30 minutes	
CAN BE GLUTEN-FREE	

6 cups water

1 pound boneless skinless chicken breasts, *cut into ½-inch pieces*

8 ounces raw dried penne (gluten-free, if necessary—for more information, see the pasta chapter introduction on page 103)

1 cup red or green salsa

1 cup drained and rinsed canned pinto beans

One 4½-ounce can hot or mild diced green chiles (½ cup)

⅓ cup stemmed, chopped, fresh cilantro leaves

4 ounces American sharp or mild cheddar cheese, shredded (1 cup)

Other Pots

- For a 3-quart Instant Pot, you *must* reduce the water in the pot to 4 *cups* and the pasta to 6 ounces while otherwise completing the recipe as stated.
- For a 10-quart Instant Pot, you *must* increase the ingredient amounts by 50 percent or you *can* even double the amounts.

Beyond

- For more crunch, add up to ½ cup thinly sliced celery and/or diced carrot with the salsa and other ingredients.
- For more flavor, add up to 1 teaspoon ground cumin and/or 1 teaspoon dried oregano with the cilantro.

Here's an easy pasta salad that'll be a hit at your next summer picnic. Note two tricks to success. One, the chicken breasts have to be cut into fairly small pieces. Don't be tempted to drop larger chunks into the pot. They won't cook in the allotted time. And two, the salad must cool a bit before you add the cheese. Otherwise, it'll melt into a stringy mess. With those two bits of advice in hand, you're ready for blue-ribbon results.

1.

	Press	Set it for	Set time for	If needed, press
In all models	SAUTÉ	MEDIUM, NORMAL, or CUSTOM 300°F	10 minutes	START

2. As the pot heats, stir the water and chicken into the insert set in a **5-, 6-, or 8-quart Instant Pot.** Continue cooking until plenty of steam wisps rise from the water. Stir in the pasta, turn off the heat, and lock the lid on the pot.

3.

	Set pot for	Set level to	Valve must be	Set time for	If needed, press
For Max pots only	PRESSURE COOK	MAX	—	5 minutes with the KEEP WARM setting off	START
For all other pots	PRESSURE COOK or MANUAL	HIGH	Closed	7 minutes with the KEEP WARM setting off	START

4. When the pot has finished cooking, use the **quick-release method** to bring the pressure back to normal. Unlatch the lid and open the cooker. Use hot pads or silicone baking mitts to pick up the (hot!) insert and drain its contents in a large colander set in the sink. Cool for 5 minutes.

5. In a large serving bowl, stir the salsa, beans, green chiles, and cilantro until combined. Add the still-warm chicken and pasta. Toss well. Set aside for 15 minutes to blend the flavors. Stir in the cheese. Serve warm or at room temperature—or cover and refrigerate for up to 2 days and serve cold.

Easy Chicken-Antipasto Pasta Salad

10 or 11 ingredients

4–6 SERVINGS

METHOD:
standard

SPECIAL EQUIPMENT:
none

PRESSURE:
max or high

TIME UNDER PRESSURE:
5 or 7 minutes

RELEASE:
quick

TOTAL TIME WITH PRESSURE:
about 30 minutes

CAN BE GLUTEN-FREE

6 cups water

1 pound boneless skinless chicken breasts, *cut into ½-inch pieces*

8 ounces raw dried ziti (gluten-free, if necessary—for more information, see the pasta chapter introduction on page 103)

3 tablespoons olive oil

2 tablespoons red wine vinegar

One 6½-ounce jar marinated *quartered* artichoke hearts (do not drain)

2 tablespoons minced red onion

8 pliable sun-dried tomatoes, cut into thin strips

2 teaspoons dried oregano

Up to ½ teaspoon red pepper flakes (optional)

1 ounce Parmigiano-Reggiano, finely grated (½ cup)

Other Pots

- For a 3-quart Instant Pot, you *must* reduce the water in the pot to 4 cups and the pasta to 6 ounces while otherwise completing the recipe as stated.

- For a 10-quart Instant Pot, you *must* increase the ingredient amounts by 50 percent or you *can* even double the amounts.

Beyond

- For a richer salad, add up to 8 halved mini *fresh* mozzarella balls (bocconcini) with the artichoke hearts.

- And/or add up to ¼ cup toasted pine nuts.

Here's how to make a pasta salad even easier: Shop the salad bar at your supermarket. This pasta salad uses standard antipasto favorites often found on that bar to make a flavorful lunch or light dinner. There's no added salt in the recipe because the marinated artichoke hearts are loaded with it.

1.

	Press	Set it for	Set time for	If needed, press
In all models	SAUTÉ	MEDIUM, NORMAL, or CUSTOM 300°F	10 minutes	START

2. As the pot heats, stir the water and chicken into the insert set in a **5-, 6-, or 8-quart Instant Pot.** Continue cooking until plenty of steam wisps rise from the water. Stir in the pasta, turn off the heat, and lock the lid on the pot.

3.

	Set pot for	Set level to	Valve must be	Set time for	If needed, press
For Max pots only	PRESSURE COOK	MAX	—	5 minutes with the KEEP WARM setting off	START
For all other pots	PRESSURE COOK or MANUAL	HIGH	Closed	7 minutes with the KEEP WARM setting off	START

4. When the pot has finished cooking, use the **quick-release method** to bring the pressure back to normal. Unlatch the lid and open the cooker. Use hot pads or silicone baking mitts to pick up the (hot!) insert and drain its contents in a large colander set in the sink. Cool for 5 minutes.

5. Whisk the olive oil and vinegar in the insert. Add the artichoke hearts (with their liquid), the onion, sun-dried tomatoes, oregano, and red pepper flakes (if using). Dump in the still-warm chicken and pasta. Toss gently but well to coat. Cool for 5 more minutes, then stir in the cheese. Serve warm or at room temperature—or cover and refrigerate for up to 2 days and serve cold.

See photo in insert.

Gingery Chicken and Cucumber Pasta Salad

13 ingredients	**SPECIAL EQUIPMENT:** none
4–6 SERVINGS	
METHOD: standard	**PRESSURE:** max or high

TIME UNDER PRESSURE: 5 or 7 minutes	**TOTAL TIME WITH PRESSURE:** about 30 minutes
RELEASE: quick	**CAN BE GLUTEN-FREE**

6 cups water

1 pound boneless skinless chicken breasts, *cut into ½-inch pieces*

8 ounces raw dried farfalle (or bow-tie) pasta (gluten-free, if necessary—for more information, see the pasta chapter introduction on page 103)

6 tablespoons toasted sesame oil

3 tablespoons tahini (sesame seed paste) or natural-style smooth peanut butter

3 tablespoons regular or low-sodium soy sauce, or gluten-free tamari sauce

1½ tablespoons Worcestershire sauce (gluten-free, if possible)

2 teaspoons white wine vinegar

Up to 2 teaspoons thick or hot red chile sauce, such as sambal oelek or Sriracha

2 teaspoons granulated white sugar

2 teaspoons minced peeled fresh ginger

1 large garden or slicing cucumber, peeled, seeded, and diced (2 cups)

3 medium scallions, trimmed and thinly sliced (1 cup)

Other Pots

- For a 3-quart Instant Pot, you *must* reduce the water in the pot to 4 cups and the pasta to 6 ounces while otherwise completing the recipe as stated. If you find the salad is now overdressed, add up to 1 cup thinly sliced celery.

- For a 10-quart Instant Pot, you *must* increase the ingredient amounts by 50 percent or you *can* even double the amounts.

Okay, we know: There are no pasta salads in authentic Chinese cooking. But we're convinced the traditional flavors of take-out sesame noodles can turn an American picnic favorite into a new classic. And since this is the next generation of Instant Pot cooking, we're here to shake things up a bit.

1.

	Press	Set it for	Set time for	If needed, press
In all models	SAUTÉ	MEDIUM, NORMAL, or CUSTOM 300°F	10 minutes	START

2. As the pot heats, stir the water and chicken into the insert set in a **5-, 6-, or 8-quart Instant Pot.** Continue cooking until plenty of steam wisps rise from the water. Stir in the pasta, turn off the heat, and lock the lid on the pot.

3.

	Set pot for	Set level to	Valve must be	Set time for	If needed, press
For Max pots only	PRESSURE COOK	MAX	—	5 minutes with the KEEP WARM setting off	START
For all other pots	PRESSURE COOK or MANUAL	HIGH	Closed	7 minutes with the KEEP WARM setting off	START

4. When the pot has finished cooking, use the **quick-release method** to bring the pressure back to normal. Unlatch the lid and open the cooker. Use hot pads or silicone baking mitts to pick up the (hot!) insert and drain its contents in a large colander set in the sink. Cool for 5 minutes.

5. Stir the sesame oil, tahini or peanut butter, soy sauce, Worcestershire sauce, vinegar, red chile sauce, sugar, and ginger in the insert until the peanut butter dissolves. Add the still-warm chicken and pasta, as well as the cucumber and scallions; toss gently but well to coat. Serve warm or at room temperature—or cover and refrigerate for up to 2 days and serve cold.

Beyond

- Add one 8-ounce can sliced bamboo shoots (drained) and/or 8-ounce can sliced water chestnuts (drained) with the cucumber and scallions.

- And/or add up to ¼ cup chopped roasted unsalted peanuts or chopped roasted unsalted cashews.

Better-Than-Classic Chicken Salad

10 ingredients	SPECIAL EQUIPMENT: steamer basket and a food processor	TIME UNDER PRESSURE: 12 or 15 minutes	TOTAL TIME WITH PRESSURE: about 40 minutes
6 SERVINGS			
METHOD: steam		RELEASE: modified natural	CAN BE GLUTEN-FREE
	PRESSURE: max or high		

1½ cups water

Four 12-ounce or three 16-ounce boneless skinless chicken breasts

½ cup regular, low-fat, or fat-free mayonnaise (gluten-free, if necessary)

½ cup regular, low-fat, or fat-free sour cream (gluten-free, if necessary)

Up to 2 tablespoons jarred prepared white horseradish

1 teaspoon Dijon or honey mustard (gluten-free, if necessary)

1 tablespoon loosely packed fresh tarragon leaves

½ teaspoon onion powder

½ teaspoon celery seeds

½ teaspoon table salt

Other Pots

- For a 3-quart Instant Pot, you *must* halve almost all of the ingredient amounts *except* you *must* use 1 cup water in the insert.

- For a 10-quart Instant Pot, you *must* use 2½ cups water in the insert. You *can* complete the recipe as stated or you *can* increase the remaining ingredient amounts by 50 percent.

Beyond

- Because of the horseradish, this chicken salad is particularly good on toasted rye bread.

- Or serve it in peeled and seeded avocado halves, topped with a nest of spicy radish sprouts.

This is not a chunky chicken salad. It's a sandwich spread, sort of like a chicken version of tuna salad. Our version has a secret whammy: prepared white horseradish. It gives the dish a nose-spanking flavor and pairs exceptionally well with our favorite herb for chicken salad: tarragon. The horseradish will mellow over a day or two as you store the chicken salad in the fridge.

The best chicken for most chicken salads comes from boneless, skinless breasts steamed in a steamer basket. The meat stays firm and juicy, far better than if it's just boiled under pressure. Since, for the sake of ease, we use a food processor to make the creamy salad, firmer meat doesn't get reduced to a horrid porridge consistency.

One more thing: The chicken breasts are larger than you might anticipate so they can stand up to the pressure without drying out. Also, you must stand them on their sides in the steamer basket without stacking them on top of each other. Overlap them end to end as little as possible, preferably thin ends over thin ends only as necessary.

1. Pour the water into the insert set in a **5-, 6-, or 8-quart Instant Pot.** Place an IP-safe steamer basket in the insert (see page 14 in the introduction for more information). Stand the chicken breasts on their sides in a single layer in basket. Lock the lid on the pot.

2.

	Set pot for	Set level to	Valve must be	Set time for	If needed, press
For Max pots only	PRESSURE COOK	MAX	—	12 minutes with the KEEP WARM setting off	START
For all other pots	PRESSURE COOK or MANUAL	HIGH	Closed	15 minutes with the KEEP WARM setting off	START

3. When the pot has finished cooking, turn it off and let the pressure **come back to normal naturally for 10 minutes.** Then use the **quick-release method** to get rid of the pot's residual pressure. Unlatch the lid and open the cooker. Use kitchen tongs to transfer the chicken breasts to a nearby cutting board. Cool for 10 minutes.

4. Use two forks to shred the meat. Put it in a food processor with the mayonnaise, sour cream, prepared horseradish, mustard, tarragon, onion powder, celery seeds, and salt. Cover and pulse several times until the mixture is spreadable but not pureed. Serve at once or transfer to a storage container, cover, and refrigerate for up to 3 days.

Better-Than-Classic Curried Chicken Salad

10 ingredients	**SPECIAL EQUIPMENT:** steamer basket	**TIME UNDER PRESSURE:** 10 or 12 minutes	**TOTAL TIME WITH PRESSURE:** about 35 minutes
4–6 SERVINGS			
METHOD: steam	**PRESSURE:** max or high	**RELEASE:** quick	**CAN BE GLUTEN-FREE**

1½ cups water

Two 12-ounce boneless skinless chicken breasts

½ cup regular, low-fat, or fat-free mayonnaise (gluten-free, if necessary)

3 medium celery stalks, thinly sliced (1 cup)

1 large single-lobe shallot, *minced* (a rounded ¼ cup)

3 tablespoons mango chutney

1 tablespoon apple cider vinegar

2 teaspoons yellow curry powder

½ teaspoon table salt

½ teaspoon ground black pepper

Other Pots

- For a 3-quart Instant Pot, you *must* reduce the amount of water in the insert to 1 cup while otherwise completing the recipe.

- For a 10-quart Instant Pot, you *must* increase the amount of water in the insert to 2½ cups. You *can* complete the recipe as stated or you *can* increase the remaining ingredient amounts by 50 percent.

Beyond

- Choose another sort of chutney: cranberry, plum, rhubarb, whatever you can find.

- Add ½ cup chopped pecans, walnuts, or pistachios in step 4.

- Serve this chicken salad in pita pockets, topped with plain yogurt and shredded cucumbers.

Rather than being a sandwich spread (as our Better-than-Classic Chicken Salad on page 165), this chicken salad is chunkier, although it would still be welcome on toasted whole-wheat bread.

The success of the salad depends on the quality of the chutney and curry powder you use. The chutney should be *minimally* chunky. Chop any large bits of mango into smaller pieces so you can get lots of flavors in each bite. And take the salad over the top by using a curry powder beyond the standard, yellow bottling. Online suppliers and spice stores offer an astounding array. Some are fiery; others, aromatic with cinnamon and nutmeg in the mix.

1. Pour the water into the insert set in a **5-, 6-, or 8-quart Instant Pot.** Place an IP-safe steamer basket in the insert (see page 14 in the introduction for more information). Stand the chicken breasts on their sides in the basket with as little overlap as possible. Lock the lid on the pot.

2.

	Set pot for	Set level to	Valve must be	Set time for	If needed, press
For Max pots only	PRESSURE COOK	MAX	—	10 minutes with the KEEP WARM setting off	START
For all other pots	PRESSURE COOK or MANUAL	HIGH	Closed	12 minutes with the KEEP WARM setting off	START

3. When the pot has finished cooking, use the **quick-release method** to bring the pressure back to normal. Unlatch the lid and open the cooker. Use kitchen tongs to transfer the chicken breasts to a nearby cutting board. Cool for 10 minutes.

4. Stir the mayonnaise, celery, shallot, chutney, vinegar, curry powder, salt, and pepper in a large bowl. Dice the chicken breasts into small pieces. Stir into the mayonnaise mixture until uniform. Serve warm or cover and refrigerate for up to 2 days.

Buffalo Chicken Salad

8 ingredients	**SPECIAL EQUIPMENT:** steamer basket
6 SERVINGS	
METHOD: steam	**PRESSURE:** max or high

TIME UNDER PRESSURE: 12 or 15 minutes

TOTAL TIME WITH PRESSURE: about 40 minutes

RELEASE: modified natural

CAN BE GLUTEN-FREE

1½ cups water

Two 12-ounce boneless skinless chicken breasts

½ cup regular, low-fat, or fat-free sour cream (gluten-free, if necessary)

2 medium celery stalks, thinly sliced (⅔ cup)

½ small red onion, diced (¼ cup)

8 ounces Monterey Jack cheese, shredded (2 cups)

6 tablespoons bottled buffalo sauce (gluten-free, if necessary)

Crumbled blue cheese, for garnishing

With bottled buffalo sauce, this chunky chicken salad couldn't be easier. And with lots of cheese and crunchy celery in the mix, it couldn't be better! Note that the large boneless skinless chicken breasts are cooked a little longer than some others in this chapter *and* given a longer time in the pot's heat with a modified natural release—which makes them softer so they can be shredded.

There's an internet trick making the rounds about shredding cooked chicken breasts with a handheld electric mixer. We find that 1) doing so is messier since chicken strands inevitably end up on the counter, and 2) it turns out to be *more* work because we have to drag out a mixer and then clean up even more utensils (presumably you already have a cutting board out for the celery and onion). We love hacks. We wrote *The Kitchen Shortcut Bible* to detail as many as we could. But frankly this shredding job is easier and faster with two forks.

1. Pour the water into the insert set in a **5-, 6-, or 8-quart Instant Pot.** Place an IP-safe steamer basket in the insert (see page 14 in the introduction for more information). Stand the chicken breasts on their sides in a single layer in the basket. Lock the lid on the pot.

2.

	Set pot for	Set level to	Valve must be	Set time for	If needed, press
For Max pots only	PRESSURE COOK	MAX	—	12 minutes with the KEEP WARM setting off	START
For all other pots	PRESSURE COOK or MANUAL	HIGH	Closed	15 minutes with the KEEP WARM setting off	START

3. When the pot has finished cooking, turn it off and let the pressure **come back to normal naturally for 10 minutes.** Then use the **quick-release method** to get rid of the pot's residual pressure. Unlatch the lid and open the cooker. Use kitchen tongs to transfer the chicken breasts to a nearby cutting board. Cool for 10 minutes.

4. Use two flatware forks to shred the meat. Place the chicken in a large serving bowl. Stir in the sour cream, celery, and red onion. Set aside for 5 minutes to blend the flavors and continue to cool the chicken. Stir in the Jack cheese and buffalo sauce until uniform. Serve at once or cover and refrigerate for up to 2 days. Garnish the servings with crumbled blue cheese.

Other Pots

- For a 3-quart Instant Pot, you *must* reduce the amount of water in the insert to 1 cup while otherwise completing the recipe.

- For a 10-quart Instant Pot, you *must* increase the amount of water in the insert to 2½ cups. You *can* complete the recipe as stated or you *can* increase the remaining ingredient amounts by 50 percent.

Beyond

- Serve the chicken salad in wraps made from large flour tortillas.

- To go all out, line peeled, pitted, and thinly sliced avocado and/or thinly sliced trimmed radishes in the wrap with the chicken salad.

Arugula, White Bean, and Chicken Salad

12 ingredients	
4–6 SERVINGS	
METHOD: steam	

| SPECIAL EQUIPMENT: steamer basket | |
| PRESSURE: max or high | |

| TIME UNDER PRESSURE: 10 or 12 minutes | |
| RELEASE: quick | |

| TOTAL TIME WITH PRESSURE: about 35 minutes | |
| CAN BE GLUTEN-FREE | |

1½ cups water

Two 12-ounce boneless skinless chicken breasts

⅓ cup olive oil

¼ cup red wine vinegar

1 medium garlic clove, minced (1 teaspoon)

1 teaspoon dried oregano

1 teaspoon table salt

½ teaspoon red pepper flakes

One 15-ounce can cannellini beans, drained and rinsed (1¾ cups)

2 cups purchased plain or seasoned salad croutons (gluten-free, if necessary)

2 cups loosely packed baby arugula (2 ounces)

1 ounce Parmigiano-Reggiano, finely grated (½ cup)

Other Pots

- For a 3-quart Instant Pot, you *must* reduce the amount of water in the insert to 1 cup while otherwise completing the recipe.

- For a 10-quart Instant Pot, you *must* increase the amount of water in the insert to 2½ cups. You *can* complete the recipe as stated or you *can* increase the remaining ingredient amounts by 50 percent.

Beyond

- For more flavor, add up to 2 teaspoons minced fresh rosemary leaves and/or 2 teaspoons fresh thyme leaves with the oregano.

This recipe is a go-to lunch at our house: a fresh, light entrée, not just a mix of chicken and other ingredients, but more like a full-meal *salad*. Two or three days in advance, we make the chicken breasts, cover them when they've cooled for 10 minutes, and refrigerate them until we're ready to dice them and make the salad. If you follow our lead, there's no need spending time cooling the meat and the salad in the final steps of this recipe. The cold chicken breasts won't melt the cheese into a stringy mess *and* won't soften the croutons.

1. Pour the water into the insert set in a **5-, 6-, or 8-quart Instant Pot.** Place an IP-safe steamer basket in the insert (see page 14 in the introduction for more information). Stand the chicken breasts on their sides in a single layer in the basket. Lock the lid on the pot.

2.

	Set pot for	Set level to	Valve must be	Set time for	If needed, press
For Max pots only	PRESSURE COOK	MAX	—	10 minutes with the KEEP WARM setting off	START
For all other pots	PRESSURE COOK or MANUAL	HIGH	Closed	12 minutes with the KEEP WARM setting off	START

3. When the pot has finished cooking, use the **quick-release method** to bring the pressure back to normal. Unlatch the lid and open the cooker. Use kitchen tongs to transfer the chicken breasts to a nearby cutting board. Cool for 10 minutes, then dice the chicken into ¼-inch pieces.

4. In a large serving bowl, whisk the oil, vinegar, garlic, oregano, salt, and red pepper flakes until uniform and emulsified. (There should be no spots of vinegar in the mix.)

5. Add the diced chicken and beans. Toss well, then set aside for another 5 minutes to continue to cool the salad. Add the croutons, arugula, and cheese. Toss well and serve at once.

Barbecue Chicken Sliders

10 ingredients	**SPECIAL EQUIPMENT:** steamer basket
8 SLIDERS	
METHOD: steam	**PRESSURE:** max or high

TIME UNDER PRESSURE: 12 or 15 minutes	**TOTAL TIME WITH PRESSURE:** about 40 minutes
RELEASE: modified natural	**CAN BE GLUTEN-FREE**

1½ cups water

Two 12-ounce boneless skinless chicken breasts

½ cup purchased barbecue sauce (gluten-free, if necessary)

One 1-pound bag shredded cabbage and carrot coleslaw mix

½ cup regular, low-fat, or fat-free mayonnaise (gluten-free, if necessary)

1 tablespoon apple cider vinegar

½ teaspoon celery seeds

¼ teaspoon table salt

At least ¼ teaspoon ground black pepper, or more to taste

8 slider buns (gluten-free, if necessary)

These little sliders are sweet, salty, and an irresistible addition to your next backyard or patio lunch (and lower in fat than hamburger sliders, too, what with chicken breasts). You'll notice that there's no sugar in our simple coleslaw. There's plenty in the barbecue sauce and even in most purchased slider buns. We didn't want the servings to get too sweet. We also went a little light on the salt because most purchased barbecue sauce is loaded with it. You can pass more when you serve the mini sandwiches.

1. Pour the water into the insert set in a **5-, 6-, or 8-quart Instant Pot.** Place an IP-safe steamer basket in the insert (see page 14 in the introduction for more information). Stand the chicken breasts on their sides in a single layer in the basket. Lock the lid on the pot.

2.

	Set pot for	Set level to	Valve must be	Set time for	If needed, press
For Max pots only	PRESSURE COOK	MAX	—	12 minutes with the KEEP WARM setting off	START
For all other pots	PRESSURE COOK or MANUAL	HIGH	Closed	15 minutes with the KEEP WARM setting off	START

3. When the pot has finished cooking, turn it off and let the pressure **come back to normal naturally for 10 minutes.** Then use the **quick-release method** to get rid of any residual pressure in the pot. Unlatch the lid and open the cooker. Use kitchen tongs to transfer the chicken breasts to a nearby cutting board. Cool for 10 minutes.

4. Use two forks to shred the chicken into threads. Scrape these into a large bowl, add the barbecue sauce, and stir until uniform. (The chicken mixture can be made up to 2 days in advance; cover and refrigerate but set the mixture on the counter for 20 minutes before continuing with the recipe.)

5. Mix the coleslaw, mayonnaise, vinegar, celery seeds, salt, and pepper in a large bowl until uniform. To serve, fill the slider buns with the chicken mixture and coleslaw.

Other Pots

- For a 3-quart Instant Pot, you *must* reduce the amount of water in the insert to 1 cup while otherwise completing the recipe.

- For a 10-quart Instant Pot, you *must* increase the amount of water in the insert to 2½ cups. You *can* complete the recipe as stated or you *can* increase the remaining ingredient amounts by 50 percent.

Beyond

- Garnish the sliders with lots of bread-and-butter pickles.

Down East Chicken Rolls

11 ingredients	
6 CHICKEN ROLLS	
METHOD: steam	

SPECIAL EQUIPMENT: steamer basket	
PRESSURE: max or high	

TIME UNDER PRESSURE: 10 or 12 minutes	
RELEASE: quick	

TOTAL TIME WITH PRESSURE: about 35 minutes	
CAN BE GLUTEN-FREE	

1½ cups water

Two 12-ounce boneless skinless chicken breasts

½ cup regular, low-fat, or fat-free mayonnaise (gluten-free, if necessary)

1 medium celery stalk, *finely chopped* (3 tablespoons)

3 tablespoons lemon juice, or to taste

2 tablespoons loosely packed, stemmed, fresh parsley leaves, finely chopped

½ teaspoon table salt

½ teaspoon ground black pepper

6 hot dog buns (gluten-free, if necessary)

Butter, to taste

6 large soft lettuce leaves, such as Boston or butter lettuce

Okay, no hate mail from Maine, please! We've ditched the lobster from the classic Maine roll, subbed in chicken, and made some satisfying deck food. The only worry? Who's staffing the bar?

One note: Bottled lemon juice is less tart than fresh. Depending on your taste, you might like to add more of the bottled stuff (or less of the fresh).

1. Pour the water into the insert set in a **5-, 6-, or 8-quart Instant Pot.** Place an IP-safe steamer basket in the insert (see page 14 in the introduction for more information). Stand the chicken breasts on their sides in a single layer in the basket. Lock the lid on the pot.

2.

	Set pot for	Set level to	Valve must be	Set time for	If needed, press
For Max pots only	PRESSURE COOK	MAX	—	10 minutes with the KEEP WARM setting off	START
For all other pots	PRESSURE COOK or MANUAL	HIGH	Closed	12 minutes with the KEEP WARM setting off	START

3. When the pot has finished cooking, use the **quick-release method** to bring the pressure back to normal. Unlatch the lid and open the cooker. Use kitchen tongs to transfer the chicken breasts to a nearby cutting board. Cool for 10 minutes, then dice the chicken into ¼-inch pieces.

4. In a large bowl, stir the mayonnaise, celery, lemon juice, parsley, salt, and pepper until uniform. Stir in the chicken until well coated and evenly distributed.

5. Open the hot dog buns and butter the inside cut parts. Heat a large skillet over medium-high heat. Set the buns cut side down one at a time in the skillet and toast until lightly browned, about 1 minute per bun. Line the toasted buns with the lettuce leaves, fill with the chicken mixture, and serve at once.

Other Pots

- For a 3-quart Instant Pot, you *must* reduce the amount of water in the insert to 1 cup while otherwise completing the recipe.

- For a 10-quart Instant Pot, you *must* increase the amount of water in the insert to 2½ cups. You *can* complete the recipe as stated or you *can* increase the remaining ingredient amounts by 50 percent.

Beyond

- Add ¼ cup sweet pickle relish or ¼ cup drained jarred diced pimientos to the chicken mixture.

Chicken Summer Rolls

13 ingredients

12 SUMMER ROLLS WITH A DIPPING SAUCE

METHOD: steam

SPECIAL EQUIPMENT: steamer basket

PRESSURE: max or high

TIME UNDER PRESSURE: 12 or 15 minutes

RELEASE: modified natural

TOTAL TIME WITH PRESSURE: about 50 minutes

CAN BE GLUTEN-FREE

1½ cups plus 2 tablespoons water, plus additional warm water as needed

Two 12-ounce boneless skinless chicken breasts

½ cup plus 1 tablespoon unseasoned rice vinegar

1 medium carrot, peeled and shredded through the large holes of a box grater

4 medium scallions, trimmed and thinly sliced (1⅓ cups)

¼ cup loosely packed, stemmed, fresh cilantro leaves, finely chopped

¼ cup loosely packed, stemmed, fresh mint leaves, finely chopped

4 teaspoons granulated white sugar

½ teaspoon table salt

½ cup smooth, natural-style peanut butter

3 tablespoons regular or low-sodium soy sauce, or gluten-free tamari sauce

2 teaspoons thin red hot sauce, such as Sriracha or Texas Pete

Twelve 8-inch dried rice paper rounds

Other Pots

- For a 3-quart Instant Pot, you *must* reduce the amount of water in the insert to 1 cup while otherwise completing the recipe.

- For a 10-quart Instant Pot, you *must* increase the amount of water in the insert to 2½ cups. You *can* complete the recipe as stated or you *can* increase the remaining ingredient amounts by 50 percent.

Beyond

- For more crunch, place a halved slice of canned water chestnut on the top of the chicken mixture before closing each roll.

Stuffed with all sorts of fresh ingredients and wrapped in softened, opaque rice "paper," summer rolls are a treat any time of the year: light, flavorful, and perfect with dry white wine. (Or champagne!) Our version keeps the traditional Southeast Asian flavors with cilantro and mint but avoids heavier flavors that might come from traditional condiments like fish sauce and hoisin sauce.

1. Pour the 1½ cups water into the insert set in a **5-, 6-, or 8-quart Instant Pot.** Place an IP-safe steamer basket in the insert (see page 14 in the introduction for more information). Stand the chicken breasts on their sides in a single layer in the basket. Lock the lid on the pot.

2.

	Set pot for	Set level to	Valve must be	Set time for	If needed, press
For Max pots only	PRESSURE COOK	MAX	—	12 minutes with the KEEP WARM setting off	START
For all other pots	PRESSURE COOK or MANUAL	HIGH	Closed	15 minutes with the KEEP WARM setting off	START

3. When the pot has finished cooking, turn it off and let the pressure **come back to normal naturally for 10 minutes.** Then use the **quick-release method** to get rid of the pot's residual pressure. Unlatch the lid and open the cooker. Use kitchen tongs to transfer the chicken breasts to a nearby cutting board. Cool for 10 minutes.

4. Use two forks to shred the chicken. Put the meat in a bowl and stir in ½ cup rice vinegar, the carrot, scallions, cilantro, mint, 2 teaspoons sugar, and the salt.

5. In a small bowl, whisk the peanut butter, soy sauce, hot sauce, the remaining 2 tablespoons water, the remaining 1 tablespoon rice vinegar, and the remaining 2 teaspoons sugar until smooth.

6. Fill a shallow soup bowl or a pie plate with warm water. Set a rice paper round in the water and soften for about 30 seconds. Set the round on your clean work surface and put about ⅓ cup of the chicken mixture in a thin oval at the center. Fold two opposite "sides" of the round up and over the filling, then roll the round closed to make a squat cigar. Set aside and continue making more summer rolls, changing the water as necessary when it gets to room temperature. Serve at once or cover the rolls on a platter with plastic wrap and refrigerate for up to 3 hours. In either case, offer the peanut sauce on the side for dipping.

Barbecue Chicken Tamale Bites

7 ingredients	SPECIAL EQUIPMENT: two seven-indentation egg-bite molds, an electric mixer, and a pressure-safe rack or trivet	PRESSURE: max or high	RELEASE: quick
14 "BITES"		TIME UNDER PRESSURE: 17 or 20 minutes	TOTAL TIME WITH PRESSURE: about 1 hour
METHOD: egg bites			CAN BE GLUTEN-FREE

1¼ cups chicken broth

1¾ cups instant masa harina, such as the Maseca brand

5 tablespoons solid vegetable shortening or lard

2 cups shredded skinned deboned rotisserie chicken (white or dark meat—or both)

½ cup purchased barbecue sauce

Vegetable oil or nonstick spray, for greasing the molds

1½ cups water

Tamales without corn husks? Impossible? Sacrilege? Not as far as we're concerned! Here's our straightforward technique, using egg-bite molds. (For vegetarian tamale bites, see pages 370 and 372.) This recipe makes a lot of tamale bites, but you can use only one egg-bite mold and halve all the ingredients as long as you maintain the stated amount of water in the pot (to create the necessary steam). Customize this recipe by using any sort of barbecue sauce you prefer.

1. Warm the broth in a microwave-safe container in the microwave set on HIGH for 20 seconds (but not until simmering).

2. Pour the broth into a large bowl. Add the instant masa harina. Use an electric mixer at medium speed to beat the two together until a soft dough forms. Beat in the shortening until the mixture is fluffy and light, not pasty. Set aside.

3. Mix the chicken and barbecue sauce in a medium bowl until uniform. Set aside.

4. Grease the seven indentations in two egg-bite molds (that is, 14 indentations). Divide the masa mixture into 14 even balls, about ⅓ cup each. Eyeballing it, place about two-thirds of one ball in a prepared indentation. Press down so the masa mixture covers the bottom and sides of the mold. Place about 2 tablespoons of the chicken mixture in the cup created by the masa in the indentation. Take the remaining third of the masa ball and use it to seal a top over the chicken mixture, making sure that the top meets the masa "sides." Repeat to make thirteen more of these bites in the remaining indentations. Cover the mold with its silicone lid or seal closed with aluminum foil.

5. Pour the water into the insert set in a **5-, 6-, or 8-quart Instant Pot.** Set a pressure-safe rack or trivet in the insert. Set one egg-bite mold in the insert, then stack the second on top so that the indentations of the upper mold sit on walls of the bottom mold, not into the bottom indentations themselves (except for the center indentation of the top mold which will now hover above the center indentation below). Lock the lid onto the cooker.

6.

	Set pot for	Set level to	Valve must be	Set time for	If needed, press
For Max pots only	PRESSURE COOK	MAX	—	17 minutes with the KEEP WARM setting off	START
For all other pots	PRESSURE COOK or MANUAL	HIGH	Closed	20 minutes with the KEEP WARM setting off	START

7. When the pot has finished cooking, use the **quick-release method** to bring the pressure back to normal. Unlatch the lid and open the cooker. Use hot pads or silicone baking mitts to transfer the (hot!) molds to a nearby wire rack. Uncover and cool for 5 minutes before turning out the tamale bites. Serve warm.

Other Pots

- For a 3-quart Instant Pot, you *must* decrease the amount of water in the insert to 1 cup and you *must* halve the remaining ingredient amounts. You *must* also use two four-indentation egg-bite molds made for this smaller pot, stacking them in the insert and using only seven of the indentations.

- For a 10-quart Instant Pot, you *must* increase the amount of water in the insert to 2½ cups while otherwise completing the recipe as stated.

Beyond

- You'll need a dip for these tamale bites. Serve them with the salsa of your choice, red or green.

- And/or sour cream.

Chicken Tortilla Casserole

6 ingredients	
4 SERVINGS	
METHOD: pot-in-pot	

SPECIAL EQUIPMENT: a 2-quart, 7-inch-round, high-sided, pressure-safe baking or soufflé dish and a pressure-safe rack or trivet

PRESSURE: max or high

TIME UNDER PRESSURE: 12 or 15 minutes

RELEASE: modified natural

TOTAL TIME WITH PRESSURE: about 45 minutes

1½ cups water

Nonstick spray

Five 6-inch corn tortillas

2 cups chopped skinned deboned rotisserie chicken meat (white or dark meat—or both)

1¼ cups jarred red or green salsa (do *not* use a super-chunky salsa)

6 ounces American cheddar or Monterey Jack cheese, shredded (1½ cups)—or a purchased Tex-Mex cheese blend (without any added spices)

This easy, family-friendly casserole is sort of like a Southwestern take on lasagna, with tortillas standing in for the noodles and jarred green salsa for the tomato sauce. Use any salsa you like, although we suggest you skip sweet salsas (like peach salsa) because the flavors will get cloying. The main recipe is rather plain, maybe better for kids. Look in the **Beyond** section for ideas to gussy it up.

1. Pour the water into the insert set in a **5-, 6-, or 8-quart Instant Pot.** Put a pressure-safe rack or trivet in the insert.

2. Coat the inside of a 2-quart, 7-inch-round, high-sided, pressure-safe baking or soufflé dish with nonstick spray. Place a tortilla in its bottom, then top with even layers of ½ cup chicken, ¼ cup salsa, and a rounded ⅓ cup cheese. Repeat that tortilla-chicken-salsa-cheese layering three more times. Top the casserole with a tortilla, the remaining ¼ cup salsa, and the remaining cheese. Cover the dish tightly with aluminum foil and set it on the rack. Lock the lid on the pot.

3.

	Set pot for	Set level to	Valve must be	Set time for	If needed, press
For Max pots only	PRESSURE COOK	MAX	—	12 minutes with the KEEP WARM setting off	START
For all other pots	PRESSURE COOK or MANUAL	HIGH	Closed	15 minutes with the KEEP WARM setting off	START

4. When the pot has finished cooking, turn it off and let the pressure **return to normal naturally for 10 minutes.** Then use the **quick-release method** to get rid of the pot's residual pressure. Unlatch the lid and open the cooker. Use hot pads or silicone baking mitts to transfer the (hot!) dish to a nearby wire rack. Uncover and cool for 5 to 10 minutes before dishing up with a big spoon.

Other Pots

- Because of ingredient ratios and sizes, this recipe cannot be completed successfully in a 3-quart Instant Pot.

- For a 10-quart Instant Pot, you *must* increase the amount of water in the insert to 2½ cups while otherwise completing the recipe as written.

Beyond

- Add jarred pickled jalapeño slices to some of the layers. Or add a little jalapeño relish.

- And/or sprinkle drained and rinsed canned beans among some of the layers.

- And/or sprinkle corn kernels (thawed if frozen) among some of the layers.

Chicken Pastrami

10 ingredients	
6 SERVINGS	

SPECIAL EQUIPMENT: steamer basket

TIME UNDER PRESSURE: 10 or 12 minutes

TOTAL TIME WITH PRESSURE: about 35 minutes

METHOD: steam

PRESSURE: max or high

RELEASE: natural

CAN BE GLUTEN-FREE

---

1 cup brine from a jar of regular or garlic dill pickles (gluten-free, if necessary—do *not* use a sweet pickle brine)

One 4-ounce bottle liquid smoke (gluten-free, if necessary)

1½ teaspoons ground coriander

1½ teaspoons ground dried mustard

1½ teaspoons mild smoked paprika

1 teaspoon ground dried ginger

1 teaspoon garlic powder

1 teaspoon table salt

1 teaspoon ground black pepper

Six 6-ounce boneless skinless chicken breasts

It's so easy to make a chicken (and low-fat!) version of pastrami with the Instant Pot: Simply use a rack and steam the breasts in an aromatic mixture of pickle brine and liquid smoke. We give these chicken breasts a natural release, even though the meat will be softer than we might prefer under normal circumstances. With the added time, the aromatics more successfully infuse the meat, yielding more flavorful pastrami.

1. Stir the brine and liquid smoke in a **5-, 6-, or 8-quart Instant Pot**. Place an IP-safe steamer basket in the insert (see page 14 in the introduction for more information).

2. Mix the coriander, mustard, smoked paprika, garlic powder, salt, and black pepper in a small bowl until uniform. Rub this mixture evenly over the chicken breasts. Stand the chicken breasts on their sides in a single layer in the steamer basket with as little overlap end to end as possible. Lock the lid on the pot.

3.

	Set pot for	Set level to	Valve must be	Set time for	If needed, press
For Max pots only	PRESSURE COOK	MAX	—	10 minutes with the KEEP WARM setting off	START
For all other pots	PRESSURE COOK or MANUAL	HIGH	Closed	12 minutes with the KEEP WARM setting off	START

4. When the pot has finished cooking, turn it off and let the pressure **return to normal naturally,** about 15 minutes. Unlatch the lid and open the cooker. Use kitchen tongs to transfer the chicken to a nearby wire rack. Cool for at least 10 minutes before slicing—or cool for 20 minutes, then store in a covered container in the fridge for up to 1 week.

Other Pots

- For a 3-quart Instant Pot, you *must* halve almost all of the ingredient amounts *except* you *must* use the originally stated amount of pickle brine and liquid smoke.

- For an 8-quart Instant Pot, you *can* increase the ingredient amounts by 50 percent or even double the spice mixture and number of chicken breasts, but you *must* keep the amount of pickle brine and liquid smoke the same as originally stated.

- For a 10-quart Instant Pot, you *must* double the amount of pickle brine and liquid smoke. You *can* complete the recipe as stated, increase the spices and chicken breasts by 50 percent, or even double those amounts.

Beyond

- Make chicken Reubens! Slice the breasts into ¼-inch-thick strips, then set them on toasted rye bread with purchased sauerkraut and Russian dressing. If you must, add a slice of Swiss cheese, although you'll make a zillion kosher butchers cry. Coat the inside of a nonstick skillet with nonstick spray, set it over medium heat, and griddle the sandwiches until toasty brown, about 2 minutes per side. (Make the butchers cry even more by using butter instead of nonstick spray.)

See photo in insert.

Perfect Roast Chicken

6 ingredients

4–6 SERVINGS

METHOD:
steam

SPECIAL
EQUIPMENT:
pressure- and
food-safe rack or
trivet

PRESSURE:
max or high

TIME UNDER
PRESSURE:
35 or 40 minutes

RELEASE:
modified natural

TOTAL TIME WITH
PRESSURE:
about 1 hour
15 minutes

GLUTEN-FREE

---

2 tablespoons butter, at room
temperature

1 teaspoon table salt

½ teaspoon poultry seasoning spice
blend

½ teaspoon ground black pepper

One 3½-pound whole chicken, any
giblets and neck removed

1½ cups water

Let's face it: A whole chicken out of an Instant Pot is inevitably too soft all around, both the skin and the meat. Sure, it's quick and easy to throw a bird in the insert. But it's not exactly what most of us consider *roast* chicken. To solve the problems, we've got a two-step technique for great chicken every time. First, undercook the chicken in the pot, just until it's *almost* done so that the meat never gets too soft. Then use the Instant Pot Air Fryer Lid and basket (or our alternate technique for broiling the pieces) to get the meat fully done and the skin crisp. Crunchy, tender, juicy, satisfying: It's finally *roast* chicken!

1. Mash the butter, salt, poultry seasoning, and pepper together in a small bowl. Make a small slit in the skin of the chicken at each thigh so the skin can be pulled loose from the meat. Use your clean fingers to loosen the skin over the breast meat and perhaps along the thighs, running first one finger and then more between the skin and meat without stretching out the skin too much. Smear the butter mixture between the meat and skin, patting the skin back into place. Wash and dry your hands.

2. Pour the water into the insert set in a **5-, 6-, or 8-quart Instant Pot.** Set a pressure- and food-safe rack or trivet in the insert. Set the chicken with its breast side up on the rack. Lock the lid on the pot.

3.

	Set pot for	Set level to	Valve must be	Set time for	If needed, press
For Max pots only	PRESSURE COOK	MAX	—	35 minutes with the KEEP WARM setting off	START
For all other pots	PRESSURE COOK or MANUAL	HIGH	Closed	40 minutes with the KEEP WARM setting off	START

4. When the pot has finished cooking, turn it off and let the pressure **return to normal naturally for 10 minutes.** Then use the **quick-release method** to get rid of the pot's residual pressure. Unlatch the lid and open the pot.

5. Use a large spatula and perhaps kitchen tongs to transfer the (hot!) chicken to a nearby large cutting board. Cool for 5 minutes, then carve the bird into quarters by 1) cutting down on each side of the spine to remove it, 2) removing each of the leg and thigh quarters, and 3) slicing the breast in half lengthwise.

6. If you've used a **6- or 8-quart Instant Pot,** use kitchen tongs to remove the rack or trivet from the insert. Use hot pads or silicone baking mitts to drain the (hot!) liquid out of the (hot!) insert. Wipe out the insert and return it to the pot. Put the air fryer basket in the insert and set the chicken pieces skin side down in it, overlapping as little as possible. Set the Instant Pot Air Fryer Lid on top. Cook at 375°F for 15 to 20 minutes, turning the chicken pieces as the lid tells you, until the chicken is well browned and crisp. Turn off the lid and use kitchen tongs to transfer the pieces to a cutting board or platter to cool for 5 minutes before serving.

Alternately, set the chicken pieces skin side down on a large, lipped baking sheet. Place the oven rack 6 to 8 inches from the broiler and heat the broiler. Slip the baking sheet into the oven and broil for 4 minutes. Turn the chicken pieces over and continue broiling for about 5 more minutes, until the pieces are well browned and crisp. Use kitchen tongs to transfer them to a cutting board or platter to cool for 5 minutes before serving.

Other Pots

- Because of the size of the chicken, this recipe cannot be done in a 3-quart Instant Pot.

- For a 10-quart Instant Pot, you *must* increase the amount of water in the insert to 2½ cups while otherwise completing the recipe as stated. Since there is no air fryer lid for a 10-quart pot as of this writing, you must crisp the chicken with the broiler method.

Beyond

- Increase the flavor by increasing the butter to 3 tablespoons and substituting 1½ teaspoons rubbed or ground sage, 1 teaspoon dried thyme, and 1 teaspoon finely grated lemon zest for the dried poultry seasoning blend.

No-Brainer Chicken Chili

10 ingredients

6 SERVINGS

METHOD:
fast/slow

SPECIAL EQUIPMENT:
none

PRESSURE:
max or high

TIME UNDER PRESSURE:
12 or 15 minutes

RELEASE:
quick

TOTAL TIME WITH PRESSURE:
about 25 minutes

TOTAL TIME WITH SLOW COOKING:
about 4 hours 15 minutes

GLUTEN-FREE

2 pounds boneless skinless chicken breast, *diced* into ¼-inch pieces

1 medium yellow or white onion, chopped (1 cup)

¼ cup standard chili powder

1 tablespoon dried oregano

1 teaspoon ground cumin

Up to 1 teaspoon garlic powder

1 teaspoon table salt

One 28-ounce can diced tomatoes *packed in juice* (3½ cups)

1½ cups chicken broth

2 tablespoons apple butter

Other Pots

- For a 3-quart Instant Pot, you *must* halve all of the ingredient amounts.

- For an 8-quart Instant Pot, you *can* increase all of the ingredient amounts by 50 percent.

- For a 10-quart Instant Pot, you *must* increase all of the ingredient amounts by 50 percent or you *can* even double the amounts.

Beyond

- Garnish the servings with jarred (hot or "tamed") pickled jalapeño rings, sour cream, pico de gallo, or sliced avocado.

- This chili is a great filling for tacos. Cover and refrigerate it overnight or up to 3 days. Scrape off any solidified fat, then heat until bubbling. Use a slotted spoon to dish it into taco shells or soft tortillas so you leave much of the "juice" behind. Top the tacos with shredded iceberg lettuce, chopped tomatoes, and shredded American cheddar cheese.

We all know that browning can be the most effective way to increase the flavor of a chili or stew, but we also know that some days just don't allow enough time for browning. Don't fret. We've got a secret that will add that complex flavor without the extra browning step: apple butter. It adds depth to this super-easy chicken chili without any fuss.

1. Stir the chicken, onion, chili powder, oregano, cumin, garlic powder, and salt in the insert set in a **5-, 6-, or 8-quart Instant Pot** until the chicken is evenly and thoroughly coated in the spices. Stir in the tomatoes with their juice and broth until uniform. Lock the lid on the pot.

2.

	Set pot for	Set level to	Valve must be	Set time for	If needed, press
For Max pots only	PRESSURE COOK	MAX	—	12 minutes with the KEEP WARM setting off	START
For all other pots	PRESSURE COOK or MANUAL	HIGH	Closed	15 minutes with the KEEP WARM setting off	START
For the slow-cook function	SLOW COOK	HIGH	Open	4 hours with the KEEP WARM setting off	START

3. When the pot has finished cooking under pressure, use the **quick-release method** to bring the pressure back to normal. Whichever cooking method you've used, unlatch the lid and open the cooker. Stir in the apple butter, then set the lid askew over the pot and set it aside for 2 to 3 minutes to blend the flavors. Serve warm.

Buffalo Chicken Chili

12 ingredients	SPECIAL EQUIPMENT: none	RELEASE: quick
6 SERVINGS	PRESSURE: max or high	TOTAL TIME WITH PRESSURE: about 20 minutes
METHOD: fast/slow	TIME UNDER PRESSURE: 5 or 7 minutes	

TOTAL TIME WITH SLOW COOKING: about 4 hours 15 minutes

CAN BE GLUTEN-FREE

---

2 pounds boneless skinless chicken breasts, *diced* into ¼-inch pieces

2 cups chicken broth

One 15-ounce can cannellini or great northern beans, drained and rinsed (1¾ cups)

One 14-ounce can diced tomatoes *packed in juice,* preferably fire-roasted tomatoes (1¾ cups)

1½ cups fresh corn kernels, drained canned kernels, or thawed frozen kernels

⅓ cup thin red hot sauce, preferably Texas Pete

½ stick (4 tablespoons or ¼ cup) butter, cut into small pieces

1 teaspoon onion powder

1 teaspoon table salt

½ teaspoon garlic powder

½ teaspoon celery seeds

8 ounces regular or low-fat cream cheese (gluten-free, if necessary—do *not* use fat-free), cut into small bits

Other Pots

- For a 3-quart Instant Pot, you *must* halve all of the ingredient amounts.

- For an 8-quart Instant Pot, you *can* increase all of the ingredient amounts by 50 percent.

- For a 10-quart Instant Pot, you *must* increase all of the ingredient amounts by 50 percent or you *can* even double the amounts.

Beyond

- Garnish the servings with lots of minced celery and perhaps minced chives or the green part of a scallion.

- For the full "buffalo" experience, also garnish the servings with crumbled blue cheese.

A stew modeled on buffalo chicken wings? Sounds like heaven! Or maybe hell, depending on your capacity for hot sauce. This recipe calls for a lot of it, but it mellows considerably under pressure. If you're worried, use only ¼ cup (!) the first time you make the chili. You can always souse the servings with more.

1. Stir the chicken, broth, beans, the tomatoes with their juice, the corn, hot sauce, butter, onion powder, salt, garlic powder, and celery seeds in the insert set in a **5-, 6-, or 8-quart Instant Pot.** Lock the lid onto the cooker.

2.

	Set pot for	Set level to	Valve must be	Set time for	If needed, press
For Max pots only	PRESSURE COOK	MAX	—	5 minutes with the KEEP WARM setting off	START
For all other pots	PRESSURE COOK or MANUAL	HIGH	Closed	7 minutes with the KEEP WARM setting off	START
For the slow-cook function	SLOW COOK	HIGH	Open	4 hours with the KEEP WARM setting off	START

3. When the pot has finished cooking under pressure, use the **quick-release method** to bring the pressure back to normal. Whichever cooking method you've used, unlatch the lid and open the cooker. Stir in the cream cheese until dissolved and uniform. Set the lid askew over the pot and set it aside for 3 to 5 minutes to blend the flavors. Stir again and serve warm.

Chicken Fajita Stew

8 ingredients

4–6 SERVINGS

METHOD:
fast/slow

SPECIAL EQUIPMENT:
none

PRESSURE:
max or high

TIME UNDER
PRESSURE:
4 or 6 minutes

RELEASE:
quick

TOTAL TIME WITH
PRESSURE:
about 20 minutes

TOTAL TIME WITH
SLOW COOKING:
about 2 hours 10
minutes

CAN BE GLUTEN-FREE

---

2 pounds chicken tenders, each halved lengthwise

1½ tablespoons fajita seasoning mix (gluten-free, if necessary)

One 10-ounce can hot or mild diced tomatoes and green chiles, such as Rotel (1¼ cups)

1½ cups chicken broth

1 medium red onion, halved and sliced into thin half-moons

One 16-ounce bag frozen bell pepper strips (no need to thaw)

One 3-inch cinnamon stick

Sour cream, for garnishing

This one's so easy: chicken tenders, a seasoning mix, frozen bell pepper strips, and canned tomatoes. Voilà: a one-pot stew modeled on fajitas. But be careful because some fajita seasonings are loaded with salt. Read the label and purchase a blend with salt later in the ingredient list, at least the fourth item, if not farther down. And some seasoning blends are not certified gluten-free. Check yours, if this is a concern.

1. Mix the chicken tenders and fajita seasoning in a large bowl until the chicken is thoroughly and evenly coated.

2. Stir the canned tomatoes and chiles, the broth, onion, bell peppers, and cinnamon stick in the insert set in a **5- or 6-quart Instant Pot.** Nestle the chicken into this mixture, scraping any additional seasoning from the bowl into the pot. Lock the lid onto the cooker.

3.

	Set pot for	Set level to	Valve must be	Set time for	If needed, press
For Max pots only	PRESSURE COOK	MAX	—	4 minutes with the KEEP WARM setting off	START
For all other pots	PRESSURE COOK or MANUAL	HIGH	Closed	6 minutes with the KEEP WARM setting off	START
For the slow-cook function	SLOW COOK	HIGH	Open	2 hours with the KEEP WARM setting off	START

4. When the pot has finished cooking under pressure, use the **quick-release method** to bring the pressure back to normal. Whichever cooking method you've used, unlatch the lid and open the cooker. Fish out and discard the cinnamon stick. Serve hot in bowls, garnished with sour cream.

Other Pots

- For a 3-quart Instant Pot, you *must* halve all of the ingredient amounts.

- For an 8-quart Instant Pot, you *must* increase all of the ingredient amounts by 50 percent.

- For a 10-quart Instant Pot, you *must* double all of the ingredient amounts.

Beyond

- For additional garnishes, try chopped tomatoes, chopped fresh cilantro leaves, jarred (hot or "tamed") pickled jalapeño rings, shredded Monterey Jack cheese, and/or torn-up flour tortillas.

Easy Chicken & Rice Casserole with Smoked Paprika and Tomatoes

15 or 16 ingredients	SPECIAL EQUIPMENT: none	TIME UNDER PRESSURE: 7 or 10 minutes	TOTAL TIME WITH PRESSURE: about 35 minutes
4–6 SERVINGS	PRESSURE: max or high	RELEASE: modified quick	GLUTEN-FREE
METHOD: standard			

2 tablespoons olive oil

1 medium yellow or white onion, chopped (1 cup)

1 medium red bell pepper, stemmed, cored, and chopped (1 cup)

2 medium garlic cloves, minced (2 teaspoons)

1 tinned anchovy fillet, minced

1 tablespoon mild smoked paprika

1½ teaspoons dried oregano

1 teaspoon fennel seeds

½ teaspoon red pepper flakes

½ teaspoon table salt

Up to ¼ teaspoon saffron (optional)

1½ pounds boneless skinless chicken breasts, cut into 1-inch pieces

1¼ cups raw long-grain white rice

One 14-ounce can diced tomatoes *packed in juice*, preferably fire-roasted tomatoes (1¾ cups)

1½ cups chicken broth

1 cup shelled fresh peas, or frozen peas (no need to thaw)

Other Pots

- For a 3-quart Instant Pot, you *must* halve all of the ingredient amounts.
- For a 10-quart Instant Pot, you *must* increase all of the ingredient amounts by 50 percent or you *can* even double the amounts.

Beyond

- Garnish the servings with drained jarred diced pimientos and/or sliced sun-dried tomatoes.
- For more flavor, reduce the chicken broth to 1 cup and add ½ cup dry sherry with it.

This casserole is a simplified version of arroz con pollo...with an extra bit of oomph: We add an anchovy fillet to the mix for briny, umami notes. The casserole can also include saffron for a musky, earthy flavor, depending (of course) on how much you want to splurge. (Even a thread or two of saffron will up the flavors considerably.) Don't use parboiled rice like Uncle Ben's or so-called "instant" rice for this or any other recipe in this book. Here, you need the standard, long-grain rice. The grains will stay distinct and toothsome. But avoid basmati rice. The grains are actually too long and dry for this casserole.

1.

	Press	Set it for	Set time for	If needed, press
In all models	SAUTÉ	MEDIUM, NORMAL, or CUSTOM 300°F	10 minutes	START

2. As the pot heats, warm the oil in the insert set in a **5-, 6-, or 8-quart Instant Pot.** Add the onion and bell pepper; cook, stirring often, until the onion softens, about 3 minutes. Add the garlic, anchovy, smoked paprika, oregano, fennel seeds, red pepper flakes, salt, and saffron (if using). Cook, stirring all the while, until fragrant, about 20 seconds.

3. Dump in the chicken and stir constantly until the meat is coated in the spice mixture. Pour in the rice and continue stirring until evenly distributed.

4. Pour in the tomatoes with their juice and the broth. Scrape up any browned bits on the pot's bottom. Turn off the heat and pour the peas on top of the casserole without stirring them in. Lock the lid on the pot.

5.

	Set pot for	Set level to	Valve must be	Set time for	If needed, press
For Max pots only	PRESSURE COOK	MAX	—	7 minutes with the KEEP WARM setting off	START
For all other pots	PRESSURE COOK or MANUAL	HIGH	Closed	10 minutes with the KEEP WARM setting off	START

6. When the pot has finished cooking, use the **quick-release method** to bring the pressure back to normal but **do not open the cooker.** Set it aside for 10 minutes. Unlatch the lid and open the pot. Stir well before serving. (If there's still too much liquid in the pot, set the lid askew over the pot and set it aside for 5 to 10 minutes for the rice to continue to absorb the sauce.)

Not-Really-Cracker-Barrel's Chicken, Broccoli, and Cheese Casserole

14 ingredients

4–6 SERVINGS

METHOD: pot-in-pot

SPECIAL EQUIPMENT: a 2-quart, 7-inch-round, high-sided, pressure-safe baking or soufflé dish and a pressure-safe rack or trivet

PRESSURE: max or high, then high

TIME UNDER PRESSURE: 24 or 29 minutes

RELEASE. quick twice

TOTAL TIME WITH PRESSURE: about 45 minutes

1½ cups water

2 pounds boneless skinless chicken breasts, cut into 1-inch pieces

2 tablespoons all-purpose flour

½ teaspoon dried sage

½ teaspoon onion powder

½ teaspoon garlic powder

½ teaspoon table salt

½ teaspoon ground black pepper

2 cups whole milk (do *not* use low-fat or fat-free milk)

½ cup heavy cream (do *not* use light cream)

½ stick (4 tablespoons or ¼ cup) butter, cut into small pieces

8 ounces (1½ cups) fresh or frozen small broccoli florets (thawed if frozen)

4 ounces American mild cheddar cheese, shredded (1 cup)

12 Ritz or Ritz knock-off crackers

Rather than using canned cream of chicken soup as many copycat recipes do, we've created a richer sauce, modeled on homemade cream of chicken soup but with a lot more flavor because of bold spices like dried sage, onion, and garlic powder. Cooking the dish twice under pressure might seem excessive. We do so to solve the problem of too much cooking producing overly soft broccoli. And don't skip the Ritz crackers! They're *crucial*.

1. Pour the water into the insert set in a **5-, 6-, or 8-quart Instant Pot**. Put a pressure-safe rack or trivet in the insert.

2. Toss the chicken, flour, sage, onion powder, garlic powder, salt, and pepper in a 2-quart, 7-inch-round, high-sided, pressure-safe baking or soufflé dish until the chicken pieces are evenly and well coated in the spice and flour mixture. The dried ingredients should stick to the chicken and *not* settle to the bottom of the baking dish.

3. Stir in the milk and cream until well blended. Dot the top evenly with bits of butter. Seal the dish tightly with aluminum foil, set the dish on the rack, and lock the lid on the pot.

4.

	Set pot for	Set level to	Valve must be	Set time for	If needed, press
For Max pots only	PRESSURE COOK	MAX	—	20 minutes with the KEEP WARM setting off	START
For all other pots	PRESSURE COOK or MANUAL	HIGH	Closed	25 minutes with the KEEP WARM setting off	START

5. When the pot has finished cooking, use the **quick-release method** to bring the pressure back to normal. Unlatch the lid and open the cooker. Uncover the (hot!) baking dish.

6. Stir the contents of the baking dish so that the sauce is smooth. Top the chicken casserole with the broccoli, then sprinkle the cheese evenly on the top. Cover the baking dish tightly once more with the foil. Lock the lid back onto the cooker.

7.

	Set pot for	Set level to	Valve must be	Set time for	If needed, press
For *all* pots	PRESSURE COOK or MANUAL	HIGH	Closed	4 minutes with the KEEP WARM setting off	START

8. When the pot has finished cooking, use the **quick-release method** to bring the pressure back to normal. Unlatch the lid and open the cooker. Use hot pads or silicone baking mitts to transfer the (hot!) dish to a nearby wire rack. Cool for 2 to 3 minutes, then crumble the Ritz crackers over the casserole before serving warm by the big spoonful.

Other Pots

- For a 3-quart Instant Pot, you *must* halve almost all of the ingredient amounts *except* you *must* use 1 cup water in the insert. You *must* also use a 1-quart, 6-inch-round, high-sided, pressure-safe baking or soufflé dish.

- For a 10-quart Instant Pot, you *must* increase the amount of water in the insert to 2½ cups while otherwise completing the recipe as stated.

Beyond

- Keep the Cracker Barrel theme going by serving this casserole with warmed corn and butter alongside steamed or roasted carrots.

Sweet-and-Sour Chicken & Rice Casserole

10 ingredients	**SPECIAL EQUIPMENT:** none
4 SERVINGS	
METHOD: standard	**PRESSURE:** max or high

TIME UNDER PRESSURE: 7 or 9 minutes	**TOTAL TIME WITH PRESSURE:** about 40 minutes
RELEASE: modified quick	**CAN BE GLUTEN-FREE**

1 pound boneless skinless chicken breasts, cut into 1-inch pieces

2 cups chicken broth

One 8-ounce can chunked pineapple *packed in juice*, drained

One 8-ounce can whole water chestnuts, drained and quartered

1 large carrot, peeled and cut into ½-inch-thick slices

¼ cup regular or low-sodium soy sauce, or gluten-free tamari sauce

¼ cup unseasoned rice vinegar

2 tablespoons light brown sugar

1½ cups raw long-grain white rice

Toasted sesame oil, for garnishing

Other Pots

- For a 3-quart Instant Pot, you *must* halve all of the ingredient amounts.
- For an 8-quart Instant Pot, you *can* increase all of the ingredient amounts by 50 percent.
- For a 10-quart Instant Pot, you *must* increase all of the ingredient amounts by 50 percent and you *can* even double the amounts.

Beyond

- Garnish the servings with trimmed and minced scallions as well as the sesame oil.
- And/or garnish with purchased crunchy wonton strips.

This isn't a fried rice variation made for an Instant Pot. Instead, it's something of a reinvention of a more familiar chicken-and-rice casserole but through the lens of take-out sweet-and-sour chicken. Confusing? Not really. It's salty and sweet, similar to the Chinese-American favorite. Better yet, it's all done in one pot. Rather than using a bottled sweet-and-sour sauce (which is inevitably *too* sweet), we build the sauce with soy (or tamari) sauce, unseasoned rice vinegar, and brown sugar.

1.

	Press	Set it for	Set time for	If needed, press
In all models	SAUTÉ	MEDIUM, NORMAL, or CUSTOM 300°F	10 minutes	START

2. As the pot heats, stir the chicken, broth, pineapple, water chestnuts, carrot, soy sauce, rice vinegar, and brown sugar in the insert set in a **5-, 6-, or 8-quart Instant Pot** until the brown sugar dissolves.

3. Continue cooking, stirring occasionally, until many wisps of steam rise off the liquid and the liquid is on the verge of simmering, about 6 minutes. Stir in the rice, turn off the heat, and lock the lid on the cooker.

4.

	Set pot for	Set level to	Valve must be	Set time for	If needed, press
For Max pots only	PRESSURE COOK	MAX	—	7 minutes with the KEEP WARM setting off	START
For all other pots	PRESSURE COOK or MANUAL	HIGH	Closed	9 minutes with the KEEP WARM setting off	START

5. When the pot has finished cooking, use the **quick-release method** to bring the pressure back to normal but **do not open the cooker.** Set it aside for 10 minutes, then unlatch the lid and open the pot. Stir well, then ladle into bowls and garnish each serving with toasted sesame oil.

Not-Really-Applebee's Fiesta Lime Chicken

10 ingredients

4 SERVINGS

METHOD:
pot-in-pot

SPECIAL EQUIPMENT:
a 2-quart, 7-inch-round, high-sided, pressure-safe baking or soufflé dish and a pressure-safe rack or trivet

PRESSURE:
max or high

TIME UNDER PRESSURE:
21 or 23 minutes

RELEASE:
quick twice

TOTAL TIME WITH PRESSURE:
about 45 minutes

CAN BE GLUTEN-FREE

1½ cups water

¼ cup jarred teriyaki sauce (gluten-free, if necessary)

3 tablespoons dark brown sugar

2 tablespoons lime juice

3 medium garlic cloves, minced (1 tablespoon)

1 tablespoon minced peeled fresh ginger

1 teaspoon ground cumin

1 teaspoon liquid smoke (gluten-free, if necessary)

Four 6- to 8-ounce boneless skinless chicken breasts

3 ounces American sharp cheddar cheese, shredded (¾ cup)

Other Pots

- For a 3-quart Instant Pot, you *must* halve almost all of the ingredient amounts *except* you *must* use 1 cup water in the insert. You *must* also use a 1-quart, 6-inch-round, high-sided, pressure-safe baking or soufflé dish.

- For a 10-quart Instant Pot, you *must* use 2½ cups water in the insert while otherwise completing the recipe as stated.

Beyond

- These breasts are traditionally served over tortilla chips and garnished with pico de gallo. To make your own pico de gallo, see the Beyond for the Not-Really-Chili's Chicken Enchilada Soup recipe on page 86.

This popular knock-off recipe uses a combo of teriyaki sauce and lime juice to make *very* flavorful chicken breasts that go great with margaritas, chips, and salsa on the deck, a quick meal when you just want to enjoy your evening. Notice that these boneless skinless chicken breasts are not the gargantuan ones we've used in earlier recipes in this chapter.

1. Pour the water into the insert set in a **5-, 6-, or 8-quart Instant Pot.** Put a pressure-safe rack or trivet in the insert.

2. Stir the teriyaki sauce, brown sugar, lime juice, garlic, ginger, cumin, and liquid smoke in a 2-quart, 7-inch-round, high-sided, pressure-safe baking or soufflé dish until the brown sugar dissolves.

3. Set the chicken breasts in this marinade and turn them repeatedly until they are well coated. Spread them out into as much of a single layer as possible. Only if necessary, put thinner ends under thicker ends. Do not cover the dish. Set it on the rack and lock the lid on the pot.

4.

	Set pot for	Set level to	Valve must be	Set time for	If needed, press
For Max pots only	PRESSURE COOK	MAX	—	20 minutes with the KEEP WARM setting off	START
For all other pots	PRESSURE COOK or MANUAL	HIGH	Closed	22 minutes with the KEEP WARM setting off	START

5. When the pot has finished cooking, use the **quick-release method** to bring the pressure back to normal. Unlatch the lid and open the cooker. Use a cooking spoon or a flatware tablespoon to remove as much liquid from around the chicken as you can. (Some left on the bottom is fine.) Sprinkle the cheese evenly over the chicken breasts. Lock the lid back on the pot.

6.

	Set pot for	Set level to	Valve must be	Set time for	If needed, press
For *all* pots	PRESSURE COOK or MANUAL	HIGH	Closed	1 minute with the KEEP WARM setting off	START

7. When the pot has finished cooking, use the **quick-release method** to bring the pressure back to normal. Unlatch the lid and open the cooker. Use hot pads or silicone baking mitts to transfer the (hot!) dish to a nearby wire rack. Cool for 2 to 3 minutes.

Not-Really-Panda-Express's Orange Chicken

11 ingredients	
4–6 SERVINGS	
METHOD: fast/slow	
SPECIAL EQUIPMENT: none	
PRESSURE: low	
TIME UNDER PRESSURE: 6 minutes	
RELEASE: quick	
TOTAL TIME WITH PRESSURE: about 20 minutes	
TOTAL TIME WITH SLOW COOKING: about 2 hours 15 minutes	
CAN BE GLUTEN-FREE	

2 pounds chicken tenders, each cut into 4 pieces

3 medium carrots, thinly sliced (1½ cups)

3 medium garlic cloves, minced (1 tablespoon)

1 tablespoon finely grated fresh orange zest (from about 2 medium oranges)

1 cup pulp-free orange juice

⅓ cup hoisin sauce (gluten-free, if necessary—see page 18 for more information)

3 tablespoons granulated white sugar

½ teaspoon table salt

½ teaspoon ground black pepper

1½ tablespoons water

1 tablespoon cornstarch

Other Pots

- For a 3-quart Instant Pot, you *must* halve all of the ingredient amounts.
- For an 8-quart Instant Pot, you *can* increase all of the ingredient amounts by 50 percent.
- Unfortunately, there's no good way to adjust this recipe for a 10-quart Instant Pot without swamping the dish with too much liquid.

Beyond

- Sprinkle servings with sesame seeds and/or the minced scallions.
- The dish needs a good batch of rice as its base. See our recipe for Perfect White Rice Every Time (page 355).

We've simplified this popular dish by using chicken tenders, which cook more quickly in the flavorful sauce—made with lots of orange juice and a little orange zest for a brighter flavor. The dish is fairly sweet, so don't stint on the garlic which will balance the flavors. You can even double the garlic, if you want! There's no soy sauce or vinegar here, just as in the original recipe. That said, you could add up to 2 tablespoons unseasoned rice vinegar with the other ingredients for a more sophisticated take.

1. Stir the chicken, carrots, garlic, zest, orange juice, hoisin sauce, sugar, salt, and pepper in the insert set in a **5-, 6-, or 8-quart Instant Pot** until the sugar dissolves and the mixture is uniform. Lock the lid onto the cooker.

2.

	Set pot for	Set level to	Valve must be	Set time for	If needed, press
For *all* pots	PRESSURE COOK or MANUAL	LOW	Closed	6 minutes with the KEEP WARM setting off	START
For the slow-cook function	SLOW COOK	HIGH	Open	2 hours with the KEEP WARM setting off	START

3. When the pot has finished cooking under pressure, use the **quick-release method** to bring the pressure back to normal. Whichever cooking method you've used, unlatch the lid and open the cooker. Whisk the water and cornstarch in a small bowl until smooth.

4.

	Press	Set it for	Set time for	If needed, press
In all models	SAUTÉ	MEDIUM, NORMAL, or CUSTOM 300°F	5 minutes	START

5. Stir quite often while the chicken mixture comes to a simmer. Stir in the cornstarch slurry and continue cooking, stirring almost constantly, until bubbling and thickened, less than 1 minute. Turn off the heat and use hot pads or silicone baking mitts to remove the (hot!) insert to a nearby wire rack. Cool for 2 to 3 minutes before serving warm.

See photo in insert.

Poached Chicken Breasts with Honey and Lemon

11 ingredients 8 small chicken breasts **METHOD:** pot-in-pot	**SPECIAL EQUIPMENT:** a 2-quart, 7-inch-round high-sided, pressure-safe baking or soufflé dish and a pressure-safe rack or trivet	**PRESSURE:** max or high **TIME UNDER PRESSURE:** 20 or 25 minutes	**RELEASE:** natural **TOTAL TIME WITH PRESSURE:** about 50 minutes

---

1½ cups water

¼ cup chicken broth

2 tablespoons red wine vinegar

2 tablespoons lemon juice

1 tablespoon honey

1 tablespoon loosely packed, stemmed, fresh oregano leaves, minced

½ teaspoon table salt

½ teaspoon ground black pepper

1½ tablespoons all-purpose flour

Eight *small* (4-ounce) boneless skinless chicken breasts

Stemmed, chopped, fresh flat-leaf parsley leaves, for garnishing

Other Pots

- For a 3-quart Instant Pot, you *must* halve almost all of the ingredient amounts *except* you *must* use 1 cup water in the insert. You *must* also use a 1-quart, 6-inch-round, high-sided, pressure-safe baking or soufflé dish.

- For a 10-quart Instant Pot, you *must* increase the amount of water in the insert to 2½ cups while otherwise completing the recipe as stated.

Beyond

- Serve with Creamy Orzo with Spinach (page 149) or Perfect Polenta Every Time (page 351).

- Prepare the chicken breasts in advance, then wrap each individually in plastic wrap and store in the refrigerator for up to 5 days. They make great sandwiches or toppers for a Caesar salad.

This is a dish with clean, simple flavors that shine. Cooking boneless skinless chicken breasts with the pot-in-pot method lets them stay moist and tender while absorbing the sweet-and-sour sauce flavorings. Whisking a little flour into the sauce lets it thicken a bit as the chicken cooks.

Note that these are *very small* chicken breasts, only 4 ounces each. You'll often find them individually wrapped in large bags, either in the fresh meat case or the frozen case, especially at big-box stores. These smaller breasts will cook quickly before the sauce has a chance to burn.

1. Pour the water into the insert set in a **5-, 6-, or 8-quart Instant Pot.** Set a pressure-safe rack or trivet in the insert.

2. Whisk the broth, vinegar, lemon juice, honey, oregano, salt, and pepper in a 2-quart, 7-inch-round, high-sided, pressure-safe baking or soufflé dish until the honey dissolves. Whisk in the flour until it dissolves.

3. Dump the chicken breasts into the dish and toss repeatedly until they're all evenly coated in the sauce. Seal the baking dish tightly with aluminum foil. Set the dish on the rack and lock the lid on the pot.

4.

	Set pot for	Set level to	Valve must be	Set time for	If needed, press
For Max pots only	PRESSURE COOK	MAX	—	20 minutes with the KEEP WARM setting off	START
For all other pots	PRESSURE COOK or MANUAL	HIGH	Closed	25 minutes with the KEEP WARM setting off	START

5. When the pot has finished cooking, turn it off and let the pressure **come back to normal naturally,** about 15 minutes. Unlatch the lid and open the cooker. Use hot pads or silicone baking mitts to transfer the (hot!) baking dish to a nearby wire rack. Uncover and cool for a couple of minutes before serving the chicken breasts with the sauce ladled over the top. Garnish each breast with chopped parsley.

Not-Really-Romano's-Macaroni-Grill's Chicken Marsala

14 ingredients	
4–6 SERVINGS	
METHOD: standard	

SPECIAL EQUIPMENT: none	TIME UNDER PRESSURE: 8 minutes	TOTAL TIME WITH PRESSURE: about 25 minutes
PRESSURE: low	RELEASE: quick	
		GLUTEN-FREE

3 tablespoons butter

3 tablespoons olive oil

6 ounces white or brown button mushrooms, cleaned and thinly sliced

1 large single-lobe shallot, halved and thinly sliced (⅓ cup)

1 medium garlic clove, minced (1 teaspoon)

½ teaspoon dried oregano

½ teaspoon table salt

½ teaspoon ground black pepper

Two extra-large (1-pound) boneless skinless chicken breasts, cut into 2-inch-wide strips

⅓ cup marsala wine

½ cup chicken broth

1 tablespoon cornstarch

1 tablespoon white wine vinegar

Finely grated Parmigiano-Reggiano, for garnishing

At Macaroni Grill, this dish is a seared chicken breast served in a marsala sauce with cheese on top. We've adapted the preparation for the Instant Pot so that it becomes a braise—which means the chicken is first cut into strips for more even cooking. Since we also cut down on the liquid levels to keep the chicken from getting swamped, we used LOW pressure for the cooking.

Marsala wine is a fortified Sicilian wine, prized in Italian-American cooking for its sweet nutty flavors. It's the *primary* flavoring in this copycat recipe—which means you should opt for a decent bottle, not just the two-buck cooking marsala at the supermarket. Recork and store the opened bottle in the fridge for up to 1 week. Or freeze it in sealed, ⅓-cup portions for up to 1 year to make future batches of this braise.

1.

	Press	Set it for	Set time for	If needed, press
In all models	SAUTÉ	MEDIUM, NORMAL, or CUSTOM 300°F	10 minutes	START

2. As the pot heats, melt the butter in the oil in the insert set in a **5- or 6-quart Instant Pot.** Add the mushrooms and shallot. Cook, stirring often, until the mushrooms give off their liquid, about 3 minutes. Stir in the garlic, oregano, salt, and pepper until aromatic, just a few seconds.

3. Add the chicken and cook, stirring almost constantly, until it loses its raw, pink color, about 2 minutes. Pour in the wine and scrape up any browned bits on the pot's bottom. Turn off the heat, stir in the broth, and lock the lid onto the cooker.

4.

	Set pot for	Set level to	Valve must be	Set time for	If needed, press
For *all* pots	PRESSURE COOK or MANUAL	LOW	Closed	8 minutes with the KEEP WARM setting off	START

5. When the pot has finished cooking, use the **quick-release method** to bring the pressure back to normal. Unlatch the lid and open the cooker. Whisk the cornstarch and vinegar in a small bowl until smooth.

6.

	Press	Set it for	Set time for	If needed, press
In all models	SAUTÉ	MEDIUM, NORMAL, or CUSTOM 300°F	5 minutes	START

7. Stir almost constantly as the sauce comes to a simmer. Stir in the cornstarch slurry and cook, stirring constantly, until somewhat thickened while bubbling, less than 1 minute. Turn off the heat and use hot pads or silicone baking mitts to transfer the (hot!) insert to a nearby wire rack to stop the cooking. Cool for 2 to 3 minutes before serving hot with each portion garnished with grated cheese.

Other Pots

- For a 3-quart Instant Pot, you *must* halve almost all of the ingredients *except* you *must* use the stated amount of broth.

- For an 8-quart Instant Pot, you *must* increase all of the ingredient amounts by 50 percent.

- For a 10-quart Instant Pot, you *must* double almost all of the ingredient amounts *except* you *must* increase the broth to 1½ cups and you *must* use 2½ tablespoons cornstarch and 2½ tablespoons vinegar for the slurry.

Beyond

- Gussy up the dish by using oyster or hen-of-the-wood mushrooms.

- Serve over No-Brainer Cauliflower Mash (page 338).

Butter-Poached Chicken and Green Bean Dinner

9 ingredients

4 SERVINGS

METHOD:
stacks

SPECIAL
EQUIPMENT:
7½-inch
stackable
insert pans

PRESSURE:
high

TIME UNDER
PRESSURE:
20 minutes

RELEASE:
natural

TOTAL
TIME WITH
PRESSURE:
about 40
minutes

GLUTEN-
FREE

1½ cups water plus ½ cup *hot* tap water

Two 12-ounce boneless skinless chicken breasts

½ teaspoon mild paprika

½ teaspoon ground black pepper

¼ teaspoon onion powder

¼ teaspoon table salt, plus more to taste

½ stick (4 tablespoons or ¼ cup) butter, cut into small bits

12 ounces green beans, trimmed

1 small lemon

Other Pots

- For a 3-quart Instant Pot, you *must* use stackable containers that fit this smaller pot and you *must* halve almost all of the ingredient amounts *except* you *must* use 1 cup water in the insert.

- For a 5-quart Instant Pot, you *must* use 7-inch stackable containers specifically made to fit this slightly smaller pot (some stacks are too tall to work).

- For a 10-quart Instant Pot, you *must* increase the amount of water in the insert to 2½ cups while otherwise completing the recipe as stated.

Beyond

- Substitute thin asparagus spears or large (3-inch) broccoli florets for the green beans.

An entire dinner? Yep, with stackable insert pans, you can make the whole meal, protein and side, right in the pot — in this case, seasoned chicken breasts and steamed green beans. But while we're at it, we might as well poach those seasoned breasts in butter, right? And then turn the juices in the pan into a light sauce so as not to waste a drop.

1. Pour 1½ cups water into the insert set in a **6- or 8-quart Instant Pot.** If your stackable containers do not include feet to lift them out of the water, set a pressure-safe rack or trivet inside the pot.

2. Put the chicken breasts in the bottom container of the stack containers. (For more information on working with stacks, see page 16 of the introduction.) Do not overlap the meat but squish it all to fit. Sprinkle the paprika, black pepper, onion powder, and salt evenly over the meat. Dot bits of butter across the chicken.

3. Set the second level of stacks on top of the first. Put the green beans and the ½ cup hot tap water in this second level. Cover this container and lower the two-tiered stack into the pot. Lock the lid on the cooker.

4.

	Set pot for	Set level to	Valve must be	Set time for	If needed, press
For *all* pots	PRESSURE COOK or MANUAL	HIGH	Closed	20 minutes with the KEEP WARM setting off	START

5. When the pot has finished cooking, turn it off and let the pressure **return to normal naturally,** about 15 minutes. Unlatch the lid and open the cooker. Use hot pads or silicone baking mitts to transfer the (hot!) stacks to a nearby wire rack (watch out for the hot liquid inside). Uncover both levels.

6. Use kitchen tongs to transfer the chicken breasts to a cutting board. Slice the meat diagonally into ½-inch slices. Squeeze the lemon to get the juice through a small strainer (to catch any seeds) and into the butter and juices in the bottom container of the stacks. Stir well, taste for salt, and spoon this sauce over the servings of chicken and green beans.

Raspberry-Chipotle Pulled Chicken

12 ingredients	
6 SERVINGS	
METHOD: fast/slow	**SPECIAL EQUIPMENT:** none
	PRESSURE: max or high
TIME UNDER PRESSURE: 18 or 25 minutes	**TOTAL TIME WITH PRESSURE:** about 1 hour
RELEASE: natural	**TOTAL TIME WITH SLOW COOKING:** about 3½ hours

One 10-ounce can hot or mild diced tomatoes and green chiles, such as Rotel (1¼ cups)

¾ cup ginger ale (do not use diet ginger ale)

½ cup raspberry jam

2 or 3 tablespoons red wine vinegar

Up to 2 canned chipotle chiles in adobo sauce, stemmed, seeded, and chopped

1 tablespoon adobo sauce from the can

1 tablespoon Worcestershire sauce

1 tablespoon mild smoked paprika

1 teaspoon ground cumin

½ teaspoon garlic powder

½ teaspoon table salt

Five medium 8-ounce boneless skinless chicken breasts

Raspberry jam is the unexpected star of this easy sweet-and-spicy pulled chicken. You can use regular or seedless jam, but do not use raspberry jelly (too mild) or raspberry preserves (too chunky). Don't be afraid of all the chipotles here. They add smoky notes without too much fire, so long as you seed the chiles before you add them to the pot.

1. Stir the canned tomatoes and chiles, the ginger ale, jam, and vinegar in the insert set in a **5- or 6-quart Instant Pot** until the jam dissolves. Stir in the chipotles, adobo sauce, Worcestershire sauce, smoked paprika, cumin, garlic powder, and salt until uniform. Nestle the chicken breasts into the sauce and lock the lid on the pot.

2.

	Set pot for	Set level to	Valve must be	Set time for	If needed, press
For Max pots only	PRESSURE COOK	MAX	—	18 minutes with the KEEP WARM setting off	START
For all other pots	PRESSURE COOK or MANUAL	HIGH	Closed	25 minutes with the KEEP WARM setting off	START
For the slow-cook function	SLOW COOK	HIGH	Open	3 hours with the KEEP WARM setting off	START

3. When the pot has finished cooking under pressure, turn it off and let its pressure **return to normal naturally,** about 35 minutes. Whichever cooking method you've used, unlatch the lid and open the cooker. Use two forks to shred the chicken into the sauce. Set aside for a couple of minutes so the meat continues to absorb the sauce. Serve warm.

Other Pots

- For a 3-quart Instant Pot, you *must* halve almost all of the ingredient amounts *except* you *must* use ½ cup ginger ale.

- For an 8-quart Instant Pot, you *must* increase the ginger ale to 1 cup or you *can* increase all of the ingredient amounts by 50 percent.

- For a 10-quart Instant Pot, you *must* double all of the ingredient amounts.

Beyond

- Because this pulled chicken is fairly sweet, consider vinegary condiments like sandwich-sliced dill pickles, a sour chowchow, or even kimchi.

Spicy Chicken and Chickpea Stew

10 ingredients

6 SERVINGS

METHOD:
fast/slow

SPECIAL EQUIPMENT:
none

PRESSURE:
max or high

TIME UNDER PRESSURE:
12 or 15 minutes

RELEASE:
quick

TOTAL TIME WITH PRESSURE:
about 35 minutes

TOTAL TIME WITH SLOW COOKING:
about 4 hours 15 minutes

GLUTEN-FREE

2 teaspoons ground coriander

1 teaspoon ground cumin

1 teaspoon mild paprika

1 teaspoon dried thyme

1 teaspoon table salt

Six 6- to 8-ounce boneless skinless chicken breasts

3 tablespoons butter

½ cup chicken broth

One 28-ounce can diced tomatoes *packed in juice* (3½ cups)

One 15-ounce can chickpeas, drained and rinsed (1¾ cups)

Other Pots

- For a 3-quart Instant Pot, you *must* halve all of the ingredient amounts.
- For a 10-quart Instant Pot, you *must* increase all of the ingredient amounts by 50 percent.

Beyond

- For more flavor, nix the dried spices and substitute 1½ to 2 tablespoons ras el hanout. Check to see if there's salt in the blend. In better bottlings, there isn't.
- Given the dish's Middle Eastern flavors, garnish the servings with tahini sauce. For six servings, whisk ⅓ cup tahini (sesame seed paste), ¼ cup lemon juice, ¼ cup plain regular or low-fat yogurt (do not use fat-free or Greek yogurt), ½ teaspoon table salt, and ½ teaspoon ground black pepper in a medium bowl until smooth. Whisk in water, 1 to 2 tablespoons at a time, until you get a pourable sauce, about like pancake batter.

Even in smaller pots, this buttery, cumin-scented stew makes enough for a crowd. Fortunately, it freezes well, too. Freeze individual cooked chicken breasts in a little sauce in separate containers for easy lunches in the days ahead. For a great weekend brunch, serve the chicken breasts in the stew topped with a poached egg, with warmed pita rounds at the ready.

1. Mix the coriander, cumin, paprika, thyme, and salt in a small bowl until uniform. Use clean hands to rub this mixture onto the chicken breasts for an even coating.

2.

	Press	Set it for	Set time for	If needed, press
In all models	SAUTÉ	LESS or LOW	20 minutes	START

3. As the pot heats, melt the butter in the insert set in a **5-, 6-, or 8-quart Instant Pot.** Add half the chicken breasts and brown well, turning once, about 8 minutes. Transfer the meat to a nearby plate. Add the remaining chicken breasts and brown these, too, turning once, about 7 minutes. Transfer these to the plate as well.

4. Pour in the broth and scrape up all the browned bits on the pot's bottom. Stir in the tomatoes with their juice and the chickpeas. Turn off the heat and nestle the chicken breasts into the sauce. Lock the lid on the pot.

5.

	Set pot for	Set level to	Valve must be	Set time for	If needed, press
For Max pots only	PRESSURE COOK	MAX	—	12 minutes with the KEEP WARM setting off	START
For all other pots	PRESSURE COOK or MANUAL	HIGH	Closed	15 minutes with the KEEP WARM setting off	START
For the slow-cook function	SLOW COOK	HIGH	Open	4 hours with the KEEP WARM setting off	START

6. When the pot has finished cooking under pressure, use the **quick-release method** to bring the pressure back to normal. Whichever cooking method you've used, unlatch the lid and open the cooker. Set aside for 2 to 3 minutes so the chicken continues to absorb some of the sauce. Serve in bowls with lots of sauce ladled over each breast.

Chicken Negimaki

8 ingredients

4 SERVINGS

METHOD:
pot-in-pot

SPECIAL EQUIPMENT:
a 2-quart, 7-inch-round, high-sided, pressure-safe baking or soufflé dish and a pressure-safe rack or trivet

PRESSURE:
high

TIME UNDER PRESSURE:
30 minutes

RELEASE:
natural

TOTAL TIME WITH PRESSURE:
about 1 hour 15 minutes

CAN BE GLUTEN-FREE

1½ cups water

½ cup regular or low-sodium soy sauce, or gluten-free tamari sauce

¼ cup honey

1 tablespoon minced peeled fresh ginger

2 medium garlic cloves, minced (2 teaspoons)

Four 6-ounce boneless skinless chicken breasts, pounded to ¼-inch thick

12 medium scallions, trimmed and cut into 4-inch sections

Sesame seeds, for garnishing

Other Pots

- For a 3-quart Instant Pot, you *must* halve almost all of the ingredient amounts except you *must* use 1 cup water in the insert. You *must* also use a 1-quart, 6-inch-round, high-sided, pressure-safe baking or soufflé dish.

- For a 10-quart Instant Pot, you *must* increase the amount of water in the insert to 2½ cups while otherwise completing the recipe as stated.

Beyond

- Make an easy carrot salad. Shred carrots into a serving bowl, then make an easy dressing with sesame oil, soy sauce, and rice vinegar in a one-to-one proportion. Add some sesame seeds and/or minced chives for more flavor.

With the pot-in-pot method, it's easy to make this tasty ginger and garlicky treat of chicken breasts rolled around scallions and lacquered in a sweet-and-salty sauce. To create the rolls, the recipe requires chicken *cutlets,* not just boneless skinless chicken breasts. You can sometimes find the cutlets in the meat case at the supermarket. You can also DIY it by putting a chicken breast between two sheets of plastic wrap, then flattening the chicken with the smooth side of a meat mallet or the bottom of a heavy saucepan. Give it forceful, straight downstrokes so that the meat doesn't thin out at its edges. (And repeat with three more breasts and clean sheets of plastic wrap each time.) Or you can ask the butcher at your supermarket to do the job for you. (Tip well!)

1. Pour the water into the insert set in a **5-, 6-, or 8-quart Instant Pot.** Put a pressure-safe rack or trivet in the insert.

2. Whisk the soy sauce, honey, ginger, and garlic in a 2-quart, 7-inch-round, high-sided, pressure-safe baking or soufflé dish.

3. Lay one pounded chicken breast on your clean work surface or cutting board with one of the two shorter sides facing you. Put a quarter of the scallion pieces along the bottom edge closest to you. Mix up green and white parts so that there are some of each. Roll up the chicken, starting at the edge with the scallions. Set this roll seam side down in the sauce and spoon some of the sauce over it. Repeat to make three more rolls and place in the baking dish. Seal it tightly with aluminum foil and set it on the rack. Lock the lid on the cooker.

4.

	Set pot for	Set level to	Valve must be	Set time for	If needed, press
For *all* pots	PRESSURE COOK or MANUAL	HIGH	Closed	30 minutes with the KEEP WARM setting off	START

5. When the pot has finished cooking, turn it off and let the pressure **return to normal naturally,** about 15 minutes. Unlatch the lid and open the cooker. Use hot pads or silicone baking mitts to transfer the (hot!) baking dish to a nearby wire rack.

6. Use a flexible metal spatula to transfer the chicken rolls to a cutting board. Slice them into 1-inch lengths. Drizzle the sauce from the baking dish over the pieces and garnish them with a sprinkling of sesame seeds.

See photo in insert.

Tikka-Spiced Chicken Kebabs

15 ingredients

4–6 SERVINGS

METHOD:
steam

SPECIAL
EQUIPMENT:
eight 6-inch
bamboo skewers
and a pressure-
and food-safe rack
or trivet

PRESSURE:
max or high

TIME UNDER
PRESSURE:
10 or 12 minutes

RELEASE:
quick

TOTAL TIME WITH
PRESSURE:
1 hour 30
minutes (includes
marinating)

GLUTEN-FREE

2 pounds boneless skinless chicken breasts, cut into 2-inch cubes

3 medium garlic cloves, minced (1 tablespoon)

1 tablespoon minced peeled fresh ginger

1 tablespoon lemon juice

1 tablespoon light brown sugar

2 teaspoons ground coriander

1 teaspoon ground cumin

1 teaspoon ground dried turmeric

1 teaspoon mild paprika

1 teaspoon onion powder

1 teaspoon table salt

½ teaspoon ground black pepper

1½ cups chicken broth

½ cup plain full-fat, low-fat, or fat-free Greek yogurt

Chopped, stemmed, fresh cilantro leaves, for garnishing

No, you can't grill in an Instant Pot. (Not yet, at least—although they're always inventing new pots!) But you can turn out some pretty fine tikka kebabs, flavored with a rub worthy of a spice bazaar. These skewers are great fare for a Super Bowl party. Invest in a package of bamboo skewers, way more skewers than needed for this recipe. They are great to have on hand for all sorts of fare off the grill and also make excellent cake and cupcake testers.

1. Stir the chicken pieces, garlic, ginger, lemon juice, brown sugar, coriander, cumin, turmeric, paprika, onion powder, salt, and pepper in a large bowl until the brown sugar dissolves and the chicken pieces are evenly coated. Cover and refrigerate for at least 1 hour, stirring once.

2. Divide the chicken cubes among eight 6-inch bamboo skewers, threading about four pieces on each skewer and leaving a little room between each piece.

3. Pour the broth into the insert set in a **5-, 6-, or 8-quart Instant Pot.** Set a pressure- and food-safe rack or trivet in the insert. Pile the skewers on the rack and lock the lid on the pot.

4.

	Set pot for	Set level to	Valve must be	Set time for	If needed, press
For Max pots only	PRESSURE COOK	MAX	—	10 minutes with the KEEP WARM setting off	START
For all other pots	PRESSURE COOK or MANUAL	HIGH	Closed	12 minutes with the KEEP WARM setting off	START

5. When the pot has finished cooking, use the **quick-release method** to bring the pressure back to normal. Unlatch the lid and open the cooker. Use kitchen tongs to transfer the skewers to a serving platter. Remove the rack or trivet from the pot.

6.

	Press	Set it for	Set time for	If needed, press
In all models	SAUTÉ	HIGH or MORE	10 minutes	START

7. Stir the liquid in the insert as it comes to a full simmer. Cook, stirring occasionally, until it's reduced to about a third of the volume before you began simmering (that is, until it's about ½ cup), about 8 minutes.

8. Turn off the heat and whisk in the yogurt until smooth. Use hot pads or silicone baking mitts to pick up the (hot!) insert and drizzle the sauce over the kebabs, pouring any extra sauce to be served on the side in a bowl. Sprinkle fresh cilantro over kebabs as a garnish.

Other Pots

- For a **3-quart Instant Pot**, you *must* halve almost all of the ingredient amounts *except* you *must* use 1 cup broth in the insert.

- For an **8-quart Instant Pot**, you *can* increase almost all of the ingredient amounts by 50 percent (using 12 skewers) *except* you *must* leave the broth in the insert at the stated 1½ cups.

- For a **10-quart Instant Pot**, you *must* increase the broth in the insert to 2½ cups. You can complete the recipe as stated, increase the remaining ingredient amounts by 50 percent (using 12 skewers), or even double the amounts (using 16 skewers).

Beyond

- Serve these with any sort of chutney you like as well as purchased na'an (Indian flatbread).

- These skewers *need* Yellow Rice (page 357) or even Not-Really-Chipotle's Chili-Lime Rice (page 358).

See photo in insert.

Bacony Barbecue Chicken Breasts

10 ingredients

4 SERVINGS

METHOD:
fast/slow

SPECIAL EQUIPMENT:
none

PRESSURE:
max or high

TIME UNDER PRESSURE:
12 or 15 minutes

RELEASE:
quick

TOTAL TIME WITH PRESSURE:
about 40 minutes

TOTAL TIME WITH SLOW COOKING:
about 3½ hours

CAN BE GLUTEN-FREE

---

1 tablespoon olive oil

Four 12-ounce bone-in skin-on chicken breasts

4 thin strips of bacon (gluten-free, if necessary), chopped

1 small yellow or white onion, chopped (½ cup)

1 medium red or green bell pepper, stemmed, cored, and chopped (1 cup)

1 canned chipotle chile in adobo sauce (gluten-free, if necessary), stemmed, seeded, and chopped

1 tablespoon adobo sauce from the can

1 teaspoon dried oregano

1 cup unsweetened apple cider

½ cup smooth, thick barbecue sauce (gluten-free, if necessary)

Other Pots

- For a 3-quart Instant Pot, you *must* halve almost all of the ingredient amounts *except* you *must* use ¾ cup unsweetened apple cider.

- For an 8-quart Instant Pot, you *must* increase all of the ingredient amounts by 50 percent.

- For a 10-quart Instant Pot, you *must* double almost all of the ingredient amounts *except* you *must* use only 1½ teaspoons dried oregano.

Beyond

- Try these chicken breasts with Smashed Potatoes with Herbs and Butter (page 348) or Wheat Berry "Risotto" (page 366).

- Garnish them with minced lemon zest and/or minced fresh oregano leaves.

The secret to this smoky chicken braise is the right barbecue sauce. If it's a chunky sauce, there won't be enough liquid to coat the bone-in chicken breasts before they go under pressure (the chunks will take up too much room in the measurement). If it's a thin sauce, it will run down into the liquid below and cause the pot to produce the BURN notice. Look for a thick but smooth barbecue sauce from a jar (a better bet than a squeeze bottle).

1.

	Press	Set it for	Set time for	If needed, press
In all models	SAUTÉ	MEDIUM, NORMAL, or CUSTOM 300°F	10 minutes	START

2. As the pot heats, warm the oil in the insert set in a **5- or 6-quart Instant Pot.** Add the chicken skin side down and brown well, about 5 minutes, without touching. Do not turn the breasts. Instead, use kitchen tongs to transfer them to a nearby plate.

3. Add the bacon to the pot and cook, stirring often, until browned at the edges. Add the onion and bell pepper; cook, stirring more frequently, until the onion softens, about 2 minutes. Stir in the chile, adobo sauce, and dried oregano until fragrant, just a few seconds.

4. Pour in the cider and scrape up any browned bits on the pot's bottom. Turn off the heat and set the chicken skin side up in the sauce. Smear the barbecue sauce over the chicken without mixing it into the sauce below. Lock the lid on the pot.

5.

	Set pot for	Set level to	Valve must be	Set time for	If needed, press
For Max pots only	PRESSURE COOK	MAX	—	12 minutes with the KEEP WARM setting off	START
For all other pots	PRESSURE COOK or MANUAL	HIGH	Closed	15 minutes with the KEEP WARM setting off	START
For the slow-cook function	SLOW COOK	HIGH	Open	3 hours with the KEEP WARM setting off	START

6. When the pot has finished cooking under pressure, use the **quick-release method** to bring the pressure back to normal. Whichever cooking method you've used, unlatch the lid and open the cooker. Serve the dish by transferring the chicken breasts to plates and ladling any sauce in the pot over them.

Fiery Coconut Curry Chicken Breasts

8 ingredients	
4–6 SERVINGS	
METHOD: standard	

SPECIAL EQUIPMENT: none	
PRESSURE: max or high	

TIME UNDER PRESSURE: 12 or 15 minutes	
RELEASE: quick	

TOTAL TIME WITH PRESSURE: about 50 minutes	
GLUTEN-FREE	

Four 12-ounce bone-in chicken breasts, the skin removed and discarded, the breasts halved widthwise

2 tablespoons Madras curry powder or other spicy curry powder blend

2 tablespoons butter

4 medium yellow or white onions, halved and sliced into thin half-moons

2 tablespoons minced peeled fresh ginger

Up to 1 teaspoon table salt

2 tablespoons orange marmalade

1 cup *light* coconut milk (see the headnote for more information)

Other Pots

- For a 3-quart Instant Pot, you *must* halve almost all of the ingredient amounts *except* you *must* use ¾ cup light coconut milk.

- For an 8-quart Instant Pot, you *must* increase almost all of the ingredient amounts by 50 percent *except* you *must* stir ½ cup chicken broth into the increased coconut milk before pouring it into the insert.

- For a 10-quart Instant Pot, you *must* double almost all of the ingredient amounts *except* you *must* stir 1 cup chicken broth into the increased coconut milk before pouring it into the insert.

Beyond

- For a more sweet-and-sour flavor, add 1 tablespoon tamarind paste with the marmalade.

- Garnish the servings with stemmed and minced fresh cilantro leaves and/or peeled, seeded, and chopped cucumber.

We have a whole chapter of curried dishes in the first *Instant Pot Bible,* but somehow we missed a basic recipe for a curried chicken dish using coconut milk as the base. Lucky for us, *and* for you, we have this opportunity to rectify our sin of omission! A rich, fiery coconut curry is one of the best pleasures from an Instant Pot.

Note two things about this recipe. First, it calls for a spicy curry powder, preferably a Madras blend. Don't be afraid of the burn; the pressure softens it. If you're worried, use 1 tablespoon Madras curry powder and 1 tablespoon standard yellow curry powder.

Second, you *must* use *light* coconut milk (sometimes spelled "lite" on the cans). Full-fat coconut milk will burn on the pot's bottom without other liquids in the mix. A lot of the added moisture will come from *so many* onions under pressure.

1. Put the chicken pieces in a large bowl, sprinkle them with the curry powder, and stir well until the pieces are evenly and thoroughly coated.

2.

	Press	Set it for	Set time for	If needed, press
In all models	SAUTÉ	MEDIUM, NORMAL, or CUSTOM 300°F	10 minutes	START

3. As the pot heats, melt the butter in the insert set in a **5- or 6-quart Instant Pot.** Add the onions and cook, stirring often, until they begin to brown at some of the edges, about 6 minutes.

4. Add the ginger and salt, cook, stirring often, until fragrant, less than 1 minute. Stir in the marmalade until melted, then add the chicken and stir until the chicken is coated in the onions and spice mixture. Pour in the *light* coconut milk, stir well, and turn off the heat. Lock the lid on the pot.

5.

	Set pot for	Set level to	Valve must be	Set time for	If needed, press
For Max pots only	PRESSURE COOK	MAX	—	12 minutes with the KEEP WARM setting off	START
For all other pots	PRESSURE COOK or MANUAL	HIGH	Closed	15 minutes with the KEEP WARM setting off	START

6. Use the **quick-release method** to bring the pressure back to normal. Unlatch the lid and open the cooker. Set the lid askew over the pot and set aside for 5 minutes to let the meat absorb more of the sauce. Serve warm.

Bistro Chicken Thighs

12 ingredients

6 SERVINGS

METHOD:
fast/slow

SPECIAL EQUIPMENT:
none

PRESSURE:
max or high

TIME UNDER PRESSURE:
12 or 15 minutes

RELEASE:
natural

TOTAL TIME WITH PRESSURE:
about 1 hour

TOTAL TIME WITH SLOW COOKING:
about 3½ hours

4 thin strips of bacon, chopped

Six 7- to 8-ounce bone-in skin-on chicken thighs

1 cup frozen pearl onions (no need to thaw)

1 cup "baby" carrots (see page 68 for more information)

½ cup dry white wine, such as Chardonnay; or unsweetened apple juice

¾ cup chicken broth

1 tablespoon packed, stemmed, fresh sage leaves, minced

½ teaspoon table salt

½ teaspoon ground black pepper

One 4-inch rosemary stalk

2 tablespoons heavy or light cream

1½ tablespoons all-purpose flour

Admittedly, this recipe for an herb-rich bistro favorite is a tad complicated, what with the extra steps of browning everything and thickening the sauce. But the reward is a perfect main course for a dinner party. If you lock the lid on the pot about 5 minutes before your guests arrive to start the pressure-cooking, you'll have plenty of time for a drink and chitchat before the natural release is finished. Then it's just a matter of thickening the sauce right before you're ready to sit down at the table.

1.

	Press	Set it for	Set time for	If needed, press
In all models	SAUTÉ	MEDIUM, NORMAL, or CUSTOM 300°F	30 minutes	START

2. As the pot heats, add the bacon to the insert set in a **5- or 6-quart Instant Pot.** Cook, stirring often, until well browned, about 4 minutes. Use a slotted spoon to transfer the bacon to a nearby large bowl.

3. Add half the chicken thighs skin side down and brown well without touching, about 5 minutes. Turn the thighs over and brown lightly on the other side, about 3 minutes. Transfer the thighs to the nearby large bowl with the bacon and brown the remaining thighs the same way before transferring them to the bowl.

4. Add the pearl onions and carrots to the pot. Cook, stirring often, until the onions begin to brown in spots, about 3 minutes. Pour in the wine or juice; scrape up all the browned bits on the pot's bottom.

5. Pour in the broth; stir in the sage, salt, and pepper. Turn off the heat and return the chicken, skin up, and the bacon bits (along with any juices in that bowl) to the pot. Nestle the rosemary stalk into the ingredients. Lock the lid on the cooker.

6.

	Set pot for	Set level to	Valve must be	Set time for	If needed, press
For Max pots only	PRESSURE COOK	MAX	—	12 minutes with the KEEP WARM setting off	START
For all other pots	PRESSURE COOK or MANUAL	HIGH	Closed	15 minutes with the KEEP WARM setting off	START
For the slow-cook function	SLOW COOK	HIGH	Open	3 hours with the KEEP WARM setting off	START

7. When the pot has finished cooking under pressure, turn it off and let the pressure **return to normal naturally,** about 35 minutes. Whichever cooking method you've used, unlatch the lid and open the cooker. Fish out and discard the rosemary spear. Use kitchen tongs to transfer the chicken thighs to a clean plate. Whisk the cream and flour in a small bowl until smooth.

8.

	Press	Set it for	Set time for	If needed, press
In all models	SAUTÉ	MEDIUM, NORMAL, or CUSTOM 300°F	10 minutes	START

9. Bring the sauce to a simmer, whisking occasionally. Then whisk in the flour slurry. Continue cooking, whisking all the while, until the sauce thickens, less than 1 minute. Turn off the heat and return the chicken to the pot. Stir gently but well to coat the meat in the sauce. Serve hot.

Other Pots

- For a **3-quart Instant Pot,** you *must* halve almost all of the ingredient amounts *except* you *must* use ½ cup broth.

- For an **8-quart Instant Pot,** you *must* use 1 cup broth if you complete the recipe as otherwise written *or* you *must* increase all of the ingredient amounts (even the broth) by 50 percent.

- For a **10-quart Instant Pot,** you *must* double all of the ingredient amounts.

Beyond

- These chicken thighs need Leek and Buttermilk Mashed Potatoes (page 349).

- Garnish the servings with minced fresh flat-leaf parsley leaves.

Buttery Chicken Thighs with Leeks and Vinegar

8 ingredients

6 SERVINGS

METHOD:
fast/slow

SPECIAL
EQUIPMENT:
none

PRESSURE:
max or high

TIME UNDER
PRESSURE:
12 or 15
minutes

RELEASE:
natural

TOTAL
TIME WITH
PRESSURE:
about 1 hour

TOTAL TIME
WITH SLOW
COOKING:
about
3 hours
45 minutes

GLUTEN-
FREE

½ stick (4 tablespoons or ¼ cup) butter

Six 7- to 8-ounce bone-in skin-on
chicken thighs

1 large leek, white and pale green part
only, halved lengthwise, washed for
internal grit, and thinly sliced (¾ cup)

3 large garlic cloves, smashed under a
small saucepan (any skins removed
and discarded)

½ cup apple cider vinegar

½ cup chicken broth

2 tablespoons water

1 tablespoon potato starch or cornstarch

This recipe serves up something like a Venetian nonna dish,
although simplified for today's pace of life (and the pressure cooker).
The butter mellows the vinegar quite a bit, yielding a savory,
sophisticated sauce alongside the leeks and garlic. Although you can
use cornstarch to thicken the sauce, potato starch is a better bet
because the texture is less slippery.

1.

	Press	Set it for	Set time for	If needed, press
In all models	SAUTÉ	MEDIUM, NORMAL, or CUSTOM 300°F	20 minutes	START

2. As the pot heats, melt 2 tablespoons of the butter in the insert set
in a **5- or 6-quart Instant Pot.** Add half the chicken thighs skin side
down and brown well without touching, about 5 minutes. Turn the
thighs over and brown lightly on the other wide, about 3 minutes.
Transfer the thighs to a nearby large bowl and brown the remaining
thighs the same way before transferring them to the bowl.

3. Melt the remaining 2 tablespoons butter in the insert. Add the
leek and cook, stirring often, until softened, about 2 minutes. Add
the garlic and stir until aromatic, about 20 seconds. Pour in the
vinegar and bring it to a boil, scraping up any browned bits on the
pot's bottom.

4. Stir in the broth and turn off the heat. Return the chicken thighs
skin side up to the sauce. Pour any juice from their bowl over them.
Lock the lid on the cooker.

5.

	Set pot for	Set level to	Valve must be	Set time for	If needed, press
For Max pots only	PRESSURE COOK	MAX	—	12 minutes with the KEEP WARM setting off	START
For all other pots	PRESSURE COOK or MANUAL	HIGH	Closed	15 minutes with the KEEP WARM setting off	START
For the slow-cook function	SLOW COOK	HIGH	Open	3 hours with the KEEP WARM setting off	START

6. When the pot has finished cooking under pressure, turn it off and let the pressure **return to normal naturally,** about 30 minutes.

7. Whichever cooking method you've used, unlatch the lid and open the cooker. Use kitchen tongs to transfer the thighs to a clean plate. Whisk the water and potato starch or cornstarch in a small bowl until smooth.

8.

	Press	Set it for	Set time for	If needed, press
In all models	SAUTÉ	MEDIUM, NORMAL, or CUSTOM 300°F	5 minutes	START

9. Whisk the sauce as it comes to a simmer. Whisk in the starch slurry. Continue cooking, whisking all the while, until thickened, less than 1 minute. *Immediately* turn off the heat, use hot pads or silicone baking mitts to transfer the (hot!) insert to a nearby wire rack, and return the chicken to the pot. Toss gently but well to coat in the sauce. Serve the thighs individually on plates with more pot sauce on the side as desired.

Other Pots

- For a 3-quart Instant Pot, you *must* halve almost all of the ingredient amounts *except* you *must* use ½ cup broth (the stated amount).

- For an 8-quart Instant Pot, you *must* use ¾ cup broth if you complete the recipe as otherwise written *or* you *must* increase all of the ingredient amounts (including the broth) by 50 percent.

- For a 10-quart Instant Pot, you *must* double all of the ingredient amounts.

Beyond

- Garnish the servings with chopped fresh flat-leaf parsley and/or oregano leaves.

- Serve the chicken and sauce over Perfect Polenta Every Time (page 351).

Pesto Chicken and Balsamic Potato Dinner

7 ingredients

4 SERVINGS

METHOD:
steam

SPECIAL EQUIPMENT:
a pressure- and food-safe rack or trivet

PRESSURE:
max or high

TIME UNDER PRESSURE:
10 or 12 minutes

RELEASE:
natural

TOTAL TIME WITH PRESSURE:
about 1 hour

GLUTEN-FREE

Four 8-ounce russet or baking potatoes, peeled and quartered widthwise

2 tablespoons balsamic vinegar

¾ cup chicken broth

½ stick (4 tablespoons or ¼ cup) butter, cut into 6 pieces

1 teaspoon table salt

Four 7- to 8-ounce bone-in but *skinless* chicken thighs

½ cup purchased pesto

Other Pots

- For a 3-quart Instant Pot, you *must* halve almost all of the ingredient amounts *except* you *must* use ¾ cup broth (the stated amount).

- For an 8-quart Instant Pot, you *must* use 1 cup broth if you complete the recipe as otherwise written *or* you *must* increase all of the ingredient amounts (including the broth) by 50 percent.

- For a 10-quart Instant Pot, you *must* double all of the ingredient amounts and you *must* use the large rack that comes with the larger cooker.

Beyond

- For homemade parsley-basil pesto, put 1 cup loosely packed fresh basil leaves, ¾ cup loosely packed fresh parsley leaves, ½ cup finely grated Parmigiano-Reggiano, ⅓ cup olive oil, ¼ cup sliced almonds, 1 peeled medium garlic clove, and 1 teaspoon table salt in a food processor. Cover and process until smooth, adding more olive oil in 1-tablespoon amounts until the sauce is thick but not paste-like. Pack any leftover pesto in a small container, cover the top with olive oil, seal, and refrigerate for up to 1 week.

We've done the research and can say that there's nothing better than opening a pot and looking down at a *complete* meal! This recipe cooks pesto-coated chicken on a rack over potatoes that poach in a balsamic sauce with lots of butter. The results are absurdly easy with nothing else to do but dig in. (Although you might have to crack open a beer and pour it yourself—sadly, they have yet to introduce an Instant Pot model that will do that for you.)

The one trick has to do with that rack. It should sit comfortably over the potatoes. The rack's feet don't have to touch the bottom of the pot, but the rack must sit fairly flat to hold the chicken breasts so as little of the pesto as possible slides off the meat under pressure.

1. Toss the potato pieces and vinegar in the insert of a **5- or 6-quart Instant Pot** until the potatoes are evenly coated. Pour in the broth, then dot the butter on the potatoes and sprinkle them with the salt.

2. Set a pressure- and food-safe rack or trivet over the potatoes. Smear the meaty side of the chicken thighs with the pesto for an even coating. Place them on the rack, separating them as much as you can while keeping them flat and in one layer. Lock the lid on the pot.

3.

	Set pot for	Set level to	Valve must be	Set time for	If needed, press
For Max pots only	PRESSURE COOK	MAX	—	10 minutes with the KEEP WARM setting off	START
For all other pots	PRESSURE COOK or MANUAL	HIGH	Closed	12 minutes with the KEEP WARM setting off	START

4. When the pot has finished cooking, turn it off and let the pressure **return to normal naturally,** about 30 minutes. Unlatch the lid and open the cooker. Use kitchen tongs to transfer the chicken thighs to a nearby platter or plates. Remove the rack from the pot, then arrange the potatoes around the thighs on the platter, drizzling everything with the sauce from the pot.

Ginger and Garlic Chicken Dinner with Couscous

13 ingredients

4 SERVINGS

METHOD:
pot-in-pot

SPECIAL EQUIPMENT:
a 1-quart, 6-inch-round high-sided, pressure-safe baking or soufflé dish

PRESSURE:
high

TIME UNDER PRESSURE:
10 minutes

RELEASE:
modified natural

TOTAL TIME WITH PRESSURE:
about 40 minutes

2 tablespoons butter

Four 7- to 8-ounce bone-in skin-on chicken thighs

1 medium yellow or white onion, chopped (1 cup)

1 tablespoon minced peeled fresh ginger

2 medium garlic cloves, minced (2 teaspoons)

1 teaspoon mild paprika

1 teaspoon ground coriander

½ teaspoon table salt

¼ teaspoon ground cinnamon

¼ teaspoon ground black pepper

2½ cups chicken broth

8 dried apricots, halved

1½ cups dried instant couscous (see the headnote on page 82)

Other Pots

- Because of the size of the baking dish on top of the chicken, this recipe cannot be made in a 3-quart Instant Pot.

- For an 8-quart Instant Pot, you *must* increase all of the ingredient amounts by 50 percent.

- For a 10-quart Instant Pot, you *must* double all of the ingredient amounts, and you *must* also use a 2-quart, 7-inch-round, high-sided, pressure-safe baking or soufflé dish for the couscous.

Beyond

- Before cooking, season the couscous mixture with ¼ cup sliced almonds, 1 tablespoon minced candied or crystallized ginger, ½ teaspoon ground dried turmeric, and/or ½ teaspoon ground cardamom.

It's so easy to make a complete couscous supper in the pot. The trick is not to brown the *skinless* side of the chicken thighs so they cook properly against the hot surface as the bowl of couscous presses them down. (In other words, this recipe's technique is the opposite of Pesto Chicken and Balsamic Potato Dinner on page 202, in which the chicken thighs cook over the potatoes.

1.

	Press	Set it for	Set time for	If needed, press
In all models	SAUTÉ	MEDIUM, NORMAL, or CUSTOM 300°F	10 minutes	START

2. As the pot heats, melt the butter in the insert set in a **5- or 6-quart Instant Pot.** Add the chicken thighs skin side down and cook without disturbing until well browned, about 5 minutes. Transfer the chicken to a nearby plate without browning the other side of the thighs.

3. Add the onion, ginger, and garlic to the pot; cook, stirring often, until aromatic, only about 2 minutes. Stir in the paprika, coriander, salt, cinnamon, and pepper.

4. Pour in 1 cup of the broth and scrape up any browned bits on the pot's bottom. Turn off the heat, stir in the apricots, and nestle the thighs skin side up in the sauce.

5. Mix the couscous and remaining 1½ cups broth in a 1-quart, 6-inch-round, high-sided, pressure-safe baking or soufflé dish. Do not cover. Set the dish on top of the chicken thighs. Lock the lid on the pot.

6.

	Set pot for	Set level to	Valve must be	Set time for	If needed, press
For *all* pots	PRESSURE COOK or MANUAL	HIGH	Closed	10 minutes with the KEEP WARM setting off	START

7. When the pot has finished cooking, turn it off and let the pressure **return to normal naturally for 5 minutes.** Then use the **quick-release method** to get rid of the pot's residual pressure. Unlatch the lid and open the cooker.

8. Use hot pads or silicone baking mitts to transfer the (hot!) baking dish to a nearby wire rack. Fluff the couscous with a fork, then divide it among serving plates. Top each serving with a chicken thigh and some of the juicy sauce from the pot.

Sweet & Spicy Chicken Thighs

14 ingredients

6 DINNER SERVINGS, AT LEAST 8 APPETIZER SERVINGS

METHOD: fast/slow

SPECIAL EQUIPMENT: none

PRESSURE: max or high

TIME UNDER PRESSURE: 10 or 12 minutes

RELEASE: quick

TOTAL TIME WITH PRESSURE: about 45 minutes

TOTAL TIME WITH SLOW COOKING: about 3½ hours

GLUTEN-FREE

1½ teaspoons dried thyme

½ teaspoon ground allspice

½ teaspoon grated nutmeg

½ teaspoon table salt

½ teaspoon ground black pepper

3 pounds boneless skinless chicken thighs, trimmed of any big fat blobs

2 tablespoons vegetable, canola, or other neutral-flavored oil

1 medium yellow or white onion, chopped (1 cup)

1 medium fresh jalapeño chile, stemmed and thinly sliced

3 medium garlic cloves, minced (1 tablespoon)

1 tablespoon minced peeled fresh ginger

2 tablespoons light brown sugar

1 cup chicken broth

1 tablespoon apple cider vinegar

Other Pots

- For a 3-quart Instant Pot, you *must* halve all of the ingredient amounts.

- For an 8-quart Instant Pot, you *must* increase the broth to 1½ cups while otherwise completing the recipe as stated—or you *must* increase all of the ingredient amounts by 50 percent.

- For a 10-quart Instant Pot, you *must* double all of the ingredient amounts.

Beyond

- For a subtler flavor, substitute 2 tablespoons pineapple jam for the brown sugar.

- For more sour in the sweet-and-sour balance, increase the vinegar to 2 tablespoons.

Although this dish may look like dinner, it would also be welcome as a substantial nibble on the patio with drinks or even at a schmancy cocktail party in the dead of winter. In those cases, slice the finished chicken thighs into bite-size bits, then serve with toothpicks.

1. Stir the thyme, allspice, nutmeg, salt, and pepper in a large bowl. Add the chicken thighs and toss until they are well coated.

2.

	Press	Set it for	Set time for	If needed, press
In all models	SAUTÉ	MEDIUM, NORMAL, or CUSTOM 300°F	10 minutes	START

3. As the pot heats, warm the oil in the insert set in a **5- or 6-quart Instant Pot.** Add the onion and cook, stirring often, until softened, about 3 minutes. Stir in the jalapeño, garlic, and ginger until aromatic, about 20 seconds.

4. Stir in the brown sugar until dissolved, then pour in the broth and vinegar. Scrape up any browned bits on the pot's bottom. Turn off the heat and nestle the chicken thighs into the sauce. Lock the lid on the pot.

5.

	Set pot for	Set level to	Valve must be	Set time for	If needed, press
For Max pots only	PRESSURE COOK	MAX	—	10 minutes with the KEEP WARM setting off	START
For all other pots	PRESSURE COOK or MANUAL	HIGH	Closed	12 minutes with the KEEP WARM setting off	START
For the slow-cook function	SLOW COOK	HIGH	Open	3 hours with the KEEP WARM setting off	START

6. When the pot has finished cooking under pressure, use the **quick-release method** to bring the pressure back to normal. Whichever cooking method you've used, unlatch the lid and open the cooker. Use kitchen tongs to transfer the chicken thighs to a serving platter or bowl.

7.

	Press	Set it for	Set time for	If needed, press
In all models	SAUTÉ	HIGH or MORE	5 minutes	START

8. Stir the liquid as it comes to a simmer. Continue cooking, stirring all the while, until the liquid has thickened to a sauce consistency. Turn off the heat and spoon the sauce over the thighs.

Lemon-Ginger Chicken Thighs

9 ingredients

6 SERVINGS

METHOD:
fast/slow

SPECIAL
EQUIPMENT:
none

PRESSURE:
max or high

TIME UNDER
PRESSURE:
10 or 12
minutes

RELEASE:
quick

TOTAL
TIME WITH
PRESSURE:
about 45
minutes

TOTAL TIME
WITH SLOW
COOKING:
about 3½
hours

CAN BE
GLUTEN-
FREE

---

3 pounds boneless skinless chicken thighs, trimmed of any big fat blobs

3 tablespoons light brown sugar

3 tablespoons minced peeled fresh ginger

3 tablespoons regular or low-sodium soy sauce, or gluten-free tamari sauce

2 teaspoons finely grated lemon zest

3 tablespoons fresh lemon juice

¾ cup plus 1½ tablespoons chicken broth

1 tablespoon cornstarch

2 medium scallions, trimmed and thinly sliced (⅔ cup)

Other Pots

- For a 3-quart Instant Pot, you *must* halve almost all of the ingredient amounts *except* you *must* use ½ cup broth.

- For an 8-quart Instant Pot, you *must* increase the broth to 1 cup while otherwise completing the recipe as stated—or you *must* increase all of the ingredient amounts by 50 percent.

- For a 10-quart Instant Pot, you *must* double all of the ingredient amounts.

Beyond

- For lots of heat, add up to 2 teaspoons red pepper flakes with the brown sugar and other ingredients.

- Serve the chicken thighs over Coconut Rice (page 359).

Very aromatic, a little spicy, a little sweet-and-sour, this chicken dish has all the makings of new-fangled comfort food. Remember that there's no real substitute for fresh lemon juice, particularly in a simple recipe like this one. The bottled stuff just doesn't have the zing.

1. Stir the chicken thighs, brown sugar, ginger, soy sauce, lemon zest, and lemon juice in the insert set in a **5- or 6-quart Instant Pot** until the chicken is thoroughly coated in the sauce mixture. Stir in ¾ cup of the broth until well combined and lock the lid on the pot.

2.

	Set pot for	Set level to	Valve must be	Set time for	If needed, press
For Max pots only	PRESSURE COOK	MAX	—	10 minutes with the KEEP WARM setting off	START
For all other pots	PRESSURE COOK or MANUAL	HIGH	Closed	12 minutes with the KEEP WARM setting off	START
For the slow-cook function	SLOW COOK	HIGH	Open	3 hours with the KEEP WARM setting off	START

3. When the pot has finished cooking under pressure, use the **quick-release method** to bring the pressure back to normal. Whichever cooking method you've used, unlatch the lid and open the cooker. Whisk the remaining 1½ tablespoons broth with the cornstarch in a small bowl until smooth.

4.

	Press	Set it for	Set time for	If needed, press
In all models	SAUTÉ	MEDIUM, NORMAL, or CUSTOM 300°F	5 minutes	START

5. Stir the sauce (with the chicken still in it) occasionally as the liquid comes to a simmer. Stir in the cornstarch slurry and continue cooking, stirring constantly, until the sauce around the chicken thickens, less than 1 minute. Turn off the heat and use hot pads or silicone baking mitts to transfer the (hot!) insert to a nearby wire rack (to stop the cooking). Cool for 2 to 3 minutes before serving hot, garnishing the servings with sliced scallions.

Sesame Chicken Wings

9 ingredients	
4–6 SERVINGS	
SPECIAL EQUIPMENT: none	
TIME UNDER PRESSURE: 12 minutes	
TOTAL TIME WITH PRESSURE: about 25 minutes	
METHOD: standard	
PRESSURE: low	
RELEASE: quick	
CAN BE GLUTEN-FREE	

3 pounds chicken wings, separated into wingettes and drumettes (the flappers discarded or saved for stock)

⅓ cup regular or low-sodium soy sauce, or gluten-free tamari sauce

¼ cup unsweetened apple juice

2 tablespoons toasted sesame oil

2 tablespoons apple cider vinegar

2 tablespoons honey

1 tablespoon minced peeled fresh ginger

3 medium garlic cloves, minced (1 tablespoon)

Scallions, trimmed and thinly sliced, for garnishing

Here's a backyard classic that we've given an Instant Pot spin. By cooking chicken wings on LOW pressure, we can reduce the amount of liquid in the pot so that the sauce doesn't swamp the meat (and turn the wings unpleasantly soft).

Buy packages of either wingettes or drumettes, depending on your preference—or buy whole wings and divide them yourself. If you want to save the little flapper sections to make chicken stock, we've got a terrific recipe in the original *Instant Pot Bible*.

1. Stir the chicken wing parts, soy sauce, apple juice, sesame oil, vinegar, honey, ginger, and garlic in a **5- or 6-quart Instant Pot** until the chicken is well coated and the honey has dissolved. Lock the lid on the pot.

2.

	Set pot for	Set level to	Valve must be	Set time for	If needed, press
For *all* pots	PRESSURE COOK or MANUAL	LOW	Closed	12 minutes with the KEEP WARM setting off	START

3. When the pot has finished cooking, use the **quick-release method** to bring the pressure back to normal. Unlatch the lid and open the cooker. Use kitchen tongs to transfer the wing pieces to a serving platter.

4.

	Press	Set it for	Set time for	If needed, press
In all models	SAUTÉ	MEDIUM, NORMAL, or CUSTOM 300°F	5 minutes	START

5. Stir the sauce in the insert as it comes to a simmer. Cook, stirring constantly to keep the sugars from burning, until reduced to a thick glaze, about 4 minutes. Turn off the heat and use hot pads or silicone baking mitts to transfer the (hot!) insert to a nearby wire rack (to stop the cooking—the sauce will continue to thicken even after you remove the insert). Spoon this glaze over the wings and garnish them with sliced scallions.

Beyond

- Crisp the wings after reducing the sauce by wiping out the (hot!) insert and returning it to the cooker. Set the air-fryer basket in the pot, return the unsauced wings to the basket, and set the Instant Pot Air Fryer Lid over the pot. Cook at 400°F, rearranging the wings twice (ignoring any TURN FOOD indicator), for 15 minutes, or until the wings are crisp and browned. Sauce and garnish the wings as directed.

- Or you can spread the cooked unsauced wings on a lipped baking sheet and broil them 4 to 6 inches from the heating element, turning a couple of times, until crunchy, about 3 minutes. Sauce and garnish the wings as directed.

Other Pots

- For a 3-quart Instant Pot, you *must* halve the amount of wings *but* you *must* keep all of the other ingredient amounts as stated. It will take up to 7 minutes to boil to a glaze in step 5. Stir constantly!

- For an 8-quart Instant Pot, you *must* increase all of the ingredient amounts by 50 percent.

- For a 10-quart Instant Pot, you *must* double all of the ingredient amounts.

Spicy Beer-Glazed Wings

9 ingredients

4–6 SERVINGS

METHOD:
standard

SPECIAL
EQUIPMENT:
none

PRESSURE:
low

TIME UNDER
PRESSURE:
12 minutes

RELEASE:
quick

TOTAL TIME WITH
PRESSURE:
about 20 minutes

CAN BE GLUTEN-
FREE

3 pounds chicken wings, separated into wingettes and drumettes (the flappers discarded or saved for stock)

⅓ cup dark beer, preferably a brown ale; or beef broth

¼ cup Worcestershire sauce (gluten-free, if necessary)

¼ cup bottled smooth chile sauce, such as Heinz

2 tablespoons dark brown sugar

½ teaspoon rubbed or ground sage

½ teaspoon ground dried cayenne

¼ teaspoon celery seeds

Sesame seeds, for garnishing

The mix of dark beer, Worcestershire sauce, and bottled chile sauce, along with a few dried spices, offers the best rendition we can imagine of spicy-sweet flavors from an Instant Pot. As with our other recipe for chicken wings (page 206), this one *must* be done on LOW pressure. The sauce here doesn't need to be boiled down but it is quite spicy. Have lots of napkins on hand because you'll do a fair amount of slurping (given the thinner sauce).

1. Mix the wing parts, beer or broth, Worcestershire sauce, chile sauce, brown sugar, sage, cayenne, and celery seeds in a **5- or 6-quart Instant Pot** until the wings are thoroughly coated. Lock the lid on the pot.

2.

	Set pot for	Set level to	Valve must be	Set time for	If needed, press
For *all* pots	PRESSURE COOK or MANUAL	LOW	Closed	12 minutes with the KEEP WARM setting off	START

3. When the pot has finished cooking, use the **quick-release method** to bring the pressure back to normal. Unlatch the lid and open the cooker. Use kitchen tongs to transfer the wing parts to a big bowl. Pour some or all of the sauce in the pot over them and toss gently but well to coat. Garnish with sesame seeds.

Other Pots

- For a 3-quart Instant Pot, you *must* halve the amount of wings *but* you *must* keep all of the other ingredient amounts as stated. (The sauce will be much thinner for the amount of wings.)

- For an 8-quart Instant Pot, you *must* increase all of the ingredient amounts by 50 percent.

- For a 10-quart Instant Pot, you *must* double all of the ingredient amounts.

Beyond

- For ideas on how to crisp the wings before they're sauced and garnished, see the Beyond to Sesame Chicken Wings on page 206.

- To enrich the sauce, whisk 3 tablespoons crumbled blue cheese into it while it's hot.

- Add thinly sliced scallions along with the sesame seeds for a garnish.

- What's with all the Worcestershire sauce in our recipes? It's a sweet-salty-umami combo that can't be beat! If you really want to go over the top, check out the video of how to make your own Worcestershire on our YouTube channel, Cooking with Bruce and Mark.

Not-Really-P.F.-Chang's Chicken Lettuce Wraps

13 ingredients	
4 SERVINGS	
METHOD: standard	

SPECIAL EQUIPMENT: none	TIME UNDER PRESSURE: 2 minutes	TOTAL TIME WITH PRESSURE: about 15 minutes	
PRESSURE: low	RELEASE: quick	CAN BE GLUTEN-FREE	

4 medium scallions, trimmed

1 tablespoon toasted sesame oil

1 tablespoon minced peeled fresh ginger

2 medium garlic cloves, minced (2 teaspoons)

1 pound ground chicken

¼ cup chicken broth

¼ cup hoisin sauce (gluten-free, if necessary—see page 18 for more information)

2 tablespoons regular or low-sodium soy sauce, or gluten-free tamari sauce

1 tablespoon unseasoned rice vinegar

1 tablespoon light brown sugar

1 tablespoon thin red chile sauce, preferably Sriracha

2 medium celery stalks, diced

Boston lettuce leaves (as many as 12), for wrapping

Other Pots

- For a 3-quart Instant Pot, you *must* halve almost all of the ingredient amounts *except* you *must* keep the broth at ¼ cup.

- For an 8-quart Instant Pot, you *must* increase all of the ingredient amounts by 50 percent.

- For a 10-quart Instant Pot, you *must* double all of the ingredient amounts.

Beyond

- A better balance to the sweet chicken mixture might be radicchio lettuce cups, rather than Boston lettuce.

- Substitute one 8-ounce can of sliced water chestnuts, drained, for the celery.

- Garnish the wraps with more hot sauce, particularly Sriracha.

The first time we tried the original at this popular chain, we knew we had to re-create the sweet, salty, aromatic dish for the Instant Pot. In truth, this copycat recipe is pretty straightforward, except it *must* be cooked on LOW pressure to keep the ground chicken from drying out and to preserve the aromatic flavors. The liquid levels may seem low, but they'll work (only!) with this pressure setting. And here's our little trick: We save the celery until *after* the dish is finished for the sake of more crunch per bite. Note that the celery is diced, not thinly sliced. Slice each stalk lengthwise into halves or even thirds, then cut these spears into ¼- to ½-inch bits.

1. Divide the scallions into the white and green parts. Thinly slice each but keep them separate.

2.

	Press	Set it for	Set time for	If needed, press
In all models	SAUTÉ	HIGH or MORE	5 minutes	START

3. As the pot heats, warm the oil in the insert set in a **5- or 6-quart Instant Pot.** Add the white parts of the scallion, the ginger, and garlic. Stir until very aromatic, about 30 seconds.

4. Crumble in the ground chicken and stir well to break it up into small bits. It should not brown. Stir in the broth, hoisin sauce, soy sauce, vinegar, brown sugar, red chile sauce, and the green parts of the scallions until the brown sugar dissolves and the ground chicken is evenly coated. Turn off the heat and lock the lid on the pot.

5.

	Set pot for	Set level to	Valve must be	Set time for	If needed, press
For *all* pots	PRESSURE COOK or MANUAL	LOW	Closed	2 minutes with the KEEP WARM setting off	START

6. When the pot has finished cooking, use the **quick-release method** to bring the pressure back to normal. Unlatch the lid and open the cooker. Stir in the celery. Set the lid askew over the pot and set it aside for 3 to 5 minutes so the chicken continues to absorb the sauce. Use a big spoon to transfer the chicken mixture to a serving bowl and serve with the lettuce leaves on the side to fill and make wraps.

See photo in insert.

Jerk Chicken and Mango Lettuce Wraps

12 ingredients	
6–8 SERVINGS	

SPECIAL EQUIPMENT: none	
METHOD: standard	**PRESSURE:** low

SPECIAL EQUIPMENT: none

TIME UNDER PRESSURE: 5 minutes

TOTAL TIME WITH PRESSURE: about 30 minutes

METHOD: standard

PRESSURE: low

RELEASE: quick

CAN BE GLUTEN-FREE

---

2 tablespoons peanut or vegetable oil

1 small red onion, chopped (½ cup)

1 small red bell pepper, stemmed, cored, and chopped (½ cup)

1½ tablespoons minced peeled fresh ginger

1½ tablespoons bottled dry jerk seasoning blend

2 pounds ground chicken

½ cup chicken broth

3 tablespoons regular or low-sodium soy sauce, or gluten-free tamari sauce

1 tablespoon honey

2 medium mangos, peeled, pitted, and chopped

¼ cup loosely packed, stemmed, fresh cilantro leaves, finely chopped

Butter lettuce leaves (as many as 24), for wrapping

Jerk chicken makes for a gingery, spicy filling for lettuce wraps, perfect for a warm night. The mango creates the balance here, a sweet finish against the fiery fare. The fruit should be quite ripe, even soft, for an even better contrast. All that said, bottled jerk blends can be unbelievably hot. If you're concerned, find one that doesn't list cayenne as the first ingredient. Or see the *Beyond* section for a way to make your own.

1.

	Press	Set it for	Set time for	If needed, press
In all models	SAUTÉ	MEDIUM, NORMAL, or CUSTOM 300°F	10 minutes	START

2. Warm the oil in the insert set in a **5-, 6-, or 8-quart Instant Pot.** Add the onion and bell pepper. Cook, stirring often, until the onion softens, about 3 minutes. Stir in the ginger and jerk seasoning until aromatic, a few seconds.

3. Crumble in the ground chicken and stir to break it up into little bits. Do not brown. Pour in the broth, soy or tamari sauce, and honey. Scrape up any browned bits on the pot's bottom. Turn off the heat and lock the lid on the pot.

4.

	Set pot for	Set level to	Valve must be	Set time for	If needed, press
For *all* pots	PRESSURE COOK or MANUAL	LOW	Closed	5 minutes with the KEEP WARM setting off	START

5. When the pot has finished cooking, use the **quick-release method** to bring the pressure back to normal. Unlatch the lid and open the cooker. Stir in the mango and cilantro. Set the lid askew over the pot and set it aside for 5 minutes to blend the flavors. Serve warm with the lettuce leaves on the side to fill and make wraps.

Other Pots

- For a **3-quart Instant Pot,** you *must* halve almost all of the ingredient amounts *except* you *must* keep the broth at ½ cup.

- For an **8-quart Instant Pot,** you *can* increase all of the ingredient amounts by 50 percent.

- For a **10-quart Instant Pot,** you *must* double all of the ingredient amounts.

Beyond

- To make your own jerk seasoning blend, mix the following together: 1 tablespoon garlic powder, 2 teaspoons onion powder, 2 teaspoons dried thyme, 2 teaspoons light brown sugar, 2 teaspoons table salt, 1 teaspoon ground dried ginger, 1 teaspoon mild paprika, 1 teaspoon ground allspice, 1 teaspoon ground dried cayenne, ½ teaspoon grated nutmeg, and ½ teaspoon ground cinnamon. Store the blend in a sealed glass jar or small container in a dry, dark place for up to 1 year.

Curried Chicken Meatballs

20 ingredients
4–6 SERVINGS
METHOD: standard

SPECIAL EQUIPMENT: none
PRESSURE: low

TIME UNDER PRESSURE: 10 minutes

RELEASE: quick
TOTAL TIME WITH PRESSURE: about 50 minutes

2 slices white sandwich bread, crusts removed

1 cup low-fat or *light* coconut milk

1½ pounds ground chicken

1 refrigerator-cold large egg, lightly beaten

¼ cup loosely packed, stemmed, fresh cilantro leaves, minced

Up to 1 medium fresh jalapeño chile, stemmed, cored, and minced

2 teaspoons garam masala

1 teaspoon table salt

2 tablespoons butter

1 large yellow or white onion, chopped (1½ cups)

3 medium garlic cloves, minced (1 tablespoon)

1 tablespoon minced peeled fresh ginger

1 teaspoon ground coriander

1 teaspoon ground dried ginger

½ teaspoon ground cinnamon

½ teaspoon ground dried turmeric

Up to ½ teaspoon ground dried cayenne

3 medium Roma or plum tomatoes, chopped (¾ cup)

2 teaspoons granulated white sugar

¾ cup chicken broth

Yes, there are a *lot* of ingredients in this recipe, but we wanted to take one chicken dish over the top to create an authentic curry for light chicken meatballs. The dish *must* be cooked on LOW pressure and you *must* use *light* coconut milk (or as it's sometimes spelled, "lite"—that is, low-fat coconut milk) to keep the sauce from burning.

Garam masala is an aromatic, "warming" spice blend—not fiery but alleged to raise the body's temperature. See the *Beyond* for a recipe to make your own.

1. Soak the bread slices in the coconut milk in a shallow soup plate or pie pan at room temperature for 15 minutes.

2. Over a small bowl, gently squeeze the coconut milk out of the bread, reserving the coconut milk that comes out.

3. Place the wet bread in a large bowl and add the ground chicken, egg, cilantro, jalapeño, garam masala, and ½ teaspoon salt. Mix until uniform (your clean hands work best). Divide the mixture into 12 equal balls. Set aside.

4.

	Press	Set it for	Set time for	If needed, press
In all models	SAUTÉ	MEDIUM, NORMAL, or CUSTOM 300°F	10 minutes	START

5. As the pot heats, melt the butter in the insert set in a **5-, 6-, or 8-quart Instant Pot.** Add the onion and cook, stirring often, until softened, about 4 minutes. Stir in the garlic, fresh ginger, coriander, ground ginger, cinnamon, turmeric, cayenne, and remaining ½ teaspoon salt until fragrant, about 20 seconds.

6. Add the tomatoes and sugar. Cook, stirring frequently, until the tomatoes begin to break down, about 1 minute. Pour in the broth and scrape up any browned bits on the pot's bottom. Turn off the heat.

7. Nestle the meatballs into the sauce. Pour the reserved coconut milk on and around them. Lock the lid on the pot.

8.

	Set pot for	Set level to	Valve must be	Set time for	If needed, press
For *all* pots	PRESSURE COOK or MANUAL	LOW	Closed	10 minutes with the KEEP WARM setting off	START

9. When the pot has finished cooking, use the **quick-release method** to bring the pressure back to normal. Unlatch the lid and open the cooker. Set the lid askew over the pot and set it aside for 2 to 3 minutes so the meatballs continue to absorb more of the sauce. Stir very gently (the meatballs are fragile) and serve warm.

Other Pots

- For a 3-quart Instant Pot, you *must* halve almost all of the ingredient amounts *except* you *must* use ½ cup broth.

- For an 8-quart Instant Pot, you *can* increase all of the ingredient amounts by 50 percent.

- For a 10-quart Instant Pot, you must double almost all of the ingredient amounts *except* you *must* use 2 cups broth.

Beyond

- To make your own garam masala, grind 2 teaspoons fennel seeds in a spice grinder until powdery, then pour this powder into a small bowl and mix it with 1 tablespoon ground coriander, 2 teaspoons ground cumin, 2 teaspoons mild paprika, 1 teaspoon ground cinnamon, 1 teaspoon ground allspice, and ¼ teaspoon grated nutmeg. Store in a sealed, small glass or plastic container in a cool, dry place for up to 1 year.

Chicken Picadillo

14 ingredients

4–6 SERVINGS

METHOD:
fast/standard

SPECIAL
EQUIPMENT:
none

PRESSURE:
max or high

TIME UNDER
PRESSURE:
3 or 5 minutes

RELEASE:
quick

TOTAL TIME
WITH PRESSURE:
about 25 minutes

GLUTEN-FREE

2 tablespoons olive oil

2 medium single-lobe shallots, *minced* (a rounded ⅓ cup)

2 medium garlic cloves, minced (2 teaspoons)

1 teaspoon ground coriander

1 teaspoon ground cumin

1 teaspoon dried oregano

½ teaspoon ground cinnamon

2 pounds ground chicken

1 cup chicken broth

½ cup pitted green olives, chopped

¼ cup golden raisins, chopped

1 tablespoon drained and rinsed capers, finely chopped

3 tablespoons tomato paste

½ cup loosely packed, stemmed, fresh parsley leaves, finely chopped

Other Pots

- For a 3-quart Instant Pot, you *must* halve all of the ingredient amounts.

- For an 8-quart Instant Pot, you *must* increase all of the ingredient amounts by 50 percent.

- For a 10-quart Instant Pot, you *must* double all of the ingredient amounts.

Beyond

- Serve the picadillo in toasted hamburger or hot dog buns with chopped lettuce and jarred (hot or "tamed") pickled jalapeño rings.

- Or serve it as a dip with whole-wheat crackers for a simple meal.

- Or toss it with drained hot ziti or penne.

Picadillo is usually an aromatic ground beef (or maybe pork) mixture, often served over cooked white rice (along with black beans in many Caribbean cultures—see one version of those beans on page 346). This chicken picadillo is then hardly authentic, but it's still quite tasty, thanks to all the spices as well as the sweet-and-salty hit from the raisins paired with olives. It might be a tad too soupy for wraps, unless you dish it up with a slotted spoon. Look for our other serving ideas in this recipe's **Beyond**.

1.

	Press	Set it for	Set time for	If needed, press
In all models	SAUTÉ	MEDIUM, NORMAL, or CUSTOM 300°F	5 minutes	START

2. Warm the oil in the insert set in a **5- or 6-quart Instant Pot.** Add the shallots and garlic. Cook, stirring often, just until aromatic, about 1 minute. Stir in the coriander, cumin, oregano, and cinnamon.

3. Crumble in the ground chicken and stir constantly to break it into small bits and coat these in the spices. Pour in the broth and scrape up any browned bits on the pot's bottom. Stir in the olives, raisins, and capers. Turn off the heat and lock the lid on the pot.

4.

	Set pot for	Set level to	Valve must be	Set time for	If needed, press
For Max pots only	PRESSURE COOK	MAX	—	3 minutes with the KEEP WARM setting off	START
For all other pots	PRESSURE COOK or MANUAL	HIGH	Closed	5 minutes with the KEEP WARM setting off	START

5. When the pot has finished cooking under pressure, use the **quick-release method** to bring the pressure back to normal.

6.

	Press	Set it for	Set time for	If needed, press
In all models	SAUTÉ	MEDIUM, NORMAL, or CUSTOM 300°F	5 minutes	START

7. As the mixture simmers, stir in the tomato paste until dissolved and uniform. Let the sauce bubble for a couple of seconds, stirring almost constantly; then turn off the heat. Use hot pads or silicone baking mitts to transfer the (hot!) insert to a nearby wire rack (to stop the cooking). Stir in the parsley. Let sit for 2 to 3 minutes to blend the flavors and allow the chicken to absorb some more of the sauce. Serve warm.

Cider-Brined Turkey Breast

7 ingredients

6–8 SERVINGS

METHOD:
steam

SPECIAL EQUIPMENT:
a pressure- and food-safe rack or trivet

PRESSURE:
max or high

TIME UNDER PRESSURE:
20 or 25 minutes

RELEASE:
natural

TOTAL TIME WITH PRESSURE:
about 3 hours 15 minutes (with brining)

GLUTEN-FREE

At least 7½ cups water

2 cups unsweetened apple juice or apple cider

½ cup packed light brown sugar

3 medium garlic cloves, minced (1 tablespoon)

½ cup kosher salt

One 4- to 4½-pound bone-in skin-on turkey breast

2 tablespoons dried poultry seasoning blend

Other Pots

- Because of the size of turkey breasts, this recipe will not work in a 3-quart Instant Pot.

- For a 10-quart Instant Pot, you *must* increase the amount of water in the insert to 2½ cups in step 3 while otherwise completing the recipe as stated.

Beyond

- The best part of a turkey is the crisp skin, right? To deliver on that promise (and only in a 6- or 8-quart pot), complete the recipe as written, then clean out the insert and return it to the pot. Set the air-fryer basket in the pot, add the turkey breast, and set the Instant Pot Air Fryer Lid over the pot. Air-fry at 400°F for about 10 minutes (ignoring any TURN FOOD indicator) to crisp the skin.

This recipe calls for brining the turkey breast right in the pot's insert. Doing so will yield moister, more flavorful meat, great either as the main course at a supper with sides and a salad or even just sliced for turkey sandwiches (particularly turkey clubs!). But you must *not* brine a kosher turkey breast (which is already salted) or a turkey breast that has been injected with a saline solution—read the label to be sure. You'll most likely need a turkey breast labeled "natural" or even an "organic," although there are standard turkey breasts that have not been injected.

1. Stir 6 cups water, the apple juice or cider, brown sugar, garlic, and salt in the insert to a **5-, 6-, or 8-quart Instant Pot.** Set the turkey breast in the insert, then add more water as needed until the meat is submerged under at least 2 inches of water. Cover the insert and set it in the fridge for 2 hours.

2. Drain the liquid out of the insert. Remove the turkey. Rub the poultry seasoning all across the exposed surfaces of the meat.

3. Wipe the insert clean and return it to the pot. Pour the remaining 1½ cups water into the insert. Set a pressure- and food-safe rack or trivet in the insert. Set the turkey skin side up on the rack and lock the lid onto the cooker.

4.

	Set pot for	Set level to	Valve must be	Set time for	If needed, press
For Max pots only	PRESSURE COOK	MAX	—	20 minutes with the KEEP WARM setting off	START
For all other pots	PRESSURE COOK or MANUAL	HIGH	Closed	25 minutes with the KEEP WARM setting off	START

5. When the pot has finished cooking, turn it off and let its pressure **return to normal naturally,** about 25 minutes. Unlatch the lid and open the cooker. Use kitchen tongs *and* a large metal spatula to transfer the turkey breast to a cutting board. Cool for 10 minutes before carving.

Bacony Turkey Thigh and Potato Dinner

11 ingredients	SPECIAL EQUIPMENT: none
4 SERVINGS	
METHOD: standard	PRESSURE: max or high

TIME UNDER PRESSURE: 30 or 40 minutes	TOTAL TIME WITH PRESSURE: about 1½ hours
RELEASE: natural	CAN BE GLUTEN-FREE

4 thick-cut slices of bacon (gluten-free, if necessary), chopped

Two 1¼- to 1½-pound bone-in skin-on turkey thighs

1 medium yellow or white onion, chopped (1 cup)

2 medium carrots, peeled and thinly sliced (1 cup)

3 medium celery stalks, thinly sliced (1 cup)

1 teaspoon dried oregano

1 teaspoon dried sage

¼ teaspoon ground allspice

1½ cups chicken broth

1 tablespoon light brown sugar

Four 6- to 8-ounce Yukon Gold potatoes, each poked with a fork in a few places

Other Pots

- For a 3-quart Instant Pot, you *must* halve all of the ingredient amounts.
- For an 8-quart Instant Pot, you *can* increase all of the ingredient amounts by 50 percent.
- For a 10-quart Instant Pot, you *must* increase all of the ingredient amounts by 50 percent or you *can* even double the amounts.

Beyond

- For a richer dish, melt up to 1 tablespoon butter in the insert before you brown the bacon, then add another 2 tablespoons butter before you add the onion and other vegetables.
- For a more sophisticated flavor, substitute 1½ cups hard apple cider for both the chicken broth and the brown sugar.

By setting potatoes on the turkey thighs, we end up with fluffy spuds steamed under pressure (rather than squishier spuds braised in a sauce). You may not be able to perfectly balance the potatoes on the meat. Close enough counts, even if some fall a bit into the liquid below.

1.

	Press	Set it for	Set time for	If needed, press
In all models	SAUTÉ	MEDIUM, NORMAL, or CUSTOM 300°F	10 minutes	START

2. As the pot heats, add the bacon to the insert in a **5-, 6-, or 8-quart Instant Pot.** Cook, stirring often, until quite crisp, about 4 minutes. Use a slotted spoon to transfer the bacon to a nearby large bowl.

3. Put the turkey thighs skin side down in the insert and brown well without disturbing, about 5 minutes. Turn them over and lightly brown the other side, about 3 minutes. Transfer the thighs to the bowl with the bacon.

4. Add the onion, carrots, and celery to the pot. Cook, stirring often, until the onion softens, about 3 minutes. Stir in the oregano, sage, and allspice until fragrant, just a few seconds. Pour in the broth and scrape up all the browned bits on the pot's bottom.

5. Stir in the brown sugar until dissolved. Turn off the heat and return the turkey thighs skin side up to the pot. Also add the bacon and any juices in the bowl. Set the potatoes on top of the turkey thighs without stirring them into the sauce. Lock the lid onto the cooker.

6.

	Set pot for	Set level to	Valve must be	Set time for	If needed, press
For Max pots only	PRESSURE COOK	MAX	—	30 minutes with the KEEP WARM setting off	START
For all other pots	PRESSURE COOK or MANUAL	HIGH	Closed	40 minutes with the KEEP WARM setting off	START

7. When the pot has finished cooking, turn it off and let the pressure **return to normal naturally,** about 35 minutes. Unlatch the lid and open the cooker. Set the lid askew over the pot and set it aside for a few minutes so the meat continues to absorb some of the sauce. Use kitchen tongs to transfer the turkey thighs to a cutting board; slice each into half or large chunks. Serve in bowls with the potatoes and some of the pot sauce ladled on top.

Turkey Tacos with Red Cabbage–Lime Slaw

21 ingredients	
6 SERVINGS	
METHOD: standard	

SPECIAL EQUIPMENT: none	
PRESSURE: low	

TIME UNDER PRESSURE: 4 minutes	
RELEASE: quick	

TOTAL TIME WITH PRESSURE: about 30 minutes	
CAN BE GLUTEN-FREE	

⅓ cup lime juice

¼ cup olive oil

1½ tablespoons honey

1½ teaspoons table salt

½ teaspoon red pepper flakes

3 cups shredded cored red cabbage (about half a medium head)

1 cup shredded peeled jicama (through the holes of a box grater—about half a medium jicama)

2 tablespoons vegetable, canola, or other neutral-flavored oil

2 pounds lean ground turkey

¼ cup packed light brown sugar

2 tablespoons mild paprika

1 tablespoon standard chili powder

2 teaspoons dried oregano

1 teaspoon dried thyme

1 teaspoon ground cumin

1 teaspoon garlic powder

1 teaspoon onion powder

1 teaspoon ground black pepper

2 bay leaves

1 cup chicken broth

Flour or corn tortillas (gluten-free, if necessary), for serving

Other Pots

- For a 3-quart Instant Pot, you *must* halve all of the ingredient amounts.

- For an 8-quart Instant Pot, you *can* increase all of the ingredient amounts by 50 percent.

- For a 10-quart Instant Pot, you *must* double all of the ingredient amounts.

We love a vinegary slaw in tacos, even better than the more standard shredded cheese and lettuce. With a light turkey filling, these tacos have a bright, almost summer flavor, not quite as heavy as the standard but just as satisfying.

Once again, by using LOW pressure we can keep the liquid level in the turkey filling to a minimum without worrying about the pot's BURN notice. Admittedly, this recipe has a long ingredient list. You can certainly serve the tacos with purchased coleslaw, although we think a vinegary slaw (rather than a creamy one) works best with the filling.

1. Whisk the lime juice, olive oil, honey, ½ teaspoon salt, and red pepper flakes in a large bowl until uniform. Add the cabbage and jicama. Toss well and set the slaw aside.

2.

	Press	Set it for	Set time for	If needed, press
In all models	SAUTÉ	MEDIUM, NORMAL, or CUSTOM 300°F	10 minutes	START

3. As the pot heats, warm the vegetable oil in the insert set in a **5-, 6-, or 8-quart Instant Pot.** Crumble in the ground turkey and cook, stirring constantly to break up the clumps, until it loses its raw, pink color.

4. Stir in the brown sugar, paprika, chili powder, oregano, thyme, cumin, garlic powder, onion powder, pepper, bay leaves, and the remaining 1 teaspoon salt until fragrant, just a few seconds. Pour in the broth and scrape up any browned bits on the pot's bottom. Turn off the heat and lock the lid on the pot.

5.

	Set pot for	Set level to	Valve must be	Set time for	If needed, press
For *all* pots	PRESSURE COOK or MANUAL	LOW	Closed	4 minutes with the KEEP WARM setting off	START

6. When the pot has finished cooking, use the **quick-release method** to bring the pressure back to normal. Unlatch the lid and open the cooker. Fish out and discard the bay leaves, then stir well. Use a slotted spoon to get some of the turkey mixture into the flour tortillas; top each with the slaw before serving.

Beyond

- Garnish the tacos with sliced pitted black olives and/or sour cream.

Cheesy-Spicy Turkey Casserole

17 ingredients	**SPECIAL EQUIPMENT:** none
4–6 SERVINGS	**PRESSURE:** high
METHOD: fast/slow	

TIME UNDER PRESSURE: 4 minutes	**TOTAL TIME WITH PRESSURE:** about 25 minutes	**TOTAL TIME WITH SLOW COOKING:** about 2 hours 20 minutes
RELEASE: quick		**CAN BE GLUTEN-FREE**

1 tablespoon olive oil

1 medium yellow or white onion, chopped (1 cup)

1 pound lean ground turkey

2 medium garlic cloves, minced (2 teaspoons)

One 4½-ounce can hot or mild diced green chiles (½ cup)

2 teaspoons ground cumin

2 teaspoons mild smoked paprika

½ teaspoon table salt

½ teaspoon ground black pepper

2 cups riced cauliflower (8 ounces)

1½ cups red salsa (any variety)

One 10-ounce can hot or mild diced tomatoes and green chiles, such as Rotel (1¼ cups)

1 cup *canned* pinto beans, drained and rinsed

1 cup fresh or frozen corn kernels (if frozen, no need to thaw)

½ cup chicken broth

¼ cup loosely packed, stemmed, fresh cilantro leaves, finely chopped

4 ounces Monterey Jack cheese, shredded (1 cup)

Other Pots

- For a **3-quart Instant Pot, you *must*** halve almost all of the ingredient amounts *except* you *must* use ½ cup broth (the original amount).
- For an **8-quart Instant Pot, you *can*** increase all of the ingredient amounts by 50 percent.
- For a **10-quart Instant Pot, you *must*** double all of the ingredient amounts.

We've swapped out the rice of classic turkey casserole in favor of riced cauliflower because we wanted a little lower carb load per serving (even with all those beans and the corn). The riced cauliflower also isn't quite as binding, so the casserole feels lighter all around. It's an ideal weeknight dinner.

1.

	Press	Set it for	Set time for	If needed, press
In all models	SAUTÉ	MEDIUM, NORMAL, or CUSTOM 300°F	10 minutes	START

2. As the pot heats, warm the oil in the insert set in a **5-, 6-, or 8-quart Instant Pot.** Add the onion and cook, stirring often, until softened, about 3 minutes.

3. Crumble in the ground turkey and garlic. Continue cooking, stirring more frequently to break up any clumps, until the meat loses its raw, pink color, about 2 minutes.

4. Stir in the canned chiles, cumin, smoked paprika, salt, and pepper until aromatic, just a few seconds. Stir in the riced cauliflower, salsa, canned tomatoes and chiles, the pinto beans, corn, broth, and cilantro until uniform. Turn off the heat and lock the lid on the pot.

5.

	Set pot for	Set level to	Valve must be	Set time for	If needed, press
For *all* pots	PRESSURE COOK or MANUAL	HIGH	Closed	4 minutes with the KEEP WARM setting off	START
For the slow-cook function	SLOW COOK	HIGH	Open	2 hours with the KEEP WARM setting off	START

6. When the pot has finished cooking under pressure, use the **quick-release method** to bring the pressure back to normal. Whichever cooking method you've used, unlatch the lid and open the cooker. Stir in the cheese, then set the lid askew over the pot and set it aside for 3 to 5 minutes to melt the cheese and blend the flavors. Stir well before serving warm.

Beyond

- You can serve this casserole in Boston or butter lettuce leaves, folded around the filling to make wraps.

Super-Easy Italian Turkey Meatballs in Cream Sauce

9 ingredients

4 SERVINGS

METHOD:
pot-in-pot

SPECIAL EQUIPMENT:
a 1-quart, 6-inch-round, high-sided, pressure-safe baking or soufflé dish and two pressure-safe racks or trivets (one food-safe as well)

PRESSURE:
high

TIME UNDER PRESSURE:
1 minute

RELEASE:
quick

TOTAL TIME WITH PRESSURE:
about 20 minutes

1½ cups water

¾ cup whole, low-fat, or fat-free milk

½ cup jarred alfredo sauce

1½ tablespoons Worcestershire sauce

1 tablespoon all-purpose flour

¼ teaspoon ground allspice

¼ teaspoon grated nutmeg

¼ teaspoon ground black pepper

1 pound purchased frozen cooked "dinner size" turkey meatballs (1 ounce each), thawed

Other Pots

- Because of the height of the double-stacked racks in this recipe, it won't work in a 3-quart Instant Pot.

- For a 10-quart Instant Pot, you *must* increase the amount of water in the insert to 2½ cups while otherwise completing the recipe as stated.

Beyond

- Serve the meatballs and sauce over cooked and drained spaghetti, ziti, or farfalle.

- Or skip the pasta and make cucumber noodles: Peel one or two *room-temperature* English cucumbers, then use a vegetable peeler to make long strips down the cucumbers (that is, the "noodles), working your way around the vegetable until you get to the seedy core. If you really want to go all out, toss these "noodles" with a little olive oil and a dried Italian seasoning blend.

This super-tasty recipe offers a shortcut way to make an easy Italian meatball dish: Use store-bought meatballs and sauce to cut down on prep time. It also requires you to use two racks: one for the baking dish and one for the meatballs. The first rack should be whatever you've been using all along in these recipes, whether a silicon rack with handles or the wire rack that comes with an Instant Pot. However, the second rack, for the meatballs, should be a small, *food-safe* wire rack to rest on top of the baking dish. It should not seal the baking dish below. The point is to let the meatballs steam over the sauce so the whole dish cooks at once.

1. Pour the water into the insert set in a **5-, 6-, or 8-quart Instant Pot.** Put a pressure-safe rack or trivet in the insert.

2. Whisk the milk, alfredo sauce, Worcestershire sauce, flour, allspice, nutmeg, and pepper in a 1-quart, 6-inch-round, high-sided, pressure-safe baking or soufflé dish until smooth. Do not cover. Set the dish on the rack.

3. Set a second, smaller, food-safe wire rack on top of the baking dish. Put the meatballs on this second rack (spread them out—but If they have to stack a bit, so be it). Lock the lid on the pot.

4.

	Set pot for	Set level to	Valve must be	Set time for	If needed, press
For *all* pots	PRESSURE COOK or MANUAL	HIGH	Closed	1 minute with the KEEP WARM setting off	START

5. When the pot has finished cooking, use the **quick-release method** to bring the pressure back to normal. Unlatch the lid and open the cooker.

6. Use kitchen tongs to gently transfer the meatballs to a serving bowl. Remove the (hot!) upper rack and whisk the sauce in the baking dish below until smooth. Use hot pads or silicone baking mitts to lift this (hot!) dish out of the pot. Pour the sauce over the meatballs and toss gently before serving.

Real-Deal Turkey Meatballs in Tomatoes and Cream

15 ingredients

4 SERVINGS

METHOD:
fast/slow

SPECIAL EQUIPMENT:
none

PRESSURE:
max or high

TIME UNDER PRESSURE:
7 or 9 minutes

RELEASE:
quick

TOTAL TIME WITH PRESSURE:
about 30 minutes

TOTAL TIME WITH SLOW COOKING:
about 2½ hours

---

1 pound lean ground turkey

1 refrigerator-cold large egg, lightly beaten

½ cup Italian-style seasoned panko bread crumbs

½ ounce Parmigiano-Reggiano, finely grated (¼ cup)

½ teaspoon table salt

½ teaspoon ground black pepper

¼ teaspoon grated nutmeg

2 tablespoons butter

1 medium yellow or white onion, chopped (1 cup)

2 medium celery stalks, thinly sliced (⅔ cup)

⅔ cup chicken broth

One 28-ounce can diced tomatoes *packed in juice* (3½ cups)

2 teaspoons dried oregano

2 teaspoons rubbed or ground sage

¼ cup heavy or light cream

Here's a recipe for turkey meatballs that's more authentic than our shortcut version on page 217. In this one, you'll make seasoned meatballs with bread crumbs, then cook them in a spiced tomato sauce that's enriched with cream just before serving. The dish's success hinges on those canned tomatoes. There are lots of inferior varieties on the market. Look for Italian plum tomatoes with a sharp-sweet flavor. (Just make sure they're packed in *juice,* not puree.)

1. Mix the ground turkey, egg, bread crumbs, cheese, salt, pepper, and nutmeg in a large bowl until the bread crumbs and cheese are evenly distributed and the mixture is uniform. Form into 12 equal balls, each about the size of a golf ball.

2.

	Press	Set it for	Set time for	If needed, press
In all models	SAUTÉ	MEDIUM, NORMAL, or CUSTOM 300°F	5 minutes	START

3. As the pot heats, melt the butter in the insert set in a **5-, 6-, or 8-quart Instant Pot.** Add the onion and celery; cook, stirring often, until the onion softens, about 3 minutes.

4. Pour in the broth and scrape up the very few browned bits on the pot's bottom. Stir in the tomatoes and their juice, the oregano, and sage. Turn off the heat and nestle the meatballs into the sauce. Lock the lid on the pot.

5.

	Set pot for	Set level to	Valve must be	Set time for	If needed, press
For Max pots only	PRESSURE COOK	MAX	—	7 minutes with the KEEP WARM setting off	START
For all other pots	PRESSURE COOK or MANUAL	HIGH	Closed	9 minutes with the KEEP WARM setting off	START
For the slow-cook function	SLOW COOK	HIGH	Open	2 hours with the KEEP WARM setting off	START

6. When the pot has finished cooking under pressure, use the **quick-release method** to bring the pressure back to normal. Whichever cooking method you've used, unlatch the lid and open the cooker.

7.

	Press	Set it for	Set time for	If needed, press
In all models	SAUTÉ	MEDIUM, NORMAL, or CUSTOM 300°F	10 minutes	START

8. As the sauce comes to a bubble, gently stir in the cream (the meatballs are fragile). Cook for 1 minute, stirring very gently. Turn off the heat and use hot pads or silicone baking mitts to transfer the (hot!) insert to a nearby wire rack. Cool for 2 to 3 minutes but serve warm.

Other Pots

- For a 3-quart Instant Pot, you *must* halve almost all of the ingredient amounts, *except* you *must* use ½ cup broth.

- For an 8-quart Instant Pot, you *can* increase all of the ingredient amounts by 50 percent.

- For a 10-quart Instant Pot, you *must* double all of the ingredient amounts.

Beyond

- If you like penne alla vodka, use ⅓ cup broth and ⅓ cup vodka instead of all broth.

- Serve the meatballs and sauce over cooked penne.

- Garnish the servings with finely chopped fresh parsley and/or oregano leaves.

Thanksgiving Turkey Meat Loaf

9 ingredients

6 SERVINGS

METHOD:
pot-in-pot

SPECIAL EQUIPMENT:
a 7-inch-round springform pan and a pressure-safe rack or trivet

PRESSURE:
max or high

TIME UNDER PRESSURE:
25 or 30 minutes

RELEASE:
natural

TOTAL TIME WITH PRESSURE:
about 1 hour

1½ cups water

Nonstick spray

1½ pounds lean ground turkey

2½ ounces (1¼ cups) seasoned *crumb-style* stuffing mix

¼ cup minced yellow or white onion (about half a small onion)

1 medium celery stalk, *minced* (about ¼ cup)

1 refrigerator-cold large egg, lightly beaten

2 tablespoons whole-berry cranberry sauce, plus more for garnishing

1 teaspoon mild paprika

Other Pots

- Because of the size of the pan and the ingredient ratios, this recipe cannot be easily sized for a 3-quart Instant Pot.

- For a 10-quart Instant Pot, you *must* increase the amount of water in the insert to 2½ cups while otherwise completing the recipe as stated.

Beyond

- Serve the meat loaf with Leek and Buttermilk Mashed Potatoes (page 349) or Scalloped Potatoes (page 350).

- The loaf makes exceptionally good meat loaf sandwiches. Cool the meat loaf to room temperature, then cover it with plastic wrap and chill in the fridge at least overnight or for up to 3 days. Cut thin pie-like wedges to pile onto toasted rye bread with lots of deli mustard.

Seasoned stuffing mix is the perfect hack for a turkey meat loaf. The mix absorbs liquid more readily than plain dried bread crumbs, thus keeping the meat loaf from drying out or (worse yet) getting gummy. Opt for the crumb-style stuffing mix, not the cubes. You'll notice that there's no salt in this recipe because the seasoned stuffing has plenty.

1. Pour the water into the insert set in a **5-, 6-, or 8-quart Instant Pot**. Set a pressure-safe rack or trivet in the insert. Generously spray the inside of a 7-inch-round springform pan with nonstick spray.

2. Mix the ground turkey, ¾ cup of the stuffing mix, the onion, celery, egg, and cranberry sauce in a large bowl until well blended and uniform. Press this mixture into the prepared pan, smoothing it to a cake batter–like evenness.

3. Mix the remaining ½ cup stuffing mix and paprika in a small bowl. Sprinkle this over the top of the "loaf" in the pan. Do not cover the pan. Set it on the rack and lock the lid on the pot.

4.

	Set pot for	Set level to	Valve must be	Set time for	If needed, press
For Max pots only	PRESSURE COOK	MAX	—	25 minutes with the KEEP WARM setting off	START
For all other pots	PRESSURE COOK or MANUAL	HIGH	Closed	30 minutes with the KEEP WARM setting off	START

5. When the pot has finished cooking, turn it off and let the pressure **return to normal naturally,** about 20 minutes. Unlatch the lid and open the cooker.

6. Use hot pads or silicone baking mitts to transfer the (hot!) springform pan to a nearby wire rack. Take extra caution: Hot juices may lap over the sides of the pan or may leak from the bottom. Consider placing a kitchen towel under that rack to catch any drips. Cool for 5 minutes, then unlatch the pan's ring side. Cut the meat loaf into pie-like wedges to serve warm with additional cranberry sauce as a garnish.

World's Easiest Shepherd's Pie

17 ingredients	**SPECIAL EQUIPMENT:** none
4–6 SERVINGS	
METHOD: standard	**PRESSURE:** low

TIME UNDER PRESSURE: 5 minutes	**TOTAL TIME WITH PRESSURE:** about 30 minutes
RELEASE: quick	**CAN BE GLUTEN-FREE**

1⅓ cups instant mashed potato flakes

1 cup whole, low-fat, or fat-free milk

¾ cup water

2 tablespoons butter, melted and cooled

1¼ teaspoons table salt

1 tablespoon olive oil

1 small yellow or white onion, chopped (½ cup)

2 medium celery stalks, thinly sliced (⅔ cup)

1½ pounds lean ground turkey

2 tablespoons Worcestershire sauce (gluten-free, if necessary)

1 tablespoon Dijon mustard (gluten-free, if necessary)

½ teaspoon rubbed or ground sage

½ teaspoon dried thyme

½ teaspoon ground black pepper

½ cup chicken broth

1 cup fresh shelled peas, or thawed frozen peas

½ teaspoon mild paprika

Other Pots

- For a 3-quart Instant Pot, you *must* halve almost all of the ingredient amounts *except* you *must* use ½ cup broth (the original amount).

- For an 8-quart Instant Pot, you *must* increase all of the ingredient amounts by 50 percent.

- For a 10-quart Instant Pot, you *must* double all of the ingredient amounts.

Beyond

- Make the dish richer by substituting half-and-half or even light cream for the milk in the potato flake mixture.

How can a recipe with seventeen ingredients be considered "the world's easiest"? One, because this shepherd's pie uses instant mashed potato flakes for a rich topping, so there's no need to make mashed potatoes. Two, because it's cooked on LOW pressure, we can get away with less liquid and not swamp the pot so much that we later have to boil down the liquid. And three, because we don't call for any special baking dishes. The shepherd's pie is baked right in the pot's insert. In other words, once you assemble this dish, there's not much else to do.

1. Stir the instant mashed potatoes, milk, water, butter, and 1 teaspoon salt in a medium bowl until smooth. Set aside.

2.

	Press	Set it for	Set time for	If needed, press
In all models	SAUTÉ	MEDIUM, NORMAL, or CUSTOM 300°F	10 minutes	START

3. Warm the oil in the insert set in a **5- or 6-quart Instant Pot**. Add the onion and celery; cook, stirring often, until the onion softens, about 3 minutes. Crumble in the ground turkey and cook, stirring to break it up into small pieces, until very lightly browned, about 2 minutes.

4. Stir in the Worcestershire sauce, mustard, sage, thyme, pepper, and remaining ¼ teaspoon salt until fragrant, just a few seconds. Pour in the broth and scrape up any browned bits on the pot's bottom. Turn off the heat and stir in the peas.

5. Smooth the turkey mixture into a fairly even layer in the insert, then spread the potato mixture evenly on top. Sprinkle with paprika and lock the lid on the pot.

6.

	Set pot for	Set level to	Valve must be	Set time for	If needed, press
For *all* pots	PRESSURE COOK or MANUAL	LOW	Closed	5 minutes with the KEEP WARM setting off	START

7. When the pot has finished cooking, use the **quick-release method** to bring the pressure back to normal. Unlatch the lid and open the cooker. Set aside to cool for a couple of minutes, then scoop up by the big spoonful.

Beef, Pork, & Lamb

Chuck roasts, beef briskets, pork butts, veal shoulders: These cuts are big and tasty, a little fatty or a bit tough without a proper braise. They were probably the reason your grandmother owned a stovetop pressure cooker. And given the popularity of Mississippi pot roast and pulled pork nowadays, these cuts may be why you bought an Instant Pot, too. Unfortunately, these cuts are no longer very economical because demand has grown, partly as a result of the speedy way the IP cooks, as well as the rise of local barbecue joints and just the tidal forces in culture that seem to wax and wane over the decades. You could go into debt over a 5-pound beef brisket.

All that is why nearly a third of this chapter's recipes call for an ingredient we used to avoid in pressure cooking: ground beef. We've come to see that pressure readily blends all sorts of spices and seasonings with ground beef (which probably explains the popularity of chili from the pot). Because of the way pressure mutes bitter and spicy notes, the pot also balances the flavors in a ground beef stew better than a stovetop simmer does.

As we've said before, use lean ground beef. In fact, use lean everything. Even chuck roasts and pork butts should get a trim. No, you don't have to cut off every speck of fat. It's flavor, after all. But you should take off the large globs. The fat has nowhere to go in a sealed pot, no way to condense to become more flavorful. Trim for better results.

In this chapter, we use the LOW pressure setting a fair amount. It helps keep a stew or a braise from needing excess liquid and turning into a soup. Even so, you might be surprised at the liquid levels in some of these recipes. "Where's the required 1½ cups for an 8-quart?" you might ask. Don't forget: It's partially in the ingredients. Meat gives off a lot of internal liquid under pressure. Vegetables, too. Everything rendered and leached counts toward the volume of liquid that brings on the necessary steam to create pressure (and avoid the BURN notice).

And one more thing, we need to clarify something about grass-fed and (more importantly) grass-*finished* beef, pork, and lamb. These cuts require a little more finesse because they are generally so much leaner. Don't trim them unless you see a significant excess of fat. They even have less interstitial fat, so they can be tougher. They may need additional time under pressure. We often figure about 10 percent more time for grass-finished short ribs or briskets. Finally, because the cuts do not have as much internal moisture to throw off and create steam, we also use about 15 to 20 percent more liquid in any given recipe. For every 1 cup of broth or wine, that's an extra 2 or 3 tablespoons.

On to the chapter itself! We start with some super-easy ground beef recipes that get a little more challenging as they roll along. We next turn to bigger cuts of beef, mostly chuck, round, and tri tip, with some brisket and short ribs thrown in for good measure. We then do the same for pork: Start simple and get crazier. And we end up with six recipes for lamb, not often used in a pressure cooker (for reasons we still don't understand).

Our grandmothers led the way to a pressure-cooking revolution with delicious pot roasts and beef stews. Let's extend the range for the next generation!

Not-Really-Taco-Bell's Taco Meat

13 ingredients

6–8 SERVINGS

METHOD:
standard

SPECIAL EQUIPMENT:
none

PRESSURE:
low

TIME UNDER PRESSURE:
6 minutes

RELEASE:
natural

TOTAL TIME WITH PRESSURE:
about 30 minutes

CAN BE GLUTEN-FREE

2 tablespoons vegetable, canola, or other neutral-flavored oil

2 pounds lean ground beef, preferably 90 percent lean or more

2 beef bouillon cubes (gluten-free, if necessary), crumbled

2 tablespoons dehydrated onion flakes

1½ tablespoons standard chili powder

2 teaspoons unsweetened cocoa powder (do *not* use a powdered cocoa mix)

2 teaspoons garlic powder

2 teaspoons mild smoked paprika

2 teaspoons granulated white sugar

1 teaspoon onion powder

½ teaspoon ground dried cayenne

¼ cup raw steel-cut oats (certified gluten-free, if necessary—do *not* use standard rolled or quick-cooking oats)

¾ cup water

If you read the ingredients in Taco Bell's taco meat, there's cocoa powder (as here) and smoky flavorings (so the smoked paprika here). But there's also an "oat isolate" which undoubtedly thickens the mixture to give it that characteristic, smooth consistency. We can match that with steel-cut oats, which absorb much of the excess liquid, especially during the natural release, to give the meat its much-beloved texture.

Many copycat recipes are also soupy and require thickening afterwards (or worse yet, draining, which removes much of the aromatic flavor you worked to get into the dish in the first place). We solve the soupiness with LOW pressure which requires much less liquid.

1.

	Press	Set it for	Set time for	If needed, press
In all models	SAUTÉ	MEDIUM, NORMAL, or CUSTOM 300°F	10 minutes	START

2. As the pot heats, warm the oil in the insert set in a **5- or 6-quart Instant Pot.** Crumble in the ground beef and cook, stirring often, until lightly browned, about 5 minutes.

3. Stir in the crumbled bouillon cubes, onion flakes, chili powder, cocoa powder, garlic powder, smoked paprika, sugar, onion powder, and cayenne until fragrant, about 30 seconds. Add the steel-cut oats and stir well. Pour in the water and scrape up any browned bits on the pot's bottom. Turn off the heat and lock the lid on the pot.

4.

	Set pot for	Set level to	Valve must be	Set time for	If needed, press
For *all* pots	PRESSURE COOK or MANUAL	LOW	Closed	6 minutes with the KEEP WARM setting off	START

5. When the pot has finished cooking, turn it off and let the pressure **return to normal naturally,** about 15 minutes. Unlatch the lid and open the cooker. Stir well and set aside for a couple of minutes so the meat continues to absorb the sauce.

Other Pots

- For a 3-quart Instant Pot, you *must* halve all of the ingredient amounts.

- For an 8-quart Instant Pot, you *must* increase all of the ingredient amounts by 50 percent.

- For a 10-quart Instant Pot, you *must* double all of the ingredient amounts.

Beyond

- Serve the taco meat in taco shells with diced tomatoes, shredded iceberg lettuce, and/or shredded Monterey Jack cheese.

- To make a copycat version of Taco Bell's quesadilla sauce for tacos, whisk these ingredients in a medium bowl until uniform: ⅔ cup regular or low-fat mayonnaise (gluten-free, if necessary), ⅔ cup regular or low-fat sour cream (gluten-free, if necessary), ¼ cup minced jarred (hot or "tamed") pickled jalapeño rings, ¼ cup brine from the jar of pickled jalapeños, 1 tablespoon mild paprika, 1 tablespoon ground cumin, 1½ teaspoons onion powder, ½ teaspoon garlic powder, and ½ teaspoon standard chili powder. Store any leftovers in a covered bowl in the refrigerator for up to 3 days.

See photo in insert.

Sloppy Joe Subs

12 ingredients

6 SANDWICHES

METHOD:
fast/slow

SPECIAL EQUIPMENT:
none

PRESSURE:
low

TIME UNDER PRESSURE:
6 minutes

RELEASE:
natural

TOTAL TIME WITH PRESSURE:
about 40 minutes

TOTAL TIME WITH SLOW COOKING:
about 2 hours 45 minutes

2 tablespoons olive oil

1½ pounds lean ground beef, preferably 90 percent lean or more

One 4½-ounce can hot or mild diced green chiles (½ cup)

One 2-ounce jar diced pimientos (with their juice, about 2 tablespoons)

3 tablespoons standard chili powder

2 tablespoons dark brown sugar

2 tablespoons Worcestershire sauce

1 teaspoon ground cumin

1 teaspoon dried thyme

¾ cup brown ale or beef broth

3 tablespoons tomato paste

6 hoagie buns

Other Pots

- For a 3-quart Instant Pot, you *must* halve all of the ingredient amounts.

- For an 8-quart Instant Pot, you *must* increase all of the ingredient amounts by 50 percent.

- For a 10-quart Instant Pot, you *must* double almost all of the ingredient amounts—*except* if using a brown ale, you *should* use ¾ cup brown ale *plus* ¾ cup beef broth (to keep the mixture from being too sweet).

Beyond

- For a somewhat less sweet filling, substitute ketchup for the brown sugar.

- Don't stop with just the sloppy joe filling in the buns. Add chopped iceberg lettuce, chopped tomatoes, and/or pickle relish.

- To go over the top, smear a little butter and/or Dijon mustard in the buns before adding the filling and any garnishes.

Imagine crossing Tex-Mex chili with a sloppy joe filling. This flavorful mixture is thick and rich, best in buns—although you could just pile it on top of cooked white rice and pile some jarred salsa or pickled jalapeño rings on top.

1.

	Press	Set it for	Set time for	If needed, press
In all models	SAUTÉ	MEDIUM, NORMAL, or CUSTOM 300°F	5 minutes	START

2. As the pot heats, warm the oil in the insert set in a **5- or 6-quart Instant Pot.** Crumble in the beef and cook, stirring often to break up any clumps, until very lightly browned, about 3 minutes.

3. Stir in the chiles, pimientos and their juice, the chili powder, brown sugar, Worcestershire sauce, cumin, and thyme until aromatic, just a few seconds. Pour in the ale or broth and scrape up any browned bits on the pot's bottom. Turn off the heat and lock the lid onto the cooker.

4.

	Set pot for	Set level to	Valve must be	Set time for	If needed, press
For *all* pots	PRESSURE COOK or MANUAL	LOW	Closed	6 minutes with the KEEP WARM setting off	START
For the slow-cook function	SLOW COOK	HIGH	Open	2½ hours with the KEEP WARM setting off	START

5. When the pot has finished cooking under pressure, turn it off and let the pressure **return to normal naturally,** about 15 minutes. Whichever cooking method you've used, unlatch the lid and open the cooker.

6.

	Press	Set it for	Set time for	If needed, press
In all models	SAUTÉ	MEDIUM, NORMAL, or CUSTOM 300°F	5 minutes	START

7. As the beef mixture comes to a bubble, stir in the tomato paste. Continue cooking, stirring almost constantly, until somewhat thickened, about 2 minutes. Turn off the heat, set the lid askew over the pot, and set the pot aside to cool for 10 minutes, stirring once in a while. Serve in the hoagie buns with plenty of napkins.

Chimichurri Ground Beef Sandwiches

14 ingredients	
6 SANDWICHES	

SPECIAL EQUIPMENT: none

METHOD: fast/slow

PRESSURE: low

TIME UNDER PRESSURE: 6 minutes

RELEASE: quick

TOTAL TIME WITH PRESSURE: about 35 minutes

TOTAL TIME WITH SLOW COOKING: about 2½ hours

---

6 tablespoons olive oil

2 pounds lean ground *sirloin*

¼ cup beef broth

1 cup canned crushed tomatoes *packed in juice*

1 cup loosely packed, stemmed, fresh parsley leaves, finely chopped

1 small yellow or white onion, chopped (½ cup)

3 tablespoons red wine vinegar

2 tablespoons Worcestershire sauce

2 tablespoons dark brown sugar

2 tablespoons loosely packed, stemmed, fresh oregano leaves, finely chopped

2 tablespoons loosely packed, stemmed, fresh thyme leaves

2 medium garlic cloves, minced (2 teaspoons)

2 teaspoons mild smoked paprika

6 ciabatta rolls, each split open into two squares

Other Pots

- For a 3-quart pot, you *must* halve almost all of the ingredient amounts *except* you must *use* the stated amount of beef broth (¼ cup).

- For an 8-quart Instant Pot, you *must* increase all of the ingredient amounts by 50 percent.

- For a 10-quart Instant Pot, you *must* double almost all of the ingredient amounts *except* you *must* increase the broth to 1 cup and use only 3 tablespoons fresh thyme leaves.

Beyond

- For a sweeter finish, add up to ¼ cup raisins, chopped, with the crushed tomatoes.

This recipe yields something like Argentinian sloppy joes—which makes no sense except to say that the meat is cooked with lots of herbs (as would be used in the classic chimichurri sauce) and only on LOW pressure (not HIGH or MAX!) so that the whole thing ends up more like a sloppy joe filling, rather than a soupy mess. That said, this dish will still have more liquid in it than some of our other ground-beef sandwich fillings, to keep the herbs from sticking to the insert's hot surface under pressure. Be sure to use a slotted spoon to get it into the ciabatta rolls.

The olive oil is added twice: once at the start to sauté the ground meat and again at the end for flavoring. Since we're adding quite a bit of olive oil to carry forward the herb flavors, use only ground sirloin.

1.

	Press	Set it for	Set time for	If needed, press
In all models	SAUTÉ	MEDIUM, NORMAL, or CUSTOM 300°F	10 minutes	START

2. As the pot heats, warm 3 tablespoons oil in the insert set in a **5- or 6-quart Instant Pot.** Crumble in the ground sirloin and cook, stirring often to break up the clumps, until it loses its raw, red color, about 2 minutes. Add the broth and stir well to scrape up any browned bits on the pot's bottom. (There should be almost none).

3. Turn off the heat and stir in the crushed tomatoes with their juice, the parsley, onion, vinegar, Worcestershire sauce, brown sugar, oregano, thyme, garlic, and smoked paprika. Lock the lid on the pot.

4.

	Set pot for	Set level to	Valve must be	Set time for	If needed, press
For *all* pots	PRESSURE COOK or MANUAL	LOW	Closed	6 minutes with the KEEP WARM setting off	START
For the slow-cook function	SLOW COOK	HIGH	Open	2 hours with the KEEP WARM setting off	START

5. When the pot has finished cooking under pressure, use the **quick-release method** to bring the pressure back to normal. Whichever cooking method you've used, unlatch the lid and open the pot. Set the lid askew over the pot and set it aside for 5 minutes so the ground beef continues to absorb some of the sauce. Use a slotted spoon to spoon the meat into the rolls. Use a flatware tablespoon to drizzle the meat with a little sauce from the pot to moisten it as well as ½ tablespoon olive oil per sandwich as a condiment.

Meatball and Spaghetti Squash Dinner

11 ingredients

4 SERVINGS

METHOD:
pot-in-pot

SPECIAL EQUIPMENT:
the bottom layer of a set of 7½-inch stackable insert pans and a pressure- and food-safe rack

PRESSURE:
max or high

TIME UNDER PRESSURE:
10 or 12 minutes

RELEASE:
quick

TOTAL TIME WITH PRESSURE:
about 1 hour

CAN BE GLUTEN-FREE

1½ cups water

1 pound lean ground beef, preferably 90 percent lean or more

¼ cup Italian-seasoned dried bread crumbs (gluten-free, if necessary)

2 tablespoons finely grated Parmigiano-Reggiano

1 teaspoon dried oregano

¼ teaspoon red pepper flakes

One 24-ounce jar plain red spaghetti or marinara sauce (3 cups—gluten-free, if necessary)

One *small* 1½-pound spaghetti squash, stemmed, split lengthwise, and seeds and membranes removed

2 tablespoons butter

¼ teaspoon table salt

⅛ teaspoon grated nutmeg

Other Pots

- Because of the size of the equipment and the height needed for the spaghetti squash, you cannot complete this recipe in a 3- or a 5-quart Instant Pot.

- For a 10-quart Instant Pot, you *must* increase the amount of water in the insert to 2½ cups while otherwise completing the recipe as stated.

Beyond

- Sprinkle lots of finely grated Parmigiano-Reggiano or finely shredded semi-firm mozzarella over the meatballs and sauce when the pan first comes out of the pot so the cheese has time to melt over the hot ingredients.

This recipe gives you a complete meal out of the pot, thanks to the techniques: a stacking pan *and* a rack over it. The meatballs simmer in the pan while the spaghetti squash steams above them. You'll end up with a pasta-free version of spaghetti and meatballs, a satisfying weeknight supper.

1. Pour the water into the insert set in a **6- or 8-quart Instant Pot**. If your stackable pans do not have feet, you'll need to put a pressure-safe rack or trivet in the insert. (Most stackable pans do have feet.)

2. Mix the ground beef, bread crumbs, cheese, oregano, and red pepper flakes in a medium bowl until well combined. Form this mixture into 12 equal balls, each about the size of a golf ball.

3. Set the balls in the bottom layer of a 7½-inch stackable insert pan. Pour the spaghetti or marinara sauce over and around the meatballs. Do not cover the pan. Set it in the insert.

4. Set a pressure- and food-safe rack on top of the pan. Put the spaghetti squash halves side by side and cut side up on the rack. They can overlap slightly but as little as possible. Lock the lid on the cooker.

5.

	Set pot for	Set level to	Valve must be	Set time for	If needed, press
For Max pots only	PRESSURE COOK	MAX	—	10 minutes with the KEEP WARM setting off	START
For all other pots	PRESSURE COOK or MANUAL	HIGH	Closed	12 minutes with the KEEP WARM setting off	START

6. When the pot has finished cooking, use the **quick-release method** to bring the pressure back to normal. Unlatch the lid and open the cooker.

7. Use kitchen tongs and a metal spatula to transfer the (hot! soft!) spaghetti squash halves to a nearby cutting board. Cool for 5 minutes. Meanwhile, use kitchen tongs to remove the rack from the pot, then use hot pads or silicone baking mitts to transfer the (hot!) pan to a nearby wire rack.

8. Use a fork to scrape the stringy flesh out of the squash halves and into a clean bowl. Add the butter, salt, and nutmeg. Stir well until the butter melts. Mound the spaghetti squash on plates or a serving platter; top with the meatballs and the sauce from the pan.

Meatball Steak

16 ingredients

4 SERVINGS

METHOD:
standard

SPECIAL
EQUIPMENT:
none

PRESSURE:
low

TIME UNDER
PRESSURE:
10 minutes

RELEASE:
modified natural

TOTAL TIME WITH
PRESSURE:
about 50 minutes

1¼ pounds lean ground beef, preferably 90 percent lean or more

¼ cup Italian-seasoned dried bread crumbs

¼ cup whole or low-fat ricotta (do not use fat-free)

2 tablespoons Worcestershire sauce

1 teaspoon ground cumin

2 tablespoons butter

1 medium yellow or white onion, chopped (1 cup)

1 pound white or brown button mushrooms, cleaned and thinly sliced

2 medium garlic cloves, minced (2 teaspoons)

1 teaspoon dried thyme

½ teaspoon rubbed or ground sage

½ teaspoon table salt

½ teaspoon ground black pepper

2 teaspoons all-purpose flour

1 cup beef or chicken broth

¼ cup heavy or light cream

Other Pots

- For a 3-quart Instant Pot, you *must* halve all of the ingredient amounts.

- For an 8-quart Instant Pot, you *must* increase all of the ingredient amounts by 50 percent.

- For a 10-quart Instant Pot, you *must* double almost all of the ingredient amounts *except* you *must* use only 3 medium garlic cloves, minced (1 tablespoon); and only 1½ teaspoons dried thyme.

Beyond

- Serve the meatballs and sauce over cooked and drained egg or no-yolk noodles.

Some of us grew up with "hamburger steak," a braise of ground beef patties in a rich, creamy sauce, usually with mushrooms in the mix. The patties needed a knife and a fork, not a bun. We can't make those patties in an Instant Pot because it's impossible to brown them properly in its narrow confines. We'd also be forced to stack the patties in the pot—which causes them to break under pressure. Still, we can replicate those retro flavors with meatballs.

1. Mix the ground beef, bread crumbs, ricotta, Worcestershire sauce, and cumin in a medium bowl until uniform and well combined. Form this mixture into 8 even balls, about ⅓ cup each.

2.

	Press	Set it for	Set time for	If needed, press
In all models	SAUTÉ	MEDIUM, NORMAL, or CUSTOM 300°F	10 minutes	START

3. As the pot heats, melt the butter in the insert set in a **5- or 6-quart Instant Pot**. Add the onion and cook, stirring often, until softened, about 3 minutes. Add the mushrooms and cook, stirring more often, until they give off their liquid and it reduces to a glaze, about 5 minutes.

4. Stir in the garlic, thyme, sage, salt, and pepper until aromatic, just a few seconds. Then stir in the flour until well combined. Pour in the broth in a slow, steady stream, stirring all the while to get up any browned bits on the pot's bottom and to dissolve the flour.

5. Stir in the cream until combined. Turn off the heat and nestle the meatballs into the sauce. Lock the lid on the pot.

6.

	Set pot for	Set level to	Valve must be	Set time for	If needed, press
For *all* pots	PRESSURE COOK or MANUAL	LOW	Closed	10 minutes with the KEEP WARM setting off	START

7. When the pot has finished cooking, turn it off and let the pressure **return to normal naturally for 10 minutes**. Then use the **quick-release method** to get rid of the pot's residual pressure. Unlatch the lid and open the cooker. Stir gently before serving hot.

One-Pot Cheese-Stuffed Meatballs

11 ingredients

7 MEATBALLS IN SAUCE

METHOD:
egg bites

SPECIAL EQUIPMENT:
one seven-indentation egg-bite mold; 1-quart, 6-inch-round, high-sided, pressure-safe baking or soufflé dish; and a pressure-safe rack or trivet

PRESSURE:
max or high

TIME UNDER PRESSURE:
17 or 20 minutes

RELEASE:
quick

TOTAL TIME WITH PRESSURE:
about 45 minutes

1½ cups water

¾ pound lean ground beef, preferably 90 percent lean or more

¼ cup Italian-seasoned dried bread crumbs

1 refrigerator-cold large egg, lightly beaten

½ ounce Parmigiano-Reggiano, finely grated (¼ cup)

2 medium garlic cloves, minced (2 teaspoons)

¼ teaspoon grated nutmeg

¼ teaspoon red pepper flakes

2 string cheese sticks, each quartered crosswise

Olive oil spray or olive oil, for greasing

1½ cups jarred alfredo sauce or your favorite red or white spaghetti sauce

Other Pots

- Because of the height of the three pieces of stacked equipment, this recipe cannot be made in a 3-quart Instant Pot.

- For a 10-quart Instant Pot, you *must* increase the amount of water in the insert to 2½ cups while otherwise completing the recipe as stated.

Beyond

- Serve these meatballs and sauce over cooked and drained spaghetti or farfalle.

- Or over Perfect Polenta Every Time (page 351).

With purchased sauce and seasoned bread crumbs, these cheesy meatballs couldn't be easier. You'll have one quarter of one stick of string cheese left over (since you'll make seven, not eight, meatballs, given the parameters of standard egg-bite molds). Consider that quarter your snack while dinner cooks.

1. Pour the water into the insert set in a **5-, 6-, or 8-quart Instant Pot.** Set a pressure-safe rack or trivet in the insert.

2. Mix the ground beef, bread crumbs, egg, cheese, garlic, nutmeg, and red pepper flakes in a medium bowl until uniform (the egg must be well distributed). Make seven equal balls (about ⅓ cup each). Push a piece of string cheese into each ball, sealing the meat around the cheese.

3. Coat the seven indentations of an egg-bite mold with olive oil spray or grease them well with olive oil. Set a meatball in each indentation. Cover the mold tightly with its lid or seal it with aluminum foil. Set the mold on the rack.

4. Pour the sauce into a 1-quart, 6-inch-round, high-sided, pressure-safe baking or soufflé dish. Cover tightly with foil and set it on top of the egg-bite mold. Lock the lid on the pot.

5.

	Set pot for	Set level to	Valve must be	Set time for	If needed, press
For Max pots only	PRESSURE COOK	MAX	—	17 minutes with the KEEP WARM setting off	START
For all other pots	PRESSURE COOK or MANUAL	HIGH	Closed	20 minutes with the KEEP WARM setting off	START

6. When the pot has finished cooking, use the **quick-release method** to bring the pressure back to normal. Unlatch the lid and open the cooker. Use hot pads or silicone baking mitts to transfer the (hot!) dish to a nearby wire rack. Uncover and stir well. Remove the egg-bite mold from the pot and uncover it. Dump the meatballs into the sauce and stir gently before serving.

The Cutest Ever Mini Meat Loaves

8 ingredients

7 MINI MEAT LOAVES

METHOD:
egg bites

SPECIAL EQUIPMENT:
one seven-indentation egg-bite mold and a pressure-safe rack or trivet

PRESSURE:
max or high

TIME UNDER PRESSURE:
17 or 20 minutes

RELEASE:
quick

TOTAL TIME WITH PRESSURE:
about 50 minutes

1½ cups water

Olive oil spray or olive oil, for greasing

½ pound lean ground beef, preferably 90 percent lean or more

6 ounces sweet Italian sausage meat (any casings removed)

3 tablespoons Italian-seasoned dried bread crumbs

1 refrigerator-cold large egg, lightly beaten

½ cup jarred plain marinara sauce (do not use a chunky variety)

Seven 4-inch-round slices of provolone cheese

Other Pots

- For a **3-quart Instant Pot**, you *must* decrease the amount of water in the insert to 1 cup and you *must* use two, four-indentation egg-bite molds specifically made for this smaller model, leaving one of the indentations empty. You *must* then stack the molds on top of each other in the insert.

- For a **10-quart Instant Pot**, you *must* increase the amount of water in the insert to 2½ cups. You *can* either complete the recipe as stated or you *can* double all of the other ingredient amounts, in which case you *must* use two egg-bite molds, stacking them on each other so that the feet of the top layer sit on the rims between the indentations of the bottom layer.

Beyond

- The meat loaves can rest at room temperature while you make Smashed Potatoes with Herbs and Butter (page 348).

These small, individual meat loaves have an Italian flair, thanks to seasoned bread crumbs and melted provolone. They make great leftovers, too! Once they come out of the cooker in step 4, unmold them, cool for 15 minutes, and store in a sealed container in the fridge for up to 3 days. When you're ready, heat the broiler as directed in step 5, then set as many mini meat loaves as you like on a lipped baking sheet *without* covering them in sauce and cheese. Broil for 1 to 2 minutes to heat them up, then add the sauce and cheese and continue broiling as directed in step 5.

1. Pour the water into the insert set in a **5-, 6-, or 8-quart Instant Pot**. Set a pressure-safe rack or trivet in the insert. Coat the inside of the seven indentations of an egg-bite mold with olive oil spray or grease them well with olive oil.

2. Mix the ground beef, sausage meat, bread crumbs, and egg in a medium bowl until uniform. Divide this mixture evenly among the indentations in the egg-bite mold, pressing it into the indentations to make flat-topped, compact loaves. Cover the mold tightly with its silicone lid or seal it with aluminum foil. Set the mold on the rack and lock the lid on the pot.

3.

	Set pot for	Set level to	Valve must be	Set time for	If needed, press
For Max pots only	PRESSURE COOK	MAX	—	17 minutes with the KEEP WARM setting off	START
For all other pots	PRESSURE COOK or MANUAL	HIGH	Closed	20 minutes with the KEEP WARM setting off	START

4. When the pot has finished cooking, use the **quick-release method** to bring the pressure back to normal. Unlatch the lid and open the cooker. Use hot pads or silicone baking mitts to transfer the (hot!) egg-bite mold to a nearby wire rack. Uncover the mold.

5. Set the oven rack 4 to 6 inches from the oven's broiler element. Heat the broiler. Unmold the mini meat loaves and set them long side down on a lipped baking sheet. Top each one with a generous 1 tablespoon marinara sauce; lay a slice of cheese on each mini meat loaf. Broil until the cheese melts, about 1 minute. Cool for just a minute or two and serve hot.

Beef Kofta with Tzatziki

20 ingredients

7 KOFTA PLUS SAUCE

METHOD:
egg bites

SPECIAL EQUIPMENT:
one seven-indentation egg-bite mold and a pressure-safe rack or trivet

PRESSURE:
max or high

TIME UNDER PRESSURE:
12 or 15 minutes

RELEASE:
natural

TOTAL TIME WITH PRESSURE:
about 50 minutes

GLUTEN-FREE

1½ cups water

2 tablespoons olive oil, plus more for greasing

1 pound lean ground beef, preferably 90 percent lean or more

1 medium single-lobe shallot, chopped (¼ cup)

3 medium garlic cloves, minced (3 teaspoons)

2 teaspoons minced peeled fresh ginger

1½ teaspoons table salt

1 teaspoon ground coriander

1 teaspoon ground cumin

½ teaspoon ground cinnamon

½ teaspoon ground cloves

Up to ½ teaspoon red pepper flakes

¼ cup loosely packed, stemmed, fresh cilantro leaves, finely chopped

¼ cup loosely packed, stemmed, fresh mint leaves, finely chopped

1 medium garden or slicing cucumber

1 cup plain regular, low-fat, or non-fat yogurt (do *not* use Greek yogurt of any sort)

¼ cup loosely packed, stemmed, fresh dill fronds, finely chopped

¼ cup loosely packed, stemmed, fresh parsley leaves, finely chopped

3 tablespoons lemon juice

½ teaspoon ground black pepper

We promised a few crazy recipes. Here's one to create a version of classic, Middle-Eastern mini "meat loaves" in egg-bite molds. While we're at it, we might as well whip up a traditional Mediterranean yogurt and cucumber sauce, tzatziki, to bump up the flavors. Leftover tzatziki can be stored in a covered container in the refrigerator for up to 2 days, although the cucumber will leach excess moisture. You can stir this back in for a thinner sauce or pour off the liquid (although you'll lose a little flavor).

Because these kofta have no bread crumbs or egg to increase the moisture in the ground beef, they are cooked for a bit shorter time than some other meat loaf and meatball recipes in this chapter. The kofta are then given a natural release to make sure the meat stays tender and juicy. The sheer force of a quick release method would push liquid out of ground beef.

1. Pour the water into the insert set in a **5-, 6-, or 8-quart Instant Pot.** Set a pressure-safe rack or trivet in the insert. Lightly grease the seven indentations of an egg-bite mold with olive oil.

2. Mix the ground beef, shallot, 2 teaspoons of the minced garlic, the ginger, 1 teaspoon of the salt, the coriander, cumin, cinnamon, cloves, and red pepper flakes in a large bowl until the spices are evenly distributed and the mixture is uniform. Form this mixture into 7 evenly sized balls, each a scant ⅓ cup.

3. Combine the cilantro and mint leaves on a plate. Roll each meatball in these herbs, coating it generously, evenly, and fully. Set the balls into the molds' indentations. Cover the mold tightly with its silicone lid or seal it tightly in aluminum foil. Set the mold on the rack and lock the lid on the pot.

4.

	Set pot for	Set level to	Valve must be	Set time for	If needed, press
For Max pots only	PRESSURE COOK	MAX	—	12 minutes with the KEEP WARM setting off	START
For all other pots	PRESSURE COOK or MANUAL	HIGH	Closed	15 minutes with the KEEP WARM setting off	START

5. *While the meatballs are cooking,* make the tzatziki: Use a vegetable peeler to peel the cucumber, then cut it in half lengthwise. Use a small spoon (preferably a grapefruit spoon) to scoop out and discard the seeds, then shred the cucumber halves through the large holes of a box grater. Squeeze these threads by the handful to remove excess liquid, then transfer them to a serving bowl. Stir in yogurt, dill, parsley, lemon juice, black pepper, 2 tablespoons olive oil, the remaining 1 teaspoon minced garlic, and the remaining ½ teaspoon salt.

6. When the pot has finished cooking, turn it off and let the pressure **return to normal naturally,** about 15 minutes. Unlatch the lid and open the cooker. Use hot pads or silicone baking mitts to transfer the (hot!) mold to a nearby wire rack. Uncover the mold. Cool 2 to 3 minutes, then unmold the meatballs and serve them with the tzatziki sauce, either as a dip or spooned over them.

Other Pots

- For a 3-quart Instant Pot, you *must* decrease the amount of water in the insert to 1 cup and you *must* use two, four-indentation egg-bite molds specifically made for this smaller model, leaving one of the indentations empty. You *must* then stack the molds on top of each other in the insert.

- For a 10-quart Instant Pot, you *must* increase the amount of water in the insert to 2½ cups. You *can* either complete the recipe as stated or you *can* double all of the other ingredient amounts, in which case you *must* use two egg-bite molds, stacking them on each other so that the feet of the top layer sit on the rims between the indentations of the bottom layer.

Beyond

- Serve the meatballs and sauce with warmed pita rounds.

- For a more assertive flavor in the tzatziki, add up to 1 tablespoon minced chives.

Miso and Scallion Meatballs and Sushi Rice Dinner

12 ingredients

7 MEATBALLS PLUS RICE

METHOD:
egg bite and pot-in-pot

SPECIAL EQUIPMENT:
a 1-quart, 6-inch-round, high-sided, pressure-safe baking or soufflé dish; a seven-indentation egg-bite mold; and a pressure-safe rack or trivet

PRESSURE:
max or high

TIME UNDER PRESSURE:
10 or 12 minutes

RELEASE:
natural

TOTAL TIME WITH PRESSURE:
about 50 minutes

---

3 cups water

Vegetable, canola, or other neutral-flavored oil, for greasing

1 pound lean ground beef, preferably 90 percent lean or more

2 medium scallions, trimmed and *very* thinly sliced (⅔ cup)

2 tablespoons light brown sugar

2 tablespoons regular or low-sodium soy sauce, or gluten-free tamari sauce

2 tablespoons white miso paste

1 tablespoon toasted sesame oil

Up to 1 tablespoon ground black pepper

1 cup raw *short-grain* white rice, sometimes called "sushi rice"

2 tablespoons unseasoned rice vinegar

2 teaspoons granulated white sugar

This meatball recipe uses a simplified version of the flavors from a Korean classic: bulgogi. Our recipe omits the more traditional, complex spice pastes because they're not easy to find in North American supermarkets; but it does call for miso paste to give the meatballs more of a fermented flavor. In short, flavorful meatballs are cooked in an egg-bite mold over a baking dish of sticky sushi rice.

Don't reverse their positions! The rice will not cook if it sits on top of the meatballs, one of the many curiosities of cooking under pressure.

Miso paste can be found in the refrigerator case of almost all North American supermarkets. Store it, covered, in the refrigerator for up to 2 months or in the freezer for up to 1 year.

1. Pour 1½ cups water into the insert set in a **5-, 6-, or 8-quart Instant Pot.** Set a pressure-safe rack or trivet in the insert. *Generously* grease the 7 indentations of an egg-bite mold with oil. (Seriously, oil it—a nonstick spray just won't get the molds greasy enough.)

2. Mix the ground beef, scallions, brown sugar, soy sauce, miso paste, sesame oil, and black pepper in a large bowl until uniform. Divide this mixture evenly among the indentations in the egg-bite mold. The mixture may mound up in the indentations. Do not cover.

3. Stir the rice, vinegar, sugar, and remaining 1½ cups water in a 1-quart, 6-inch-round, high-sided, pressure-safe baking or soufflé dish. Do not cover. Set this baking dish on the rack in the pot, then set the egg-bite mold over this bowl, centering the mold so it balances on the rim over the baking dish. Lock the lid on the pot.

4.

	Set pot for	Set level to	Valve must be	Set time for	If needed, press
For Max pots only	PRESSURE COOK	MAX	—	10 minutes with the KEEP WARM setting off	START
For all other pots	PRESSURE COOK or MANUAL	HIGH	Closed	12 minutes with the KEEP WARM setting off	START

5. When the pot has finished cooking, turn it off and let the pressure **return to normal naturally,** about 15 minutes. Unlatch the lid and open the cooker.

6. Use hot pads or silicone baking mitts to transfer the (hot!) mold to a nearby wire rack. Also transfer the (hot!) baking dish to that rack. Cool for a couple of minutes, then lift the meatballs out of the mold with a flatware fork (and maybe a metal spatula for balance). Set the meatballs on a serving platter. Fluff the rice with that fork and drizzle any liquid from the meatballs into the rice. Stir again and mound on the platter next to the meatballs.

Other Pots

- Because of the height of all the stacked equipment in this recipe, it will not work in a 3-quart Instant Pot.

- For a 10-quart Instant Pot, you *must* increase the amount of water in the insert to 2½ cups while otherwise completing the recipe as stated.

Beyond

- Garnish the servings with toasted sesame oil, minced scallions, and/ or sesame seeds.

- For a more authentic flavor, substitute doenjang, a Korean chile paste, for the miso paste.

- To get even closer to the original, substitute gochugaru, a dried hot pepper (sometimes called "tae-kyung Korean red pepper flakes") for the black pepper.

Not-Really-Wendy's Chili

16 ingredients

6–8 SERVINGS

METHOD:
fast/slow

SPECIAL EQUIPMENT:
none

PRESSURE:
high

TIME UNDER PRESSURE:
6 minutes

RELEASE:
quick

TOTAL TIME WITH PRESSURE:
about 30 minutes

TOTAL TIME WITH SLOW COOKING:
about 3 hours 15 minutes

GLUTEN-FREE

---

2 tablespoons vegetable, canola, or other neutral-flavored oil

1½ pounds lean ground beef, preferably 90 percent lean or more

1 medium yellow or white onion, chopped (1 cup)

2 medium celery stalks, thinly sliced (⅔ cup)

½ cup standard chili powder

1 teaspoon ground cumin

1 teaspoon garlic powder

1 teaspoon granulated white sugar

1 teaspoon table salt

1 teaspoon ground black pepper

½ cup chicken broth

One 28-ounce can *stewed* tomatoes (3½ cups)

One 15-ounce can pinto beans, drained and rinsed (1¾ cups)

One 15-ounce can red kidney beans, drained and rinsed (1¾ cups)

One 10-ounce can hot or mild diced tomatoes and green chiles, such as Rotel (1¼ cups)

1¼ cups canned tomato juice (do *not* use V8)

Other Pots

- For a 3-quart Instant Pot, you *must* halve almost all of the ingredient amounts *except* you *must* use ⅓ cup broth.

- For a 10-quart Instant Pot, you *must* increase all of the ingredient amounts by 50 percent or you *can* even double the amounts.

We worked and worked to get this copycat recipe right. Along the way, we discovered two secrets. One is canned *stewed* tomatoes, which give the chili a more "cooked" flavor. The other secret comes into play in part of the cooking technique: The onion is *not* first softened in the pot. Doing so sweetens the chili and modifies the taste of this savory favorite.

1.

	Press	Set it for	Set time for	If needed, press
In all models	SAUTÉ	MEDIUM, NORMAL, or CUSTOM 300°F	10 minutes	START

2. As the pot heats, warm the oil in the insert set in a **5-, 6-, or 8-quart Instant Pot.** Crumble in the ground beef and cook until browned, stirring often to break up the clumps, about 5 minutes. Don't stint on the browning.

3. Stir in the onion and celery; cook for 30 seconds, stirring frequently, just to warm the vegetables. Stir in the chili powder, cumin, garlic powder, sugar, salt, and pepper until fragrant, just a few seconds.

4. Pour in the broth and scrape up *all* of the browned bits on the pot's bottom. Turn off the heat, then stir in the stewed tomatoes, pinto beans, red kidney beans, canned tomatoes and chiles, and the tomato juice. Lock the lid on the pot.

5.

	Set pot for	Set level to	Valve must be	Set time for	If needed, press
For *all* pots	PRESSURE COOK or MANUAL	HIGH	Closed	6 minutes with the KEEP WARM setting off	START
For the slow-cook function	SLOW COOK	HIGH	Open	3 hours with the KEEP WARM setting off	START

6. When the pot has finished cooking under pressure, use the **quick-release method** to bring the pressure back to normal. Whichever cooking method you've used, unlatch the lid and open the cooker. Stir well, then set the lid askew over the pot and set it aside for 5 minutes to blend the flavors before serving warm.

Beyond

- Garnish the servings with sour cream or plain yogurt, as well as shredded American cheddar cheese or even a shredded Tex-Mex cheese blend.

BEEF, PORK, & LAMB

Real-Deal Texas Chili

14 ingredients

6–8 SERVINGS

METHOD:
fast/standard

SPECIAL
EQUIPMENT:
a blender

PRESSURE:
max or high

TIME UNDER
PRESSURE:
16 or 20 minutes

RELEASE:
natural

TOTAL TIME WITH
PRESSURE:
about 1½ hours

CAN BE GLUTEN-
FREE

---

12 dried New Mexican red chiles

Boiling water

4 medium garlic cloves, minced
(4 teaspoons)

1 canned chipotle chile in adobo sauce
(gluten-free, if necessary), stemmed
and chopped (seeded, if desired)

1½ teaspoons adobo sauce from the can

2 teaspoons dried oregano

2 teaspoons mild smoked paprika

1½ teaspoons ground cumin

1 teaspoon table salt

½ teaspoon ground cinnamon

4 ounces slab bacon (gluten-free, if
necessary), diced

2 large yellow or white onions, chopped
(3 cups)

3 pounds boneless beef sirloin, cut into
¼-inch pieces

1 cup beef broth

Other Pots

- For a 3-quart Instant Pot, you *must*
  halve almost all of the ingredient
  amounts *except* you *must* use
  ¾ cup broth.

- For an 8-quart Instant Pot, you
  must increase all of the ingredient
  amounts by 50 percent.

- For a 10-quart Instant Pot, you
  must increase almost all of the
  ingredient amounts *except* you
  must double the amount of broth to
  2 cups—or you *can* just double all
  of the ingredient amounts.

Beyond

- Garnish with pickled jalapeño rings,
  sour cream, and shredded cheese.

Honest-to-God Texas chili is something of a religious creed. So here
are its tenets. First, there are no beans. Ever. Second, there are no
tomatoes. Ever. And third, dried chiles have to be soaked and turned
into a paste with spices. Listen, you can either do real Texas chili right
or you can enjoy any of the other chili recipes in this book.

1. Split each dried chile lengthwise over a garbage can and discard
the seeds and any white membrane inside. Tear the chiles into
chunks and put them in a large bowl. Cover with boiling water and
set aside for 20 minutes.

2. Use a slotted spoon to transfer the softened chiles from the bowl
to a blender. (Do not discard the water in that bowl.) Add the garlic,
chipotle, adobo sauce, oregano, smoked paprika, cumin, salt, and
cinnamon to the blender. Put about 1 tablespoon of the soaking
liquid in the blender, cover, and blend until a smooth paste, stopping
the blend at least once to scrape down the inside of the canister *and*
adding more soaking liquid if the ingredients do not blend smoothly.

3.

	Press	Set it for	Set time for	If needed, press
In all models	SAUTÉ	MEDIUM, NORMAL, or CUSTOM 300°F	15 minutes	START

4. Add the bacon to the insert set in a **5- or 6-quart Instant Pot.** Cook,
stirring often, until quite crisp, about 5 minutes. Add the onions; cook,
stirring more frequently, until the onions soften, about 4 minutes.

5. Stir in the prepared chile paste (every last drop!) and cook, stirring
constantly, for 1 minute. Add the beef and stir until it is evenly coated
in the paste mixture. Pour in the broth and scrape up *all* of the browned
bits on the pot's bottom. Turn off the heat and lock the lid on the pot.

6.

	Set pot for	Set level to	Valve must be	Set time for	If needed, press
For Max pots only	PRESSURE COOK	MAX	—	16 minutes with the KEEP WARM setting off	START
For all other pots	PRESSURE COOK or MANUAL	HIGH	Closed	20 minutes with the KEEP WARM setting off	START

7. When the pot has finished cooking, turn it off and let the pressure
return to normal naturally, about 35 minutes. Unlatch the lid and
stir well before serving hot.

French-Onion-Soup Meat Loaf

16 ingredients	
4–6 SERVINGS	
METHOD: fast/slow	

SPECIAL EQUIPMENT: a pressure- and food-safe rack or trivet

PRESSURE: max or high

TIME UNDER PRESSURE: 20 or 25 minutes

RELEASE: natural

TOTAL TIME WITH PRESSURE: about 1½ hours

TOTAL TIME WITH SLOW COOKING: about 4 hours

---

2 tablespoons butter

4 medium yellow or white onions, chopped (4 cups)

1 teaspoon granulated white sugar

1 teaspoon table salt

1½ pounds lean ground beef, preferably 90 percent lean or more

1 refrigerator-cold large egg, lightly beaten

6 tablespoons plain panko bread crumbs

2 teaspoons bottled dried Provençal seasoning blend

½ teaspoon ground black pepper

4 ounces Swiss cheese, shredded (1 cup)

2 tablespoons brandy or unsweetened apple cider

2 tablespoons Worcestershire sauce

1 cup beef broth

½ teaspoon mild paprika

2 tablespoons water

1 tablespoon cornstarch

We've stuffed a meat loaf with shredded cheese, then cooked it over a rich onion mixture that tastes like French onion soup. Wow! Brown those onions well. Stop short of burning them black, of course; but they must be deeply colored—a rich, dark brown.

One note: Because you have to pick up and remove the hot meat loaf (on its rack) from the pot to then thicken the sauce, it's best to use a rack with arms that can stand up in the insert—or even a silicone rack with flexible, silicone arms (so long as it doesn't have wide gaps between the slats).

1.

	Press	Set it for	Set time for	If needed, press
In all models	SAUTÉ	MEDIUM, NORMAL, or CUSTOM 300°F	20 minutes	START

2. As the pot heats, melt the butter in the insert set in a **5-, 6-, or 8-quart Instant Pot.** Add the onions, sugar, and ½ teaspoon salt. Cook, stirring *quite often*, until the onions soften and even brown, about 15 minutes.

3. Meanwhile, mix the ground beef, egg, bread crumbs, seasoning blend, pepper, and remaining ½ teaspoon salt in a large bowl until uniform. The egg should be thoroughly blended in the mixture.

4. Divide the ground beef mixture in half. Form each into a flat, 7-inch-long oval. Put the cheese down the middle of one of the ovals. Top with the other oval and press the edges to seal well. Compact the mixture gently into a meat loaf without breaking through to the cheese.

5. When the onions are ready, add the brandy and Worcestershire sauce to the pot; scrape up any browned bits on the insert's bottom. Stir in the broth and turn off the heat.

6. Set a pressure- and food-safe rack or trivet in the pot over the onions. Set the meat loaf on the rack. Sprinkle the meat loaf with the paprika and lock the lid onto the cooker.

7.

	Set pot for	Set level to	Valve must be	Set time for	If needed, press
For Max pots only	PRESSURE COOK	MAX	—	20 minutes with the KEEP WARM setting off	START
For all other pots	PRESSURE COOK or MANUAL	HIGH	Closed	25 minutes with the KEEP WARM setting off	START
For the slow-cook function	SLOW COOK	HIGH	Open	3½ hours with the KEEP WARM setting off	START

8. When the pot has finished cooking, turn it off and let the pressure **return to normal naturally,** about 35 minutes. Whichever cooking method you used, unlatch the lid and open the cooker. Remove the meat loaf from the pot by using silicone baking mitts to pick up the (hot!) rack it's sitting on. Transfer to a nearby cutting board. Whisk the water and cornstarch in a small bowl until smooth.

9.

	Press	Set it for	Set time for	If needed, press
In all models	SAUTÉ	MEDIUM, NORMAL, or CUSTOM 300°F	5 minutes	START

10. As the onion mixture comes to a simmer, whisk in the cornstarch slurry. Continue cooking, whisking constantly, until somewhat thickened, less than 1 minute. Turn off the heat and use hot pads or silicone baking mitts to transfer the (hot!) insert from the pot to a nearby wire rack. Cut the meat loaf into 1-inch-thick slices and serve in bowls with the onion sauce ladled over the top.

Other Pots

- For a 3-quart Instant Pot, you *must* halve all of the ingredient amounts (to form 5-inch ovals in step 4). You *must* also reduce the cooking time to 20 minutes at HIGH pressure (there is no MAX setting for 3-quart pots as of this writing).

- For a 10-quart Instant Pot, you *must* increase all of the ingredient amounts by 50 percent (to form 9-inch ovals). You *must* also increase the cooking time to 35 minutes at HIGH pressure (there is no MAX setting for 10-quart pots as of this writing).

Beyond

- For even more French-onion-soup flavor, substitute shredded Gruyère for the Swiss cheese.

- To make your own Provençal seasoning blend, stir together 1 teaspoon dried marjoram, ½ teaspoon dried sage, and ½ teaspoon dried thyme.

See photo in insert.

Barbecue Meat Loaf and Sour-Cream Mashed Potato Dinner

12 ingredients	**SPECIAL EQUIPMENT:** 7-inch-round cake pan and a pressure- and food-safe rack or trivet
4–6 SERVINGS	**PRESSURE:** max or high
METHOD: steam and pot-in-pot	**TIME UNDER PRESSURE:** 25 or 32 minutes
	RELEASE: natural
	TOTAL TIME WITH PRESSURE: about 1 hour 15 minutes

2 pounds yellow potatoes, such as Yukon Golds, cut into 2-inch pieces (peeled or not, your choice)

1½ cups chicken broth

3 tablespoons butter, cut into small pieces

1¾ pounds lean ground beef, preferably 90 percent lean or more

1 refrigerator-cold large egg, lightly beaten

⅓ cup Italian-seasoned dried bread crumbs

¼ cup barbecue sauce

1 tablespoon dried barbecue seasoning blend or rub

2 teaspoons table salt

1 teaspoon ground black pepper

¼ cup heavy or light cream, or half-and-half

¼ cup regular or low-fat sour cream (do not use fat-free)

Other Pots

- Because of the height of the stacked ingredients, this recipe cannot be made in a 3-quart Instant Pot.

- For a 10-quart Instant Pot, you *must* increase all of the ingredient amounts by 50 percent or you *can* even double the amounts. You *must* also use a 9-inch cake pan. You *must* increase the cooking time to 35 minutes at HIGH pressure if you increased by 50 percent or to 38 minutes at HIGH pressure if you doubled the amounts. (There is no MAX pressure setting in 10-quart pots as of this writing.)

This recipe gives you both mashed potatoes and a meat loaf made with barbecue seasonings. It's actually pretty simple, so long as the rack is set in a flat position over the potatoes in step 1. The meat loaf should also be fairly squat (even more so if you're working with a 5-quart pot). Make sure it's truly oval without tapered ends (so the thinner parts don't overcook).

One note: Many barbecue seasoning blends include salt. If yours does, consider nixing any in the meat loaf (but not, of course, in the mashed potatoes).

1. Gently stir the potato pieces, broth, and butter bits in a **5-, 6-, or 8-quart Instant Pot.** Set a pressure- and food-safe rack or trivet over the potatoes, arranging the potatoes so that the rack is fairly flat, not tilted.

2. Mix the ground beef, egg, bread crumbs, barbecue sauce, seasoning blend, 1 teaspoon salt, and ½ teaspoon pepper in a large bowl until uniform. The egg should be evenly and well distributed.

3. Shape this mixture into a meat "lump," oval in shape, maybe a little squatter than a perfect oval for geometry class, mostly so it fits into a 7-inch-round cake pan. Set the lump in that pan. Set the pan on the rack over the potatoes and lock the lid onto the cooker.

4.

	Set pot for	Set level to	Valve must be	Set time for	If needed, press
For Max pots only	PRESSURE COOK	MAX	—	25 minutes with the KEEP WARM setting off	START
For all other pots	PRESSURE COOK or MANUAL	HIGH	Closed	32 minutes with the KEEP WARM setting off	START

5. When the pot has finished cooking, turn it off and let the pressure **return to normal naturally,** about 35 minutes. Unlatch the lid and open the cooker. Use hot pads or silicone baking mitts to lift the meat loaf—on its (hot!) rack—out of the pot. Set on a nearby cutting board.

6. Add the cream or half-and-half, sour cream, the remaining 1 teaspoon salt, and the remaining ½ teaspoon pepper to the pot. Use a potato masher or a handheld electric mixture at low speed to mash the potatoes in the insert. Slice the meat loaf and serve with (or over) the mashed potatoes.

Ballpark Meat Loaf and Buttery Potato Dinner

12 ingredients	**SPECIAL EQUIPMENT:** 7½-inch-round stackable insert pans
4–6 SERVINGS	
METHOD: stacks	**PRESSURE:** high

TIME UNDER PRESSURE: 50 minutes	**TOTAL TIME WITH PRESSURE:** about 1½ hours
RELEASE: natural	

- 1½ pounds lean ground beef, preferably 90 percent lean or more
- ¾ pound lean ground pork
- ¾ cup Italian-seasoned *panko* bread crumbs
- 2 refrigerator-cold large eggs, lightly beaten
- 3 tablespoons sweet pickle relish
- 2 tablespoons yellow mustard
- ½ teaspoon garlic powder
- 1½ teaspoons table salt
- 1 pound small yellow potatoes (1½ to 2 inches in diameter), halved
- ½ stick (4 tablespoons or ¼ cup) butter, cut into small bits
- 1½ cups water
- 3 tablespoons ketchup

Other Pots

- For a 3-quart Instant Pot, you *must* use stackable containers that fit this smaller pot and you *must* halve almost all of the ingredient amounts *except* you *must* use 1 cup water in the insert.
- For a 5-quart Instant Pot, you *must* use 7-inch stackable containers specifically made to fit this slightly smaller pot. (FYI, some standard stacking containers are too tall to work in these pots).
- For a 10-quart Instant Pot, you *must* increase the amount of water in the insert to 2½ cups while otherwise completing the recipe as stated.

Beyond

- Add herbs to the potatoes: up to 1 tablespoon minced fresh tarragon, thyme, sage, and/or parsley leaves.

This recipe's name came about because we wanted to create a beef-and-pork meat loaf with the seasonings and condiments reminiscent of ballpark hot dogs.

1. Mix the ground beef, ground pork, bread crumbs, eggs, pickle relish, mustard, garlic powder, and ½ teaspoon salt in a large bowl until uniform with the eggs and pickle relish distributed throughout the mixture. Pat and press this mixture evenly into the top container of a 7½-inch-round stackable insert pan set. (For more information on working with stacks, see page 16 of the introduction.)

2. Stir the potato pieces, butter, and remaining 1 teaspoon salt in the bottom stack container of that set. Set the meat loaf container over the potatoes and cover the meat loaf tin with its lid or aluminum foil (sealed tightly).

3. Pour the water into the insert set in **6- or 8-quart Instant Pot.** If your stacks set doesn't include feet, set a pressure-safe rack or trivet in the insert. Set the stacked containers into the pot. Lock the lid onto the cooker.

4.

	Set pot for	Set level to	Valve must be	Set time for	If needed, press
For *all* pots	PRESSURE COOK or MANUAL	HIGH	Closed	50 minutes with the KEEP WARM setting off	START

5. When the pot has finished cooking, turn it off and let the pressure **return to normal naturally,** about 20 minutes. Unlatch the lid and open the cooker. Use hot pads or silicone baking mitts to transfer the (hot!) stacking pans to a nearby wire rack. Uncover the top layer, unstack the containers, and smear the ketchup over the meat loaf.

6. If you've used a **6- or 8-quart Instant Pot,** empty out the insert in the pot and wipe it clean. Set the air-fryer basket in the insert and set the stacks container with the meat loaf in the cooker. Fit it with the Instant Pot Air Fryer Lid. Air-fry at 400°F for 10 minutes to caramelize the top of the meat loaf.

Alternatively, use a large metal spatula to transfer the coated meat loaf to a small, lipped baking sheet. Broil 4 to 6 inches from the heat source until caramelized, 3 to 4 minutes.

In either case, let the meat loaf rest for 5 minutes before slicing and serving with the buttery potatoes.

Stuffed Cabbage

14 ingredients

12 CABBAGE
ROLLS

METHOD:
standard

SPECIAL
EQUIPMENT:
a pressure- and
food-safe rack or
trivet

PRESSURE:
max or high

TIME UNDER
PRESSURE:
30 or 35 minutes

RELEASE:
natural

TOTAL TIME WITH
PRESSURE:
about 1 hour
45 minutes

CAN BE GLUTEN-
FREE

2 pounds lean ground beef, preferably 90 percent lean or more

½ cup raw long-grain white rice

1½ teaspoons dried dill

1½ teaspoons dried thyme

1 teaspoon table salt

½ teaspoon ground black pepper

Lots of water

12 large Savoy cabbage leaves

One 28-ounce can diced tomatoes *packed in juice* (3½ cups)

2 tablespoons red wine vinegar

2 tablespoons honey

2 tablespoons regular or low-sodium soy sauce, or gluten-free tamari sauce

2 teaspoons fennel seeds

½ teaspoon red pepper flakes

In one of our companion volumes, *From Freezer To Instant Pot: The Cookbook,* we have a recipe for Unstuffed Cabbage, a deconstructed version of this old-school, Eastern European recipe. But we've always wanted to include the standard in our collections, mostly because we love it as a hearty, winter dinner: lots of dill, plenty of tomatoes, a real rib-sticker. In fact, this recipe is our standard, welcome-home meal when one of us is on the road.

That all sounds great, but there's always been a problem with stuffed cabbage in the Instant Pot. Most recipes ask you to braise the rolls in the sauce. Easy, right? But the results are not very good. The cabbage overcooks and turns mushy, particularly on the rolls' undersides. In our technique, the rolls steam on a rack above the sauce. The cabbage still has a bit of bite to it. Now it's right. Now it can welcome anyone home.

One final note: You might be anxious about the soy as tamari sauce in this recipe. Because the pot offers little reduction, we snuck this ingredient into the tomato sauce to give it an umami richness.

1. Mix the ground beef, rice, dill, thyme, salt, and pepper in a big bowl until uniform. Fill another big bowl with cold tap water and set it near the cooker.

2.

	Press	Set it for	Set time for	If needed, press
In all models	SAUTÉ	HIGH or MORE	20 minutes	START

3. Fill the insert set in a **5-, 6-, or 8-quart Instant Pot** about three-quarters full of hot tap water and bring the water to the point where it's quite hot, almost simmering, not boiling. Reduce the heat level if it starts to boil.

4. Dunk 4 cabbage leaves into the water, gently pressing them down with a wooden spoon to submerge them. Cook for 2 minutes, then transfer the leaves to the cold water and carry on, dunking the remaining leaves and transferring them to that bowl in two more batches. If the water in the bowl gets warm, drain it and refresh with more cold water.

5. When all the cabbage leaves have been softened, turn off the heat and pour the water out of the (hot!) insert. Return it to the machine and stir in the diced tomatoes with their juice, the vinegar, honey, soy sauce, fennel seeds, and red pepper flakes until the honey dissolves. Set a pressure- and food-safe rack or trivet above this mixture. It may be submerged (the point is to keep the cabbage rolls off the insert's bottom).

6. Drain the cabbage leaves. Lay one on a clean, dry work surface. Cut out the thick stem at one end in a V pattern, the wide part of the V at the edge of the leaf where the stem was. Only cut out enough stem so that the leaf can be rolled. Discard this stemmy part. Set the leaf so the cut-out part is closest to you. Put about ⅓ cup of the ground beef mixture on the leaf just above the pointy end of the V cut. Fold the two sides over the filling, then roll up the leaf starting at the V section. Set the filled roll on the rack seam side down and continue making the remaining cabbage rolls. When they're all done, lock the lid on the pot.

7.

	Set pot for	Set level to	Valve must be	Set time for	If needed, press
For Max pots only	PRESSURE COOK	MAX	—	30 minutes with the KEEP WARM setting off	START
For all other pots	PRESSURE COOK or MANUAL	HIGH	Closed	35 minutes with the KEEP WARM setting off	START

8. When the pot has finished cooking, turn it off and let the pressure **return to normal naturally,** about 35 minutes. Unlatch the lid and open the cooker. Use kitchen tongs to transfer the delicate but hot cabbage rolls to a serving platter. Use hot pads or silicone baking mitts to remove the (hot!) rack from the insert. Ladle the tomato sauce in the pot over the rolls.

Other Pots

- For a **3-quart Instant Pot,** you *must* halve all of the ingredient amounts.
- For a **10-quart Instant Pot,** you *must* increase all of the ingredient amounts by 50 percent or you *can* even double the amounts.

Beyond

- Substitute lean ground turkey for the ground beef.
- Serve the rolls over plain mashed potatoes.
- Or over cooked and drained egg or no-yolk noodles.

Un-Stuffed-Pepper Stew

13 ingredients

4–6 SERVINGS

METHOD:
fast/slow

SPECIAL
EQUIPMENT:
none

PRESSURE:
max or high

TIME UNDER
PRESSURE:
8 or 10 minutes

RELEASE:
modified natural

TOTAL TIME
WITH PRESSURE:
about 40 minutes

TOTAL TIME
WITH SLOW
COOKING:
about 3 hours
45 minutes

GLUTEN-FREE

---

2 tablespoons olive oil

1 pound lean ground beef, preferably 90 percent lean or more

One 1-pound bag frozen mixed-color bell pepper strips (no need to thaw)

1 large yellow or white onion, chopped (1½ cups)

2 medium garlic cloves, minced (2 teaspoons)

One 4½-ounce can hot or mild diced green chiles (½ cup)

One 4-ounce jar (or two 2-ounce jars) diced pimientos (with their juice—about ¼ cup)

2 teaspoons dried oregano

1 teaspoon rubbed or ground sage

½ teaspoon table salt

4 cups (1 quart) chicken broth

One 28-ounce can diced tomatoes *packed in juice* (3½ cups)

1 cup raw long-grain white rice

This stew tastes like stuffed peppers without any of the work, since we call for a bag of frozen bell pepper strips that don't need to be thawed. (To make things really easy, you can also use 1½ cups of frozen chopped onions—which also don't need to be thawed.) We add canned diced green chiles and jarred diced pimientos to boost the peppery flavor of the stew.

1.

	Press	Set it for	Set time for	If needed, press
In all models	SAUTÉ	MEDIUM, NORMAL, or CUSTOM 300°F	15 minutes	START

2. As the pot heats, warm the oil in the insert set in a **5-, 6-, or 8-quart Instant Pot.** Crumble in the ground beef and cook, stirring often to break up the clumps, until the meat loses its raw, pink color, about 2 minutes.

3. Add the pepper strips and onion. Continue cooking until the onion begins to soften, about 3 minutes. Stir in the garlic until aromatic, just a few seconds.

4. Add the chiles, pimientos, oregano, sage, and salt. Stir well, then pour in the broth and scrape up any browned bits on the pot's bottom. Continue cooking, stirring occasionally, until the broth is quite hot, not simmering, but with wisps of steam rising from it, about 4 minutes. Stir in the tomatoes with their juice and the rice. Turn off the heat and lock the lid onto the cooker.

5.

	Set pot for	Set level to	Valve must be	Set time for	If needed, press
For Max pots only	PRESSURE COOK	MAX	—	8 minutes with the KEEP WARM setting off	START
For all other pots	PRESSURE COOK or MANUAL	HIGH	Closed	10 minutes with the KEEP WARM setting off	START
For the slow-cook function	SLOW COOK	HIGH	Open	3½ hours with the KEEP WARM setting off	START

6. When the pot has finished cooking under pressure, turn it off and let its pressure **return to normal naturally for 12 minutes.** Then use the **quick-release method** to get rid of any residual pressure in the pot. Whichever cooking method you've used, unlatch the lid and open the cooker. Stir well and set the lid askew over the pot. Set it aside for 2 to 3 minutes to blend the flavors before serving hot.

Other Pots

- For a 3-quart Instant Pot, you *must* halve all of the ingredient amounts.

- For an 8-quart Instant Pot, you *can* increase all of the ingredient amounts by 50 percent.

- For a 10-quart Instant Pot, you *must* increase all of the ingredient amounts by 50 percent or you *can* even double the amounts.

Gingery Beef, Rice, and Scallion Casserole

12 ingredients	SPECIAL EQUIPMENT:	TIME UNDER PRESSURE:	TOTAL TIME WITH PRESSURE:
6 SERVINGS	none	8 or 10 minutes	about 45 minutes
METHOD: standard	PRESSURE: max or high	RELEASE: modified quick	CAN BE GLUTEN-FREE

2 tablespoons toasted sesame oil

6 medium scallions, trimmed and thinly sliced (2 cups)

2 tablespoons minced peeled fresh ginger

¾ pound lean ground beef, preferably 90 percent lean or more

2 cups raw long-grain white rice

⅓ cup low-sodium soy sauce or gluten-free tamari sauce

2 tablespoons unseasoned rice vinegar

2 tablespoons granulated white sugar

Up to 1 tablespoon thick red chile sauce, such as sambal oelek

½ teaspoon ground cinnamon

¼ teaspoon ground cloves

4 cups (1 quart) chicken broth

Other Pots

- For a 3-quart Instant Pot, you *must* halve all of the ingredient amounts.
- For an 8-quart Instant Pot, you *can* increase all of the ingredient amounts by 50 percent.
- For a 10-quart Instant Pot, you *must* increase all of the ingredient amounts by 50 percent or you *can* even double almost all of the amounts *except* for the cinnamon which *should* only be ¾ teaspoon.

Beyond

- Substitute ½ teaspoon five-spice powder for the cinnamon and cloves.
- Substitute the beyond-fabulous Lao Gan Ma spicy chili crisp for the sambal oelek.

This recipe yields a truly robust meal, much more like a North American beef-and-rice casserole than any notion of take-out fried rice. There are lots of aromatics, even cinnamon and cloves, all to pack as much flavor into every bite as we could. Because there's *so much* soy sauce, you'll get the best results with low-sodium.

1.

	Press	Set it for	Set time for	If needed, press
In all models	SAUTÉ	MEDIUM, NORMAL, or CUSTOM 300°F	10 minutes	START

2. As the pot heats, warm the sesame oil in the insert set in a **5-, 6-, or 8-quart Instant Pot**. Add the scallions and cook, stirring often, until wilted a bit, about 2 minutes.

3. Crumble in the ground beef and cook, stirring often to break up the clumps, until lightly browned, about 4 minutes. Add the rice and stir well until the grains are evenly distributed.

4. Add the soy sauce, rice vinegar, sugar, chile sauce, cinnamon, and cloves, stirring until almost all of this liquid has been absorbed, about 1 minute. Pour in the broth and scrape up any browned bits on the pot's bottom. Continue cooking until the liquid in the pot is hot (but not simmering), stirring occasionally, about 3 minutes. Turn off the heat and lock the lid on the pot.

5.

	Set pot for	Set level to	Valve must be	Set time for	If needed, press
For Max pots only	PRESSURE COOK	MAX	—	8 minutes with the KEEP WARM setting off	START
For all other pots	PRESSURE COOK or MANUAL	HIGH	Closed	10 minutes with the KEEP WARM setting off	START

6. When the pot has finished cooking, use the **quick-release method** to bring the pressure back to normal **but do not open the cooker.** Set aside for 10 minutes, then unlatch the lid and open the cooker. Fluff the rice with a fork. If there's still too much liquid in the pot, cover it and set it aside for 5 minutes so the rice continues to absorb the liquid. Serve warm.

Ground Beef and Eggplant Stew

17 ingredients	
4–6 SERVINGS	
METHOD: fast/slow	

SPECIAL EQUIPMENT: none	
PRESSURE: low	

TIME UNDER PRESSURE: 5 minutes	
RELEASE: quick	

TOTAL TIME WITH PRESSURE: about 40 minutes	

TOTAL TIME WITH SLOW COOKING: about 2 hours 45 minutes	
GLUTEN-FREE	

¼ cup pine nuts

2 tablespoons olive oil

1 medium yellow or white onion, chopped (1 cup)

1 medium green bell pepper, stemmed, cored, and chopped (1 cup)

Up to 3 medium garlic cloves, minced (1 tablespoon)

½ teaspoon rubbed or ground sage

½ teaspoon ground allspice

½ teaspoon ground cinnamon

Up to ½ teaspoon grated nutmeg

½ teaspoon salt

½ teaspoon ground black pepper

1 pound lean ground beef, preferably 90 percent lean or more

6 medium Roma or plum tomatoes, chopped (1½ cups)

½ cup chicken broth

One 1¼- to 1½-pound eggplant, stemmed, peeled, and cut into 1½- to 2-inch cubes

½ cup loosely packed, stemmed, fresh parsley leaves, chopped

2 tablespoons tomato paste

This stew's flavors are inspired by the Greek pantry: sage, allspice, cinnamon, and nutmeg. We like to serve it over cooked and drained penne, although it's wetter than a standard pasta sauce and perhaps not to everyone's taste over pasta. It's also great over cooked white or brown rice, as well as spooned into an open baked potato.

This stew needs LOW pressure 1) to keep the eggplant from turning to mush, and 2) to let us keep the liquid level lower so it doesn't become a soup.

1.

	Press	Set it for	Set time for	If needed, press
In all models	SAUTÉ	MEDIUM, NORMAL, or CUSTOM 300°F	15 minutes	START

2. As the pot heats, pour the pine nuts into the insert set in a **5-, 6-, or 8-quart Instant Pot.** Toast them, stirring occasionally, until lightly browned, about 3 minutes. Use a cooking spoon to transfer the pine nuts to a nearby bowl. Set aside.

3. Add the oil to the insert, then the onion and bell pepper. Cook, stirring often, until the onion softens, about 3 minutes. Stir in the garlic, sage, allspice, cinnamon, nutmeg, salt, and pepper until fragrant, just a few seconds.

4. Crumble in the ground beef and cook, stirring almost constantly to break up any clumps, until the meat loses its raw, red color, about 3 minutes.

5. Add the tomatoes and continue cooking, stirring fairly often, until they begin to break down, about 2 minutes. Pour in the broth and scrape up any browned bits on the pot's bottom. Turn off the heat. Stir in the eggplant cubes. Lock the lid on the pot.

6.

	Set pot for	Set level to	Valve must be	Set time for	If needed, press
For *all* pots	PRESSURE COOK or MANUAL	LOW	Closed	5 minutes with the KEEP WARM setting off	START
For the slow-cook function	SLOW COOK	HIGH	Open	2½ hours with the KEEP WARM setting off	START

7. When the pot has finished cooking under pressure, use the **quick-release method** to bring the pressure back to normal. Whichever cooking method you've used, unlatch the lid and open the cooker.

8. Add the parsley and tomato paste. Stir gently to keep the eggplant from breaking up. Set the lid askew over the pot and set aside for 2 to 3 minutes to let the parsley wilt and the tomato paste dissolve. Stir in the toasted pine nuts and serve warm.

Other Pots

- For a **3-quart Instant Pot**, you *must* halve almost all of the ingredient amounts *except* you *must* use ⅓ cup broth.

- For a **10-quart Instant Pot**, you *must* double almost all of the ingredient amounts *except* you *must* use 1½ cups broth.

Beyond

- For heat, add up to 1 teaspoon red pepper flakes with the spices.

- Serve this soup with warmed pita rounds.

- Even better, sprinkle crunchy pita chips over the servings.

Ground Beef, Dried Fig, and Jalapeño Picadillo

15 ingredients

6 SERVINGS

METHOD:
fast/slow

SPECIAL EQUIPMENT:
none

PRESSURE:
max or high

TIME UNDER PRESSURE:
3 or 5 minutes

RELEASE:
quick

TOTAL TIME WITH PRESSURE:
about 45 minutes

TOTAL TIME WITH SLOW COOKING:
about 3½ hours

CAN BE GLUTEN-FREE

2 tablespoons olive oil

1 medium red onion, chopped (1 cup)

1 medium red bell pepper, stemmed, cored, and chopped (1 cup)

2 medium fresh jalapeño chiles, stemmed, cored, and chopped (seeded, if desired)

4 medium garlic cloves, minced (4 teaspoons)

2 teaspoons dried oregano

2 teaspoons mild smoked paprika

1 teaspoon cumin seeds

2 pounds lean ground beef, preferably 90 percent lean or more

¼ cup Worcestershire sauce (gluten-free, if necessary)

1 cup beef broth

1 pound globe tomatoes, chopped (2 cups)

6 dried figs, stemmed and finely chopped

2 tablespoons dark brown sugar

¼ cup tomato paste

We have a recipe for Picadillo-Style Ragù in the first *Instant Pot Bible*, but we wanted to offer a more traditional picadillo here (along with a new take on Chicken Picadillo, page 212). This one is sweet with dried figs and uses *fresh* chiles, rather than dried, for their slightly citrus bite. However, ours lacks olives and capers, traditional briny additives. We felt they deaden the flavors a bit under pressure. We were looking for a brighter, lighter mélange.

1.

	Press	Set it for	Set time for	If needed, press
In all models	SAUTÉ	MEDIUM, NORMAL, or CUSTOM 300°F	10 minutes	START

2. As the pot heats, warm the oil in the insert set in a **5- or 6-quart Instant Pot.** Add the onion, bell pepper, and jalapeño. Cook, stirring occasionally, until the onion softens, about 3 minutes. (The chile oils can volatilize and burn your eyes. Stand back.)

3. Stir in the garlic, oregano, smoked paprika, and cumin seeds until fragrant, just a few seconds. Crumble in the ground beef and continue cooking, stirring often to break up the clumps, just until the meat is well coated in the spices.

4. Pour in the Worcestershire sauce and scrape up any browned bits on the pot's bottom. Turn off the heat and stir in the broth, tomatoes, dried figs, and brown sugar until the brown sugar dissolves. Lock the lid on the pot.

5.

	Set pot for	Set level to	Valve must be	Set time for	If needed, press
For Max pots only	PRESSURE COOK	MAX	—	3 minutes with the KEEP WARM setting off	START
For all other pots	PRESSURE COOK or MANUAL	HIGH	Closed	5 minutes with the KEEP WARM setting off	START
For the slow-cook function	SLOW COOK	HIGH	Open	3 hours with the KEEP WARM setting off	START

6. When the pot has finished cooking under pressure, use the **quick-release method** to bring the pressure back to normal. Whichever cooking method you've used, unlatch the lid and open the cooker.

7.

	Press	Set it for	Set time for	If needed, press
In all models	SAUTÉ	MEDIUM, NORMAL, or CUSTOM 300°F	5 minutes	START

8. As the liquid comes to a full simmer, stir in the tomato paste. Continue cooking, stirring all the while, until the tomato paste dissolves and the picadillo thickens. Turn off the heat and set the lid askew over the pot. Set it aside for 2 to 3 minutes to blend the flavors. Serve warm.

Other Pots

- For a 3-quart Instant Pot, you *must* halve all of the ingredient amounts.

- For an 8-quart Instant Pot, you *must* increase almost all of the ingredient amounts by 50 percent *except* you *must* use only 2½ tablespoons dark brown sugar.

- For a 10-quart Instant Pot, you *must* double almost all of the ingredient amounts *except* you *must* use only 3 tablespoons dark brown sugar.

Beyond

- Serve the picadillo over cooked white rice and warmed canned black beans.

- Or offer it with Romaine lettuce or radicchio leaves, like spades to scoop it up.

Good-for-What-Ails-You Beef and Stout Stew

15 ingredients	
6–8 SERVINGS	
METHOD: fast/slow	
SPECIAL EQUIPMENT: none	
PRESSURE: max or high	
TIME UNDER PRESSURE: 40 or 45 minutes	
RELEASE: natural	
TOTAL TIME WITH PRESSURE: about 2 hours	
TOTAL TIME WITH SLOW COOKING: about 5 hours	
CAN BE GLUTEN-FREE	

1 tablespoon butter

4 ounces thin strips of bacon (gluten-free, if necessary), chopped

1 small yellow or white onion, chopped (½ cup)

2 medium garlic cloves, minced (2 teaspoons)

1 pound white or brown button mushrooms, cleaned and thinly sliced

1 teaspoon caraway seeds

1 teaspoon dried thyme

½ teaspoon ground allspice

½ teaspoon table salt

½ teaspoon ground black pepper

1 tablespoon Dijon mustard (gluten-free, if necessary)

1 tablespoon Worcestershire sauce (gluten-free, if necessary)

1 tablespoon dark brown sugar

2 pounds boneless beef top or bottom round, cut into 1-inch pieces

One 12-ounce bottle stout (*not* a chocolate or coffee stout); or beef broth as a gluten-free alternative

This well-stocked stew is a hands-down favorite winter warmer. The stout will add a bitter-and-sweet accent, a nice match to the earthy mushrooms and the (perhaps unusual) blend of spices that includes caraway seeds and thyme.

The difference between top and bottom round is pronounced. Top round will give you a much less fatty stew. The meat may be too dry for some tastes, although others may be happy to spend less time on the cross-trainer. Bottom round will give you a richer stew with softer chunks of meat.

1.

	Press	Set it for	Set time for	If needed, press
In all models	SAUTÉ	MEDIUM, NORMAL, or CUSTOM 300°F	15 minutes	START

2. As the pot heats, melt the butter in the insert set in a **5-, 6-, or 8-quart Instant Pot.** Add the bacon and cook, stirring often, until lightly browned, about 3 minutes. Add the onion and continue cooking, stirring often, until softened, about 2 minutes.

3. Stir in the garlic until aromatic, just a few seconds. Add the mushrooms and cook, stirring more frequently, until they give off their liquid and it reduces to a glaze, about 5 minutes.

4. Stir in the caraway seeds, thyme, allspice, salt, and pepper until aromatic, just a few seconds. Stir in the mustard, Worcestershire sauce, and brown sugar. Stir until the brown sugar melts, then add the beef. Stir well to coat in the spices and any sauce in the pot.

5. Pour in the stout and scrape up any browned bits on the pot's bottom. Turn off the heat and lock the lid on the pot.

6.

	Set pot for	Set level to	Valve must be	Set time for	If needed, press
For Max pots only	PRESSURE COOK	MAX	—	40 minutes with the KEEP WARM setting off	START
For all other pots	PRESSURE COOK or MANUAL	HIGH	Closed	45 minutes with the KEEP WARM setting off	START
For the slow-cook function	SLOW COOK	HIGH	Open	4½ hours with the KEEP WARM setting off	START

7. When the pot has finished cooking under pressure, turn it off and let the pressure **return to normal naturally,** about 40 minutes. Whichever cooking method you've used, unlatch the lid and open the cooker. Set the lid askew over the pot and set it aside for 5 minutes so the beef continues to absorb some of the sauce. Stir well before serving warm.

Other Pots

- For a 3-quart Instant Pot, you *must* halve all of the ingredient amounts.

- For a 10-quart Instant Pot, you *must* increase all of the ingredient amounts by 50 percent or you *can* even double the amounts.

Beyond

- For a deeper flavor, substitute strong coffee, even espresso, for some or all of the stout (or beef broth).

- Garnish the servings with minced chives or the green part of a scallion.

- Serve the stew over No-Brainer Cauliflower Mash (page 338).

Kalimotxo Beef Stew

13 ingredients

6 SERVINGS

METHOD: fast/slow

SPECIAL EQUIPMENT: none

PRESSURE: max or high

TIME UNDER PRESSURE: 32 or 40 minutes

RELEASE: natural

TOTAL TIME WITH PRESSURE: about 2 hours

TOTAL TIME WITH SLOW COOKING: about 5 hours

GLUTEN-FREE

2 tablespoons olive oil

3 pounds boneless beef chuck, trimmed and cut into 1½-inch cubes; or beef stew meat, cut into 1½-inch cubes

1 medium yellow or white onion, chopped (1 cup)

4 medium Roma or plum tomatoes, chopped (1 cup)

3 medium garlic cloves, minced (1 tablespoon)

2 teaspoons mild smoked paprika

1½ teaspoons dried oregano

1 teaspoon table salt

½ teaspoon ground allspice

½ teaspoon ground black pepper

½ cup dry red wine, preferably a dry Spanish Rioja

1 cup carbonated cola (do not use diet, low-sugar, or sugar-free)

1½ pounds yellow fingerling or very small potatoes (do not peel)

A kalimotxo (or sometimes spelled "calimocho") is an original Spanish quaff: a drink of half red wine and half carbonated cola. We decided to revamp that classic as the base for a sweet and aromatic beef stew. Notice that you don't stir the potatoes into the stew; rather, you place them on top of the other ingredients so they steam and retain better texture in the finished dish.

1.

	Press	Set it for	Set time for	If needed, press
In all models	SAUTÉ	MEDIUM, NORMAL, or CUSTOM 300°F	20 minutes	START

2. As the pot heats, warm the oil in the insert set in a **5-, 6-, or 8-quart Instant Pot.** Add about half of the beef. (No crowding!) Brown the pieces *well,* turning occasionally, about 6 minutes. Use a slotted spoon to transfer these to a nearby large bowl, then continue browning the remainder of the beef in the same way before getting it into the bowl.

3. Add the onion to the pot and cook, stirring often, until softened, about 3 minutes. Add the tomatoes and garlic; cook, stirring often, until the tomatoes begin to break down, about 2 minutes. Stir in the smoked paprika, oregano, salt, allspice, and pepper until aromatic, just a few seconds.

4. Pour in the wine and scrape up any browned bits on the pot's bottom. Turn off the heat and stir in the cola. Return the beef and any accumulated juice to the pot. Stir well again, then pile the potatoes on top of the other ingredients without stirring them in. Lock the lid onto the cooker.

5.

	Set pot for	Set level to	Valve must be	Set time for	If needed, press
For Max pots only	PRESSURE COOK	MAX	—	32 minutes with the KEEP WARM setting off	START
For all other pots	PRESSURE COOK or MANUAL	HIGH	Closed	40 minutes with the KEEP WARM setting off	START
For the slow-cook function	SLOW COOK	HIGH	Open	4½ hours with the KEEP WARM setting off	START

6. When the pot has finished cooking under pressure, turn it off and let its pressure **return to normal naturally,** about 35 minutes. Whichever cooking method you've used, unlatch the lid and open the cooker. Set the lid askew over the pot and set it aside for 2 to 3 minutes so that the beef tenderizes a bit as it absorbs some of the sauce. Stir gently (so the potatoes don't break apart) before serving warm.

Other Pots

- For a 3-quart Instant Pot, you *must* halve all of the ingredient amounts.

- For an 8-quart Instant Pot, you *can* increase all of the ingredient amounts by 50 percent.

- For a 10-quart Instant Pot, you *must* increase all of the ingredient amounts by 50 percent or you *can* even double the amounts.

Beyond

- Add complexity to the stew's sweetness by drizzling servings with olive oil—or better yet, smoked olive oil.

- Or sprinkle the servings with lots of stemmed and minced fresh oregano leaves or trimmed and thinly sliced scallions.

- And serve it with a more savory side like Wheat Berry "Risotto" (page 366).

Beef Enchilada Stew

13 ingredients	**SPECIAL EQUIPMENT:** none	**TIME UNDER PRESSURE:** 10 minutes	**TOTAL TIME WITH PRESSURE:** about 30 minutes
4–6 SERVINGS			
METHOD: fast/slow	**PRESSURE:** low	**RELEASE:** quick	**TOTAL TIME WITH SLOW COOKING:** about 2 hours 15 minutes

1 tablespoon dark brown sugar

2 teaspoons ground cumin

1 teaspoon mild smoked paprika

½ teaspoon onion powder

½ teaspoon garlic powder

½ teaspoon table salt

½ teaspoon ground black pepper

2 pounds beef cube steak, cut into 1-inch-wide strips

1 cup canned crushed tomatoes

½ cup dark beer, such as Dos Equis

2 tablespoons lime juice

1 tablespoon standard chili powder

6 ounces American mild cheddar or Monterey Jack cheese, shredded (1½ cups); or a packaged Tex-Mex blend

Other Pots

- For a 3-quart Instant Pot, you *must* halve all of the ingredient amounts.

- For an 8-quart Instant Pot, you *must* increase almost all of the ingredient amounts by 50 percent *except* you *must* use only 2½ tablespoons lime juice.

- For a 10-quart Instant Pot, you *must* double almost all of the ingredient amounts *except* you *must* use 1½ cups beer (a 12-ounce bottle) and only 3 tablespoons lime juice.

Beyond

- The stew is not super wet, so you can serve it *in* flour tortillas, if you use a slotted spoon to keep even the small amount of liquid out of the tortillas.

- Garnish the servings with thinly sliced scallions.

- Or pickled red onions.

What if we undid beef enchiladas, got rid of the tortillas, and made a meal out of the filling and the sauce? We'd have this easy stew! It uses cube steak with all its little holes and indentations, which let the meat 1) hold onto the spices and 2) cook in no time so you can have the flavors of enchiladas without much work at all.

1. Stir the brown sugar, cumin, smoked paprika, onion powder, garlic powder, salt, and pepper in a large bowl until uniform. Add the beef strips and toss until they are thoroughly coated in the spice mixture.

2. Stir the crushed tomatoes, beer, lime juice, and chili powder in the insert set in a **5- or 6-quart Instant Pot.** Add the coated meat (and any remaining spices in the bowl) and stir gently until the meat is coated in the sauce. Lock the lid on the pot.

3.

	Set pot for	Set level to	Valve must be	Set time for	If needed, press
For *all* pots	PRESSURE COOK or MANUAL	LOW	Closed	10 minutes with the KEEP WARM setting off	START
For the slow-cook function	SLOW COOK	HIGH	Open	2 hours with the KEEP WARM setting off	START

4. When the pot has finished cooking under pressure, use the **quick-release method** to bring the pressure back to normal. Whichever cooking method you've used, unlatch the lid and open the cooker.

5. Sprinkle the cheese over the top of the stew. Set the lid askew over the pot and set it aside for 5 minutes to melt the cheese. Serve warm.

Throwback Takeout Pepper Steak

11 ingredients	
4–6 SERVINGS	
METHOD: fast/slow	
SPECIAL EQUIPMENT: none	
PRESSURE: max or high	
TIME UNDER PRESSURE: 3 or 4 minutes	
RELEASE: quick	
TOTAL TIME WITH PRESSURE: about 30 minutes	
TOTAL TIME WITH SLOW COOKING: about 2 hours 15 minutes	
CAN BE GLUTEN-FREE	

2¼ pounds boneless beef sirloin, cut against the grain into ½-inch-wide strips (see the headnote for more information)

3 tablespoons hoisin sauce (gluten-free, if necessary—see page 18 for more information)

2 tablespoons minced peeled fresh ginger

2 medium garlic cloves, minced (2 teaspoons)

1½ tablespoons regular or low-sodium soy sauce, or gluten-free tamari sauce

1½ tablespoons unseasoned rice vinegar

4 medium green bell peppers, stemmed, cored, and sliced into ½-inch-wide strips

6 medium scallions, trimmed and thinly sliced (2 cups)

1 cup beef or chicken broth

1 tablespoon water

2 teaspoons cornstarch or potato starch

Other Pots

- For a 3-quart Instant Pot, you *must* halve almost all of the ingredient amounts *except* you *must* use ¾ cup broth.

- For an 8-quart Instant Pot, you *must* increase all of the ingredient amounts by 50 percent.

- For a 10-quart Instant Pot, you *must* double almost all of the ingredient amounts *except* you *must* use 2⅓ cups broth.

Beyond

- For a sweeter and more colorful dish, substitute red and/or yellow bell peppers for the green.

- For a slightly less sweet and saltier dish, substitute oyster sauce for the hoisin sauce.

We don't mean "pepper" as in ground pepper. Nor do we mean a version of Salisbury steak. Instead, we mean "pepper" as in bell pepper strips. This dish was popular in Chinese-American restaurants in the 1960s and '70s, and it's still a big batch of comfort food: salty, aromatic, and satisfying. Use only fresh bell pepper strips. Frozen ones don't have so bright a flavor and become a bit too soft in this dish.

To slice the beef against the grain, run your fingers across the meat, pressing down gently to reveal the strips (or fibers) that make up the cut. Slice the steak at a 90-degree angle to the direction of these strips (that is, *not* parallel with them but "against the grain.")

1. Mix the beef, hoisin sauce, ginger, garlic, soy or tamari sauce, and rice vinegar in the insert set in a **5- or 6-quart Instant Pot** until the beef is evenly and thoroughly coated in the sauce mixture.

2. Sprinkle the bell pepper strips and scallions over the top of the beef mixture without stirring them in. Pour the broth on top and lock the lid on the pot.

3.

	Set pot for	Set level to	Valve must be	Set time for	If needed, press
For Max pots only	PRESSURE COOK	MAX	—	3 minutes with the KEEP WARM setting off	START
For all other pots	PRESSURE COOK or MANUAL	HIGH	Closed	4 minutes with the KEEP WARM setting off	START
For the slow-cook function	SLOW COOK	HIGH	Open	2 hours with the KEEP WARM setting off	START

4. When the pot has finished cooking under pressure, use the **quick-release method** to bring the pressure back to normal. Whichever cooking method you've used, unlatch the lid and open the cooker. Whisk the water and cornstarch or potato starch in a small bowl until smooth.

5.

	Press	Set it for	Set time for	If needed, press
In all models	SAUTÉ	MEDIUM, NORMAL, or CUSTOM 300°F	5 minutes	START

6. As the sauce comes to a simmer, stir in the starch slurry. Cook, stirring constantly, until somewhat thickened, less than 1 minute. Turn off the heat and use hot pads or silicone baking mitts to transfer the (hot!) insert to a nearby wire rack. Cool for 2 to 3 minutes, then serve hot.

Not-Really-Chipotle's Barbacoa Beef

13 ingredients

4–6 SERVINGS

METHOD: fast/slow

SPECIAL EQUIPMENT: none

PRESSURE: high

TIME UNDER PRESSURE: 35 minutes

RELEASE: natural

TOTAL TIME WITH PRESSURE: about 1½ hours

TOTAL TIME WITH SLOW COOKING: about 4½ hours

CAN BE GLUTEN-FREE

1 tablespoon olive oil

2 pounds boneless beef chuck, cut into 2-inch pieces; or beef stew meat, cut into 2-inch pieces

Up to 6 medium garlic cloves, minced (2 tablespoons)

2 canned chipotle chiles in adobo sauce, stemmed, cored, and minced (seeded, if desired—and gluten-free, if necessary)

1 tablespoon mild paprika

2 teaspoons ground cumin

2 teaspoons onion powder

1 teaspoon ground black pepper

2 tablespoons adobo sauce from the can or a chipotle-flavored hot sauce, such as Cholula (either gluten-free, if necessary)

2 tablespoons apple cider vinegar

2 tablespoons lime juice

2 tablespoons regular or low-sodium soy sauce, or gluten-free tamari sauce

¾ cup beef broth

On the road, we've been known to drive out of the way (unheard of!) to find a Chipotle's and wolf down the barbacoa. In an online forum recently, we discovered we weren't the only ones. So here we are: a copycat recipe for the IP. There are three secrets to success—which happen to be three simple ingredients: 1) lots of garlic (seriously!), 2) canned chipotle chiles in adobo sauce (for the smokiness), and 3) apple cider vinegar (for zip). We upped the game a bit by using olive oil for a slightly sweeter finish and by giving the stew a heavy splash of soy sauce for greater umami flavor.

A new can of chipotles in adobo sauce should have about the 2 tablespoons sauce you need here. If you're using a can you've already opened or if your can is scant on sauce, you can make up the difference with a chipotle-flavored hot sauce like Cholula. If you skip the hot sauce and use a reduced amount of adobo sauce from the can, you *must* make up the liquid difference with more broth.

1.

	Press	Set it for	Set time for	If needed, press
In all models	SAUTÉ	MEDIUM, NORMAL, or CUSTOM 300°F	10 minutes	START

2. As the pot heats, warm the oil in the insert set in a **5- or 6-quart Instant Pot.** Add the meat and cook, stirring often, until it browns, about 6 minutes. Get good color on some of the pieces (although there will be a lot of boiling juices in the pot). Stir in the garlic and minced chipotle until aromatic, just a few seconds.

3. Stir in the paprika, cumin, onion powder, and pepper. Warm by stirring a few times, then stir in the adobo sauce, vinegar, lime juice, and soy or tamari sauce. Scrape up any browned bits on the pot's bottom and turn off the heat. Stir in the broth until uniform. Lock the lid on the pot.

4.

	Set pot for	Set level to	Valve must be	Set time for	If needed, press
For *all* pots	PRESSURE COOK or MANUAL	HIGH	Closed	35 minutes with the KEEP WARM setting off	START
For the slow-cook function	SLOW COOK	HIGH	Open	4 hours with the KEEP WARM setting off	START

5. When the pot has finished cooking under pressure, turn it off and let the pressure **return to normal naturally,** about 35 minutes. Whichever cooking method you've used, unlatch the lid and open the cooker.

6. Use two forks to shred the beef right in the pot. Stir it into the sauce and set the pot aside for 2 to 3 minutes so that the meat continues to absorb the juices. Serve warm.

Other Pots

- For a 3-quart Instant Pot, you *must* halve almost all of the ingredient amounts *except* you *must* use ½ cup broth.

- For an 8-quart Instant Pot, you must increase almost all of the ingredient amounts by 50 percent *except* you *must* use 1¼ cups broth.

- For a 10-quart Instant Pot, you *must* double almost all of the ingredient amounts *except* you *must* use 2 cups broth.

Beyond

- For a complete take on the original, serve the stew in bowls over Not-Really-Chipotle's Cilantro-Lime Rice (page 358).

- Or serve in flour or corn tortillas with hot sauce (or salsa), sliced avocado, sliced radishes, and/or diced mango.

See photo in insert.

Balsamic Beef Stew

10 ingredients	
6 SERVINGS	
METHOD: fast/slow	

SPECIAL EQUIPMENT: none	
PRESSURE: max or high	

TIME UNDER PRESSURE: 40 or 45 minutes	
RELEASE: natural	

TOTAL TIME WITH PRESSURE: about 1 hour 45 minutes	

TOTAL TIME WITH SLOW COOKING: about 5 hours	
GLUTEN-FREE	

---

2 tablespoons butter

4 large single-lobe shallots, each lobe peeled and halved widthwise

2½ pounds boneless beef chuck, cut into 1½-inch pieces; or beef stew meat, cut into 1½-inch pieces

1 cup beef broth

¼ cup balsamic vinegar

1 teaspoon table salt

1 teaspoon ground black pepper

One 3- to 4-inch fresh rosemary sprig

1 multi-stemmed fresh thyme sprig

2 tablespoons tomato paste

If you're a fan of super-savory stews and braises, this recipe is for you! The sweet notes from the tomato paste will be almost overwhelmed by the balsamic vinegar. If you've never braised beef in it, you haven't lived your best life. The vinegar mellows and becomes a gentle, slightly sour, somewhat woodsy note against the beef. Don't use an aged, syrupy balsamic vinegar. A sturdy one for everyday salad dressings is best here.

1.

	Press	Set it for	Set time for	If needed, press
In all models	SAUTÉ	MEDIUM, NORMAL, or CUSTOM 300°F	10 minutes	START

2. As the pot heats, melt the butter in the insert set in a **5- or 6-quart Instant Pot.** Add the shallots and cook, stirring gently but often, until a little softened, about 3 minutes.

3. Add the beef and continue cooking, stirring often but gently (to preserve the shallots) until the meat loses its raw, red color, about 2 minutes. Pour in the broth and scrape up any browned bits on the pot's bottom. Turn off the heat.

4. Stir in the vinegar, salt, and pepper. Tuck the herb sprigs into the stew and lock the lid on the pot.

5.

	Set pot for	Set level to	Valve must be	Set time for	If needed, press
For Max pots only	PRESSURE COOK	MAX	—	40 minutes with the KEEP WARM setting off	START
For all other pots	PRESSURE COOK or MANUAL	HIGH	Closed	45 minutes with the KEEP WARM setting off	START
For the slow-cook function	SLOW COOK	HIGH	Open	4 hours with the KEEP WARM setting off	START

6. When the pot has finished cooking under pressure, turn it off and let the pressure **return to normal naturally,** about 35 minutes. Whichever cooking method you've used, unlatch the lid and open the cooker. Fish out and discard the herb sprigs.

7.

	Press	Set it for	Set time for	If needed, press
In all models	SAUTÉ	MEDIUM, NORMAL, or CUSTOM 300°F	20 minutes	START

8. As the stew comes to a simmer, stir in the tomato paste. Continue cooking until it dissolves into the sauce, about 1 minute. Turn off the heat, set the lid askew over the pot, and set it aside for 5 minutes to let the beef tenderize as it continues to absorb the sauce. Serve warm.

Other Pots

- For a 3-quart Instant Pot, you *must* halve all of the ingredient amounts.

- For an 8-quart Instant Pot, you *must* increase almost all of the ingredient amounts by 50 percent *except* you *must* use the stated amount of rosemary (1 sprig).

- For a 10-quart Instant Pot, you *must* double almost all of the ingredient amounts *except* you *must* use 2¼ cups broth.

Beyond

- If you want to thicken the sauce after you open the pot in step 6, turn the machine to its SAUTÉ setting set to MEDIUM, NORMAL, or CUSTOM 300°F. Whisk 1½ tablespoons water and 1 tablespoon potato starch in a small bowl until smooth (this is for the 5- or 6-quart versions, adjust as necessary for other pot sizes). When the sauce is bubbling, stir this slurry into the pot and cook, stirring constantly, until somewhat thickened, less than 1 minute. Turn off the heat and use hot pads or silicone baking mitts to transfer the (hot!) insert to a wire rack (to stop the cooking and keep the potato starch from breaking).

Make-Your-Own-Curry Beef Stew

12 or 13 ingredients	SPECIAL EQUIPMENT: none	TIME UNDER PRESSURE: 40 or 45 minutes	TOTAL TIME WITH PRESSURE: about 1 hour 45 minutes	TOTAL TIME WITH SLOW COOKING: about 5 hours
6 SERVINGS	PRESSURE: max or high			
METHOD: fast/slow		RELEASE: natural		GLUTEN-FREE

2½ pounds boneless beef top or bottom round, cut into 1½-inch cubes; or beef stew meat, cut into 1½-inch cubes

1½ to 2½ teaspoons ground coriander

1 to 2 teaspoons ground cardamom

1 to 1½ teaspoons ground dried ginger

Up to 1 teaspoon ground cumin

Up to 1 teaspoon fennel seeds (optional)

Up to ½ teaspoon ground cloves

Up to ½ teaspoon ground dried cayenne

½ teaspoon table salt

½ stick (4 tablespoons or ¼ cup) butter

2 large yellow or white onions, halved and sliced into thin half-moons

¼ cup golden raisins

1½ cups chicken broth

This recipe's the real deal: a heady mix of spices blends with sweet raisins to balance the flavors perfectly. In fact, you can customize the spice blend quite a bit. The ratio of the spices listed highlights a certain warming, comforting feel, but you might prefer a little more musky flavor with more cumin or a few more aromatic notes with more cardamom in the mix. Chicken broth might be a bit of a surprise in a beef stew but its lighter flavor doesn't dull the many spices that go into the stew.

1. Stir the beef, coriander, cardamom, ginger, cumin, fennel seeds (if using), cloves, cayenne, and salt in a large bowl until the beef is evenly coated in the spices. Set aside.

2.

	Press	Set it for	Set time for	If needed, press
In all models	SAUTÉ	MEDIUM, NORMAL, or CUSTOM 300°F	10 minutes	START

3. As the pot heats, melt the butter in the insert set in a **5-, 6-, or 8-quart Instant Pot**. Add the onions and cook, stirring often, until softened, about 5 minutes.

4. Add the beef and any leftover spices in its bowl. Stir over the heat until aromatic but not browned, about 2 minutes. Stir in the raisins, then pour in the broth. Scrape up any browned bits on the pot's bottom. Turn off the heat and lock the lid onto the cooker.

5.

	Set pot for	Set level to	Valve must be	Set time for	If needed, press
For Max pots only	PRESSURE COOK	MAX	—	40 minutes with the KEEP WARM setting off	START
For all other pots	PRESSURE COOK or MANUAL	HIGH	Closed	45 minutes with the KEEP WARM setting off	START
For the slow-cook function	SLOW COOK	HIGH	Open	4½ hours with the KEEP WARM setting off	START

6. When the pot has finished cooking under pressure, turn it off and let the pressure **return to normal naturally,** about 35 minutes. Whichever cooking method you've used, unlatch the lid and open the cooker. Stir well before serving hot.

Other Pots

- For a 3-quart Instant Pot, you *must* halve all of the ingredient amounts.

- For an 8-quart Instant Pot, you *can* increase all of the ingredient amounts by 50 percent.

- For a 10-quart Instant Pot, you *must* increase all of the ingredient amounts by 50 percent or you *can* even double the amounts.

Beyond

- To thicken the sauce, whisk 1 tablespoon water and 2 teaspoons cornstarch in a small bowl until smooth (this is for a 5-, 6-, or 8-quart pot; adjust as necessary for other pot sizes). After you open the pot in step 6, set it on SAUTÉ at the MEDIUM, NORMAL, or CUSTOM 300°F setting. Stir the cornstarch slurry into the bubbling stew and cook, stirring constantly, until a bit thickened, less than 1 minute. Turn off the heat and remove the (hot!) insert from the pot to stop the cooking. Set aside for a couple of minutes to blend the flavors.

- To get rid of the slightly bitter notes from the butter's milk solids, substitute ghee for the butter.

Braised Brisket

13 ingredients

6–8 SERVINGS

METHOD: fast/slow

SPECIAL EQUIPMENT: none

PRESSURE: max or high

TIME UNDER PRESSURE: 70 or 80 minutes

RELEASE: natural

TOTAL TIME WITH PRESSURE: about 2½ hours

TOTAL TIME WITH SLOW COOKING: about 5½ hours

CAN BE GLUTEN-FREE

1 tablespoon olive oil

One 3½-pound beef brisket, preferably a first- or flat-cut brisket, trimmed of any excess fat (although a thin layer of fat should be left over the meat)

1 large yellow or white onion, chopped (1½ cups)

1½ cups dry but light red wine, such as Pinot Noir; or 1¼ cups beef broth and ¼ cup unsweetened cranberry juice

One 14-ounce can diced tomatoes *packed in juice* but drained (about 1¼ cups)

½ cup beef or chicken broth

2 tablespoons Worcestershire sauce (gluten-free, if necessary)

½ teaspoon table salt

½ teaspoon ground black pepper

One 3- to 4-inch fresh rosemary sprig

One multi-stemmed fresh thyme sprig

2 tablespoons water

1 tablespoon potato starch

If you only know barbecue brisket, you might not be familiar with the cut braised in wine with tomatoes. In fact, this is the traditional main course in some homes at Passover and other holidays. The brisket becomes soft and tender, not as firm as smoked brisket from a barbecue joint, but sliceable nonetheless. If you prefer a *super*-soft, falling-apart braised brisket, add 10 minutes to the pressure-cooking time (for either MAX or HIGH) or another hour to the slow-cooking time. (If you're observant of kosher laws and celebrating Passover, you'll have to use a Worcestershire sauce that's kosher for Passover — that is, not thickened with a wheat derivative. A gluten-free Worcestershire sauce should fit the bill, but check the label.)

1.

	Press	Set it for	Set time for	If needed, press
In all models	SAUTÉ	MEDIUM, NORMAL, or CUSTOM 300°F	15 minutes	START

2. As the pot heats, warm the oil in the insert set in a **6- or 8-quart Instant Pot.** Add the brisket and brown well undisturbed for 4 minutes. Turn it over and continue browning undisturbed for 4 minutes. Transfer the brisket to a nearby cutting board.

3. Add the onion to the pot and cook, stirring often, until fragrant but not quite softened, about 2 minutes. Pour in the wine and scrape up any browned bits on the pot's bottom. Turn off the heat.

4. Stir in the tomatoes, broth, Worcestershire sauce, salt, and pepper. Return the beef to the pot and turn it to coat. Tuck the fresh herb sprigs around the beef and lock the lid onto the cooker.

5.

	Set pot for	Set level to	Valve must be	Set time for	If needed, press
For Max pots only	PRESSURE COOK	MAX	—	1 hour 10 minutes with the KEEP WARM setting off	START
For all other pots	PRESSURE COOK or MANUAL	HIGH	Closed	1 hour 20 minutes with the KEEP WARM setting off	START
For the slow-cook function	SLOW COOK	HIGH	Open	5 hours with the KEEP WARM setting off	START

6. When the pot has finished cooking under pressure, turn it off and let the pressure **return to normal naturally,** about 45 minutes. Whichever cooking method you've used, unlatch the lid and open the cooker. Fish out and discard the herb sprigs. Use a meat fork and a metal spatula to transfer the brisket to a nearby cutting board. Whisk the water and potato starch in a small bowl.

7.

	Press	Set it for	Set time for	If needed, press
In all models	SAUTÉ	MEDIUM, NORMAL, or CUSTOM 300°F	5 minutes	START

8. As the sauce comes to a simmer, stir in the potato starch slurry. Continue cooking, stirring constantly, until the sauce thickens somewhat, less than 1 minute. Turn off the heat and use hot pads or silicone baking mitts to transfer the (hot!) insert to a nearby wire rack (to stop the cooking and to keep the potato starch from breaking). Cool for 2 to 3 minutes.

9. Run your clean fingers across the brisket to determine which way the meat's fibers lie. Slice the brisket into ½-inch-thick strips at a 90-degree angle to this grain. Ladle the sauce from the insert over each serving.

Other Pots

- For a 3-quart Instant Pot, you *must* halve all of the ingredient amounts.

- For a 5-quart Instant Pot, you *must* use a 3-pound brisket while leaving the other ingredient amounts as stated.

- For a 10-quart Instant Pot, you *must* increase all of the ingredient amounts by 50 percent—or you *can* use two 3½-pound briskets, overlapping them slightly in the pot, along with a 50-percent increase of all of the remaining ingredients. In either case, you *must* increase the cooking time to 1½ hours under HIGH pressure (there is no MAX setting in the larger cooker as of this writing) or 6 hours with slow cooking.

Beyond

- Braised brisket is sometimes sweeter than this recipe's. If you want that more traditional flavor, add up to ½ cup raisins with the fresh herb sprigs.

Dinner-Party-Worthy Corned Beef & Cabbage

4 ingredients

6 SERVINGS

METHOD:
steam

SPECIAL EQUIPMENT:
a pressure- and food-safe rack or trivet

PRESSURE:
max or high twice

TIME UNDER PRESSURE:
54 or 65 minutes

RELEASE:
natural, then quick

TOTAL TIME WITH PRESSURE:
about 1 hour 45 minutes

CAN BE GLUTEN-FREE

1½ cups beer (preferably an IPA), unsweetened apple cider, or chicken broth

One 3½-pound corned beef, preferably the flat or point cut, and preferably low-sodium corned beef (gluten-free, if necessary), the seasoning packet *reserved*

¼ cup jarred prepared white horseradish (gluten-free, if necessary)

1 medium green cabbage, cut into six wedges through the core (to hold them together)

What's so special about this corned beef recipe? For one thing, the beef is smeared in horseradish, which sweetens under pressure, becoming a sophisticated, salty coating. For another, the cabbage is cooked separately so it doesn't become mushy. Our timing yields cabbage that's still *al dente*. If you like softer cabbage, add 2 minutes to the cooking time in step 6.

Prepared horseradish is salty and pressure-cooking exacerbates the saltiness of most ingredients, so this recipe works best with low-sodium corned beef. If you can't find a low-sodium cut, consider soaking a standard corned beef in a big bowl of water in the fridge for 4 to 8 hours, changing the water once, to remove some of that salt.

1. Pour the beer or its substitute into the insert set in a **5-, 6-, or 8-quart Instant Pot**. Sprinkle the seasonings from the seasoning packet with the corned beef into this liquid. Set a pressure- and food-safe rack or trivet in the insert.

2. Rinse the corned beef under cool water to remove some of the salt. Set it on the rack fat side up and smear the horseradish over the corned beef. Lock the lid on the pot.

3.

	Set pot for	Set level to	Valve must be	Set time for	If needed, press
For Max pots only	PRESSURE COOK	MAX	—	50 minutes with the KEEP WARM setting off	START
For all other pots	PRESSURE COOK or MANUAL	HIGH	Closed	1 hour with the KEEP WARM setting off	START

4. When the pot has finished cooking, turn it off and let the pressure **return to normal naturally,** about 35 minutes. Unlatch the lid and open the cooker.

5. Use a meat fork and a large metal spatula to transfer the corned beef to a nearby cutting board. Use kitchen tongs to remove the (hot!) rack from the pot. Set the cabbage wedges into the liquid in the pot. Lock the lid back onto the cooker.

6.

	Set pot for	Set level to	Valve must be	Set time for	If needed, press
For Max pots only	PRESSURE COOK	MAX	—	4 minutes with the KEEP WARM setting off	START
For all other pots	PRESSURE COOK or MANUAL	HIGH	Closed	5 minutes with the KEEP WARM setting off	START

7. When the pot has finished cooking, use the **quick-release method** to bring the pressure back to normal. Unlatch the lid and open the cooker. Slice the corned beef into strips against the grain and serve with the cabbage wedges as well as some of the "sauce" in the pot.

Other Pots

- For a **3-quart Instant Pot,** you *must* halve almost all of the ingredient amounts *except* you *must* use 1 cup beer, cider, or broth in the insert.

- For a **10-quart Instant Pot,** you *must* use 2½ cups beer, cider, or broth in the insert while otherwise completing the recipe as stated.

Beyond

- Miss the potatoes? Raw potatoes won't cook in the quick time the cabbage takes. Instead, sprinkle thawed frozen hash-brown potato cubes over the cabbage and into the broth before cooking the cabbage under pressure.

Not-Really-P.F.-Chang's Mongolian Beef

10 ingredients	SPECIAL EQUIPMENT: none
4–6 SERVINGS	PRESSURE: high
METHOD: fast/slow	TIME UNDER PRESSURE: 3 minutes
	RELEASE: natural
	TOTAL TIME WITH PRESSURE: about 30 minutes
	TOTAL TIME WITH SLOW COOKING: about 3 hours 15 minutes
	CAN BE GLUTEN-FREE

2 pounds beef flank steak, cut lengthwise in half, then across the grain into ½-inch-wide slices

½ cup low-sodium soy sauce or gluten-free tamari sauce

½ cup beef broth

½ cup packed dark brown sugar

2 tablespoons unseasoned rice vinegar

6 medium garlic cloves, minced (2 tablespoons)

1 tablespoon minced peeled fresh ginger

3 tablespoons water

2 tablespoons cornstarch

Medium scallions, trimmed and cut into 1-inch sections, for garnishing

Other Pots

- For a 3-quart Instant Pot, you *must* halve almost all of the ingredient amounts *except* you *must* use ⅓ cup broth.

- For an 8-quart Instant Pot, you *must* increase all of the ingredient amounts by 50 percent.

- For a 10-quart Instant Pot, you *must* double all of the ingredient amounts.

Beyond

- Serve the beef over cooked long-grain white rice, particularly jasmine rice.

- For a fancier presentation, slice the scallions lengthwise into long, thin strips, maybe five or six per scallions. Slice these strips into 1-inch pieces for garnishing.

Sure, there are many Mongolian beef recipes for the Instant Pot. But since P. F. Chang's version is such a crowd-pleaser, here's our copycat recipe. Our version uses flank steak, which has a distinctly beefier flavor than some other cuts. The dish is also fairly sweet, so we must use a natural release to keep all that hot, sugary sauce in the pot (and not on the counter). There's so much soy sauce that a low-sodium bottling is best.

1. Stir the beef, soy sauce, broth, brown sugar, vinegar, garlic, and ginger in a **5- or 6-quart Instant Pot** until the beef is evenly coated in the sauce and the brown sugar has dissolved. Lock the lid on the pot.

2.

	Set pot for	Set level to	Valve must be	Set time for	If needed, press
For *all* pots	PRESSURE COOK or MANUAL	HIGH	Closed	3 minutes with the KEEP WARM setting off	START
For the slow-cook function	SLOW COOK	HIGH	Open	3 hours with the KEEP WARM setting off	START

3. When the pot has finished cooking under pressure, turn it off and let its pressure **return to normal naturally,** about 20 minutes. Whichever cooking method you've used, unlatch the lid and open the cooker. Whisk the water and cornstarch in a small bowl until smooth.

4.

	Press	Set it for	Set time for	If needed, press
In all models	SAUTÉ	MEDIUM, NORMAL, or CUSTOM 300°F	5 minutes	START

5. As the sauce comes to a simmer, stir in the cornstarch slurry. Cook, stirring constantly, until somewhat thickened, less than 1 minute. Turn off the heat and use hot pads or silicone baking mitts to transfer the (hot!) insert to a nearby wire rack (to stop the cooking). Cool for 2 to 3 minutes, then garnish the servings with sliced scallions.

Braised Beef Bottom Round with Tomatoes and Cinnamon

11 ingredients	
6 SERVINGS	
METHOD: standard	

SPECIAL INGREDIENTS: none	
PRESSURE: max or high	

TIME UNDER PRESSURE: 70 or 90 minutes	
RELEASE: natural	

TOTAL TIME WITH PRESSURE: about 2 hours 45 minutes	
CAN BE GLUTEN-FREE	

2 tablespoons butter

One 3- to 3½-pound beef bottom round roast

2 medium yellow or white onions, chopped (2 cups)

½ cup beef or chicken broth

One 28-ounce can whole tomatoes *packed in juice* (3½ cups)

1 teaspoon ground cinnamon

1 teaspoon table salt

½ teaspoon ground allspice

Up to ½ teaspoon grated nutmeg

Up to ½ teaspoon ground cloves

½ teaspoon ground black pepper

Other Pots

- For a 3-quart Instant Pot, you *must* halve almost all of the ingredient amounts *except* you *must* use ⅓ cup broth.
- For an 8-quart Instant Pot, you *must* increase the broth to ¾ cup, while completing the recipe as otherwise stated.
- This recipe with these ratios does not work well in a 10-quart Instant Pot.

Beyond

- Serve the beef and sauce over cooked and drained egg or no-yolk noodles.
- For an even better meal, toss the hot noodles with butter and perhaps minced thyme leaves before serving.

Tomatoes and cinnamon are a match made in heaven! The spice skews the tomatoes toward the savory, a great partner to sweet, braised beef. To keep those tomatoes from breaking down into a sauce, use *whole* canned tomatoes (packed in juice, not puree). Yes, you must crush them by hand. Even so, they stay in pieces after cooking under pressure. (Diced tomatoes tend to melt into a sauce.)

1.

	Press	Set it for	Set time for	If needed, press
In all models	SAUTÉ	MEDIUM, NORMAL, or CUSTOM 300°F	10 minutes	START

2. As the pot heats, melt the butter in the insert set in a **5- or 6-quart Instant Pot.** Set the meat in the pot and brown well on both sides, turning only once, for about 8 minutes. The butter may well begin to brown. No worries! When done, transfer the beef to a nearby cutting board.

3. Add the onions to the pot and cook, stirring often, until they begin to soften, about 3 minutes. Pour in the broth and scrape up any browned bits on the pot's bottom. Turn off the heat.

4. Add the whole tomatoes by crushing them one by one in your clean hand. Add their juice from the can as well. Also stir in the cinnamon, salt, allspice, nutmeg, cloves, and pepper. Return the beef and any collected juices to the pot, nestling the meat into the sauce. Lock the lid on the pot.

5.

	Set pot for	Set level to	Valve must be	Set time for	If needed, press
For Max pots only	PRESSURE COOK	MAX	—	1 hour 10 minutes with the KEEP WARM setting off	START
For all other pots	PRESSURE COOK or MANUAL	HIGH	Closed	1 hour 30 minutes with the KEEP WARM setting off	START

6. When the pot has finished cooking under pressure, turn it off and let its pressure **return to normal naturally,** about 40 minutes. Unlatch the pot and open the cooker.

7. Use a meat fork and a heavy metal spatula to transfer the roast to a cutting board. Cool for 5 minutes, then carve the meat into ½-inch-thick slices against the grain. Serve with the sauce from the pot ladled over the meat.

No-Brainer Orange Beef with Broccoli

14 ingredients

4–6 SERVINGS

METHOD:
standard

SPECIAL EQUIPMENT:
none

PRESSURE:
low, then high

TIME UNDER PRESSURE:
4 minutes

RELEASE:
quick, then modified natural

TOTAL TIME WITH PRESSURE:
about 30 minutes

CAN BE GLUTEN-FREE

2 pounds boneless beef sirloin, cut against the grain into ½-inch-wide strips (for more information on cutting meat against the grain, see the headnote on page 255)

One 11-ounce can mandarin orange sections *packed in juice* (not in syrup)

4 medium scallions, trimmed and thinly sliced (1⅓ cups)

¼ cup beef or chicken broth

3 tablespoons regular or low-sodium soy sauce, or gluten-free tamari sauce

2 tablespoons minced peeled fresh ginger

1 tablespoon finely grated orange zest

1 tablespoon granulated white sugar

1 tablespoon hot red chile sauce, preferably Sriracha

½ teaspoon ground coriander

½ teaspoon ground cinnamon

1 pound medium fresh broccoli florets (3 cups)

1 tablespoon water

2 teaspoons cornstarch or potato starch

Here's a fairly easy dump-and-stir version of a favorite take-out stir-fry. Everything's stirred in the pot without browning. However, we do add an extra step for cooking the broccoli. In essence, we want to cook it as little as possible to keep it as fresh and crunchy. Other than that, there's nothing much easier than this tasty dinner. Have the beer cold or the iced tea fresh.

1. Gently stir the beef, orange sections with their juice, scallions, broth, soy or tamari sauce, ginger, orange zest, sugar, red chile sauce, coriander, and cinnamon in a **5- or 6-quart Instant Pot** until the beef is coated in the spices and the sugar has dissolved. Lock the lid on the pot.

2.

	Set pot for	Set level to	Valve must be	Set time for	If needed, press
For *all* pots	PRESSURE COOK or MANUAL	LOW	Closed	4 minutes with the KEEP WARM setting off	START

3. When the pot has finished cooking, use the **quick-release method** to bring the pressure back to normal. Unlatch the lid and open the cooker. Stir well, then sprinkle the broccoli florets over everything. Lock the lid on the pot again.

4.

	Set pot for	Set level to	Valve must be	Set time for	If needed, press
For *all* pots	PRESSURE COOK or MANUAL	HIGH	Closed	0 or 1 minute with the KEEP WARM setting off	START

5. *Do not* let the machine come to full pressure. Instead, **the moment the pin pops up** to lock the lid on the pot, turn it off and let the pressure **return to normal naturally for 1 minute.** Then use the **quick-release method** to get rid of the pot's residual pressure. Unlatch the lid and open the cooker. Whisk the water and cornstarch or potato starch in a small bowl until smooth.

6.

	Press	Set it for	Set time for	If needed, press
In all models	SAUTÉ	MEDIUM, NORMAL, or CUSTOM 300°F	5 minutes	START

7. As the sauce comes to a simmer, stir in the starch slurry. Continue cooking, stirring constantly, until somewhat thickened, less than 1 minute. Turn off the heat and use hot pads or silicone baking mitts to transfer the (hot!) insert to a nearby wire rack (to stop the cooking). Set aside for 2 to 3 minutes to blend the flavors. Serve warm.

Other Pots

- For a 3-quart Instant Pot, you *must* halve almost all of the ingredient amounts *except* you *must* use ¼ cup broth.

- For an 8-quart Instant Pot, you *must* increase almost all of the ingredient amounts by 50 percent *except* you *must* use ¾ cup broth.

- For a 10-quart Instant Pot, you *must* double almost all of the ingredient amounts *except* you *must* use 1 cup broth.

Beyond

- Substitute ¾ teaspoon five-spice powder for the ground coriander and ground cinnamon.

- Garnish the servings with toasted sesame oil, sesame seeds, minced fresh celery leaves, sliced almonds, and/or more Sriracha.

- Rather than serving this dish over cooked white rice, try it over softened and drained glass noodles, particularly mung bean or sweet potato noodles.

Jalapeño-Braised Beef Bottom Round

8 ingredients	SPECIAL EQUIPMENT: none	TIME UNDER PRESSURE: 70 or 90 minutes	TOTAL TIME WITH PRESSURE: about 2 hours 35 minutes	TOTAL TIME WITH SLOW COOKING: about 5½ hours
6 SERVINGS				
METHOD: fast/slow	PRESSURE: max or high	RELEASE: natural		CAN BE GLUTEN-FREE

---

2 tablespoons vegetable, canola, or other neutral-flavored oil

One 3½-pound beef bottom round roast

1 cup hard apple cider (gluten-free, if necessary) or unsweetened (non-alcoholic) apple cider

½ cup sweet pickle relish (gluten-free, if necessary)

½ cup drained jarred (hot or "tamed") pickled jalapeño rings (gluten-free, if necessary)

¼ cup brine from the jar of pickled jalapeño rings

¼ cup jarred barbecue sauce, preferably a smooth sauce (gluten-free, if necessary)

1½ tablespoons yellow mustard (gluten-free, if necessary)

Make sure you get a big bottle of pickled jalapeño rings for this recipe. You'll use a lot of them as well as some of the brine from the jar. It all may seem as if it would produce an ungodly hot dish. But the pressure softens the burn, leaving you with a sweet-sour-and-spicy roast.

Unfortunately, when we tried this dish in a **10-quart Instant Pot,** we got very poor results: Increasing the liquid only left a small piece of meat swamped in sauce. And increasing the size of the cut (almost impossible to find in most supermarkets, to be honest) changed the timings dramatically and resulted in sections of the cut becoming too dried out. If you're looking to cook a large hunk of beef in a 10-quart machine, check out our chuck roast recipe on page 271.

1.

	Press	Set it for	Set time for	If needed, press
In all models	SAUTÉ	MEDIUM, NORMAL, or CUSTOM 300°F	10 minutes	START

2. As the pot heats, warm the oil in the insert set in a **5-, 6-, or 8-quart Instant Pot.** Add the beef and brown well on both sides, turning once, about 8 minutes. Transfer the beef to a nearby cutting board.

3. Pour in the cider or juice and scrape up any browned bits on the pot's bottom. Turn off the heat and stir in the relish, jalapeños, brine, barbecue sauce, and mustard until smooth. Return the beef to the pot (as well as any collected juices), nestling the meat into the sauce. Lock the lid on the pot.

4.

	Set pot for	Set level to	Valve must be	Set time for	If needed, press
For Max pots only	PRESSURE COOK	MAX	—	1 hour 10 minutes with the KEEP WARM setting off	START
For all other pots	PRESSURE COOK or MANUAL	HIGH	Closed	1 hour 30 minutes with the KEEP WARM setting off	START
For the slow-cook function	SLOW COOK	HIGH	Open	5 hours with the KEEP WARM setting off	START

5. When the pot has finished cooking under pressure, turn it off and let its pressure **return to normal naturally,** about 40 minutes. Whichever cooking method you've used, unlatch the lid and open the cooker.

6. Use a meat fork and a heavy metal spatula to transfer the bottom round to a cutting board. Cool for 5 minutes, then slice into ½-inch-thick strips against the grain (for more information on slicing beef against the grain, see the headnote on page 255). Serve with the sauce from the pot ladled over the meat.

Other Pots

- For a 3-quart Instant Pot, you *must* use a 2-pound beef bottom round roast and halve the remaining ingredients. Reduce the cooking time under pressure on HIGH to 1 hour 5 minutes (there is no MAX setting in these smaller pots). Maintain the same timing for slow cooking.

- This recipe is not easily adaptable for a 10-quart Instant Pot.

Beyond

- You can substitute a boneless beef chuck roast for the bottom round. The results will definitely be richer—but not sliceable: You'll need to carve the cooked chuck into chunks. Cook under pressure at 1 hour at MAX pressure or 1 hour 15 minutes at HIGH pressure, followed by a natural release. Or reduce the slow-cooking time to 4½ hours.

Spicy-Sweet Beef Short Ribs

14 ingredients

6 SERVINGS

METHOD:
fast/slow

SPECIAL EQUIPMENT:
none

PRESSURE:
max or high

TIME UNDER PRESSURE:
35 or 45 minutes

RELEASE:
natural

TOTAL TIME WITH PRESSURE:
about 1 hour 45 minutes

TOTAL TIME WITH SLOW COOKING:
about 5½ hours

CAN BE GLUTEN-FREE

2 tablespoons peanut oil (or vegetable oil, if necessary)

Six 8- to 9-ounce bone-in beef short ribs

1 medium yellow or white onion, chopped (1 cup)

Up to 8 large garlic cloves, *thinly* sliced

2 tablespoons minced peeled fresh ginger

1 cup beef broth

½ cup regular or low-sodium soy sauce, or gluten-free tamari sauce

¼ cup packed dark brown sugar

2 tablespoons unseasoned rice vinegar

2 tablespoons thick red chile sauce, such as sambal oelek

2 tablespoons water

1 tablespoon cornstarch

12 medium scallions, trimmed and cut into 1½- to 2-inch pieces

1 tablespoon toasted sesame oil

We love Korean-style barbecued short ribs. Unfortunately, since these "cross-cut" short ribs are cut across the bones (rather than with them) to create strips of meat with bone ovals along the length, they don't do very well under pressure. The meat gets too soft and the bones fall out to make a mess in the pot. So we've morphed the flavors of Korean barbecue into a braise with more standard North American short ribs (sometimes called "English short ribs"—that is, long bones with meat mounded at one end).

Beef short ribs with exceptionally long bones will not fit in an Instant Pot. Have the butcher trim them down so the bone is only a little longer than the lump of meat.

1.

	Press	Set it for	Set time for	If needed, press
In all models	SAUTÉ	MEDIUM, NORMAL, or CUSTOM 300°F	20 minutes	START

2. As the pot heats, warm the oil in the insert set in a **5-, 6-, or 8-quart Instant Pot.** Add the short ribs and brown *well* on all sides, turning occasionally, about 12 minutes. Don't get impatient! Brown is flavor. Transfer the short ribs to a nearby big bowl.

3. Spoon out and discard all but 1 tablespoon of the (hot!) fat in the insert. Add the onion and cook, stirring often, until barely softened, about 2 minutes. Stir in the garlic and ginger until fragrant, about 20 seconds.

4. Pour in the broth and scrape up any browned bits on the pot's bottom. Stir in the soy sauce, brown sugar, vinegar, and chile sauce until the brown sugar dissolves. Turn off the heat and return the shorts ribs and any accumulated juices to the pot. Lock the lid onto the cooker.

5.

	Set pot for	Set level to	Valve must be	Set time for	If needed, press
For Max pots only	PRESSURE COOK	MAX	—	35 minutes with the KEEP WARM setting off	START
For all other pots	PRESSURE COOK or MANUAL	HIGH	Closed	45 minutes with the KEEP WARM setting off	START
For the slow-cook function	SLOW COOK	HIGH	Open	5 hours with the KEEP WARM setting off	START

6. When the pot has finished cooking under pressure, turn it off and let its pressure **return to normal naturally,** about 40 minutes. Whichever cooking method you've used, unlatch the lid and open the cooker. Use kitchen tongs to transfer the short ribs to a nearby cutting board. Whisk the water and cornstarch in a small bowl until smooth.

7.

	Press	Set it for	Set time for	If needed, press
In all models	SAUTÉ	MEDIUM, NORMAL, or CUSTOM 300°F	10 minutes	START

8. As the sauce comes to a simmer, stir in the scallions. When the sauce is bubbling, stir in the cornstarch slurry and sesame oil. Cook, stirring constantly, until a little thickened, less than 1 minute. Turn off the heat.

9. Use hot pads or silicone baking mitts to transfer the (hot!) insert to a nearby wire rack. Return the short ribs to the pot, turning to coat them in the sauce. Let sit for 2 to 3 minutes to blend the flavors before serving warm.

Other Pots

- For a 3-quart Instant Pot, you *must* halve all of the ingredient amounts.

- For a 10-quart Instant Pot, you *must* increase all of the ingredient amounts by 50 percent or you *can* even double almost all of the amounts (making twelve short ribs!) *except* you *might* consider tripling the chile sauce.

Beyond

- For a more authentic flavor, substitute gochujang (a Korean chile paste) for the sambal oelek.

- Serve the short ribs over cooked white short-grain or "sushi" rice.

Sauerbraten-Style Tri Tip Roast

10 or 11 ingredients

6 SERVINGS

METHOD:
fast/slow

SPECIAL EQUIPMENT:
none

PRESSURE:
max or high

TIME UNDER PRESSURE:
32 or 40 minutes

RELEASE:
natural

TOTAL TIME WITH PRESSURE:
about 1½ hours

TOTAL TIME WITH SLOW COOKING:
about 3½ hours

CAN BE GLUTEN-FREE

2 tablespoons unsalted butter

One 2½-pound beef tri tip roast

1 cup drained jarred pepperoncini (gluten-free, if necessary)

1 small leek, white and pale green parts only, trimmed, halved lengthwise, washed for internal grit, and thinly sliced (⅓ cup)

1 medium garlic clove, minced (1 teaspoon)

One 3- to 4-inch fresh rosemary sprig

1 multi-stemmed fresh thyme sprig

8 juniper berries (optional)

¼ cup dry red wine, such as Cabernet Sauvignon; or unsweetened cranberry juice

¼ cup red wine vinegar

½ cup beef or chicken broth

Consider this a simpler version of sauerbraten. There's no extra step of marinating the meat because of the way the pressure blends the flavors (and tenderizes the cut). Even better, a tri tip roast is a luxurious cut, from the sirloin with the flavor of a chuck roast but the leanness of a round steak.

The juniper berries in this recipe are optional, but they will give the sauce that true "sauerbraten" flavor. Store a jar of juniper berries in a cool, dry cupboard for up to 6 months or in the freezer for up to 2 years.

1.

	Press	Set it for	Set time for	If needed, press
In all models	SAUTÉ	MEDIUM, NORMAL, or CUSTOM 300°F	10 minutes	START

2. As the pot heats, melt the butter in the insert set in a **5- or 6-quart Instant Pot**. Add the beef and brown it *well* on both sides, turning as little as possible, about 10 minutes. Transfer the beef to a nearby bowl.

3. Add the pepperoncini, leek, garlic, thyme, rosemary, and juniper berries (if using) to the pot. Stir until aromatic, about 30 seconds; then pour in the wine and vinegar. Scrape up any browned bits on the pot's bottom and turn off the heat.

4. Stir in the broth and return the meat to the pot, nestling it into the sauce. Add any accumulated juices in its bowl as well. Lock the lid onto the cooker.

5.

	Set pot for	Set level to	Valve must be	Set time for	If needed, press
For Max pots only	PRESSURE COOK	MAX	—	32 minutes with the KEEP WARM setting off	START
For all other pots	PRESSURE COOK or MANUAL	HIGH	Closed	40 minutes with the KEEP WARM setting off	START
For the slow-cook function	SLOW COOK	HIGH	Open	3 hours with the KEEP WARM setting off	START

6. When the pot has finished cooking under pressure, turn it off and let its pressure **return to normal naturally,** about 35 minutes. Whichever cooking method you've used, unlatch the lid and open the cooker. Transfer the roast to a nearby cutting board and cool for 5 minutes.

7. Use a flatware tablespoon to skim the fat off the surface of the sauce in the pot. Fish out and discard the herb sprigs and the juniper berries (if you've used them). Carve the meat into ½-inch-thick slices against the grain (for more information about cutting beef against the grain, see page 255). Serve with the sauce from the pot.

Other Pots

- For a 3-quart Instant Pot, you *must* halve all of the ingredient amounts.

- For an 8-quart Instant Pot, you *must* increase all of the ingredient amounts by 50 percent and you *must* increase the cooking time at HIGH pressure to 45 minutes (there is no Max 8-quart model as of this writing).

- For a 10-quart Instant Pot, you *must* double all of the ingredient amounts, using *two* 2½-pound tri tip roasts side by side (with no change in the cooking time).

Beyond

- Serve the roast and sauce over cooked and drained egg or no-yolk noodles that have been tossed while hot with butter and poppy seeds.

Tri Tip Stew with Mushrooms and Sour Cream

11 ingredients

4–6 SERVINGS

METHOD: fast/slow

SPECIAL EQUIPMENT: none

PRESSURE: max or high

TIME UNDER PRESSURE: 16 or 20 minutes

RELEASE: quick

TOTAL TIME WITH PRESSURE: about 1 hour

TOTAL TIME WITH SLOW COOKING: about 3½ hours

CAN BE GLUTEN-FREE

One 2-pound beef tri tip roast, cut into 1½-inch pieces

2 tablespoons mild paprika

1 teaspoon rubbed or ground sage

1 teaspoon table salt

½ teaspoon caraway seeds

½ teaspoon ground black pepper

1 tablespoon butter

1 medium yellow or white onion, chopped (1 cup)

8 ounces white or brown button mushrooms, cleaned and thinly sliced

1 cup beef or chicken broth

½ cup regular or low-fat sour cream (gluten-free, if necessary—do not use fat-free)

Here's a rich stew made from a tasty, luxurious tri tip roast (rather than stew meat), all flavored with sage and caraway seeds. If you can't find tri tip, use a sirloin roast that you cut into 1½-inch pieces. The stew is best on a chilly weekend night with lots of beer on hand. The sour cream *must* be added *after* the cooking; otherwise, it can break and cause a mess.

1. Stir the beef pieces, paprika, sage, salt, caraway seeds, and black pepper in a large bowl until the meat is evenly and thoroughly coated with the spices.

2.

	Press	Set it for	Set time for	If needed, press
In all models	SAUTÉ	MEDIUM, NORMAL, or CUSTOM 300°F	10 minutes	START

3. As the pot heats, melt the butter in the insert set in a **5- or 6-quart Instant Pot.** Add the onion and mushrooms; cook, stirring often, until the onion softens, about 4 minutes.

4. Add the beef and any spices in its bowl. Stir over the heat until the meat loses its raw, red color, about 2 minutes. Pour in the broth and scrape up any browned bits on the pot's bottom. Turn off the heat and lock the lid onto the cooker.

5.

	Set pot for	Set level to	Valve must be	Set time for	If needed, press
For Max pots only	PRESSURE COOK	MAX	—	16 minutes with the KEEP WARM setting off	START
For all other pots	PRESSURE COOK or MANUAL	HIGH	Closed	20 minutes with the KEEP WARM setting off	START
For the slow-cook function	SLOW COOK	HIGH	Open	3 hours with the KEEP WARM setting off	START

6. When the pot has finished cooking under pressure, use the **quick-release method** to bring the pressure back to normal. Whichever cooking method you've used, unlatch the lid and open the cooker. Use a slotted spoon or kitchen tongs to transfer the pieces of meat to a nearby big bowl.

7.

	Press	Set it for	Set time for	If needed, press
In all models	SAUTÉ	MEDIUM, NORMAL, or CUSTOM 300°F	15 minutes	START

8. Stir as the sauce comes to a full simmer. Cook, stirring often, until the sauce has reduced to about half the volume it was when you opened the pot, about 10 minutes.

9. Turn off the heat and use hot pads or silicone baking mitts to transfer the (hot!) insert to a nearby wire rack. Wait until all bubbling stops, then stir in the sour cream until smooth. Return the beef and any juices to the insert. Stir well and set aside for a minute or two to blend the flavors before serving warm.

Other Pots

- For a 3-quart Instant Pot, you *must* halve all of the ingredient amounts.
- For an 8-quart Instant Pot, you *must* increase all of the ingredient amounts by 50 percent.
- For a 10-quart Instant Pot, you *must* double all of the ingredient amounts.

Beyond

- Add 1 teaspoon fennel seeds with the other spices.
- Use a 50-50 split of broth and beer, preferably a brown ale.
- Serve with warm potato or pretzel rolls.

Tri Tip Kebabs with Easy Garlic Aioli

12 ingredients

4 SERVINGS

METHOD:
steam

SPECIAL EQUIPMENT:
a pressure- and food-safe rack or trivet and eight 6-inch bamboo skewers

PRESSURE:
max or high

TIME UNDER PRESSURE:
12 or 15 minutes

RELEASE:
quick

TOTAL TIME WITH PRESSURE:
at least 2 hours (with marinating)

CAN BE GLUTEN-FREE

2 pounds beef tri tip, cut into 2-inch pieces

¼ cup regular or low-sodium soy sauce, or gluten-free tamari sauce

8 medium garlic cloves, minced (2 tablespoons plus 2 teaspoons)

1 tablespoon honey

1 tablespoon mild smoked paprika

½ teaspoon onion powder

1½ cups beef broth

1 cup regular or low-fat mayonnaise (gluten-free, if necessary)

3 tablespoons lemon juice

3 tablespoons minced chives or the green part of a scallion

½ teaspoon table salt

½ teaspoon ground black pepper

A beef tri tip roast is just fatty enough to make tender, mild kebabs without being too soft or greasy! Without an Instant Pot, you could never get pieces of a tri tip roast tender enough on a grill before they burned up. But by pressure-cooking the beef, you get wonderfully tender bits on each skewer.

1. Mix the beef, soy sauce, 2 teaspoons minced garlic, honey, smoked paprika, and onion powder in a large bowl until the beef is evenly and thoroughly coated with the marinade. Cover and refrigerate for at least 1 hour or up to 3 hours, stirring at least once.

2. Take the meat out of the fridge and set it on the counter for 20 minutes. Meanwhile, pour the broth into the insert set in a **5-, 6-, or 8-quart Instant Pot.** Put a pressure- and food-safe rack or trivet in the insert.

3. Divide the meat cubes among eight 6-inch bamboo skewers, threading about 4 pieces on each. Pile these skewers onto the rack and lock the lid on the pot.

4.

	Set pot for	Set level to	Valve must be	Set time for	If needed, press
For Max pots only	PRESSURE COOK	MAX	—	12 minutes with the KEEP WARM setting off	START
For all other pots	PRESSURE COOK or MANUAL	HIGH	Closed	15 minutes with the KEEP WARM setting off	START

5. When the pot has finished cooking, use the **quick-release method** to bring the pressure back to normal. Unlatch the lid and open the cooker.

6. Pile the skewers onto a serving platter. Whisk the mayonnaise, lemon juice, chives, salt, pepper, and remaining 2 tablespoons minced garlic in a bowl until uniform. Serve as a dipping sauce alongside the skewers.

Beyond

- To get some crunch on the cooked meat (if you've used a 6- or 8-quart Instant Pot), drain the liquid out of the (hot!) insert, wipe it out, return it to the pot, and put the air-frying basket attachment in the insert. Pile the skewers inside. Set the Instant Pot Air Fryer Lid over the pot and air-fry at 400°F until crisp, turning several times, for at least 5 minutes.

- Alternatively, you can grill the finished skewers over high heat until the meat has a crisp coating, turning the skewers occasionally, for 1 to 2 minutes.

Other Pots

- For a 3-quart Instant Pot, you *must* halve all of the ingredient amounts.

- For a 10-quart Instant Pot, you *must* increase the amount of broth in the insert to 2½ cups. You *can* complete the recipe as stated, you *can* increase all of the remaining ingredient amounts by 50 percent, or you *can* even double the amounts.

Tomatoey Sausage and Polenta Dinner

9 ingredients

4 SERVINGS

METHOD:
stacks

SPECIAL EQUIPMENT:
7½-inch-round stackable insert pans

PRESSURE:
high

TIME UNDER PRESSURE:
30 minutes

RELEASE:
quick

TOTAL TIME WITH PRESSURE:
about 1 hour

CAN BE GLUTEN-FREE

1½ cups water

3 cups chicken broth

¾ cup *instant* polenta

2 tablespoons butter, cut into small bits

2 pounds Italian sausages in their casings, cut into 1-inch pieces (see headnote for more information)

1 cup jarred plain marinara or spaghetti sauce

¼ cup tomato paste

1 tablespoon balsamic vinegar

One 2-inch fresh rosemary sprig

Other Pots

- For a 3-quart Instant Pot, you *must* use stackable containers that fit this smaller pot and you *must* halve almost all of the ingredient amounts *except* you *must* use 1 cup water in the insert.

- For a 5-quart Instant Pot, you *must* use 7-inch stackable containers specifically made to fit this slightly smaller pot. (FYI, some standard stacking containers are too tall to work in these pots).

- For a 10-quart Instant Pot, you *must* increase the amount of water in the insert to 2½ cups while otherwise completing the recipe as stated.

Beyond

- Stir up to 3 ounces shredded semi-firm mozzarella (¾ cup) into the polenta after it comes out of the pot.

- Garnish the servings with stemmed and minced fresh oregano and/or parsley leaves.

- And/or sprinkle them with red pepper flakes.

Here's an easy recipe to make a full meal using stacks, one layer for sausages in a tomato sauce and one layer for polenta. We need to add tomato paste to the sausage mixture because the pieces will give off so much, um, "liquid" (that is, fat) that the sauce needs thickening in some way.

As to the sausages, use any you like: mild or hot; beef, pork, turkey, or chicken; cheese-stuffed or herb-laced. And here's a tip: The easiest way to cut sausages still in their casings is with kitchen shears, rather than a knife. (Do the operation over the pan and the pieces will fall right in.)

1. Pour the water into the insert set in a **6- or 8-quart Instant Pot.** If your stacks set doesn't come with a bottom layer that has feet to lift it up, set a pressure-safe rack or trivet in the insert.

2. In the bottom layer of stacks set, mix the broth, polenta, and butter. Set this in the insert (on the rack, if necessary). In the top layer of the stacks, stir the sausage, sauce, tomato paste, and vinegar until the tomato paste dissolves and the sausage pieces are coated. Tuck the rosemary sprig among the sausage pieces. (For more information on working with stacks, see page 16 of the introduction.)

3. Set the top layer on the bottom one in the insert. Cover the top layer or seal it tightly with aluminum foil. Lock the lid on the pot.

4.

	Set pot for	Set level to	Valve must be	Set time for	If needed press
For *all* pots	PRESSURE COOK or MANUAL	HIGH	Closed	30 minutes with the KEEP WARM setting off	START

5. When the pot has finished cooking, use the **quick-release method** to bring the pressure back to normal. Unlatch the lid and open the cooker. Use hot pads or silicone baking mitts to transfer the (hot!) stack layers to a wire rack (watch out for hot liquid inside). Uncover, separate the layer, and cool for a couple of minutes. Discard the rosemary sprig. Stir the polenta, then serve it as a bed for the sausages in their tomato sauce.

Osso Buco with Red Cabbage and Dill

12 ingredients

4 SERVINGS

METHOD: fast/slow

SPECIAL EQUIPMENT: butchers' twine

PRESSURE: max or high

TIME UNDER PRESSURE: 35 or 45 minutes

RELEASE: natural

TOTAL TIME WITH PRESSURE: about 2 hours

TOTAL TIME WITH SLOW COOKING: about 5 hours

CAN BE GLUTEN-FREE

3 thin strips of bacon (gluten-free, if necessary), chopped

Four 12- to 14-ounce osso buco, tied (see the headnote for more information)

1 teaspoon table salt

1 teaspoon ground black pepper

1 large red onion, chopped (1½ cups)

4 cups cored and shredded red cabbage (about half a large head)

¼ cup loosely packed, stemmed, fresh dill fronds, finely chopped

2 tablespoons red wine vinegar

½ teaspoon ground allspice

1 cup beef broth

2 tablespoons potato starch

1 tablespoon water

Why stick with the ordinary when you can use the pressure cooker to make an extraordinary, new version of a braising favorite? Admittedly, this osso buco recipe isn't very Italian! It's savory and smoky, with delicate, sweet notes from the cabbage and a nosy finish from all the dill.

The raw osso buco should be tied so the meat still adheres to the bone after pressure-cooking. Loop butchers' twine around the circumference of each piece, knotting the twine so that the meat is held securely but not tightly.

1.

	Press	Set it for	Set time for	If needed, press
In all models	SAUTÉ	MEDIUM, NORMAL, or CUSTOM 300°F	20 minutes	START

2. Put the bacon in the insert set in a **5- or 6-quart Instant Pot.** Cook, stirring often, until quite crisp, about 4 minutes. Use a slotted spoon to transfer the bacon bits to a nearby large bowl.

3. Season the osso buco with the salt and pepper on all sides. Put two of them in the pot and brown well, turning once, about 5 minutes. Transfer these two to the bowl with the bacon and brown the other two pieces of osso buco in the same way before getting them into the bowl.

4. Add the onion to the pot and cook, stirring often, until softened, about 3 minutes. Stir in the cabbage and continue cooking, stirring almost constantly, until just wilted, about 2 minutes.

5. Stir in the dill, vinegar, and allspice. Scrape up any browned bits on the pot's bottom. Stir in the broth and turn off the heat. Return the osso buco, bacon, and any accumulated juices in the bowl to the pot, nestling the meat into the sauce (one or two pieces may be wedged up on an angle in a 5- or 6-quart pot). Lock the lid on the cooker.

6.

	Set pot for	Set level to	Valve must be	Set time for	If needed, press
For Max pots only	PRESSURE COOK	MAX	—	35 minutes with the KEEP WARM setting off	START
For all other pots	PRESSURE COOK or MANUAL	HIGH	Closed	45 minutes with the KEEP WARM setting off	START
For the slow-cook function	SLOW COOK	HIGH	Open	4½ hours with the KEEP WARM setting off	START

7. When the pot has finished cooking under pressure, turn it off and let its pressure **return to normal naturally,** about 40 minutes. Whichever cooking method you've used, unlatch the lid and open the cooker.

8. Use kitchen tongs and perhaps a metal spatula to transfer the osso buco pieces to a big serving platter or serving plates. Snip off and remove the string around each. Use a large spoon to skim and discard the surface fat from the sauce. Whisk the potato starch and water in a small bowl until smooth.

9.

	Press	Set it for	Set time for	If needed, press
In all models	SAUTÉ	MEDIUM, NORMAL, or CUSTOM 300°F	5 minutes	START

10. As the sauce comes to a simmer, stir in the potato starch slurry. Continue cooking, stirring constantly, until somewhat thickened, less than 1 minute. Turn off the heat and use hot pads or silicone baking mitts to transfer the (hot!) insert to a nearby wire rack (so the potato starch doesn't fall out of suspension). Cool for 1 or 2 minutes, then spoon the sauce generously over the osso buco pieces.

Other Pots

- For a 3-quart Instant Pot, you *must* halve almost all of the ingredient amounts *except* you *must* use ¾ cup broth.

- For an 8-quart Instant Pot, you *must* increase almost all of the ingredient amounts by 50 percent *except* you *must* use only 5 tablespoons chopped dill.

- For a 10-quart Instant Pot, you *must* double almost all of the ingredient amounts *except* you *must* use only 6 tablespoons chopped dill.

Beyond

- Garnish the servings with a drizzle of very syrupy, aged balsamic vinegar.

- And maybe a fine finishing olive oil, too.

Osso Buco with Fennel and Green Olives

12 ingredients	SPECIAL EQUIPMENT: butchers' twine	TIME UNDER PRESSURE: 35 or 45 minutes	TOTAL TIME WITH PRESSURE: about 2 hours	TOTAL TIME WITH SLOW COOKING: about 5 hours	
4 SERVINGS					
METHOD: fast/slow	PRESSURE: max or high	RELEASE: natural		GLUTEN-FREE	

2 tablespoons olive oil

Four 12- or 14-ounce osso buco, tied with butchers' twine (for more information, see the headnote on page 280)

1 teaspoon table salt

1 teaspoon ground black pepper

1 large yellow or white onion, chopped (1½ cups)

1 large fennel bulb, trimmed of both its woody bottom as well as its stalks and fronds, then chopped (2½ cups)

½ cup pitted green olives

3 medium garlic cloves, minced (1 tablespoon)

1 tablespoon packed, stemmed, fresh oregano leaves, minced

1 tablespoon finely grated lemon zest

½ cup dry white wine, such as Chardonnay; or unsweetened apple juice

1 cup chicken broth

If our other recipe for osso buco on page 280 was unexpected, here's a more traditional preparation, although we nixed the tomatoes from the Italian original so that the fennel and olive mixture can yield a savory and salty sauce without tomatoes' distracting sweetness. We recommend chicken broth as a lighter addition to the sauce with the white wine.

The sauce is fairly thin, but we don't recommend thickening it. It adds a soft touch to the final dish. That said, you might choose to boil it down in the pot for a minute or two—but remember: The more you boil a sauce with olives, the saltier it gets.

1.

	Press	Set it for	Set time for	If needed, press
In all models	SAUTÉ	MEDIUM, NORMAL, or CUSTOM 300°F	20 minutes	START

2. As the pot heats, warm the oil in the insert set in a **5-, 6-, or 8-quart Instant Pot.** Season the osso buco with the salt and pepper on all sides. Put two of them in the insert and brown well, turning once, about 5 minutes. Transfer these two to the bowl with the bacon and brown the other two pieces of osso buco in the same way before getting them into the bowl.

3. Add the onion and fennel to the pot. Cook, stirring often, until the onion softens, about 4 minutes. Stir in the olives, garlic, oregano, and lemon zest until very fragrant, less than 1 minute. Pour in the wine and scrape up any browned bits on the pot's bottom. Turn off the heat.

4. Pour in the broth, then return the osso buco pieces to the pot (as well as any accumulated juices in their bowl), nestling the meat into the sauce. Lock the lid on the pot.

5.

	Set pot for	Set level to	Valve must be	Set time for	If needed, press
For Max pots only	PRESSURE COOK	MAX	—	35 minutes with the KEEP WARM setting off	START
For all other pots	PRESSURE COOK or MANUAL	HIGH	Closed	45 minutes with the KEEP WARM setting off	START
For the slow-cook function	SLOW COOK	HIGH	Open	4½ hours with the KEEP WARM setting off	START

6. When the pot has finished cooking under pressure, turn it off and let its pressure **return to normal naturally,** about 40 minutes. Whichever cooking method you've used, unlatch the lid and open the cooker. Use kitchen tongs and perhaps a metal spatula to transfer the osso buco to serving bowls. Snip off the twine, then ladle lots of the sauce from the pot over each serving.

Other Pots

- For a 3-quart Instant Pot, you *must* halve all of the ingredient amounts.

- For an 8-quart Instant Pot, you *can* increase all of the ingredient amounts by 50 percent.

- For a 10-quart Instant Pot, you *must* increase all of the ingredient amounts by 50 percent or you *can* even double the amounts.

Beyond

- Serve the osso buco over cooked and drained penne or ziti.

- Or cut kaiser rolls in half, coat the cut sides with olive oil, and toast them very well (or even grill them). Put half a kaiser roll in the bottom of each bowl before you add the meat and sauce.

Smoked Sausage and Lentil Stew

13 ingredients

4 SERVINGS

METHOD:
fast/slow

SPECIAL EQUIPMENT:
none

PRESSURE:
max or high

TIME UNDER PRESSURE:
25 or 30 minutes

RELEASE:
quick

TOTAL TIME WITH PRESSURE:
about 50 minutes

TOTAL TIME WITH SLOW COOKING:
about 3½ hours

CAN BE GLUTEN-FREE

2 tablespoons olive oil

2 medium yellow or white onions, chopped (2 cups)

2 medium carrots, peeled and chopped (1 cup)

1½ pounds smoked pork (or beef) kielbasa (gluten-free, if necessary), thinly sliced

2 medium garlic cloves, minced (2 teaspoons)

1 teaspoon mild smoked paprika

½ teaspoon dried thyme

½ teaspoon table salt

¼ teaspoon ground dried cayenne

One 14-ounce can diced tomatoes *packed in juice*, preferably fire-roasted tomatoes (1¾ cups)

1½ cups chicken broth

½ cup green lentils (that is, *lentilles du Puy*)

½ cup brown lentils, picked over for small stones and rinsed

Other Pots

- For a 3-quart Instant Pot, you *must* halve all of the ingredient amounts.

- For a 10-quart Instant Pot, you *must* increase all of the ingredient amounts by 50 percent or you *can* even double them.

Beyond

- Add more flavor to the stew by stirring in ½ teaspoon ground cinnamon and/or ¼ teaspoon ground cardamom with the other spices.

- Give the stew a deeper finish by substituting a 50-50 ratio of dark beer (such as a porter or a stout) and beef broth for the chicken broth.

We love it when classic French bistros serve sausage on a bed of lentils. Naturally, we wanted to morph that entrée into a stew for the Instant Pot. However, we opted for *two* types of lentils, green and brown, to keep the dish from turning into wallpaper paste. Brown lentils break down more quickly than the green do under pressure. In other words, the brown ones will thicken the stew while the green will hold their shape and offer a soft but chewy texture.

1.

	Press	Set it for	Set time for	If needed, press
In all models	SAUTÉ	MEDIUM, NORMAL, or CUSTOM 300°F	10 minutes	START

2. As the pot heats, warm the oil in the insert set in a **5-, 6-, or 8-quart Instant Pot.** Add the onion and carrots; cook, stirring often, until the onion softens, about 4 minutes.

3. Add the kielbasa and cook, stirring often, until it begins to give off some fat, about 2 minutes. Stir in the garlic, smoked paprika, thyme, salt, and cayenne until aromatic, just a few seconds.

4. Pour in the tomatoes with their juice and scrape up any browned bits on the pot's bottom. Turn off the heat and stir in the broth, then the green and brown lentils. Lock the lid onto the cooker.

5.

	Set pot for	Set level to	Valve must be	Set time for	If needed, press
For Max pots only	PRESSURE COOK	MAX	—	25 minutes with the KEEP WARM setting off	START
For all other pots	PRESSURE COOK or MANUAL	HIGH	Closed	30 minutes with the KEEP WARM setting off	START
For the slow-cook function	SLOW COOK	HIGH	Open	3 hours with the KEEP WARM setting off	START

6. When the pot has finished cooking under pressure, use the **quick-release method** to bring the pressure back to normal. Whichever cooking method you've used, unlatch the lid and open the cooker. Set the lid askew over the pot and set it aside for 2 to 3 minutes to blend the flavors. Stir well and serve warm.

No-Brainer Pierogi and Sausage Salad

12 ingredients

4–6 SERVINGS

METHOD:
steam

SPECIAL
EQUIPMENT:
steamer basket

PRESSURE:
high

TIME UNDER
PRESSURE:
5 minutes

RELEASE:
quick

TOTAL TIME WITH
PRESSURE:
about 25 minutes

1½ cups water

1 pound smoked pork (or beef) kielbasa, cut into 1-inch sections

1 pound fresh potato pierogi; or frozen potato pierogi, thawed

1 large yellow or orange bell pepper, stemmed, cored, and cut into 1-inch squares

4 medium scallions, trimmed and thinly sliced (1⅓ cups)

Up to 2 tablespoons chipotle hot sauce, such as Cholula

1 tablespoon olive oil

1 tablespoon apple cider vinegar

½ teaspoon mild smoked paprika

½ teaspoon caraway seeds

½ teaspoon table salt

½ teaspoon ground black pepper

Other Pots

- For a 3-quart Instant Pot, you *must* halve almost all of the ingredient amounts *except* you *must* use 1 cup water in the insert.

- For a 10-quart Instant Pot, you *must* increase the amount of water in the insert to 2½ cups. You *can* complete the recipe as stated or you *can* double all of the remaining ingredient amounts if you have a very large steamer basket.

Beyond

- Although this is already a full meal, you can add sliced radishes, halved grape tomatoes, halved seedless grapes, and/or thinly sliced celery to the salad. If you do, it's best to also increase the oil and vinegar by at least 50 percent, if not a little more.

By using purchased pierogi (savory Polish dumplings, usually filled with potato) and kielbasa, you can make an easy salad for a picnic or a light meal on the patio. The only trick is making sure the hot pierogi (right out of the pot) get into the salad ingredients quickly so they can absorb some of the dressing.

1. Pour the water into the insert set in a **5-, 6-, or 8-quart Instant Pot**. Set a pressure-safe steamer basket in the insert.

2. Arrange the sausage pieces in as close to one layer as you can in the basket. Lay the pierogi on top. Lock the lid on the pot.

3.

	Set pot for	Set level to	Valve must be	Set time for	If needed, press
For *all* pots	PRESSURE COOK or MANUAL	HIGH	Closed	5 minutes with the KEEP WARM setting off	START

4. As the pot cooks, toss the bell pepper, scallion, chipotle hot sauce, oil, vinegar, smoked paprika, caraway seeds, salt, and black pepper in a large bowl until well combined. Set aside.

5. When the pot has finished cooking, use the **quick-release method** to bring the pressure back to normal. Unlatch the lid and open the cooker.

6. Use kitchen tongs and perhaps a metal spatula to transfer the filled steamer basket to a nearby cutting board. Use those tongs to peel the (hot!) pierogi off the pile (they'll be sticky but shouldn't tear). Drop the pierogi into the bowl with the bell pepper ingredients. Stir gently, then add the sausages and toss very gently to combine. Serve warm or at room temperature.

Pork Spiedies

11 ingredients

4 OR 6 SERVINGS

METHOD:
steam

SPECIAL EQUIPMENT:
a pressure- and food-safe rack or trivet and eight 6-inch bamboo skewers

PRESSURE:
max or high

TIME UNDER PRESSURE:
12 or 15 minutes

RELEASE:
quick

TOTAL TIME WITH PRESSURE:
about 2 hours (includes marinating)

CAN BE GLUTEN-FREE

2 pounds pork loin, trimmed and cut into 1½-inch cubes

¼ cup plus 3 tablespoons white wine vinegar

2 tablespoons dried Italian seasoning blend

1 tablespoon lemon juice

1 teaspoon table salt

½ teaspoon red pepper flakes

1½ cups chicken broth

2 tablespoons liquid smoke (gluten-free, if necessary)

1 cup regular, low-fat, or fat-free mayonnaise (gluten-free, if necessary)

1 tablespoon ground black pepper

4 toasted hoagie rolls or 6 toasted hot dog buns (gluten-free, if necessary)

A Binghamton, New York, favorite, spiedies (*SPEE-deez*) are traditionally grilled meat sandwiches. The chunks are usually skewered—and sometimes even served on their skewers when they're in the bun! We decided to go for an all-pork meal in our version. (Because why not?) But how in the world can we get that classic, grilled, smoky flavor in a skewer out of an IP? By adding a little liquid smoke to the broth!

Although hoagie rolls might be traditional, you can serve these spiedies in hot dog buns (with maybe some pickle relish smeared on the inside of the bun before you add the pork).

1. Stir the pork, ¼ cup vinegar, Italian seasoning blend, lemon juice, salt, and red pepper flakes in a large bowl until the meat is coated in the marinade. Cover and refrigerate for 1 hour (but no more because of the vinegar), stirring once or twice.

2. Take the bowl with the pork out of the fridge and set it on the counter for 20 minutes. Meanwhile, pour the broth and liquid smoke into the insert set in a **5-, 6-, or 8-quart Instant Pot.** Put a pressure- and food-safe rack or trivet in the insert.

3. Thread the pork cubes onto eight 6-inch bamboo skewers, 4 or 5 pieces per skewer. Pile the skewers onto the rack and lock the lid on the pot.

4.

	Set pot for	Set level to	Valve must be	Set time for	If needed, press
For Max pots only	PRESSURE COOK	MAX	—	12 minutes with the KEEP WARM setting off	START
For all other pots	PRESSURE COOK or MANUAL	HIGH	Closed	15 minutes with the KEEP WARM setting off	START

5. When the pot has finished cooking, use the **quick-release method** to bring the pressure back to normal. Unlatch the lid and open the cooker. Cool right in the pot for a few minutes. Meanwhile, whisk the mayonnaise, black pepper, and remaining 3 tablespoons vinegar in a small bowl until uniform.

6. Pull the pork pieces off the skewers and line them in the toasted hoagie rolls or buns. Top with the mayonnaise sauce to serve.

Other Pots

- For a **3-quart Instant Pot**, you *must* halve almost all of the ingredient amounts *except* you *must* use 1 cup chicken broth (with 1 tablespoon liquid smoke) in the insert.

- For a **10-quart Instant Pot**, you *must* use 2½ cups broth and 3 tablespoons liquid smoke in the insert while otherwise completing the recipe as stated.

Beyond

- Add chopped lettuce (particularly iceberg lettuce), chopped tomatoes, and/or sprouts (particularly radish sprouts) to the hoagies with the pork.

- If you've used a 6- or 8-quart Instant Pot, you can crunch the meat as it would be on a grill. Remove the skewers as directed in step 6, then remove the rack from the (hot!) insert, pour out any liquid in it, and wipe it out. Return it to the pot and set the air-frying basket attachment in the insert. Set the Instant Pot Air Fryer Lid over the pot and air-fry at 400°F for 5 minutes, rearranging the skewers once to allow even browning.

- Alternatively, set the cooked skewers in a nonstick grill pan set over medium-high heat or on a grill grate over high heat. Grill for about 2 minutes, turning several times, until browned.

See photo in insert.

Falling-off-the-Bone Pork Ribs

6 ingredients

6 SERVINGS

METHOD:
steam

SPECIAL EQUIPMENT:
a pressure- and food-safe rack or trivet

PRESSURE:
max or high

TIME UNDER PRESSURE:
19 or 25 minutes

RELEASE:
natural

TOTAL TIME WITH PRESSURE:
about 1 hour 20 minutes

CAN BE GLUTEN-FREE

---

1 cup light-colored beer, preferably a pilsner; or beef broth

One 4-ounce bottle liquid smoke (gluten-free, if necessary)

Two 3-pound racks of Saint Louis–style or baby-back pork ribs, membranes removed (see the headnote for more information)

2 tablespoons Worcestershire sauce (gluten-free, if necessary)

3½ tablespoons dried barbecue spice rub blend

1 cup purchased barbecue sauce (gluten-free, if necessary)

Racks of ribs from the grill are an all-day affair. Racks from an Instant Pot are a relatively quick and certainly easy pleasure. This recipe is *super* easy because it uses both a purchased barbecue seasoning blend and bottled barbecue sauce. (Or you can make your own seasoning blend—see the **Beyond** section.)

Here's a clarification of exactly the sort of pork ribs you need. There are three types available at most supermarkets. *Spare ribs* are from a spot near the pig's belly, so they're quite fatty. Although these are the classic barbecue ribs, the bones are too large to fit in most sizes of Instant Pot. The other two types of pork ribs, however, will work: *Saint Louis–style ribs* are actually traditional spare ribs except the bones have been squared off (or trimmed). *Baby-back ribs* (sometimes called "loin ribs") are from higher up on the pig, so they're shorter and meatier (and will fit as well). Note that you can *only* use baby-back ribs in a **3-quart Instant Pot** because of the shorter length of the bones.

To remove the membrane from a rack of ribs, set the rack meat side down on a large cutting board. Use a paring knife to lift about 1 inch of the milky membrane off the short end of the rib meat. Grab that little bit of membrane and zip the rest of it off the rack.

1. Stir the beer and liquid smoke in the insert set in a **5-, 6-, or 8-quart Instant Pot.** Set a pressure- and food-safe rack or trivet into the insert.

2. Rub the pork racks with the Worcestershire sauce, then sprinkle them with the dried seasoning mix (the Worcestershire sauce will help the spices stick). Coil one rib rack into a spiral (like the start of crazy cartoon eyes) and set that spiral cut side down on the rack or trivet in the insert so that you look down into the cooker and see the coiling spiral. Release the spiral and let it uncoil a bit. Now coil up the second rack the same way and set it right in the middle of the first rack of ribs, releasing it and letting it, too, uncoil a bit inside the first coil. If you're unsure how to do this, check out the video for Sticky-Sweet Soy Pork Ribs on our YouTube channel, Cooking with Bruce and Mark. Lock the lid on the pot.

3.

	Set pot for	Set level to	Valve must be	Set time for	If needed, press
For Max pots only	PRESSURE COOK	MAX	—	19 minutes with the KEEP WARM setting off	START
For all other pots	PRESSURE COOK or MANUAL	HIGH	Closed	25 minutes with the KEEP WARM setting off	START

4. When the pot has finished cooking, turn it off and let the pressure **return to normal naturally,** about 20 minutes. Unlatch the lid and open the cooker. Use kitchen tongs to transfer the (hot!) rib racks to a large, lipped baking sheet. Unfold them and spread them flat on the sheet. Spread the barbecue sauce over both sides of the racks.

5. Set the oven rack 8 inches from the broiler element and heat the broiler. Broil the ribs until bubbling and crisp, 4 to 6 minutes, turning once. Watch out that the ribs don't burn. Remove the baking sheet from the oven and cool for 2 to 3 minutes before slicing the ribs between the bones to serve.

Other Pots

- For a 3-quart Instant Pot, you *must* halve all of the ingredient amounts (using only one rack of ribs). And you *must* only use baby-back ribs.

- For an 8-quart Instant Pot, you *can* increase the amount of ribs, Worcestershire sauce, rub, and barbecue sauce by 50 percent but you *must* leave the amount of liquid in the insert the same as in the stated recipe. (Follow the technique for setting one rib spiral in another from the main recipe, then set the third spiral of ribs in the center and let it uncoil a bit, too.)

- For a 10-quart Instant Pot, you *must* increase the amount of beer or broth in the insert to 2½ cups, even if you complete the recipe as otherwise stated. However, you *can* also increase almost all of the other ingredient amounts by 50 percent or you *can* even double the amounts but do not increase the amount of liquid smoke. (See further instructions about coiling the racks in the above note for 8-quart pots.)

Beyond

- To make your own barbecue spice blend, stir 1 tablespoon mild smoked paprika, 2 teaspoons dark brown sugar, 2 teaspoons table salt, 1 teaspoon onion powder, 1 teaspoon garlic powder, ½ teaspoon celery seeds, ½ teaspoon ground dried mustard, and ½ teaspoon ground black pepper in a small bowl. Store in a sealed container in a cool, dark pantry for up to 6 months.

Sticky-Sweet Soy Pork Ribs

10 or 11 ingredients

6 SERVINGS

METHOD: steam

SPECIAL EQUIPMENT: a pressure- and food-safe rack or trivet

PRESSURE: max or high

TIME UNDER PRESSURE: 19 or 25 minutes
Release: natural

TOTAL TIME WITH PRESSURE: about 5½ hours (includes marinating)

CAN BE GLUTEN-FREE

½ cup hoisin sauce (gluten-free, if necessary—see page 18 for more information)

¼ cup regular or low-sodium soy sauce, or gluten-free tamari sauce

3 tablespoons dark brown sugar

2 tablespoons honey

1 tablespoon minced peeled fresh ginger

3 medium garlic cloves, minced (1 tablespoon)

½ teaspoon ground cinnamon

4 drops red food coloring (optional)

Two 3-pound racks of Saint Louis–style or baby-back pork ribs, membranes removed (see the headnote on page 288)

1½ cups chicken broth

1 cup purchased duck sauce or sweet chili sauce (gluten-free, if necessary)

Most North American Chinese restaurants use racks of pork *spare ribs* for this dish, which unfortunately won't fit in the Instant Pot because the bones are too long. But we can get that favorite flavor into the ribs by using Saint Louis–style or baby-back ribs and marinating the racks to get the most flavor into the meat before they undergo pressure. For more information about the types of pork ribs and for instructions on how to remove the membrane over the ribs, see the headnote to Falling-off-the-Bone Pork Ribs on page 288.

1. Stir the hoisin sauce, soy or tamari sauce, the brown sugar, honey, ginger, garlic, cinnamon, and food coloring (if using) in a small bowl until uniform. Brush this mixture all over all sides of the rib racks. If you've used food coloring, wear rubber gloves to save your hands.

2. Coil each rack up, wrap each separately in plastic wrap, and place them in a 9 x 13-inch baking pan. Cover the pan with more plastic wrap and refrigerate for at least 3 hours or up to 24 hours.

3. Set the racks of ribs out on the counter for 20 minutes. Pour the broth into the insert set in a **5-, 6-, or 8-quart Instant Pot.** Set a pressure- and food-safe rack or trivet into the pot.

4. Unwrap the baking dish, then the ribs. Coil one rib rack into a spiral (like the start of crazy cartoon eyes) and set that spiral cut side down on the rack or trivet in the insert so that you look down into the cooker and see the coiling spiral. Release the spiral and let it uncoil a bit. Now coil up the second rack the same way and set it right in the middle of the first rack of ribs, releasing it and letting it, too, uncoil a bit inside the first coil. If you're unsure how to do this, check out the video for this recipe on our YouTube channel, Cooking with Bruce and Mark. Lock the lid on the pot.

5.

	Set pot for	Set level to	Valve must be	Set time for	If needed, press
For Max pots only	PRESSURE COOK	MAX	—	19 minutes with the KEEP WARM setting off	START
For all other pots	PRESSURE COOK or MANUAL	HIGH	Closed	25 minutes with the KEEP WARM setting off	START

6. When the pot has finished cooking, turn it off and let the pressure **return to normal naturally,** about 20 minutes. Unlatch the lid and open the cooker. Use kitchen tongs to transfer the (hot!) rib racks to a large, lipped baking sheet. Unfold them and spread them flat on the sheet. Spread the duck sauce or sweet chili sauce over both sides of the racks

7. Set the oven rack 8 inches from the broiler element and heat the broiler. Broil the ribs until bubbling and crisp, 4 to 6 minutes, turning once. Watch out that the ribs don't burn. Remove the baking sheet from the oven and cool for 2 to 3 minutes before slicing the ribs between the bones to serve.

Other Pots

- For a 3-quart Instant Pot, you *must* halve all of the ingredient amounts (using only one rack of ribs). And you *must* only use baby-back ribs.

- For an 8-quart Instant Pot, you *can* increase the amount of marinade, ribs, and duck sauce by 50 percent but you *must* leave the amount of liquid in the insert the same as the original recipe. (Follow the technique for setting one rib spiral in another from the main recipe, then set the third spiral of ribs in the center and let it uncoil a bit, too.)

- For a 10-quart Instant Pot, you *must* increase the amount of liquid in the insert to 2½ cups, even if you complete the recipe as otherwise stated. However, you *can* also increase the other ingredient amounts by 50 percent or you *can* even double the other amounts. (See further instructions about coiling the racks in the above note for 8-quart pots.)

Beyond

- Substitute 1 teaspoon five-spice powder for the ground cinnamon.

- Garnish the ribs with sesame seeds and/or finely minced scallions.

- Or drizzle with toasted sesame oil and unseasoned rice vinegar.

- Have extra duck sauce or sweet chile sauce for dipping.

See photo in insert.

Honey-Orange Pork Ribs

14 ingredients	**SPECIAL EQUIPMENT:** a pressure- and food-safe rack or trivet	**TIME UNDER PRESSURE:** 19 or 25 minutes	**TOTAL TIME WITH PRESSURE:** about 1 hour 20 minutes
6 SERVINGS		**RELEASE:** natural	
METHOD: steam	**PRESSURE:** max or high		**CAN BE GLUTEN-FREE**

1½ cups chicken broth

1 tablespoon dried parsley

1½ teaspoons table salt

1 teaspoon granulated white sugar

1 teaspoon ground coriander

1 teaspoon ground cumin

1 teaspoon ground black pepper

½ teaspoon onion powder

½ teaspoon garlic powder

Up to ½ teaspoon ground dried cayenne

Two 3-pound racks of Saint Louis–style or baby-back pork ribs, membranes removed (see the headnote on page 288)

2 tablespoons orange juice

¾ cup orange marmalade, preferably bitter (or Seville) orange marmalade (gluten-free, if necessary)

¼ cup honey

If you're a fan of sweet, aromatic pork ribs, you've come to the best place. However, even sweetaholics need some balance among the flavors. For the best success, search for *bitter* orange marmalade (sometimes called "Seville orange marmalade," not the standard, North American variety). The bitter stuff is still sweet, no worries; but it's made from oranges that have a punch against the pork. Look for a jar of marmalade without a lot of chunks (and certainly without stacks of little orange rings—which is lovely on toast but not successful here).

For more information about the types of pork ribs and for instructions on how to remove the membrane over the ribs, see the headnote to Falling-off-the-Bone Pork Ribs on page 288.

1. Pour the broth into the insert set in a **5-, 6-, or 8-quart Instant Pot.** Set a pressure- and food-safe rack or trivet in the insert. Stir the parsley, salt, sugar, coriander, cumin, black pepper, onion powder, garlic powder, and cayenne in a small bowl until uniform.

2. Rub the pork racks with the orange juice. Sprinkle them with the dried seasoning mix (the juice will help the spices stick to the ribs). Coil one rib rack into a spiral (like the start of crazy cartoon eyes) and set that spiral cut side down on the rack or trivet in the insert so that you look down into the cooker and see the coiling spiral. Release the spiral and let it uncoil a bit. Now coil up the second rack the same way and set it right in the middle of the first rack of ribs, releasing it and letting it, too, uncoil a bit inside the first coil. If you're unsure how to do this, check out the video for Sticky-Sweet Soy Pork Ribs on our YouTube channel, Cooking with Bruce and Mark. Lock the lid on the pot.

3.

	Set pot for	Set level to	Valve must be	Set time for	If needed, press
For Max pots only	PRESSURE COOK	MAX	—	19 minutes with the KEEP WARM setting off	START
For all other pots	PRESSURE COOK or MANUAL	HIGH	Closed	25 minutes with the KEEP WARM setting off	START

4. When the pot has finished cooking, turn it off and let the pressure **return to normal naturally,** about 20 minutes. Unlatch the lid and open the cooker. Use kitchen tongs to transfer the (hot!) rib racks to a large, lipped baking sheet. Unfold them and spread them flat on the sheet. Whisk the marmalade and honey until uniform in a small bowl. Spread this mixture over both sides of the racks.

5. Set the oven rack 8 inches from the broiler element and heat the broiler. Broil the ribs until bubbling and crisp, 4 to 6 minutes, turning once. Watch out that the ribs don't burn. Remove the baking sheet from the oven and cool for 2 to 3 minutes before slicing the ribs between the bones to serve.

Other Pots

- For a 3-quart Instant Pot, you *must* halve all of the ingredient amounts (using only one rack of ribs). And you *must* only use baby-back ribs.

- For an 8-quart Instant Pot, you *can* increase the amount of ribs, juice, and rub by 50 percent but you *must* leave the amount of liquid in the insert the same as in the stated recipe. (Follow the technique for setting one rib spiral in another from the main recipe, then set the third spiral of ribs in the center and let it uncoil a bit, too.)

- For a 10-quart Instant Pot, you *must* increase the amount of broth in the insert to 2½ cups, even if you complete the recipe as otherwise stated. However, you *can* also increase the other ingredient amounts by 50 percent or you *can* even double the other amounts. (See further instructions about coiling the racks in the above note for 8-quart pots.)

Beyond

- Substitute lemon marmalade and lemon juice for the orange marmalade and orange juice.

- Or substitute ginger marmalade for the orange marmalade but keep the orange juice as stated.

Barbecue Country-Style Pork Ribs

12 ingredients	SPECIAL EQUIPMENT: a pressure- and food-safe rack or trivet	TIME UNDER PRESSURE: 20 minutes	TOTAL TIME WITH PRESSURE: about 9 hours (includes marinating)
4–6 SERVINGS			
METHOD: steam		RELEASE: quick	
	PRESSURE: high		CAN BE GLUTEN-FREE

2 tablespoons Worcestershire sauce (gluten-free, if necessary)

2 tablespoons dark brown sugar

2 tablespoons mild smoked paprika

Up to 1 tablespoon thin red hot sauce, such as Texas Pete

1 teaspoon ground cumin

1 teaspoon onion powder

½ teaspoon garlic powder

½ teaspoon table salt

½ teaspoon ground black pepper

3½ pounds country-style pork ribs

1½ cups beef broth

½ cup purchased barbecue sauce (gluten-free, if necessary)

Country-style pork ribs are a knife-and-fork affair (as opposed to fingers and napkins with other pork ribs). Country-style ribs are cut from the blade end of the loin, close to the pork shoulder. Some may have bits of shoulder bone in them. Remember: the more bone, the less meat. Examine the packages at the market for the meatiest cuts, especially for this relatively easy barbecue classic.

1. Combine the Worcestershire sauce, brown sugar, smoked paprika, hot sauce, cumin, onion powder, garlic powder, salt, and pepper in a large, zip-top plastic bag. Seal and massage the ingredients through the plastic to combine them. Open the bag, add the country-style ribs, seal again, and massage the spice mixture evenly and thoroughly across the meat. Refrigerate for at least 8 hours or even (preferably) 24 hours, turning the bag occasionally to redistribute the marinade.

2. Pour the broth into the insert set in a **5-, 6-, or 8-quart Instant Pot.** Set a pressure- and food-safe rack or trivet in the insert.

3. Unseal the bag with the ribs and engage your inner kid by building them on the rack in the pot like Lincoln Logs—that is, two set this way, then two set at 90 degrees, then maybe another layer at a diagonal. The point is to get space between the ribs so that the heat (and pressure) circulates freely and evenly between and among them. Lock the lid on the pot.

4.

	Set pot for	Set level to	Valve must be	Set time for	If needed, press
For *all* pots	PRESSURE COOK or MANUAL	HIGH	Closed	20 minutes with the KEEP WARM setting off	START

5. When the pot has finished cooking, use the **quick-release method** to bring the pressure back to normal. Unlatch the lid and open the pot. Use kitchen tongs to transfer the ribs to a nearby cutting board and smear them evenly with the barbecue sauce.

6. If you've used a **6- or 8-quart pot,** remove the (hot!) rack from the pot, pour out the liquid in the (still hot!) insert, and wipe it clean. Set it back in the insert, put the air-fryer basket attachment in the insert, and pile the ribs into the basket. Set the Instant Pot Air Fryer Lid on the pot and air-fry at 400°F for 10 minutes, turning the ribs repeatedly, or until crisp and brown.

Alternatively, line a large, lipped baking sheet with aluminum foil (so the burned sauce won't make a mess on the sheet). Set the oven rack 8 inches from the broiler element and heat the broiler. Line the ribs on the prepared baking sheet and broil until browned and crisp, turning once, about 4 minutes.

In either case, cool a few minutes to help the meat reabsorb some of its juices but serve hot.

Other Pots

- In a 3-quart Instant Pot, you *must* halve almost all of the ingredient amounts *except* you *must* use 1 cup broth in the insert.

- In an 8-quart Instant Pot, you *can* increase almost all of the ingredient amounts by 50 percent *but* you *must* leave the amount of broth in the insert at 1½ cups.

- In a 10-quart Instant Pot, you *must* increase the amount of broth to 2½ cups in the insert. You *can* complete the recipe as otherwise stated, or you *can* increase all of the remaining ingredient amounts by 50 percent, or you *can* even double them.

Beyond

- Serve these meaty pork ribs with Cauliflower Cheese Grits (page 330).

Pork Tenderloins with Herbs and Garlic

12 ingredients

6 SERVINGS

METHOD:
standard

SPECIAL EQUIPMENT:
none

PRESSURE:
low

TIME UNDER PRESSURE:
10 minutes

RELEASE:
natural

TOTAL TIME WITH PRESSURE:
about 40 minutes

GLUTEN-FREE

1 teaspoon dried oregano

1 teaspoon rubbed or ground sage

1 teaspoon dried thyme

1 teaspoon mild paprika

1 teaspoon table salt

1 teaspoon ground black pepper

Two 1- to 1¼-pound pork tenderloins

2 tablespoons olive oil

3 medium garlic cloves, minced (1 tablespoon)

⅔ cup chicken broth

1 tablespoon cornstarch

1 tablespoon water

We've never gotten good results with pork tenderloins in an Instant Pot... until now! Listen, we've tried lots of recipes on HIGH or MAX pressure. The meat ended up unpleasantly mushy *and* dried out, somehow at the same time. To add insult to injury, the pork was sitting in a too-soupy sauce. Then we tried the tenderloins on LOW pressure. Ta da! We can create a real sauce with less liquid (because LOW requires less steam) and the meat can be more protected as it cooks, as here with a simple mix of dried herbs.

1. Stir the oregano, sage, thyme, paprika, salt, and pepper in a small bowl until uniform. Massage this mixture evenly all over the pork.

2.

	Press	Set it for	Set time for	If needed, press
In all models	SAUTÉ	MEDIUM, NORMAL, or CUSTOM 300°F	10 minutes	START

3. As the pot heats, warm the oil in the insert set in a **5- or 6-quart Instant Pot.** Add the pork and brown well, turning occasionally, about 5 minutes. Transfer the pork to a nearby cutting board.

4. Add the garlic to the pot and cook, stirring constantly, just until aromatic, about 10 seconds. Pour in the broth and scrape up any brown bits on the pot's bottom. Turn off the heat. Return the pork tenderloins to the sauce, as well as any accumulated juices on the cutting board. Lock the lid on the pot.

5.

	Set pot for	Set level to	Valve must be	Set time for	If needed, press
For *all* pots	PRESSURE COOK or MANUAL	LOW	Closed	10 minutes with the KEEP WARM setting off	START

6. When the pot has finished cooking, turn it off and let the pressure **return to normal naturally,** about 15 minutes. Unlatch the lid and open the cooker. Use kitchen tongs to transfer the pork tenderloins to a clean cutting board. Whisk the cornstarch and water in a small bowl until smooth.

7.

	Press	Set it for	Set time for	If needed, press
In all models	SAUTÉ	MEDIUM, NORMAL, or CUSTOM 300°F	5 minutes	START

8. As the sauce comes to a simmer, stir in the cornstarch slurry. Cook, stirring constantly, until somewhat thickened, less than 1 minute. Turn off the heat and use hot pads or silicone baking mitts to transfer the (hot!) insert to a nearby wire rack (to stop the cooking). Carve the pork tenderloins into 1-thick-inch rounds and serve with the pot sauce spooned on top.

Other Pots

- You can do this recipe as stated in a 3-quart Instant Pot, but you *must* cut each of the tenderloins in half widthwise so they'll fit.

- In an 8-quart Instant Pot, you *must* increase the broth to 1¼ cups if you complete the recipe as stated. Or you *can* increase all of the ingredient amounts by 50 percent.

- For a 10-quart Instant Pot, you *must* double almost all of the ingredient amounts *except* you *must* use 2¼ cups broth.

Beyond

- Although mashed potatoes might seem the way to go, we actually prefer this dish over baked potatoes. Split them open, give them a generous drizzle of olive oil and/or some butter, as well as salt and pepper, then spoon the meat and sauce right into the potatoes.

Pork Tenderloins with Mushrooms and Cream

12 ingredients

6 SERVINGS

METHOD:
standard

SPECIAL EQUIPMENT:
none

PRESSURE:
low

TIME UNDER PRESSURE:
10 minutes

RELEASE:
natural

TOTAL TIME WITH PRESSURE:
about 40 minutes

CAN BE GLUTEN-FREE

2 tablespoons butter

Two 1- to 1¼-pound pork tenderloins

1 large single-lobe shallot, chopped (⅓ cup)

8 ounces white or brown button mushrooms, cleaned and thinly sliced

1 teaspoon dried dill

1 teaspoon table salt

1 teaspoon ground black pepper

½ cup chicken broth

¼ cup heavy or light cream

1 tablespoon water

2 teaspoons cornstarch

1 teaspoon Dijon mustard (gluten-free, if necessary)

The secret to this recipe—and any pork tenderloin recipe in the Instant Pot—is to brown the meat well. Since pork tenderloin is so mild tasting, it only stands to reason that the main culinary point is to get as much flavor into the cut as possible. And because this recipe uses LOW pressure, we're able to add the cream to the sauce for a richer flavor when the dish is done.

1.

	Press	Set it for	Set time for	If needed, press
In all models	SAUTÉ	MEDIUM, NORMAL, or CUSTOM 300°F	15 minutes	START

2. As the pot heats, melt the butter in the insert set in a **5- or 6-quart Instant Pot.** Add the pork tenderloins and brown them *well*, turning occasionally, about 6 minutes. Transfer the pork to a nearby cutting board.

3. Add the shallot to the pot and cook, stirring constantly, just until softened, less than 30 seconds. Stir in the mushrooms and cook, stirring often, until they give off their liquid and it reduces to a thick glaze, about 5 minutes.

4. Stir in the dill, salt, and pepper. Then pour in the broth and scrape up any browned bits on the pot's bottom. Turn off the heat. Stir in the cream. Return the pork tenderloins to the sauce, as well as any accumulated juices on the cutting board. Lock the lid on the pot.

5.

	Set pot for	Set level to	Valve must be	Set time for	If needed, press
For *all* pots	PRESSURE COOK or MANUAL	LOW	Closed	10 minutes with the KEEP WARM setting off	START

6. When the pot has finished cooking, turn it off and let the pressure **return to normal naturally,** about 15 minutes. Unlatch the lid and open the cooker. Use kitchen tongs to transfer the pork tenderloins to a cleaned cutting board. Whisk the water and cornstarch in a small bowl until smooth.

7.

	Press	Set it for	Set time for	If needed, press
In all models	SAUTÉ	MEDIUM, NORMAL, or CUSTOM 300°F	5 minutes	START

8. As the sauce comes to a simmer, stir in the cornstarch slurry. Cook, stirring constantly, until somewhat thickened, less than 1 minute. Turn off the heat and stir in the mustard. Use hot pads or silicone baking mitts to transfer the (hot!) insert to a nearby wire rack (to stop the cooking). Slice the pork tenderloins into 1-thick-inch rounds and serve with the pot sauce spooned on top.

Other Pots

- You can do this recipe as stated in a 3-quart Instant Pot, but you *must* cut each of the tenderloins in half widthwise so they'll fit.

- In an 8-quart Instant Pot, you *must* increase the broth to 1 cup if you complete the recipe as stated. Or you *can* increase all of the ingredient amounts by 50 percent.

- For a 10-quart Instant Pot, you *must* double almost all of the ingredient amounts *except* you *must* use 1¾ cups broth.

Beyond

- Rather than potatoes, try this dish over cooked and drained egg or no-yolk noodles. If they've been tossed with butter and a little salt, so much the better!

Pork Tenderloins with Spiced Cherry Sauce

13 ingredients	
6 SERVINGS	
METHOD: standard	

SPECIAL EQUIPMENT: none	PRESSURE: low

TIME UNDER PRESSURE: 10 minutes	TOTAL TIME WITH PRESSURE: about 40 minutes

RELEASE: natural	GLUTEN-FREE

1 teaspoon table salt

1 teaspoon ground black pepper

½ teaspoon ground coriander

½ teaspoon ground cinnamon

½ teaspoon ground dried ginger

Two 1- to 1¼-pound pork tenderloins

2 tablespoons butter

1 small red onion, chopped (½ cup)

1 medium garlic clove, minced (1 teaspoon)

⅔ cup chicken broth

2 tablespoons cherry jam

1 tablespoon water

2 teaspoons cornstarch

Pork in a spiced cherry sauce is no doubt a classic. But if we added all of these aromatic spices like coriander and dried ginger directly to the sauce that cooks around the meat *under pressure*, they would begin to overpower the delicate cherry flavors. By turning those spices into a rub and browning them *onto* the meat, we actually mute them a bit and keep this sweet and fragrant meal more, well, cherry-focused. Beyond that, the dish is pretty simple and can only be made better with a high-quality cherry jam, not one stocked with artificial flavors—what we call "Robitussin jam."

1. Mix the salt, pepper, coriander, cinnamon, and ginger in a small bowl until uniform. Massage this mixture evenly all over the pork tenderloins.

2.

	Press	Set it for	Set time for	If needed, press
In all models	SAUTÉ	MEDIUM, NORMAL, or CUSTOM 300°F	10 minutes	START

3. As the pot heats, melt the butter in the insert set in a **5- or 6-quart Instant Pot.** Add the pork tenderloins and brown them well, turning occasionally, about 6 minutes. Transfer to a nearby cutting board.

4. Add the onion to the pot and cook, stirring often, until softened, about 2 minutes. Add the garlic and cook until just aromatic, for a few seconds. Pour in the broth and scrape up any browned bits on the pot's bottom. Stir in the cherry jam until dissolved, then turn off the heat.

5. Return the pork tenderloins to the sauce, as well as any accumulated juices on the cutting board. Lock the lid on the pot.

6.

	Set pot for	Set level to	Valve must be	Set time for	If needed, press
For *all* pots	PRESSURE COOK or MANUAL	LOW	Closed	10 minutes with the KEEP WARM setting off	START

7. When the pot has finished cooking, turn it off and let the pressure **return to normal naturally,** about 15 minutes. Unlatch the lid and open the cooker. Use kitchen tongs to transfer the pork tenderloins to a cleaned cutting board. Whisk the water and cornstarch in a small bowl until smooth.

8.

	Press	Set it for	Set time for	If needed, press
In all models	SAUTÉ	MEDIUM, NORMAL, or CUSTOM 300°F	5 minutes	START

9. As the sauce comes to a simmer, stir in the cornstarch slurry. Cook, stirring constantly, until somewhat thickened, less than 1 minute. Turn off the heat and use hot pads or silicone baking mitts to transfer the (hot!) insert to a nearby wire rack (to stop the cooking). Slice the pork tenderloins into 1-thick-inch rounds and serve with the pot sauce spooned on top.

Other Pots

- You can do this recipe as stated in a 3-quart Instant Pot, but you must cut each of the tenderloins in half widthwise so they'll fit.

- In an 8-quart Instant Pot, you *must* increase the broth to 1 cup if you complete the recipe as stated. Or you *can* increase all of the ingredient amounts by 50 percent.

- For a 10-quart Instant Pot, you *must* double almost all of the ingredient amounts *except* you *must* use 2 cups broth.

Beyond

- For a richer sauce, stir up to ¼ cup heavy or light cream into the sauce along with the cornstarch slurry.

Teriyaki Pork Tenderloin and Rice Dinner

11 ingredients	**SPECIAL EQUIPMENT:** a 1-quart, 6-inch-round, high-sided, pressure-safe baking or soufflé dish
4 SERVINGS	
METHOD: pot-in-pot	

PRESSURE: high

TIME UNDER PRESSURE: 4 minutes

RELEASE: modified natural

TOTAL TIME WITH PRESSURE: about 40 minutes

CAN BE GLUTEN-FREE

½ cup regular or low-sodium soy sauce, or gluten-free tamari sauce

½ cup unsweetened apple juice

2 tablespoons honey

1 tablespoon minced peeled fresh ginger

2 medium scallions, trimmed and thinly sliced (⅔ cup)

1 medium garlic clove, minced (1 teaspoon)

One 1½-pound pork tenderloin, cut into 2 pieces

1½ cups water

1 cup raw long-grain white rice

½ teaspoon ground dried ginger

½ teaspoon table salt

Let's skip the bottled teriyaki sauce for this one and make an aromatic blend that ups the game a bit and makes this one-pot dinner even more flavorful. The technique here is really for "modified stacks": The pork cooks in an aromatic soy/ginger/honey mixture with the baking dish of rice set right on top of the meat. During recipe testing, we found that cooking the pork right *in* the rice resulted in mushy rice and overdone pork. But this way, we get a better one-pot meal all around.

1. Stir the soy sauce, apple juice, honey, fresh ginger, scallions, and garlic in the insert set in a **5- or 6-quart Instant Pot.** Add the pork tenderloin pieces and turn several times to coat well.

2. Mix the water, rice, ground ginger, and salt in a 1-quart, 6-inch-round, high-sided, pressure-safe baking or soufflé dish. Do not cover. Set this dish right on top of the pork pieces, balancing it so it doesn't tip over. Lock the lid on the pot.

3.

	Set pot for	Set level to	Valve must be	Set time for	If needed, press
For *all* pots	PRESSURE COOK or MANUAL	HIGH	Closed	4 minutes with the KEEP WARM setting off	START

4. When the pot has finished cooking, turn it off and let its pressure **return to normal naturally for 10 minutes.** Then use the **quick-release method** to get rid of the pot's residual pressure. Unlatch the lid and open the pot.

5. Use hot pads or silicone baking mitts to transfer the (hot!) baking dish to a nearby wire rack. Fluff the rice with a fork. Use kitchen tongs to transfer the pork tenderloins to a nearby cutting board.

6.

	Press	Set it for	Set time for	If needed, press
In all models	SAUTÉ	MEDIUM, NORMAL, or CUSTOM 300°F	5 minutes	START

7. Stir often as the sauce in the insert comes to a simmer. Then cook, stirring quite frequently, until it has reduced to half the volume it had when you opened the pot in step 4, about 3 minutes. Turn off the heat. Serve the pork pieces on a bed of rice with the pot sauce spooned on top.

Other Pots

- For a 3-quart Instant Pot, you *must* reduce the amount of pork tenderloin to 1 pound while otherwise completing the recipe as stated (thereby reducing the servings to 3).

- For an 8-quart Instant Pot, you *must* increase the ingredient amounts by 50 percent and you *must* use a 2-quart, 7-inch-round, high-sided, pressure-safe baking or soufflé dish.

- Because of ingredient ratios, this recipe cannot be easily adapted for a 10-quart Instant Pot.

Beyond

- Garnish the servings with toasted sesame oil, more thinly sliced scallions, pickled "sushi" ginger, and/or a dark rich *smoked* soy sauce.

Bone-In Pork Chop and Buttery Cauliflower Rice Dinner

9 ingredients

4 SERVINGS

METHOD:
stacks

SPECIAL
EQUIPMENT:
7½-inch-
round
stackable
insert pans

PRESSURE:
high

TIME UNDER
PRESSURE:
20 minutes

RELEASE:
natural

TOTAL
TIME WITH
PRESSURE:
about 50
minutes

GLUTEN-
FREE

1½ cups water

½ teaspoon mild paprika

½ teaspoon onion powder

½ teaspoon table salt

½ teaspoon ground black pepper

Four ½-inch-thick 6- to 8-ounce bone-in pork chops

2 tablespoons plus 4 teaspoons butter

3 cups riced cauliflower (¾ pound)

1 teaspoon lemon pepper seasoning blend

Here's another whole meal right out of the pot, made with old-fashioned, better-for-gnawing bone-in pork chops. These have more interstitial fat to keep them moist during the longer cooking that a stack set requires. We've given them a simple rub so that they pair better with the buttery side dish, a low-carb pot of cauliflower rice.

1. Pour the water into the insert set in a **6- or 8-quart Instant Pot.** If your two-stack containers do not include feet to lift them out of the water, set a pressure-safe rack or trivet inside the pot. (For more information on working with stacks, see page 16 of the introduction.)

2. Combine the paprika, onion powder, salt, and pepper in a small bowl. Sprinkle this mixture evenly over the pork chops. Set them in the bottom container of a stack set, overlapping as necessary, but only as thin end under thicker part. Dot each chop with 1 teaspoon butter and set the stack container in the insert (on the rack, if necessary).

3. Mix the riced cauliflower and lemon pepper seasoning in the top layer of a stacks set. Cut the remaining 2 tablespoons butter into small pieces and stir them into the cauliflower mixture. Cover and set on top of the bottom layer in the insert. Lock the lid onto the cooker.

Other Pots

- For a 3-quart Instant Pot, you *must* use stackable containers that fit this smaller pot and you *must* halve almost all of the ingredient amounts *except* you *must* use 1 cup water in the insert.

- For a 5-quart Instant Pot, you *must* use 7-inch stackable containers specifically made to fit this slightly smaller pot. (FYI, some standard stacking containers are too tall to work in these pots.)

- For a 10-quart Instant Pot, you *must* increase the amount of water in the insert to 2½ cups while otherwise completing the recipe as stated.

4.

	Set pot for	Set level to	Valve must be	Set time for	If needed, press
For *all* pots	PRESSURE COOK or MANUAL	HIGH	Closed	20 minutes with the KEEP WARM setting off	START

5. When the pot has finished cooking, turn it off and let the pressure **return to normal naturally,** about 20 minutes. Unlatch the lid and open the cooker. Use hot pads or silicone baking mitts to transfer the stack containers to a nearby cutting board. (Be careful because there are hot juices in the bottom container.) Uncover and unstack to cool for 2 to 3 minutes before serving hot.

Beyond

- Add more flavor to the cauliflower rice by stirring in up to 1 tablespoon stemmed and minced fresh parsley leaves and/or 2 teaspoons stemmed, fresh thyme leaves with the lemon pepper seasoning.

Mini Lion's Head Meatballs with Steamed Bok Choy

17 ingredients	SPECIAL EQUIPMENT: a seven-indentation egg-bite mold; a small, 2-cup, heat-and-pressure-safe bowl; and a pressure-safe rack or trivet	PRESSURE: max or high, then high	RELEASE: quick twice
3–4 SERVINGS			TOTAL TIME WITH PRESSURE: about 1 hour
METHOD: egg bites		TIME UNDER PRESSURE: 18 or 21 minutes	CAN BE GLUTEN-FREE

1½ cups plus 2 tablespoons water

Nonstick spray, or vegetable, canola, or other neutral-flavored oil, for greasing

1 pound lean ground pork

5 canned whole water chestnuts, drained and *minced*

2 medium scallions, trimmed and *very* thinly sliced (a rounded ½ cup), plus more for garnishing

1 tablespoon minced peeled fresh ginger

1 refrigerator-cold large egg white

2 tablespoons dry white wine, dry sherry, or dry vermouth; or chicken broth

1 teaspoon table salt

½ teaspoon ground black pepper

2 tablespoons regular or low-sodium soy sauce, or gluten-free tamari sauce

2 tablespoons hoisin sauce (gluten-free, if necessary—see page 18 for more information)

1 tablespoon unseasoned rice vinegar

1 tablespoon toasted sesame oil

2 teaspoons granulated white sugar

2 teaspoons cornstarch

1 pound baby bok choy (4 to 5 heads), washed and separated into their leaves

Lion's head meatballs are a large "meatball" (sometimes more like a half-sphere meat loaf) surrounded by lots of wilted Chinese water spinach or other leafy greens so that the whole dish looks like a lion's head with a mane. We've altered the proportions to make the dish easier in an Instant Pot, thanks to egg-bite molds which can shape and hold mini versions of this classic. As to the greens, we've used baby bok choy for a fresher, lighter flavor to complement the pork meatballs.

1. Pour 1½ cups water into the insert set in a **5-, 6-, or 8-quart Instant Pot.** Set a pressure-safe rack or trivet in the insert. *Generously* coat the inside of the seven indentations in an egg-bite mold with nonstick spray or use oil to grease them.

2. Mix the ground pork, water chestnuts, scallions, ginger, egg white, wine or its substitutes, the salt, and pepper in a medium bowl until uniform but sticky. Divide this mixture evenly among the egg-bite mold indentations, packing it in and rounding the top a bit (the amount will probably rise up higher than the indentations). Do not cover the mold.

3. Mix the soy sauce, hoisin sauce, vinegar, sesame oil, sugar, cornstarch, and the remaining 2 tablespoons water in a small, 2-cup, pressure- and heat-safe bowl until smooth. Cover tightly with aluminum foil. Set this covered bowl on the rack. Center the egg-bite mold on top of this bowl, balancing the bowl so it's stable. Lock the lid on the pot.

4.

	Set pot for	Set level to	Valve must be	Set time for	If needed, press
For Max pots only	PRESSURE COOK	MAX	—	17 minutes with the KEEP WARM setting off	START
For all other pots	PRESSURE COOK or MANUAL	HIGH	Closed	20 minutes with the KEEP WARM setting off	START

5. When the pot has finished cooking, use the **quick-release method** to bring the pressure back to normal. Unlatch the lid and open the cooker.

6. Use hot pads or silicone baking mitts to transfer the (hot!) egg-bite mold to a nearby cutting board. Also transfer the bowl to a wire rack. Use kitchen tongs to remove the (hot!) rack from the insert, leaving the liquid in place. Load the bok choy into the pot and lock the lid back on the cooker.

7.

	Set pot for	Set level to	Valve must be	Set time for	If needed, press
For *all* pots	PRESSURE COOK	HIGH	—	1 minute with the KEEP WARM setting off	START

8. When the pot has finished cooking, use the **quick-release method** to bring the pressure back to normal. Unlatch the lid and open the cooker.

9. Remove the meatballs from their mold, draining off and discarding any surrounding liquid (or fat). Arrange the meatballs on a platter and pour the sauce from the bowl over them. Pick up the bok choy with kitchen tongs and arrange the wilted vegetable around the meatballs, sort of like a lion's mane. Garnish the whole platter with more thinly sliced scallions.

Other Pots

- Because of the height of the stacked ingredients, this recipe will not work in a 3-quart Instant Pot.

- For a 10-quart Instant Pot, you *must* increase the amount of water in the insert to 2½ cups while otherwise completing the recipe as stated.

Beyond

- For a less sweet flavor, substitute oyster sauce for the hoisin sauce.

- Serve over cooked and drained soba noodles, dressed with a little unseasoned rice vinegar.

Boneless Pork Loin Chops in a Creamy Mustard Sauce

13 ingredients

4 SERVINGS

METHOD:
steam

SPECIAL EQUIPMENT:
a steamer basket or rack

PRESSURE:
max or high

TIME UNDER PRESSURE:
8 or 10 minutes

RELEASE:
natural

TOTAL TIME WITH PRESSURE:
about 45 minutes

CAN BE GLUTEN-FREE

---

1 teaspoon dried dill

½ teaspoon celery seeds

½ teaspoon table salt

½ teaspoon ground black pepper

¼ teaspoon grated nutmeg

Four ½- to ¾-inch-thick, 6- to 8-ounce boneless center-cut pork loin chops

1 tablespoon butter

4 large single-lobe shallots, cut widthwise into ½-inch-thick slices

¼ cup dry white wine, such as Chardonnay; or dry vermouth; or unsweetened apple juice

¾ cup chicken broth

2 tablespoons Dijon mustard (gluten-free, if necessary)

¼ cup heavy or light cream

2 teaspoons cornstarch

Mustard and cream are a classic French-bistro combo, a rich and slightly sour pairing that can't be beat when paired with sweet pork. Here, we call for boneless pork loin chops because we don't want excess fat leaching into the sauce and turning it dull. Don't dare use standard yellow mustard for this sauce. It needs the pop of Dijon.

1. Mix the dill, celery seeds, salt, pepper, and nutmeg in a small bowl until uniform. Massage this mixture onto the pork chops.

2.

	Press	Set it for	Set time for	If needed, press
In all models	SAUTÉ	MEDIUM, NORMAL, or CUSTOM 300°F	10 minutes	START

3. As the pot heats, melt the butter in the insert set in a **5- or 6-quart Instant Pot.** Add the shallots and cook, stirring often, just until they begin to soften, about 2 minutes. Pour in the wine or its substitute and scrape up any browned bits on the pot's bottom. (There should be almost none.) Stir in the broth and mustard, then turn off the heat.

4. Set an IP-safe steamer basket or steamer rack in the insert. Place the pork chops in the basket, overlapping them as little as possible, only thin end under thicker part as necessary. You can even stand some up on an edge. Lock the lid onto the cooker.

5.

	Set pot for	Set level to	Valve must be	Set time for	If needed, press
For Max pots only	PRESSURE COOK	MAX	—	8 minutes with the KEEP WARM setting off	START
For all other pots	PRESSURE COOK or MANUAL	HIGH	Closed	10 minutes with the KEEP WARM setting off	START

6. When the pot has finished cooking, turn it off and let the pressure **return to normal naturally,** about 15 minutes. Unlatch the lid and open the cooker. Use hot pads or silicone baking mitts to transfer the (hot!) steamer basket to a nearby cutting board. Whisk the cream and cornstarch in a small bowl until smooth.

7.

	Press	Set it for	Set time for	If needed, press
In all models	SAUTÉ	MEDIUM, NORMAL, or CUSTOM 300°F	5 minutes	START

8. Stir well as the sauce comes to a simmer, then whisk in the cream slurry. Continue cooking, whisking constantly, until somewhat thickened, less than 1 minute. Turn off the heat and use hot pads or silicone baking mitts to transfer the (hot!) insert to a nearby wire rack (to stop the cooking). Serve the pork chops with this sauce ladled on top.

Other Pots

- For a 3-quart Instant Pot, you *must* halve almost all of the ingredient amounts *except* you *must* use ⅔ cup broth.

- For an 8-quart Instant Pot, you *must* increase all of the ingredient amounts by 50 percent.

- For a 10-quart Instant Pot, you *must* double all of the ingredient amounts (and use a very large steaming basket).

Beyond

- For more flavor, use a coarse-grained Dijon mustard, particularly a nose-spanking kind like Maille.

- Serve alongside Butter-and-Herb Israeli Couscous (page 331) or Mashed Butternut Squash (page 342).

Braised Pork T-Bone Chops with Artichokes

12 ingredients	**SPECIAL EQUIPMENT:** none
4 SERVINGS	**PRESSURE:** max or high
METHOD: standard	**TIME UNDER PRESSURE:** 10 or 12 minutes
	RELEASE: natural
	TOTAL TIME WITH PRESSURE: about 45 minutes
	GLUTEN-FREE

1 tablespoon butter

1 tablespoon olive oil

Four 1¼-inch-thick 12-ounce bone-in pork loin T-bone chops

1 teaspoon ground black pepper

½ teaspoon table salt

3 ounces pancetta, chopped

1 tablespoon packed, stemmed, fresh oregano leaves, minced

2 medium garlic cloves, minced (2 teaspoons)

2 teaspoons finely minced lemon zest

½ cup dry but light white wine, such as Pinot Grigio; or dry vermouth; or unsweetened white grape juice

½ cup chicken broth

One 14-ounce can artichoke heart quarters packed in water, drained

Other Pots

- For a 3-quart Instant Pot, you *must* halve all of the ingredient amounts.
- For an 8-quart Instant Pot, you *must* increase all of the ingredient amounts by 50 percent.
- For a 10-quart Instant Pot, you *must* double all of the ingredient amounts.

Beyond

- Serve this over cooked white rice (for our notion of how to make it perfect every time, see page 355), cooked brown rice (page 356), or Barley "Risotto" (page 368).
- Offer extra lemon wedges for squeezing over the servings.

Meaty T-bone pork chops are expensive enough that they deserve a royal treatment. In this technique, each chop will stand up on its bony edge so the meat doesn't sit in the sauce and get spongy as it cooks. Consider this the right technique any time you want to make pork T-bones in an IP.

We've used jarred artichoke heart quarters because they just about melt into the lemony sauce, offering a bit of body to the sauce without our having to thicken it.

1.

	Press	Set it for	Set time for	If needed, press
In all models	SAUTÉ	MEDIUM, NORMAL, or CUSTOM 300°F	15 minutes	START

2. As the pot heats, melt the butter in the olive oil in the insert set in a **5- or 6-quart Instant Pot.** Season the chops with the pepper and salt, then add two of them to the pot. Brown well, turning as little as possible, about 5 minutes. Transfer the chops to a nearby large bowl and brown the other two chops in the same way before getting them into that bowl.

3. Add the pancetta to the pot and cook, stirring often, until crisp at the edges, about 3 minutes. Stir in the oregano, garlic, and lemon zest until fragrant, just a few seconds. Pour in the wine or its substitute and scrape up any browned bits on the pot's bottom. Stir in the broth and turn off the heat.

4. Stir in the artichoke heart quarters, then stand the pork chops in the sauce on their bony sides. Add any accumulated juices from their bowl and lock the lid onto the cooker.

5.

	Set pot for	Set level to	Valve must be	Set time for	If needed, press
For Max pots only	PRESSURE COOK	MAX	—	10 minutes with the KEEP WARM setting off	START
For all other pots	PRESSURE COOK or MANUAL	HIGH	Closed	12 minutes with the KEEP WARM setting off	START

6. When the pot has finished cooking under pressure, turn it off and let the pressure **return to normal naturally,** about 20 minutes. Unlatch the lid and open the cooker. Serve the chops in bowls with the sauce ladled generously over them.

Oregano-and-Butter Pork Loin

12 ingredients	SPECIAL EQUIPMENT: none	TIME UNDER PRESSURE: 12 or 15 minutes	TOTAL TIME WITH PRESSURE: about 50 minutes
4–6 SERVINGS			
METHOD: standard	PRESSURE: max or high	RELEASE: natural	GLUTEN-FREE

½ stick (4 tablespoons or ¼ cup) butter, melted and cooled for a few minutes

3 medium garlic cloves, minced (1 tablespoon)

1 tablespoon honey

1 teaspoon dried oregano

1 teaspoon table salt

½ teaspoon mild paprika

½ teaspoon onion powder

½ teaspoon ground black pepper

One 2½-pound boneless pork loin roast

1 tablespoon olive oil

1 cup chicken broth

1 tablespoon balsamic vinegar

Other Pots

- This pork loin will not fit in a 3-quart Instant Pot—and a smaller cut will not cook evenly with the given timings.

- For an 8-quart Instant Pot, you *must* increase the broth in the insert to 1½ cups while otherwise completing the recipe as stated.

- The amount of liquid required will swamp the pork in a 10-quart Instant Pot. For a pork loin recipe designed for this larger pot, see page 461.

Beyond

- For a richer sauce, remove the meat from the pot, then set the SAUTÉ setting on HIGH or MORE. Reduce the liquid in the pot to half the original volume, stirring constantly, about 6 minutes. Add 2 to 3 tablespoons butter, turn off the heat, and stir until smooth.

This buttery paste smeared on a pork loin makes a relatively low-fat meat so flavorful. Even so, the real secret to success is properly browning the meat. Leave it alone in the pot. TV chefs are always fussing with food over the heat. What's with them? Let the pork loin get a good crust for better color *and* flavor.

1. Stir the melted butter, garlic, honey, oregano, salt, paprika, onion powder, and pepper in a small bowl until uniform. Rub this mixture evenly over the pork loin.

2.

	Press	Set it for	Set time for	If needed, press
In all models	SAUTÉ	MEDIUM, NORMAL, or CUSTOM 300°F	15 minutes	START

3. As the pot heats, warm the oil in the insert set in a **5- or 6-quart Instant Pot.** Add the pork loin and brown well on all sides, turning once in a while, about 10 minutes. Use kitchen tongs to transfer the pork loin to a nearby cutting board.

4. Add the broth and vinegar to the pot. Stir well to get up any browned bits on the pot's bottom. Turn off the heat and return the pork loin to the pot. Lock the lid onto the cooker.

5.

	Set pot for	Set level to	Valve must be	Set time for	If needed, press
For Max pots only	PRESSURE COOK	MAX		12 minutes with the KEEP WARM setting off	START
For all other pots	PRESSURE COOK or MANUAL	HIGH	Closed	15 minutes with the KEEP WARM setting off	START

6. When the pot has finished cooking, turn it off and let the pressure **return to normal naturally,** about 20 minutes. Unlatch the lid and open the cooker. Use cleaned kitchen tongs and perhaps a metal spatula to transfer the pork loin to a cleaned nearby cutting board. Set aside for 5 minutes, then slice the meat into ½-inch-thick rounds. Serve them with some of the pot's juices drizzled on top.

Smoky Pulled Pork with Alabama White Sauce

14 ingredients	
6–8 SERVINGS	

SPECIAL EQUIPMENT: none

METHOD: fast/slow

PRESSURE: max or high

TIME UNDER PRESSURE: 55 or 70 minutes

RELEASE: natural

TOTAL TIME WITH PRESSURE: about 2 hours

TOTAL TIME WITH SLOW COOKING: about 6 hours

CAN BE GLUTEN-FREE

---

3 tablespoons mild paprika

2 tablespoons dark brown sugar

1 tablespoon ground cumin

1 tablespoon plus 2 teaspoons ground black pepper

1½ teaspoons table salt

1 teaspoon ground dried mustard

1 teaspoon garlic powder

½ teaspoon ground cloves

One 2-pound boneless pork butt or shoulder (sometimes called "Boston butt")

2 cups chicken broth

Two 12-ounce smoked ham hocks

1 cup regular, low-fat, or fat-free mayonnaise (gluten-free, if necessary)

¼ cup distilled white vinegar

1 tablespoon jarred prepared white horseradish (gluten-free, if necessary)

By "seasoning" pork butt with smoked ham hocks, rather than liquid smoke or smoked paprika, we can craft an alternate version of pulled pork that's super simple *and* super porky. You'll find smoked ham hocks in the meat case of almost all North American supermarkets.

We didn't add much sugar to this recipe, to keep the dish savory. Alabama white sauce, a mayonnaise-based barbecue sauce, doesn't often include horseradish; but we like that nose-tingling flavor alongside the pulled pork.

1. Mix the paprika, brown sugar, cumin, 2 teaspoons pepper, salt, ground mustard, garlic powder, and cloves in a small bowl until uniform. Massage this mixture evenly and well over the exterior of the pork shoulder or butt.

2. Pour the broth into the insert set in a **5-, 6-, or 8-quart Instant Pot.** Set the coated shoulder or butt in the insert. Add the hocks. Lock the lid onto the cooker.

3.

	Set pot for	Set level to	Valve must be	Set time for	If needed, press
For Max pots only	PRESSURE COOK	MAX	—	55 minutes with the KEEP WARM setting off	START
For all other pots	PRESSURE COOK or MANUAL	HIGH	Closed	1 hour 10 minutes with the KEEP WARM setting off	START
For the slow-cook function	SLOW COOK	HIGH	Open	5½ hours with the KEEP WARM setting off	START

4. When the pot has finished cooking under pressure, turn it off and let the pressure **return to normal naturally,** about 40 minutes. Whichever cooking method you've used, unlatch the lid and open the cooker.

5. Use kitchen tongs and a slotted spoon to transfer the hocks to a nearby cutting board. Make sure you catch any small bones that fall into the pot. Cool a few minutes, then remove the skin from the hocks. You can discard the skin or you can finely chop it to add it back to the pot, a very chewy texture that some adore and others don't. In any event, use two forks to shred the meat off the hocks, discarding any bones and hard cartilage.

6. Use those forks to shred the shoulder or butt right in the insert. Stir the hock meat (and the chopped skin, if desired) into the sauce and meat in the pot. Set the lid askew over the pot and set aside for 5 minutes.

7. Meanwhile, whisk the mayonnaise, vinegar, horseradish, and remaining 1 tablespoon pepper in a bowl until uniform. Use kitchen tongs to pick up wads of warm meat to serve with the white sauce on the side, keeping the remainder of the pork in the juices to maintain the flavor.

Other Pots

- For a **3-quart Instant Pot,** you *must* use only one 12-ounce hock and halve the remaining ingredient amounts.

- For a **10-quart Instant Pot,** you *must* double almost all of the ingredient amounts *except* you *must* use only 3 hocks.

Beyond

- Serve the pulled pork in toasted hoagie or hot dog buns.

- Even with the white sauce, pickle relish makes a great condiment.

- Or try the pulled pork sandwiches garnished with kimchi.

Salty-Sweet Pulled Pork

5 ingredients	**SPECIAL EQUIPMENT:** none
6–8 SERVINGS	**PRESSURE:** max or high
METHOD: fast/slow	

TIME UNDER PRESSURE: 60 or 75 minutes	**TOTAL TIME WITH PRESSURE:** about 2 hours 10 minutes	**TOTAL TIME WITH SLOW COOKING:** about 6 hours
RELEASE: natural		**CAN BE GLUTEN-FREE**

8 ounces thick-cut double-smoked slab bacon (gluten-free, if necessary), diced; or thick-cut doubled-smoked strips of bacon (gluten-free, if necessary), chopped

One 3-pound boneless pork shoulder, cut into 3 pieces

1 tablespoon kosher salt

1 cup unsweetened pineapple juice

½ cup water

Other Pots

- For a 3-quart Instant Pot, you *must* halve all of the ingredient amounts.

- For a 10-quart Instant Pot, you *must* increase all of the ingredient amounts by 50 percent or you *can* even double the amounts.

Beyond

- For a more authentic flavor, substitute Hawaiian black (or so-called "lava") salt for the kosher salt.

- Serve the pulled pork in lettuce wraps with this simple pineapple salsa: Stir together 2 cups peeled, cored, and diced fresh pineapple; 1 medium red bell pepper, stemmed, cored, and chopped; 1 small red onion, finely chopped; 1 small fresh jalapeño chile, stemmed, cored, and finely chopped; and 3 tablespoons lime juice. Since the pork is fairly salty, check it before adding any salt to the salsa.

Here's our take on kālua pork, a Hawaiian favorite. If we were to go the traditional route, a piece of pork would be salted and cooked in an underground pit for an unbelievably earthy, smoky flavor. Since we can't do any of that (and aren't willing to bury an Instant Pot), we use double-smoked bacon to get the maximum amount of smokiness into the pulled pork.

1.

	Press	Set it for	Set time for	If needed, press
In all models	SAUTÉ	MEDIUM, NORMAL, or CUSTOM 300°F	20 minutes	START

2. As the pot heats, add the bacon to the insert set in a **5-, 6-, or 8-quart Instant Pot.** Cook, stirring often, until browned, about 5 minutes. Use a slotted spoon to transfer the bacon to a nearby large bowl.

3. Rub the pork pieces with the salt. Brown them in two batches (two pieces in one, one piece in the other), turning occasionally, about 6 minutes per batch, eventually getting all the pork into the bowl with the bacon.

4. Pour the pineapple juice into the pot and scrape up any browned bits on the pot's bottom. Stir in the water, then turn off the heat. Return the pork, bacon, and any accumulated juices to the insert. Lock the lid on the pot.

5.

	Set pot for	Set level to	Valve must be	Set time for	If needed, press
For Max pots only	PRESSURE COOK	MAX	—	1 hour with the KEEP WARM setting off	START
For all other pots	PRESSURE COOK or MANUAL	HIGH	Closed	1 hour 15 minutes with the KEEP WARM setting off	START
For the slow-cook function	SLOW COOK	HIGH	Open	5½ hours with the KEEP WARM setting off	START

6. When the pot has finished cooking under pressure, turn it off and let its pressure **return to normal naturally,** about 40 minutes. Whichever cooking method you've used, unlatch the lid and open the cooker. Use two forks to shred the meat into the juices in the pot. Set the lid askew over the pot and set aside for 5 minutes to blend the flavors before serving.

No-Brainer Pork Posole

11 ingredients

4–6 SERVINGS

METHOD: fast/slow

SPECIAL EQUIPMENT: none

PRESSURE: max or high

TIME UNDER PRESSURE: 25 or 30 minutes

RELEASE: natural

TOTAL TIME WITH PRESSURE: about 1 hour 20 minutes

TOTAL TIME WITH SLOW COOKING: about 3 hours 15 minutes

GLUTEN-FREE

1½ pounds boneless pork shoulder, cut into 2-inch pieces, any chunks of fat removed

One 29-ounce can hominy, drained and rinsed (3½ cups)

1½ cups chicken broth

1 medium yellow or white onion, chopped (1 cup)

One 10-ounce can hot or mild diced tomatoes and green chiles, such as Rotel (1¼ cups)

One 4½-ounce can hot or mild diced green chiles (½ cup)

2 tablespoons *pure* chile powder, preferably pure ancho chile powder

3 medium garlic cloves, minced (1 tablespoon)

1 tablespoon ground cumin

1 teaspoon dried oregano

½ cup loosely packed, stemmed, fresh cilantro leaves, finely chopped

It can't get much easier: canned staples turned into the base for an otherwise fairly traditional pork and hominy stew. The only trick to this recipe is that you must wait patiently for that natural release to work its magic, tenderizing the pork as it sits in the pot.

There's no added salt because canned products, even low-sodium versions, can be quite salty. Pass extra at the table, preferably a coarse, crunchy salt.

1. Stir the pork, hominy, broth, onion, canned tomatoes and chiles, the canned green chiles, chile powder, garlic, cumin, and oregano in the insert set in a **5-, 6-, or 8-quart Instant Pot** until well combined. Lock the lid onto the cooker.

2.

	Set pot for	Set level to	Valve must be	Set time for	If needed, press
For Max pots only	PRESSURE COOK	MAX	—	25 minutes with the KEEP WARM setting off	START
For all other pots	PRESSURE COOK or MANUAL	HIGH	Closed	30 minutes with the KEEP WARM setting off	START
For the slow-cook function	SLOW COOK	HIGH	Open	3 hours with the KEEP WARM setting off	START

3. When the pot has finished cooking under pressure, turn it off and let the pressure **return to normal naturally,** about 40 minutes. Whichever cooking method you've used, unlatch the lid and open the cooker. Stir in the cilantro. Set the lid askew over the pot and set it aside for 5 minutes to blend the flavors. Stir again and serve warm.

Other Pots

- For a 3-quart Instant Pot, you *must* halve all of the ingredient amounts.

- For a 10-quart Instant Pot, you *must* double all of the ingredient amounts.

Beyond

- The best condiments for this posole are peeled, pitted, and chopped avocado; thinly sliced radishes; and/or fresh lime wedges for squeezing over the servings.

See photo in insert.

Lamb Gyros

15 ingredients

8 SERVINGS

METHOD:
fast/slow

PRESSURE:
max or high

TIME UNDER
PRESSURE:
10 or 12 minutes

RELEASE:
quick

TOTAL TIME WITH
PRESSURE:
at least 1½ hours
(includes
marinating)

TOTAL TIME WITH
SLOW COOKING:
at least 3 hours
15 minutes
(includes
marinating)

CAN BE GLUTEN-
FREE

2 pounds *butterflied* boneless leg of lamb, opened out and cut across the length of the meat into ¼-inch-wide strips

1 small red onion, halved and sliced into thin half-moons

3 tablespoons olive oil

Up to 6 medium garlic cloves, minced (2 tablespoons)

1 tablespoon dried marjoram

1 tablespoon dried oregano

1 tablespoon dried thyme

1½ teaspoons table salt

1½ cups chicken broth

1½ cups plain full-fat Greek yogurt

1 medium cucumber, peeled, halved lengthwise, seeded, and shredded through the large holes of a box grater

1 tablespoon distilled white vinegar

1 tablespoon packed stemmed fresh dill fronds, minced

8 pita pockets (gluten-free, if necessary), warmed (see the headnote for more information)

1 pound Roma or plum tomatoes, chopped (2 cups)

Other Pots

- For a 3-quart Instant Pot, you *must* halve all of the ingredient amounts.

- For a 10-quart Instant Pot, you *must* increase all of the ingredient amounts by 50 percent or you *can* even double the amounts.

Beyond

- Add shredded iceberg lettuce, thinly sliced radishes, and/or sprouts to the pockets.

You need a lot of dried herbs to make a successful filling for gyros as the meat should be highly flavored to stand up to the yogurt sauce in the pita pockets. Note that the lamb is butterflied, so that it's a flat piece. If you can't find a butterflied cut at your market, ask the butcher to help out.

To warm the pitas, place them on a large, lipped baking sheet and set them in a 350°F oven for about 5 minutes (they should be just warmed, not hot). Or microwave the pockets individually on HIGH for 1 minute each. (If you stack them, some brands will stick together.)

1. Stir the lamb strips, onion, 1 tablespoon of the olive oil, 1 tablespoon of the minced garlic, the marjoram, oregano, thyme, and 1 teaspoon of the salt in the insert for a **5-, 6-, or 8-quart Instant Pot** until the meat is evenly and well coated in the spices. Cover the pot's insert and refrigerate for at least 1 hour or up to 3 hours, stirring once or twice.

2. Set the filled insert into its pot. Pour in the broth and stir well. Lock the lid on the cooker.

3.

	Set pot for	Set level to	Valve must be	Set time for	If needed, press
For Max pots only	PRESSURE COOK	MAX	—	10 minutes with the KEEP WARM setting off	START
For all other pots	PRESSURE COOK or MANUAL	HIGH	Closed	12 minutes with the KEEP WARM setting off	START
For the slow-cook function	SLOW COOK	HIGH	Open	2 hours with the KEEP WARM setting off	START

4. *While the lamb cooks,* stir the yogurt, cucumber, vinegar, dill, the remaining 2 tablespoons olive oil, up to the remaining 1 tablespoon minced garlic (you can use less), and the remaining ½ teaspoon salt in a medium bowl until well combined.

5. When the pot has finished cooking under pressure, use the **quick-release method** to bring the pressure back to normal. Whichever cooking method you've used, unlatch the lid and open the cooker. Stir well and set aside for a couple of minutes so the meat continues to absorb the sauce.

6. Use kitchen tongs to pick up (and partly drain) some lamb strips before adding them to the pita pockets along with the chopped tomatoes and cucumber sauce.

Old-School Irish Lamb Stew

12 ingredients	
4–6 SERVINGS	
METHOD: fast/slow	

SPECIAL EQUIPMENT: none

PRESSURE: max or high

TIME UNDER PRESSURE: 25 or 35 minutes

RELEASE: natural

TOTAL TIME WITH PRESSURE: about 1 hour 15 minutes

TOTAL TIME WITH SLOW COOKING: about 3 hours 15 minutes

1½ pounds boneless leg of lamb, cut into 1½-inch chunks

3 medium or 2 large leeks, white and pale green parts only, halved lengthwise, washed well for internal grit, and thinly sliced (1½ cups)

4 large red-skinned potatoes, quartered (do not peel)

2 medium turnips (8 ounces total weight), peeled and cubed (1½ cups)

1 cup stout beer, preferably Guinness

½ cup beef broth

1 tablespoon Worcestershire sauce

One 3-inch fresh rosemary sprig

1 multi-stemmed fresh thyme sprig

2 bay leaves

2 tablespoons butter, softened to room temperature

2 tablespoons all-purpose flour

Other Pots

- For a 3-quart Instant Pot, you *must* halve all of the ingredient amounts.
- For an 8-quart Instant Pot, you *can* increase all of the ingredient amounts by 50 percent.
- For a 10-quart Instant Pot, you *must* double all of the ingredient amounts.

Beyond

- Stir up to ⅓ cup heavy cream into the pot before you begin adding the butter mixture.

The problem with lamb in stews, particularly in a pressure cooker, is that the meat gives off a great deal of liquid as it cooks. Without the benefit of the evaporation and condensation that would occur in a stovetop or oven, lamb creates a watery stew in the IP—*unless* the liquid is thickened in some way. The best way is an old French method, a butter-and-flour paste, to make the stew incredibly silky and rich. Add the paste in small bits, stirring constantly, so that the flour doesn't fall out of suspension and burn on the pot's bottom before it has dissolved into the liquid.

1. Stir the lamb, leeks, potatoes, turnips, beer, broth, Worcestershire sauce, rosemary, thyme, and bay leaves in a **5-, 6-, or 8-quart Instant Pot.** Lock the lid onto the cooker.

2.

	Set pot for	Set level to	Valve must be	Set time for	If needed, press
For Max pots only	PRESSURE COOK	MAX	—	25 minutes with the KEEP WARM setting off	START
For all other pots	PRESSURE COOK or MANUAL	HIGH	Closed	35 minutes with the KEEP WARM setting off	START
For the slow-cook function	SLOW COOK	HIGH	Open	3 hours with the KEEP WARM setting off	START

3. When the pot has finished cooking under pressure, turn it off and let the pressure **return to normal naturally,** about 10 minutes. Whichever cooking method you've used, unlatch the lid and open the cooker. Fish out and discard the herbs sprigs and the bay leaves.

4.

	Press	Set it for	Set time for	If needed, press
In all models	SAUTÉ	MEDIUM, NORMAL, or CUSTOM 300°F	5 minutes	START

5. As the sauce comes to a simmer, use a flatware fork to mash the butter and flour into a paste in a small bowl. When the sauce is bubbling, add this butter mixture in small dribs and drabs, *stirring constantly,* until the sauce is slightly thickened, about 2 minutes. Turn off the heat and use hot pads or silicone baking mitts to transfer the (hot!) insert to a nearby wire rack (to stop the cooking). Set aside for 2 to 3 minutes to blend the flavors. Stir again and serve hot.

Spiced Lamb and White Bean Stew

14 ingredients

6 SERVINGS

METHOD:
fast/slow

SPECIAL EQUIPMENT:
none

PRESSURE:
max or high

TIME UNDER PRESSURE:
25 or 35 minutes

RELEASE:
natural

TOTAL TIME WITH PRESSURE:
about 1½ hours

TOTAL TIME WITH SLOW COOKING:
about 3 hours 15 minutes

GLUTEN-FREE

2 tablespoons olive oil

1 large yellow or white onion, halved and sliced into thin half-moons

3 medium garlic cloves, minced (1 tablespoon)

1 teaspoon ground coriander

1 teaspoon ground cumin

1 teaspoon table salt

1 teaspoon ground black pepper

½ teaspoon ground cinnamon

2 pounds boneless leg of lamb, cut into 1½-inch pieces

2 tablespoons dark brown sugar

¼ cup apple cider vinegar

One 15-ounce can cannellini beans, drained and rinsed (1¾ cups)

1¼ cups chicken broth

2 tablespoons tomato paste

This recipe is not a curry but uses the technique of a curry—toasting spices in fat and then adding meat without browning it—to create a rich and satisfying stew. Use only leg of lamb, not shoulder or stew meat, both of which will make the stew too oily. The canned beans get super soft under pressure and help to thicken the stew, particularly if you stir it well before you set it aside for a couple of minutes in the last step.

1.

	Press	Set it for	Set time for	If needed, press
In all models	SAUTÉ	MEDIUM, NORMAL, or CUSTOM 300°F	10 minutes	START

2. As the pot heats, warm the oil in the insert set in a **5- or 6-quart Instant Pot.** Add the onion and cook, stirring often, until it softens and even starts to brown in spots, about 5 minutes.

3. Stir in the garlic, coriander, cumin, salt, pepper, and cinnamon. Toast until quite fragrant, about 15 seconds. Add the meat and stir well to coat it in the onions and spices without browning it.

4. Stir in the brown sugar until uniform. Add the vinegar and scrape up any browned bits on the pot's bottom. Turn off the heat. Stir in the beans and broth. Lock the lid on the pot.

5.

	Set pot for	Set level to	Valve must be	Set time for	If needed, press
For Max pots only	PRESSURE COOK	MAX	—	25 minutes with the KEEP WARM setting off	START
For all other pots	PRESSURE COOK or MANUAL	HIGH	Closed	35 minutes with the KEEP WARM setting off	START
For the slow-cook function	SLOW COOK	HIGH	Open	3 hours with the KEEP WARM setting off	START

6. When the pot has finished cooking under pressure, turn it off and let the pressure **return to normal naturally,** about 40 minutes. Whichever cooking method you've used, unlatch the lid and open the cooker.

7.

	Press	Set it for	Set time for	If needed, press
In all models	SAUTÉ	MEDIUM, NORMAL, or CUSTOM 300°F	5 minutes	START

8. As the sauce comes to a bubble, stir in the tomato paste. Continue cooking, stirring almost constantly, until slightly thickened, about 1 minute. Turn off the heat and set the lid askew over the pot. Set it aside for 5 minutes so the meat can continue to absorb some of the juices. Stir well again and serve hot.

Other Pots

- For a 3-quart Instant Pot, you *must* halve all of the ingredient amounts.
- For an 8-quart Instant Pot, you *must* increase all of the ingredient amounts by 50 percent.
- For a 10-quart Instant Pot, you *must* double all of the ingredient amounts.

Beyond

- Garnish the servings with stemmed and minced fresh cilantro leaves.
- And/or sliced almonds.

Nonna-Worthy Braised Leg of Lamb

12 ingredients	
8 SERVINGS	
METHOD: fast/slow	

SPECIAL EQUIPMENT: butchers' twine

PRESSURE: max or high

TIME UNDER PRESSURE: 50 or 60 minutes

RELEASE: natural

TOTAL TIME WITH PRESSURE: about 2 hours

TOTAL TIME WITH SLOW COOKING: about 6 hours

GLUTEN-FREE

---

3 medium garlic cloves, peeled

3 tablespoons packed, stemmed, fresh rosemary leaves

1 teaspoon kosher or coarse-grained sea salt

2 tablespoons olive oil

1 teaspoon fennel seeds

½ teaspoon ground black pepper

One 4-pound boneless leg of lamb, any netting removed, but the meat tied (see the headnote for more information)

2 tablespoons unsalted butter

1 large yellow or white onion, chopped (1½ cups)

1 large fennel bulb, trimmed of its fronds and hard bottom, then chopped (2½ cups)

½ cup dry and big-flavored red wine, such as Sangiovese; or beef broth

One 28-ounce can whole tomatoes *packed in juice* (3½ cups)

Many people roast or even grill leg of lamb these days. That's because they're buying younger (and more tender) lamb than our grandmothers did. But many of these venerable women knew the pleasures of braising a leg of lamb to soften the cartilage, enrich the meat, and get the most flavor into every bite.

To tie a boneless leg of lamb, compact the cut into a rather round roast (not perfect, of course), pushing the cut sides of the meat against each other. Wrap butchers' twine around both its "equator" and around the north-south pole axis to keep it closed. Or ask the butcher at your supermarket to do this deed for you.

1. Put the garlic, rosemary, and salt on a cutting board. Rock a chef's knife or sturdy kitchen knife through these ingredients, repeatedly changing the blade's direction. It helps to balance one hand on the back of the handle while using the other hand to move the blade up and down. Gather the ingredients together and continue rocking the knife until the ingredients are finely chopped. Add 1 tablespoon of the olive oil and the fennel seeds; continue that rocking action until minced. Add the remaining 1 tablespoon olive oil and the pepper. Keep rocking the knife through the ingredients, gathering them together and changing the blade's direction repeatedly, until you've made a thick paste.

2. Make eighteen 1-inch-deep slits all over the leg of lamb with the point of a paring knife. Fill each of these slits with some of the garlic paste you've made. Rub the meat with any remaining paste.

3.

	Press	Set it for	Set time for	If needed, press
In all models	SAUTÉ	MEDIUM, NORMAL, or CUSTOM 300°F	20 minutes	START

4. As the pot heats, melt the butter in the insert set in a **5-, 6-, or 8-quart Instant Pot.** Add the meat and brown it well on all sides, turning it only occasionally to let it really sear against the hot surface, about 10 minutes. Transfer the meat to a nearby cutting board.

5. Add the onion and fennel to the pot; cook, stirring often, until the onion softens, about 4 minutes. Pour in the wine and scrape up any browned bits on the pot's bottom.

6. Crush the canned tomatoes over the pot one by one with your clean hand, letting the pieces fall into the pot. Add the juices from the can, stir well, and turn off the heat. Nestle the leg of lamb into the sauce, adding any accumulated juice around it. Lock the lid on the pot.

7.

	Set pot for	Set level to	Valve must be	Set time for	If needed, press
For Max pots only	PRESSURE COOK	MAX	—	50 minutes with the KEEP WARM setting off	START
For all other pots	PRESSURE COOK or MANUAL	HIGH	Closed	1 hour with the KEEP WARM setting off	START
For the slow-cook function	SLOW COOK	HIGH	Open	5½ hours with the KEEP WARM setting off	START

8. When the pot has finished cooking under pressure, turn it off and let the pressure **return to normal naturally,** about 40 minutes. Whichever cooking method you used, unlatch the lid and open the cooker. Use kitchen tongs and perhaps a metal spatula to transfer the leg of lamb to a nearby cutting board. Be careful: It can come apart. Set aside for 5 minutes.

9. Use a flatware tablespoon to skim the fat off the top of the sauce in the pot. Slice the lamb into small chunks and serve in bowls with the pot sauce ladled on top.

Other Pots

- For a 3-quart Instant Pot, you *must* halve almost all of the ingredient amounts *except* you *must* use a 1½-pound boneless leg of lamb, tied.

- For a 10-quart Instant Pot, you *must* increase all of the ingredient amounts by 50 percent (it's fine to use *two* 3-pound boneless legs of lamb, each tied).

Beyond

- Serve the lamb and its pot juices over cooked and drained pasta, particularly fettuccine, even spinach fettuccine.

- For a richer sauce, bring the pot juices to a boil after you remove the lamb by setting the pot on its SAUTÉ setting at HIGH or MORE. Cook, stirring often, until the juices have reduced to about half their volume when you opened the pot, about 6 minutes. If desired, stir up to 2 tablespoons butter into the sauce, then turn off the heat and let the sauce sit for a couple of minutes to blend the flavors.

Smoky, Spicy, and Sweet Lamb Shanks

12 ingredients

4 SERVINGS

METHOD: fast/slow

SPECIAL EQUIPMENT: none

PRESSURE: max or high

TIME UNDER PRESSURE: 35 or 45 minutes

RELEASE: natural

TOTAL TIME WITH PRESSURE: about 1 hour 50 minutes

TOTAL TIME WITH SLOW COOKING: about 4½ hours

CAN BE GLUTEN-FREE

2 tablespoons olive oil

Four ¾-pound lamb shanks (each no more than 8 inches long)

1 medium yellow or white onion, chopped (1 cup)

¼ cup apricot jam (gluten-free, if necessary)

1 canned chipotle chile in adobo sauce (gluten-free, if necessary), stemmed, cored, and chopped (seeded, if desired)

1 tablespoon adobo sauce from the can

1½ teaspoons ground coriander

1½ teaspoons ground cumin

1 teaspoon table salt

1 teaspoon ground black pepper

½ cup whole toasted unsalted almonds

1 cup chicken broth

Lamb shanks are an all-afternoon affair in the oven. Not anymore! With an Instant Pot, they're within reach for a weekend meal—and you still get your weekend. The combo of apricot jam and canned chipotle chiles in adobo sauce can't be beat: sweet and hot, salty and a little vinegary. It makes a beautifully complex sauce for strongly flavored lamb shanks.

1.

	Press	Set it for	Set time for	If needed, press
In all models	SAUTÉ	MEDIUM, NORMAL, or CUSTOM 300°F	20 minutes	START

2. As the pot heats, warm the oil in the insert set in a **6-quart Instant Pot.** Set two lamb shanks in the insert and brown them well, turning only occasionally, about 6 minutes. Transfer the shanks to a nearby large bowl, then brown the other shanks the same way before getting them into that bowl.

3. Add the onion to the pot and cook, stirring often, until softened, about 3 minutes. Stir in the jam, chipotle chile, adobo sauce, coriander, cumin, salt, and pepper until fragrant, just a few seconds.

4. Stir in the almonds, then pour in the broth. Scrape up any browned bits on the pot's bottom. Turn off the heat. Return the shanks to the pot, along with any accumulated juices in their bowl, making them fit in the pot by placing them fat ends over skinny ends, with some perhaps in a second layer. Lock the lid onto the cooker.

5.

	Set pot for	Set level to	Valve must be	Set time for	If needed, press
For Max pots only	PRESSURE COOK	MAX	—	35 minutes with the KEEP WARM setting off	START
For all other pots	PRESSURE COOK or MANUAL	HIGH	Closed	45 minutes with the KEEP WARM setting off	START
For the slow-cook function	SLOW COOK	HIGH	Open	4 hours with the KEEP WARM setting off	START

6. When the pot has finished cooking under pressure, turn it off and let the pressure **return to normal naturally,** about 40 minutes. Whichever cooking method you've used, unlatch the lid and open the cooker. Use kitchen tongs and maybe a slotted spoon to transfer the shanks to serving bowls. Use a flatware spoon to skim the surface fat off the sauce in the pot.

7.

	Press	Set it for	Set time for	If needed, press
In all models	SAUTÉ	HIGH or MORE	5 minutes	START

8. Bring the sauce to a high simmer, stirring constantly. Cook, stirring quite frequently, until the sauce has reduced to about half the volume it was when you opened the pot, about 5 minutes. Turn off the heat and let the sauce cool for 2 to 3 minutes before ladling it over the shanks.

Other Pots

- Unfortunately, lamb shanks will not fit in a 3-quart Instant Pot.

- For a 5-quart Instant Pot, you *must* use lamb shanks no more than 5 inches long while otherwise completing the recipe as stated.

- For an 8-quart Instant Pot, you *must* increase all of the ingredient amounts by 50 percent.

- For a 10-quart Instant Pot, you *must* double all of the ingredient amounts. You *can* even triple (!) the chipotles used in the recipe.

Beyond

- Serve the shanks over Leek and Buttermilk Mashed Potatoes (page 349) or your favorite mashed potatoes.

- Or try them over Rice Pilaf with Mushrooms (page 361).

Orange-Sage Braised Lamb Shanks

12 ingredients	SPECIAL EQUIPMENT: none	TIME UNDER PRESSURE: 35 or 45 minutes	TOTAL TIME WITH PRESSURE: about 1 hour 50 minutes	TOTAL TIME WITH SLOW COOKING: about 4½ hours
4 SERVINGS	PRESSURE: max or high			
METHOD: fast/slow		RELEASE: natural		

2 tablespoons butter, plus 1½ tablespoons butter at room temperature

2 ounces pancetta (gluten-free, if necessary), diced

Four ¾-pound lamb shanks (each no more than 8 inches long)

1 large yellow or white onion, chopped (1½ cups)

1 tablespoon loosely packed, stemmed, fresh sage leaves, finely chopped

1 tablespoon finely grated orange zest

1 teaspoon table salt

1 teaspoon ground black pepper

Up to ½ teaspoon grated nutmeg

⅓ cup orange juice, preferably fresh orange juice

1 cup chicken broth

1½ tablespoons all-purpose flour

The other lamb shank recipe on page 320 is simpler, but this one takes the shanks over the top with a bold mix of flavors. The sage and orange give the sauce a sophisticated finish, herbaceous and sweet. The sauce is thickened with a traditional French technique, a butter-and-flour paste, to give it a silky smooth finish.

1.

	Press	Set it for	Set time for	If needed, press
In all models	SAUTÉ	MEDIUM, NORMAL, or CUSTOM 300°F	20 minutes	START

2. As the pot heats, melt the 2 tablespoons butter in the insert set in a **6-quart Instant Pot.** Add the pancetta and cook, stirring often, until well browned and crisp at the edges, about 5 minutes. Use a slotted spoon to transfer the pancetta to a nearby large bowl.

3. Set two lamb shanks in the pot and brown them well, turning occasionally, about 6 minutes. Transfer the shanks to the nearby large bowl, then brown the other shanks the same way before getting them into that bowl.

4. Add the onion to the pot and cook, stirring often, until softened, about 3 minutes. Stir in the sage, orange zest, salt, pepper, and nutmeg until fragrant, just a few seconds. Pour in the orange juice and scrape up any browned bits on the pot's bottom. Stir in the broth, then turn off the heat.

5. Return the pancetta and shanks to the pot, along with any accumulated juices in their bowl, making the shanks fit in the pot by placing them fat ends over skinny ends, with some perhaps in a second layer. Lock the lid onto the cooker.

6.

	Set pot for	Set level to	Valve must be	Set time for	If needed, press
For Max pots only	PRESSURE COOK	MAX	—	35 minutes with the KEEP WARM setting off	START
For all other pots	PRESSURE COOK or MANUAL	HIGH	Closed	45 minutes with the KEEP WARM setting off	START
For the slow-cook function	SLOW COOK	HIGH	Open	4 hours with the KEEP WARM setting off	START

7. When the pot has finished cooking under pressure, turn it off and let the pressure **return to normal naturally,** about 40 minutes. Whichever cooking method you've used, unlatch the lid and open the cooker.

8. Use kitchen tongs and maybe a slotted spoon to transfer the shanks to serving bowls. Use a flatware spoon to skim the surface fat off the sauce in the pot. Use a flatware fork to mash the 1½ tablespoons room-temperature butter and the flour into a smooth paste in a small bowl.

9.

	Press	Set it for	Set time for	If needed, press
In all models	SAUTÉ	HIGH or MORE	5 minutes	START

10. As the sauce comes to a full simmer, add the butter paste in very small bits, *whisking all the while*. Each bit of butter and flour must dissolve before the next gets added, although it should only take a few seconds per bit if it's small enough and you're whisking vigorously enough. Continue whisking until the sauce thickens somewhat, less than 1 minute. Turn off the heat and use hot pads or silicone baking mitts to immediately transfer the (hot!) insert to a nearby wire rack (to stop the cooking). Set aside for 2 to 3 minutes, whisking occasionally, to cool the sauce. Ladle it over the shanks.

Other Pots

- Unfortunately, lamb shanks will not fit in a 3-quart Instant Pot.

- For a 5-quart Instant Pot, you *must* use lamb shanks no more than 5 inches long while otherwise completing the recipe as stated.

- For an 8-quart Instant Pot, you *must* increase all of the ingredient amounts by 50 percent.

- For a 10-quart Instant Pot, you *must* double all of the ingredient amounts.

Beyond

- Serve the shanks over cooked and drained Israeli couscous that's been tossed with butter and a little more finely grated orange zest.

- Drizzle a little aged, syrupy balsamic vinegar and/or a high-quality finishing olive oil over each serving.

6

Sides, Grains, & Vegetable Mains

Here's a chapter of recipes that are too often overlooked by Instant Pot cooks: vegetable dishes, from appetizers all the way to main courses. Yes, we all know about big hunks of meat out of the pot. And creamy soups. And smooth porridges. But a cauliflower mash? It may not quicken the pulse.

It should. Side dishes are a great way to use your IP, *even when* you're not "cooking with pressure" for your meal. If you've got a roast in the oven, fish fillets on the grill, or a wokful of stir-fry on the stovetop, you ought to consider setting up your IP on the side to handle whatever else you need for the meal. What could be better with the turkey at your holiday feast than a pot of Smashed Potatoes with Herbs and Butter (page 348)? Or what could be better with your next Italian braise than a pot of Risi e Bisi (page 360)? Even for more mundane meals, our pot-in-pot method for white rice and other grains gives you perfect results every time.

Then there are the vegetarian and vegan main courses that round out this chapter: Quinoa and Cauliflower Bowls (page 378), an insane Vegan Pot Roast (page 382), and Vegan Cassoulet (page 381), a mushroom stew that will satisfy even the doubtful and give the vegans in your life a great meal to be savored. Or for a full, vegetable-centered meal, combine a couple of our sides into one plate of deliciousness: Try Stewed Beans and Greens (page 343) with Rice Pilaf with Mushrooms (page 361); or From-Scratch No-Cheat Hummus (page 326) with Smoky Brown Rice and Green Lentils (page 363).

Many fresh vegetables don't need intense pressure to get them done quickly. But the pressure makes them more flavorful, particularly bringing forward natural sweet notes and forcing their internal moisture into the sauce. To that end, *fresh* is more important here than perhaps elsewhere in this book because mushy vegetables become even more so in

the pot. You can often buy a cut of beef and keep it in your fridge for several days before you prepare it. Not so with leafy greens, cauliflower, and sometimes even mushrooms. These need to be as fresh as you can get them for the best results out of the cooker.

In this chapter, you'll also find a host of grain dishes, many of them cooked PIP (pot-in-pot). Yes, a lot of models have a RICE button. And yes, there are lots of ways to make it work more efficiently. Frankly, we think none of them compares to cooking rice PIP. The grains are kept off the insert's hot surface so they don't need to be flooded with liquid or larded with fat. They steam in their own baking dish, actually an ancient way of cooking rice and other grains that ensures a tender, light texture, rather than a soggy mush. Cooking grains PIP is an easy way to up your culinary creds!

Sometimes, however, it's necessary to put those grains right in the insert—as in risotto or particularly our "faux" risottos made with wheat berries (page 366) or barley (page 368). In these cases, we actually want the grains to soften at their edges so they can thicken the surrounding liquid into a sauce with leached starches. The only way to achieve those results is to let the grains rest right against the insert's hot surface.

Given everything we just mentioned, don't think of this as a chapter of also-rans. Think of vegetables and grains as a perfect use for the pot, even when you're cooking something else on the grill, in the oven, or at the stove.

From-Scratch No-Cheat Hummus

9 ingredients	
10–12 APPETIZER SERVINGS	
METHOD: standard	

SPECIAL EQUIPMENT: a food processor	
PRESSURE: max or high	

TIME UNDER PRESSURE: 10 or 15 minutes	
RELEASE: natural	

TOTAL TIME WITH PRESSURE: about 11½ hours (includes soaking)	
VEGAN	
GLUTEN-FREE	

12 ounces dried chickpeas

Water, as needed

½ cup tahini (sesame seed paste)

¼ cup olive oil

¼ cup lemon juice

3 medium garlic cloves, roughly chopped

1½ teaspoons table salt, or more to taste

½ teaspoon ground cumin

½ teaspoon ground black pepper

Sometimes, we just want to give it our all. So here's our hummus recipe, made from dried chickpeas. It's so much easier to get super-creamy results from an IP, rather than from cooking the chickpeas all afternoon on the stovetop.

We use some of the chickpea cooking liquid as well as the more traditional olive oil to make a rich, thick hummus that's not quite as heavy as some standard versions. However, there's no hummus without tahini, a paste of ground sesame seeds. Look for it in the health-food section of your supermarket or sometimes with the alternative nut butters. Store it, covered, in the fridge for at least 1 month or in the freezer indefinitely. Always stir tahini before use, mixing the solids that have settled to the bottom into the liquid above.

1. Pour the chickpeas into a pot's insert or a large bowl. Add enough cold tap water to cover the chickpeas by about 2 inches. (Some may float.) Set aside at room temperature for 10 to 12 hours to soak.

2. Drain the chickpeas in a large colander set in the sink. Do not rinse. Pour the chickpeas into the insert set in a **5-, 6-, or 8-quart Instant Pot.** Add enough water to cover them by about 2 inches. Lock the lid onto the cooker.

3.

	Set pot for	Set level to	Valve must be	Set time for	If needed, press
For Max pots only	PRESSURE COOK	MAX	—	10 minutes with the KEEP WARM setting off	START
For all other pots	PRESSURE COOK or MANUAL	HIGH	Closed	15 minutes with the KEEP WARM setting off	START

4. When the pot has finished cooking, turn it off and let the pressure **return to normal naturally,** about 40 minutes. Unlatch the lid and open the cooker.

5. Scoop out and discard any skins that are floating in the pot. Then scoop out and reserve 1 cup of the liquid in the pot. Use hot pads or silicone baking mitts to drain the (hot!) insert with the chickpeas through a large colander set in the sink.

6. While the chickpeas are hot, put them in a food processor. Add the tahini, olive oil, lemon juice, garlic, salt, cumin, and pepper. Cover and process for 1 minute.

7. Stop the machine and scrape down the inside of the canister. Cover and continue processing, adding some of the reserved cooking water through the feed tube in 1-tablespoon increments, until you have a creamy, rich puree. You'll probably end up using between ⅓ and ⅔ cup of the reserved liquid, depending on the chickpeas' and the tahini's moisture content. Check the hummus's consistency by stopping the machine and scooping up a little with a rubber spatula. Honestly, you can't process it enough. Let the machine run and run. And check for salt when the consistency is right, adding a little more if the hummus needs it. Scoop the hummus into a serving bowl and serve at once or cover and refrigerate for up to 4 days.

Other Pots

- For a 3-quart Instant Pot, you *must* halve all of the ingredient amounts.
- For a 10-quart Instant Pot, you *can* increase all of the ingredient amount by 50 percent or you *can* even double the amounts.

Beyond

- Garnish the hummus with ground black pepper, red pepper flakes, minced scallions, and/or balsamic vinegar.
- Or go all out and top it with ground urfa biber (or Turkish isot pepper), ground Aleppo pepper, or Ethiopian berbere (a very aromatic blend of spices).

Not-Really-Chili's Queso Dip

10 ingredients

6–8 APPETIZER SERVINGS

METHOD:
pot-in-pot

SPECIAL EQUIPMENT:
a 2-quart, 7-inch-round, high-sided, pressure-safe baking or soufflé dish and a pressure-safe rack or trivet

PRESSURE:
max or high

TIME UNDER PRESSURE:
17 or 20 minutes

RELEASE:
quick

TOTAL TIME WITH PRESSURE:
about 35 minutes

1½ cups water

One 15-ounce can chili without beans (2 cups), such as Wolf Brand Chili No Beans or Skyline Original Chili

8 ounces Velveeta cheese, shredded

8 ounces American sharp cheddar cheese, shredded (2 cups)

1 cup whole or low-fat milk (do not use fat-free)

1 tablespoon mild smoked paprika

2 teaspoons ground cumin

1 teaspoon dried oregano

Up to ½ teaspoon thin red hot sauce, such as Texas Pete

1 tablespoon lime juice

Other Pots

- For a 3-quart Instant Pot, you *must* halve almost all of the ingredient amounts *except* you *must* use 1 cup water in the insert. You *must* also use a 1-quart, 6-inch-round, high-sided, pressure-safe baking or soufflé dish.

- For a 10-quart Instant Pot, you *must* increase the amount of water in the insert to 2½ cups while otherwise completing the recipe as stated.

Beyond

- Garnish the dip with stemmed and minced fresh cilantro leaves.

- For more flavor (and color), stir one 4-ounce jar diced pimientos, drained and rinsed, into the mixture with the cheese.

It's hard to make a copycat version of this restaurant favorite on a stovetop, given the way the cheese can burn, even with constant stirring. The only way to make a smooth, creamy dip every time is with the PIP (pot-in-pot) method in an Instant Pot. Even so, we still wanted to up the game (as you well know by now). Most copycat recipes use 100 percent Velveeta; we supplement it with sharp American cheddar for better flavor. The smoked paprika offers a bit of "hearth" or "grill" flavor. And we save the lime juice for the end for a brighter, fresher taste.

1. Pour the water into the insert set in a **5-, 6-, or 8-quart Instant Pot.** Set a pressure-safe rack or trivet into the pot.

2. Stir the chili, Velveeta, cheddar, milk, smoked paprika, cumin, oregano, and hot sauce in a 2-quart, 7-inch-round, high-sided, pressure-safe baking or soufflé dish. Cover the dish tightly with aluminum foil and set it on the rack. Lock the lid on the cooker.

3.

	Set pot for	Set level to	Valve must be	Set time for	If needed, press
For Max pots only	PRESSURE COOK	MAX	—	17 minutes with the KEEP WARM setting off	START
For all other pots	PRESSURE COOK or MANUAL	HIGH	Closed	20 minutes with the KEEP WARM setting off	START

4. When the pot has finished cooking, use the **quick-release method** to bring the pressure back to normal. Unlatch the lid and open the cooker. Use hot pads or silicone baking mitts to transfer the (hot!) baking dish to a nearby wire rack. Stir in the lime juice (perhaps also re-emulsifying the dip). Let sit for 5 minutes to blend the flavors and thicken slightly before serving.

See photo in insert.

Perfect Grits Every Time

6 ingredients

6 SERVINGS

METHOD:
pot-in-pot

SPECIAL
EQUIPMENT:
a 2-quart, 7-inch-
round, high-sided,
pressure-safe
baking or soufflé
dish and a
pressure-safe rack
or trivet

PRESSURE:
max or high

TIME UNDER
PRESSURE:
10 or 12 minutes

RELEASE:
natural

TOTAL TIME WITH
PRESSURE:
about 35 minutes

VEGETARIAN

GLUTEN-FREE

1½ cups water

3 cups whole milk (do not use low-fat or fat-free)

1 cup plus 2 tablespoons raw white grits (do not use quick-cooking or instant grits)

2 tablespoons butter, cut into small bits

1 tablespoon granulated white sugar

½ teaspoon table salt

These creamy, buttery grits are modeled after those served in some cafeterias in Texas. (We're mostly looking at you, Luby's.) These, however, are not so sweet. They're a better side to grilled chicken or pork. If you insist on them for breakfast, you'll want maple syrup on the side. With the PIP (pot-in-pot) method, the grits can be cooked right in milk for a richer flavor without risking a BURN notice.

1. Pour the water into the insert set in a **5-, 6-, or 8-quart Instant Pot.** Set a pressure-safe rack or trivet in the insert.

2. Stir the milk, grits, butter, sugar, and salt in a 2-quart, 7-inch-round, high-sided, pressure-safe baking or soufflé dish. Do not cover. Set the dish on the rack and lock the lid on the pot.

3.

	Set pot for	Set level to	Valve must be	Set time for	If needed, press
For Max pots only	PRESSURE COOK	MAX	—	10 minutes with the KEEP WARM setting off	START
For all other pots	PRESSURE COOK or MANUAL	HIGH	Closed	12 minutes with the KEEP WARM setting off	START

4. When the pot has finished cooking, turn it off and let the pressure **return to normal naturally,** about 15 minutes. Unlatch the lid and open the cooker. Use hot pads or silicone baking mitts to transfer the (hot!) baking dish to a nearby wire rack. Stir the grits until smooth, then cool for 1 or 2 minutes to firm up a bit. Serve warm.

Other Pots

- For a 3-quart Instant Pot, you *must* halve almost all of the ingredient amounts *except* you *must* use 1 cup water in the insert. You *must* also use a 1-quart, 6-inch-round, high-sided, pressure-safe baking or soufflé dish.

- For a 10-quart Instant Pot, you *must* increase the amount of water in the insert to 2½ cups while completing the recipe as stated.

Beyond

- Ever had grits for dessert? Increase the sugar to 2 tablespoons, then serve the grits warm in bowls, topped with strawberry or raspberry sauce and crumbled shortbread cookies.

Cauliflower Cheese Grits

7 ingredients

4–6 SERVINGS

METHOD:
pot-in-pot

SPECIAL
EQUIPMENT:
a 2-quart, 7-inch-
round, high-sided,
pressure-safe
baking or soufflé
dish and a
pressure-safe rack
or trivet

PRESSURE:
max or high

TIME UNDER
PRESSURE:
16 or 20 minutes

RELEASE:
natural

TOTAL TIME WITH
PRESSURE:
about 45 minutes

VEGETARIAN

1½ cups water

Butter, for greasing

3 cups riced cauliflower (¾ pound)

3 tablespoons all-purpose flour

½ teaspoon table salt

¾ cup half-and-half or light cream

4 ounces Swiss, American sharp cheddar,
or semi-firm mozzarella cheese,
shredded (1 cup)

Other Pots

- For a 3-quart Instant Pot, you *must*
halve almost all of the ingredient
amounts *except* you *must* use
1 cup water in the insert. You *must*
also use a 1-quart, 6-inch-round,
high-sided, pressure-safe baking or
soufflé dish.

- For a 10-quart Instant Pot, you
must increase the amount of
water in the insert to 2½ cups
but otherwise make the recipe as
stated.

Beyond

- Add *fresh* herbs to the cauliflower
mix—maybe stemmed, fresh
thyme leaves or stemmed and
finely chopped fresh parsley
leaves—either before or after
cooking. If adding them before
cooking, the grits will have a more
herbaceous flavor (and maybe a
green tint).

- For an easy dinner, spoon the grits
into bowls and top each serving
with one or two poached eggs.

These low-carb grits swap out the traditional corn grits for riced
cauliflower. Yes, this side dish is great if you're on a special diet. But
consider it as well if you want something a little out of the ordinary
to go along with almost any roasted or grilled beef, pork, or lamb.

Look for riced cauliflower either in the produce section of almost
all supermarkets or in the freezer case. If you buy a frozen bag, you
must thaw it before you can use it.

1. Pour the water into the insert set in a **5-, 6-, or 8-quart Instant
Pot.** Set a pressure-safe rack or trivet in the insert. Use butter to
generously grease the inside of a 2-quart, 7-inch-round, high-sided,
pressure-safe baking or soufflé dish.

2. Toss the riced cauliflower, flour, and salt in a large bowl until well
combined. Stir in the half-and-half or light cream and the cheese
until uniform. Pack this mixture into the prepared baking dish. Do
not cover. Set the dish on the rack and lock the lid on the cooker.

3.

	Set pot for	Set level to	Valve must be	Set time for	If needed, press
For Max pots only	PRESSURE COOK	MAX	—	16 minutes with the KEEP WARM setting off	START
For all other pots	PRESSURE COOK or MANUAL	HIGH	Closed	20 minutes with the KEEP WARM setting off	START

4. When the pot has finished cooking, turn it off and let the pressure
return to normal naturally, about 15 minutes. Unlatch the lid and
open the cooker. Use hot pads or silicone baking mitts to transfer the
(hot!) baking dish to a nearby wire rack. Cool for 2 to 3 minutes to
firm up a bit before serving.

Butter and Herb Israeli Couscous

11 ingredients	
4–6 SERVINGS	
METHOD: standard	

SPECIAL EQUIPMENT: none	

PRESSURE: max or high	
TIME UNDER PRESSURE: 5 or 6 minutes	
RELEASE: quick	

TOTAL TIME WITH PRESSURE: about 30 minutes	
VEGETARIAN	

5 tablespoons butter

1 medium yellow or white onion, chopped (1 cup)

1 medium celery stalk, thinly sliced (⅓ cup)

2 cups dried Israeli couscous

½ teaspoon dried thyme

½ teaspoon rubbed or ground sage

½ teaspoon onion powder

½ teaspoon garlic powder

½ teaspoon table salt

½ teaspoon ground black pepper

2½ cups vegetable broth

We have other main-course Israeli couscous dishes in this book (see pages 150, 151, and 152). This recipe, however, makes a tasty side dish for grilled fish fillets, roast turkey, or even pan-fried veal scaloppini. The dish is pretty simple—so much so that it uses dried herbs, not fresh. Because the dried herbs have a slightly earthier flavor, they're a better match in this rather straightforward side to the naturally sweet pasta.

1.

	Press	Set it for	Set time for	If needed, press
In all models	SAUTÉ	MEDIUM, NORMAL, or CUSTOM 300°F	10 minutes	START

2. As the pot heats, melt 2 tablespoons butter in the insert set in a **5-, 6-, or 8-quart Instant Pot.** Add the onion and celery; cook, stirring often, until softened, about 3 minutes.

3. Add the Israeli couscous and stir well to coat it in the butter and vegetables. Stir in the thyme, sage, onion powder, garlic powder, salt, and pepper until aromatic, just a few seconds.

4. Pour in the broth and scrape up any browned bits on the pot's bottom. Continue cooking, stirring occasionally, until wisps of steam rise from the liquid, about 5 minutes. Turn off the heat and lock the lid onto the cooker.

5.

	Set pot for	Set level to	Valve must be	Set time for	If needed, press
For Max pots only	PRESSURE COOK	MAX	—	5 minutes with the KEEP WARM setting off	START
For all other pots	PRESSURE COOK or MANUAL	HIGH	Closed	6 minutes with the KEEP WARM setting off	START

6. When the pot has finished cooking, use the **quick-release method** to bring the pressure back to normal. Unlatch the lid and open the cooker. Add the remaining 3 tablespoons butter, stir the pot's contents, and set the lid askew over it so the couscous can continue to absorb the excess liquid for 3 to 5 minutes. Stir again and serve warm.

Other Pots

- For a 3-quart Instant Pot, you *must* halve all of the ingredient amounts.
- For a 10-quart Instant Pot, you *must* increase all of the ingredient amounts by 50 percent or you *can* even double the amounts.

Beyond

- For a richer (and not vegetarian) side dish, substitute chicken broth for the vegetable broth.

Buckwheat and Noodles

9 ingredients	**SPECIAL EQUIPMENT:** none
4–6 SERVINGS	
METHOD: standard	**PRESSURE:** high

TIME UNDER PRESSURE: 4 minutes	**TOTAL TIME WITH PRESSURE:** about 25 minutes
RELEASE: quick	**VEGETARIAN**

---

3 tablespoons vegetable, canola, or other neutral-flavored oil

2 large yellow or white onions, chopped (3 cups)

2 medium garlic cloves, minced (2 teaspoons)

½ teaspoon ground coriander

½ teaspoon table salt

½ teaspoon ground black pepper

1 cup plus 2 tablespoons raw buckwheat groats

5 cups (1 quart plus 1 cup) vegetable broth

12 ounces dried egg or no-yolk noodles

Other Pots

- For a 3-quart Instant Pot, you *must* halve all of the ingredient amounts.

- For an 8-quart Instant Pot, you *can* increase all of the ingredient amounts by 50 percent.

- For a 10-quart Instant Pot, you *must* increase all of the ingredient amounts by 50 percent or you *can* even double the amounts.

Beyond

- For a richer (but not a vegetarian) dish, substitute chicken broth for the vegetable broth.

- To go more old-world, substitute chicken fat or even duck fat for the oil.

Something of a New York deli staple, a version of this dish called kasha varnishkes is traditionally made with bow-tie pasta and toasted buckwheat (aka kasha). Toasted buckwheat has a distinctly bitter edge that becomes even more pronounced under pressure. Plain buckwheat, by contrast, stays mild and sweet with pleasant, grassy notes. Unfortunately, it also cooks more quickly than bow-tie pasta; so in a bid to make a one-pot dish, we substituted egg noodles for the more traditional pasta. In other words, we totally revamped the deli classic and hope we've morphed it into a new classic.

1.

	Press	Set it for	Set time for	If needed, press
In all models	SAUTÉ	MEDIUM, NORMAL, or CUSTOM 300°F	10 minutes	START

2. As the pot heats, warm the oil in the insert set in a **5-, 6-, or 8-quart Instant Pot.** Add the onions and cook, stirring often, until softened and even a little browned at the edges, about 7 minutes.

3. Stir in the garlic, coriander, salt, and pepper until aromatic, just a few seconds. Add the buckwheat groats and stir until they are coated in the spices and onions.

4. Pour in the broth and scrape up any browned bits on the pot's bottom. Continue cooking, stirring occasionally, until many wisps of steam rise from the liquid in the pot. Stir in the noodles, making sure most are submerged although many will sit above the water line. Turn off the heat and lock the lid on the pot.

5.

	Set pot for	Set level to	Valve must be	Set time for	If needed, press
For *all* pots	PRESSURE COOK or MANUAL	HIGH	Closed	4 minutes with the KEEP WARM setting off	START

6. When the pot has finished cooking, use the **quick-release method** to bring the pressure back to normal. Unlatch the lid and open the cooker. Stir well, then set aside for 2 to 3 minutes so the pasta can continue to absorb the liquid. Stir again and serve warm.

Home-Style Thanksgiving Dressing

7 ingredients	SPECIAL EQUIPMENT: a 2-quart, 7-inch-round, high-sided, pressure-safe baking or soufflé dish and a pressure-safe rack or trivet
6 SERVINGS	
METHOD: pot-in-pot	

PRESSURE: max or high	TOTAL TIME WITH PRESSURE: about 40 minutes
TIME UNDER PRESSURE: 12 or 15 minutes	VEGETARIAN
RELEASE: quick	

2 tablespoons butter, plus more for greasing

1 small yellow or white onion, chopped (½ cup)

2 medium celery stalks, chopped (⅔ cup)

1½ cups water

1 cup vegetable broth

1 refrigerator-cold large egg

3 cups seasoned dry *bread-cube-style* stuffing mix, such as Arnold's or Pepperidge Farm, any variety except cornbread

Other Pots

- For a 3-quart Instant Pot, you *must* halve almost all of the ingredient amounts *except* you *must* use 1 cup water in the insert. You *must* also use a 1-quart, 6-inch-round, high-sided, pressure-safe baking or soufflé dish.

- For a 10-quart Instant Pot, you *must* increase the amount of water in the insert to 2½ cups but otherwise make the recipe as stated.

Beyond

- Add up to 1 cup packed, cleaned, and thinly sliced white or brown button mushrooms to the pot with the onion and celery. Cook for at least 2 additional minutes to soften properly.

- If you've used a 6- or 8-quart Instant Pot and a broiler-safe baking dish, you can get a crunchy top on the dressing: Open the pot as instructed in step 6. Uncover the baking dish and replace the pot's lid with the Instant Pot Air Fryer Lid. Air-fry at 375°F for 5 minutes, or until well browned.

With purchased stuffing mix and the PIP method, this recipe is super easy, a great side dish that you don't have to wait for Thanksgiving to enjoy. Try it with grilled steaks or broiled chicken breasts. The stuffing mix *must* be bread-cube-style, not powdered or ground. Do not use cornbread stuffing mix because the cubes dissolve into a paste under pressure.

1.

	Press	Set it for	Set time for	If needed, press
In all models	SAUTÉ	MEDIUM, NORMAL, or CUSTOM 300°F	5 minutes	START

2. As the pot heats, melt the butter in the insert set in a **5-, 6-, or 8-quart Instant Pot.** Add the onion and celery; cook, stirring often, until softened, about 2 minutes. Turn off the heat, use hot pads or silicone baking mitts to remove the (hot!) insert, and scrape the vegetables and any remaining butter into a small bowl.

3. Wipe out the (still hot!) insert and return it to the pot. Pour in the water and set a pressure-safe rack or trivet in the insert. Use more butter to grease the inside of a 2-quart, 7-inch-round, high-sided, pressure-safe baking or soufflé dish.

4. Whisk the broth and egg in a large bowl until well combined. Add the bread-cube stuffing mix as well as all the vegetables and any juices in the small bowl. Stir until uniform.

5. Dump the stuffing mix into the prepared baking dish and press down gently to flatten the top and compact the ingredients. Cover the dish with aluminum foil and set it on the rack. Lock the lid on the cooker.

	Set pot for	Set level to	Valve must be	Set time for	If needed, press
For Max pots only	PRESSURE COOK	MAX	—	12 minutes with the KEEP WARM setting off	START
For all other pots	PRESSURE COOK or MANUAL	HIGH	Closed	15 minutes with the KEEP WARM setting off	START

6. When the pot has finished cooking, use the **quick-release method** to bring the pressure back to normal. Unlatch the lid and open the cooker. Use hot pads or silicone baking mitts to transfer the (hot!) baking dish to a nearby wire rack. Uncover and cool 2 to 3 minutes before dishing up warm by the big spoonful.

No-Brainer Savory Cornbread Pudding

6 ingredients

4–6 SERVINGS

METHOD:
pot-in-pot

SPECIAL EQUIPMENT:
a 1-quart, 6-inch-round, high-sided, pressure-safe baking or soufflé dish and a pressure-safe rack or trivet

PRESSURE:
max or high

TIME UNDER PRESSURE:
12 or 15 minutes

RELEASE:
natural

TOTAL TIME WITH PRESSURE:
about 45 minutes

VEGETARIAN

CAN BE GLUTEN-FREE

1½ cups water

Butter, for greasing

1½ cups whole milk (do not use low-fat or fat-free)

2 refrigerator-cold large eggs

1 medium celery stalk, diced

6 ounces (2½ cups) seasoned cornbread dressing mix (gluten-free, if necessary)

Other Pots

- For a 3-quart Instant Pot, you *must* use only 1 cup water in the insert while otherwise completing the recipe as stated.

- For an 8-quart Instant Pot, you *can* double almost all of the ingredient amounts except you *must* use the stated 1½ cups water in the insert. In this case, you *must* use a 2-quart, 7-inch-round, high-sided, pressure-safe baking or soufflé dish and you *must* increase the cooking time to 18 minutes at HIGH pressure (there is no Max 8-quart as of this writing).

- For a 10-quart Instant Pot, you *must* increase the amount of water in the insert to 2½ cups while otherwise completing the recipe as stated. You *can* also double all of the other ingredient amounts but you then *must* use a 2-quart, 7-inch-round, high-sided, pressure-safe baking or soufflé dis. You *must* also increase the cooking time to 18 minutes at HIGH pressure (there is no Max 10-quart as of this writing).

Talk about easy! All the seasoning in this easy PIP side dish comes from the cornbread stuffing mix. We don't even sauté the celery first so it retains a bit of its crunch. Other than that, you'll just need some pork chops off the grill or a meat loaf out of a second Instant Pot (or the oven, if you must).

1. Pour the water into the insert set in a **5-, 6-, or 8-quart Instant Pot.** Set a pressure-safe rack or trivet in the insert. Use butter to generously grease the inside of a 1-quart, 6-inch-round, high-sided, pressure-safe baking or soufflé dish.

2. Whisk the milk and eggs in a large bowl until well blended. There should be no floating bits of egg white in the mix. Stir in the celery, then add the cornbread stuffing mix and stir well until uniform and almost all the liquid has been absorbed.

3. Pour and pack this mixture into the prepared baking dish. Do not cover. Set the dish on the rack and lock the lid on the pot.

4.

	Set pot for	Set level to	Valve must be	Set time for	If needed, press
For Max pots only	PRESSURE COOK	MAX	—	12 minutes with the KEEP WARM setting off	START
For all other pots	PRESSURE COOK or MANUAL	HIGH	Closed	15 minutes with the KEEP WARM setting off	START

5. When the pot has finished cooking, turn it off and let the pressure **return to normal naturally,** about 15 minutes. Unlatch the lid and open the cooker. Use hot pads or silicone baking mitts to transfer the (hot!) baking dish to a nearby wire rack. Cool for 2 to 3 minutes before dishing up by the big spoonful.

Beyond

- If you cool the casserole for 10 minutes, you can turn it out of its baking dish. Set a wooden cutting board over the baking dish, turn it all upside down, then jostle the baking dish until the cornbread pudding comes free. Remove the baking dish and slice the pudding into wedges to serve.

From-Scratch Holiday Green Bean Casserole

12 ingredients

6 SERVINGS

METHOD:
pot-in-pot

SPECIAL EQUIPMENT:
a 2-quart, 7-inch-round, high-sided, pressure-safe baking or soufflé dish and a pressure-safe rack or trivet

PRESSURE:
high

TIME UNDER PRESSURE:
20 minutes

RELEASE:
natural

TOTAL TIME WITH PRESSURE:
about 1 hour 15 minutes

VEGETARIAN

1½ cups water

12 ounces white button mushrooms, brushed clean

1 pound frozen French-style cut green beans, thawed

¼ cup all-purpose flour (dip and level—do not pack)

1 teaspoon table salt

½ teaspoon rubbed or ground sage

½ teaspoon onion powder

½ teaspoon garlic powder

½ teaspoon ground black pepper

½ cup heavy or light cream

¼ cup whole milk (do not use low-fat or fat-free)

4 ounces Monterey Jack cheese, shredded (1 cup)

Other Pots

- For a 3-quart Instant Pot, you *must* halve almost all of the ingredient amounts *except* you *must* use 1 cup water in the insert and you *must* use a 1-quart, 6-inch-round, high-sided, pressure-safe baking or soufflé dish.

- For a 10-quart Instant Pot, you *must* increase the amount of water in the insert to 2½ cups while otherwise completing the recipe as stated.

Beyond

- Top the casserole with canned fried onions, such as French's, just before serving.

- Or skip the fried onions and crumble thick-cut potato chips on top.

- Or go over the top with thick-cut sour-cream-and-onion potato chips.

We're playing with fire! We set out to adapt a US holiday favorite. Maybe the casserole didn't need our tinkering; but we dared the odds, skipped the canned cream of mushroom soup, and crafted an easy, homemade version of a creamy mushroom sauce for a rich, tasty side dish that we couldn't stop eating at the photo shoot for this book! Admittedly, ours doesn't have a crunchy topping, the part most people love. Check out the **Beyond** section for our ideas to solve this problem.

1. Pour the water into the insert set in a **5-, 6-, or 8-quart Instant Pot.** Set a pressure-safe rack or trivet in the insert.

2. Finely chop half of the mushrooms, then thinly slice the remainder. Transfer them to a large bowl and stir in the green beans, flour, salt, sage, onion powder, garlic powder, and pepper until uniform. Stir in the cream and milk until well combined.

3. Pour and pack this mixture into a 2-quart, 7-inch-round, high-sided, pressure-safe baking or soufflé dish. Do not cover. Set the dish on the rack and lock the lid on the pot.

4.

	Set pot for	Set level to	Valve must be	Set time for	If needed, press
For *all* pots	PRESSURE COOK or MANUAL	HIGH	Closed	20 minutes with the KEEP WARM setting off	START

5. When the pot has finished cooking, turn it off and let the pressure **return to normal naturally,** about 15 minutes. Unlatch the lid and open the cooker. Use hot pads or silicone baking mitts to transfer the (hot!) baking dish to a nearby wire rack. Stir in the cheese, then set aside for 5 minutes to let the cheese melt. Stir again before serving warm.

See photo in insert.

Artichoke and Spinach Casserole

8 ingredients	
6 SERVINGS	
METHOD: pot-in-pot	**SPECIAL EQUIPMENT:** a 2-quart, 7-inch-round, high-sided, pressure-safe baking or soufflé dish and a pressure-safe rack or trivet
PRESSURE: max or high	**TIME UNDER PRESSURE:** 12 or 15 minutes
RELEASE: quick	**TOTAL TIME WITH PRESSURE:** about 35 minutes
VEGETARIAN	**CAN BE GLUTEN-FREE**

1½ cups water

Butter, for greasing

Two 14-ounce cans artichoke hearts packed in water, drained

One 10-ounce box frozen chopped spinach, thawed

⅔ cup Italian-seasoned dried bread crumbs (gluten-free, if necessary)

4 ounces *white* American cheddar cheese, shredded (1 cup)

3 refrigerator-cold large eggs, lightly beaten

½ cup half-and-half or light cream

Other Pots

- For a **3-quart Instant Pot**, you *must* halve almost all of the ingredient amounts *except* you *must* use 1 cup water in the insert and you *must* use a 1-quart, 6-inch-round, high-sided, pressure-safe baking or soufflé dish.

- For a **10-quart Instant Pot**, you *must* increase the amount of water in the insert to 2½ cups while otherwise completing the recipe as stated.

Beyond

- For a crisp top, use a broiler-proof baking dish and a 6- or 8-quart Instant Pot. Pour the water out of the insert after you've removed the baking dish in step 6. Also remove the rack. Return the baking dish to the pot, set the air-frying basket in the insert, and replace the pot's lid with the Instant Pot Air Fryer Lid. Air-fry at 400°F for about 10 minutes, or until the casserole is browned and crisp. Cool for a few minutes before serving.

Consider this cheese-laden, creamy casserole a twofer: maybe a side dish, maybe an appetizer. Or maybe just deck food after a busy day. Serve it with pita chips. Or here's an idea: Use it as a condiment on a grilled hamburger for sheer decadence!

1. Pour the water into the insert set in a **5-, 6-, or 8-quart Instant Pot**. Set a pressure-safe rack or trivet in the insert. Use butter to generously grease the inside of a 2-quart, 7-inch-round, high-sided, pressure-safe baking or soufflé dish.

2. Pick up a small handful of the drained artichoke hearts with your clean hand and squeeze them over the sink to remove excess liquid. Put these squeezed bits in a big bowl and continue squeezing more handfuls of the artichoke hearts until they're all in the bowl.

3. Do the same with the thawed chopped spinach: Squeeze it over the sink by the handful until all of it is in that bowl, too.

4. Stir in the bread crumbs and cheese, breaking up the artichoke hearts and spinach until the mixture is a uniform amalgam. Stir in the eggs and half-and-half until uniform. Pour and pack this mixture into the prepared baking dish. Do not cover. Set the dish on the rack and lock the lid on the pot.

5.

	Set pot for	Set level to	Valve must be	Set time for	If needed, press
For Max pots only	PRESSURE COOK	MAX	—	12 minutes with the KEEP WARM setting off	START
For all other pots	PRESSURE COOK or MANUAL	HIGH	Closed	15 minutes with the KEEP WARM setting off	START

6. When the pot has finished cooking, use the **quick-release method** to bring the pressure back to normal. Unlatch the lid and open the cooker. Use hot pads or silicone baking mitts to transfer the (hot!) baking dish to a nearby wire rack. Cool for a few minutes before serving.

Creamy Hominy and Cheese Casserole

10 ingredients

4–6 SERVINGS

METHOD:
pot-in-pot

SPECIAL
EQUIPMENT:
a 2-quart, 7-inch-
round high-sided,
pressure-safe
baking or soufflé
dish and a
pressure-safe rack
or trivet

PRESSURE:
max or high

TIME UNDER
PRESSURE:
15 or 18 minutes

RELEASE:
natural

TOTAL TIME WITH
PRESSURE:
about 45 minutes

VEGETARIAN

1½ cups water

One 29-ounce can hominy, drained and
rinsed (3½ cups)

2 tablespoons all-purpose flour

6 ounces Jarlsberg or white American
cheddar cheese, shredded (1½ cups)

One 4½-ounce can hot or mild diced
green chiles (½ cup)

1 teaspoon dried oregano

½ teaspoon onion powder

½ teaspoon table salt

½ teaspoon ground black pepper

1 cup half-and-half or light cream

Here's something like a pasta-free version of mac-and-cheese. It's a hearty, cheesy side casserole, made better with the earthy-sweet taste of hominy. Canned hominy also makes this dish super easy. And the PIP method keeps it rich without the threat of burning.

One note: When we tested the recipe, heavy cream took it too far over the top. We didn't know that was possible! Use half-and-half or light cream for still-decadent but less-heavy results.

1. Pour the water into the insert set in a **5-, 6-, or 8-quart Instant Pot.** Set a pressure-safe rack or trivet in the insert.

2. Stir the hominy and flour in a 2-quart, 7-inch-round, high-sided, pressure-safe baking or soufflé dish until the hominy is evenly coated in the flour. Stir in ¾ cup of the shredded cheese, the chiles, oregano, onion powder, salt, and pepper until uniform.

3. Stir in the half-and-half, then sprinkle the remaining ¾ cup shredded cheese over the top of the casserole. Cover the baking dish with aluminum foil and set it on the rack. Lock the lid on the pot.

4.

	Set pot for	Set level to	Valve must be	Set time for	If needed, press
For Max pots only	PRESSURE COOK	MAX	—	15 minutes with the KEEP WARM setting off	START
For all other pots	PRESSURE COOK or MANUAL	HIGH	Closed	18 minutes with the KEEP WARM setting off	START

5. When the pot has finished cooking, turn it off and let the pressure **return to normal naturally,** about 15 minutes. Unlatch the lid and open the cooker. Use hot pads or silicone baking mitts to transfer the (hot!) baking dish to a nearby wire rack. Uncover and cool for a few minutes before scooping it up by the big spoonful.

Other Pots

- For a 3-quart Instant Pot, you *must* halve almost all of the ingredient amounts *except* you *must* use 1 cup water in the insert and you *must* use a 1-quart, 6-inch-round, high-sided, pressure-safe baking or soufflé dish.

- For a 10-quart Instant Pot, you *must* increase the amount of water in the insert to 2½ cups while otherwise completing the recipe as stated.

Beyond

- For a sweeter flavor, substitute drained and rinsed jarred diced pimientos for the green chiles.

No-Brainer Cauliflower Mash

8 ingredients

4–6 SERVINGS

METHOD:
standard

SPECIAL
EQUIPMENT:
a potato masher
or an electric
mixer

PRESSURE:
low

TIME UNDER
PRESSURE:
6 minutes

RELEASE:
quick

TOTAL TIME WITH
PRESSURE:
about 20 minutes

VEGETARIAN

GLUTEN-FREE

One 2-pound cauliflower head, cored
   and the remainder broken into
   3-inch pieces; or 1¾ pounds frozen
   cauliflower florets (no need to thaw)

1 cup vegetable broth

One 8-ounce yellow potato, such as
   Yukon Gold

2 tablespoons butter, cut into bits

1 teaspoon table salt, plus more to taste

½ teaspoon ground black pepper

¼ teaspoon grated nutmeg

¼ cup heavy or light cream

Cauliflower mash is a terrific substitute for mashed potatoes,
except cauliflower can be pretty watery when cooked. So here's our
compromise: Add a grated potato to give the mash a little more body
(because of the potato's natural starches). This small tweak makes
this "new-standard" dish so much better: a buttery cauliflower side
dish that doesn't run all over the plate.

1. Stir the cauliflower chunks and broth in a **5- or 6-quart Instant
Pot.** Shred the potato through the large holes of a box grater right
into the pot. Stir in the butter, salt, pepper, and nutmeg. Lock the lid
onto the cooker.

2.

	Set pot for	Set level to	Valve must be	Set time for	If needed, press
For *all* pots	PRESSURE COOK or MANUAL	LOW	Closed	6 minutes with the KEEP WARM setting off	START

3. When the pot has finished cooking, use the **quick-release
method** to bring the pressure back to normal. Unlatch the lid
and open the cooker. Add the cream and use a potato masher
or a handheld electric mixer at medium-low speed to mash the
vegetables into a rather smooth puree. Taste to see if it needs more
salt before serving.

Other Pots

- For a 3-quart Instant Pot, you *must*
  halve almost all of the ingredient
  amounts *except* you *must* use
  ⅔ cup broth.

- For an 8-quart Instant Pot, you
  must increase all of the ingredient
  amounts by 50 percent.

- For a 10-quart Instant Pot, see
  our alternate recipe with changed
  proportions and thickening agents
  on page 476.

Beyond

- Skip the cream and add up to ⅓ cup
  regular or low-fat sour cream. Or
  add both cream and sour cream!

Butter-Bathed Corn on the Cob

6 ingredients		
6 SERVINGS Method: standard		

SPECIAL EQUIPMENT:	TIME UNDER PRESSURE:	TOTAL TIME WITH PRESSURE:
none	1 minute	about 25 minutes
PRESSURE:	RELEASE:	VEGETARIAN
low	natural	GLUTEN-FREE

One 12-ounce can regular or low-fat evaporated milk (1½ cups—do not use fat-free)

2 cups water

3 tablespoons granulated white sugar

1 teaspoon table salt

1 stick (8 tablespoons or ½ cup) butter

6 medium corn ears, husked and de-silked, then cut in half widthwise

Here's an old-school method for cooking corn on the cob: poaching the ears in milk and butter. Standard milk will often curdle under pressure, so we use evaporated milk and thin it out with water for perfect results. We also use LOW pressure, both to preserve the milk and to keep the corn from getting overcooked. The results are rich and sweet, a summertime treat.

1.

	Press	Set it for	Set time for	If needed, press
In all models	SAUTÉ	MEDIUM, NORMAL, or CUSTOM 300°F	10 minutes	START

2. As the pot heats, stir the water, evaporated milk, sugar, and salt in the insert set in a **5-, 6-, 8-, or 10-quart Instant Pot** until the sugar dissolves. Add the butter and cook, stirring once in a while, until the butter melts, about 3 minutes. Turn off the heat. Pile the corn in the pot. Lock the lid on the cooker.

3.

	Set pot for	Set level to	Valve must be	Set time for	If needed, press
For *all* pots	PRESSURE COOK or MANUAL	LOW	Closed	1 minute with the KEEP WARM setting off	START

4. When the pot has finished cooking, turn it off and let the pressure **return to normal naturally,** about 12 minutes. Unlatch the lid and open the cooker. Use kitchen tongs to transfer the corn ears to a serving platter. Cool for a couple of minutes before serving.

Other Pots

- For a **3-quart Instant Pot,** you *must* halve all of the ingredient amounts.

- For a **10-quart Instant Pot,** you *can* double all of the ingredient amounts.

Beyond

- Sprinkle the cooked ears with finely grated Parmigiano-Reggiano and lots of ground black pepper.

- Or drizzle with Sriracha before sprinkling with a little ground cinnamon and grated nutmeg.

Cauliflower and Cheese Sauce

9 ingredients

6 SERVINGS

METHOD:
pot-in-pot

SPECIAL EQUIPMENT:
a pressure- and food-safe rack or trivet and a 7-inch-round cake pan or the top layer of a set of 7½-inch-round stackable insert pans

PRESSURE:
high

TIME UNDER PRESSURE:
0 or 1 minute

RELEASE:
quick

TOTAL TIME WITH PRESSURE:
about 20 minutes

VEGETARIAN

GLUTEN-FREE

1½ cups water

One 1½-pound (medium) cauliflower head, cored but left whole

8 ounces American sharp cheddar cheese, shredded (2 cups)

1 cup whole milk (do not use low-fat or fat-free)

1½ teaspoons cornstarch

½ teaspoon onion powder

½ teaspoon garlic powder

½ teaspoon table salt

½ teaspoon ground black pepper

Talk about a way to get your kids to eat cauliflower! How about a rich cheese sauce poured over a soft, luxurious head of cauliflower? What could be better?

This side dish is made in two parts—that is, the vegetable and the cheese sauce are made separately but all at once in the pot. The only trick is to make sure the cake pan or the stackable insert pan with the cheese sauce balances well on the cauliflower. Give everything a test run: Cut the cauliflower as directed, then set the empty cake pan on top of the cauliflower to make sure it's stable before you fill that pan with cheese sauce (or the insert with water). Finding the right balance is actually more a matter of getting the bottom, cored side of the cauliflower head to sit flat, than endlessly adjusting the trim of the top.

1. Pour the water into the insert set in a **5-, 6-, or 8-quart Instant Pot.** Set a pressure- and food-safe rack or trivet in the pot.

2. Slice about ½ inch off the top of the cauliflower head so that when it sits on its cored bottom it has a flat surface on top. This may take a little jimmying and adjusting of the top and bottom to get a flat surface (see the headnote for more information). Set the cauliflower head on the rack.

3. Make an even layer with the cheese in a 7-inch-round cake pan or the top layer of a set of 7½-inch-round stackable insert pans. Whisk the milk, cornstarch, onion powder, garlic powder, salt, and pepper in a medium bowl until smooth. Pour the milk mixture over the cheese.

4. Seal the pan tightly with aluminum foil or its own cover. Set the pan on the trimmed cauliflower head in the pot. Lock the lid onto the cooker.

5.

	Set pot for	Set level to	Valve must be	Set time for	If needed, press
For *all* pots	PRESSURE COOK or MANUAL	HIGH	Closed	0 or 1 minute with the KEEP WARM setting off	START

6. *Do not* let the machine come to full pressure. Instead, **the moment the pin pops up** to lock the lid on the pot, turn it off and use the **quick-release method** to bring the pressure back to normal. Unlatch the lid and open the cooker.

7. Use hot pads or silicone baking mitts to transfer the (hot!) cake pan to a nearby wire rack. Whisk the sauce until smooth. Use a large spatula and kitchen tongs to transfer the cauliflower head to a deep serving bowl. Pour the cheese sauce over the cauliflower. Serve warm.

Other Pots

- Because of the ratio of pan sizes and cauliflower sizes, this recipe cannot be completed successfully in a 3-quart Instant Pot.

- For a 5-quart Instant Pot, if you use stackable insert pans, you *must* use 7-inch stackable containers specifically made to fit this slightly smaller pot.

- For a 10-quart Instant Pot, you *must* use 2½ cups water in the insert while otherwise completing the recipe as stated. You must make sure the pan is level on the cauliflower since the sides of the insert will not help balance it.

Beyond

- After you pour the cheese sauce over the cauliflower, garnish it with stemmed and minced fresh parsley leaves and/or red pepper flakes.

- Substitute Gruyère or fontina for the sharp cheddar cheese. Or make a blend of one of these and the sharp cheddar in a 50-50 proportion.

Mashed Butternut Squash

6 ingredients

4–6 SERVINGS

METHOD:
pot-in-pot

SPECIAL EQUIPMENT:
a 2-quart, 7-inch-round, high-sided, pressure-safe baking or soufflé dish; a potato masher or an electric mixer; and a pressure-safe rack or trivet

PRESSURE:
high

TIME UNDER PRESSURE:
45 minutes

RELEASE:
natural

TOTAL TIME WITH PRESSURE:
about 1 hour 10 minutes

VEGETARIAN

GLUTEN-FREE

1½ cups water

1½ pounds butternut squash, stemmed, peeled, seeded, and chopped into 1-inch pieces

½ stick (4 tablespoons or ¼ cup) butter, cut into small bits

½ teaspoon table salt, plus more as needed

¼ teaspoon ground cinnamon

¼ teaspoon grated nutmeg

Skip the mashed potatoes and try something different like this buttery mash made from our favorite sweet autumn vegetable. This side is pretty easy, but you can make it even easier by buying cut-up butternut squash at the supermarket. (FYI, you'll still need to cut the chunks into smaller pieces for this recipe.) There's no need to add any water to the baking dish. The squash will throw off some as it cooks and the resulting mash will be all the richer and thicker.

1. Pour the water into the insert set in a **5-, 6-, or 8-quart Instant Pot.** Set a pressure-safe rack or trivet in the insert.

2. Put the squash, butter, salt, cinnamon, and nutmeg in a 2-quart, 7-inch-round, high-sided, pressure-safe baking or soufflé dish. Cover the dish with aluminum foil and set it on the rack. Lock the lid on the cooker.

3.

	Set pot for	Set level to	Valve must be	Set time for	If needed, press
For *all* pots	PRESSURE COOK or MANUAL	HIGH	Closed	45 minutes with the KEEP WARM setting off	START

4. When the pot has finished cooking, turn it off and let the pressure **return to normal naturally,** about 15 minutes. Unlatch the lid and open the cooker. Use hot pads or silicone baking mitts to transfer the (hot!) baking dish to a nearby wire rack.

5. Uncover the baking dish. Use a potato masher or a handheld electric mixer at medium-low speed to mash the butternut squash right in the dish. Check for salt to taste and serve warm.

Other Pots

- For a 3-quart Instant Pot, you *must* halve almost all of the ingredient amounts except you must use 1 cup water in the insert. You *must* also use a 1-quart, 6-inch-round, high-sided, round, pressure-safe baking or soufflé dish.

- For a 10-quart Instant Pot, you *must* increase the amount of water in the insert to 2½ cups while otherwise completing the recipe as stated.

Beyond

- For a richer dish, add up to 2 tablespoons heavy or light cream to the cooked squash before mashing it, taking care that the dish doesn't get soupy. (Butternut squash will not thicken cream with natural starches the way potatoes will.)

Stewed Beans and Greens

12 ingredients

6 SERVINGS

METHOD:
standard

SPECIAL EQUIPMENT:
none

PRESSURE:
max or high

TIME UNDER PRESSURE:
4 or 5 minutes

RELEASE:
quick

TOTAL TIME WITH PRESSURE:
about 25 minutes

GLUTEN-FREE

¼ cup olive oil

4 tinned anchovy fillets, minced

3 medium garlic cloves, minced (1 tablespoon)

1 teaspoon red pepper flakes

1 large yellow or white onion, halved and sliced into thin half-moons

3 cups vegetable or chicken broth

Two 15-ounce cans cannellini beans, drained and rinsed (3½ cups)

1 tablespoon stemmed and minced fresh rosemary leaves

10 cups stemmed and roughly chopped mixed leafy greens—choose among or mix together kale (*not* baby kale), spinach (*not* baby spinach), collard, mustard, or turnip greens

2 tablespoons lemon juice

1 teaspoon granulated white sugar

½ teaspoon table salt

Other Pots

- For a 3-quart Instant Pot, you *must* halve all of the ingredient amounts.
- For a 10-quart Instant Pot, you *can* increase all of the ingredient amounts by 50 percent.

Beyond

- Garnish the servings generously with finely grated Parmigiano-Reggiano or aged Asiago.
- And drizzle them with a syrupy, aged balsamic vinegar.
- Or go all out and add a poached egg to each serving.

We think this side dish should become a new American classic: a satisfying stew of leafy greens and white beans that gets a lot of flavor from an Italian-inspired combo of anchovies, garlic, and red pepper flakes. Frankly, this dish can be an easy vegetarian main course, especially if you take our suggestions in the **Beyond** section.

1.

	Press	Set it for	Set time for	If needed, press
In all models	SAUTÉ	MEDIUM, NORMAL, or CUSTOM 300°F	5 minutes	START

2. As the pot heats, warm the oil in the insert set in a **5-, 6-, 8-, or 10-quart Instant Pot.** Add the anchovy, garlic, and red pepper flakes; cook, stirring occasionally, until sizzling and fragrant, about 1 minute. Add the onion and cook, stirring much more frequently, until just starting to soften, about 2 minutes.

3. Carefully pour in the broth (there's a lot of oil that can spatter) and scrape up any browned bits on the pot's bottom. Stir in the beans and rosemary until well combined. Then turn off the heat. Add the greens and toss a bit, pressing them down into the broth and vegetable mixture. Lock the lid on the cooker.

4.

	Set pot for	Set level to	Valve must be	Set time for	If needed, press
For Max pots only	PRESSURE COOK	MAX	—	4 minutes with the KEEP WARM setting off	START
For all other pots	PRESSURE COOK or MANUAL	HIGH	Closed	5 minutes with the KEEP WARM setting off	START

5. When the pot has finished cooking, use the **quick-release method** to bring the pressure back to normal. Unlatch the lid and open the cooker. Stir in the lemon juice, sugar, and salt. Serve warm.

Easy Red Beans & Rice

10 ingredients

4 SERVINGS

METHOD:
pot-in-pot

SPECIAL EQUIPMENT:
a 2-quart, 7-inch-round, high-sided, pressure-safe baking or soufflé dish and a pressure-safe rack or trivet

PRESSURE:
max or high

TIME UNDER PRESSURE:
4 or 5 minutes

RELEASE:
modified natural

TOTAL TIME WITH PRESSURE:
about 25 minutes

VEGAN

GLUTEN-FREE

1½ cups water

1½ cups vegetable broth

1 cup raw long-grain white rice

¾ cup drained canned red kidney beans, rinsed

2 medium scallions, trimmed and thinly sliced (⅔ cup)

Up to 2 tablespoons drained jarred diced pimientos

2 medium garlic cloves, minced (2 teaspoons)

2 teaspoons ground cumin

2 teaspoons mild smoked paprika

½ teaspoon table salt

Other Pots

- For a 3-quart Instant Pot, you *must* halve almost all of the ingredient amounts except you must use 1 cup water in the insert. You *must* also use a 1-quart, 6-inch-round, high-sided, round, pressure-safe baking or soufflé dish.

- For a 10-quart Instant Pot, you *must* increase the amount of water in the insert to 2½ cups while otherwise completing the recipe as stated.

Beyond

- For heat, stir up to 1 teaspoon ground dried cayenne into the mixture with the cumin. Or use hot smoked paprika rather than mild.

- For a heartier dish, omit the salt and stir up to 1 cup finely diced ham into the rice mixture before cooking.

Some of our efforts to take things to the next generation have been about simplifying classics. As an example, we've here streamlined a Louisiana favorite with canned beans (which can be cooked with the rice under pressure, rather than in the second, longer step that dried beans would require), with scallions (which don't need to be sautéed before they're added to the rice mixture), and with canned diced pimientos (which only need to be drained). Otherwise, we've maintained the standard flavorings (except perhaps for the heat—see the **Beyond** section if you want more). By cooking the dish pot-in-pot, we avoid swamped, soggy rice and create perfectly tender grains to go with the beans.

1. Pour the water into the insert set in a **5-, 6-, or 8-quart Instant Pot.** Set a pressure-safe rack or trivet in the insert.

2. Stir the broth, rice, beans, scallions, pimientos, garlic, cumin, smoked paprika, and salt in a 2-quart, 7-inch-round, high-sided, pressure-safe baking or souffle dish until well combined. Do not cover. Set the dish on the rack and lock the lid on the pot.

3.

	Set pot for	Set level to	Valve must be	Set time for	If needed, press
For Max pots only	PRESSURE COOK	MAX	—	4 minutes with the KEEP WARM setting off	START
For all other pots	PRESSURE COOK or MANUAL	HIGH	Closed	5 minutes with the KEEP WARM setting off	START

4. When the pot has finished cooking, turn it off and let the pressure **return to normal naturally for 10 minutes.** Then use the **quick-release method** to get rid of the pot's residual pressure. Unlatch the lid and open the cooker. Use hot pads or silicone baking mitts to transfer the (hot!) baking dish to a nearby wire rack. Fluff the mixture with a fork and set aside for a minute or two as the rice continues to absorb the liquid. Serve warm.

Easy Barbecue Baked Beans

15 ingredients	
6 SERVINGS	
METHOD: pot-in-pot	

SPECIAL EQUIPMENT: a 2-quart, 7-inch-round high-sided, pressure-safe baking or soufflé dish and a pressure-safe rack or trivet

PRESSURE: max or high

TIME UNDER PRESSURE: 20 or 25 minutes

RELEASE: quick

TOTAL TIME WITH PRESSURE: about 45 minutes

VEGETARIAN

CAN BE GLUTEN-FREE

1½ cups water

One 10-ounce can hot or mild diced tomatoes and green chiles, such as Rotel (1¼ cups)

1 cup canned refried beans (gluten-free, if necessary)

Two 15-ounce cans pinto, pink, white, cannellini, red kidney, and/or great northern beans, drained and rinsed (3½ cups)

6 medium scallions, trimmed and thinly sliced (2 cups)

One 4½-ounce can hot or mild diced green chiles (½ cup)

¼ cup barbecue sauce (choose your favorite—gluten-free, if necessary)

3 tablespoons apple cider vinegar

2 tablespoons honey

1 tablespoon Worcestershire sauce (gluten-free, if necessary)

1 tablespoon molasses

1 teaspoon dried oregano

Up to 1 teaspoon ground dried mustard

½ teaspoon ground cloves

½ teaspoon ground cumin

Other Pots

- For a 3-quart Instant Pot, you *must* halve almost all of the ingredient amounts *except* you *must* use 1 cup water in the insert. You *must* also use a 1-quart, 6-inch-round, high-sided, pressure-safe baking or soufflé dish.

- For a 10-quart Instant Pot, you *must* increase the amount of water in the insert to 2½ cups while otherwise completing the recipe as stated.

We have a no-cheat version of barbecue baked beans in the first *Instant Pot Bible,* made from dried beans that are cooked slowly with lots of liquid to prevent scorching. In contrast, this is our *simplified* take on the classic. It uses canned beans and canned tomatoes for much less work (and time under pressure). And perhaps as a bit of a surprise, we've used canned refried beans as our thickener, all to turn out a tasty but fast version of a barbecue favorite.

1. Pour the water into the insert set in a **5-, 6-, or 8-quart Instant Pot.** Set a pressure-safe rack or trivet in the insert.

2. Stir the canned tomatoes with chiles and the refried beans in a large bowl until fairly smooth. The refried beans shouldn't be a clump but be smoothed out in the mixture. Stir in the canned beans, scallions, green chiles, barbecue sauce, vinegar, honey, Worcestershire sauce, molasses, oregano, ground mustard, cloves, and cumin until well combined.

3. Pour and pack this bean mixture into a 2-quart, 7-inch-round, high-sided, pressure-safe baking or soufflé dish. Cover the dish tightly with aluminum foil, set it on the rack, and lock the lid on the pot.

4.

	Set pot for	Set level to	Valve must be	Set time for	If needed, press
For Max pots only	PRESSURE COOK	MAX	—	20 minutes with the KEEP WARM setting off	START
For all other pots	PRESSURE COOK or MANUAL	HIGH	Closed	25 minutes with the KEEP WARM setting off	START

5. When the pot has finished cooking, use the **quick-release method** to bring the pressure back to normal. Unlatch the lid and open the cooker. Use hot pads or silicone baking mitts to transfer the (hot!) baking dish to a nearby wire rack. Uncover the baking dish, stir the baked beans, and set aside for 2 to 3 minutes to blend the flavors and thicken a little bit before serving warm.

No-Brainer Chile and Cilantro Black Beans

16 ingredients	
8 SERVINGS	
METHOD: standard	

SPECIAL EQUIPMENT: none	
PRESSURE: max or high	

TIME UNDER PRESSURE: 32 or 40 minutes	
RELEASE: natural	

TOTAL TIME WITH PRESSURE: about 1½ hours	
VEGAN	
GLUTEN-FREE	

5 cups (1 quart plus 1 cup) vegetable broth

1 pound dried black beans

1 medium yellow or white onion, chopped (1 cup)

1 medium celery stalk, thinly sliced (⅓ cup)

1 fresh poblano chile, stemmed, cored (seeded, if desired), and chopped

¼ cup loosely packed, stemmed, fresh cilantro leaves, chopped

3 medium garlic cloves, minced (1 tablespoon)

1 tablespoon finely grated orange zest

1 tablespoon dried oregano

2 teaspoons ground cumin

1 teaspoon ground coriander

1 teaspoon mild smoked paprika

1 teaspoon table salt

One 3-inch cinnamon stick

2 tablespoons lime juice

2 teaspoons granulated white sugar

Although this is a no-brainer recipe (because almost everything is dumped right in the pot's insert), it's *not* a shortcut recipe. In fact, we use dried beans for great texture and a load of fresh ingredients and dried spices (like onion, chile, orange zest, cinnamon, and oregano) to give you much more flavor in every spoonful. The results are a pot of somewhat thickened stewed beans, best served in small bowls, not a pasty bean puree but also not a thin bean soup. We save the lime juice and sugar for last for a bright, light finish to this wide but melded array of flavors.

1. Stir the broth, beans, onion, celery, chile, cilantro, garlic, orange zest, oregano, cumin, coriander, smoked paprika, salt, and cinnamon stick in the insert set in a **5-, 6-, 8-, or 10-quart Instant Pot.** Lock the lid onto the cooker.

2.

	Set pot for	Set level to	Valve must be	Set time for	If needed, press
For Max pots only	PRESSURE COOK	MAX	—	32 minutes with the KEEP WARM setting off	START
For all other pots	PRESSURE COOK or MANUAL	HIGH	Closed	40 minutes with the KEEP WARM setting off	START

3. When the pot has finished cooking, turn it off and let the pressure **return to normal naturally,** about 40 minutes. Unlatch the lid and open the cooker. Fish out and discard the cinnamon stick. Stir in the lime juice and sugar, then set the pot aside for 2 to 3 minutes to blend the flavors before serving warm.

Other Pots

- For a 3-quart Instant Pot, you *must* halve all of the ingredient amounts.
- For a 10-quart Instant Pot, you *can* increase all of the ingredient amounts by 50 percent.

Beyond

- For a vegetarian main course, spoon the beans over cooked long-grain white rice and top with a poached egg.
- And/or top them with chimichurri sauce. To make your own, mix the following in a medium bowl: ¼ cup olive oil; 1 cup packed, stemmed, chopped, fresh parsley leaves; 3 tablespoons packed, stemmed, chopped, fresh oregano leaves; 2 tablespoons red wine vinegar; 2 to 4 teaspoons minced garlic; 1 teaspoon table salt; ½ teaspoon ground black pepper; and ¼ teaspoon red pepper flakes (or more to taste). After use, press plastic wrap right against the remaining sauce in the bowl to seal it and store in the fridge for up to 3 days. Let the sauce come back to room temperature before serving.

Cheesy Baked Beans

10 ingredients

4–6 SERVINGS

METHOD:
pot-in-pot

SPECIAL EQUIPMENT:
a 2-quart, 7-inch-round, high-sided pressure-safe baking or soufflé dish and a pressure-safe rack or trivet

PRESSURE:
max or high

TIME UNDER PRESSURE:
10 or 12 minutes

RELEASE:
quick

TOTAL TIME WITH PRESSURE:
about 35 minutes

CAN BE GLUTEN-FREE

1½ cups water

Two 15-ounce cans cannellini beans, drained and rinsed (3½ cups)

One 14-ounce can diced tomatoes *packed in either juice or puree but drained* (1¼ cups)

4 ounces hard Italian salami, sopressata, or pepperoni (gluten-free, if necessary), diced

1 tablespoon loosely packed, stemmed, fresh sage leaves, minced

2 medium garlic cloves, minced (2 teaspoons)

¼ teaspoon fennel seeds

¼ teaspoon red pepper flakes

¼ teaspoon table salt

6 ounces purchased, shredded Italian cheese blend (with no seasonings—1½ cups)

Other Pots

- For a 3-quart Instant Pot, you *must* halve almost all of the ingredient amounts *except* you *must* use 1 cup water in the insert. You *must* also use a 1-quart, 6-inch-round, high-sided, pressure-safe baking or soufflé dish.

- For a 10-quart Instant Pot, you *must* increase the amount of water in the insert to 2½ cups while otherwise completing the recipe as stated.

Beyond

- Substitute minced fresh oregano leaves for the sage.

- Or add up to 1 tablespoon loosely packed, stemmed, minced parsley leaves with the sage (or oregano).

These are not barbecued baked beans for an American cookout. Instead, this pot of baked beans has a ton of Italian flavors: There are tomatoes, melty cheese, and even sausage in the mix. The dish would be welcome with stuffed peppers or a veal chop, but it could stand on its own for dinner with a chopped salad on the side.

1. Pour the water into the insert set in a **5-, 6-, or 8-quart Instant Pot.** Set a pressure-safe rack or trivet in the insert.

2. Stir the beans, *drained* diced tomatoes, salami, sage, garlic, fennel seeds, red pepper flakes, and salt in a 2-quart, 7-inch-round, high-sided, pressure-safe baking or soufflé dish. Cover the dish tightly with aluminum foil. Set the dish on the rack and lock the lid on the pot.

3.

	Set pot for	Set level to	Valve must be	Set time for	If needed, press
For Max pots only	PRESSURE COOK	MAX	—	10 minutes with the KEEP WARM setting off	START
For all other pots	PRESSURE COOK or MANUAL	HIGH	Closed	12 minutes with the KEEP WARM setting off	START

4. When the pot has finished cooking, use the **quick-release method** to bring the pressure back to normal. Unlatch the lid and open the cooker. Use hot pads or silicone baking mitts to transfer the (hot) baking dish to a nearby wire rack. Uncover and stir in the cheese. Set aside for 2 to 3 minutes to melt the cheese and blend the flavors. Stir again before serving warm.

Smashed Potatoes with Herbs and Butter

8 ingredients	
4–6 SERVINGS	
METHOD: standard	

SPECIAL EQUIPMENT: none

PRESSURE: max or high

TIME UNDER PRESSURE: 6 or 8 minutes

RELEASE: quick

TOTAL TIME WITH PRESSURE: about 20 minutes

VEGETARIAN

GLUTEN-FREE

---

2 pounds small red-skinned potatoes (about 4 ounces each), halved (do not peel)

2 cups water

½ stick (4 tablespoons or ¼ cup) butter

1 tablespoon loosely packed, stemmed, fresh rosemary leaves, minced

2 teaspoons loosely packed, stemmed, fresh oregano leaves, minced

Up to 2 medium garlic cloves, minced (2 teaspoons)

1 teaspoon table salt

½ teaspoon ground black pepper

Other Pots

- For a 3-quart Instant Pot, you *must* halve all of the ingredient amounts.
- For an 8-quart Instant Pot, you *can* increase all of the ingredient amounts by 50 percent.
- For a 10-quart Instant Pot, you *must* increase all of the ingredient amounts by 50 percent or you *can* even double the amounts.

Beyond

- If you miss the flavor of milk with potatoes, add 2 tablespoons heavy or light cream when you smash the potatoes in step 5.
- For a richer dish, substitute vegetable or chicken broth for the water in the pot.

This is not a smooth puree of potatoes. Instead, it's a chunky side dish, more like boiled potatoes, broken up so they can be slathered in butter with every bite. To that end, we leave the skin on the potatoes and don't add any extra liquid when we smash them, all to create more chunkiness. If you're looking for super-creamy mashed potatoes, see the recipe for Leek and Buttermilk Mashed Potatoes on page 349.

1. Stir the potatoes and water in the insert set in a **5-, 6-, or 8-quart Instant Pot.** Lock the lid on the pot.

2.

	Set pot for	Set level to	Valve must be	Set time for	If needed, press
For Max pots only	PRESSURE COOK	MAX	—	6 minutes with the KEEP WARM setting off	START
For all other pots	PRESSURE COOK or MANUAL	HIGH	Closed	8 minutes with the KEEP WARM setting off	START

3. When the pot has finished cooking, use the **quick-release method** to bring the pressure back to normal. Unlatch the lid and open the cooker. Use hot pads or silicone baking mitts to drain the (hot!) insert of potatoes into a colander set in the sink. Return the insert to the pot.

4.

	Press	Set it for	Set time for	If needed, press
In all models	SAUTÉ	MEDIUM, NORMAL, or CUSTOM 300°F	5 minutes	START

5. Add the butter to the insert and melt it a bit more than halfway. Stir in the rosemary, oregano, and garlic until fragrant, just a few seconds. Pour in the potatoes and stir well to coat in the butter and herbs. Use a potato masher or the back of a wooden spoon to break up the potatoes into smaller clumps and bits, all coated with butter. Turn off the heat; stir in the salt and pepper before serving warm.

Leek and Buttermilk Mashed Potatoes

9 ingredients

6–8 SERVINGS

METHOD:
standard

SPECIAL EQUIPMENT:
a potato masher or an electric mixer

PRESSURE:
max or high

TIME UNDER PRESSURE:
8 or 10 minutes

RELEASE:
modified natural

TOTAL TIME WITH PRESSURE:
about 25 minutes

VEGETARIAN

GLUTEN-FREE

½ stick (4 tablespoons or ¼ cup) butter

2 large leeks, white and pale green parts only, halved lengthwise, washed to remove internal grit, and thinly sliced (1½ cups)

Up to 3 medium garlic cloves, minced (1 tablespoon)

3 pounds russet or baking potatoes, peeled and cut into 2-inch chunks

½ cup dry but light white wine, such as Pinot Gris; or dry vermouth; or additional broth

¾ cup vegetable broth

1½ teaspoons table salt, plus more to taste

½ cup uncultured buttermilk (see page 17 for more information), plus more to taste

Up to ½ teaspoon ground black pepper

Other Pots

- For a 3-quart Instant Pot, you *must* halve the ingredient amounts.

- For an 8-quart Instant Pot, you *must* increase almost all of the ingredient amounts by 50 percent *except* you *must* use only 2 teaspoons table salt.

- For a 10-quart Instant Pot, you *must* double almost all of the ingredient amounts *except* you *must* use only 2½ teaspoons table salt.

Beyond

- Serve the potatoes with extra butter on top.

- And/or garnish the servings with minced chives (or the green part of a scallion).

- And/or crumbled, well-cooked bacon (gluten-free, if necessary).

We have a recipe for holiday-worthy, creamy mashed potatoes in the first *Instant Pot Bible*. But this recipe is even more sumptuous! The buttermilk adds a tangy richness which is balanced by the natural sweetness of the leeks and wine. If you substitute broth for the wine or vermouth, consider also adding 1 tablespoon unsweetened apple juice for just a touch of extra sweetness to balance that buttermilk.

1.

	Press	Set it for	Set time for	If needed, press
In all models	SAUTÉ	MEDIUM, NORMAL, or CUSTOM 300°F	5 minutes	START

2. As the pot heats, melt the butter in the insert set in a **5- or 6-quart Instant Pot.** Add the leeks and garlic. Cook, stirring quite often, until the leeks have begun to soften, about 2 minutes.

3. Add the potatoes and stir well to coat in the butter and vegetables. Pour in the wine and scrape up any browned bits on the pot's bottom. (There should be almost none.) Turn off the heat. Stir in the broth and salt. Lock the lid on the cooker.

4.

	Set pot for	Set level to	Valve must be	Set time for	If needed, press
For Max pots only	PRESSURE COOK	MAX	—	8 minutes with the KEEP WARM setting off	START
For all other pots	PRESSURE COOK or MANUAL	HIGH	Closed	10 minutes with the KEEP WARM setting off	START

5. When the pot has finished cooking, turn it off and let the pressure **return to normal naturally for 10 minutes.** Then use the **quick-release method** to get rid of any residual pressure in the pot. Unlatch the lid and open the cooker.

6. Add the buttermilk and pepper. Use a potato masher or a handheld electric mixer at medium-low speed to mash or beat the potatoes into velvety richness, adding more buttermilk if you want a thinner puree. Taste for salt and adjust for your taste before serving warm.

Scalloped Potatoes

10 ingredients

4–6 SERVINGS

METHOD:
pot-in-pot

SPECIAL EQUIPMENT:
a 2-quart, 7-inch-round, high-sided, pressure-safe baking or soufflé dish and a pressure-safe rack or trivet

PRESSURE:
max or high

TIME UNDER PRESSURE:
35 or 40 minutes

RELEASE:
natural

TOTAL TIME WITH PRESSURE:
about 1 hour 20 minutes

VEGETARIAN

GLUTEN-FREE

1½ cups water

Butter, for greasing

1 teaspoon dried thyme

1 teaspoon table salt

½ teaspoon mild paprika, plus additional for the top of the casserole

½ teaspoon onion powder

½ teaspoon ground black pepper

Two 8- to 10-ounce russet or baking potatoes, peeled and very thinly sliced

¾ cup heavy or light cream

4 ounces American sharp or mild cheddar cheese, shredded (1 cup)

Other Pots

- For a 3-quart Instant Pot, you *must* halve almost all of the ingredient amounts *except* you *must* use 1 cup water in the insert. You *must* also use a 1-quart, 6-inch-round, high-sided, pressure-safe baking or soufflé dish.

- For a 10-quart Instant Pot, you *must* increase the amount of water in the insert to 2½ cups while otherwise completing the recipe as stated.

Beyond

- Add *finely* shredded Brussels sprouts between the potato layers, a scant 2 tablespoons Brussels sprouts threads per layer. If you do, increase the cream or half-and-half to 1 cup.

Let's go old school! In fact, we're old enough to remember that no holiday table was complete without scalloped potatoes. So in a tribute to our childhoods, we wanted to create an IP version of this creamy, rich casserole, one we could pull out any Thanksgiving when we were feeling nostalgic. But you don't have to follow our lead. Don't save it for a special day. The potatoes would be great this weekend alongside steaks off the grill. The only way it all works is with the pot-in-pot method: There's no danger of scorching the potato layer right against the pot's hot insert.

1. Pour the water into the insert set in a **5-, 6-, or 8-quart Instant Pot.** Put a pressure-safe rack or trivet in the insert. Mix the thyme, salt, paprika, onion powder, and black pepper in a small bowl.

2. Use butter to generously grease the inside of a 2-quart, 7-inch-round, high-sided, pressure-safe baking or soufflé dish. Make an even, single layer of some of the potato slices in the dish. Sprinkle with a little of the thyme mixture, then continue on, making lots of layers with the thyme mixture between them. Work to keep the layers from mounding up in the middle of the baking dish.

3. Pour the cream over the top of the potato layers, then sprinkle the cheese evenly on top. Sprinkle the top of the casserole lightly with additional mild paprika. Cover the dish tightly with aluminum foil. Set the dish on the rack and lock the lid on the pot.

4.

	Set pot for	Set level to	Valve must be	Set time for	If needed, press
For Max pots only	PRESSURE COOK	MAX	—	35 minutes with the KEEP WARM setting off	START
For all other pots	PRESSURE COOK or MANUAL	HIGH	Closed	45 minutes with the KEEP WARM setting off	START

5. When the pot has finished cooking, turn it off and let the pressure **return to normal naturally,** about 15 minutes. Unlatch the lid and open the cooker. Use hot pads or silicone baking mitts to transfer the (hot!) baking dish to a nearby wire rack. Uncover the baking dish and cool for 2 to 3 minutes before scooping up by the big spoonful to serve warm.

Perfect Polenta Every Time

5 ingredients

4–6 SERVINGS

METHOD:
pot-in-pot

SPECIAL EQUIPMENT:
a 2-quart, 7-inch-round, high-sided, pressure-safe baking or soufflé dish and a pressure-safe rack or trivet

PRESSURE:
high

TIME UNDER PRESSURE:
15 minutes

RELEASE:
natural

TOTAL TIME WITH PRESSURE:
about 40 minutes

VEGETARIAN

GLUTEN-FREE

1½ cups water plus 4 cups (one quart) hot tap water

1 cup regular dried polenta (do not use instant polenta or premade polenta available in tubes)

2 tablespoons butter, cut into small bits

1 teaspoon table salt

1 ounce Parmigiano-Reggiano, finely grated (½ cup)

Making polenta in an Instant Pot can be an exercise in frustration... or in the BURN notice. If you make polenta right in the insert, you have to douse it with too much water, then either boil it down after cooking (and risk scorching) or let it sit forever to absorb all that water, only to eventually serve it tepid (at best) and not very flavorful—more like water-logged. The PIP method to the rescue! You can make creamy polenta quickly without so much liquid. More importantly, you can finally make perfect polenta without standing over a hot stove and stirring, stirring, stirring, stirring....

1. Pour 1½ cups of the water into the insert set in a **5-, 6-, or 8-quart Instant Pot.** Set a pressure-safe rack or trivet in the insert.

2. Stir 4 cups (1 quart) hot water, the polenta, butter, and salt in a 2-quart, 7-inch-round, high-sided, pressure-safe baking or soufflé dish. Do not cover. Set the baking dish on the rack and lock the lid on the pot.

3.

	Set pot for	Set level to	Valve must be	Set time for	If needed, press
For *all* pots	PRESSURE COOK or MANUAL	HIGH	Closed	15 minutes with the KEEP WARM setting off	START

4. When the pot has finished cooking, turn it off and let the pressure **return to normal naturally,** about 15 minutes. Unlatch the lid and open the cooker. Use hot pads or silicone baking mitts to transfer the (hot!) baking dish to a nearby wire rack. Stir the polenta until smooth, then stir in the cheese and set aside for 2 to 3 minutes until melted.

Other Pots

- For a 3-quart Instant Pot, you *must* halve almost all of the ingredient amounts *except* you *must* use 1 cup water in the insert. You *must* also use a 1-quart, 6-inch-round, high-sided, pressure-safe baking or soufflé dish.

- For a 10-quart Instant Pot, you *must* increase the amount of water in the insert to 2½ cups while otherwise completing the recipe as stated.

Beyond

- Up the game by substituting 4 cups (1 quart) vegetable or chicken broth for the water mixed with the polenta. (You *must* first warm the broth.)

- Up the game even more by using other cheeses: shredded Asiago or Pecorino Romano come to mind, but there's no reason to stand on (Italian) ceremony. Try Gruyère; an aged, hard goat cheese; a semi-firm goat cheese like Cypress Grove's Midnight Moon; or an aged Gouda like boerenkaas.

Dal

13 Ingredients	SPECIAL EQUIPMENT: None	TIME UNDER PRESSURE: 10 Minutes	TOTAL TIME WITH PRESSURE: About 45 Minutes	TOTAL TIME WITH SLOW COOKING: About 3 Hours 15 Minutes
6 SERVINGS				
METHOD: Fast/Slow	PRESSURE: High	RELEASE: Natural		VEGETARIAN
				GLUTEN-FREE

1 cup dried yellow lentils (sometimes called "pigeon peas")

2 tablespoons butter or ghee

1 small yellow or white onion, *diced* (a rounded ⅓ cup)

1 small fresh jalapeño chile, stemmed, cored (seeded, if desired), and minced

Up to 3 medium garlic cloves, minced (1 tablespoon)

1 tablespoon minced peeled fresh ginger

1 teaspoon table salt

½ teaspoon ground coriander

½ teaspoon ground dried turmeric

Up to ½ teaspoon ground dried cayenne

One 3-inch cinnamon stick

3 cups vegetable broth

½ cup loosely packed, stemmed, fresh cilantro leaves, finely chopped

How can you even think about having a curry without dal, made from lentils, garlic, chiles, and lots of spices? In our house, we serve curries in a three-part division in the bowl: one third curry, one third cooked long-grain white rice, and one third dal.

Dal is made from *yellow* lentils, which break down a bit under pressure. Starch from their softened edges thickens the dish a bit. And one more thing: Don't confuse yellow lentils with yellow split peas.

1. Pour the yellow lentils into a large bowl and cover them with cool tap water. Set them aside as you prepare this recipe.

2.

	Press	Set it for	Set time for	If needed, press
In all models	SAUTÉ	MEDIUM, NORMAL, or CUSTOM 300°F	5 minutes	START

3. As the pot heats, melt the butter or ghee in the insert set in a **5-, 6-, or 8-quart Instant Pot.** Add the onion, jalapeño, garlic, and ginger. Cook, stirring quite often, until the onion just begins to soften, about 2 minutes.

4. Stir in the salt, coriander, turmeric, cayenne, and cinnamon stick until fragrant, just a few seconds. Pour in the broth and scrape up any browned bits on the pot's bottom. (There should be almost none.)

5. Drain the lentils in a large colander set in the sink. Stir the lentils into the pot. Turn off the heat and lock the lid on the pot.

6.

	Set pot for	Set level to	Valve must be	Set time for	If needed, press
For *all* pots	PRESSURE COOK or MANUAL	HIGH	Closed	10 minutes with the KEEP WARM setting off	START
For the slow-cook function	SLOW COOK	HIGH	Open	3 hours with the KEEP WARM setting off	START

7. When the pot has finished cooking under pressure, turn it off and let the pressure **return to normal naturally,** about 20 minutes. If by 20 minutes the pressure valve has not dropped and released the lid, use the **quick-release method** to get rid of any residual pressure in the pot. Whichever cooking method you used, unlatch the lid and open the cooker. Stir well.

8.

	Press	Set it for	Set time for	If needed, press
In all models	SAUTÉ	MEDIUM, NORMAL, or CUSTOM 300°F	5 minutes	START

9. As the liquid comes to a simmer, cook, stirring almost constantly, until the dal thickens somewhat, about 4 minutes. It should still have some residual liquid. In fact, dal will tighten as it sits at room temperature (that is, as the lentils absorb more moisture).

10. Turn off the heat and use hot pad or silicone baking mitts to transfer the (hot!) insert to a nearby wire rack (to stop the cooking). Fish out and discard the cinnamon stick. Stir in the cilantro and set aside for 2 to 3 minutes to blend the flavors.

Other Pots

- For a 3-quart Instant Pot, you *must* halve all of the ingredient amounts.

- For an 8-quart Instant Pot, you *can* increase all of the ingredient amounts by 50 percent.

- For a 10-quart Instant Pot, you *must* increase all of the ingredient amounts by 50 percent or you *can* even double the amounts.

Beyond

- Top the servings with chopped unsalted roasted peanuts or cashews.

- Or toast mustard, fennel, and cumin seeds in a little vegetable oil in a small nonstick skillet set over medium heat, stirring until the seeds start to pop. Spoon this hot mixture (oil and all) over the servings of dal.

Perfect Quinoa Every Time

3 ingredients

4 SERVINGS

METHOD:
pot-in-pot

SPECIAL EQUIPMENT:
a 1-quart, 6-inch-round, high-sided, pressure-safe baking or soufflé dish and a pressure-safe rack or trivet

PRESSURE:
high

TIME UNDER PRESSURE:
4 minutes

RELEASE:
natural

TOTAL TIME WITH PRESSURE:
about 30 minutes

VEGAN

GLUTEN-FREE

---

3 cups water

1 cup raw white (or beige) quinoa (certified gluten-free, if necessary), rinsed (for more information about rinsing the grains, see the headnote for Quinoa Porridge on page 27)

½ teaspoon table salt

Quinoa grains are surprisingly delicate. Although you can cook them directly in the insert, you have to wait a long time for the pot to come to pressure because you must heat all that excess water; you have to then drain the grains, thereby losing some of their flavor in the lost cooking water; and you will find that many of the grains have blown apart under pressure. All these problems are solved by cooking quinoa with the PIP method.

One note: Although quinoa is naturally gluten-free, it is often grown near or even with wheat or processed in facilities that process wheat. There can be cross-contamination. Buy certified gluten-free quinoa if this is a concern.

1. Pour 1½ cups of the water into the insert set in a **5-, 6-, or 8-quart Instant Pot.** Set a pressure-safe rack or trivet in the insert.

2. Stir the remaining 1½ cups water, quinoa, and salt in a 1-quart, 6-inch-round, high-sided, pressure-safe baking or soufflé dish. Do not cover. Set the dish on the rack and lock the lid on the pot.

Other Pots

- For a 3-quart Instant Pot, you *must* use only 1 cup water in the insert while otherwise completing the recipe as stated.

- For a 10-quart Instant Pot, you *must* increase the amount of water in the insert to 2½ cups while otherwise completing the recipe as stated.

3.

	Set pot for	Set level to	Valve must be	Set time for	If needed, press
For *all* pots	PRESSURE COOK or MANUAL	HIGH	Closed	4 minutes with the KEEP WARM setting off	START

4. When the pot has finished cooking, turn it off and let the pressure **return to normal naturally,** about 15 minutes. Unlatch the lid and open the cooker. Use hot pads or silicone baking mitts to transfer the (hot!) dish to a nearby wire rack. Fluff the quinoa with a fork, then set aside 2 to 3 minutes so the grains can absorb the excess liquid.

Beyond

- Make a richer dish by using vegetable or even chicken broth instead of water in the baking dish with the quinoa.

- Add herbs or spices. Dried work best against the grassy flavor of quinoa: dried basil, parsley, sage, and/or thyme, no more than 1 teaspoon each. Or try hot red pepper flakes, ground cinnamon, and/or ground allspice, no more than ½ teaspoon each.

Perfect White Rice Every Time

3 ingredients

4–6 SERVINGS

METHOD:
pot-in-pot

SPECIAL EQUIPMENT:
a 2-quart, 7-inch-round, high-sided, pressure-safe baking or soufflé dish and a pressure-safe rack or trivet

PRESSURE:
max or high

TIME UNDER PRESSURE:
4 or 5 minutes

RELEASE:
modified natural

TOTAL TIME WITH PRESSURE:
about 25 minutes

VEGAN

GLUTEN-FREE

4½ cups water

2 cups raw long-grain white rice

½ teaspoon table salt

Although many models of Instant Pots have a rice button, and although we certainly have plenty of risotto recipes in the original *Instant Pot Bible* that are cooked directly in the pot's insert, we feel the best *long-grain white* rice is made with the PIP (pot-in-pot) method. There's less chance for the grains to stick on the pot's bottom. Even better, the cooked rice will have a better overall texture (that is, not nearly so mushy) because the grains are essentially simmered *and* steamed at the same moment in the pot.

1. Pour 1½ cups of the water into the insert set in a **5-, 6-, or 8-quart Instant Pot**. Set a pressure-safe rack or trivet in the insert.

2. Stir the remaining 3 cups water, the rice, and salt in a 2-quart, 7-inch-round, high-sided, pressure-safe baking or soufflé dish. Do not cover. Set the dish on the rack and lock the lid on the pot.

3.

	Set pot for	Set level to	Valve must be	Set time for	If needed, press
For Max pots only	PRESSURE COOK	MAX	—	4 minutes with the KEEP WARM setting off	START
For all other pots	PRESSURE COOK or MANUAL	HIGH	Closed	5 minutes with the KEEP WARM setting off	START

4. When the pot has finished cooking, turn it off and let the pressure **return to normal naturally for 10 minutes**. Then use the **quick-release method** to get rid of any residual pressure in the pot. Unlatch the lid and open the cooker. Use hot pads or silicone baking mitts to transfer the (hot!) baking dish to a nearby wire rack. Fluff the rice with a fork and set aside for a couple of minutes so the rice absorbs any remaining liquid.

Other Pots

- For a 3-quart Instant Pot, you *must* halve almost all of the ingredient amounts *except* you *must* use 1 cup water in the insert. You *must* also use a 1-quart, 6-inch-round, high-sided, baking or soufflé dish.

- For a 10-quart Instant Pot, you *must* increase the amount of water in the insert to 2½ cups while otherwise completing the recipe as stated.

Beyond

- Enrich the rice by using 3 cups vegetable or chicken broth in place of the water in the baking dish. (Or altered amounts in proportion for other-sized pots.)

- And/or add up to 2 tablespoons butter, cut into small bits, to the baking dish with the raw rice.

Perfect Brown Rice Every Time

3 ingredients

4–6 SERVINGS

METHOD:
pot-in-pot

SPECIAL EQUIPMENT:
a 2-quart, 7-inch-round, high-sided, pressure-safe baking or soufflé dish and a pressure-safe rack or trivet

PRESSURE:
high

TIME UNDER PRESSURE:
25 minutes

RELEASE:
natural

TOTAL TIME WITH PRESSURE:
about 55 minutes

VEGAN

GLUTEN-FREE

---

4 cups (1 quart) water

2 cups raw long-grain brown rice

1 teaspoon table salt

By cooking brown rice with the PIP (pot-in-pot) method, there's no way the grains will end up gummy or soggy. Instead, they will still have their characteristic, slightly firmer (than white rice) texture, as well as a nutty, mellow flavor.

Because brown rice is a whole grain with the bran and germ intact, it can go rancid in your pantry. Store the raw grains in a sealed container in a dark, cool place for up to 4 months or in the freezer for up to 1 year. If you've taken the rice out of the freezer for this recipe, you'll need to let it come to room temperature, probably by setting it on the counter for at least 3 hours or even overnight.

1. Pour 1½ cups of the water into the insert set in a **5-, 6-, or 8-quart Instant Pot.** Set a pressure-safe rack or trivet in the insert.

2. Mix the remaining 2½ cups water, the brown rice, and salt in a 2-quart, 7-inch-round, high-sided, pressure-safe baking or soufflé dish. Do not cover. Set the dish on the rack and lock the lid on the pot.

Other Pots

- For a 3-quart Instant Pot, you *must* halve almost all of the ingredient amounts *except* you *must* use 1 cup water in the insert. You *must* also use a 1-quart, 6-inch-round, high-sided, baking or soufflé dish.

- For a 10-quart Instant Pot, you *must* increase the amount of water in the insert to 2½ cups while otherwise completing the recipe as stated.

3.

	Set pot for	Set level to	Valve must be	Set time for	If needed, press
For *all* pots	PRESSURE COOK or MANUAL	HIGH	Closed	25 minutes with the KEEP WARM setting off	START

4. When the pot has finished cooking, turn it off and let the pressure **return to normal naturally,** about 20 minutes. Unlatch the lid and open the cooker. Use hot pads or silicone baking mitts to transfer the (hot!) baking dish to a nearby wire rack. Fluff the rice with a fork and set aside for 2 to 3 minutes so the rice absorbs the remaining liquid.

Beyond

- Enrich brown rice by using ½ cup beef broth and ¾ cup water for the liquid in the baking dish (although it will no longer be a vegan side dish).

- Brown rice can be dry. Enhance it with added fat. Although butter may seem the norm, try a toasted nut oil: walnut, pecan, or even hazelnut.

Yellow Rice

9 ingredients

4–6 SERVINGS

METHOD:
pot-in-pot

SPECIAL
EQUIPMENT:
a 2-quart, 7-inch-
round, high-sided,
pressure-safe
baking or soufflé
dish and a
pressure-safe rack
or trivet

PRESSURE:
max or high

TIME UNDER
PRESSURE:
4 or 5 minutes

RELEASE:
modified natural

TOTAL TIME WITH
PRESSURE:
about 25 minutes

VEGETARIAN

GLUTEN-FREE

1½ cups water

3 cups vegetable broth

2 cups raw long-grain white rice

½ stick (4 tablespoons or ¼ cup) butter,
cut into small bits

1 teaspoon onion powder

1 teaspoon ground dried turmeric

1 teaspoon table salt

½ teaspoon garlic powder

½ teaspoon ground black pepper

Why buy those packages of yellow rice mix, loaded with *too* much salt and *not* much flavor besides the musk of inferior turmeric? This yellow rice recipe comes out perfect every time, thanks both to the PIP (pot-in-pot) method and the blend of dried aromatics and spices. This flavorful side can stand up to any Caribbean or Spanish fare. It's also great with grilled chicken!

1. Pour 1½ cups of the water into the insert set in a **5-, 6-, or 8-quart Instant Pot.** Set a pressure-safe rack or trivet in the insert.

2. Mix the broth, rice, butter, onion powder, turmeric, salt, garlic powder, and pepper in a 2-quart, 7-inch-round, high-sided, pressure-safe baking or soufflé dish. Do not cover. Set the dish on the rack and lock the lid on the pot.

3.

	Set pot for	Set level to	Valve must be	Set time for	If needed, press
For Max pots only	PRESSURE COOK	MAX	—	4 minutes with the KEEP WARM setting off	START
For all other pots	PRESSURE COOK or MANUAL	HIGH	Closed	5 minutes with the KEEP WARM setting off	START

4. When the pot has finished cooking, turn it off and let the pressure **return to normal naturally for 10 minutes**. Then use the **quick-release method** to get rid of the pot's residual pressure. Unlatch the lid and open the cooker. Use hot pads or silicone baking mitts to transfer the (hot!) baking dish to a nearby wire rack. Fluff the rice with a fork. Set aside for 2 to 3 minutes as the rice continues to absorb any excess liquid.

Other Pots

- For a 3-quart Instant Pot, you *must* halve almost all of the ingredient amounts *except* you *must* use 1 cup water in the insert. You *must* also use a 1-quart, 6-inch-round, high-sided, baking or soufflé dish.

- For a 10-quart Instant Pot, you *must* increase the amount of water in the insert to 2½ cups while otherwise completing the recipe as stated.

Beyond

- For a richer (and not a vegetarian) side dish, substitute chicken broth for the vegetable broth.

- For much more flavor, stir in up to ¼ teaspoon saffron threads with the dried spices.

- This rice would be best alongside No-Brainer Chile and Cilantro Black Beans (page 346).

Not-Really-Chipotle's Cilantro-Lime Rice

8 ingredients

4–6 SERVINGS

METHOD:
pot-in-pot

SPECIAL EQUIPMENT:
a 2-quart, 7-inch-round, high-sided, pressure-safe baking or soufflé dish and a pressure-safe rack or trivet

PRESSURE:
max or high

TIME UNDER PRESSURE:
4 or 5 minutes

RELEASE:
modified natural

TOTAL TIME WITH PRESSURE:
about 25 minutes

GLUTEN-FREE

1½ cups water

3 cups chicken broth

2 cups raw long-grain white rice

½ teaspoon table salt

2 tablespoons lime juice

1 teaspoon olive oil

1 medium garlic clove, minced (1 teaspoon)

¼ cup loosely packed, stemmed, fresh cilantro leaves, finely chopped

To make this copycat favorite, you must cook white rice in broth, not water. And you must save the relatively few aromatics (lime juice, garlic, even olive oil) until *after* the rice has cooked in a bid to preserve their bright flavors. Don't stir the cilantro into the rice; sprinkle it all across the top of the dish so it retains its appealing, fresh look.

1. Pour the water into the insert set in a **5-, 6-, or 8-quart Instant Pot.** Put a pressure-safe rack or trivet in the insert.

2. Mix the broth, rice, and salt in a 2-quart, 7-inch-round, high-sided, pressure-safe baking or soufflé dish. Do not cover. Set the dish on the rack and lock the lid on the pot.

3.

	Set pot for	Set level to	Valve must be	Set time for	If needed, press
For Max pots only	PRESSURE COOK	MAX	—	4 minutes with the KEEP WARM setting off	START
For all other pots	PRESSURE COOK or MANUAL	HIGH	Closed	5 minutes with the KEEP WARM setting off	START

4. When the pot has finished cooking, turn it off and let the pressure **return to normal naturally for 10 minutes.** Then use the **quick-release method** to get rid of the pot's residual pressure. Unlatch the lid and open the cooker.

5. Use hot pads or silicone baking mitts to transfer the (hot!) dish to a nearby wire rack. Fluff the rice with a fork, then stir in the lime juice, olive oil, and garlic. Sprinkle the cilantro over the top and set aside for 2 to 3 minutes to blend the flavors. Serve by the big spoonful.

Other Pots

- For a 3-quart Instant Pot, you *must* halve almost all of the ingredient amounts *except* you *must* use 1 cup water in the insert. You *must* also use a 1-quart, 6-inch-round, high-sided, baking or soufflé dish.

- For a 10-quart Instant Pot, you *must* increase the amount of water in the insert to 2½ cups while otherwise completing the recipe as stated.

Beyond

- Serve with Not-Really-Chipotle's Barbacoa Beef (page 256).

Coconut Rice

5 ingredients	SPECIAL EQUIPMENT: a 2-quart, 7-inch-round, high-sided, pressure-safe baking or soufflé dish and a pressure-safe rack or trivet	PRESSURE: max or high	TOTAL TIME WITH PRESSURE: about 25 minutes
4–6 SERVINGS		TIME UNDER PRESSURE: 4 or 5 minutes	VEGAN
METHOD: pot-in-pot		RELEASE: modified natural	GLUTEN-FREE

3½ cups water

2 cups raw long-grain white rice

1 cup full-fat coconut milk (do not use low-fat)

2 teaspoons granulated white sugar

½ teaspoon table salt

Cooking white rice in coconut milk is a genius way to make the creamiest side dish imaginable. You probably know about coconut rice alongside Thai fare, but you might not have considered pairing it with grilled steaks or chops. It makes an excellent, full-flavored accompaniment, particularly if the meat has a bold seasoning like a spicy, lemongrass, or herb-rich rub, or even a curry blend.

1. Pour 1½ cups of the water into the insert set in a **5-, 6-, or 8-quart Instant Pot.** Set a pressure-safe rack or trivet in the insert.

2. Mix the remaining 2 cups water, the rice, coconut milk, sugar, and salt in a 2-quart, 7-inch-round, high-sided, pressure-safe baking or soufflé dish. Do not cover. Set the dish on the rack and lock the lid on the pot.

3.

	Set pot for	Set level to	Valve must be	Set time for	If needed, press
For Max pots only	PRESSURE COOK	MAX	—	4 minutes with the KEEP WARM setting off	START
For all other pots	PRESSURE COOK or MANUAL	HIGH	Closed	5 minutes with the KEEP WARM setting off	START

4. When the pot has finished cooking, turn it off and let the pressure **return to normal naturally for 10 minutes.** Then use the **quick-release method** to get rid of the pot's residual pressure. Unlatch the lid and open the cooker. Use hot pads or silicone baking mitts to transfer the (hot!) baking dish to a nearby wire rack. Fluff the rice with a fork. Set aside for 2 to 3 minutes so the rice can absorb the excess liquid.

Other Pots

- For a 3-quart Instant Pot, you must halve almost all of the ingredient amounts *except* you *must* use 1 cup water in the insert. You *must* also use a 1-quart, 6-inch-round, high-sided, baking or soufflé dish.

- For a 10-quart Instant Pot, you *must* increase the amount of water in the insert to 2½ cups while otherwise completing the recipe as stated.

Beyond

- Serve the rice with Chicken Tikka Kebabs (page 194) or Curried Chicken Meatballs (page 210).

Risi e Bisi

9 ingredients

6 SERVINGS

METHOD:
standard

SPECIAL EQUIPMENT:
none

PRESSURE:
max or high

TIME UNDER PRESSURE:
7 or 10 minutes

RELEASE:
quick

TOTAL TIME WITH PRESSURE:
about 45 minutes

CAN BE GLUTEN-FREE

2 tablespoons butter

1 medium yellow or white onion, chopped (1 cup)

3 ounces slab bacon (gluten-free, if necessary), diced

1½ cups raw white Arborio rice

¼ cup dry but light white wine, such as Pinot Grigio; or unsweetened apple juice

4 cups (1 quart) chicken broth

1½ cups fresh shell peas or frozen peas (no need to thaw)

1 ounce Parmigiano-Reggiano, finely grated (½ cup)

¼ cup loosely packed, stemmed, fresh parsley leaves, finely chopped

Other Pots

- For a 3-quart Instant Pot, you *must* halve all of the ingredient amounts.

- For a 10-quart Instant Pot, you *must* increase all of the ingredient amounts by 50 percent or you *can* even double the amounts.

Beyond

- For a more traditional flavor, substitute pancetta (gluten-free, if necessary) for the bacon.

- For a more professional look, don't stir in the parsley in step 7. Sprinkle it over each serving.

- For a richer dish, stir in ¼ cup heavy cream with the cheese and parsley. Cook, stirring *constantly,* for 1 additional minute to help the rice absorb the excess liquid.

This side of rice and peas is an Italian classic, here made simpler with a more common cheese than is usually used and a streamlined set of flavors. But we couldn't leave well enough alone. Bacon, rather than the more traditional pancetta, gives the dish a smokier, bolder flavor. Let's call it a North American adaptation of the classic. Bacon is salty (as is cheese), so save adding any salt for the table.

1.

	Press	Set it for	Set time for	If needed, press
In all models	SAUTÉ	MEDIUM, NORMAL, or CUSTOM 300°F	10 minutes	START

2. As the pot heats, melt the butter in the insert set in a **5-, 6-, or 8-quart Instant Pot.** Add the onion and cook, stirring often, until softened, about 3 minutes. Add the bacon; continue cooking, stirring even more often, until the meat has browned around the edges, about 3 minutes.

3. Stir in the rice to coat it in the fat. Pour in the wine and scrape up any browned bits on the pot's bottom. Stir in the broth and peas, then turn off the heat. Lock the lid on the cooker.

4.

	Set pot for	Set level to	Valve must be	Set time for	If needed, press
For Max pots only	PRESSURE COOK	MAX	—	7 minutes with the KEEP WARM setting off	START
For all other pots	PRESSURE COOK or MANUAL	HIGH	Closed	10 minutes with the KEEP WARM setting off	START

5. When the pot has finished cooking, use the **quick-release method** to bring the pressure back to normal. Unlatch the lid and open the cooker.

6.

	Press	Set it for	Set time for	If needed, press
In all models	SAUTÉ	MEDIUM, NORMAL, or CUSTOM 300°F	5 minutes	START

7. Without waiting for the pot to register нот, stir in the cheese and parsley. Cook, stirring often, until much of the liquid has been absorbed and the dish has thickened a bit, about 3 minutes. Turn off the heat. Use hot pads or silicone baking mitts to transfer the (hot!) insert to a nearby rack. Set aside for 5 minutes to allow the rice to absorb more of the liquid. Stir well and serve warm.

Rice Pilaf with Mushrooms

10 ingredients

4–6 SERVINGS

METHOD:
pot-in-pot

SPECIAL EQUIPMENT:
a 2-quart, 7-inch-round, high-sided, pressure-safe baking or soufflé dish and a pressure-safe rack or trivet

PRESSURE:
max or high

TIME UNDER PRESSURE:
4 or 5 minutes

RELEASE:
modified natural

TOTAL TIME WITH PRESSURE:
about 35 minutes

VEGETARIAN

GLUTEN-FREE

2 tablespoons butter

6 ounces white or brown button mushrooms, cleaned and thinly sliced

3 medium scallions, trimmed and minced (1 cup)

2 medium garlic cloves, minced (2 teaspoons)

1½ cups water

1¼ cups raw long-grain white rice

1¾ cups vegetable broth

1 teaspoon dried thyme

½ teaspoon table salt

½ teaspoon ground black pepper

Other Pots

- For a 3-quart Instant Pot, you *must* halve almost all of the ingredient amounts *except* you *must* use 1 cup water in the insert. You *must* also use a 1-quart, 6-inch-round, high-sided, baking or soufflé dish.

- For a 10-quart Instant Pot, you *must* increase the amount of water in the insert to 2½ cups while otherwise completing the recipe as stated.

Beyond

- For a heartier (and not vegetarian) side dish, substitute chicken broth for the vegetable broth.

- And/or add up to 2 ounces thin strips of bacon, chopped, with the mushrooms. Use gluten-free bacon, if necessary.

- Add more dried herbs with the thyme: 1 teaspoon dried basil, oregano, and/or parsley.

We have several, simpler rice pilafs in the original *Instant Pot Bible*, but we wanted to feature one here with the PIP method because of the way the rice grains retain a firmer texture when they're not put straight over the heat. This recipe is a tad more work because you have to sauté those ingredients. Trust us: The payoff is worth it.

1.

	Press	Set it for	Set time for	If needed, press
In all models	SAUTÉ	MEDIUM, NORMAL, or CUSTOM 300°F	10 minutes	START

2. As the pot heats, melt the butter in the insert set in a **5-, 6-, or 8-quart Instant Pot.** Add the mushrooms and cook, stirring often, until they give off their liquid and it evaporates to a glaze, about 4 minutes. Add the scallions and garlic; cook, stirring almost constantly, until the scallions *start* to soften, less than 1 minute.

3. Turn off the heat and use hot pads or silicone baking mitts to pick up the (hot!) insert and scrape its contents into a 2-quart, 7-inch-round, high-sided, pressure-safe baking or soufflé dish.

4. Clean and dry the (still hot!) insert and return it to the machine. Pour the water into the insert, then set a pressure-safe rack or trivet in the insert.

5. Stir the rice, broth, thyme, salt, and pepper into the ingredients in the baking dish until well combined. Do not cover. Set the baking dish on the rack and lock the lid onto the cooker.

6.

	Set pot for	Set level to	Valve must be	Set time for	If needed, press
For Max pots only	PRESSURE COOK	MAX	—	4 minutes with the KEEP WARM setting off	START
For all other pots	PRESSURE COOK or MANUAL	HIGH	Closed	5 minutes with the KEEP WARM setting off	START

7. When the pot has finished cooking, turn it off and let the pressure **return to normal naturally for 10 minutes.** Then use the **quick-release method** to get rid of the pot's residual pressure. Unlatch the lid and open the cooker. Use hot pads or silicone baking mitts to transfer the (hot!) baking dish to a nearby wire rack. Stir well, then let sit for 2 to 3 minutes so the rice can absorb some of the liquid.

Easy Dirty Rice

10 ingredients	SPECIAL EQUIPMENT: none	TIME UNDER PRESSURE: 7 or 10 minutes	TOTAL TIME WITH PRESSURE: about 45 minutes
4–6 SERVINGS			
METHOD: standard	PRESSURE: max or high	RELEASE: modified quick	CAN BE GLUTEN-FREE

2 tablespoons vegetable, canola, or other neutral-flavored oil

1 pound bulk breakfast sausage meat, or breakfast sausages with the casings removed (gluten-free, if necessary)

1 small yellow or white onion, chopped (½ cup)

1 small green bell pepper, stemmed, cored, and chopped (½ cup)

2 medium celery stalks, chopped (½ cup)

2 medium garlic cloves, minced (2 teaspoons)

1 tablespoon bottled dried Cajun seasoning blend

3 cups chicken broth

1½ cups raw long-grain white rice

2 bay leaves

Other Pots

- For a 3-quart Instant Pot, you *must* halve all of the ingredient amounts.
- For an 8-quart Instant Pot, you *can* increase all of the ingredient amounts by 50 percent.
- For a 10-quart Instant Pot, you *must* increase all of the ingredient amounts by 50 percent and you *can* even double them.

Beyond

- For a more authentic flavor, substitute peanut oil for the vegetable oil.
- For a still more authentic flavor, use 1 pound smoked Cajun andouille, diced or thinly sliced. Since the sausage is already cooked, only warm it up in the oil in step 2 for a minute or two.

This recipe for dirty rice won't win any authenticity awards from the Louisiana Chamber of Commerce. Where are the chicken gizzards? The chicken livers? The cayenne? Not here. Instead, we've used sausage meat and a purchased seasoning blend, all to make this a hearty, fast version of the Cajun classic. The flavors are spot on; the effort, much less. Isn't that the whole point of an IP?

1.

	Press	Set it for	Set time for	If needed, press
In all models	SAUTÉ	MEDIUM, NORMAL, or CUSTOM 300°F	10 minutes	START

2. As the pot heats, warm the oil in the insert set in a **5-, 6-, or 8-quart Instant Pot.** Crumble in the sausage meat and cook, stirring occasionally, until it's no longer clumped together and has lost its raw, pink color, about 3 minutes.

3. Stir in the onion, bell pepper, and celery. Cook, stirring more often, until the onion starts to soften, about 3 minutes. Stir in the garlic and seasoning blend until aromatic, just a few seconds.

4. Pour in the broth and scrape up any browned bits on the pot's bottom. Stir in the rice and bay leaves. Turn off the heat and lock the lid on the pot.

5.

	Set pot for	Set level to	Valve must be	Set time for	If needed, press
For Max pots only	PRESSURE COOK	MAX	—	7 minutes with the KEEP WARM setting off	START
For all other pots	PRESSURE COOK or MANUAL	HIGH	Closed	10 minutes with the KEEP WARM setting off	START

6. When the pot has finished cooking, use the **quick-release method** to bring the pressure back to normal but **do not open the pot.** Instead, set it aside for 10 minutes. Unlatch the lid and open the cooker. Find and discard the bay leaves. Fluff the rice before serving hot.

Smoky Brown Rice and Green Lentils

10 ingredients	SPECIAL EQUIPMENT: none	TIME UNDER PRESSURE: 23 or 30 minutes	TOTAL TIME WITH PRESSURE: about 1 hour 20 minutes	
4–6 SERVINGS				
METHOD: standard	PRESSURE: max or high	RELEASE: natural	VEGAN	
			GLUTEN-FREE	

4½ cups (1 quart plus ½ cup) vegetable broth

2 cups raw long-grain brown rice

1 cup green lentils (that is, *lentilles du Puy*)

2 tablespoons mild smoked paprika

2 teaspoons fennel seeds

1 teaspoon onion powder

1 teaspoon garlic powder

1 teaspoon table salt

1 teaspoon ground black pepper

1 tablespoon apple cider vinegar

With smoked paprika, this dish is a Southwestern take on the Middle Eastern side of rice and lentils called *mujadara*. Confusing, right? Don't worry. It's flavorful enough to go great with anything off the grill. *And* it even makes a terrific burrito filling. In a tortilla wrap, top the rice concoction with diced tomatoes, purchased pickled jalapeño rings or jarred salsa, maybe some sour cream, and perhaps the pickled onions found in the **Beyond** section of this recipe.

1. Stir the broth, rice, lentils, smoked paprika, fennel seeds, onion powder, garlic powder, salt, and pepper in a **5-, 6-, 8-, or 10-quart Instant Pot.** Lock the lid onto the cooker.

2.

	Set pot for	Set level to	Valve must be	Set time for	If needed, press
For Max pots only	PRESSURE COOK	MAX	—	23 minutes with the KEEP WARM setting off	START
For all other pots	PRESSURE COOK or MANUAL	HIGH	Closed	30 minutes with the KEEP WARM setting off	START

3. When the pot has finished cooking, turn it off and let the pressure **return to normal naturally,** about 35 minutes. Unlatch the lid and open the cooker. Use hot pads or silicone baking mitts to transfer the (hot!) insert to a nearby wire rack. Fluff the rice with a fork, then stir in the vinegar. Set aside for 5 minutes so the rice and lentils absorb most of the remaining liquid. Serve warm.

Other Pots

- For a 3-quart Instant Pot, you *must* halve all of the ingredient amounts.

- For an 8-quart Instant Pot, you *can* increase all of the ingredient amounts by 50 percent.

- For a 10-quart Instant Pot, you *can* increase all of the ingredient amounts by 50 percent or you *can* even double them.

Beyond

- This side dish is terrific topped with pickled onions. To make your own, whisk ½ cup apple cider vinegar, 1 tablespoon granulated white sugar, and 1½ teaspoons kosher salt in a large glass or other nonreactive container. Halve a large red onion and slice it into *very* thin half-moons. Put these in the jar, add enough water to cover them, stir well, seal, and refrigerate for at least 1 hour or up to 2 weeks.

Butternut Squash Risotto

11 ingredients

4–6 SERVINGS

METHOD:
standard

SPECIAL EQUIPMENT:
none

PRESSURE:
max or high

TIME UNDER PRESSURE:
7 or 10 minutes

RELEASE:
quick

TOTAL TIME WITH PRESSURE:
about 35 minutes

VEGETARIAN

GLUTEN-FREE

2 tablespoons butter

1 medium yellow or white onion, chopped (1 cup)

1½ cups raw white Arborio rice

1 teaspoon dried thyme

½ teaspoon ground dried turmeric

½ teaspoon table salt

½ teaspoon ground black pepper

¼ cup dry white wine, such as Chardonnay; dry vermouth; or unsweetened apple juice

4 cups (1 quart) vegetable broth

1½ pounds butternut squash, peeled, seeded, and cut into 2-inch cubes

1 ounce Parmigiano-Reggiano or Pecorino Romano, finely grated (½ cup)

Other Pots

- For a 3-quart Instant Pot, you *must* halve all of the ingredient amounts.

- For a 10-quart Instant Pot, you *must* increase all of the ingredient amounts by 50 percent or you *can* even double the amounts.

Beyond

- Add up to ½ teaspoon red pepper flakes with the other spices.

- To go over the top, substitute ¼ teaspoon saffron threads for the ground dried turmeric.

- For a richer (but not a vegetarian) risotto, substitute chicken broth for the vegetable broth and stir in up to 3 tablespoons heavy cream with the cheese.

Risotto from a pressure cooker is what first brought us back to the pots in the mid-'90s, long after we'd watched our grandmothers wrestle big pot roasts out of stovetop models. With purchased, cut-up butternut squash, this recipe couldn't be better: creamy, light, and very flavorful. It's even a great meal on its own when the day's been rushed and all you really want is something satisfying to go with a glass of wine.

1.

	Press	Set it for	Set time for	If needed, press
In all models	SAUTÉ	MEDIUM, NORMAL, or CUSTOM 300°F	10 minutes	START

2. As the pot heats, melt the butter in the insert set in a **5-, 6-, or 8-quart Instant Pot.** Add the onion and cook, stirring often, until softened, about 3 minutes. Stir in the rice, thyme, turmeric, salt, and pepper until the rice is thoroughly coated in the butter and spices, less than 1 minute.

3. Pour in the wine and scrape up any browned bits on the pot's bottom. Stir in the broth, then the butternut squash until well combined. Turn off the heat and lock the lid on the pot.

4.

	Set pot for	Set level to	Valve must be	Set time for	If needed, press
For Max pots only	PRESSURE COOK	MAX	—	7 minutes with the KEEP WARM setting off	START
For all other pots	PRESSURE COOK or MANUAL	HIGH	Closed	10 minutes with the KEEP WARM setting off	START

5. When the pot has finished cooking, use the **quick-release method** to bring the pressure back to normal. Unlatch the lid and open the cooker. Stir in the cheese, set the lid askew over the pot, and set it aside for 5 minutes to let the rice absorb the remaining liquid. Serve warm.

Lemon, Baby Kale, and Goat Cheese Risotto

11 ingredients

4–6 SERVINGS

METHOD:
standard

SPECIAL EQUIPMENT:
none

PRESSURE:
max or high

TIME UNDER PRESSURE:
7 or 10 minutes

RELEASE:
quick

TOTAL TIME WITH PRESSURE:
about 35 minutes

VEGETARIAN

GLUTEN-FREE

2 tablespoons butter

1 small leek, white and pale green part only, halved lengthwise, washed well for internal grit, and thinly sliced (⅓ cup)

1½ cups raw white Arborio rice

2 teaspoons stemmed and minced fresh oregano leaves

2 teaspoons finely grated lemon zest

1 teaspoon table salt

½ teaspoon ground black pepper

¼ cup dry white wine, such as Chardonnay; dry vermouth; or unsweetened apple juice

4 cups (1 quart) vegetable broth

2 ounces soft goat cheese (¼ cup)

2 cups loosely packed chopped baby kale leaves (2 ounces)

Other Pots

- For a 3-quart Instant Pot, you *must* halve all of the ingredient amounts.

- For a 10-quart Instant Pot, you *must* increase all of the ingredient amounts by 50 percent or you can even double them.

Beyond

- For more pop, garnish the servings with more finely grated lemon zest.

- Leftovers make great risotto cakes: Refrigerate what's left in a covered container for at least 24 hours. Stir in 1 refrigerator-cold large egg for 2 cups of leftovers and form the mixture into 4-inch patties. Fry in olive oil in a nonstick skillet set over medium heat, turning once, until browned and crisp, about 6 minutes in all.

Our recipe for Butternut Squash Risotto (page 364) is definitely weeknight fare. But here's a dinner-party-worthy risotto, way beyond the norm. The lemon zest is added *before* cooking, rather than after, to soften the flavor. (If you miss the pop, see our **Beyond** suggestions.) The baby kale, by contrast, is added *after* cooking so it just wilts while retaining its fresh, herbaceous flavor.

1.

	Press	Set it for	Set time for	If needed, press
In all models	SAUTÉ	MEDIUM, NORMAL, or CUSTOM 300°F	10 minutes	START

2. As the pot heats, melt the butter in the insert set in a **5-, 6-, or 8-quart Instant Pot**. Add the leek and cook, stirring often, until softened, about 1 minute. Stir in the rice, oregano, lemon zest, salt, and pepper until the rice is thoroughly coated in the butter and spices.

3. Pour in the wine and scrape up any browned bits on the pot's bottom. Stir in the broth and turn off the heat. Lock the lid onto the cooker.

4.

	Set pot for	Set level to	Valve must be	Set time for	If needed, press
For Max pots only	PRESSURE COOK	MAX	—	7 minutes with the KEEP WARM setting off	START
For all other pots	PRESSURE COOK or MANUAL	HIGH	Closed	10 minutes with the KEEP WARM setting off	START

5. When the pot has finished cooking, use the **quick-release method** to bring the pressure back to normal. Unlatch the lid and open the cooker. Crumble in the cheese and add the baby kale. Stir well, then set the lid askew over the pot and set it aside for 5 minutes to let the rice continue to absorb the liquid. Serve warm.

See photo in insert.

Wheat Berry "Risotto"

13 ingredients

4–6 SERVINGS

METHOD:
standard

SPECIAL EQUIPMENT:
none

PRESSURE:
max or high

TIME UNDER PRESSURE:
30 or 35 minutes

RELEASE:
natural

TOTAL TIME WITH PRESSURE:
about 1½ hours

VEGETARIAN

---

2 tablespoons butter

2 tablespoons olive oil

2 medium single-lobe shallots, chopped (½ cup)

8 ounces brown button (or cremini or baby bella) mushrooms, cleaned and thinly sliced

4 ounces shiitake mushrooms, stems discarded, the caps thinly sliced

2 medium garlic cloves, minced (2 teaspoons)

1½ cups raw soft white (or "spring") wheat berries

1 teaspoon dried basil

½ teaspoon dried thyme

½ teaspoon table salt

½ cup dry red wine, such as Cabernet Sauvignon; or extra broth

2½ cups vegetable broth

1 ounce Parmigiano-Reggiano, finely grated (½ cup)

Wheat berries are actually raw grains of wheat, processed so their hulls have been removed but are otherwise intact (with their germ and bran). In other words, they're packed with a lot of wheaty flavor and solid nutrition. There are soft, white (or "spring") and hard, red (or "winter") varieties. The soft white wheat berries can be cooked (or really, overcooked as here) into something like a risotto with a nutty wheat flavor—a hearty side dish to a roast on a cold night. Use only soft, white (or "spring") wheat berries in this recipe.

All wheat berries go rancid quickly. Smell your package to make sure the grains don't have an acrid tang. (If they do and the package is new, take it back to the store for a refund!) Store wheat berries in a sealed container in a cool, dark pantry for up to 2 months or in the freezer for up to 1 year.

1.

	Press	Set it for	Set time for	If needed, press
In all models	SAUTÉ	MEDIUM, NORMAL, or CUSTOM 300°F	10 minutes	START

2. As the pot heats, melt the butter in the olive oil inside the insert set in a **5-, 6-, or 8-quart Instant Pot.** Add the shallot and cook, stirring often, until softened, about 2 minutes. Add both types of mushrooms and cook, stirring more often, until they give off their liquid and it reduces to a glaze, about 4 minutes.

3. Stir in the garlic until aromatic, just a few seconds. Then stir in the wheat berries, basil, thyme, and salt until the grains are thoroughly coated in the spices and other ingredients. Pour in the wine and scrape up any browned bits on the pot's bottom. Stir in the broth and turn off the heat. Lock the lid onto the cooker.

4.

	Set pot for	Set level to	Valve must be	Set time for	If needed, press
For Max pots only	PRESSURE COOK	MAX	—	30 minutes with the KEEP WARM setting off	START
For all other pots	PRESSURE COOK or MANUAL	HIGH	Closed	35 minutes with the KEEP WARM setting off	START

5. When the pot has finished cooking, turn it off and let the pressure **return to normal naturally,** about 30 minutes. Unlatch the lid and open the cooker.

6.

	Press	Set it for	Set time for	If needed, press
In all models	SAUTÉ	MEDIUM, NORMAL, or CUSTOM 300°F	5 minutes	START

7. Stir the risotto as it comes to a simmer. Cook, stirring constantly, until the excess liquid boils down to a thickened sauce, like a thick porridge, about 2 minutes. Turn off the heat and stir in the cheese. Set the lid askew over the pot and set it aside for 5 minutes to blend the flavors. Serve warm.

Other Pots

- For a 3-quart Instant Pot, you *must* halve all of the ingredient amounts.
- For a 10-quart Instant Pot, you *must* double all of the ingredient amounts.

Beyond

- For a richer (and not vegetarian) version of this dish, substitute beef broth for the vegetable broth.
- Rather than adding red pepper flakes to the dish, garnish the servings with Sriracha.

Barley "Risotto"

11 ingredients

4–6 SERVINGS

METHOD:
standard

SPECIAL
EQUIPMENT:
none

PRESSURE:
max or high

TIME UNDER
PRESSURE:
15 or 18 minutes

RELEASE:
natural

TOTAL TIME WITH
PRESSURE:
about 1 hour

VEGETARIAN

1 tablespoon butter

1 tablespoon olive oil

1 medium leek, white and pale green part only, halved lengthwise, washed well to remove internal grit, and thinly sliced (½ cup)

8 ounces brown button (or cremini or baby bella) mushrooms, cleaned and thinly sliced

1 teaspoon dried basil

½ teaspoon dried oregano

½ teaspoon table salt

½ teaspoon ground black pepper

1⅓ cups raw pearled barley

4 cups (1 quart) vegetable broth

2 ounces Gruyère or Jarlsberg cheese, shredded (½ cup)

Other Pots

- For a 3-quart Instant Pot, you *must* halve all of the ingredient amounts.

- For a 10-quart Instant Pot, you *must* increase all of the ingredient amounts by 50 percent or you *can* even double the amounts.

Beyond

- For a richer (and not vegetarian) dish, substitute chicken broth for the vegetable broth.

- For a much richer dish, double the cheese and add 3 tablespoons heavy or light cream with it.

- For a sweeter dish, use 3 cups broth and 1 cup dry white wine (with ratio proportions for other size pots).

Pearled barley can be turned into a creamy risotto-like side dish without much work by essentially overcooking it in an Instant Pot. In fact, it's easy to overcook it because pearled barley has already been stripped of its germ and bran, leaving just the sweet, mild endosperm.

One note: In this recipe you'll only cook the mushrooms until they begin to soften, *not* until they release their liquid (as we often have you do). The excess liquid that comes out under pressure is necessary for the success of the dish.

1.

	Press	Set it for	Set time for	If needed, press
In all models	SAUTÉ	MEDIUM, NORMAL, or CUSTOM 300°F	10 minutes	START

2. As the pot heats, melt the butter in the olive oil in the insert set in a **5-, 6-, or 8-quart Instant Pot.** Add the leek and cook, stirring often, until softened, about 2 minutes. Add the mushrooms and cook, stirring even more often, just until barely softened, about 2 minutes.

3. Stir in the basil, oregano, salt, and pepper until aromatic, just a few seconds. Then stir in the pearled barley until it is coated in the spices and well combined with the vegetables. Pour in the broth and scrape up any browned bits on the pot's bottom. Turn off the heat and lock the lid onto the cooker.

4.

	Set pot for	Set level to	Valve must be	Set time for	If needed, press
For Max pots only	PRESSURE COOK	MAX	—	15 minutes with the KEEP WARM setting off	START
For all other pots	PRESSURE COOK or MANUAL	HIGH	Closed	18 minutes with the KEEP WARM setting off	START

5. When the pot has finished cooking, turn it off and let the pressure **return to normal naturally,** about 30 minutes. Unlatch the lid and open the cooker. Stir in the cheese, then set the lid askew over the pot and set it aside for 5 minutes to melt the cheese. Stir again before serving.

No-Brainer Low-Carb Stuffed Peppers

9 ingredients

4 STUFFED PEPPERS

METHOD: pot-in-pot

SPECIAL EQUIPMENT: a 2-quart, 7-inch-round, high-sided, pressure-safe baking or soufflé dish and a pressure-safe rack or trivet

PRESSURE: max or high

TIME UNDER PRESSURE: 16 or 18 minutes

RELEASE: natural

TOTAL TIME WITH PRESSURE: about 1 hour 15 minutes

VEGETARIAN

CAN BE GLUTEN-FREE

1½ cups water

2 cups riced cauliflower (8 ounces)

4 ounces American mild or sharp cheddar cheese, shredded (1 cup)

One 4½-ounce can hot or mild diced green chiles (½ cup)

1 teaspoon dried oregano

1 teaspoon ground cumin

½ teaspoon table salt

4 large, long bell peppers of any color (green, red, yellow, or orange), stemmed and cored (that is, hollowed out—see the headnote for more information)

One 10-ounce can hot or mild red enchilada sauce (1 cup plus 2 tablespoons—gluten-free, if necessary)

Other Pots

- For a 3-quart Instant Pot, you *must* halve almost all of the ingredient amounts *except* you *must* use 1 cup water in the insert. You *must* also use a 1-quart, 6-inch-round, high-sided, pressure-safe baking or soufflé dish.

- For a 10-quart Instant Pot, you *must* increase the amount of water in the insert to 2½ cups while otherwise completing the recipe as stated.

Beyond

- This recipe yields bell peppers that still need to be cut with a knife. If you want softer bell peppers, cook under pressure for 18 at MAX or 25 at HIGH.

- Garnish with red pepper flakes.

Here, you'll stuff bell peppers with riced cauliflower (rather than rice) for a lower-carb take on the classic. (But don't worry: There's plenty of cheese.) Look for bell peppers that are longer than wide so they'll stand up in the baking dish.

Here's our hack to prepare the bell peppers. Cut about ½ inch off the stem end, thereby removing that stem and opening a "lid" into the pepper. Run a serrated grapefruit spoon (or a paring knife—but take care not to cut the pepper) around the inside to loosen the white, fibrous membranes from the interior walls. Discard all that stuff and you're ready to stuff the pepper.

1. Pour the water into the insert set in a **5-, 6-, or 8-quart Instant Pot**. Set a pressure-safe rack or trivet in the insert.

2. Stir the riced cauliflower, cheese, chiles, oregano, cumin, and salt in a large bowl until uniform. Divide this mixture among and pack it evenly into the bell peppers. Stand them up in a 2-quart, 7-inch round, high-sided, pressure-safe baking or soufflé dish.

3. Pour the enchilada sauce over and around the peppers. Do not cover. Set the baking dish on the rack and lock the lid on the pot.

4.

	Set pot for	Set level to	Valve must be	Set time for	If needed, press
For Max pots only	PRESSURE COOK	MAX	—	16 minutes with the KEEP WARM setting off	START
For all other pots	PRESSURE COOK or MANUAL	HIGH	Closed	18 minutes with the KEEP WARM setting off	START

5. When the pot has finished cooking, turn it off and let the pressure **return to normal naturally,** about 20 minutes. Unlatch the lid and open the cooker. Use hot pads or silicone baking mitts to transfer the (hot!) baking dish to a nearby wire rack. Cool for a few minutes, then serve the peppers in bowls with the sauce ladled around and over them.

See photo in insert.

Chile & Cheese Tamale Bites

8 ingredients

14 MINI TAMALES

METHOD:
egg bites

SPECIAL EQUIPMENT:
two seven-indentation egg-bite molds, an electric mixer, and a pressure-safe rack or trivet

PRESSURE:
max or high

TIME UNDER PRESSURE:
17 or 20 minutes

RELEASE:
quick

TOTAL TIME WITH PRESSURE:
about 45 minutes

CAN BE VEGETARIAN

GLUTEN-FREE

1½ cups water

Vegetable oil, for greasing

1¼ cups vegetable or chicken broth, *warmed*

1¾ cups instant masa harina, such as Maseca

5 tablespoons solid vegetable shortening, preferably expeller-pressed shortening

¾ cup fresh corn kernels (or thawed frozen kernels)

2 ounces Monterey Jack cheese, shredded (½ cup)

One 4½-ounce can hot or mild diced green chiles (½ cup)

These little husk-less, corn-laced tamales can be either an appetizer or a light meal. The recipe is actually another of our "cheat" ways to make a quick version of tamales in egg-bite molds. (For a chicken version of tamale bites, see page 172.)

Two notes: One, the broth must be warm to make the dough soft and pliable. Heat it up in a microwave-safe container in a microwave on HIGH in 10-second increments until it's warm but not hot (certainly not boiling).

And two, the mini tamales freeze exceptionally well after they've cooled to room temperature. Heat them up by setting the frozen bites in a steamer basket in the pot, adding 1½ to 2 cups water, and putting the pot on its SAUTÉ function at HIGH or MORE. Set the lid askew over the pot and steam for 10 minutes.

1. Pour the water into the insert set in a **5-, 6-, or 8-quart Instant Pot.** Set a pressure-safe rack or trivet in the pot. Generously grease the insides of all of the indentations of two 7-indentation egg-bite molds. (For more information about cooking with these molds, see page 15 of the introduction.)

2. Pour the warmed broth into a large bowl. Add the instant masa harina. Use an electric mixer at medium speed to beat the two together until a soft dough forms. Beat in the shortening until the mixture is fluffy and light, not pasty. Beat in the corn, cheese, and chiles until well combined. Turn off the mixer and scrape down and remove the beaters.

3. Fill the prepared indentations in the molds with about ½ cup of the masa mixture each. Cover the molds tightly with their silicone lids or seal them with aluminum foil. Stack the two molds on the rack, setting one egg-bite mold in the insert, then the second on top so that the indentations of the upper mold sit on the walls of the bottom mold, not into the bottom indentations themselves (except for the center indentation of the top mold which will now hover above the center indentation below it). Lock the lid onto the cooker.

4.

	Set pot for	Set level to	Valve must be	Set time for	If needed, press
For Max pots only	PRESSURE COOK	MAX	—	17 minutes with the KEEP WARM setting off	START
For all other pots	PRESSURE COOK or MANUAL	HIGH	Closed	20 minutes with the KEEP WARM setting off	START

5. When the pot has finished cooking, use the **quick-release method** to bring the pressure back to normal. Unlatch the lid and open the cooker. Use hot pads or silicone baking mitts to transfer the (hot!) molds to a nearby wire rack. Uncover the molds and cool for 5 minutes before unmolding the tamale bites and serving warm.

Other Pots

- Because of the height of the stacked equipment in this recipe, it will not work in a 3-quart Instant Pot.

- For a 10-quart Instant Pot, you *must* increase the amount of water in the insert to 2½ cups while otherwise completing the recipe as stated.

Beyond

- Serve the tamales topped with green or red salsa.

- Or with pico de gallo—see the Beyond for the Not-Really-Chili's Chicken Enchilada Soup on page 86.

- Or with Not-Really-Wendy's Chili (page 236) and lots of shredded American sharp cheddar cheese.

Refried Bean Tamale Bites

7 ingredients

14 TAMALE BITES

METHOD:
egg bites

SPECIAL EQUIPMENT:
two seven-indentation egg-bite molds, an electric mixer, and a pressure-safe rack or trivet

PRESSURE:
max or high

TIME UNDER PRESSURE:
17 or 20 minutes

RELEASE:
quick

TOTAL TIME WITH PRESSURE:
about 45 minutes

CAN BE VEGETARIAN

CAN BE GLUTEN-FREE

1½ cups water

Vegetable oil, for greasing

1¼ cups chicken or vegetable broth, *warmed*

1¾ cups instant masa harina, such as Maseco

5 tablespoons solid vegetable shortening, preferably expeller-pressed

1 ounce Monterey Jack cheese, shredded (¼ cup)

1¼ cups canned refried beans (gluten-free and vegetarian, if necessary)

With canned refried beans and shredded cheese, you can make easy tamales (or a husk-less version of tamales, if you're a purist) for snacks or a light meal. Although canned refried beans have gotten a bad rap over the years, there are flavorful varieties that still taste like beans, often available at Latin American markets. There are even fat-free versions that will stand up well with this technique. Check out the headnote to the Chile & Cheese Tamale Bites (page 370) for a couple of notes about how to make a success out of tamale bites from egg-bite molds.

1. Pour the water into the insert set in a **5-, 6-, or 8-quart Instant Pot.** Set a pressure-safe rack or trivet into the pot. Generously grease the insides of all of the indentations of two 7-indentation egg-bite molds. (For more information about cooking with these molds, see page 15 of the introduction.)

2. Pour the warmed broth into a large bowl. Add the instant masa harina. Use an electric mixer at medium speed to beat the two together until a soft dough forms. Beat in the shortening until the mixture is fluffy and light, not pasty. Beat in the cheese until well combined. Turn off the mixer and scrape down and remove the beater(s).

3. Divide the masa mixture into fourteen balls, about ⅓ cup each. Take one ball and place about two-thirds in one of the egg-bite mold indentations, pressing it down to the bottom and up the sides of the mold to conform to the contours of the indentation. Fill this with about 2 tablespoons refried beans. Top with the remaining third of the ball and seal the filling inside the masa shell. Repeat with the remaining thirteen balls.

4. Cover the molds with their silicone lids or with aluminum foil. Stack the two molds on the rack, setting one egg-bite mold in the insert, then the second on top so that the indentations of the upper mold sit on the walls of the bottom mold, not into the bottom indentations themselves (except for the center indentation of the top mold which will now hover above the center indentation below it). Lock the lid onto the cooker.

5.

	Set pot for	Set level to	Valve must be	Set time for	If needed, press
For Max pots only	PRESSURE COOK	MAX	—	17 minutes with the KEEP WARM setting off	START
For all other pots	PRESSURE COOK or MANUAL	HIGH	Closed	20 minutes with the KEEP WARM setting off	START

6. When the pot has finished cooking, use the **quick-release method** to bring the pressure back to normal. Unlatch the lid and open the cooker. Use hot pads or silicone baking mitts to transfer the (hot!) molds to a nearby wire rack. Uncover the molds and cool for 5 minutes before unmolding and serving warm.

Other Pots

- Because of the height of the stacked equipment in this recipe, it will not work in a 3-quart Instant Pot.
- For a 10-quart Instant Pot, you *must* increase the amount of water in the insert to 2½ cups while otherwise completing the recipe as stated.

Beyond

- For more fire, stir a minced stemmed (and seeded, if desired) *fresh* jalapeño chile into the refried beans before you use it as a filling.
- Garnish these tamale bites with sour cream and stemmed and chopped fresh cilantro leaves.
- Or serve them with Not-Really-Chili's Queso Dip (page 328).

Pumpkin Nut Chili

14 ingredients

6–8 SERVINGS

METHOD: fast/slow

SPECIAL EQUIPMENT: none

PRESSURE: max or high

TIME UNDER PRESSURE: 12 or 15 minutes

RELEASE: modified natural

TOTAL TIME WITH PRESSURE: about 40 minutes

TOTAL TIME WITH SLOW COOKING: about 3 hours 15 minutes

VEGAN

7 cups (1 quart plus 3 cups) vegetable broth

One 28-ounce diced tomatoes *packed in juice,* preferably fire-roasted tomatoes (3½ cups)

1 cup finely chopped walnuts

1 cup dried red lentils

1 cup dried brown lentils, picked over for stones

½ cup raw golden bulgur

1 large single-lobe shallot, chopped (⅓ cup)

1 canned chipotle chile in adobo sauce, stemmed, cored (seeded, if desired), and minced

2 teaspoons adobo sauce from the can

3 medium garlic cloves, minced (1 tablespoon)

3 tablespoons standard chili powder

1 tablespoon mild smoked paprika

2 teaspoons ground cumin

1 cup canned solid-pack pumpkin puree (do not use pumpkin pie filling)

Other Pots

- For a 3-quart Instant Pot, you *must* halve all of the ingredient amounts.

- For a 10-quart Instant Pot, you *can* increase all of the ingredient amounts by 50 percent.

Beyond

- Sprinkle the servings with toasted shelled pumpkin seeds (also called "pepitas." If you can only find raw shelled pumpkin seeds, toast them in a nonstick skillet with a little vegetable oil over medium-low heat.

This unusual vegan chili has a base of nuts and lentils (rather than the more common beans and maybe rice). It also includes bulgur, which helps thicken the chili as it cooks, giving it the more familiar texture of ground beef chili. The canned pumpkin is stirred in at the end to thicken the stew and add sweet notes to the earthy and spicy ingredients. All in all, you don't need much more than a glass of iced tea or maybe a cold beer.

1. Stir the broth, tomatoes (with their juice), walnuts, red lentils, brown lentils, bulgur, shallot, chipotle chile, adobo sauce, garlic, chili powder, smoked paprika, and cumin in a **5-, 6-, 8-, or 10-quart Instant Pot.** Lock the lid on the cooker.

2.

	Set pot for	Set level to	Valve must be	Set time for	If needed, press
For Max pots only	PRESSURE COOK	MAX	—	12 minutes with the KEEP WARM setting off	START
For all other pots	PRESSURE COOK or MANUAL	HIGH	Closed	15 minutes with the KEEP WARM setting off	START
For the slow-cook function	SLOW COOK	HIGH	Open	3 hours with the KEEP WARM setting off	START

3. When the pot has finished cooking under pressure, turn it off and let the pressure **return to normal naturally for 10 minutes.** Then use the **quick-release method** to remove the pot's residual pressure. Whichever cooking method you've used, unlatch the lid and open the cooker.

4.

	Press	Set it for	Set time for	If needed, press
In all models	SAUTÉ	MEDIUM, NORMAL, or CUSTOM 300°F	5 minutes	START

5. As the liquid comes to a simmer, stir in the pumpkin puree. Cook, stirring *constantly,* for 1 minute. Turn off the heat and use hot pads or silicone baking mitts to transfer the (hot!) insert to a wire rack. Cool for 5 minutes, stirring several times, to blend the flavors. Serve warm.

No-Brainer Burrito Dinner

6 ingredients	
6 SERVINGS	
METHOD: stacks	

SPECIAL EQUIPMENT: 7½-inch-round stackable insert pans	
PRESSURE: high	

TIME UNDER PRESSURE: 20 minutes	
RELEASE: natural	

TOTAL TIME WITH PRESSURE: about 50 minutes	
VEGETARIAN	

1½ cups water

Six 4½-inch-long frozen bean and cheese burritos, thawed

One 16-ounce jar salsa verde or green enchilada sauce (2 cups)

4 ounces American mild cheddar cheese, shredded (1 cup)

One 14- to 15-ounce can refried beans (vegetarian, if necessary)

2 cups fresh corn kernels or thawed frozen kernels

Other Pots

- For a **3-quart Instant Pot,** you *must* use stackable containers that fit this smaller pot and you *must* halve almost all of the ingredient amounts *except* you *must* use 1 cup water in the insert.

- For a **5-quart Instant Pot,** you *must* use 7-inch stackable containers specifically made to fit this slightly smaller pot. (FYI, some standard stacking containers are too tall to work in these pots.)

- For a **10-quart Instant Pot,** you *must* increase the amount of water in the insert to 2½ cups while otherwise completing the recipe as stated.

Beyond

- Substitute any purchased burrito you like, as long as the size remains the same.

- Substitute red salsa or even red enchilada sauce for the salsa verde.

This super-easy recipe uses frozen burritos, jarred sauce, and canned refried beans in stacks (or stackable insert pans) to make a kid-friendly Tex-Mex meal in no time. To get the right-size burritos, an 8-pack should weigh 32 ounces (or 2 pounds).

1. Pour the water into the insert set in a **6- or 8-quart Instant Pot.** If your two-stack containers do not include feet to lift them out of the water, set a pressure-safe rack or trivet inside the pot. (For more information on working with stacks, see page 16 of the introduction.)

2. Arranging the burritos on their thinner sides, like envelopes in a box, put the burritos in one layer on the bottom layer of the stack set. Pour the salsa verde or green enchilada sauce over them and sprinkle the cheese evenly over the top. Set this layer in the pot (on the rack, if necessary).

3. Put the refried beans in the top layer of the stack set, then push the beans to the side and fill in the space with the corn. Cover tightly and set the top layer on the bottom layer. Lock the lid on the pot.

4.

	Set pot for	Set level to	Valve must be	Set time for	If needed, press
For *all* pots	PRESSURE COOK or MANUAL	HIGH	Closed	20 minutes with the KEEP WARM setting off	START

5. When the pot has finished cooking, turn it off and let the pressure **return to normal naturally,** about 20 minutes. Unlatch the lid and open the cooker. Use hot pads or silicone baking mitts to transfer the (hot!) stack set to a nearby cutting board. Uncover and unstack the layers, then cool for a few minutes before serving.

Brown Rice Burritos

16 ingredients

8 LARGE BURRITOS

METHOD: standard

SPECIAL EQUIPMENT: none

PRESSURE: max or high

TIME UNDER PRESSURE: 20 or 24 minutes

RELEASE: modified quick

TOTAL TIME WITH PRESSURE: about 45 minutes

VEGAN

---

2 cups vegetable broth

One 15-ounce can pinto beans, drained and rinsed (1¾ cups)

1½ cups jarred red salsa

1½ cups fresh corn kernels or thawed frozen kernels

1½ cups raw *medium*-grain *brown* rice, such as *brown* Arborio

1 large yellow or white onion, chopped (1½ cups)

1 large green bell pepper, stemmed, cored, and chopped (1 cup)

3 medium garlic cloves, minced (1 tablespoon)

2 teaspoons standard chili powder

1 teaspoon ground cumin

1 teaspoon mild smoked paprika

1 teaspoon table salt

1 cup loosely packed chopped baby spinach or baby kale leaves (1 ounce)

8 large flour tortillas, preferably whole wheat tortillas

4 ripe medium avocados, peeled, pitted, and thinly sliced

Jarred (hot or "tamed") pickled jalapeño rings, to taste

Admittedly, this recipe really makes just a burrito filling of corn, beans, salsa, and rice. You have to then fill the tortillas with that mixture as well as a few condiments. But the recipe does make a lot of that filling! (Who can eat just one burrito?) If you have a small household or just don't want to carb out in one sitting, the filling freezes exceptionally well. Store it in individual 1-cup containers so that you can heat one portion in the microwave and make a vegan burrito any time you want.

1. Stir the broth, beans, salsa, corn, brown rice, onion, bell pepper, garlic, chili powder, cumin, smoked paprika, and salt in a **5-, 6-, or 8-quart Instant Pot.** Lock the lid on the pot.

2.

	Set pot for	Set level to	Valve must be	Set time for	If needed, press
For Max pots only	PRESSURE COOK	MAX	—	20 minutes with the KEEP WARM setting off	START
For all other pots	PRESSURE COOK or MANUAL	HIGH	Closed	24 minutes with the KEEP WARM setting off	START

3. When the pot has finished cooking, use the **quick-release method** to bring the pressure back to normal but **do not open the cooker.** Set aside for 10 minutes, then unlatch the lid and open the cooker.

4. Stir in the baby spinach or kale. Set the lid askew over the pot and set it aside for 5 minutes to blend the flavors and wilt the greens.

5. To serve, spread the rice mixture down the center of the tortillas, top with the avocado slices and pickled jalapeño, and roll up the burritos.

Other Pots

- For a 3-quart Instant Pot, you *must* halve all of the ingredient amounts.
- For an 8-quart Instant Pot, you *can* increase all of the ingredient amounts by 50 percent.
- For a 10-quart Instant Pot, you *must* double all of the ingredient amounts.

Beyond

- If you've used a 6- or 8-quart Instant Pot, you can turn these burritos into vegan chimichangas. Complete the recipe as stated, then pour out the water in the insert and wipe it clean. Return it to the pot and set the air-frying basket in the insert. Generously coat the rolled-up burritos with nonstick spray, then set two in the basket. Set the Instant Pot Air Fryer Lid on top and air-fry at 400°F for about 10 minutes, or until browned and crisp. Repeat with the remaining burritos.

Black Bean Tortilla Casserole

8 ingredients	**SPECIAL EQUIPMENT:** a 2-quart, 7-inch-round, high-sided, pressure-safe baking or soufflé dish and a pressure-safe rack or trivet	**PRESSURE:** max or high
4 SERVINGS		**TIME UNDER PRESSURE:** 12 or 15 minutes
METHOD: pot-in-pot		**RELEASE:** modified natural

TOTAL TIME WITH PRESSURE: about 45 minutes

VEGETARIAN

1½ cups water

Nonstick spray

One 15-ounce can black beans, drained and rinsed (1¾ cups)

One 10-ounce can hot or mild red enchilada sauce (1 cup plus 2 tablespoons)

One 4½-ounce can hot or mild diced green chiles (½ cup)

½ cup fresh corn kernels, drained canned kernels, or thawed frozen kernels

Five 6-inch flour tortillas

6 ounces American mild cheddar or Monterey Jack cheese, shredded (1½ cups)—or an equal combination of the two

Other Pots

- For a 3-quart Instant Pot, you *must* halve almost all of the ingredient amounts *except* you *must* use 1 cup water in the insert. You *must* also use a 1-quart, 6-inch-round, high-sided, pressure-safe baking or soufflé dish.

- For a 10-quart Instant Pot, you *must* increase the amount of water in the insert to 2½ cups while otherwise completing the recipe as stated.

Beyond

- For more flavor, add up to 1 teaspoon ground cumin and/or 1 teaspoon dried oregano to the bean mixture.

This dish is something like a sloppy, overstuffed burrito turned into a casserole, no wrapping or folding necessary. In other words, it's a newfangled version of Tex-Mex comfort food. It's also very easy, thanks to canned beans, enchilada sauce, and chiles. Control the heat by using mild or hot enchilada sauce as well as hot or mild canned green chiles.

1. Pour the water into the insert set in a **5-, 6-, or 8-quart Instant Pot.** Put a pressure-safe rack or trivet in the insert.

2. Spray the inside of a 2-quart, 7-inch-round, high-sided, pressure-safe baking or soufflé dish with nonstick spray. Stir the black beans, enchilada sauce, green chiles, and corn in a medium bowl until uniform.

3. Place one tortilla in the bottom of the prepared baking dish. Spread about ½ cup of the bean mixture over the tortilla, then sprinkle a scant ⅓ cup of the cheese on top. Repeat this layering (tortilla, then bean mixture, then cheese) four times, ending with the cheese at the top of the fifth layer. The layers should be flat and even so the casserole doesn't mound in the middle. Cover the baking dish with aluminum foil. Set it on the rack and lock the lid on the pot.

4.

	Set pot for	Set level to	Valve must be	Set time for	If needed, press
For Max pots only	PRESSURE COOK	MAX	—	12 minutes with the KEEP WARM setting off	START
For all other pots	PRESSURE COOK or MANUAL	HIGH	Closed	15 minutes with the KEEP WARM setting off	START

5. When the pot has finished cooking, turn it off and let its pressure **return to normal naturally for 10 minutes.** Then use the **quick-release method** to get rid of any residual pressure in the pot. Unlatch the lid and open the cooker. Use hot pads or silicone baking mitts to transfer the (hot!) baking dish to a nearby wire rack. Uncover and cool for 5 minutes before dishing up by the big spoonful.

Quinoa and Cauliflower Bowls

16 ingredients

6 SERVINGS

METHOD:
pot-in-pot

SPECIAL EQUIPMENT:
a 2-quart, 7-inch-round, high-sided, pressure-safe baking or soufflé dish and a pressure-safe rack or trivet

PRESSURE:
high

TIME UNDER PRESSURE:
4 minutes

RELEASE:
natural

TOTAL TIME WITH PRESSURE:
about 30 minutes

VEGAN

CAN BE GLUTEN-FREE

1½ cups water

3 cups vegetable broth

1 cup raw white (or beige) quinoa, rinsed (see the headnote for Quinoa Porridge on page 27 for more information)

2 medium garlic cloves, minced (2 teaspoons)

2 teaspoons minced peeled fresh ginger

1 teaspoon ground coriander

1 teaspoon ground cumin

½ teaspoon ground cinnamon

½ teaspoon table salt

½ teaspoon ground black pepper

1 pound plain extra-firm tofu (gluten-free, if necessary), drained and cut into 1-inch cubes

2 cups riced cauliflower (8 ounces)

1 medium red bell pepper, stemmed, cored, and chopped (1 cup)

½ cup chopped pecan pieces

3 tablespoons olive oil

2 tablespoons red wine vinegar

Here's the perfect healthy bowl for lunch or dinner. The quinoa is cooked with tons of aromatics. It's also done PIP (pot-in-pot), so the grains stay fluffy, light, and super tasty. While still hot, the quinoa is then tossed with vegetables, tofu, and a simple oil-and-vinegar dressing, thereby warming the vegetables for a softer, mellow flavor and letting those warm ingredients absorb more of the dressing. It's a great grab-and-go lunch. Save it back in smaller, sealed containers in the fridge for up to 3 days. The leftovers may need a little additional olive oil and vinegar, given that the quinoa will continue to absorb the dressing in storage.

1. Pour the water into the insert set in a **5-, 6-, or 8-quart Instant Pot.** Put a pressure-safe rack or trivet in the insert.

2. Mix the broth, quinoa, garlic, ginger, coriander, cumin, cinnamon, salt, and pepper in a 2-quart, 7-inch-round, high-sided, pressure-safe baking or soufflé dish. Do not cover. Set the dish on the rack and lock the lid on the pot.

3.

	Set pot for	Set level to	Valve must be	Set time for	If needed, press
For *all* pots	PRESSURE COOK or MANUAL	HIGH	Closed	4 minutes with the KEEP WARM setting off	START

4. When the pot has finished cooking, turn it off and let the pressure **return to normal naturally,** about 15 minutes. Unlatch the lid and open the cooker.

5. Put the tofu, riced cauliflower, bell pepper, pecans, oil, and vinegar in a large heat-safe serving bowl. Use hot pads or silicone baking mitts to pick up the (hot!) baking dish in the pot. Dump and scrape the quinoa mixture on top of the ingredients in the bowl. Toss very gently to combine but keep the tofu intact. Set aside for 5 minutes to blend the flavors. Toss very gently again and serve warm in bowls.

Other Pots

- For a 3-quart Instant Pot, you *must* halve almost all of the ingredient amounts except you *must* use 1 cup water in the insert. You *must* also use a 1-quart, 6-inch-round, high-sided, pressure-safe baking or soufflé dish.

- For a 10-quart Instant Pot, you *must* increase the amount of water to 2½ cups in the insert while otherwise completing the recipe as stated.

Beyond

- Garnish the servings with chopped tomatoes, chopped cucumbers, sprouts of any sort, and/or pico de gallo (see the **Beyond** for the Not-Really-Chili's Chicken Enchilada Soup on page 86 for a recipe to make your own).

Curry-Spiced *Butter* Squash

15 ingredients	**SPECIAL EQUIPMENT:** none	**TIME UNDER PRESSURE:** 6 minutes
6 SERVINGS		
METHOD: standard	**PRESSURE:** low	**RELEASE:** natural

TOTAL TIME WITH PRESSURE: about 30 minutes

VEGETARIAN

CAN BE GLUTEN-FREE

3 tablespoons butter

1 medium yellow or white onion, chopped (1 cup)

3 medium garlic cloves, minced (1 tablespoon)

1 tablespoon minced peeled fresh ginger

1 teaspoon ground cumin

1 teaspoon ground dried turmeric

½ teaspoon ground cinnamon

½ teaspoon table salt

¼ teaspoon ground dried cayenne

One 14-ounce can diced tomatoes *packed in juice* (1¾ cups)

1 cup vegetable broth

½ cup heavy cream

4 cups peeled, seeded, and 2-inch-cubed butternut squash (2 pounds)

1 pound plain extra-firm tofu (gluten-free, if necessary), drained and cut into 1-inch cubes

Stemmed and finely chopped fresh cilantro leaves, for garnishing

Other Pots

- For a 3-quart Instant Pot, you *must* halve almost all of the ingredient amounts *except* you *must* use ¾ cup broth.
- For an 8-quart Instant Pot, you *must* increase all of the ingredient amounts by 50 percent.
- For a 10-quart Instant Pot, you *must* double all of the ingredient amounts.

Butter Chicken is an Instant Pot rage. (Find our version in the first *Instant Pot Bible.*) But it's high time for a Butter Chicken vegetarian makeover. Butternut squash does the trick! It's sweet and flavorful, a good match to the curry blend. We've even added tofu for more protein (but see the **Beyond** section if you're a tofuphobe).

1.

	Press	Set it for	Set time for	If needed, press
In all models	SAUTÉ	MEDIUM, NORMAL, or CUSTOM 300°F	10 minutes	START

2. As the pot heats, melt the butter in the insert set in a **5- or 6-quart Instant Pot.** Add the onion and cook, stirring often, until softened, about 3 minutes. Stir in the garlic, ginger, cumin, turmeric, cinnamon, salt, and cayenne until fragrant, just a few seconds.

3. Stir in the tomatoes with their juice and the broth; scrape up any browned bits on the pot's bottom. (There should be almost none.) Stir in the cream, then add the squash and stir well to combine.

4. Turn off the heat. Lay the tofu cubes evenly across the top of the other ingredients without stirring. Lock the lid onto the cooker.

5.

	Set pot for	Set level to	Valve must be	Set time for	If needed, press
For *all* pots	PRESSURE COOK or MANUAL	LOW	Closed	6 minutes with the KEEP WARM setting off	START

6. When the pot has finished cooking, turn it off and let the pressure **return to normal naturally,** about 15 minutes. Unlatch the lid and open the cooker. Stir gently, preferably with a rubber spatula, to keep from breaking up the tofu. Spoon the hot mixture into bowls and garnish with cilantro.

Beyond

- If you can't stand tofu, substitute 1 pound medium parsnips, peeled and cut into 1-inch pieces. Don't use large, fat parsnips—or if those are the only sort you can find, cut the large ends into ½-inch-thick rounds, then cut these rounds into quarters.

Sweet Potato and Plantain Stew

15 ingredients

4–6 SERVINGS

METHOD: standard

SPECIAL EQUIPMENT: none

PRESSURE: max or high

TIME UNDER PRESSURE: 7 or 10 minutes

RELEASE: natural

TOTAL TIME WITH PRESSURE: about 1 hour 15 minutes

VEGAN

GLUTEN-FREE

---

2 tablespoons vegetable, canola, or other neutral-flavored oil

1 large red onion, halved and sliced into thin half-moons

1 small fresh jalapeño chile, stemmed, cored (seeded, if desired), and thinly sliced

3 medium garlic cloves, minced (1 tablespoon)

1 tablespoon minced peeled fresh ginger

1 tablespoon packed, stemmed, fresh thyme leaves

1 teaspoon ground cumin

1 teaspoon mild smoked paprika

1 teaspoon table salt

2 cups vegetable broth

One 28-ounce can diced tomatoes *packed in juice* (3½ cups)

One 15-ounce can kidney beans, drained and rinsed (1¾ cups)

1 large sweet potato (about 1 pound), peeled and cut into 1-inch cubes

2 medium green bell peppers, stemmed, cored, and chopped (2 cups)

2 yellow plantains, peeled and sliced into 1-inch sections

This one's pure comfort, even if you're a carnivore. It's a rich, thick stew, stocked with vegetables—a hearty meal after a day of yardwork. Look for plantains that are yellow without too many brown spots. Green plantains will be too astringent; brown (or darker) ones will be too soft (they break down to mush). Check out the **Beyond** section for a list of garnishes.

1.

	Press	Set it for	Set time for	If needed, press
In all models	SAUTÉ	MEDIUM, NORMAL, or CUSTOM 300°F	10 minutes	START

2. As the pot heats, warm the oil in the insert set in a **5-, 6-, or 8-quart Instant Pot.** Add the onion and cook, stirring often, until softened, about 4 minutes. Stir in the jalapeño, garlic, and ginger until aromatic, about 20 seconds.

3. Stir in the thyme, cumin, smoked paprika, and salt until well combined. Pour in the broth and scrape up any browned bits on the pot's bottom. Stir in the tomatoes with their juice, the kidney beans, sweet potato, bell peppers, and plantains. Turn off the heat and lock the lid onto the cooker.

4.

	Set pot for	Set level to	Valve must be	Set time for	If needed, press
For Max pots only	PRESSURE COOK	MAX	—	7 minutes with the KEEP WARM setting off	START
For all other pots	PRESSURE COOK or MANUAL	HIGH	Closed	10 minutes with the KEEP WARM setting off	START

5. When the pot has finished cooking, turn it off and let the pressure **return to normal naturally,** about 25 minutes. Unlatch the lid and open the cooker. Stir well, then set aside uncovered for 2 to 3 minutes to blend the flavors.

Other Pots

- For a 3-quart Instant Pot, you *must* halve all of the ingredient amounts.

- For an 8-quart Instant Pot, you *can* increase all of the ingredient amounts by 50 percent.

- For a 10-quart Instant Pot, you *must* increase all of the ingredient amounts by 50 percent or you *can* even double the amounts.

Beyond

- Garnish the stew with coconut milk yogurt (to keep it vegan).

- And/or chopped, salted, roasted peanuts.

- And/or a drizzle of a hot red pepper sauce, such as Sriracha.

- And/or a smattering of minced chives.

Vegan Cassoulet

14 ingredients	**SPECIAL EQUIPMENT:** none
4–6 SERVINGS	**PRESSURE:** max or high
METHOD: fast/slow	

TIME UNDER PRESSURE: 10 or 12 minutes	**TOTAL TIME WITH PRESSURE:** about 30 minutes
RELEASE: quick	**TOTAL TIME WITH SLOW COOKING:** about 3 hours 15 minutes

VEGAN

GLUTEN-FREE

One 28-ounce can diced tomatoes *packed in juice* (3½ cups)

Two 15-ounce cans great northern or cannellini beans, drained and rinsed (3½ cups)

1 cup vegetable broth

2 medium celery stalks, thinly sliced (⅔ cup)

1 small red onion, chopped (½ cup)

1 large carrot, peeled, halved lengthwise, and thinly sliced (½ cup)

1 large parsnip, peeled, halved lengthwise, and thinly sliced (⅓ cup)

2 medium garlic cloves, minced (2 teaspoons)

1 tablespoon molasses

1½ teaspoons dried rosemary

1½ teaspoons dried thyme

1½ teaspoons fennel seeds

1 teaspoon table salt

½ teaspoon red pepper flakes

Other Pots

- For a 3-quart Instant Pot, you *must* halve all of the ingredient amounts.

- For an 8-quart Instant Pot, you *can* increase all of the ingredient amounts by 50 percent.

- For a 10-quart Instant Pot, you *must* increase all of the ingredient amounts by 50 percent or you *can* even double the amounts.

Beyond

- Add 1 medium or large fennel bulb, trimmed and chopped, along with the carrot and parsnip.

- Serve the stew over big croutons. (Make sure the bread is vegan, if a concern.) To make your own, see page 65.

In essence, this vegan recipe includes all of the classic ingredients of a big pot of the French favorite, cassoulet—*except*, of course, it ups the vegetables and beans while skipping the duck and pork. We also make up for the meat by 1) adding a little molasses for a complex sweetness, and 2) increasing the spice blend's game in the dish. This vegan entrée is about as easy as they come: Dump it all in, lock the lid on the pot, and go!

1. Stir everything in a **5-, 6-, or 8-quart Instant Pot**. (Do not drain those tomatoes—the dish needs the juice.) Lock the lid onto the cooker.

2.

	Set pot for	Set level to	Valve must be	Set time for	If needed, press
For Max pots only	PRESSURE COOK	MAX	—	10 minutes with the KEEP WARM setting off	START
For all other pots	PRESSURE COOK or MANUAL	HIGH	Closed	12 minutes with the KEEP WARM setting off	START
For the slow-cook function	SLOW COOK	HIGH	Open	3 hours with the KEEP WARM setting off	START

3. When the pot has finished cooking under pressure, use the **quick-release method** to bring the pressure back to normal. Whichever cooking method you've used, unlatch the lid and open the cooker. Stir well, then set the lid askew over the pot and set it aside for 5 minutes to blend the flavors before serving warm.

Vegan Pot Roast

14 ingredients	
4–6 SERVINGS	
METHOD: standard	
SPECIAL EQUIPMENT: none	
PRESSURE: max or high	
TIME UNDER PRESSURE: 6 or 8 minutes	
RELEASE: quick	
TOTAL TIME WITH PRESSURE: about 35 minutes	
VEGAN	
CAN BE GLUTEN-FREE	

2 tablespoons olive oil

1½ cups frozen pearl onions (8 ounces— no need to thaw)

2 pounds large *baby* bella mushrooms, each about 1½ inches across the cap, halved through the caps and stems

Up to 3 medium garlic cloves, minced (1 tablespoon)

½ cup dry but fruit-forward red wine, such as Zinfandel; or tomato juice (do not use V8)

3 cups vegetable broth

2 tablespoons *vegan* Worcestershire sauce (gluten-free, if necessary), such as Annie's organic Worcestershire sauce

4 large carrots, peeled and cut into 1-inch sections

4 medium parsnips, peeled and cut into 1-inch sections

4 fresh multi-stemmed thyme sprigs

½ teaspoon ground black pepper

2 tablespoons cornstarch

2 tablespoons water

3 tablespoons tomato paste

We use baby bella mushrooms as a substitute for the beef in this hearty winter warmer that includes lots of root vegetables, a splash of red wine, and a little tomato paste to thicken it at the end. Don't substitute portobello caps for the baby bellas. The portobellos will discolor the stew with their black gills. Instead, handpick brown baby bella mushrooms from the bin at the supermarket, looking for ones that are the right size (about 1½ inches across the caps) to provide the best texture in the final dish.

One note: The timings here will give you rather chewy carrots and parsnips, pieces that may need a knife and a fork at the table. For softer vegetables, add 3 minutes to either the MAX or the HIGH pressure cooking time.

1.

	Press	Set it for	Set time for	If needed, press
In all models	SAUTÉ	MEDIUM, NORMAL, or CUSTOM 300°F	15 minutes	START

2. As the pot heats, warm the oil in the insert set in a **5-, 6-, or 8-quart Instant Pot.** Add the pearl onions and cook, stirring often, until they are lightly browned in places, about 5 minutes if they were frozen (about 3 minutes if they were thawed).

3. Add the mushrooms and garlic. Cook, stirring more often, until the mushrooms give off their liquid and it evaporates to a glaze, about 5 minutes. Pour in the wine and scrape up all the browned bits off the pot's bottom.

4. Stir in the broth and vegan Worcestershire sauce until well combined. Turn off the heat and stir in the carrots, parsnips, thyme, and pepper. Lock the lid onto the cooker.

5.

	Set pot for	Set level to	Valve must be	Set time for	If needed, press
For Max pots only	PRESSURE COOK	MAX	—	6 minutes with the KEEP WARM setting off	START
For all other pots	PRESSURE COOK or MANUAL	HIGH	Closed	8 minutes with the KEEP WARM setting off	START

6. When the pot has finished cooking, use the **quick-release method** to bring the pressure back to normal. Unlatch the lid and open the cooker. Whisk the cornstarch and water in a small bowl until smooth.

7.

	Press	Set it for	Set time for	If needed, press
In all models	SAUTÉ	MEDIUM, NORMAL, or CUSTOM 300°F	5 minutes	START

8. As the liquid comes to a simmer, stir in the cornstarch slurry and the tomato paste. Cook, stirring constantly, until the tomato paste has dissolved and the sauce has somewhat thickened, less than 1 minute. Turn off the heat and use hot pads or silicone baking mitts to transfer the (hot!) insert to a nearby wire rack (to stop the cooking). Cool for 2 to 3 minutes and serve warm.

Other Pots

- For a **3-quart Instant Pot**, you *must* halve all of the ingredient amounts.
- For an **8-quart Instant Pot**, you *can* increase all of the ingredient amounts by 50 percent.
- For a **10-quart Instant Pot**, you *must* increase all of the ingredient amounts by 50 percent or you *can* even double the amounts.

Beyond

- Serve this vegan stew over mashed potatoes made with vegetable broth, a little Dijon mustard, and perhaps some plain almond yogurt for richness.
- Or serve over cooked and drained noodles that you've tossed with toasted walnut or pecan oil.
- Or serve the stew in split-open baked potatoes.

Desserts

If life's so short that you're supposed to eat sweets first, how come a chapter on desserts always falls near the end of a cookbook? We can't figure it out, but here are forty-eight recipes for the carpe diem part of the meal. We start with fondue and lemon curd, move to fruit desserts, work through traditional cakes, and finish up with eighteen (!) cake and cake bite recipes that are all shortcuts in some way.

Almost all of those cakes are made in either a 6-inch pressure-safe Bundt pan or a 7-inch springform pan. Don't confuse the two. And make sure that you carefully grease the insides of the pans.

Most of the doctored-mix batters are made with 2 cups of cake mix, about half of a 15¼-ounce box of standard cake mix. But be careful: Cake mixes are sold in many different sizes and varieties. Do not use a sugar-free, gluten-free, or pudding cake mix unless a recipe calls for such. And one more note: Not all cake mixes are vegan or even vegetarian. Check the ingredient label if this matters.

Most of the time, we stick with baking or nonstick spray to coat the inside of the pans. Of course, you can do the job old-school—that is, butter the inside of the pan and add some all-purpose flour, tilt the pan this way and that to get the flour into every inch, then tap out the excess flour over the garbage.

Unlike many ingredients in earlier parts of this book, those here must often be at room temperature before you can start "baking" in the pot. Believe it or not, this fussy, almost clichéd culinary advice is even more important now than when you bake in an oven. Inside the pot, the pressure works to puff up batters quickly, almost immediately, long before they would in an oven. If the cream cheese or the eggs are not at room temperature, they will impede that rise, resulting in a fallen cake or one that's undercooked in spots. To bring eggs to room temperature, leave them on the counter for 20 to 30 minutes or submerge

them in their shells in a bowl of lukewarm tap water for 10 minutes. Leave cream cheese on the counter for up to 8 hours. However, because of safety issues and the popularity of raw or low-pasteurized milk among Instant Pot users, all of these recipes were tested with *cold* milk or cream.

Pay close attention to the visual cues. Batters should be thick *or* grainy, depending on the structure of the cake. Beaten eggs should be lightly mixed, smooth, *or* fluffy, depending on how light the crumb or how dense the curd will be.

Truth is, pressure-cooked cakes and other desserts don't last long because the moisture slowly falls out of suspension and flattens a cake's crumb or loosens a pudding's set. With the exception of the curds and cheesecakes, every dessert here will be best the day you make it.

Finally, two niggles. In some cakes, we ask you to lay a paper towel over the pan to protect the batter from drips off the lid. Depending on the brand of paper towels you buy, one sheet may not do the job. The paper towel needs to drape over the sides. Do *not* seal it to the pan.

And two, you'll note that we don't cover cheesecakes. Doing so alters the pressure currents and results in weird, wiggly tops. Better to let the thing set properly, then blot off a few drips when you open the cooker. Use the corner of a paper towel. Don't go nuts. Just be careful. Because everyone wants dessert first. They just want it to look right.

Chocolate Fondue

4 ingredients	
6 SERVINGS	
METHOD: pot-in-pot	

SPECIAL EQUIPMENT:
a 1-quart, 6-inch-round, high-sided, pressure-safe baking or soufflé dish and a pressure-safe rack or trivet

PRESSURE:
high

TIME UNDER PRESSURE:
less than 1 minute

RELEASE:
modified natural

TOTAL TIME WITH PRESSURE:
about 15 minutes

VEGETARIAN

CAN BE GLUTEN-FREE

1½ cups water

8 ounces 60 percent or up to 75 percent bittersweet or dark chocolate, chopped

1 cup half-and-half or light cream

2 tablespoons hazelnut-flavored liqueur, such as Frangelico; or a nonalcoholic hazelnut-flavored syrup (gluten-free, if necessary)

Any self-respecting book of next generation recipes better include one for fondue since the IP makes it so easy! And here's the truth of the matter: A better chocolate fondue is made with better chocolate, which lists the proportion of cocoa solids *and* cocoa butter to sugar on the package. Higher numbers indicate more bitter, sophisticated chocolate, prized by those in the know. Our personal favorite for fondue is 72 percent.

1. Pour the water into the insert set in a **5-, 6-, or 8-quart Instant Pot.** Set a pressure-safe rack or trivet in the insert.

2. Mix the chocolate, half-and-half, and liqueur in a 1-quart, 6-inch-round, high-sided, pressure-safe baking or soufflé dish. Do not cover. Set the dish on the rack and lock the lid on the pot.

3.

	Set pot for	Set level to	Valve must be	Set time for	If needed, press
For *all* pots	PRESSURE COOK or MANUAL	HIGH	Closed	1 minute with the KEEP WARM setting off	START

4. *The moment the machine reaches high pressure, beyond the pin's popping up but actually the pot's switching from "on" to "1" to count down,* turn the pot off and let it **return to normal pressure naturally for 1 minute.** Then use the **quick-release method** to get rid of the pot's residual pressure. Unlatch the lid and open the cooker. Whisk the chocolate mixture until smooth. Either use hot pads or silicone baking mitts to transfer the (hot!) dish to a nearby wire rack or a serving trivet. Serve hot.

Other Pots

- For a 3-quart Instant Pot, you *must* reduce the amount of water in the insert to 1 cup while otherwise completing the recipe as stated.

- For a 10-quart Instant Pot, you *must* increase the amount of water in the insert to 2½ cups while otherwise completing the recipe as stated.

Beyond

- Use fondue forks or bamboo skewers to dip marshmallows, hulled strawberries, or peeled and sliced bananas into the chocolate fondue.

- Or dip in pretzels, pretzel rods, thick-cut potato chips, sugar cookies, or graham crackers.

Lemon Curd

6 or 7 ingredients

6 SERVINGS

METHOD:
pot-in-pot

SPECIAL
EQUIPMENT:
a 2-quart, 7-inch-round, high-sided, pressure-safe baking or soufflé dish and a pressure-safe rack or trivet

PRESSURE:
max or high

TIME UNDER
PRESSURE:
4 or 5 minutes

RELEASE:
modified natural

TOTAL TIME WITH
PRESSURE:
about 30 minutes

VEGETARIAN

GLUTEN-FREE

1½ cups water

1 cup granulated white sugar

3 large eggs *plus* 3 large egg yolks, *at room temperature*

1 tablespoon finely grated lemon zest (optional)

½ cup lemon juice, *at room temperature*

¼ teaspoon table salt

¾ stick (6 tablespoons) butter, melted and cooled *to room temperature*

There are many recipes for lemon curd in the Instant Pot. They garner the same complaint: They look curdled. Or *are* curdled. The problem is that the delicate curd cannot be cooked directly against the hot bottom of the pot. Once again, the PIP (pot-in-pot) method for the win!

One important note: The curd ingredients *must* be at room temperature before cooking. If you keep bottled lemon juice (or fresh lemons) in the fridge, the juice must be at room temperature, not cool to the touch. The same goes for the eggs: You can either submerge six eggs in room-temperature water for 10 minutes or leave them on the counter for 20 or 30 minutes. When you make this recipe, you'll have three egg whites left over to add to omelets for dinner.

1. Pour the water into the insert set in a **5-, 6-, or 8-quart Instant Pot.** Put a pressure-safe rack or trivet in the insert.

2. Whisk the sugar, eggs, egg yolks, lemon zest (if using), lemon juice, and salt in a 2-quart, 7-inch-round, high-sided, pressure-safe baking or soufflé dish until smooth. Whisk in the butter until uniform. Do not cover the baking dish. Set it on the rack and lock the lid on the pot.

3.

	Set pot for	Set level to	Valve must be	Set time for	If needed, press
For Max pots only	PRESSURE COOK	MAX	—	4 minutes with the KEEP WARM setting off	START
For all other pots	PRESSURE COOK or MANUAL	HIGH	Closed	5 minutes with the KEEP WARM setting off	START

4. When the pot has finished cooking, turn it off and let the pressure **return to normal naturally for 10 minutes.** Then use the **quick-release method** to get rid of the pot's residual pressure. Unlatch the lid and open the cooker. Whisk the curd in the baking dish until smooth, then use hot pads or silicone baking mitts to transfer the (hot!) dish to a nearby wire rack. Cool for 5 minutes or to room temperature before serving. To store, cover the room-temperature curd with plastic wrap and refrigerate for up to 1 week.

Other Pots

- These ingredient ratios do not work well for a 3-quart Instant Pot.
- For a 10-quart Instant Pot, you *must* increase the amount of water in the insert to 2½ cups while otherwise completing the recipe as stated.

Beyond

- Spoon the lemon curd over vanilla ice cream.
- Or scoop it up with shortbread or sugar cookies.
- Or put it over raspberries and blackberries (with sweetened whipped cream, too).

See photo in insert.

Coconut Lime Curd

7 ingredients

6 SERVINGS

METHOD:
pot-in-pot

SPECIAL EQUIPMENT:
a 2-quart, 7-inch-round, high-sided, pressure-safe baking or soufflé dish and a pressure-safe rack or trivet

PRESSURE:
max or high

TIME UNDER PRESSURE:
4 or 5 minutes

RELEASE:
modified natural

TOTAL TIME WITH PRESSURE:
about 30 minutes

VEGAN

GLUTEN-FREE

1½ cups water

One 13½-ounce can full-fat coconut milk (do not use low-fat or "lite" coconut milk)

3 tablespoons coconut oil

¾ cup plus 2 tablespoons granulated white sugar

½ cup lime juice, *at room temperature*

2 large eggs *plus* 3 large egg yolks, *at room temperature*

¼ teaspoon table salt

Other Pots

- These ingredient ratios do not work well for a 3-quart Instant Pot.

- For a 10-quart Instant Pot, you *must* increase the amount of water in the insert to 2½ cups while otherwise completing the recipe as stated.

Beyond

- This curd is best as a bed for fresh raspberries, dusted with a little confectioners' sugar or topped with a dollop of sweetened whipped cream (to make your own, see the Beyond for Chocolate Pots de Crème on page 395).

- While the curd is warm, spread it into a purchased graham cracker crust, then refrigerate for at least 4 hours or until set. Top with a dairy-free whipped topping (such as Cool Whip) or with sweetened whipped cream (if you don't mind the dairy) before slicing.

If you want a dairy-free curd, you've come to the right recipe—which is admittedly a tad unusual because it calls for a whole can of coconut milk without actually using it all. Instead, you'll use *only* the thick cream at the top of the can. That cream may even be solid. Do not shake the can before opening it to preserve the cream. The remainder of the coconut milk can be stored in a covered container in the fridge for 1 week or in the freezer for up to 1 year to be used in stews and braises.

As with the recipe for Lemon Curd (page 387), the ingredients must be at room temperature for the curd to set properly.

1. Pour the water into the insert set in a **5-, 6-, or 8-quart Instant Pot.** Put a pressure-safe rack or trivet in the insert.

2. Scoop ¼ cup of the coconut cream off the top of a can of coconut milk. The cream may be solid and you may need to use a bit of the coconut milk underneath to make up the volume. Put the coconut cream in a large microwave-safe bowl with the coconut oil. Microwave on HIGH in 10-second bursts, stirring after each, until the fat has melted. Stir until smooth, then cool for 5 minutes.

3. Whisk the sugar and lime juice into the coconut mixture until the sugar dissolves. Whisk in the eggs, egg yolks, and salt until very smooth, no bits of floating egg white. Pour this mixture into a 2-quart, 7-inch-round, high-sided, pressure-safe baking or soufflé dish. Do not cover. Set the baking dish on the rack and lock the lid on the pot.

4.

	Set pot for	Set level to	Valve must be	Set time for	If needed, press
For Max pots only	PRESSURE COOK	MAX	—	4 minutes with the KEEP WARM setting off	START
For all other pots	PRESSURE COOK or MANUAL	HIGH	Closed	5 minutes with the KEEP WARM setting off	START

5. When the pot has finished cooking, turn it off and let the pressure **return to normal naturally for 10 minutes.** Then use the **quick-release method** to get rid of the pot's residual pressure. Unlatch the lid and open the cooker. Whisk the curd until smooth, then use hot pads or silicone baking mitts to transfer the (hot!) baking dish to a nearby wire rack. Cool for 5 minutes or to room temperature before serving. To store, cover the room-temperature curd with plastic wrap and refrigerate for up to 1 week.

Not-Really-Cracker-Barrel's Cinnamon Apples

9 ingredients

4–6 SERVINGS

METHOD:
pot-in-pot

SPECIAL EQUIPMENT:
a 2-quart, 7-inch-round, high-sided, pressure-safe baking or soufflé dish and a pressure-safe rack or trivet

TIME UNDER PRESSURE:
max or high

TIME UNDER PRESSURE:
20 or 25 minutes

RELEASE:
quick

TOTAL TIME WITH PRESSURE:
about 50 minutes

VEGETARIAN

GLUTEN-FREE

1½ cups water

2 pounds baking apples, such as Granny Smith, Cortland, or Rome apples, peeled, cored, and *thinly* sliced

½ stick (4 tablespoons or ¼ cup) butter, melted and cooled *for 10 minutes*

3 tablespoons granulated white sugar

2 tablespoons dark brown sugar

1 tablespoon cornstarch

½ teaspoon ground cinnamon

Up to ½ teaspoon grated nutmeg

½ teaspoon table salt

This copycat favorite essentially gives you apple pie filling without the crust. The trick is to slice the apples very thinly, not quite paper-thin but certainly thinner than the wedges you might find already cut at the supermarket. (If you buy those to make this recipe easier, slice each wedge into two or three thinner ones.) The thin slices will partially melt, giving the dessert its smooth texture.

1. Pour the water into the insert set in a **5-, 6-, or 8-quart Instant Pot.** Put a pressure-safe rack or trivet in the insert.

2. Mix the apple slices, melted butter, white sugar, brown sugar, cornstarch, cinnamon, nutmeg, and salt in a large bowl until the apple slices are evenly coated in the sugars, butter, and spices.

3. Pour and pack this mixture into a 2-quart, 7-inch-round, high-sided, pressure-safe baking or soufflé dish. Cover tightly with aluminum foil and set the dish on the rack. Lock the lid onto the cooker.

4.

	Set pot for	Set level to	Valve must be	Set time for	If needed, press
For Max pots only	PRESSURE COOK	MAX	—	20 minutes with the KEEP WARM setting off	START
For all other pots	PRESSURE COOK or MANUAL	HIGH	Closed	25 minutes with the KEEP WARM setting off	START

5. When the pot has finished cooking, use the **quick-release method** to bring the pressure back to normal. Unlatch the lid and open the cooker. Use hot pads or silicone baking mitts to transfer the (hot!) baking dish to a nearby wire rack. Uncover and cool for 5 minutes to serve warm; or cool to room temperature, cover, and store in the refrigerator for up to 1 week.

Other Pots

- For a 3-quart Instant Pot, you *must* halve almost all of the ingredient amounts *except* you *must* use 1 cup water in the insert. You *must* use a 1-quart, 6-inch-round, high-sided, pressure-safe baking or soufflé dish.

- For a 10-quart Instant Pot, you *must* increase the amount of water in the insert to 2½ cups while otherwise completing the recipe as stated.

Beyond

- Spoon these apples over pound cake. (Vanilla ice cream would be a necessity, no?)

- Or layer them with ladyfinger cookies, sweetened whipped cream, and fresh blackberries in a glass serving bowl for an easy trifle.

Spiced Poached Pears

7 ingredients

4 SERVINGS

METHOD:
fast/slow

SPECIAL
EQUIPMENT:
none

PRESSURE:
max or high

TIME UNDER
PRESSURE:
3 or 4 minutes

RELEASE:
natural

TOTAL TIME
WITH PRESSURE:
about 1 hour 15
minutes (includes
cooling)

TOTAL TIME
WITH SLOW
COOKING:
about 3 hours
(includes cooling)

VEGAN

GLUTEN-FREE

3½ cups unsweetened apple cider

2 cups granulated white sugar

1 tablespoon vanilla extract

8 whole cloves

1 small orange

One 3-inch cinnamon stick

4 firm, ripe bosc or Anjou pears,
stemmed, peeled, cored, and halved
from top to bottom (see the headnote
for more information)

Poached pears are a make-ahead dream: a dessert as good cold out of the fridge as warm out of the pot. Make sure the pears are firm, not mushy, certainly with no brown spots—maybe not the best for eating but a little harder and so better able to stand up to the pressure.

To prepare the pears, cut off the stem ends by about ¼ inch to get rid of the woody bits in the flesh. Peel the pears, then cut them in half through their former stem ends. Use a melon baller to scoop out the seeds and their fibrous membranes in the middle of each half. If you don't work quickly, the peeled and cut pears can brown. To stop that, drop the prepared pear halves in a bowl of cool water mixed with the juice of 1 lemon as you prepare the remainder of the pears.

1. Stir the cider, sugar, and vanilla extract in the insert set in a **5-, 6-, or 8-quart Instant Pot** until the sugar dissolves. Push the "stem" ends of the cloves into the orange and drop it into the pot. Add the cinnamon stick, too. Nestle the pear halves into this liquid and lock the lid on the pot.

2.

	Set pot for	Set level to	Valve must be	Set time for	If needed, press
For Max pots only	PRESSURE COOK	MAX	—	3 minutes with the KEEP WARM setting off	START
For all other pots	PRESSURE COOK or MANUAL	HIGH	Closed	4 minutes with the KEEP WARM setting off	START
For the slow-cook function	SLOW COOK	HIGH	Open	2 hours with the KEEP WARM setting off	START

3. When the pot has finished cooking under pressure, turn it off and let the pressure **return to normal naturally,** about 25 minutes. Whichever cooking method you've used, unlatch the pot and open the cooker. Use a slotted spoon to transfer the pear halves to a heat-safe, glass, or other non-reactive storage bowl (do not use plastic). Remove and discard the orange, any cloves that have fallen out, and the cinnamon stick.

4.

	Press	Set it for	Set time for	If needed, press
In all models	SAUTÉ	HIGH or MORE	10 minutes	START

5. Stir constantly as the sauce comes to a simmer. Continue cooking, stirring almost constantly, until the sauce has reduced to a thick syrup, about half the volume it was after you removed the pears, about 10 minutes. Turn off the heat and pour this hot syrup over the pears. Cool to room temperature, about 45 minutes, before serving. Or cool to room temperature, cover, and store in the refrigerator for up to 4 days (when you can serve them cold or let them come back to room temperature).

Other Pots

- For a **3-quart Instant Pot**, you *must* halve all of the ingredient amounts (using half a small orange with the cloves stuck into the peel).

- For a **10-quart Instant Pot**, you *must* increase all of the ingredient amounts by 50 percent.

Beyond

- This dish is something of a French tradition, although not with apple cider. To go the bistro route, substitute a bold red wine, such as Cabernet Sauvignon, for the cider.

- Or switch things up and use a sweet Riesling instead of the apple cider.

- We spoon the pears and syrup over vanilla ice cream, because why not?

See photo in insert.

Coconut Tapioca Pudding

5 ingredients

4 SERVINGS

METHOD:
pot-in-pot

SPECIAL EQUIPMENT:
a 1-quart, 6-inch-round, high-sided, pressure-safe baking or soufflé dish and a pressure-safe rack or trivet

PRESSURE:
high twice

TIME UNDER PRESSURE:
13 minutes

RELEASE:
quick, then natural

TOTAL TIME WITH PRESSURE:
about 40 minutes

VEGAN

GLUTEN-FREE

½ cup raw small tapioca pearls (see headnote for more information)

2 cups water

1½ cups low-fat or "lite" coconut milk

½ cup granulated white sugar

½ teaspoon table salt

This recipe gives you old-school tapioca pudding with a new twist: coconut milk. It's so warm, sweet, and comforting that it's become the go-to ask at our house when one of us is under the weather.

The recipe *only* works with low-fat (or "lite") coconut milk. Full-fat coconut milk clumps under pressure with the tapioca pearls—which by the way are the standard (small) ones found in the baking aisle of most North American supermarkets. Do not substitute instant tapioca (a ground product used as a thickener in pie fillings) or the large tapioca balls used in bubble teas.

Two notes: One, the pudding undergoes pressure twice (with different pressure-release mechanisms) because we have to stop the cooking to stir the mixture and keep it from sticking in the dish. And two, the pudding will only set up as it cools to room temperature.

1. Pour the tapioca pearls into a fine-mesh strainer or a small-holed colander. Rinse under warm water repeatedly until the water runs clear, about 2 minutes. Set aside.

2. Pour 1½ cups water into the insert set in a **5-, 6-, or 8-quart Instant Pot.** Put a pressure-safe rack or trivet in the insert.

3. Mix the rinsed tapioca pearls, coconut milk, sugar, salt, and remaining ½ cup water in a 1-quart, 6-inch-round, high-sided, pressure-safe baking or soufflé dish until the sugar dissolves. Do not cover the baking dish. Set it on the rack and lock the lid on the pot.

4.

	Set pot for	Set level to	Valve must be	Set time for	If needed, press
For *all* pots	PRESSURE COOK or MANUAL	HIGH	Closed	8 minutes with the KEEP WARM setting off	START

5. When the pot has finished cooking, use the **quick-release method** to bring the pressure back to normal. Unlatch the lid and open the cooker. Use a fork to stir the tapioca mixture, breaking it up. There will be some clumping on the bottom of the baking dish—make sure everything is again loose. Lock the lid back onto the pot.

6.

	Set pot for	Set level to	Valve must be	Set time for	If needed, press
For *all* pots	PRESSURE COOK or MANUAL	HIGH	Closed	5 minutes with the KEEP WARM setting off	START

7. When the pot has finished cooking, turn it off and let the pressure **return to normal naturally,** about 15 minutes. Unlatch the lid and open the cooker. Again stir the tapioca mixture with a fork to smooth it out and break up any clumps. Use hot pads or silicone baking mitts to transfer the (hot!) baking dish to a nearby wire rack. Cool to room temperature, about 40 minutes, allowing the pudding to thicken and firm as it cools. Serve immediately or cover and refrigerate for up to 4 days.

Other Pots

- For a **3-quart Instant Pot,** you *must* reduce the amount of water in the insert to 1 cup while otherwise completing the recipe as stated.

- For a **10-quart Instant Pot,** you *must* increase the amount of water in the insert to 2½ cups while otherwise completing the recipe as stated.

Beyond

- Substitute almond milk or low-fat or fat-free dairy milk for the coconut milk. Do not use a thick creamy liquid like cream, half-and-half, whole milk, or oat milk.

- Serve the pudding with peeled, pitted, and sliced mango on top.

True Rice Pudding

8 ingredients

4–6 SERVINGS

METHOD:
pot-in-pot

SPECIAL EQUIPMENT:
a 2-quart, 7-inch-round, high-sided, pressure-safe baking or soufflé dish and a pressure-safe rack or trivet

PRESSURE:
max or high

TIME UNDER PRESSURE:
38 or 40 minutes

RELEASE:
modified natural

TOTAL TIME WITH PRESSURE:
about 1 hour

VEGETARIAN

GLUTEN-FREE

1½ cups water

3½ cups whole milk (do not use low-fat or fat-free)

1 cup raw long-grain white rice

½ cup granulated white sugar

2 teaspoons vanilla extract

2 refrigerator-cold large eggs

½ cup heavy or light cream

½ teaspoon table salt

Other Pots

- For a 3-quart Instant Pot, you *must* halve almost all of the ingredient amounts *except* you *must* use 1 cup water in the insert. You *must* use a 1-quart, 6-inch-round, high-sided, pressure-safe baking or soufflé dish.

- For a 10-quart Instant Pot, you *must* increase the amount of water in the insert to 2½ cups while otherwise completing the recipe as stated.

Beyond

- Add dried fruit *after* the pudding has cooked. When you whisk the combined rice-and-egg mixture into the baking dish, also whisk in up to ½ cup chopped raisins, chopped dried cranberries, dried blueberries, or chopped dried peaches.

- Spice the rice pudding by adding up to ½ teaspoon ground cinnamon, ¼ teaspoon ground cardamom, ¼ teaspoon ground allspice, and/or ¼ teaspoon grated nutmeg into the cream mixture before you begin adding the cooked rice mixture. Or whisk in up to 1 teaspoon dried pumpkin pie spice blend.

Why "true"? Because we have a recipe for rice pudding in *The Instant Pot Bible* that's essentially a sweetened risotto, made with medium-grain white Arborio rice right in the pot's insert. But with the PIP (pot-in-pot) method, we can get the more traditional rice pudding results with long-grain white rice and no worry of the BURN notice. Don't use converted or instant rice; you need the real deal for this old-fashioned favorite.

Note that you must work quickly at the end of the recipe to whisk the rice pudding into the egg mixture while the rice is still very hot.

1. Pour the water into the insert set in a **5-, 6-, or 8-quart Instant Pot.** Put a pressure-safe rack or trivet in the insert.

2. Stir the milk, rice, sugar, and vanilla extract in a 2-quart, 7-inch-round, high-sided, pressure-safe baking or soufflé dish until the sugar dissolves. Do not cover the baking dish. Set it on the rack and lock the lid on the pot.

3.

	Set pot for	Set level to	Valve must be	Set time for	If needed, press
For Max pots only	PRESSURE COOK	MAX	—	38 minutes with the KEEP WARM setting off	START
For all other pots	PRESSURE COOK or MANUAL	HIGH	Closed	40 minutes with the KEEP WARM setting off	START

4. *As the rice pudding cooks,* whisk the eggs, cream, and salt in a *large* bowl until very smooth. Set aside.

5. When the pot has finished cooking, turn it off and let the pressure **return to normal naturally for 10 minutes.** Then use the **quick-release method** to get rid of the pot's residual pressure. Unlatch the lid and open the cooker. Use a fork to break up and stir the rice in the baking dish.

6. Without delay, whisk about half of the very hot rice mixture into the cream mixture in small amounts, scooping out about ⅓ cup at a time. Then whisk this combined mixture into the remaining hot rice mixture in the baking dish until uniform. Use hot pads or silicone baking mitts to transfer the (hot!) baking dish to a nearby wire rack. Cool for 5 minutes before enjoying warm—or cool for 20 minutes before covering and refrigerating for up to 3 days.

Chocolate Pots de Crème

6 ingredients

6 POTS DE CRÈME

METHOD:
pot-in-pot

SPECIAL
EQUIPMENT:
six 6-ounce
pressure-safe
ramekins or
custard cups and a
pressure-safe rack
or trivet

PRESSURE:
max or high

TIME UNDER
PRESSURE:
4 or 5 minutes

RELEASE:
modified natural

TOTAL TIME WITH
PRESSURE:
about 45 minutes

VEGETARIAN

GLUTEN-FREE

1½ cups water

6 ounces dark chocolate, preferably
70 or 72 percent (or even a bit more)
cocoa solids, chopped

2 cups half-and-half

2 tablespoons granulated white sugar

½ teaspoon table salt

4 large egg yolks, *at room temperature*

Other Pots

- For a 3-quart Instant Pot, you *must* halve almost all of the ingredients (making 3 ramekins) except you *must* use 1 cup water in the insert.

- For a 10-quart Instant Pot, you *must* use 2½ cups water in the insert while otherwise completing the recipe as stated.

Beyond

- Serve the pots de crème with sweetened whipped cream. To make the best, chill a bowl and the beaters to a mixer (or a whisk if you're old school) in the refrigerator for at least 1 hour. Pour 1 cup cold heavy cream into the chilled bowl and beat with a mixer at high speed (or kill your arm by beating with a whisk) until thickened. Add 3 tablespoons confectioners' sugar in 1-tablespoon increments, beating (or whisking) after each addition to incorporate it. Add 1 teaspoon vanilla extract and continue beating (or whisking) until you have a thick sauce, not a meringue. Spoon the whipped cream over the pots de crème only after they've come to room temperature.

These little desserts are hardly like pudding and more like a rich but light chocolate frosting turned into a treat on its own. They'll be even firmer if you store them in the fridge before serving. At that point, they're best with sugar cookies or shortbread. Don't be tempted to use semi-sweet chocolate. The results will be too sweet and cloying.

1. Pour the water into the insert set in a **5-, 6-, or 8-quart Instant Pot.** Put a pressure-safe rack or trivet in the insert. Put the chocolate in a medium bowl.

2. Pour the half-and-half into a microwave-safe Pyrex measuring vessel or a microwave-safe small bowl. Microwave on HIGH in 15-second increments until very hot but not simmering.

3. Pour the hot half-and-half over the chocolate and stir until the chocolate melts. Stir in the sugar and salt until the sugar dissolves and the mixture is smooth. Cool at room temperature for 10 minutes.

4. Whisk in the egg yolks one at a time, adding the next after the previous is fully incorporated. Divide this mixture among six 6-ounce pressure-safe ramekins or custard cups. Cover each tightly with aluminum foil. Stack them on the rack in the pot, putting three in the bottom layer and balancing the other three on top, so that each top one sits on parts of the rim of at least two below. Lock the lid onto the cooker.

5.

	Set pot for	Set level to	Valve must be	Set time for	If needed, press
For Max pots only	PRESSURE COOK	MAX	—	4 minutes with the KEEP WARM setting off	START
For all other pots	PRESSURE COOK or MANUAL	HIGH	Closed	5 minutes with the KEEP WARM setting off	START

6. When the pot has finished cooking, turn it off and let the pressure **return to normal naturally for 10 minutes.** Then use the **quick-release method** to get rid of the pot's residual pressure. Unlock the lid and open the cooker. Use hot pads or silicone baking mitts to transfer the (hot!) ramekins to a nearby wire rack. Uncover and cool for at least 10 minutes before serving. Or cool to room temperature, about 40 minutes, before serving. Or cover the room-temperature ramekins and refrigerate for up to 3 days.

White Chocolate Pots de Crème

7 ingredients

6 POTS DE CRÈME

SPECIAL EQUIPMENT: six 6-ounce pressure-safe ramekins or custard cups and a pressure-safe rack or trivet

PRESSURE: max or high

TIME UNDER PRESSURE: 4 or 5 minutes

RELEASE: modified natural

TOTAL TIME WITH PRESSURE: about 45 minutes

VEGETARIAN

GLUTEN-FREE

1½ cups water

7 ounces white chocolate, broken into pieces

2 cups half-and-half

3 large egg yolks, *at room temperature*

2 tablespoons honey

1 teaspoon vanilla extract

½ teaspoon table salt

These delicate pots de crème, flavored with honey and vanilla extract, are best as a light dessert after a heavy stew or braise.

There are many varieties of white chocolate on the market, some no more than solid vegetable shortening flavored to be reminiscent of better white chocolate. Read the labels and make sure you get white chocolate made with real cocoa butter.

1. Pour the water into the insert set in a **5-, 6-, or 8-quart Instant Pot.** Put a pressure-safe rack or trivet in the insert.

2. Stir the white chocolate and half-and-half in a microwave-safe medium bowl. Microwave on HIGH in 10-second increments, stirring after each, until the white chocolate melts and the mixture is smooth. (It'll take about 1 minute of heating, depending on the wattage of your microwave.) Cool for 5 minutes.

3. Whisk in the egg yolks one at a time; then whisk in the honey, vanilla, and salt. Divide this mixture among six 6-ounce pressure-safe ramekins or custard cups. Cover each tightly with aluminum foil. Stack them on the rack in the pot, putting three in the bottom layer, then balancing the other three on top, so that each top one sits on parts of the rim of at least two below. Lock the lid onto the cooker.

4.

	Set pot for	Set level to	Valve must be	Set time for	If needed, press
For Max pots only	PRESSURE COOK	MAX	—	4 minutes with the KEEP WARM setting off	START
For all other pots	PRESSURE COOK or MANUAL	HIGH	Closed	5 minutes with the KEEP WARM setting off	START

5. When the pot has finished cooking, turn it off and let the pressure **return to normal naturally for 15 minutes.** Then use the **quick-release method** to get rid of the pot's residual pressure. Unlatch the lid and open the cooker. Use hot pads or silicone baking mitts to transfer the (hot!) ramekins to a nearby wire rack. Uncover and cool for at least 10 minutes before serving. Or cool for 30 minutes, then cover and refrigerate for up to 3 days.

Other Pots

- For a **3-quart Instant Pot, you** *must* halve almost all of the ingredients (making 3 ramekins) except you *must* use 1 cup water in the insert, then 2 large egg yolks, at room temperature, in the custard.

- For a **10-quart Instant Pot, you** *must* increase the amount of water in the insert to 2½ cups while otherwise completing the recipe as stated.

Beyond

- Top the pots de crème with fresh raspberries, fresh blackberries, or even a tablespoon of blackberry jam.

- Or shave semi-sweet or bittersweet chocolate over each serving.

Melted-Ice-Cream Crème Brûlée

5 ingredients

4 SERVINGS

METHOD:
pot-in-pot

SPECIAL EQUIPMENT:
four 6-ounce pressure- and broiler-safe ramekins or custard cups and a pressure-safe rack or trivet

PRESSURE:
low

TIME UNDER PRESSURE:
12 minutes

RELEASE:
natural

TOTAL TIME WITH PRESSURE:
about 5 hours (includes refrigerating)

VEGETARIAN

CAN BE GLUTEN-FREE

1½ cups water

1 pint smooth vanilla *premium* ice cream (gluten-free, if necessary), melted

4 large egg yolks, *at room temperature*

¼ teaspoon table salt

3 tablespoons granulated white sugar

Other Pots

- For a 3-quart Instant Pot, you *must* reduce the amount of water in the insert to 1 cup while otherwise completing the recipe as stated.

- For a 10-quart Instant Pot, you *must* increase the amount of water in the insert to 2½ cups while otherwise completing the recipe as stated.

Beyond

- Serve with shortbread cookies, pecan sandies, or other plain, crisp vanilla cookies.

Melted ice cream is the perfect base for crème brûlée: The rich mixture of cream and sugar morphs into the classic bistro dessert with very little fuss. You'll need to buy a premium ice cream (which doesn't have as much air suspended in the mixture). And you'll need plain vanilla; chunks of cookie dough or ribbons of chocolate sauce will prevent the custard from setting.

Please note: This dessert must be made in ramekins or custard cups that are both pressure *and broiler* safe. And be sure to broil the custards while they're still chilled from the fridge so the sugar melts on top but the pudding below doesn't.

1. Pour the water into the insert set in a **5-, 6-, or 8-quart Instant Pot.** Put a pressure-safe rack or trivet in the insert.

2. Whisk the melted ice cream, eggs, and salt in a large bowl until smooth with no bits of floating egg white.

3. Divide this mixture among four 6-ounce pressure- *and broiler*-safe ramekins or custard cups. Cover each tightly with aluminum foil. Stack them on the rack in the pot, putting three on the bottom layer, then balancing the remaining one on top so that it sits on parts of the rim of at least two (if not all three) of the ones below. Lock the lid onto the cooker.

4.

	Set pot for	Set level to	Valve must be	Set time for	If needed, press
For *all* pots	PRESSURE COOK or MANUAL	LOW	Closed	12 minutes with the KEEP WARM setting off	START

5. When the pot has finished cooking, turn it off and let the pressure **return to normal naturally,** about 15 minutes. Unlatch the lid and open the cooker. Use hot pads or silicone baking mitts to transfer the (hot!) ramekins to a nearby wire rack. Uncover and cool for 20 minutes. Then cover with plastic wrap and refrigerate for at least 4 hours or up to 3 days.

6. When you're ready to serve the dessert, uncover each ramekin and sprinkle the top of each with 2¼ teaspoons sugar. Position the oven rack 4 to 6 inches from the broiler element and heat the broiler. Set the ramekins on a lipped baking sheet and broil until the sugar melts, browns, and caramelizes, about 1 minute. Set aside at room temperature for 5 minutes so the sugar hardens before serving.

Hazelnut Crème Caramel

7 ingredients

6 SERVINGS

METHOD:
pot-in-pot

SPECIAL EQUIPMENT:
six 6-ounce pressure-
and heat-safe ramekins
or custard cups and a
pressure-safe rack or
trivet

PRESSURE:
max or high

**TIME UNDER
PRESSURE:**
5 or 7 minutes

RELEASE:
natural

**TOTAL TIME WITH
PRESSURE:**
about 3 hours 15
minutes (includes
refrigerating)

VEGETARIAN

CAN BE GLUTEN-FREE

1½ cups plus 3 tablespoons water

½ cup plus ⅓ cup granulated white
sugar

3 large eggs, *at room temperature*

1 cup heavy cream

¾ cup whole milk (do not use low-fat or
fat-free)

¼ cup hazelnut coffee creamer (gluten-
free, if necessary)

½ teaspoon table salt

Other Pots

- For a 3-quart Instant Pot, you *must*
halve almost all of the ingredient
amounts (thereby making
3 ramekins) *except* you *must* use
1 cup water in the insert.

- For a 10-quart Instant Pot, you
must increase the amounts of water
in the insert to 2½ cups while
otherwise completing the recipe as
stated.

Beyond

- When unmolded, dust the tops of
the puddings with a dried apple
pie spice blend or a little finely
grated semi-sweet or bittersweet
chocolate.

Although we make these crème caramels with a fairly traditional
technique (well, sort of traditional, what with the Instant Pot), we
cheat with the flavorings by using a hazelnut coffee creamer to give
them a big boost of deliciousness.

Please note: You must use heat-safe ramekins or custard cups
since you'll pour a super-hot sugar syrup into each one.

1. Pour 1½ cups water into the insert set in a **5-, 6-, or 8-quart
Instant Pot.** Put a pressure-safe rack or trivet in the insert.

2. Melt the ½ cup sugar and the remaining 3 tablespoons water in
a small saucepan or skillet set over medium heat, stirring until the
sugar melts and turns very light brown. Divide this hot sugar syrup
evenly among six 6-ounce pressure- *and heat*-safe ramekins or
custard cups. Use hot pads or silicone baking mitts to gently tip each
ramekin so the hot sugar syrup evenly coats the bottom and spreads
a bit up the sides. Cool for 15 minutes.

3. Whisk the remaining ⅓ cup sugar, the eggs, cream, milk, coffee
creamer, and salt in a large bowl until very smooth.

4. Divide this mixture evenly among the ramekins, then cover each
tightly with aluminum foil. Stack them on the rack in the pot, putting
three in the bottom layer, then balancing the other three on top, so
that each top one sits on parts of the rim of at least two below. Lock
the lid onto the cooker.

5.

	Set pot for	Set level to	Valve must be	Set time for	If needed, press
For Max pots only	PRESSURE COOK	MAX	—	5 minutes with the KEEP WARM setting off	START
For all other pots	PRESSURE COOK or MANUAL	HIGH	Closed	7 minutes with the KEEP WARM setting off	START

6. When the pot has finished cooking, turn it off and let the pressure
return to normal naturally, about 15 minutes. Unlatch the lid and
open the cooker. Use hot pads or silicone baking mitts to transfer the
(hot!) ramekins to a nearby wire rack. Uncover and cool for 15 minutes.
Then cover the ramekins with plastic wrap and refrigerate for at least
2 hours or up to 3 days. When you're ready to serve them, run a thin
knife around the inside edge of each ramekin, then invert it onto a
lipped plate, letting the caramel flow over the pudding.

Banana Bread Pudding

11 ingredients

4–6 SERVINGS

METHOD:
pot-in-pot

SPECIAL EQUIPMENT:
a 2-quart, 7-inch-round, high-sided, pressure-safe baking or soufflé dish and a pressure-safe rack or trivet

PRESSURE:
max or high

TIME UNDER PRESSURE:
10 or 12 minutes

RELEASE:
quick

TOTAL TIME WITH PRESSURE:
about 30 minutes

VEGETARIAN

1½ cups water

Baking spray

2 large eggs, *at room temperature*

¾ cup whole or low-fat milk (do not use fat-free)

¼ cup heavy or light cream

¼ cup granulated white sugar

½ teaspoon vanilla extract

½ teaspoon table salt

1 large very ripe banana, peeled and diced

8 ounces country-style sliced white bread, such as Pepperidge Farm, cut into 1-inch squares

½ cup purchased caramel ice cream topping

Other Pots

- For a 3-quart Instant Pot, you *must* halve almost all of the ingredient amounts *except* you *must* use 1 cup water in the insert. You *must* use a 1-quart, 6-inch-round, high-sided, pressure-safe baking or soufflé dish.

- For a 10-quart Instant Pot, you *must* increase the amount of water in the insert to 2½ cups while otherwise completing the recipe as stated.

Beyond

- Add up to ½ cup semi-sweet chocolate chips with the bread.

- Add more flavor by whisking up to 1 teaspoon ground cinnamon, ½ teaspoon ground cardamom, and/or ¼ teaspoon grated nutmeg into the egg mixture.

Although we're offering this caramel-swirled bread pudding as a dessert, you could make it for a weekend brunch, especially if the weather's cold and you've got a hot pot of coffee ready to go. For the best results, make sure the banana is quite ripe, more so than if you were just to slice it onto cereal. And use real caramel sauce: Look for butter, sugar, and cream among the ingredients.

1. Pour the water into the insert set in a **5-, 6-, or 8-quart Instant Pot.** Put a pressure-safe rack or trivet in the insert. Generously coat the inside of a 2-quart, 7-inch-round, high-sided, pressure-safe baking or soufflé dish with baking spray.

2. Whisk the eggs, milk, cream, sugar, vanilla, and salt in a large bowl until the sugar dissolves and the mixture is uniform. Add the banana and bread; stir well but gently to coat the bread in the liquid.

3. Drizzle the caramel sauce over the bread mixture and stir once to barely mix, giving the dish a swirl effect. Pour and gently pack the bread mixture into the prepared baking dish. Cover it with aluminum foil and set it on the rack. Lock the lid on the cooker.

4.

	Set pot for	Set level to	Valve must be	Set time for	If needed, press
For Max pots only	PRESSURE COOK	MAX	—	10 minutes with the KEEP WARM setting off	START
For all other pots	PRESSURE COOK or MANUAL	HIGH	Closed	12 minutes with the KEEP WARM setting off	START

5. When the pot has finished cooking, use the **quick-release method** to bring the pressure back to normal. Unlatch the lid and open the cooker. Use hot pads or silicone baking mitts to transfer the (hot!) dish to a nearby wire rack. Uncover and cool for 5 minutes before dishing up by the big spoonful.

Cranberry-Nut Bread Pudding

8 ingredients

4–6 SERVINGS

METHOD: pot-in-pot

SPECIAL EQUIPMENT: a 2-quart, 7-inch-round, high-sided, pressure-safe baking or soufflé dish and a pressure-safe rack or trivet

PRESSURE: max or high

TIME UNDER PRESSURE: 12 or 15 minutes

RELEASE: natural

TOTAL TIME WITH PRESSURE: about 45 minutes

VEGETARIAN

1½ cups water

Baking spray

2 cups whole or low-fat milk (do not use fat-free)

4 large eggs, *at room temperature*

2 tablespoons honey

½ teaspoon almond extract

¼ teaspoon table salt

10 ounces cranberry-nut bread, sliced and cut into 1-inch squares

Other Pots

- For a 3-quart Instant Pot, you *must* halve almost all of the ingredient amounts *except* you *must* use 1 cup water in the insert. You *must* use a 1-quart, 6-inch-round, high-sided, pressure-safe baking or soufflé dish.

- For a 10-quart Instant Pot, you *must* increase the amount of water in the insert to 2½ cups while otherwise completing the recipe as stated.

Beyond

- Substitute almond or oat milk for the dairy milk.

- For a spiced bread pudding, whisk ½ teaspoon ground cardamom and ¼ teaspoon grated nutmeg into the egg mixture before you add the bread squares. If you do this, substitute ¼ teaspoon rum extract for the almond extract.

Purchased cranberry-nut bread makes this bread pudding so easy. Most of the flavor comes from the bread with a little assist from the honey and almond extract. Note that you must use baking spray (a fat and flour mixture), so the bread pudding easily comes out of the baking dish. We tested this recipe with various gluten-free cranberry-nut breads and unfortunately none made a successful bread pudding.

1. Pour the water into an insert set in a **5-, 6-, or 8-quart Instant Pot.** Put a pressure-safe rack or trivet in the insert. Coat the inside of a 2-quart, 7-inch-round, high-sided, pressure-safe baking dish or ramekin with baking spray.

2. Whisk the milk, eggs, honey, almond extract, and salt in a large bowl until very smooth with no bits of egg white floating in the mix. Add the bread and stir gently until moistened. Set aside for 10 minutes to let the dense cranberry-nut bread absorb more of the liquid.

3. Pour and gently pack the bread mixture into the prepared baking dish. Cover the dish tightly with aluminum foil and set it on the rack. Lock the lid onto the cooker.

4.

	Set pot for	Set level to	Valve must be	Set time for	If needed, press
For Max pots only	PRESSURE COOK	MAX	—	12 minutes with the KEEP WARM setting off	START
For all other pots	PRESSURE COOK or MANUAL	HIGH	Closed	15 minutes with the KEEP WARM setting off	START

5. When the pot has finished cooking, turn it off and let the pressure **return to normal naturally,** about 15 minutes. Unlatch the lid and open the cooker. Use hot pads or silicone baking mitts to transfer the (hot!) baking dish to a nearby wire rack. Uncover and cool for 10 minutes before dishing up by the big spoonfuls into bowls.

Cherry-Vanilla-Ice-Cream Bread Pudding

5 ingredients

4–6 SERVINGS

METHOD:
pot-in-pot

SPECIAL EQUIPMENT:
a 2-quart, 7-inch-round, high-sided, pressure-safe baking or soufflé dish and a pressure-safe rack or trivet

PRESSURE:
max or high

TIME UNDER PRESSURE:
20 or 26 minutes

RELEASE:
modified natural

TOTAL TIME WITH PRESSURE:
about 1 hour 10 minutes

VEGETARIAN

1½ cups water

Butter, for greasing

1 pint *premium* cherry vanilla ice cream, melted

4 large eggs, *at room temperature*

8 ounces country-style sliced white bread, such as Pepperidge Farm, cut into 1-inch squares

Melted premium ice cream makes the easiest bread pudding! The ice cream's got almost everything you need (except more eggs for richness—and, of course, the bread). Better yet, cherry vanilla gelato will yield an even more decadent dessert. A pint of premium ice cream will take about 36 hours to melt in the fridge or about 6 hours to melt on the counter at room temperature.

1. Pour the water into the insert set in a **5-, 6-, or 8-quart Instant Pot.** Put a pressure-safe rack or trivet in the insert. Generously butter the inside of a 2-quart, 7-inch-round, high-sided, pressure-safe baking or soufflé dish.

2. Whisk the melted ice cream and eggs in a large bowl until smooth. Add the bread squares and toss gently to moisten and coat.

3. Pour and gently pack this mixture into the prepared baking dish. Butter a piece of aluminum foil and use it buttered side down to cover and seal the baking dish. Set the dish on the rack and lock the lid on the cooker.

4.

	Set pot for	Set level to	Valve must be	Set time for	If needed, press
For Max pots only	PRESSURE COOK	MAX	—	20 minutes with the KEEP WARM setting off	START
For all other pots	PRESSURE COOK or MANUAL	HIGH	Closed	26 minutes with the KEEP WARM setting off	START

5. When the pot has finished cooking, turn it off and let the pressure **return to normal naturally for 20 minutes.** Then use the **quick-release method** to get rid of the pot's residual pressure. Unlatch the lid and open the cooker. Use hot pads or silicone baking mitts to transfer the (hot!) baking dish to a nearby wire rack. Uncover and cool for 10 minutes before dishing up by big spoonfuls into bowls.

Other Pots

- For a 3-quart Instant Pot, you *must* halve almost all of the ingredient amounts *except* you *must* use 1 cup water in the insert. You *must* use a 1-quart, 6-inch-round, high-sided, pressure-safe baking or soufflé dish.

- For a 10-quart Instant Pot, you *must* increase the amount of water in the insert to 2½ cups while otherwise completing the recipe as stated.

Beyond

- For a decadent topping, warm heavy cream in a small saucepan set over medium-low heat, just until puffs of steam come off the cream. Whisk in a little vanilla extract and a pinch of table salt, then pour this warmed cream over the servings.

Caramel and Chocolate Chip Bread Pudding

6 ingredients

4–6 SERVINGS

METHOD:
pot-in-pot

SPECIAL EQUIPMENT:
a 2-quart, 7-inch-round, high-sided, pressure-safe baking or soufflé dish and a pressure-safe rack or trivet

PRESSURE:
max or high

TIME UNDER PRESSURE:
20 or 26 minutes

RELEASE:
modified natural

TOTAL TIME WITH PRESSURE:
about 1 hour 10 minutes

VEGETARIAN

1½ cups water

Butter, for greasing

1 pint *premium* caramel gelato, melted

3 large eggs, *at room temperature*

8 ounces country-style sliced white bread, such as Pepperidge Farm, cut into 1-inch squares

½ cup mini chocolate chips

Caramel + chocolate = OMG, the best bread pudding! And yes, melted ice cream makes for very easy bread puddings. But remember: The dessert is only going to be as good as the ice cream you use. For the best results, pop for a high-end gelato.

1. Pour the water into the insert set in a **5-, 6-, or 8-quart Instant Pot.** Put a pressure-safe rack or trivet in the insert. Generously butter the inside of a 2-quart, 7-inch-round high-sided, pressure-safe baking or soufflé dish.

2. Whisk the melted gelato and eggs in a large bowl until smooth. Add the bread squares and mini chocolate chips. Toss gently to moisten and coat the bread.

3. Pour and gently pack this mixture into the prepared baking dish. Butter a piece of aluminum foil and use it buttered side down to cover and tightly seal the baking dish. Set the dish on the rack and lock the lid on the cooker.

4.

	Set pot for	Set level to	Valve must be	Set time for	If needed, press
For Max pots only	PRESSURE COOK	MAX	—	20 minutes with the KEEP WARM setting off	START
For all other pots	PRESSURE COOK or MANUAL	HIGH	Closed	26 minutes with the KEEP WARM setting off	START

5. When the pot has finished cooking, turn it off and let the pressure **return to normal naturally for 20 minutes.** Then use the **quick-release method** to get rid of the pot's residual pressure. Unlatch the lid and open the cooker. Use hot pads or silicone baking mitts to transfer the (hot!) baking dish to a nearby wire rack. Uncover and cool for 10 minutes before dishing up by big spoonfuls into bowls.

Other Pots

- For a **3-quart Instant Pot, you** *must* halve almost all of the ingredient amounts *except* you *must* use 1 cup water in the insert. You *must* use a 1-quart, 6-inch-round, high-sided, pressure-safe baking or soufflé dish.

- For a **10-quart Instant Pot, you** *must* increase the amount of water in the insert to 2½ cups while otherwise completing the recipe as stated.

Beyond

- For an over-the-top treat, use melted, premium *salted* caramel gelato.

Peanut Butter Cheesecake

13 ingredients	SPECIAL EQUIPMENT: a 7-inch-round springform pan, a food processor, and a pressure-safe rack or trivet	PRESSURE: high	TOTAL TIME WITH PRESSURE: about 2½ hours (includes refrigerating)
ONE 7-INCH CHEESECAKE		TIME UNDER PRESSURE: 25 minutes	
METHOD: pot-in-pot		RELEASE: natural	VEGETARIAN

1½ cups water

Baking spray, for greasing

10 standard cream-filled chocolate sandwich cookies, such as Oreos, crushed (see headnote for more information)

1 pound regular cream cheese (do not use low-fat or fat-free), *at room temperature*

⅔ cup natural-style creamy peanut butter

⅓ cup granulated white sugar

⅓ cup packed dark brown sugar

⅓ cup heavy cream

2 large eggs, *at room temperature*

2 tablespoons all-purpose flour

2 teaspoons vanilla extract

2 teaspoons unsweetened cocoa powder

2 teaspoons confectioners' sugar

Other Pots

- Because of the size of the pan and the ratios of the ingredients, this recipe will not work in a 3-quart Instant Pot.

- For a 10-quart Instant Pot, you *must* increase the amount of water in the insert to 2½ cups while otherwise completing the recipe as stated.

Beyond

- For a peanut butter and jelly cheesecake, skip the cocoa powder and confectioners' sugar. Instead, stir 1 teaspoon water into 2 tablespoons strawberry, raspberry, or blackberry jam until smooth. If the jam is too thick, microwave the mixture on HIGH for 5 seconds, just to loosen it up. Use a rubber spatula or offset icing spatula to spread this mixture over the top of the cooled cheesecake.

We can't resist cheesecakes in the Instant Pot because they're light, velvety, and perfect every time. This one's a peanut butter lover's dream, best in smaller slices because it's so rich.

There are two ways to make the Oreo cookie crumbs for the crust. You can pulse the cookies in a food processor (but make sure you create crumbs, not dust). Or you can put them in a zip-top plastic bag, seal it, and crush them with a rolling pin.

1. Pour the water into the insert set in a **5-, 6-, or 8-quart Instant Pot.** Put a pressure-safe rack or trivet in the insert.

2. Generously coat the inside of a 7-inch-round springform pan with baking spray. Pour the cookie crumbs into the pan and press them into an even layer across the bottom and about halfway up the sides of the pan.

3. Put the cream cheese, peanut butter, white sugar, brown sugar, cream, eggs, flour, and vanilla in a food processor. Cover and process until smooth, stopping the machine at least once to scrape down the inside of the canister. Use a rubber spatula to gently pour this mixture into the prepared pan (be gentle so as to keep the crust intact). Smooth the top and rap the pan on the counter once or twice to get rid of any air bubbles. Set the pan on the rack and lock the lid on the pot.

4.

	Set pot for	Set level to	Valve must be	Set time for	If needed, press
For *all* pots	PRESSURE COOK or MANUAL	HIGH	Closed	25 minutes with the KEEP WARM setting off	START

5. When the pot has finished cooking, turn it off and let the pressure **return to normal naturally,** about 20 minutes. Unlatch the lid and open the cooker. Use a paper towel to blot any drips off the top of the cheesecake. Use hot pads or silicone baking mitts to transfer the (hot!) pan to a nearby wire rack. Cool for 15 minutes, then unlatch the ring side from the springform pan but do not remove the ring side. Cover the cheesecake with plastic wrap and refrigerate for at least 1 hour or up to 3 days.

6. Remove the side ring and uncover the cheesecake. Mix the cocoa powder and confectioners' sugar in a small bowl until uniform. Dust over the top of the cheesecake. Slice the cheesecake into wedges to serve.

Salt Caramel Cheesecake

11 ingredients	
ONE 7-INCH CHEESECAKE	
METHOD: pot-in-pot	SPECIAL EQUIPMENT: a 7-inch-round springform pan, a food processor, and a pressure-safe rack or trivet
PRESSURE: high	TOTAL TIME WITH PRESSURE: about 2½ hours (includes refrigerating)
TIME UNDER PRESSURE: 35 minutes	VEGETARIAN
RELEASE: natural	

1½ cups water

Baking spray

1¼ cups graham cracker crumbs

5 tablespoons butter, melted and cooled *for 10 minutes*

1 pound regular cream cheese (do not use low-fat or fat-free), *at room temperature*

⅔ cup purchased dulce de leche (see the headnote for more information)

½ cup regular or low-fat sour cream (do not use fat-free), *at room temperature*

2 large eggs, *at room temperature*

1 tablespoon all-purpose flour

1 teaspoon vanilla extract

1 teaspoon table salt

Other Pots

- Because of the size of the pan and the ratios of the ingredients, this recipe will not work in a 3-quart Instant Pot.

- For a 10-quart Instant Pot, you *must* increase the amount of water in the insert to 2½ cups while otherwise completing the recipe as stated.

Beyond

- To spice up the cheesecake, add up to 1 teaspoon ground cinnamon, ½ teaspoon ground allspice, and/or ¼ teaspoon grated nutmeg with the other ingredients in the food processor.

The only sugar in this smooth, silky cheesecake comes from purchased dulce de leche—which we combine with a healthy bit of salt to create a salt caramel flavor that's a little deeper than it would be if we'd used plain caramel sauce. Look for dulce de leche near the ice cream toppings or perhaps the jams and preserves at your supermarket. And look for a brand made with real cream and sugar, not just corn syrup.

1. Pour the water into the insert set in a **5-, 6-, or 8-quart Instant Pot.** Put a pressure-safe rack or trivet in the insert.

2. Generously coat the inside of a 7-inch-round springform pan with baking spray. Mix the graham cracker crumbs and butter in a medium bowl until well moistened, then pour this mixture into the prepared pan. Press the crumbs into an even crust across the bottom of the pan and about halfway up the sides.

3. Put the cream cheese, dulce de leche, sour cream, eggs, flour, vanilla, and salt in a food processor. Cover and process until smooth, stopping the machine at least once to scrape down the inside of the canister.

4. Use a rubber spatula to gently pour this mixture into the prepared pan (be gentle so as to keep the crust intact). Smooth the top and rap the pan on the counter once or twice to get rid of any air bubbles. Set the pan on the rack and lock the lid on the pot.

5.

	Set pot for	Set level to	Valve must be	Set time for	If needed, press
For *all* pots	PRESSURE COOK or MANUAL	HIGH	Closed	35 minutes with the KEEP WARM setting off	START

6. When the pot has finished cooking, turn it off and let the pressure **return to normal naturally,** about 20 minutes. Unlatch the lid and open the cooker. Use a paper towel to blot any drips off the top of the cheesecake. Use hot pads or silicone baking mitts to transfer the (hot!) pan to a nearby wire rack. Cool for 15 minutes, then unlatch the ring side from the springform pan but do not remove the ring side. Cover the cheesecake with plastic wrap and refrigerate for at least 1 hour or up to 3 days. Uncover and remove the side ring before slicing and serving.

Butterscotch Cheesecake

14 ingredients

ONE 7-INCH CHEESECAKE

METHOD: pot-in-pot

SPECIAL EQUIPMENT: a 7-inch-round springform pan, a food processor, and a pressure-safe rack or trivet

PRESSURE: high

TIME UNDER PRESSURE: 25 minutes

RELEASE: natural

TOTAL TIME WITH PRESSURE: about 2½ hours (includes refrigerating)

VEGETARIAN

1½ cups water

Baking spray

1½ cups graham cracker crumbs

½ stick (4 tablespoons or ¼ cup) butter, melted and cooled *for 10 minutes*

1 tablespoon molasses

1 pound regular cream cheese (do not use low-fat or fat-free), *at room temperature*

¼ cup packed dark brown sugar

¼ cup purchased butterscotch ice cream topping

2 large eggs, *at room temperature*

3 tablespoons heavy cream

2 tablespoons all-purpose flour

1 teaspoon vanilla extract

¼ teaspoon grated nutmeg

¼ teaspoon table salt

Other Pots

- Because of the size of the pan and the ratios of the ingredients, this recipe will not work in a 3-quart Instant Pot.

- For a 10-quart Instant Pot, you *must* increase the amount of water in the insert to 2½ cups while otherwise completing the recipe as stated.

Beyond

- Once the cheesecake has been properly chilled, spread about ½ cup butterscotch ice cream topping over the cheesecake, then top with 1 cup caramel corn (that is, caramel coated popcorn).

Butterscotch is made for cream cheese! Okay, well, it should be. It's got the rich level of sweetness to match the slightly sour flavor of the cheese. But rather than making butterscotch from scratch for this cheesecake, we use a butterscotch ice cream topping, which also makes for a rich, dense dessert. We've added nutmeg to the batter, perhaps a surprise, because it lightens the flavors slightly and foregrounds the molasses notes found in the crust and the dark brown sugar.

1. Pour the water into the insert set in a **5-, 6-, or 8-quart Instant Pot.** Put a pressure-safe rack or trivet in the insert.

2. Generously coat the inside of a 7-inch-round springform pan with baking spray. Mix the graham cracker crumbs, butter, and molasses in a medium bowl until uniform and well moistened. Pour this mixture into the prepared pan and press an even crust across the bottom of the pan and about halfway up the sides.

3. Put the cream cheese, brown sugar, butterscotch topping, eggs, cream, flour, vanilla, nutmeg, and salt in a food processor. Cover and process until smooth, stopping the machine at least once to scrape down the inside of the canister.

4. Use a rubber spatula to gently pour this mixture into the prepared pan (be gentle so as to keep the crust intact). Smooth the top and rap the pan on the counter once or twice to get rid of any air bubbles. Set the pan on the rack and lock the lid on the pot.

5.

	Set pot for	Set level to	Valve must be	Set time for	If needed, press
For *all* pots	PRESSURE COOK or MANUAL	HIGH	Closed	25 minutes with the KEEP WARM setting off	START

6. When the pot has finished cooking, turn it off and let the pressure **return to normal naturally,** about 20 minutes. Unlatch the lid and open the cooker. Use a paper towel to blot any drips off the top of the cheesecake. Use hot pads or silicone baking mitts to transfer the (hot!) pan to a nearby wire rack. Cool for 15 minutes, then unlatch the ring side from the springform pan but do not remove the ring side. Cover the cheesecake with plastic wrap and refrigerate for at least 1 hour or up to 3 days. Uncover and remove the side ring before slicing and serving.

See photo in insert.

Coconut Custard Cheesecake

10 ingredients

ONE 7-INCH CHEESECAKE

METHOD:
pot-in-pot

SPECIAL EQUIPMENT:
a 7-inch-round springform pan, a food processor, and a pressure-safe rack or trivet

PRESSURE:
high

TIME UNDER PRESSURE:
32 minutes

RELEASE:
natural

TOTAL TIME WITH PRESSURE:
about 2½ hours (includes refrigerating)

VEGETARIAN

1½ cups water

Baking spray

1¼ cups vanilla cookie crumbs

5 tablespoons butter, melted and cooled *for 10 minutes*

1¾ cups full-fat coconut milk

1 cup full-fat, low-fat, or fat-free sweetened condensed milk

2 large eggs *plus* 3 large egg yolks, *at room temperature*

3 tablespoons honey

1 teaspoon vanilla extract

¼ teaspoon table salt

This cheesecake isn't really a cheesecake—at least not in the traditional sense. It's made with coconut milk and sweetened condensed milk for a texture that's actually a cross between a dense cheesecake and a lighter flan. Although you can use low-fat or even fat-free sweetened condensed milk, use only full-fat coconut milk—the richer the better.

The best way to tell if you have a can of rich coconut milk in hand at the store is to shake the can. If you hear only liquid, you know it's thin and watery. If you feel some solids moving around, you know you've got the right can!

1. Pour the water into the insert set in a **5-, 6-, or 8-quart Instant Pot.** Put a pressure-safe rack or trivet in the insert.

2. Generously coat the inside of a 7-inch-round springform pan with baking spray. Mix the cookie crumbs and butter in a medium bowl until uniform. Pour this mixture into the prepared pan and press an even crust across the bottom of the pan and about halfway up the sides.

3. Put the coconut milk, sweetened condensed milk, eggs, egg yolks, honey, vanilla, and salt in a food processor. Cover and process until smooth, stopping the machine at least once to scrape down the inside of the canister.

4. Use a rubber spatula to gently pour this mixture into the prepared pan (be gentle so as to keep the crust intact). Smooth the top and rap the pan on the counter once or twice to get rid of any air bubbles. Set the pan on the rack and lock the lid on the pot.

5.

	Set pot for	Set level to	Valve must be	Set time for	If needed, press
For *all* pots	PRESSURE COOK or MANUAL	HIGH	Closed	32 minutes with the KEEP WARM setting off	START

6. When the pot has finished cooking, turn it off and let the pressure **return to normal naturally,** about 20 minutes. Unlatch the lid and open the cooker. Use a paper towel to blot any drips off the top of the cheesecake. Use hot pads or silicone baking mitts to transfer the (hot!) pan to a nearby wire rack. Cool for 15 minutes, then unlatch the ring side from the springform pan but do not remove the ring side. Cover the cheesecake with plastic wrap and refrigerate for at least 1 hour or up to 3 days. Uncover and remove the side ring before slicing and serving.

Other Pots

- Because of the size of the pan and the ratios of the ingredients, this recipe will not work in a 3-quart Instant Pot.

- For a 10-quart Instant Pot, you *must* increase the amount of water in the insert to 2½ cups while otherwise completing the recipe as stated.

Beyond

- Substitute chocolate cookie crumbs for the vanilla cookie crumbs.

- Add up to ¼ teaspoon rum extract to the batter.

Mini Double-Chocolate Cheesecakes

12 ingredients

6 MINI CHEESECAKES

METHOD:
pot-in-pot

SPECIAL EQUIPMENT:
six ½-cup (4-ounce)
pressure-safe
ramekins, custard
cups, or canning jars;
a food processor; and
a pressure-safe rack
or trivet

PRESSURE:
high

TIME UNDER
PRESSURE:
15 minutes

RELEASE:
natural

TOTAL TIME WITH
PRESSURE:
about 3 hours
(includes
refrigerating)

VEGETARIAN

1½ cups water

Butter, for greasing

6 standard cream-filled chocolate
sandwich cookies, such as Oreos,
crushed (for information, see the
headnote on page 403)

½ pound regular cream cheese (do
not use low-fat or fat-free), *at room
temperature*

¼ cup packed dark brown sugar

4 ounces (70 or 72 percent) bittersweet
chocolate, melted (see the headnote
for more information) and cooled

2 large egg yolks, *at room temperature*

2 tablespoons regular or low-fat sour
cream (do not use fat-free), *at room
temperature*

1 teaspoon all-purpose flour

1 teaspoon unsweetened cocoa powder

1 teaspoon vanilla extract

½ teaspoon table salt

Other Pots

- For a 3-quart Instant Pot, you
  must halve the ingredient amounts
  (making 3 ramekins).

- For a 10-quart Instant Pot, you
  must increase the amount of water
  in the insert to 2½ cups while
  otherwise completing the recipe
  as stated—or you *can* use that
  amount of water and increase the
  ingredient amounts by 50 percent,
  thereby making 9 ramekins.

Beyond

- Drizzle the top of each cooled
  cheesecake with purchased caramel
  sauce.

These little, hand-size cheesecakes have two hits of chocolate,
thanks to both melted bittersweet chocolate and cocoa powder.

Melting chocolate is easy with an Instant Pot. Put about 1½ cups
water in the insert, then set a heat-safe rack or trivet in it. Put the
chopped chocolate in a heat-safe bowl. Turn the pot on to its SAUTÉ
mode at HIGH or MORE. Heat the water to just below simmering,
then turn off the heat and set the bowl with the chocolate on the
rack or trivet. Stir until about three-quarters of the chocolate melts,
then remove the bowl and continue stirring until fully melted.

1. Pour the water into the insert set in a **5-, 6-, or 8-quart Instant
Pot.** Put a pressure-safe rack or trivet in the insert.

2. Grease the insides of six ½-cup (4-ounce) pressure-safe ramekins,
custard cups, or canning jars with butter, making sure it gets generously down into the joint between the side and the bottom of each.

3. Divide the crushed cookies evenly among the prepared ramekins.
Press *lightly* to form a bottom crust in each.

4. Put the cream cheese, brown sugar, melted chocolate, egg yolks,
sour cream, flour, cocoa powder, vanilla, and salt in a food processor.
Cover and process until smooth, stopping the machine at least once
to scrape down the inside of the canister. Divide this mixture evenly
among the prepared ramekins, a generous ¼ cup in each. Do not
cover.

5. Stack the ramekins on the rack, placing three on the bottom level,
then three on the top level with each sitting on a part of the rim of at
least two below. Lock the lid on the cooker.

6.

	Set pot for	Set level to	Valve must be	Set time for	If needed, press
For *all* pots	PRESSURE COOK or MANUAL	HIGH	Closed	15 minutes with the KEEP WARM setting off	START

7. When the pot has finished cooking, turn it off and let the pressure
return to normal naturally, about 20 minutes. Unlatch the lid and
open the cooker. Cool for 5 minutes.

8. Use hot pads or silicone baking mitts to transfer the (still hot!)
ramekins to a nearby wire rack. Cool to room temperature, about
1 hour. Cover and refrigerate for at least 1 hour before serving.

Mini Cheesecakes

12 ingredients

6 MINI
CHEESECAKES

METHOD:
pot-in-pot

SPECIAL
EQUIPMENT:
six ½-cup
(4-ounce)
pressure-safe
ramekins, custard
cups, or canning
jars; a food
processor; and a
pressure-safe rack
or trivet

PRESSURE:
high

TIME UNDER
PRESSURE:
15 minutes

RELEASE:
natural

TOTAL TIME WITH
PRESSURE:
about 3 hours
(includes
refrigerating)

VEGETARIAN

1½ cups water

3 tablespoons butter, melted and cooled
for 10 minutes, plus additional cold
butter for greasing

⅔ cup graham cracker crumbs

½ pound regular cream cheese (do
not use low-fat or fat-free), *at room
temperature*

¼ cup granulated white sugar

1 large egg, *at room temperature*

2 tablespoons regular or low-fat sour
cream (do not use fat-free), *at room
temperature*

2 teaspoons all-purpose flour

1 teaspoon finely grated lemon zest

2 teaspoons lemon juice

¼ teaspoon vanilla extract

⅛ teaspoon table salt

Make these simple, lemony cheesecakes in ½-cup canning jars,
then seal them when cool and tote them to picnics and cookouts
as a treat after the meal. They're super festive, guaranteed to bring
on the smiles. The only trick is to make an even crust in each jar (or
ramekin). Don't compact the crumbs into a tight mass. Press gently
just until they're an even layer without any loose bits.

If you want a gluten-free version, skip the crust entirely,
substitute cornstarch for the flour, and make sure you also use
gluten-free cream cheese and sour cream.

1. Pour the water into the insert set in a **5-, 6-, or 8-quart Instant
Pot.** Put a pressure-safe rack or trivet in the insert.

2. Grease the insides of six ½-cup (4-ounce) pressure-safe ramekins,
custard cups, or canning jars with cold butter, making sure it gets
generously down into the joint between the side and the bottom of
each.

3. Mix the graham cracker crumbs and melted butter in a small bowl
until uniform. Divide this mixture among the prepared ramekins,
about 1½ tablespoons per container. *Gently* press to form an even
bottom crust in each.

4. Put the cream cheese, sugar, egg, sour cream, flour, lemon zest,
lemon juice, vanilla, and salt in a food processor. Cover and process
until smooth, stopping the machine at least once to scrape down the
inside of the canister. Divide this mixture evenly among the prepared
ramekins, a generous ¼ cup in each. Do not cover.

5. Stack the ramekins on the rack, placing three on the bottom level, then three on the top level with each sitting on a part of the rim of at least two below. Lock the lid onto the cooker.

6.

	Set pot for	Set level to	Valve must be	Set time for	If needed, press
For *all* pots	PRESSURE COOK or MANUAL	HIGH	Closed	15 minutes with the KEEP WARM setting off	START

7. When the pot has finished cooking, turn it off and let the pressure **return to normal naturally,** about 20 minutes. Unlatch the lid and open the cooker. Cool for 5 minutes.

8. Use hot pads or silicone baking mitts to transfer the (still hot!) ramekins to a nearby wire rack. Cool to room temperature, about 1 hour. Cover and refrigerate for at least 1 hour before serving—or up to 3 days.

Other Pots

- For a 3-quart Instant Pot, you *must* halve the ingredient amounts (making 3 ramekins).

- For a 10-quart Instant Pot, you *must* increase the amount of water in the insert to 2½ cups while otherwise completing the recipe as stated—or you *can* use that amount of water and increase the ingredient amounts by 50 percent, making 9 ramekins.

Beyond

- Top each chilled mini cheesecake with 1 tablespoon of your favorite preserves or canned pie filling.

- Use this recipe to make one 7-inch cheesecake in a 5-, 6-, or 8-quart Instant Pot with four notes: 1) keep the water in the insert at 1½ cups; 2) use a 7-inch-round springform pan; 3) increase the crust amounts to 1 cup crumbs and 5 tablespoons melted and cooled butter; and 4) double the ingredient amounts for the cheesecake batter. Press the crust into the buttered or sprayed pan for an even bottom and up the sides by 1 inch. Cook at HIGH pressure for 25 minutes, followed by a natural release, a 1-hour cooling at room temperature, then a 1-day storage in the refrigerator.

See photo in insert.

Mini Ricotta Cheesecakes

11 ingredients

6 MINI CHEESECAKES

METHOD:
pot-in-pot

SPECIAL EQUIPMENT:
six ½-cup (4-ounce) pressure-safe ramekins, custard cups, or canning jars; a food processor; and a pressure-safe rack or trivet

PRESSURE:
high

TIME UNDER PRESSURE:
15 minutes

RELEASE:
natural

TOTAL TIME WITH PRESSURE:
about 3 hours (includes refrigerating)

VEGETARIAN

1½ cups water

3 tablespoons butter, melted and cooled *for 10 minutes*, plus additional cold butter for greasing

Six 2- to 3-inch gingersnap crumbs, ground to crumbs (for more information on grinding or crushing cookies, see the headnote on page 403)

4 ounces regular cream cheese (do not use low-fat or fat-free), *at room temperature*

½ cup (4 ounces) whole-milk ricotta cheese (do not use low-fat or fat-free), *at room temperature*

¼ cup granulated white sugar

1 large egg, *at room temperature*

1 tablespoon heavy cream

1½ teaspoons all-purpose flour

½ teaspoon vanilla extract

¼ teaspoon table salt

Ricotta adds a creamy lightness to any cheesecake, giving it a mousse-like texture. In fact, it became a popular addition to cheesecake in the mid-twentieth century in Italian-American bakeries, especially during the winter holidays. Those ricotta cheesecakes often had chopped candied fruit in them, although we've opted to keep our hand-size versions purer, spiking the flavors instead with a ginger cookie crust. (If you miss the chopped candied fruit, see the **Beyond** section.)

1. Pour the water into the insert set in a **5-, 6-, or 8-quart Instant Pot.** Put a pressure-safe rack or trivet in the insert.

2. Grease the insides of six ½-cup (4-ounce) pressure-safe ramekins, custard cups, or canning jars with cold butter, making sure it gets generously down into the joint between the side and the bottom of each.

3. Stir the cookie crumbs and melted butter in a medium bowl until moistened. Divide this mixture among the ramekins, about 1½ tablespoons in each. *Gently* press it into an even crust in the bottom of each.

4. Put the cream cheese, ricotta, sugar, egg, cream, flour, vanilla, and salt in a food processor. Cover and process until smooth, stopping the machine at least once to scrape down the inside of the canister. Divide this mixture evenly among the ramekins, a generous ¼ cup in each. Do not cover.

5. Stack the ramekins on the rack, placing three on the bottom level, then three on the top level with each sitting on a part of the rim of at least two below. Lock the lid onto the cooker.

6.

	Set pot for	Set level to	Valve must be	Set time for	If needed, press
For *all* pots	PRESSURE COOK or MANUAL	HIGH	Closed	15 minutes with the KEEP WARM setting off	START

7. When the machine has finished cooking, turn it off and let the pressure **return to normal naturally,** about 20 minutes. Unlatch the lid and open the cooker. Cool for 5 minutes.

8. Use hot pads or silicone baking mitts to transfer the still hot ramekins to a nearby wire rack. Cool to room temperature, about 1 hour. Cover and refrigerate for at least 1 hour before serving—or up to 3 days.

Other Pots

- For a **3-quart Instant Pot,** you *must* halve the ingredient amounts (making 3 ramekins).

- For a **10-quart Instant Pot,** you *must* increase the amount of water in the insert to 2½ cups while otherwise completing the recipe as stated—or you *can* use that amount of water and increase the ingredient amounts by 50 percent, thereby making 9 ramekins.

Beyond

- Add up to 2 tablespoons minced candied citron or orange peel to the cream cheese ingredients once they've been blended. Pulse once or twice to combine.

- To make one 7-inch ricotta cheesecake in a 5-, 6-, or 8-quart Instant Pot, you *must* keep the water in the insert the same, but you *must* double all of the other ingredient amounts and use a 7-inch-round springform pan for the cheesecake. Cook at HIGH pressure for 25 minutes, followed by a natural release, a 1-hour cooling on a rack, and then a 1-day cooling in the refrigerator before serving.

Orange Ricotta Pudding Cake

11 ingredients

4–6 SERVINGS

METHOD:
pot-in-pot

SPECIAL EQUIPMENT:
a 2-quart, 7-inch-round, high-sided, pressure-safe baking or soufflé dish; a food processor; and a pressure-safe rack or trivet

PRESSURE:
max or high

TIME UNDER PRESSURE:
15 or 18 minutes

RELEASE:
natural

TOTAL TIME WITH PRESSURE:
about 1 hour

VEGETARIAN

1½ cups water

Butter, for greasing

1 pound whole-milk ricotta (do not use low-fat or fat-free), *at room temperature*

4 large eggs, *at room temperature*

½ cup granulated white sugar

1 tablespoon finely grated orange zest

2 tablespoons orange juice

½ teaspoon orange extract

¼ teaspoon table salt

¼ cup all-purpose flour (dip and level— do not pack)

¼ cup finely chopped walnuts

Other Pots

- For a 3-quart Instant Pot, you *must* halve almost all of the ingredient amounts *except* you *must* use 1 cup water in the insert. You *must* also use a 1-quart, 6-inch-round, high-sided, pressure-safe baking or soufflé dish.

- For a 10-quart Instant Pot, you *must* increase the amount of water in the insert to 2½ cups while otherwise completing the recipe as stated.

Beyond

- The cake is so rich that it doesn't need ice cream, but a drizzle of warm caramel sauce wouldn't hurt.

- Or skip that and drizzle warmed heavy cream over each serving.

This cake is a true *pudding* cake, not just a really moist cake. You might think of it as a cross between a cheesecake and custard— which means you won't be able to cut it very well. Instead, you'll need to dish it up warm by the spoonful. Rich and decadent, it's best just a few minutes out of the cooker. It gets gummy if it sits too long—which means you can't be caught with leftovers. You'll manage.

1. Pour the water into the insert set in a **5-, 6-, or 8-quart Instant Pot.** Put a pressure-safe rack or trivet into the pot. Generously butter the inside of a 2-quart, 7-inch-round, high-sided, pressure-safe baking or soufflé dish.

2. Put the ricotta, eggs, sugar, orange zest, orange juice, orange extract, and salt in a food processor. Cover and process until smooth, stopping the machine at least once to scrape down the inside of the canister. Add the flour and walnuts. Pulse a few times to combine, just until all the flour has been moistened.

3. Pour and scrape this mixture into the prepared pan. Cover the pan with aluminum foil. Lower it onto the rack and lock the lid on the cooker.

4.

	Set pot for	Set level to	Valve must be	Set time for	If needed, press
For Max pots only	PRESSURE COOK	MAX	—	15 minutes with the KEEP WARM setting off	START
For all other pots	PRESSURE COOK or MANUAL	HIGH	Closed	18 minutes with the KEEP WARM setting off	START

5. When the pot has finished cooking, turn it off and let the pressure **return to normal naturally,** about 20 minutes. Unlatch the lid and open the cooker. Use hot pads or silicone baking mitts to transfer the (hot!) baking dish to a nearby wire rack. Cool for 10 minutes before serving up in bowls by big spoonfuls.

Apricot-Almond Pudding Cake

12 ingredients

4–6 SERVINGS

METHOD:
pot-in-pot

SPECIAL EQUIPMENT:
a 2-quart, 7-inch-round, high-sided, pressure-safe baking or soufflé dish; an electric mixer; and a pressure-safe rack or trivet

PRESSURE:
max or high

TIME UNDER PRESSURE:
25 or 35 minutes

RELEASE:
natural

TOTAL TIME WITH PRESSURE:
about 1 hour

VEGETARIAN

1½ cups water

Baking spray

⅓ cup apricot jam (do not use sugar-free)

1 stick (8 tablespoons or ½ cup) butter

½ cup packed light brown sugar

2 large eggs, *at room temperature*

3 tablespoons Southern Comfort, apricot brandy, or apricot nectar

1 tablespoon vanilla extract

1 cup whole almonds, finely ground; or ¾ cup purchased ground almonds

½ cup all-purpose flour (dip and level—do not pack)

½ teaspoon baking powder

¼ teaspoon table salt

Other Pots

- For a 3-quart Instant Pot, you *must* halve almost all of the ingredient amounts *except* you *must* use 1 cup water in the insert. You *must* also use a 1-quart, 6-inch-round, high-sided, pressure-safe baking or soufflé dish.

- For a 10-quart Instant Pot, you *must* increase the amount of water in the insert to 2½ cups while otherwise completing the recipe as stated.

Beyond

- Top the servings with an easy hard sauce: Use an electric mixer at medium speed to beat 1 stick (8 tablespoons) room-temperature butter in a medium bowl until airy, scraping down the inside of the bowl several times. Add 1½ cups confectioners' sugar and beat until smooth. Beat in 2 tablespoons whisky until uniform.

This pudding cake is more like a steamed Christmas pudding, especially with the apricots, almonds, and brandy in the mix, although it is not quite as compact and dense as the British classic.

1. Pour the water into the insert set in a **5-, 6-, or 8-quart Instant Pot.** Put a pressure-safe rack or trivet in the insert. Generously coat the inside of a 2-quart, 7-inch-round, high-sided, pressure-safe baking or soufflé dish with baking spray.

2. Loosen the jam up by stirring it in a small bowl with a fork, then use a rubber spatula to spread an even layer of the jam across the bottom of the baking dish.

3. With a handheld electric mixer or a stand mixer fitted with the paddle attachment, beat the butter and brown sugar in a large bowl at medium speed until light and creamy, about 5 minutes. Beat in the eggs one at a time, stopping the beaters and scraping down the inside of the bowl with a rubber spatula before you beat in the second egg.

4. Beat in the brandy and vanilla until smooth. Then turn off the beaters and add the almonds, flour, baking powder, and salt. Beat a low speed just until combined and all the flour has been moistened (the batter will still be grainy). Scrape down and remove the beaters.

5. Gently pour and scrape this batter into the prepared baking dish, taking care to keep the apricot jam in place. Cover the dish tightly with aluminum foil, lower it onto the rack, and lock the lid on the pot.

6.

	Set pot for	Set level to	Valve must be	Set time for	If needed, press
For Max pots only	PRESSURE COOK	MAX	—	25 minutes with the KEEP WARM setting off	START
For all other pots	PRESSURE COOK or MANUAL	HIGH	Closed	35 minutes with the KEEP WARM setting off	START

7. When the pot has finished cooking, turn it off and let the pressure **return to normal naturally,** about 20 minutes. Unlatch the lid and open the cooker. Use hot pads or silicone baking mitts to transfer the (hot!) baking dish to a nearby wire rack. Cool for 10 minutes.

8. Set a serving platter over the baking dish, then invert the still hot baking dish and platter so that the cake falls out onto the platter. Remove the baking dish and serve at once or within about 20 minutes.

Super Easy Caramel Lava Cakes

5 ingredients

6 SMALL CAKES

METHOD:
pot-in-pot

SPECIAL EQUIPMENT:
six 6-ounce pressure-safe ramekins or custard cups, an electric mixer, and a pressure-safe rack or trivet

PRESSURE:
max or high

TIME UNDER PRESSURE:
6 or 8 minutes

RELEASE:
quick

TOTAL TIME WITH PRESSURE:
about 25 minutes

VEGETARIAN

1½ cups water

Baking spray

1 large egg *plus* 2 large egg yolks, *at room temperature*

1¾ cups purchased dulce de leche (for more information, see the headnote on page 404)

¼ cup all-purpose flour

Other Pots

- For a 3-quart Instant Pot, you *must* halve the ingredient amounts (making 3 ramekins).

- For a 10-quart Instant Pot, you *must* increase the amount of water in the insert to 2½ cups while otherwise completing the recipe as stated—or you *can* use that amount of water and increase the ingredient amounts by 50 percent, thereby making 9 ramekins.

Beyond

- The cakes are so hot that they'll melt whipped cream or ice cream. Instead, drizzle each with warmed heavy cream.

- For a little kick, add up to ¼ teaspoon ground dried cayenne to the eggs before beating.

Here's a caramel version of the more famous chocolate lava cakes. These caramel ones must be served quite hot so they almost melt on the plates. Despite the recipe's name, use only dulce de leche, not jarred caramel ice cream topping. Dulce de leche is thicker and will help the cakes retain their shape until they're served—but not for long!

1. Pour the water into the insert set in a **5-, 6-, or 8-quart Instant Pot.** Put a pressure-safe rack or trivet in the insert. Coat the inside of six 6-ounce pressure-safe ramekins or custard cups with baking spray.

2. Use a handheld electric mixer at medium speed to beat the egg and egg yolks in a medium bowl until thick and light colored, about 3 minutes. Add the dulce de leche and beat until well combined. Turn off the beaters, scrape them down, and remove them.

3. Use a rubber spatula to fold in the flour just until uniform, no dry specks anywhere. Divide this mixture among the prepared ramekins. Cover each tightly with aluminum foil.

4. Stack the ramekins on the rack, placing three on the bottom level, then three on the top level with each sitting on a part of the rim of at least two below. Lock the lid onto the cooker.

5.

	Set pot for	Set level to	Valve must be	Set time for	If needed, press
For Max pots only	PRESSURE COOK	MAX	—	6 minutes with the KEEP WARM setting off	START
For all other pots	PRESSURE COOK or MANUAL	HIGH	Closed	8 minutes with the KEEP WARM setting off	START

6. When the pot has finished cooking, use the **quick-release method** to bring the pressure back to normal. Unlatch the lid and open the cooker. Use hot pads or silicone baking mitts to transfer the (hot!) ramekins to a nearby wire rack. Cool for 1 minute, then invert the ramekins onto serving plates, remove the ramekins, and serve right away, while still quite hot.

Classic Apple Cake

13 ingredients

6 SERVINGS

METHOD:
pot-in-pot

SPECIAL
EQUIPMENT:
a 7-inch-round
springform pan
and a pressure-
safe rack or trivet

PRESSURE:
max or high

TIME UNDER
PRESSURE:
45 or 50 minutes

RELEASE:
natural

TOTAL TIME WITH
PRESSURE:
about 3½
hours (includes
macerating and
cooling)

VEGETARIAN

---

2 medium tart baking apples, such as Granny Smiths, peeled, cored, and diced (2 cups)

⅔ cup plus ¼ cup granulated white sugar

2 teaspoons ground cinnamon

1½ cups water

Baking spray

1½ cups all-purpose flour (dip and level—do not pack)

1½ teaspoons baking powder

½ teaspoon baking soda

½ teaspoon table salt

1 stick (8 tablespoons or ½ cup) butter, melted and cooled *to room temperature*

2 large eggs, *at room temperature*

2 tablespoons brandy, apple brandy, or unsweetened apple cider

1½ teaspoons vanilla extract

Other Pots

- Because of the size of the pan and the delicate ingredient ratios, this recipe cannot easily be made in a 3-quart Instant Pot.

- For a 10-quart Instant Pot, you *must* increase the amount of water in the insert to 2½ cups while otherwise completing the recipe as stated.

Beyond

- Add more spice to the cake. Either stir up to ½ teaspoon ground allspice, ½ teaspoon ground cardamom, and/or ¼ teaspoon grated nutmeg into the apples with the cinnamon or substitute 2 teaspoons dried apple pie spice blend for the cinnamon.

Here's an Instant Pot version of a traditional apple cake, super light and tender when it comes out of the cooker. It's made by macerating diced apples in sugar until they release much of their internal moisture, which then becomes part of the very structure of the cake itself. We love to serve this one on the weekends for brunch when we have houseguests.

1. Stir the apples, ¼ cup sugar, and the cinnamon in a medium bowl until the apples are well coated in the sugar. Set aside on the counter for 20 minutes, stirring once.

2. Pour the water into the insert set in a **5-, 6-, or 8-quart Instant Pot.** Put a pressure-safe rack or trivet in the insert. Coat the inside of a 7-inch-round springform pan with baking spray.

3. Whisk the flour, baking powder, baking soda, and salt in a second medium bowl until uniform.

4. Whisk the melted butter, eggs, brandy or its substitutes, vanilla, and the remaining ⅔ cup sugar in a large bowl until smooth and almost creamy. Use a wooden spoon or a rubber spatula to stir in the flour mixture, just until there are no specks of dry flour. Stir in the apples and any sugar or liquid in their bowl until uniform.

5. Scrape and spread the batter into the prepared pan. Set the pan on the rack and cover the pan loosely with a paper towel. Lock the lid onto the cooker.

6.

	Set pot for	Set level to	Valve must be	Set time for	If needed, press
For Max pots only	PRESSURE COOK	MAX	—	45 minutes with the KEEP WARM setting off	START
For all other pots	PRESSURE COOK or MANUAL	HIGH	Closed	50 minutes with the KEEP WARM setting off	START

7. When the pot has finished cooking, turn it off and let the pressure **return to normal naturally,** about 20 minutes. Unlatch the lid and open the cooker. Remove and discard the paper towel. Use hot pads or silicone baking mitts to transfer the (hot!) pan to a nearby wire rack. Cool for 30 minutes, then unlatch the ring side from the springform pan. Cool for at least another 20 minutes or up to 2 hours at room temperature before removing the ring and slicing the cake into wedges.

Cranberry-Nut Cake

13 or 14 ingredients

6 SERVINGS

METHOD:
pot-in-pot

SPECIAL EQUIPMENT:
a 7-inch-round springform pan and a pressure-safe rack or trivet

PRESSURE:
max or high

TIME UNDER PRESSURE:
43 or 50 minutes

RELEASE:
natural

TOTAL TIME WITH PRESSURE:
about 2 hours (includes cooling)

VEGETARIAN

1½ cups water

Baking spray

1½ cups all-purpose flour (dip and level—do not pack)

½ teaspoon baking powder

½ teaspoon baking soda

½ teaspoon ground cinnamon

½ teaspoon table salt

One 14-ounce can *whole berry* cranberry sauce

⅓ cup packed dark brown sugar

¼ cup vegetable, canola, or other neutral-flavored oil

1 large egg, *at room temperature*

½ teaspoon vanilla extract

½ teaspoon orange extract (optional)

1 cup chopped walnuts or pecans

Other Pots

- Because of the size of the pan and the delicate ingredient ratios, this recipe cannot easily be made in a 3-quart Instant Pot.
- For a 10-quart Instant Pot, you *must* increase the amount of water in the insert to 2½ cups while otherwise completing the recipe as stated.

Beyond

- After the cake cools, add a glaze by mixing 1¼ cups confectioners' sugar with about 1 tablespoon milk, then more milk in small dribs and drabs to make a thick drizzle.
- Gussy up this glaze by adding up to 2 teaspoons finely grated orange zest with the milk.

Looking for an IP dessert this holiday season? Or looking for a little snack some weekend when you've got friends dropping by mid-afternoon? We've got you covered with this lightly spiced cake. Use only whole berry cranberry sauce. The jellied sauce has too much sugar (and will not allow the cake to set with this amount of flour).

1. Pour the water into the insert set in a **5-, 6-, or 8-quart Instant Pot.** Put a pressure-safe rack or trivet in the insert. Coat the inside of a 7-inch-round springform pan with baking spray.

2. Whisk the flour, baking powder, baking soda, cinnamon, and salt in a medium bowl until uniform.

3. Whisk the cranberry sauce, brown sugar, oil, egg, vanilla, and orange extract (if using) in a large bowl until smooth and almost creamy (except for the cranberries). Use a wooden spoon or a rubber spatula to stir in the flour mixture and the nuts just until there are no dry specks (the batter will still be grainy).

4. Pour and scrape the batter into the prepared pan. Set it on the rack and lay a paper towel over the top. Lock the lid onto the cooker.

5.

	Set pot for	Set level to	Valve must be	Set time for	If needed, press
For Max pots only	PRESSURE COOK	MAX	—	43 minutes with the KEEP WARM setting off	START
For all other pots	PRESSURE COOK or MANUAL	HIGH	Closed	50 minutes with the KEEP WARM setting off	START

6. When the pot has finished cooking, turn it off and let the pressure **return to normal naturally,** about 20 minutes. Unlatch the lid and open the cooker. Remove and discard the paper towel. Use hot pads or silicone baking mitts to transfer the (hot!) pan to a nearby wire rack. Cool for 15 minutes, then unlatch the ring side from the springform pan. Cool for at least another 15 minutes before removing the ring and slicing the cake into wedges. Lightly covered with a clean kitchen towel, the cake can keep at room temperature for up to 1 day.

Shakshuka (page 36)
with black pepper and basil

Breakfast Fruit Cobbler
(page 43)

Cinnamon-Sugar Pancake-Mix Bites (page 44) with butter and maple syrup

Blueberry Pancake-Mix Cake (page 55)

Cheddar Ale Soup with
Bacony Croutons (page 71)

Buttery Carrot-Ginger Soup
(page 61) in a bread bowl and
garnished with chives

Not-Really-Olive-
Garden's Zuppa
Toscana (page 84)

Ginger-Garlic Beef and Noodle Soup (page 92) with baby corn and toasted sesame oil

Pasta with Easy Buttery Tomato Sauce (page 108) with basil, olive oil, and red pepper flakes

Meat and Mushroom Manicotti (page 121)
with crumbled Parmigiano-Reggiano

One-Pot Barbecue Brisket
Ragù with Noodles (page 138)
as spaghetti sandwiches

One-Pot Chicken Pad Thai
(page 153) with cilantro
and more peanuts

Easy Chicken-
Antipasto
Pasta Salad
(page 163)

Chicken Pastrami (page 175)
as a reuben sandwich

Not-Really-
Panda-Express's
Orange Chicken
(page 186)

Tikka-Spiced Chicken
Kebabs (page 194)

Chicken Negimaki (page 193)
with easy carrot salad

Not-Really-P.F.-Chang's Chicken Lettuce Wraps (page 208) with hot sauce

Not-Really-Taco-Bell's Taco Meat (page 224) with all the fixings

French-Onion-Soup Meat Loaf
(page 238)

Not-Really-Chipotle's Barbacoa Beef (page 256) in flour tortillas with avocado and salsa

Pork Spiedies (page 286)
in hot dog buns with
lettuce and tomato

Sticky-Sweet
Soy Pork Ribs
(page 290)

No-Brainer Pork Posole
(page 313)

Not-Really-Chili's Queso Dip
(page 328)

From-Scratch Holiday Green Bean Casserole (page 335) and Mashed Butternut Squash (page 342)

Lemon, Baby Kale, and Goat Cheese Risotto (page 365) with more lemon zest and black pepper

No-Brainer
Low-Carb
Stuffed
Peppers
(page 369)

Lemon Curd (page 387)
with fresh berries

Spiced Poached Pears
(page 390) with vanilla
ice cream

Butterscotch Cheesecake (page 405) topped with
a caramel sauce and caramel corn

Mini Cheesecakes
(page 408) topped with
canned cherry pie filling

Cake-Mix Cinnamon-Swirl Bundt (page 428)

Cake-Mix Lemon–Poppyseed Two-Layer Cake (page 484)

Spaghetti for a Crowd (page 442)

Orange–Sour Cream Bundt

12 ingredients

6 SERVINGS

METHOD:
pot-in-pot

SPECIAL
EQUIPMENT:
a 6-cup pressure-
safe Bundt pan,
a food processor,
and a pressure-
safe rack or trivet

PRESSURE:
max or high

TIME UNDER
PRESSURE:
18 or 25 minutes

RELEASE:
natural

TOTAL TIME WITH
PRESSURE:
about 1 hour
(includes cooling)

VEGETARIAN

1½ cups water

Baking spray

⅔ cup packed light brown sugar

¾ stick (6 tablespoons) butter, *at room temperature*

¼ cup regular sour cream (do not use low-fat or fat-free), *at room temperature*

1 large egg *plus* 1 large egg white, *at room temperature*

3 tablespoons thawed frozen orange juice concentrate

2 teaspoons vanilla extract

1 cup all-purpose flour (dip and level— do not pack)

½ teaspoon baking powder

½ teaspoon baking soda

¼ teaspoon table salt

Other Pots

- For a 3-quart Instant Pot, you *must* decrease the amount of water in the insert to 1 cup while otherwise completing the recipe as stated.

- For a 10-quart Instant Pot, you *must* increase the amount of water in the insert to 2½ cups while otherwise completing the recipe as stated.

Beyond

- To make a glaze, put ¼ cup orange marmalade in a microwave-safe bowl and microwave on HIGH in 10-second increments, stirring after each, until melted. Stir in 2 tablespoons bourbon, if desired. Drizzle over the cake when the cake is out of its pan but still warm.

Thanks to sour cream, the texture of this Bundt cake is more like a sponge cake: light and airy. The brown sugar gives it slight "molasses notes," a nice pairing with the vanilla and orange juice. Make sure you save a couple of pieces for breakfast!

1. Pour the water into the insert set in a **5-, 6-, or 8-quart Instant Pot.** Put a pressure-safe rack or trivet in the insert. Coat the inside of a 6-cup pressure-safe Bundt pan with baking spray, taking care to get the coating into all the crevasses.

2. Put the brown sugar, butter, sour cream, egg, egg white, orange juice concentrate, and vanilla in a food processor. Cover and process until smooth. Scrape down the inside of the canister, then add the flour, baking powder, baking soda, and salt. Cover and process until smooth.

3. Pour and scrape the batter evenly into the prepared pan. Set it on the rack and lay a paper towel over the top of the pan. Lock the lid onto the cooker.

4.

	Set pot for	Set level to	Valve must be	Set time for	If needed, press
For Max pots only	PRESSURE COOK	MAX	—	18 minutes with the KEEP WARM setting off	START
For all other pots	PRESSURE COOK or MANUAL	HIGH	Closed	25 minutes with the KEEP WARM setting off	START

5. When the pot has finished cooking, turn it off and let the pressure **return to normal naturally,** about 20 minutes. Unlatch the lid and open the cooker. Remove and discard the paper towel. Use hot pads or silicone baking mitts to transfer the (hot!) pan to a nearby wire rack. Cool for 10 minutes, then set a serving plate or platter over the top of the pan. Invert everything, remove the pan, and cool the cake on the plate for at least another 15 minutes before slicing and serving. Or cool to room temperature and store on the counter, loosely covered, for up to 12 hours.

Spiced Pumpkin Bundt

15 ingredients

6 SERVINGS

METHOD:
pot-in-pot

SPECIAL
EQUIPMENT:
a 6-cup pressure-
safe Bundt pan, an
electric mixer, and
a pressure-safe
rack or trivet

PRESSURE:
max or high

TIME UNDER
PRESSURE:
25 or 30 minutes

RELEASE:
natural

TOTAL TIME WITH
PRESSURE:
about 1½ hours
(includes cooling)

VEGETARIAN

1½ cups water

Baking spray

1½ cups all-purpose flour (dip and
level—do not pack)

½ teaspoon baking powder

½ teaspoon baking soda

1 teaspoon ground cinnamon

½ teaspoon ground dried ginger

¼ teaspoon ground cloves

¼ teaspoon table salt

1 stick (8 tablespoons or ½ cup)
refrigerator-cold butter, cut into bits

1 cup granulated white sugar

2 large eggs, *at room temperature*

1 cup canned solid-pack pumpkin (do not
use pumpkin-pie filling)

2 teaspoons molasses

½ cup chopped walnuts or pecans

This spiced cake has a texture like a quick bread, a bit denser than a traditional cake (as well as many a cake that comes out of an IP). It might be a welcome addition to a weekend brunch as much as a great dessert with a glass of aged rum in front of the fireplace on a cold night.

You'll note that the recipe asks you to beat *cold* butter and sugar. That's the secret to the cake's crumb. Cold butter can trap more air molecules as it's beaten, resulting in a lighter cake. Yes, it takes much longer to beat it until it's smooth and light. And yes, the butter warms up as it's beaten—but it's capturing air the whole time. Beaten, room-temperature butter often results in a flatter cake. (See the Orange–Sour Cream Bundt—page 417—for one recipe that actually needs room-temperature butter for a denser cake.)

1. Pour the water into the insert set in a **5-, 6-, or 8-quart Instant Pot.** Put a pressure-safe rack or trivet in the insert. Coat the inside of a 6-cup pressure-safe Bundt pan with baking spray, taking care to get the coating into all the crevasses.

2. Whisk the flour, baking powder, baking soda, cinnamon, ginger, cloves, and salt in a medium bowl until uniform.

3. Use a stand mixer fitted with the paddle attachment or a handheld electric mixer at medium speed to beat the butter and sugar in a large bowl until creamy and smooth, about 5 minutes. Don't stint. Beat and beat, even if it takes longer than suggested.

4. Beat in the eggs one at a time, stopping the mixer to scrape down the inside of the bowl after each addition. Beat in the pumpkin and molasses until smooth.

5. Turn off the beaters; add the flour mixture and nuts. Beat at low speed *just* until well combined, no dry specks in the still-grainy mix.

6. Pour and scrape this mixture evenly into the prepared pan. Set it on the rack and lay a paper towel over the top of the pan. Lock the lid on the cooker.

7.

	Set pot for	Set level to	Valve must be	Set time for	If needed, press
For Max pots only	PRESSURE COOK	MAX	—	25 minutes with the KEEP WARM setting off	START
For all other pots	PRESSURE COOK or MANUAL	HIGH	Closed	30 minutes with the KEEP WARM setting off	START

8. When the pot has finished cooking, turn it off and let the pressure **return to normal naturally,** about 20 minutes. Unlatch the lid and open the cooker. Remove and discard the paper towel. Use hot pads or silicone baking mitts to transfer the (hot!) pan to a nearby wire rack. Cool for 10 minutes, then set a serving plate or platter over the top of the pan. Invert everything, remove the pan, and cool the cake on the plate for at least another 15 minutes before slicing and serving. Or cool to room temperature and store on the counter, loosely covered, for up to 1 day.

Other Pots

- For a **3-quart Instant Pot,** you *must* decrease the amount of water in the insert to 1 cup while otherwise completing the recipe as stated.

- For a **10-quart Instant Pot,** you *must* increase the amount of water in the insert to 2½ cups while otherwise completing the recipe as stated.

Beyond

- When cooled, the cake can be dusted with confectioners' sugar.

- Serve the slices with cream cheese for smearing (or with butter, if you've saved some cake for breakfast).

Classic
Carrot Cake

14 ingredients	
6 SERVINGS	
METHOD: pot-in-pot	

SPECIAL EQUIPMENT: a 7-inch-round springform pan and a pressure-safe rack or trivet

PRESSURE: max or high

TIME UNDER PRESSURE: 53 or 60 minutes

RELEASE: natural

TOTAL TIME WITH PRESSURE: about 3 hours (includes cooling)

VEGETARIAN

1½ cups water

Baking spray

1½ cups all-purpose flour (dip and level—do not pack)

½ teaspoon baking powder

½ teaspoon baking soda

½ teaspoon ground cinnamon

¼ teaspoon grated nutmeg

¼ teaspoon table salt

2 large eggs, *at room temperature*

¾ cup packed dark brown sugar

½ cup granulated white sugar

½ cup vegetable, canola, or other neutral-flavored oil

½ pound carrots, peeled and grated through the large holes of a box grater (1½ packed cups)

¼ cup raisins (black or golden)

Other Pots

- Because of the size of the pan and the delicate ingredient ratios, this recipe cannot easily be made in a 3-quart Instant Pot.

- For a 10-quart Instant Pot, you *must* increase the amount of water in the insert to 2½ cups while otherwise completing the recipe as stated.

Beyond

- Stir in up to ¼ cup chopped pecans or walnuts with the carrots and raisins.

- Miss the cream cheese frosting? Serve the cake with dollops of crème fraîche.

Well, this is as classic a carrot cake as we can make in an Instant Pot! Don't expect that characteristic dense crumb. As with most cakes under pressure, this one's really light, thanks to the way the pressure inflates the batter.

Do not use julienned carrots, sometimes found in the produce section of the supermarket. They will be slightly thicker than grated carrots and won't soften appropriately in the cake. And because the cake is so light, it's almost impossible to frost it. See the **Beyond** for a way to fix that deficit.

1. Pour the water into the insert set in a **5-, 6-, or 8-quart Instant Pot.** Put a pressure-safe rack or trivet in the insert. Coat the inside of a 7-inch-round springform pan with baking spray.

2. Whisk the flour, baking powder, baking soda, cinnamon, nutmeg, and salt in a medium bowl until uniform.

3. Whisk the eggs, brown sugar, white sugar, and oil in a large bowl until smooth and just about creamy. Use a wooden spoon to stir in the carrots and raisins until uniform. Add the flour mixture and stir just until there are no dry specks anywhere.

4. Pour and scrape this batter into the prepared pan. Set it on the rack and lay a paper towel over the top of the pan. Lock the lid on the cooker.

5.

	Set pot for	Set level to	Valve must be	Set time for	If needed, press
For Max pots only	PRESSURE COOK	MAX	—	53 minutes with the KEEP WARM setting off	START
For all other pots	PRESSURE COOK or MANUAL	HIGH	Closed	1 hour with the KEEP WARM setting off	START

6. When the pot has finished cooking, turn it off and let the pressure **return to normal naturally,** about 20 minutes. Unlatch the lid and open the cooker. Remove and discard the paper towel. Use hot pads or silicone baking mitts to transfer the (hot!) pan to a nearby wire rack. Cool for 30 minutes, then unlatch the ring side from the springform pan. Cool for at least another 20 minutes or up to 2 hours at room temperature before removing the ring and slicing the cake into wedges.

Melted-Vanilla-Ice-Cream Bundt

9 ingredients	
6 SERVINGS	
METHOD: pot-in-pot	

SPECIAL EQUIPMENT: a 6-cup pressure-safe Bundt pan and a pressure-safe rack or trivet

PRESSURE: max or high

TIME UNDER PRESSURE: 20 or 24 minutes

RELEASE: natural

TOTAL TIME WITH PRESSURE: about 1½ hours (includes cooling)

VEGETARIAN

1½ cups water

Baking spray

1 pint *premium* vanilla ice cream, melted

½ cup granulated white sugar

1 large egg, *at room temperature*

½ teaspoon vanilla extract

1½ cups all-purpose flour (dip and level—do not pack)

1 teaspoon baking powder

¼ teaspoon table salt

By now, you probably know we're nuts about using melted ice cream as a baking ingredient. We got hooked while we were writing *The Kitchen Shortcut Bible* and we've never looked back.

Use only a smooth vanilla ice cream here, without any nuts, shaved chocolate, or butterscotch ribbons. And use only a premium ice cream. The resulting cake is quite sweet and a little dense, thanks to all those rich ingredients in premium ice cream. It's best with a strong cup of tea or even a shot of espresso.

1. Pour the water into the insert set in a **5-, 6-, or 8-quart Instant Pot.** Put a pressure-safe rack or trivet in the insert. Coat the inside of a 6-cup pressure-safe Bundt pan with baking spray, taking care to get the coating into all the crevasses.

2. Whisk the melted ice cream, sugar, egg, and vanilla in a large bowl until quite smooth and creamy. Whisk in the flour, baking powder, and salt just until there are no dry specks of flour.

3. Scrape and pour the batter into the prepared pan. Set it on the rack and lay a paper towel over the pan. Lock the lid on the cooker.

4.

	Set pot for	Set level to	Valve must be	Set time for	If needed, press
For Max pots only	PRESSURE COOK	MAX	—	20 minutes with the KEEP WARM setting off	START
For all other pots	PRESSURE COOK or MANUAL	HIGH	Closed	24 minutes with the KEEP WARM setting off	START

5. When the pot has finished cooking, turn it off and let the pressure **return to normal naturally,** about 20 minutes. Unlatch the lid and open the cooker. Remove and discard the paper towel. Use hot pads or silicone baking mitts to transfer the (hot!) pan to a nearby wire rack. Cool for 10 minutes, then set a serving plate or platter over the top of the pan. Invert everything, remove the pan, and cool the cake on the plate for at least another 15 minutes before slicing and serving. Or cool to room temperature and store on the counter, loosely covered, for up to 12 hours.

Other Pots

- For a 3-quart Instant Pot, you *must* decrease the amount of water in the insert to 1 cup while otherwise completing the recipe as stated.

- For a 10-quart Instant Pot, you *must* increase the amount of water in the insert to 2½ cups while otherwise completing the recipe as stated.

Beyond

- Substitute any flavoring extract for the vanilla: rum, almond, orange, or lemon. Or use vanilla and another extract together.

Cake-Mix Lemon Pound Cake

11 ingredients	**SPECIAL EQUIPMENT:** a 6-cup pressure-safe Bundt pan and a pressure-safe rack or trivet
6 SERVINGS	
METHOD: pot-in-pot	

PRESSURE: max or high	**TOTAL TIME WITH PRESSURE:** about 1½ hours (includes cooling)
TIME UNDER PRESSURE: 19 or 24 minutes	**CAN BE VEGETARIAN**
RELEASE: natural	

1½ cups water

Baking spray

2 cups standard yellow cake mix (half of a 15¼-ounce box—vegetarian, if necessary—do not use a sugar-free, gluten-free, or pudding cake mix)

¼ cup *instant* lemon pudding mix (half of a 3.4-ounce box—vegetarian, if necessary)

6 tablespoons regular or low-fat sour cream (do not use fat-free), *at room temperature*

¼ cup uncultured buttermilk (see page 17 for more information)

1 large egg, *at room temperature*

2 teaspoons finely grated lemon zest

1 tablespoon lemon juice

½ teaspoon baking powder

Confectioners' sugar, for garnishing

After we wrote the first *Instant Pot Bible,* we started playing in the kitchen with boxed cake mixes—and we couldn't believe we had missed out on so many great but easy cakes in that book! In fact, by using both a cake mix and *instant* pudding, we can create a cake that's so tender and light, it's almost better with a spoon rather than a fork. Because of the way pressure inflates a batter, even a pound cake still has a fairly light crumb. However, it's still a bit dense and velvety. In other words, it's about as close to a pound cake as you can make in an Instant Pot. Do not substitute a pudding cake mix for the more standard cake mix. And use only instant pudding mix, not the more standard pudding mixes available at the supermarket.

1. Pour the water into the insert set in a **5-, 6-, or 8-quart Instant Pot.** Put a pressure-safe rack or trivet in the insert. Coat the inside of a 6-cup pressure-safe Bundt pan with baking spray, taking care to get the coating into all the crevasses.

2. Whisk the cake mix, pudding mix, sour cream, buttermilk, egg, lemon zest, lemon juice, and baking powder in a large bowl until smooth. Pour and scrape into the prepared pan. Set it on the rack, lay a paper towel over the pan, and lock the lid on the pot.

3.

	Set pot for	Set level to	Valve must be	Set time for	If needed, press
For Max pots only	PRESSURE COOK	MAX	—	19 minutes with the KEEP WARM setting off	START
For all other pots	PRESSURE COOK or MANUAL	HIGH	Closed	24 minutes with the KEEP WARM setting off	START

4. When the pot has finished cooking, turn it off and let the pressure **return to normal naturally,** about 20 minutes. Unlatch the lid and open the cooker. Remove and discard the paper towel. Use hot pads or silicone baking mitts to transfer the (hot!) pan to a nearby wire rack. Cool for 10 minutes, then set a serving plate or platter over the top of the pan. Invert everything, remove the pan, and cool the cake on the plate for at least another 15 minutes before slicing and serving, garnished with a dusting of confectioners' sugar. Or cool the cake to room temperature, garnish with the confectioners' sugar, and store on the counter, loosely covered, for up to 12 hours.

Other Pots

- For a 3-quart Instant Pot, you *must* decrease the amount of water in the insert to 1 cup while otherwise completing the recipe as stated.

- For a 10-quart Instant Pot, you *must* increase the amount of water in the insert to 2½ cups while otherwise completing the recipe as stated.

Cake-Mix Four-Chocolate Bundt

10 ingredients	
6 SERVINGS	
METHOD: pot-in-pot	

SPECIAL EQUIPMENT: a 6-cup pressure-safe Bundt pan and a pressure-safe rack or trivet

PRESSURE: max or high

TIME UNDER PRESSURE: 22 or 25 minutes

RELEASE: natural

TOTAL TIME WITH PRESSURE: about 1½ hours (includes cooling)

CAN BE VEGETARIAN

1½ cups water

Baking spray

2 cups standard chocolate cake mix (half of a 15¼-ounce box—vegetarian, if necessary—do not use a sugar-free, gluten-free, or pudding cake mix)

A slightly rounded ¼ cup *instant* chocolate pudding mix (half of a 3.9-ounce box—vegetarian, if necessary)

¾ cup semi-sweet chocolate chips

½ cup regular or low-fat sour cream (do not use fat-free), *at room temperature*

⅓ cup whole or low-fat milk (do not use fat-free)

¼ cup vegetable, canola, or other neutral-flavored oil

1 large egg, *at room temperature*

2 tablespoons unsweetened cocoa powder (do not use hot-chocolate mix)

Count 'em: four kinds of chocolate in one cake. There's a chocolate cake mix, instant chocolate pudding mix, chocolate chips, and unsweetened cocoa powder. All together, they yield a dense, fudgy cake that's got an intense kick in every bite. This one's a chocolate lover's dream!

1. Pour the water into the insert set in a **5-, 6-, or 8-quart Instant Pot.** Put a pressure-safe rack or trivet in the insert. Coat the inside of a 6-cup pressure-safe Bundt pan with baking spray, taking care to get the coating into all the crevasses.

2. Whisk the cake mix, pudding mix, chocolate chips, sour cream, milk, oil, egg, and cocoa powder in a large bowl until smooth. Pour and scrape into the prepared pan. Set it on the rack, lay a paper towel over the pan, and lock the lid on the pot.

3.

	Set pot for	Set level to	Valve must be	Set time for	If needed, press
For Max pots only	PRESSURE COOK	MAX	—	22 minutes with the KEEP WARM setting off	START
For all other pots	PRESSURE COOK or MANUAL	HIGH	Closed	25 minutes with the KEEP WARM setting off	START

4. When the pot has finished cooking, turn it off and let the pressure **return to normal naturally,** about 20 minutes. Unlatch the lid and open the cooker. Remove and discard the paper towel. Use hot pads or silicone baking mitts to transfer the (hot!) pan to a nearby wire rack. Cool for 10 minutes, then set a serving plate or platter over the top of the pan. Invert everything, remove the pan, and cool the cake on the plate for at least another 15 minutes before slicing and serving. Or cool to room temperature and store on the counter, loosely covered, for up to 1 day.

Other Pots

- For a 3-quart Instant Pot, you *must* decrease the amount of water in the insert to 1 cup while otherwise completing the recipe as stated.
- For a 10-quart Instant Pot, you *must* increase the amount of water in the insert to 2½ cups while otherwise completing the recipe as stated.

Beyond

- Serve slices of the cake with vanilla (or chocolate) ice cream and lots of sprinkles.

Cake-Mix Red Velvet Bundt

10 ingredients

6 SERVINGS

METHOD:
pot-in-pot

SPECIAL EQUIPMENT:
a 6-cup pressure-safe Bundt pan and a pressure-safe rack or trivet

PRESSURE:
max or high

TIME UNDER PRESSURE:
19 or 24 minutes

RELEASE:
natural

TOTAL TIME WITH PRESSURE:
about 1½ hours (includes cooling)

CAN BE VEGETARIAN

1½ cups water

Baking spray

2 cups standard white cake mix (half of a 15¼-ounce box—vegetarian, if necessary—do not use a sugar-free, gluten-free, or pudding cake mix)

1½ tablespoons unsweetened cocoa powder

½ teaspoon baking powder

⅔ cup regular evaporated milk (do not use low-fat or fat-free)

½ stick (4 tablespoons or ¼ cup) butter, melted and cooled *to room temperature*

1 large egg, *at room temperature*

1 teaspoon vanilla extract

4 to 5 drops red food coloring

We're inviting the ire of Southerners but we can't resist this super-easy cake-mix variation on the classic chocolate cake with a red tint. Because of the food coloring, don't make this cake while wearing a white shirt. (Trust us.)

1. Pour the water into the insert set in a **5-, 6-, or 8-quart Instant Pot.** Put a pressure-safe rack or trivet in the insert. Coat the inside of a 6-cup pressure-safe Bundt pan with baking spray, taking care to get the coating into all the crevasses.

2. Whisk the cake mix, cocoa powder, and baking powder in a large bowl until uniform. Whisk in the evaporated milk, melted butter, egg, vanilla, and food coloring until smooth.

3. Pour and scrape into the prepared pan. Set it on the rack, lay a paper towel over the pan, and lock the lid on the cooker.

4.

	Set pot for	Set level to	Valve must be	Set time for	If needed, press
For Max pots only	PRESSURE COOK	MAX	—	19 minutes with the KEEP WARM setting off	START
For all other pots	PRESSURE COOK or MANUAL	HIGH	Closed	24 minutes with the KEEP WARM setting off	START

5. When the pot has finished cooking, turn it off and let the pressure **return to normal naturally,** about 20 minutes. Unlatch the lid and open the cooker. Remove and discard the paper towel. Use hot pads or silicone baking mitts to transfer the (hot!) pan to a nearby wire rack. Cool for 10 minutes, then set a serving plate or platter over the top of the pan. Invert everything, remove the pan, and cool the cake on the plate for at least another 15 minutes before slicing and serving. Or cool to room temperature and store on the counter, loosely covered, for up to 1 day.

Beyond

- For a cream cheese frosting, beat 8 ounces room-temperature regular cream cheese (do not use low-fat or fat-free) and ¼ cup room-temperature butter with a handheld electric mixer in a medium bowl until creamy and light. (The amounts are too small to be effective in a stand mixer.) Beat in 2¼ cups confectioners' sugar, 1½ teaspoons heavy cream, 1 teaspoon vanilla extract, and ⅛ teaspoon table salt until smooth. Increase the speed to high and beat until creamy and thick, about 2 minutes. If you need, add more confectioners' sugar in 2-tablespoon increments until the frosting is thick but spreadable. Smear and spread the icing over the cooled cake—or simply dollop alongside slices of the cake.

Other Pots

- For a **3-quart Instant Pot,** you *must* decrease the amount of water in the insert to 1 cup while otherwise completing the recipe as stated.

- For a **10-quart Instant Pot,** you *must* increase the amount of water in the insert to 2½ cups while otherwise completing the recipe as stated.

Cake-Mix Coconut Bundt

7 ingredients

6 SERVINGS

METHOD:
pot-in-pot

SPECIAL EQUIPMENT:
a 6-cup pressure-safe Bundt pan and a pressure-safe rack or trivet

PRESSURE:
max or high

TIME UNDER PRESSURE:
20 or 24 minutes

RELEASE:
natural

TOTAL TIME WITH PRESSURE:
about 1½ hours (includes cooling)

CAN BE VEGETARIAN

1½ cups water

Baking spray

2 cups standard white cake mix (half of a 15¼-ounce box—vegetarian, if necessary—do not use a sugar-free, gluten-free, or pudding cake mix)

½ cup *low-fat* or "lite" coconut milk

½ cup *sweetened* shredded coconut

¼ cup vegetable, canola, or other neutral-flavored oil

1 large egg *plus* 1 large egg white, *at room temperature*

Other Pots

- For a 3-quart Instant Pot, you *must* decrease the amount of water in the insert to 1 cup while otherwise completing the recipe as stated.

- For a 10-quart Instant Pot, you *must* increase the amount of water in the insert to 2½ cups while otherwise completing the recipe as stated.

Beyond

- For more coconut flavor, substitute coconut oil for the vegetable oil. If your coconut oil is solid, microwave the ¼ cup in a small, microwave-safe bowl, on HIGH in 10-second increments, stirring after each. Cool *to room temperature* before using.

- To make a glaze for the cake, whisk ½ cup confectioners' sugar, 2 tablespoons regular or low-fat coconut milk, and ¼ teaspoon coconut extract in a medium bowl until smooth, then whisk in more confectioners' sugar in 1- to 2-tablespoon increments until the mixture can be drizzled but holds its shape a bit. Drizzle this mixture from the tines of a flatware fork over the cake once it has cooled.

If you're a coconut-phobe, you should turn the page fast—because we're not fooling around. We don't add pineapple or other junk to get in the way of the coconut flavor of this light and simple cake. Because of the fat in the shredded coconut, use only *low-fat* (or "lite") coconut milk to keep this dense, flavorful Bundt from becoming too greasy.

Note that this recipe is made with a *white* cake mix, not a coconut cake mix, because the latter is too stocked with artificial flavors. We instead wanted to doctor the mix with shredded coconut for the best flavor possible.

1. Pour the water into the insert set in a **5-, 6-, or 8-quart Instant Pot.** Put a pressure-safe rack or trivet in the insert. Coat the inside of a 6-cup pressure-safe Bundt pan with baking spray, taking care to get the spray into the crevasses.

2. Whisk the cake mix, coconut milk, shredded coconut, oil, egg, and egg white in a large bowl until smooth. Pour and scrape this mixture evenly into the prepared pan. Set it on the rack, lay a paper towel over the pan, and lock the lid on the pot.

3.

	Set pot for	Set level to	Valve must be	Set time for	If needed, press
For Max pots only	PRESSURE COOK	MAX	—	20 minutes with the KEEP WARM setting off	START
For all other pots	PRESSURE COOK or MANUAL	HIGH	Closed	24 minutes with the KEEP WARM setting off	START

4. When the pot has finished cooking, turn it off and let the pressure **return to normal naturally,** about 20 minutes. Unlatch the lid and open the cooker. Remove and discard the paper towel. Use hot pads or silicone baking mitts to transfer the (hot!) pan to a nearby wire rack. Cool for 10 minutes, then set a serving plate or platter over the top of the pan. Invert everything, remove the pan, and cool the cake on the plate for at least another 15 minutes before slicing and serving. Or cool to room temperature and store on the counter, loosely covered, for up to 1 day.

Cake-Mix Piña Colada Bundt

5 ingredients	**SPECIAL EQUIPMENT:** a 6-cup pressure-safe Bundt pan and a pressure-safe rack or trivet
6 SERVINGS	
METHOD: pot-in-pot	

PRESSURE: max or high

TIME UNDER PRESSURE: 20 or 24 minutes

RELEASE: natural

TOTAL TIME WITH PRESSURE: about 1 hour 45 minutes (includes cooling)

CAN BE VEGETARIAN

1½ cups water

Baking spray

2 cups plus 1½ tablespoons angel food cake mix (about half a 1-pound box—vegetarian, if necessary)

One 10-ounce can crushed pineapple *packed in juice* (1 cup plus 2 tablespoons)

⅓ cup *sweetened* shredded coconut

Hands down, this recipe is the easiest cake in this chapter. It uses an angel food cake mix, canned crushed pineapple, and sweetened shredded coconut to make a satisfying, flavorful dessert, best maybe when the weather's hot and you just don't want to expend much effort in the kitchen. Don't expect the traditional texture of an angel food cake. The added ingredients give the cake a denser texture, more like a traditional sponge cake.

1. Pour the water into the insert set in a **5-, 6-, or 8-quart Instant Pot.** Put a pressure-safe rack or trivet in the insert. Coat the inside of a 6-cup pressure-safe Bundt pan with baking spray, taking care to get the spray into the crevasses.

2. Use a wooden spoon to stir the cake mix, crushed pineapple with its juice, and the shredded coconut in a large bowl until smooth. Pour and scrape the mixture evenly into the prepared pan. Set it on the rack and lay a paper towel over the pan. Lock the lid on the pot.

Other Pots

- For a 3-quart Instant Pot, you *must* use only 1 cup water in the insert while otherwise completing the recipe as stated.

- For a 10-quart Instant Pot, you *must* increase the amount of water in the insert to 2½ cups while otherwise completing the recipe as stated.

3.

	Set pot for	Set level to	Valve must be	Set time for	If needed, press
For Max pots only	PRESSURE COOK	MAX	—	20 minutes with the KEEP WARM setting off	START
For all other pots	PRESSURE COOK or MANUAL	HIGH	Closed	24 minutes with the KEEP WARM setting off	START

4. When the pot has finished cooking, turn it off and let the pressure **return to normal naturally,** about 20 minutes. Unlatch the lid and open the cooker. Remove and discard the paper towel. Use hot pads or silicone baking mitts to transfer the (hot!) pan to a nearby wire rack. Cool for 5 minutes, then set a large plate or a serving platter over the pan, invert it all, remove the pan, and cool for at least another 10 minutes before slicing. Or cool to room temperature, about 1 hour, then cover loosely with a towel and store on the counter at room temperature for up to 1 day.

Beyond

- To make a rum glaze for the cake, combine ½ cup packed light brown sugar, ½ stick (4 tablespoons or ¼ cup) butter, ¼ cup uncultured buttermilk, 2½ tablespoons dark rum (such as Myers's), ¼ teaspoon baking soda, and ¼ teaspoon table salt in a small saucepan. Bring to a low simmer over medium-low heat, stirring until smooth. Set aside to cool for at least 5 minutes. Spoon the glaze over slices of cake on serving plates.

Cake-Mix Eggnog Bundt

8 ingredients

6 SERVINGS

METHOD:
pot-in-pot

SPECIAL EQUIPMENT:
a 6-cup pressure-safe Bundt pan and a pressure safe rack or trivet

PRESSURE:
max or high

TIME UNDER PRESSURE:
19 or 24 minutes

RELEASE:
natural

TOTAL TIME WITH PRESSURE:
about 1½ hours (includes cooling)

CAN BE VEGETARIAN

1½ cups plus 2 tablespoons water

Baking spray

2 cups standard yellow cake mix (half of a 15¼-ounce box—vegetarian, if necessary—do not use a sugar-free, gluten-free, or pudding cake mix)

½ cup regular eggnog (do not use alcoholic, low-fat, or fat-free eggnog)

1 large egg, *at room temperature*

3 tablespoons vegetable, canola, or other neutral-flavored oil

1 teaspoon vanilla extract

¼ teaspoon grated nutmeg

Other Pots

- For a 3-quart Instant Pot, you *must* use only 1 cup water in the insert while otherwise completing the recipe as stated.

- For a 10-quart Instant Pot, you *must* increase the amount of water in the insert to 2½ cups while otherwise completing the recipe as stated.

Beyond

- To make a glaze for this cake, stir 2 tablespoons eggnog and 2 tablespoons butter, melted and cooled, in a medium bowl until smooth. Stir in ¾ cup confectioners' sugar and ¼ teaspoon grated nutmeg. Stir in more confectioners' sugar in 1- to 2-tablespoon increments until the glaze is thick but pourable, so it will cling to the cake without running off. Drizzle the glaze over the cake when it has cooled to room temperature.

What in the world is wrong with eggnog makers? How come they don't sell it all year? It's a great treat on a fall day—or even in the early spring (especially with a shot of brandy or rum in the glass). We wanted to craft an easy, cake-mix dessert that could also be a holiday treat any time of the year—if only you can find eggnog. Oh, well. Make this cake over the holidays and dream of the summer. The pieces are super moist and even a bit dense, great with rum-raisin ice cream. Make it the day you'd like to serve it because the cake will (unfortunately) turn gummy after the next day as the pressure-forced steam condenses into the crumb.

1. Pour the 1½ cups water into the insert set in a **5-, 6-, or 8-quart Instant Pot.** Put a pressure-safe rack or trivet in the insert. Coat the inside of a 6-cup pressure-safe Bundt pan with baking spray, taking care to get the spray into the crevasses.

2. Whisk the cake mix, eggnog, egg, oil, vanilla, nutmeg, and the remaining 2 tablespoons water in a large bowl until smooth. Pour and spread this mixture evenly into the prepared pan. Set it on the rack and lay a paper towel over the pan. Lock the lid on the cooker.

3.

	Set pot for	Set level to	Valve must be	Set time for	If needed, press
For Max pots only	PRESSURE COOK	MAX	—	19 minutes with the KEEP WARM setting off	START
For all other pots	PRESSURE COOK or MANUAL	HIGH	Closed	24 minutes with the KEEP WARM setting off	START

4. When the pot has finished cooking, turn it off and let the pressure **return to normal naturally,** about 20 minutes. Unlatch the lid and open the cooker. Remove and discard the paper towel. Use hot pads or silicone baking mitts to transfer the (hot!) pan to a nearby wire rack. Cool for 10 minutes, then set a serving plate or platter over the top of the pan. Invert everything, remove the pan, and cool the cake on the plate for at least another 15 minutes before slicing and serving. Or cool to room temperature and store on the counter, loosely covered, for up to 1 day.

Cake-Mix Cinnamon-Swirl Bundt

11 ingredients

6 SERVINGS

METHOD:
pot-in-pot

SPECIAL EQUIPMENT:
a 6-cup pressure-safe Bundt pan and a pressure-safe rack or trivet

PRESSURE:
max or high

TIME UNDER PRESSURE:
27 or 32 minutes

RELEASE:
natural

TOTAL TIME WITH PRESSURE:
about 1½ hours (includes cooling)

CAN BE VEGETARIAN

1½ cups water

Baking spray

2 cups standard white cake mix (half of a 15¼-ounce box—vegetarian, if necessary—do not use a sugar-free, gluten-free, or pudding cake mix)

¼ cup *instant* vanilla pudding mix (half of a 3.4-ounce box—vegetarian, if necessary)

½ cup regular sour cream (do not use low-fat or fat-free), *at room temperature*

⅓ cup whole or low-fat milk (do not use fat-free)

⅓ cup vegetable, canola, or other neutral-flavored oil

1 large egg, *at room temperature*

1 teaspoon vanilla extract

3 tablespoons light brown sugar

2 teaspoons ground cinnamon

Other Pots

- For a 3-quart Instant Pot, you *must* use only 1 cup water in the insert while otherwise completing the recipe as stated.

- For a 10-quart Instant Pot, you *must* increase the amount of water in the insert to 2½ cups while otherwise completing the recipe as stated.

Beyond

- Stir up to 3 tablespoons *finely* chopped walnuts into the brown sugar mixture.

- To make an icing for the cake, put 1 cup confectioners' sugar in a medium bowl, then whisk in 1 tablespoon whole milk, followed by more milk in 1-teaspoon increments until you have a thick icing that can be drizzled.

This Bundt is not a dense cake but more like a classic pudding cake, thanks to the instant pudding mix in the batter (natch!) *and* to the added sour cream. It can definitely be cut into slices (rather than dished up with a spoon as the Orange Ricotta Pudding Cake on page 412) but it's very tender and flavorful. We love it with butter pecan ice cream!

1. Pour the water into the insert set in a **5-, 6-, or 8-quart Instant Pot.** Put a pressure-safe rack or trivet in the insert. Coat the inside of a 6-cup pressure-safe Bundt pan with baking spray, taking care to get the spray into the crevasses.

2. Whisk the cake mix and pudding mix in a large bowl until uniform. Whisk in the sour cream, milk, oil, egg, and vanilla until smooth.

3. Use a fork to mix the brown sugar and cinnamon in a small bowl. Sprinkle this in a rather thick, swirling circle across the top of the batter, then fold very gently with a rubber spatula so that there are big streaks in the batter. If you want to see exactly how to do this, check out the video for this recipe on our YouTube channel, Cooking with Bruce and Mark.

4. Gently pour and scrape the batter evenly around the prepared pan, trying to preserve those streaks in the best way you can. Set the pan on the rack and lay a paper towel on top. Lock the lid on the pot.

5.

	Set pot for	Set level to	Valve must be	Set time for	If needed, press
For Max pots only	PRESSURE COOK	MAX	—	27 minutes with the KEEP WARM setting off	START
For all other pots	PRESSURE COOK or MANUAL	HIGH	Closed	32 minutes with the KEEP WARM setting off	START

6. When the pot has finished cooking, turn it off and let the pressure **return to normal naturally,** about 20 minutes. Unlatch the lid and open the cooker. Remove and discard the paper towel. Use hot pads or silicone baking mitts to transfer the (hot!) pan to a nearby wire rack. Cool for 10 minutes, then set a serving plate or platter over the top of the pan. Invert everything, remove the pan, and cool the cake on the plate for at least another 15 minutes before slicing and serving. Or cool to room temperature and store on the counter, loosely covered, for up to 8 hours.

See photo in insert.

Cake-Mix Jelly Donut Bundt

8 ingredients	**SPECIAL EQUIPMENT:** a 6-cup pressure-safe Bundt pan, a pressure-safe rack or trivet, and a standard straw or two bamboo skewers
6 SERVINGS	
METHOD: pot-in-pot	

PRESSURE: max or high

TIME UNDER PRESSURE: 20 or 24 minutes

RELEASE: natural

TOTAL TIME WITH PRESSURE: about 1½ hours (includes cooling)

CAN BE VEGETARIAN

1½ cups water

Baking spray

2 cups standard yellow cake mix (half of a 15¼-ounce box—vegetarian, if necessary—do not use a sugar-free, gluten-free, or pudding cake mix)

½ cup regular or low-fat milk (do not use fat-free)

½ stick (4 tablespoons or ¼ cup) butter, melted and cooled *to room temperature*

2 large eggs, *at room temperature*

¼ cup strawberry jelly

Confectioners' sugar, for garnishing

Because of the melted butter and increased number of eggs, this cake has the texture of a cake donut, a bit denser than some others in this chapter and better able to hold all the jelly. No, it's not a tunnel of jelly in the cake. Rather, the jelly gets spooned into holes poked all across the cake. This cake needs to be cooled to room temperature before it's served so both the crumb and the jelly have time to set. One note: The cake will absorb a lot of the jelly—it won't ooze out when cut.

1. Pour the water into the insert set in a **5-, 6-, or 8-quart Instant Pot.** Put a pressure-safe rack or trivet in the insert. Coat the inside of a 6-cup pressure-safe Bundt pan with baking spray, taking care to get the spray into the crevasses.

2. Whisk the cake mix, milk, butter, and eggs in a large bowl until smooth. Spread this mixture evenly into the prepared pan. Set it on the rack and cover with a paper towel. Lock the lid on the pot.

3.

	Set pot for	Set level to	Valve must be	Set time for	If needed, press
For Max pots only	PRESSURE COOK	MAX	—	20 minutes with the KEEP WARM setting off	START
For all other pots	PRESSURE COOK or MANUAL	HIGH	Closed	24 minutes with the KEEP WARM setting off	START

Other Pots

- For a 3-quart Instant Pot, you *must* use only 1 cup water in the insert while otherwise completing the recipe as stated.

- For a 10-quart Instant Pot, you *must* increase the amount of water in the insert to 2½ cups while otherwise completing the recipe as stated.

Beyond

- You can substitute any jelly, but don't use jam (which will be too thick) or preserves (which will have larger bits of fruit).

4. When the pot has finished cooking, turn it off and let the pressure **return to normal naturally,** about 20 minutes. Unlatch the lid and open the cooker. Remove and discard the paper towel. Use hot pads or silicone baking mitts to transfer the (hot!) pan to a nearby wire rack. Cool for 10 minutes.

5. Microwave the jelly on HIGH in a small, microwave-safe bowl in 5-second increments, stirring after each, just until pourable but certainly not bubbling. Use a standard straw or two bamboo skewers to make lots and lots of holes across the cake in the pan, going about two-thirds of the way down into the cake. Pour the jelly into these holes. Cool for another 15 minutes.

6. Set a platter or a large plate or a serving platter over the cake, invert the whole thing, jiggle to loosen, and remove the pan. Cool to room temperature, about 45 more minutes. Dust the cake with confectioners' sugar before slicing and serving.

Cake-Mix Banana Cake with Maple Glaze

12 ingredients

6 SERVINGS

METHOD:
pot-in-pot

SPECIAL EQUIPMENT:
a 7-inch-round springform pan and a pressure-safe rack or trivet

PRESSURE:
max or high

TIME UNDER PRESSURE:
34 or 40 minutes

RELEASE:
natural

TOTAL TIME WITH PRESSURE:
about 2½ hours (includes cooling)

CAN BE VEGETARIAN

1½ cups water

Baking spray

2 cups standard white cake mix (half of a 15¼-ounce box—vegetarian, if necessary—do not use a sugar-free, gluten-free, or pudding cake mix)

1 cup whole or low-fat milk (do not use fat-free)

¼ cup vegetable, canola, or other neutral-flavored oil

1 large egg, *at room temperature*

1 large banana, peeled and *diced* (see headnote for more information)

3 tablespoons all-purpose flour

6 tablespoons maple syrup, preferably dark amber (do not use pancake syrup)

½ stick (4 tablespoons or ¼ cup) butter

1 teaspoon vanilla extract

1 cup confectioners' sugar

Doctoring a cake mix with bananas and maple syrup gives you the best cross between banana cake and banana bread. However, unlike with traditional banana bread, the banana here is diced so that there are small bits throughout every slice. Although we'd usually call for a banana that's quite soft in a batter, this one should be sliceable, the sort you'd use on cereal. The peel should have no green color but the banana should be firm while smelling sweet.

To dice a banana, peel it, then slice it lengthwise in half, then slice each half again in half but this time crosswise. Now slice each of these flour sections lengthwise into several smaller spears, each about ¼ inch thick. Finally, slice these crosswise into ¼-inch bits.

1. Pour the water into the insert set in a **5-, 6-, or 8-quart Instant Pot.** Put a pressure-safe rack or trivet in the insert. Coat the inside of a 7-inch-round springform pan with baking spray.

2. Whisk the cake mix, milk, oil, egg, banana, and flour in a large bowl until smooth. Use a rubber spatula to pour and scrape this mixture into the prepared pan. Smooth the top of the thick batter. Set the pan on the rack and lock the lid on the pot.

3.

	Set pot for	Set level to	Valve must be	Set time for	If needed, press
For Max pots only	PRESSURE COOK	MAX	—	34 minutes with the KEEP WARM setting off	START
For all other pots	PRESSURE COOK or MANUAL	HIGH	Closed	40 minutes with the KEEP WARM setting off	START

4. When the pot has finished cooking, turn it off and let the pressure **return to normal naturally,** about 20 minutes. Unlatch the lid and open the cooker. Use hot pads or silicone baking mitts to transfer the (hot!) pan to a nearby wire rack. Cool for 10 minutes, then unlatch and remove the ring side of the pan. Cool to room temperature, about 1 hour.

5. As the cake cools, make the maple glaze. Combine the maple syrup, butter, and vanilla in a small saucepan and set it over medium-low heat. Cook, stirring occasionally, until the butter melts. Remove from the heat and whisk in the confectioners' sugar until smooth. Set aside at room temperature. The glaze will thicken as it cools.

6. When the cake has cooled to room temperature, put wax paper sheets underneath it on the wire rack (to protect your counter from a mess). Slowly pour the thickened glaze over the cake, allowing it to run down the sides (and onto the wax paper). Set aside for 5 minutes before transferring the cake to a platter or cutting board and slicing it into wedges to serve. (Discard the wax paper sheets that have caught the drips.)

Other Pots

- Because of the size of the pan and the delicate ingredient ratios, this recipe cannot be made in a 3-quart Instant Pot.

- For a 10-quart Instant Pot, you *must* increase the amount of water in the insert to 2½ cups while otherwise completing the recipe as stated.

Beyond

- Spice the cake by adding up to 1½ teaspoons pumpkin pie spice or apple pie spice to the batter.

Cake-Mix Peach Upside-Down Cake

7 ingredients

6 SERVINGS

METHOD:
pot-in-pot

SPECIAL EQUIPMENT:
a 7-inch-round springform pan and a pressure-safe rack or trivet

PRESSURE:
max or high

TIME UNDER PRESSURE:
24 or 30 minutes

RELEASE:
natural

TOTAL TIME WITH PRESSURE:
about 1½ hours (includes cooling)

CAN BE VEGETARIAN

1½ cups water

Baking spray

One 29-ounce can sliced peaches *packed in juice* (not sugar syrup—do not drain)

½ cup juice from the can of sliced peaches

2 cups standard white cake mix (half of a 15¼-ounce box—vegetarian, if necessary—do not use a sugar-free, gluten-free, or pudding cake mix)

¼ cup vegetable, canola, or other neutral-flavored oil

1 large egg *plus* 1 large egg white, *at room temperature*

Other Pots

- Because of the size of the pan and the delicate ingredient ratios, this recipe cannot be made in a 3-quart Instant Pot.

- For a 10-quart Instant Pot, you *must* increase the amount of water in the insert to 2½ cups while otherwise completing the recipe as stated.

Beyond

- Add up to 1 teaspoon minced fresh thyme leaves to the batter.

- Sprinkle ground cinnamon or ground cardamom lightly over the peach slices in the pan.

Unfortunately, a true upside-down cake won't work in an Instant Pot. A traditional round cake pan is too shallow for the taller upside-down cake, and a springform pan poses problems because the pressure *forces* sticky syrup out of the cracks in the pan's joint. Our solution is to indeed use that springform pan but to limit the sticky syrup by using canned, sliced peaches to offer moisture to the "upside-down" part of the cake. (We also use some of the juice from the can in the batter.)

1. Pour the water into the insert set in a **5-, 6-, or 8-quart Instant Pot.** Put a pressure-safe rack or trivet in the insert. Coat the inside of a 7-inch-round springform pan with baking spray.

2. Lay 12 peach slices on their sides in the bottom of the pan, fanning them around the pan in a spiral around the center. Reserve the remaining peach slices for another use—the point of the large can is the extra juice (used in the next step).

3. Whisk the juice from the can, the cake mix, oil, egg, and egg white in a large bowl until smooth. Gently and evenly pour this mixture over the peaches, taking care not to dislodge them. Put the pan on the rack and lock the lid on the cooker.

4.

	Set pot for	Set level to	Valve must be	Set time for	If needed, press
For Max pots only	PRESSURE COOK	MAX	—	24 minutes with the KEEP WARM setting off	START
For all other pots	PRESSURE COOK or MANUAL	HIGH	Closed	30 minutes with the KEEP WARM setting off	START

5. When the pot has finished cooking, turn it off and let the pressure **return to normal naturally,** about 20 minutes. Unlatch the lid and open the cooker. Use hot pads or silicone baking mitts to transfer the (hot!) pan to a nearby wire rack. Cool for 15 minutes.

6. Do not unlatch the pan's side ring. Run a flexible, thin knife (even a thin flatware knife will work) around the inside perimeter of the pan. Put a large plate or a serving platter over the top of the pan and invert everything. Jiggle gently to turn the cake out of the pan while the side ring stays in place. Remove the baking pan and cool for at least 5 more minutes before slicing and serving. Or cool to room temperature, about 1 hour, then cover with plastic wrap and store in the refrigerator for up to 2 days.

Cake-Mix Melted-Ice-Cream Chocolate Cake

6 ingredients	**SPECIAL EQUIPMENT:** a 7-inch-round springform pan and a pressure-safe rack or trivet
6 SERVINGS	
METHOD: pot-in-pot	

PRESSURE: max or high

TIME UNDER PRESSURE: 23 or 28 minutes

RELEASE: natural

TOTAL TIME WITH PRESSURE: about 1 hour 25 minutes (includes cooling)

CAN BE VEGETARIAN

1½ cups water

Baking spray

2 cups standard chocolate cake mix (half of a 15¼-ounce box—vegetarian, if necessary—do not use a sugar-free, gluten-free, or pudding cake mix)

⅔ cup melted *premium* chocolate ice cream (from about ¾ cup frozen ice cream)

½ stick (4 tablespoons or ¼ cup) butter, melted and cooled *to room temperature*

1 large egg, *at room temperature*

Other Pots

- Because of the size of the pan and the ingredient ratios, this recipe cannot be made in a 3 quart Instant Pot.

- For a 10-quart Instant Pot, you *must* increase the amount of water in the insert to 2½ cups while otherwise completing the recipe as stated.

Beyond

- To make an easy chocolate glaze, whisk ¾ cup confectioners' sugar and 2 tablespoons unsweetened cocoa powder in a small bowl until uniform. Whisk in 1 tablespoon whole milk and ½ teaspoon vanilla extract until smooth, adding more milk in dribs and drabs just until the glaze is smooth and pourable, but still thick. Drizzle the glaze only over the cake once it has cooled to room temperature—or over slices on serving plates.

Seriously, could this get easier? There are only four ingredients in the batter! That said, you must use *premium* chocolate ice cream. And it must be a smooth chocolate ice cream without nuts, marshmallows, or swirls. With that, it's hard to beat how easy and decadent the cake is. You'll need the rest of that pint of ice cream to serve as a dip with the cake.

1. Pour the water into the insert set in a **5-, 6-, or 8-quart Instant Pot.** Set a pressure-safe rack or trivet in the insert. Coat the inside of a 7-inch-round springform pan with baking spray.

2. Whisk the cake mix, melted ice cream, butter, and egg in a large bowl until smooth. Pour and spread this mixture evenly into the prepared pan. Set it on the rack and lock the lid on the pot.

3.

	Set pot for	Set level to	Valve must be	Set time for	If needed, press
For Max pots only	PRESSURE COOK	MAX	—	23 minutes with the KEEP WARM setting off	START
For all other pots	PRESSURE COOK or MANUAL	HIGH	Closed	28 minutes with the KEEP WARM setting off	START

4. When the pot has finished cooking, turn it off and let the pressure **return to normal naturally,** about 20 minutes. Unlatch the lid and open the cooker. Use hot pads or silicone baking mitts to transfer the (hot!) pan to a nearby wire rack. Cool for 5 minutes, then unlatch the ring side to the pan and remove it. Cool for at least another 10 minutes before slicing and serving. Or cool to room temperature, about 1 hour, then cover loosely with a clean kitchen towel and set aside on the counter for up to 1 day.

Cake-Mix Orange Layer Cake

10 ingredients

6–8 SERVINGS

METHOD:
pot-in-pot

SPECIAL EQUIPMENT:
a 7-inch-round springform pan, an electric mixer (maybe), and a pressure-safe rack or trivet

PRESSURE:
max or high

TIME UNDER PRESSURE:
25 or 30 minutes

RELEASE:
natural

TOTAL TIME WITH PRESSURE:
about 2 hours (includes cooling)

CAN BE VEGETARIAN

1½ cups water

Baking spray

2 cups standard white cake mix (half of a 15¼-ounce box—vegetarian, if necessary—do not use a sugar-free, gluten-free, or pudding cake mix)

½ cup all-purpose flour (dip and level—do not pack)

¼ cup orange marmalade

¼ cup vegetable, canola, or other neutral-flavored oil

2 large eggs, *at room temperature*

½ teaspoon orange extract

¾ cup heavy cream

2 tablespoons confectioners' sugar

Other Pots

- Because of the size of the pan and the ingredient ratios, this recipe cannot be made in a **3-quart Instant Pot.**

- For a **10-quart Instant Pot,** you *must* increase the amount of water in the insert to 2½ cups while otherwise completing the recipe as stated.

Beyond

- Garnish the top of the frosted cake with finely grated orange zest or finely diced candied orange peel.

Yes, you can make a layer cake in an Instant Pot! Can you believe it? We couldn't until we tried it. By using a 7-inch-round springform pan, we created a fairly tall cake under pressure. Admittedly, it falls once it cools; but it will still be tall enough that you can slice it into two disks, add the icing to one layer, and stack the top back on to make a true layer cake.

Take note: The cake is quite fragile. It must be cooled to room temperature so the crumb can fully set before you dare slice it into two disks. A long, thin, flexible knife works best—along with the courage of your convictions.

1. Pour the water into the insert set in a **5-, 6-, or 8-quart Instant Pot.** Put a pressure-safe rack or trivet in the insert. Coat the inside of a 7-inch-round springform pan with baking spray.

2. Whisk the cake mix, flour, marmalade, oil, eggs, and orange extract in a large bowl until fairly smooth (the marmalade will leave bits of peel in the batter). Use a rubber spatula to pour and scrape this batter into the prepared pan. Smooth the top of the batter in the pan. Set the pan on the rack and lock the lid on the pot.

3.

	Set pot for	Set level to	Valve must be	Set time for	If needed, press
For Max pots only	PRESSURE COOK	MAX	—	25 minutes with the KEEP WARM setting off	START
For all other pots	PRESSURE COOK or MANUAL	HIGH	Closed	30 minutes with the KEEP WARM setting off	START

4. When the pot has finished cooking, turn it off and let the pressure **return to normal naturally,** about 20 minutes. Unlatch the lid and open the cooker. Use hot pads or silicone baking mitts to transfer the (hot!) pan to a nearby wire rack. Cool for 10 minutes, then unlatch the pan and remove the side ring. Cool the cake *to room temperature,* at least 1 hour or up to 3 hours. In the meantime, put a medium bowl and the beaters to a handheld electric mixer or a whisk in the refrigerator.

5. With a handheld electric mixer at high speed or (old school!) with a whisk, whip the cream and confectioners' sugar in that cold bowl until the cream is stiff and holds its shape when mounded.

6. Use a long, thin knife to split the cake into two layers. Remove the top layer. Spread the whipped cream evenly across the cut side of the bottom layer. Set the other layer back on top.

Cake-Mix Carrot Layer Cake

11 ingredients

6–8 SERVINGS

METHOD:
pot-in-pot

SPECIAL EQUIPMENT:
a 7-inch-round springform pan, a handheld electric mixer, and a pressure-safe rack or trivet

PRESSURE:
max or high

TIME UNDER PRESSURE:
24 or 30 minutes

RELEASE:
natural

TOTAL TIME WITH PRESSURE:
about 1 hour 45 minutes (includes cooling)

CAN BE VEGETARIAN

---

2 cups water

Baking spray

2 cups standard *spice* cake mix (half of a 15¼-ounce box—vegetarian, if necessary—do not use a sugar-free, gluten-free, or pudding cake mix)

1 large carrot, peeled and shredded through the large holes of a box grater (1 cup)

½ cup chopped pecans

1 large egg *plus* 1 large egg white, *at room temperature*

2 tablespoons vegetable, canola, or other neutral-flavored oil

4 ounces regular cream cheese (do not use low-fat or fat-free), *at room temperature*

2 tablespoons butter, *at room temperature*

1 teaspoon vanilla extract

1½ cups confectioners' sugar, plus more as needed

Other Pots

- Because of the size of the pan and the ingredient ratios, this recipe cannot be made in a 3-quart Instant Pot.

- For a 10-quart Instant Pot, you *must* increase the amount of water in the insert to 2½ cups while otherwise completing the recipe as stated.

Beyond

- Sprinkle finely chopped pecans over the top of the cake.

- And/or sprinkle a small amount finely chopped candied orange peel over the top.

Although we have a recipe for Classic Carrot Cake earlier in this chapter (page 429), we wanted to include an easy layer cake, made with a boxed mix and given the royal treatment with a rich frosting. It's a fine treat after school or yard work. Notice that the recipe calls for a box of *spice* cake mix, a real shortcut.

1. Pour 1½ cups of the water into the insert set in a **5-, 6-, or 8-quart Instant Pot.** Put a pressure-safe rack or trivet in the insert. Coat the inside of a 7-inch-round springform pan with baking spray.

2. Whisk the cake mix, carrot, pecans, egg, egg white, oil, and the remaining ½ cup water in a large bowl until smooth. Use a rubber spatula to pour and scrape this batter evenly into the prepared pan. Smooth the top of the batter and set the pan on the rack. Lay a paper towel over the pan and lock the lid on the cooker.

3.

	Set pot for	Set level to	Valve must be	Set time for	If needed, press
For Max pots only	PRESSURE COOK	MAX	—	24 minutes with the KEEP WARM setting off	START
For all other pots	PRESSURE COOK or MANUAL	HIGH	Closed	30 minutes with the KEEP WARM setting off	START

4. When the pot has finished cooking, turn it off and let the pressure **return to normal naturally,** about 20 minutes. Unlatch the lid and open the cooker. Use hot pads or silicone baking mitts to transfer the (hot!) pan to a nearby wire rack. Cool for 10 minutes, then unlatch and remove the ring side from the pan. Cool the cake *to room temperature,* for at least 1 hour or up to 3 hours.

5. Using a handheld electric mixer, beat the cream cheese, butter, and vanilla at medium speed until smooth and velvety, about 3 minutes. Scrape down the inside of the bowl, then beat in the confectioners' sugar at low speed until smooth. Continue beating, adding confectioners' sugar in 1- to 2-tablespoon increments, until the frosting is thick enough to hold its shape without appearing dry.

6. Use a long, thin knife to slice the cake into two, round, even layers. Spread half the frosting over the bottom half of the cake, then stack the top layer back on the cake. Spread the remaining frosting over the top. Serve at once or keep the cake uncovered at room temperature for up to 4 hours.

Cake-Mix Mini Wedding Cake

13 ingredients

6–8 SERVINGS

METHOD:
pot-in-pot

SPECIAL EQUIPMENT:
a 7-inch-round springform pan, an electric mixer, and a pressure-safe rack or trivet

PRESSURE:
max or high

TIME UNDER PRESSURE:
25 or 30 minutes

RELEASE:
natural

TOTAL TIME WITH PRESSURE:
about 2½ hours (includes cooling)

CAN BE VEGETARIAN

1½ cups water

Baking spray

2 cups standard white cake mix (half of a 15¼-ounce box—vegetarian, if necessary—do not use a sugar-free, gluten-free, or pudding cake mix)

½ cup all-purpose flour

½ cup granulated white sugar

¾ cup regular sour cream (do not use low-fat or fat-free), *at room temperature*

½ cup whole or low-fat milk (do not use fat-free)

2 large egg whites, *at room temperature*

2 cups confectioners' sugar

1½ sticks (12 tablespoons or ¾ cup) butter, *at room temperature*

1 teaspoon vanilla extract

⅛ teaspoon table salt

1 to 2 tablespoons heavy cream

Other Pots

- Because of the size of the pan and the ingredient ratios, this recipe cannot be made in a 3-quart Instant Pot.
- For a 10-quart Instant Pot, you *must* increase the amount of water in the insert to 2½ cups while otherwise completing the recipe as stated.

Beyond

- Fold 1 tablespoon mini chocolate chips into half the frosting before you spread it on the bottom layer.
- Decorate the top of the cake with chocolate or rainbow sprinkles.

Okay, don't make this cake for your wedding. Let the professionals handle that. But make this cake for an anniversary in your life. Or in your friend's life. Or any other small celebration that needs a fancy cake. It's got the flavor of classic white wedding cake with a butter-filled frosting. Could celebrations get any easier?

1. Pour the water into an insert set in a **5-, 6-, or 8-quart Instant Pot.** Put a pressure-safe rack or trivet in the insert. Coat the inside of a 7-inch-round springform pan with baking spray.

2. Whisk the cake mix, flour, and white sugar in a large bowl until uniform. Whisk in the sour cream, milk, and egg whites until smooth. Use a rubber spatula to pour and scrape the batter into the prepared pan. Smooth the top of the batter. Put the pan on the rack and lock the lid on the pot.

3.

	Set pot for	Set level to	Valve must be	Set time for	If needed, press
For Max pots only	PRESSURE COOK	MAX	—	25 minutes with the KEEP WARM setting off	START
For all other pots	PRESSURE COOK or MANUAL	HIGH	Closed	30 minutes with the KEEP WARM setting off	START

4. When the pot has finished cooking, turn it off and let the pressure **return to normal naturally,** about 20 minutes. Unlatch the lid and open the cooker. Use hot pads or silicone baking mitts to transfer the (hot!) pan to a nearby wire rack. Cool for 10 minutes, then unlatch and remove the ring side for the pan. Cool the cake *to room temperature,* for at least 1 hour or up to 3 hours.

5. Using a stand mixer fitted with the paddle attachment or a handheld electric mixer, beat the confectioners' sugar and butter in a large bowl until fluffy and smooth, about 3 minutes, scraping down the inside of the bowl at least once. Beat in the vanilla and salt until uniform, then beat in the cream in 1-teaspoon increments until the frosting has a rich, spreadable consistency.

6. Use a long, thin knife to slice the cake into two, round, even layers. Spread half the frosting over the bottom half of the cake, then stack the top layer back on the cake. Spread the remaining frosting over the top. Serve at once or keep the cake uncovered at room temperature for up to 4 hours.

Fudgy Brownie-Mix Bites

6 ingredients

7 BROWNIE BITES

METHOD:
egg bites

SPECIAL
EQUIPMENT:
one seven-
indentation egg-
bite mold and a
pressure-safe rack
or trivet

PRESSURE:
high

TIME UNDER
PRESSURE:
15 minutes

RELEASE:
modified natural

TOTAL TIME WITH
PRESSURE:
about 1 hour 10
minutes

CAN BE
VEGETARIAN

1½ cups water

Baking spray

1⅓ cups boxed traditional-, supreme-, or original-style brownie mix (vegetarian, if necessary—do not use a mix with the word "fudge" in the title)

⅓ cup *quick-cooking* rolled oats (do not use standard or steel-cut oats)

⅓ cup uncultured buttermilk (see page 17 for more information)

2 tablespoons vegetable oil

Boxed brownie mix + egg-bite mold = easy, chocolate bliss! These bites are more like mini brownies with a hint of buttermilk for a sour tang behind the chocolate. They're so fudgy that the oats help hold them together. The bites are best with a glass of milk when the kids come home from school. Or in the evening for the adults, alongside a glass of aged rum.

1. Pour the water into the insert set in a **5-, 6-, or 8-quart Instant Pot.** Put a pressure-safe rack or trivet in the insert. Coat the seven indentations of an egg-bite mold with baking spray.

2. Stir the brownie mix, oats, buttermilk, and oil in a medium bowl until well combined, no dry bits anywhere. Divide this mixture among the prepared indentations in the mold. Cover the mold with its silicone lid, or cover and seal it with aluminum foil. Set the mold on the rack and lock the lid on the pot.

3.

	Set pot for	Set level to	Valve must be	Set time for	If needed, press
For *all* pots	PRESSURE COOK or MANUAL	HIGH	Closed	15 minutes with the KEEP WARM setting off	START

4. When the pot has finished cooking, turn it off and let the pressure **return to normal naturally for 10 minutes.** Then use the **quick-release method** to get rid of the pot's residual pressure. Unlatch the lid and open the cooker. Use hot pads or silicone baking mitts to transfer the (hot!) egg-bite mold to a nearby wire rack. Uncover the mold and cool until barely warm, about 30 minutes. Unmold the bites and enjoy warm.

Other Pots

- For a 3-quart Instant Pot, you *must* decrease the amount of water in the insert to 1 cup and you *must* use two, four-indentation egg-bite molds specifically made for this smaller model. You *must* then stack the molds on top of each other in the pot. If you fill all eight indentations, the individual bites will be slightly smaller than those made in a seven-indentation mold.

- For an 8-quart Instant Pot, you *can* double almost all of the ingredient amounts except you *must* use the stated 1½ cups water in the insert. You *must* then use *two* egg-bite molds, one stacked on top of the other in the pot so that the indentations of the top mold sit on walls of the bottom mold, not into the bottom indentations themselves.

- For a 10-quart Instant Pot, you *must* increase the amount of water in the insert to 2½ cups. You *can* either complete the recipe as stated or you *can* double the other ingredient amounts, in which case you *must* use two egg-bite molds, stacking them as directed above for the 8-quart pot.

Beyond
- Add more flavor to the bites by stirring up to 1 teaspoon vanilla extract into the batter.
- Or try rum extract.
- Or even orange extract.

Vanilla–Peanut Butter Cake Bites

10 ingredients

7 CAKE BITES

METHOD:
egg bites

SPECIAL EQUIPMENT:
one seven-indentation egg-bite mold, a handheld electric mixer, and a pressure-safe rack or trivet

PRESSURE:
max or high

TIME UNDER PRESSURE:
12 or 15 minutes

RELEASE:
modified natural

TOTAL TIME WITH PRESSURE:
about 45 minutes

CAN BE VEGETARIAN

1½ cups water

Baking spray

1 cup standard yellow cake mix (vegetarian, if necessary—do not use a sugar-free, gluten-free, or pudding cake mix)

¼ cup whole or low-fat milk (do not use fat-free)

¼ cup smooth natural-style peanut butter

1 large egg, *at room temperature*

1 tablespoon honey

½ teaspoon vanilla extract

1 cup Marshmallow Fluff or Marshmallow Creme

4 ounces regular cream cheese (do not use low-fat or fat-free), *at room temperature*

Other Pots

- For a **3-quart Instant Pot,** you *must* decrease the amount of water in the insert to 1 cup and you *must* use two, four-indentation egg-bite molds specifically made for this smaller model. Because these cakes puff up, you cannot stack the molds. You'll have to work in batches. If you fill all eight indentations, the individual bites will be slightly smaller than those made in a seven-indentation mold.

- For a **10-quart Instant Pot,** you *must* increase the amount of water in the insert to 2½ cups while otherwise completing the recipe as stated.

Beyond

- Flavor the marshmallow dip with up to 1 teaspoon vanilla extract—or ¼ teaspoon of orange extract.

With a boxed cake mix and an egg-bite mold, you can create little cake bites that would be the best-ever treat for those weary from school. Or you can knock these out just before your adult friends arrive, pour some bourbon, and settle in for the evening.

1. Pour the water into the insert set in a **5-, 6-, or 8-quart Instant Pot.** Set a pressure-safe rack or trivet in the insert. Coat the seven indentations of a standard egg-bite mold with baking spray.

2. Put the cake mix, milk, peanut butter, egg, honey, and vanilla in a medium bowl. Use a handheld electric mixer at medium speed (the amounts are too small to be successful in a stand mixer) to beat the ingredients until smooth, stopping the machine at least once to scrape down the inside of the bowl.

3. Scraping up every last drop of the batter, divide it evenly among the egg-bite mold indentations (about a rounded ¼ cup in each). Do not cover. Set the mold on the rack and lock the lid on the pot.

4.

	Set pot for	Set level to	Valve must be	Set time for	If needed, press
For Max pots only	PRESSURE COOK	MAX	—	12 minutes with the KEEP WARM setting off	START
For all other pots	PRESSURE COOK or MANUAL	HIGH	Closed	15 minutes with the KEEP WARM setting off	START

5. When the pot has finished cooking, turn off the heat and let the pressure **return to normal naturally for 3 minutes.** Then use the **quick-release method** to get rid of the pot's residual pressure. Unlatch the lid and open the cooker. Use hot pads or silicone baking mitts to transfer the (hot!) egg-bite mold to a nearby wire rack. Cool for 5 minutes, then unmold the cake bites and continue cooling on the rack for at least 15 minutes or to room temperature, about 1 hour.

6. Using a handheld electric mixer at medium speed, beat the Marshmallow Fluff or Creme and the cream cheese in a medium bowl until smooth. Use this mixture as dip for the cake bites—or for the true be-a-kid experience, slather them with the marshmallow mixture bite by bite.

Pineapple Upside-Down Cake Bites

7 ingredients

7 CAKE BITES

METHOD:
egg bites

SPECIAL EQUIPMENT:
one seven-indentation egg-bite mold and a pressure-safe rack or trivet

PRESSURE:
max or high

TIME UNDER PRESSURE:
12 or 15 minutes

RELEASE:
natural

TOTAL TIME WITH PRESSURE:
about 50 minutes

CAN BE VEGETARIAN

1½ cups water

Baking spray

One 8-ounce can pineapple chunks *packed in juice*

1 cup standard white cake mix (vegetarian, if necessary—do not use a sugar-free, gluten-free, or pudding cake mix)

1 large egg white, *at room temperature*

7 teaspoons light brown sugar

7 teaspoons granulated white sugar

These exceptionally light (and actually low-fat) cake bites are not for the elementary-school set. They're a bit fancy, maybe the right thing for a party on the deck. They're also a bit messy because the pineapple sugar syrup drips over the cakes. They're probably best with knives and forks on plates. (Rule: Be an animal with ribs, not with cake.)

1. Pour the water into the insert set in a **5-, 6-, or 8-quart Instant Pot.** Set a pressure-safe rack or trivet in the insert. Coat the seven indentations of a standard egg-bite mold with baking spray.

2. Pour ⅓ cup of the juice from the can of pineapple chunks into a large bowl. Add the cake mix and egg white; whisk until smooth.

3. Put 1 teaspoon brown sugar, 1 teaspoon granulated white sugar, and 1 pineapple chunk from the can in the bottom of each prepared indentation. (Reserve any other pineapple chunks and juice for a snack as the cake bites bake.) If you want to see how this is done, check out the video for this recipe on our YouTube channel, Cooking with Bruce and Mark.

4. Scraping up every last drop of the cake batter, divide the batter evenly among the indentations (about ¼ cup in each). Set the mold on the rack and lock the lid on the pot.

5.

	Set pot for	Set level to	Valve must be	Set time for	If needed, press
For Max pots only	PRESSURE COOK	MAX	—	12 minutes with the KEEP WARM setting off	START
For all other pots	PRESSURE COOK or MANUAL	HIGH	Closed	15 minutes with the KEEP WARM setting off	START

6. When the pot has finished cooking, turn it off and let the pressure **return to normal naturally,** about 20 minutes. Unlatch the lid and open the cooker. Use hot pads or silicone baking mitts to transfer the (hot!) egg-bite mold to a nearby wire rack. Cool for 15 minutes, then unmold the little cakes onto a platter, letting the pineapple chunks sit on top of each and any syrup run down the cake. Serve warm or within the next hour.

Other Pots

- For a 3-quart Instant Pot, you *must* decrease the amount of water in the insert to 1 cup and you *must* use two, four-indentation egg-bite molds specifically made for this smaller model. Because these cakes puff up, you cannot stack the molds. You'll have to work in batches. If you fill all eight indentations, the individual bites will be slightly smaller than those made in a seven-indentation mold.

- For a 10-quart Instant Pot, you *must* increase the amount of water in the insert to 2½ cups while otherwise completing the recipe as stated.

Beyond

- Whisk up to ¼ teaspoon rum extract into the cake batter before adding it to the molds.

8

THE 10-QUART BONANZA:

Meals & Desserts for the Biggest Instant Pot

This chapter represents a game-changer for us. Yes, we're only two. Yes, we freeze a lot. But we love to cook for our friends and family. Our house rule is this: *If everyone invited takes seconds and there isn't food left over, we didn't make enough.* We also love to bring supper to our neighbors when we know they're stressed at work or have a sick kid at home.

The 10-quart pot to the rescue! Throughout this book, we give you simple ways to prepare most dishes in the big cooker—for example, by upping the water in the insert but otherwise using the stated 2-quart, 7-inch-round baking dish. In this chapter, however, we go all out with mounds of spaghetti or half a ham. Even more shocking, we can make full-size, 9-inch cheesecakes.

We should note that in many of these recipes, the super-fast cooking that's a hallmark of using an IP is a tad compromised. The 10-quart pot takes a *long* time to come to pressure. Think about how much steam needs to fill it. And it takes even longer to come *down* from pressure during a natural release. No doubt, a couple (!) of pork loins in the big pot cook faster than they would in the oven. But the process is not as speedy as it would be for a 1½-pound pork roast in a 6-quart pot.

Because the space inside the insert is large, every recipe requires more liquid than you might expect. You're already familiar with the necessary 2½ cups water in the bigger insert, an adaptation in the **Other Pots** section of so many recipes in this book. As you'll see, when we scale up for the 10-quart, we can use more than just more liquid—maybe more onions or more chicken breasts!—to produce that steam.

That said, the indicated cooking times under pressure may be *shorter* than you expect. Why? Because it takes time for the big pot to get to pressure *and* to come off high pressure. Both are still part of the overall cooking time, even if they're not the stated cooking time under pressure. For example, in our recipe for Chickens (Plural!) for Dinner (page 445), two chickens are cooked in seemingly less time in a 10-quart pot than one chicken would be in a 6-quart pot. This is because the actual time under pressure does not include both the run-up to HIGH and the natural release afterward.

And don't be tempted to add more cooking time, just because you see more spaghetti or more beef. A larger cut doesn't necessarily take any longer than a smaller one in a pressure cooker, the way it might in an oven or on a grill. Pressure is constant from all directions simultaneously. The timing question is not about the poundage of an ingredient. It's about its thickness and density. A 3-pound and a 6-pound beef brisket will cook in the pot in exactly the same time *if* they are both the same thickness. That said, a 5-pound chuck roast will most likely be thicker than a 2-pound one and so will take longer to cook, even under pressure.

As of this writing, there is no MAX pressure setting for a 10-quart pot. All of these recipes are cooked on more traditional HIGH or LOW pressure, from a simple spaghetti supper all the way through layer cakes.

Yep, you can make a layer cake in a 10-quart pot. Amazing, no? We don't know how we lived without one. Neither do our family, friends, and neighbors.

Spaghetti for a Crowd

10 ingredients	
12–16 SERVINGS	
METHOD: standard	

SPECIAL EQUIPMENT: none	TIME UNDER PRESSURE: 5 minutes	TOTAL TIME WITH PRESSURE: about 35 minutes
PRESSURE: low	RELEASE: quick	CAN BE GLUTEN-FREE

2 tablespoons olive oil

1 pound mild or hot bulk Italian sausage meat, or mild or hot Italian sausages with the casings removed (gluten-free, if necessary)

1½ pounds lean ground beef, preferably 90 percent lean or more

7 cups (1 quart plus 3 cups) chicken broth

Two 24-ounce jars plain marinara sauce (6 cups—gluten-free, if necessary)

1 teaspoon table salt

1 teaspoon ground black pepper

2 pounds raw dried spaghetti (gluten-free, if necessary—for more information on gluten-free dried pasta, see the introduction to the pasta chapter on page 103)

One 6-ounce can tomato paste

Lots of finely grated Parmigiano-Reggiano, for garnishing

How about a trough of spaghetti? We cook it with LOW pressure so that we can steer clear of the soupy pasta that comes from too much liquid. This dish is so easy that its success will turn on the quality of the marinara sauce and the cheese (for garnishing). Buy a block of Parmigiano-Reggiano to grate over the servings. There's no substitute.

1.

	Press	Set it for	Set time for	If needed, press
In all 10-quart pots	SAUTÉ	MEDIUM, NORMAL, or CUSTOM 300°F	15 minutes	START

2. As the pot heats, warm the oil in the insert set in a **10-quart Instant Pot.** Crumble in the sausage meat, stir over the heat for 1 minute, then crumble in the ground beef. Cook, stirring often, until lightly browned, breaking up any clumps, about 5 minutes.

3. Add the broth and scrape up any browned bits on the pot's bottom. Stir in the marinara sauce, salt, and pepper. Continue heating until wisps of steam rise from the liquids, about 5 minutes.

4. Turn off the heat and lay the spaghetti in a crosshatch pattern on top of the sauce. Lock the lid on the pot.

5.

	Set pot for	Set level to	Valve must be	Set time for	If needed, press
For all 10-quart pots	PRESSURE COOK or MANUAL	LOW	Closed	5 minutes with the KEEP WARM setting off	START

6. When the pot has finished cooking, use the **quick-release method** to bring the pressure back to normal. Unlatch the lid and open the cooker.

7.

	Press	Set it for	Set time for	If needed, press
In all 10-quart pots	SAUTÉ	MEDIUM, NORMAL, or CUSTOM 300°F	5 minutes	START

8. As the sauce comes to a simmer, stir in the tomato paste. Simmer for 1 minute, stirring constantly; then turn off the heat. Use hot pads or silicone baking mitts to transfer the (hot!) insert to a nearby wire rack. Cool for 5 minutes so the pasta can continue to absorb more sauce, *stirring once or twice to prevent sticking.* Serve in bowls with finely grated Parmigiano-Reggiano piled on top.

Beyond

- For heat, add up to 2 teaspoons red pepper flakes with the salt and pepper.

- For a creamy pasta, substitute one 24-ounce jar of alfredo sauce for one of the jars of marinara sauce.

See photo in insert.

Lots and Lots of Mac & Cheese

11 ingredients

8–10 SERVINGS

METHOD:
standard

SPECIAL
EQUIPMENT:
none

PRESSURE:
low

TIME UNDER
PRESSURE:
6 minutes

RELEASE:
quick

TOTAL TIME WITH
PRESSURE:
about 35 minutes

VEGETARIAN

CAN BE GLUTEN-
FREE

---

6 cups (1½ quarts) vegetable broth

2 cups heavy or light cream

2 cups whole or low-fat milk (do not use fat-free)

½ stick (4 tablespoons or ¼ cup) butter, cut into small bits

2 teaspoons onion powder

1 teaspoon table salt

1 teaspoon ground black pepper

½ teaspoon dried thyme

½ teaspoon ground dried mustard

Two 16-ounce packages raw large elbow macaroni or medium shells (can be gluten-free—for more information on gluten-free dried pasta, see the introduction to the pasta chapter on page 103)

1½ pounds American mild or sharp cheddar cheese, shredded (6 cups)

Sometimes, you need enough creamy, decadent mac-and-cheese for the neighborhood. Or a family reunion. Or a divorce. As with Spaghetti for a Crowd (page 442), we use LOW pressure, but this time it's so the pot doesn't take so long to come to pressure. Make sure you let the liquid in the pot get quite hot so the pasta has a chance to start cooking almost the moment it hits the liquid *and* so the pot comes to LOW pressure more quickly.

1.

	Press	Set it for	Set time for	If needed, press
In all 10-quart pots	SAUTÉ	MEDIUM, NORMAL, or CUSTOM 300°F	10 minutes	START

2. As the pot heats, stir the broth, cream, milk, butter, onion powder, salt, pepper, thyme, and ground mustard in the insert set in a **10-quart Instant Pot.** Cook, stirring once in a while, until the butter melts and the mixture begins to steam (without simmering), about 8 minutes. Stir in the pasta and turn off the heat. Lock the lid onto the cooker.

3.

	Set pot for	Set level to	Valve must be	Set time for	If needed, press
For all 10-quart pots	PRESSURE COOK	LOW	—	6 minutes with the KEEP WARM setting off	START

4. When the pot has finished cooking, use the **quick-release method** to bring the pressure back to normal. Unlatch the lid and open the cooker. Stir in the cheese, then set the lid over the pot and set it aside for 5 minutes so the pasta can continue to absorb some of the sauce, *stirring once or twice to prevent sticking*. Serve warm.

Beyond

- For a richer (but not vegetarian) dish, substitute chicken broth for some or all of the vegetable broth.

- Mix and match all sorts of semi-firm cheese: Monterey Jack, Jarlsberg, Gruyère, or a purchased combo (so long as it does not include any spices or flavorings).

Tuna Noodle Casserole for Days

13 ingredients	
8–10 SERVINGS	
METHOD: standard	

SPECIAL EQUIPMENT: none	TIME UNDER PRESSURE: 5 minutes	TOTAL TIME WITH PRESSURE: about 30 minutes
PRESSURE: low	RELEASE: quick	

4 cups (1 quart) chicken broth

2 cups whole or low-fat milk (do not use fat-free)

1 medium yellow or white onion, chopped (1 cup)

3 medium celery stalks, thinly sliced (1 cup)

½ stick (4 tablespoons or ¼ cup) butter, cut into small bits

2 teaspoons dried dill

1 teaspoon ground black pepper

½ teaspoon table salt

Up to ½ teaspoon grated nutmeg

Two 12-ounce packages raw dried egg or no-yolk noodles

2 cups heavy or light cream

Four 6-ounce cans tuna, preferably yellow-fin tuna, drained

1 pound Swiss cheese, shredded (4 cups)

This casserole is go-to comfort food in our house. We left the recipe fairly traditional—with the exception of some dried dill, which pairs so nicely with canned tuna and the creamy sauce. Some recipes for this classic include mushrooms, but we left them out because we feel they muddy the sauce with their black gills (even under LOW pressure). We stir in the cream right at the end because we want a richer, fresher, less "cooked" taste (although we do let it bubble just a bit to blend the flavors).

1.

	Press	Set it for	Set time for	If needed, press
In all 10-quart pots	SAUTÉ	MEDIUM, NORMAL, or CUSTOM 300°F	15 minutes	START

2. As the pot heats, mix the broth, milk, onion, celery, butter, dill, pepper, salt, and nutmeg in the insert set in a **10-quart Instant Pot**. Cook, stirring once in a while, until the butter melts and lots of steam comes off the liquid (but not until it boils), about 8 minutes. Stir in the pasta and turn off the heat. Lock the lid on the pot.

3.

	Set pot for	Set level to	Valve must be	Set time for	If needed, press
For all 10-quart pots	PRESSURE COOK or MANUAL	LOW	Closed	5 minutes with the KEEP WARM setting off	START

4. When the pot has finished cooking, use the **quick-release method** to bring the pressure back to normal. Unlatch the lid and open the cooker.

5.

	Press	Set it for	Set time for	If needed, press
In all 10-quart pots	SAUTÉ	MEDIUM, NORMAL, or CUSTOM 300°F	5 minutes	START

6. As the liquid begins to bubble, stir in the cream. Cook for 1 minute, stirring constantly. Turn off the heat, then stir in the tuna and cheese. Use hot pads or silicone baking mitts to transfer the (hot!) insert to a nearby wire rack. Let sit for 5 minutes, *stirring twice to prevent sticking*. Serve warm.

Beyond

- For a brinier casserole, use 1 cup fish stock and 3 cups chicken broth. Look for fish stock in the freezer case at larger supermarkets, or make your own with the recipe in the first *Instant Pot Bible*.

- For more vegetables, add up to 2 cups fresh shelled peas or thawed frozen peas with the onion and celery in step 2.

Chickens (Plural!) for Dinner

7 ingredients

8–10 SERVINGS

METHOD:
steam

SPECIAL EQUIPMENT:
a pressure- and food-safe rack or trivet

PRESSURE:
high

TIME UNDER PRESSURE:
30 minutes

RELEASE:
natural

TOTAL TIME WITH PRESSURE:
about 1½ hours

GLUTEN-FREE

2½ cups water

½ stick (4 tablespoons or ¼ cup) butter, *at room temperature*

2 tablespoons dried poultry seasoning blend, *preferably salt-free*

1 tablespoon mild paprika

2 teaspoons table salt, or to taste (check if there's salt in the seasoning blend)

2 teaspoons ground black pepper, or to taste

Two 3½- to 4-pound whole chickens, any giblets and the necks removed

Back in the day, we'd go to the Second Avenue Deli in New York City just to get their pot of stewed chicken, a ridiculously comforting but simple meal. So we crafted this big recipe as a nostalgia bump for us, who long left the city for rural New England, and for all those fans of soft, juicy chicken in the IP social-media groups. These chickens are not browned. They're steamed, almost stewed, for this old-world comfort food. They're best served over cooked noodles (see the **Beyond** section).

1. Pour the water into the insert set in a **10-quart Instant Pot.** Set a large, pressure- and food-safe rack or trivet in the insert.

2. Mash the butter, poultry seasoning, paprika, salt, and pepper in a small bowl. Rub this mixture all over the outside of both chickens. Set them on the rack back to back, one turned the opposite direction from the other, so they fit in one level. Lock the lid on the pot.

3.

	Set pot for	Set level to	Valve must be	Set time for	If needed, press
For all 10-quart pots	PRESSURE COOK or MANUAL	HIGH	Closed	30 minutes with the KEEP WARM setting off	START

4. When the pot has finished cooking, turn it off and let the pressure **return to normal naturally,** about 35 minutes. Unlatch the lid and open the cooker. Cool for 5 minutes.

5. Use a large metal spatula and kitchen tongs (or silicone baking mitts) to transfer the chickens to a nearby cutting board. Be careful: They can come to pieces. Cool for 2 to 3 minutes before slicing them into pieces, preferably two breasts with wings from each and two leg-and-thigh sections from each.

Beyond

- The stock in the pot can help make an excellent noodle side dish. Use a flatware tablespoon to skim its surface fat. Measure the remaining amount of stock, then set the pot's SAUTÉ setting on HIGH or MORE until the stock is steaming. For every 1 cup of stock, stir in 1 tablespoon butter and 4 ounces dried egg or no-yolk noodles. Turn off the heat, lock the lid on the pot, and cook at HIGH pressure for 4 minutes, followed by a quick release. Stir well before serving.

- If you really miss the crisp skin, you can carve the chicken into big chunks and set the pieces skin side up on a large, lipped baking sheet. (To transfer them, you'll need a large metal spatula, not kitchen tongs.) Broil them 4 to 6 inches from the heating element for a few minutes, no more than 4 or 5, just until the skin browns (but the meat will still be quite tender).

Family-Size Chicken Stew with Mushrooms and Cream

15 ingredients

8–10 SERVINGS

METHOD:
fast/slow

SPECIAL
EQUIPMENT:
none

PRESSURE:
low

TIME UNDER
PRESSURE:
10 minutes

RELEASE:
modified natural

TOTAL TIME WITH
PRESSURE:
about 45 minutes

TOTAL TIME WITH
SLOW COOKING:
about 3½ hours

GLUTEN-FREE

1 stick (8 tablespoons or ½ cup) butter

2 pounds white or brown button mushrooms, cleaned and thinly sliced

3 medium or 2 large leeks, white and pale green parts only, halved lengthwise, washed well to remove internal grit, and thinly sliced (1½ cups)

3 medium garlic cloves, minced (1 tablespoon)

2 tablespoons loosely packed, stemmed, fresh sage leaves, minced

2 tablespoons loosely packed, stemmed, fresh thyme leaves

2 teaspoons finely grated lemon zest

1½ teaspoons table salt

1 teaspoon ground black pepper

1 cup dry white wine, such as Chardonnay; or unsweetened apple juice

1½ cups chicken broth

Twelve 8-ounce boneless skinless chicken breasts, halved widthwise

3 tablespoons water

1½ tablespoons cornstarch or potato starch

½ cup heavy or light cream

This recipe makes a fairly simple stew, an easy crowd meal because it doesn't even require browning the chicken breasts. Doing so almost cooks them through anyway *and* would add a brown cast to the creamy sauce. The fresh herbs are crucial because their more present flavors will readily enhance the sauce during the quick cooking time. But the real hero is that little bit of lemon zest. It will soften and mellow under pressure for the slightest, pleasant spark among the flavors. (Don't worry: It won't curdle the cream that you add at the end because the zest has been so thoroughly cooked.)

1.

	Press	Set it for	Set time for	If needed, press
In all 10-quart pots	SAUTÉ	MEDIUM, NORMAL, or CUSTOM 300°F	15 minutes	START

2. As the pot heats, melt the butter in the insert set in a **10-quart Instant Pot.** Add the mushrooms and cook, stirring often, until they give off their liquid and it evaporates to a glaze, about 6 minutes.

3. Add the leeks and continue cooking, stirring more often, until they wilt, about 2 minutes. Stir in the garlic, sage, thyme, lemon zest, salt, and pepper until aromatic, about 20 seconds.

4. Pour in the wine and scrape up any browned bits on the pot's bottom. Stir in the broth and turn off the heat. Add the chicken breasts, stir well, and lock the lid on the pot.

5.

	Set pot for	Set level to	Valve must be	Set time for	If needed, press
For all 10-quart pots	PRESSURE COOK or MANUAL	LOW	Closed	10 minutes with the KEEP WARM setting off	START
For the slow-cook function	SLOW COOK	HIGH	Open	3 hours with the KEEP WARM setting off	START

6. When the pot has finished cooking under pressure, turn it off and let the pressure **return to normal naturally for 10 minutes.** Then use the **quick-release method** to bring the pot's residual pressure. Whichever cooking method you've used, unlatch the lid and open the cooker. Whisk the water and cornstarch or potato starch in a small bowl until smooth.

7.

	Press	Set it for	Set time for	If needed, press
In all 10-quart pots	SAUTÉ	MEDIUM, NORMAL, or CUSTOM 300°F	5 minutes	START

8. As the liquid comes to a simmer, stir in the cream and the starch slurry. Continue cooking, stirring constantly, until somewhat thickened, about 1 minute. Turn off the heat and use hot pads or silicone baking mitts to transfer the (hot!) insert to a nearby wire rack (to stop the cooking). Cool for 2 to 3 minutes before serving hot.

Beyond

- Add more herbs: up to 1 tablespoon stemmed, minced, fresh parsley leaves and/or 1 tablespoon stemmed, minced, fresh oregano leaves.

- Or get more "French bistro" by substituting stemmed, fresh tarragon leaves for the sage leaves.

Better — and Lots More — Chicken Marbella

14 ingredients

10–12 SERVINGS

METHOD: fast/slow

SPECIAL EQUIPMENT: none

PRESSURE: high

TIME UNDER PRESSURE: 12 minutes

RELEASE: natural

TOTAL TIME WITH PRESSURE: about 1 hour 20 minutes

TOTAL TIME WITH SLOW COOKING: about 3½ hours

GLUTEN-FREE

¼ cup olive oil

7 pounds cut-up chicken, 12 to 14 pieces, a mixture of breasts, thighs, and legs

Up to 9 medium garlic cloves, minced (3 tablespoons)

⅓ cup red wine vinegar

2 cups chicken broth

1 cup pitted prunes

1 cup pitted green olives

¼ cup drained and rinsed capers

2 tablespoons brine from the jar of capers

2 tablespoons loosely packed, stemmed, fresh oregano leaves, minced

1 teaspoon table salt

1 teaspoon ground black pepper

3 or 4 bay leaves

½ cup packed dark brown sugar

Chicken Marbella was a 1980s phenomenon, made famous by *The Silver Palate Cookbook.* You can find plenty of takes on the standard, but we felt it was in need of an update. To be honest, most recipes yield a greasy mess that's just too darn sweet. We've cut down on the oil (even draining most of it from the pot after browning the chicken) and balanced the brown sugar (and admittedly sweet prunes) with a bit more garlic and vinegar, as well as even more briny olives and capers, all of which give our version a more sweet-and-sour flavor: less cloying and (we feel) more satisfying for today's tastes.

1.

	Press	Set it for	Set time for	If needed, press
In all 10-quart models	SAUTÉ	MEDIUM, NORMAL, or CUSTOM 300°F	30 minutes	START

2. As the pot heats, warm the olive oil in the insert set in a **10-quart Instant Pot.** Add four or five pieces of chicken skin side down and brown them well without turning, about 4 minutes. Turn them over and brown the other sides, about 3 minutes. Transfer the pieces to a nearby large bowl and continue browning the chicken in two more batches until all the pieces are in the bowl.

3. Spoon out and discard almost all the rendered fat in the pot, leaving about 1 tablespoon (or so) in the pot. (Don't pour the grease down your drain!) Add the garlic to the pot and stir until fragrant, just a few seconds. Add the vinegar and scrape up all the browned bits on the pot's bottom.

4. Stir in the broth, prunes, olives, capers, their brine, the oregano, salt, pepper, and bay leaves until well combined. Turn off the heat and nestle the chicken pieces into this sauce, keeping as many of the pieces skin side up as you can. Add any accumulated juices from the bowl, sprinkle the brown sugar over the chicken pieces, and lock the lid on the pot.

5.

	Set pot for	Set level to	Valve must be	Set time for	If needed, press
For all 10-quart pots	PRESSURE COOK or MANUAL	HIGH	Closed	12 minutes with the KEEP WARM setting off	START
For the slow-cook function	SLOW COOK	HIGH	Open	3 hours with the KEEP WARM setting off	START

6. When the pot has finished cooking under pressure, turn it off and let the pressure **return to normal naturally,** about 40 minutes. Whichever cooking method you used, unlatch the lid and open the cooker. Fish out and discard the bay leaves. Stir gently and set aside, uncovered, to cool for 2 to 3 minutes before serving hot.

Beyond

- If you want to go over the top for a crowd, pour this stew into a large casserole or baking dish, then cover it and set it in a 300°F oven while you make A Big Pot of Cheesy Cauliflower Mash (page 476) as a bed for the individual servings (in bowls, of course).

A 9-Pound Capon Because You Can

9 ingredients

6–8 SERVINGS

METHOD:
steam

SPECIAL EQUIPMENT:
a pressure- and food-safe rack or trivet and butchers' twine

PRESSURE:
high

TIME UNDER PRESSURE:
1 hour

RELEASE:
natural

TOTAL TIME WITH PRESSURE:
about 2 hours 15 minutes

GLUTEN-FREE

2½ cups chicken broth

One 9-pound capon, any giblets removed, the neck reserved

1 small yellow or white onion, peeled and halved

1 large carrot, peeled and cut into thirds widthwise

1 medium celery stalk, halved widthwise

Half of a medium lemon, cut into two pieces (that is, two lemon quarters)

1½ teaspoons table salt

½ teaspoon ground black pepper

½ stick (4 tablespoons or ¼ cup) butter

A capon's a big bird, a rooster that's been, well, de-roostered. It's got lots of meat with a slightly more "chickeny" flavor, somewhere between turkey and chicken. It's also surprisingly lean, certainly more so than chicken.

You can skip making the sauce in steps 6 and 7, but we encourage you to then save the stock from the pot, freezing it in small, ½- or 1-cup containers to easily add to soups and stews for a big hit of flavor.

1. Pour the broth into the insert set in a **10-quart Instant Pot.** Set a large pressure- and food-safe rack or trivet in the insert. Put the capon's neck into the broth.

2. Stuff the bird's large cavity with the onion, carrot, celery, and lemon. (These items will round up the bird, giving it a taller shape.) Use butchers' twine to tie the bird in two places: once around the body to hold the wings against it and once around the thighs to hold the legs closer together.

3. Season the bird with the salt and pepper. Set it breast side up on the rack. Lock the lid on the pot.

4.

	Set pot for	Set level to	Valve must be	Set time for	If needed, press
For all 10-quart pots	PRESSURE COOK or MANUAL	HIGH	Closed	1 hour with the KEEP WARM setting off	START

5. When the pot has finished cooking, turn it off and let the pressure **return to normal naturally,** about 35 minutes. Unlatch the lid and open the cooker. Cool for 5 minutes, then use a large metal spatula and kitchen tongs (or silicone baking mitts) to transfer the hot bird to a nearby large cutting board. Watch out: The capon does have hot juices in the inner cavities. Cool for 10 minutes. As the bird rests, remove the rack and the neck from the pot, then use a flatware tablespoon or a large cooking spoon to skim any surface fat from the juices in the pot.

6.

	Press	Set it for	Set time for	If needed, press
In all 10-quart models	SAUTÉ	HIGH or MORE	15 minutes	START

7. Stir occasionally until the liquid is at a full boil. Continue boiling, stirring occasionally, until the liquid has reduced to about half the volume of when you removed the capon, about 10 minutes. Stir in the butter and continue to boil until thickened somewhat, about 4 minutes. Turn off the heat.

8. Remove and discard the vegetables from the bird. Carve it into several pieces: most likely four breast sections, two legs, two thighs, and the wings. Serve with the buttery sauce ladled on top.

Beyond

- If you want crunchy skin on the capon pieces, arrange them skin side up on a large lipped baking sheet and broil about 8 inches from the broiler element until browned and crisp, about 4 minutes (but watch carefully!).

Turkey Leg Cacciatore

14 ingredients	
8 SERVINGS	
METHOD: fast/slow	

SPECIAL EQUIPMENT: none	
PRESSURE: high	

TIME UNDER PRESSURE: 32 minutes	
RELEASE: natural	

TOTAL TIME WITH PRESSURE: about 1½ hours	
TOTAL TIME WITH SLOW COOKING: about 4½ hours	
GLUTEN-FREE	

¼ cup olive oil

Eight ¾- to 1-pound turkey legs

2 large yellow or white onions, chopped (3 cups)

2 large green bell peppers, stemmed, cored, and chopped (3 cups)

1 pound white or brown button mushrooms, cleaned and thinly sliced

At least 3 medium garlic cloves, minced (1 tablespoon), or more to taste

1 cup dry red wine, or additional chicken broth

One 28-ounce can diced tomatoes *packed in juice* (3½ cups)

1 cup chicken broth

1 tablespoon dried basil

1 tablespoon dried oregano

1 tablespoon dried rosemary

1½ teaspoons table salt

½ teaspoon red pepper flakes, or more to taste

Beyond

- For more flavor, add up to 1 ounce crushed, dried porcini mushrooms with the garlic.

- For a turkey stew, remove the cooked turkey legs from the pot in step 6 and cool them on a big cutting board for 10 minutes. Shred the meat off the legs, picking out and discarding any long, hard tendons. Stir the meat back into the sauce in the pot. Heat it to simmering using the SAUTÉ function on HIGH or MORE. Turn off the heat and serve the stew over mashed potatoes or cooked polenta.

Here's a hearty, Italian-style braise with a lot of spices to get as much flavor as we can into the turkey legs. They should be piled in the sauce to absorb the most flavor. Don't stand them up on their thick ends like books on shelves. Instead, set them all sorts of crossways on top of each other in as few layers as possible for the most even cooking.

1.

	Press	Set it for	Set time for	If needed, press
In all 10-quart models	SAUTÉ	MEDIUM, NORMAL, or CUSTOM 300°F	35 minutes	START

2. As the pot heats, warm the oil in the insert set in a **10-quart Instant Pot.** Put four turkey legs in the insert and brown them well, turning only occasionally, over about 12 minutes. The less you mess with them, the better they'll brown (and they need to *brown* to keep from sticking to the pot under pressure). Transfer them to a nearby large bowl and brown the other turkey legs the same way before getting them into the bowl.

3. Add the onions and bell peppers to the pot. Cook, stirring often, until the onions soften, about 4 minutes. Stir in the mushrooms and cook, stirring even more often, until they give off their liquid and it evaporates to a glaze, about 5 minutes.

4. Stir in the garlic until aromatic, then pour in the wine and scrape up all the browned bits on the pot's bottom. Stir in the tomatoes, broth, basil, oregano, rosemary, salt, and red pepper flakes until well combined. Turn off the heat. Nestle the legs into the pot and pour in any accumulated juices from their bowl. Lock the lid onto the cooker.

5.

	Set pot for	Set level to	Valve must be	Set time for	If needed, press
For all 10-quart pots	PRESSURE COOK or MANUAL	HIGH	Closed	32 minutes with the KEEP WARM setting off	START
For the slow-cook function	SLOW COOK	HIGH	Open	4 hours with the KEEP WARM setting off	START

6. When the pot has finished cooking under pressure, turn it off and let the pressure **return to normal naturally,** about 40 minutes. Whichever cooking method you've used, unlatch the lid and open the cooker. Cool for 2 to 3 minutes, then serve the legs in bowls with lots of the pot sauce ladled over them.

Smoky Beef & Bean Chili (for a Horde)

15 ingredients	
10–12 SERVINGS	
METHOD: fast/slow	
SPECIAL EQUIPMENT: none	**PRESSURE:** high
TIME UNDER PRESSURE: 5 minutes	**RELEASE:** quick
TOTAL TIME WITH PRESSURE: about 40 minutes	
TOTAL TIME WITH SLOW COOKING: about 3 hours 15 minutes	
CAN BE GLUTEN-FREE	

¼ cup vegetable, canola, or other neutral-flavored oil

2 large yellow or white onions, chopped (3 cups)

3½ pounds lean ground beef, preferably 90 percent lean or more

Two 4½-ounce cans hot or mild diced green chiles (1 cup)

½ cup drained jarred (hot or "tamed") pickled jalapeño rings

2 canned chipotle chiles in adobo sauce (gluten-free, if necessary), stemmed, cored (seeded, if desired), and chopped

1 tablespoon adobo sauce from the can

½ cup standard chili powder

2 tablespoons mild paprika

2 tablespoons ground cumin

2 tablespoons dried oregano

½ teaspoon ground cinnamon

1 cup dark beer, preferably Dos Equis; or beef broth

Two 28-ounce cans diced tomatoes *packed in juice*, preferably fire-roasted tomatoes (7 cups)

Three 15-ounce cans red kidney beans, drained and rinsed (5¼ cups)

Beyond

- For smokier flavor, substitute mild smoked paprika for the regular paprika.

- For more chile flavor, substitute a *pure* ground and dried chile powder, such as ancho chile powder or New Mexican red chile powder, for some or all of the standard chili powder. One warning: The chili will be much spicier.

- Garnish the servings with chopped avocado, grated American sharp cheddar or Monterey Jack cheese, diced tomatoes, sliced radishes, pickle relish, chow chow, and/or pickled onions.

Feed your family. Feed your crew. Feed both at once. The hot bite in this chili comes from pickled jalapeño rings, although you can use the "tamed" ones that now show up in most North American supermarkets.

A couple of notes: One, there's no additional salt in the recipe because the canned products can contain tons. Pass extra at the table. And two, a lot of liquid comes from the canned tomatoes. Make *sure* they're packed in juice, not puree.

1.

	Press	Set it for	Set time for	If needed, press
In all 10-quart models	SAUTÉ	MEDIUM, NORMAL, or CUSTOM 300°F	10 minutes	START

2. As the pot warms, heat the oil in the insert set in a **10-quart Instant Pot.** Add the onions and cook, stirring often, until softened, about 5 minutes.

3. Crumble in the ground beef and continue cooking, stirring frequently and breaking up all the clumps, until all the meat loses its raw, red color, about 3 minutes. Stir in the canned green chiles, jalapeño rings, chipotles, and adobo sauce until aromatic, about 20 seconds.

4. Stir in the chili powder, paprika, cumin, oregano, and cinnamon until fragrant, just a few seconds. Pour in the beer and scrape up all the browned bits on the pot's bottom. Stir in the tomatoes with their juice and the beans. Turn off the heat and lock the lid on the pot.

5.

	Set pot for	Set level to	Valve must be	Set time for	If needed, press
For all 10-quart pots	PRESSURE COOK or MANUAL	HIGH	Closed	5 minutes with the KEEP WARM setting off	START
For the slow-cook function	SLOW COOK	HIGH	Open	3 hours with the KEEP WARM setting off	START

6. When the pot has finished cooking under pressure, use the **quick-release method** to bring the pressure back to normal. Whichever cooking method you've used, unlatch the lid and open the cooker. Stir well, then set aside for 2 to 3 minutes to blend the flavors before serving hot.

Beef, Cranberry, and Root Vegetable Stew (for Everyone)

17 ingredients	**SPECIAL EQUIPMENT:** none
10–12 SERVINGS	**PRESSURE:** high
METHOD: fast/slow	**TIME UNDER PRESSURE:** 35 minutes
	RELEASE: natural
	TOTAL TIME WITH PRESSURE: about 1 hour 40 minutes
	TOTAL TIME WITH SLOW COOKING: about 5 hours
	CAN BE GLUTEN-FREE

3 tablespoons butter

8 ounces thin strips of bacon (gluten-free, if necessary), chopped

2 medium yellow or white onions, chopped (2 cups)

Up to 6 medium garlic cloves, minced (2 tablespoons)

2½ tablespoons loosely packed, stemmed, fresh thyme leaves

1½ teaspoons ground allspice

½ teaspoon table salt

2 bay leaves

2 tablespoons Dijon mustard (gluten-free, if necessary)

1 tablespoon Worcestershire sauce (gluten-free, if necessary)

½ cup packed dried cranberries, chopped

One 28-ounce can diced tomatoes *packed in juice*, preferably fire-roasted tomatoes (3½ cups)

1½ cups beef broth

One 5½-pound boneless beef chuck roast, cut into 2-inch pieces, any large globs of fat discarded

1 pound medium carrots, peeled and cut into 1-inch pieces

1 pound medium parsnips, peeled and cut into 1-inch pieces

2 tablespoons potato starch

Even for professional cookbook writers, browning more than 5 pounds of beef is a pain in the...neck. So we altered this giant pot of beef stew so we could skip that step by instead upping the spices and flavor boosters (like mustard and Worcestershire sauce), all to give the stew as much flavor as possible. Don't worry: There'll still be caramelized bits in the pot from the bacon (which will get scraped up with the juice from the tomatoes and the broth).

1.

	Press	Set it for	Set time for	If needed, press
In all 10-quart models	SAUTÉ	MEDIUM, NORMAL, or CUSTOM 300°F	15 minutes	START

2. As the pot heats, melt the butter in the insert set in a **10-quart Instant Pot**. Add the bacon and cook, stirring often, until browned and crisp, about 6 minutes.

3. Add the onions and continue cooking, stirring quite often, until softened, about 3 minutes. Stir in the garlic, thyme, allspice, salt, and bay leaves until aromatic, about 20 seconds.

4. Stir in the mustard and Worcestershire sauce to coat everything. Stir in the cranberries, then the tomatoes (with their juice), and the broth. Scrape up all the browned bits on the pot's bottom.

5. Stir in the beef, carrots, and parsnips until all the pieces are coated in the sauce. Turn off the heat and lock the lid on the pot.

6.

	Set pot for	Set level to	Valve must be	Set time for	If needed, press
For all 10-quart pots	PRESSURE COOK or MANUAL	HIGH	Closed	35 minutes with the KEEP WARM setting off	START
For the slow-cook function	SLOW COOK	HIGH	Open	4½ hours with the KEEP WARM setting off	START

7. When the pot has finished cooking under pressure, turn it off and let the pressure **return to normal naturally,** about 45 minutes. Whichever cooking method you've used, unlatch the lid and open the cooker. Fish out and discard the bay leaves. Scoop about ¼ cup of the liquid in the pot into a small bowl, then whisk in the potato starch to make a slurry.

8.

	Press	Set it for	Set time for	If needed, press
In all 10-quart models	SAUTÉ	MEDIUM, NORMAL, or CUSTOM 300°F	5 minutes	START

0. As the stew comes to a simmer, stir in the starch slurry. Continue cooking, stirring constantly, until somewhat thickened, less than 1 minute. Immediately turn off the heat and use hot pads or silicone baking mitts to transfer the (hot!) insert to a nearby wire rack (to stop the cooking). Cool for 5 minutes, stirring occasionally, before serving hot.

Beyond

- For a sweeter stew, substitute tamarind paste for the Worcestershire sauce (and increase the table salt to 1½ teaspoons).

- For a more savory stew, decrease the Dijon mustard to 1 tablespoon, use the Worcestershire sauce as directed, and add 1 tablespoon soy sauce *and* 1 minced tinned anchovy fillet with it.

- Don't like carrots or parsnips? Or want a larger selection of vegetables? You can add an additional 2 pounds of peeled and cubed root vegetables with the carrots and parsnips. Choose yellow-fleshed potatoes, golden turnips, turnips, or rutabaga.

All the Midwestern Goulash

16 ingredients

10–12 SERVINGS

METHOD:
standard

SPECIAL
EQUIPMENT:
none

PRESSURE:
high

TIME UNDER
PRESSURE:
4 minutes

RELEASE:
quick

TOTAL TIME WITH
PRESSURE:
about 30 minutes

CAN BE GLUTEN-
FREE

2 tablespoons butter

2 tablespoons olive oil

2 *large* yellow or white onions, chopped (3 cups)

2 *large* green bell peppers, stemmed, cored, and chopped (3 cups)

2½ pounds lean ground beef, preferably 90 percent lean or more

2 cups beef broth

One 28-ounce can diced tomatoes *packed in juice* (3½ cups)

One 28-ounce can crushed tomatoes (3½ cups)

1 tablespoon dried basil

1 tablespoon mild paprika

2 teaspoons dried thyme

1 teaspoon rubbed or ground sage

1 teaspoon table salt, or more to taste

½ teaspoon ground black pepper, or more to taste

2 pounds raw dried large elbow pasta (can be gluten-free—for more information on gluten-free dried pasta, see the introduction to the pasta chapter on page 103)

4 ounces regular or low-fat cream cheese (gluten-free, if necessary—do not use low-fat or fat-free), cut into ½-inch cubes

Beyond

- Substitute an herbed cream cheese for the plain cream cheese.
- Garnish servings with pickle relish or even jalapeño relish.

No, not Hungarian goulash. Rather, this is the goulash served at Midwestern diners in bygone days: a tomato and pasta dish with ground beef. Long ago, canned Beefaroni tried to copy the original. Forget that stuff! We can do it better and faster in an Instant Pot. But do note: the onions and bell pepper should be quite large because they add lots of necessary moisture to the stew.

Many versions, including those from the old Betty Crocker cookbooks, added cream cheese to the stew. If we *stirred* it in with the other ingredients, it would burn as the stew cooks. But by setting it over the stew as it cooks with pressure and thus letting it melt on top, we can get that old-school flavor without any worries.

1.

	Press	Set it for	Set time for	If needed, press
In all 10-quart models	SAUTÉ	MEDIUM, NORMAL, or CUSTOM 300°F	15 minutes	START

2. As the pot heats, melt the butter in the olive oil in the insert set in a **10-quart Instant Pot.** Add the onions and bell peppers. Cook, stirring often, until softened, about 4 minutes. Crumble in the ground beef and cook, stirring quite frequently to break up any clumps, until the meat loses its raw, red color, about 2 minutes.

3. Pour in the broth and scrape up all the browned bits on the pot's bottom. Stir in the diced tomatoes (with their juice), the crushed tomatoes, basil, paprika, thyme, sage, salt, and pepper until well combined.

4. Continue cooking, stirring occasionally, until wisps of steam rise from the liquid in the pot, about 5 minutes. Stir in the pasta and turn off the heat. Dot the top of the stew with the cream cheese cubes without stirring them in. Lock the lid on the pot.

5.

	Set pot for	Set level to	Valve must be	Set time for	If needed, press
For all 10-quart pots	PRESSURE COOK or MANUAL	HIGH	Closed	4 minutes with the KEEP WARM setting off	START

6. When the pot has finished cooking, use the **quick-release method** to bring the pressure back to normal. Unlatch the lid and open the cooker. Stir well, then set the lid askew over the pot and set it aside for 2 to 3 minutes to blend the flavors and let the pasta thicken the stew slightly. Serve warm.

Holiday-Size Un-Stuffed-Cabbage Stew

16 ingredients	SPECIAL EQUIPMENT:	TIME UNDER PRESSURE:	TOTAL TIME WITH PRESSURE:
10–12 SERVINGS	none	12 minutes	about 1 hour
METHOD:	PRESSURE:	RELEASE:	TOTAL TIME WITH SLOW COOKING:
fast/slow	high	modified quick	about 3½ hours
			GLUTEN-FREE

3 pounds lean ground beef, preferably 90 percent lean or more

⅔ cup raw long-grain white rice

1½ teaspoons dried thyme

1½ teaspoons onion powder

2 teaspoons table salt, or more to taste

1 teaspoon ground black pepper, or more to taste

½ teaspoon ground cinnamon

2 tablespoons olive oil

1 large yellow or white onion, chopped (1½ cups)

1 large green cabbage, cored and chopped (8 cups)

One 28-ounce can diced tomatoes *packed in juice* (3½ cups)

1½ cups chicken or beef broth

½ cup loosely packed stemmed fresh dill fronds, finely chopped

2 tablespoons granulated white sugar

2 tablespoons apple cider vinegar

½ teaspoon garlic powder

Beyond

- For heat, add up to 1 teaspoon red pepper flakes with the dill.
- Or change the flavor profile by using oregano instead of dill.

This stew offers up the flavors of stuffed cabbage in a pot to feed a crowd—all without having to go to the trouble of stuffing a zillion cabbage leaves. The traditional meat stuffing has been turned into meatballs that are made with raw rice (rather than bread crumbs and egg) because rice will yield slightly firmer meatballs that can endure the longer time it takes the big pot to come to pressure.

1. Mix the ground beef, rice, thyme, onion powder, 1 teaspoon of the salt, the pepper, and cinnamon in a large bowl until uniform.

2.

	Press	Set it for	Set time for	If needed, press
In all 10-quart models	SAUTÉ	MEDIUM, NORMAL, or CUSTOM 300°F	10 minutes	START

3. As the pot heats, warm the oil in the insert set in a **10-quart Instant Pot.** Add the onion and cook, stirring often, until softened, about 4 minutes.

4. Add the cabbage and use two wooden spoons or kitchen tongs to toss it until it begins to wilt over the heat, about 2 minutes. Stir in the tomatoes with their juice and scrape up any browned bits in the pot. (There should be almost none.) Stir in the broth, dill, sugar, vinegar, garlic powder, and remaining 1 teaspoon salt until well combined.

5. Form the ground beef mixture into 24 compact meatballs, each made from a scant ¼ cup of the mixture. Nestle most into the sauce, then layer some out of the sauce as necessary. Turn off the heat and lock the lid on the pot.

6.

	Set pot for	Set level to	Valve must be	Set time for	If needed, press
For all 10-quart pots	PRESSURE COOK or MANUAL	HIGH	Closed	12 minutes with the KEEP WARM setting off	START
For the slow-cook function	SLOW COOK	HIGH	Open	3 hours with the KEEP WARM setting off	START

7. When the pot has finished cooking under pressure, use the **quick-release method** to bring the pressure back to normal but **do not open the cooker.** Set it aside for 10 minutes. Whichever cooking method you've used, unlatch the lid and open the pot. Stir very gently to keep the meatballs intact, then set the pot aside for 2 or 3 minutes to blend the flavors before serving hot.

Family-Size Southwestern Meat Loaf with Noodles

15 ingredients

10 SERVINGS

METHOD: standard

SPECIAL EQUIPMENT: a 9-inch-round springform pan

PRESSURE: high twice

TIME UNDER PRESSURE: 34 minutes

RELEASE: natural, then quick

TOTAL TIME WITH PRESSURE: about 1½ hours

One 28-ounce can crushed tomatoes (3½ cups)

2½ cups chicken or beef broth

One 15-ounce can black beans, drained and rinsed (1¾ cups)

3 tablespoons standard chili powder

4 pounds lean ground beef, preferably 90 percent lean or more

1 cup Italian-seasoned *panko* bread crumbs

6 medium scallions, trimmed and thinly sliced (2 cups)

3 medium celery stalks, halved lengthwise and diced (1 cup)

One 4½-ounce can hot or mild diced green chiles (½ cup)

⅓ cup ketchup

3 refrigerator-cold large eggs, well beaten in a small bowl

2 teaspoons dried oregano

1½ teaspoons table salt

1 teaspoon ground cumin

18 ounces dried egg or no-yolk noodles (1½ twelve-ounce bags)

This is *almost* a one-pot meal, although with a technique that's a little unusual. First, you'll build a Southwestern tomato-and-black-bean sauce in the pot, then form a big meat loaf in a 9-inch springform pan. But the meat loaf won't cook in that pan. Instead, the pan's just a way to form a giant patty (meat cake?) that gets turned upside down *into* the sauce for cooking under pressure. After transferring the meat loaf to a cutting board to cut it into wedges, you quickly cook noodles right in the pot with the same Southwestern sauce. It still needs a vinegary salad, right? (Not exactly something we can pull out of the pot.)

1. Stir the tomatoes, broth, beans, and chili powder in the insert set in a **10-quart Instant Pot** until well combined.

2. Stir the ground beef, panko bread crumbs, scallions, celery, green chiles, ketchup, eggs, oregano, salt, and cumin in a large bowl until uniform. (Your clean hands work best!) *Pack* this mixture into a 9-inch-round springform pan, making a compact and even loaf.

3. Turn the pan upside down into the sauce in the pot. Unlatch the pan and remove the ring side as well as the bottom, thus leaving a circular loaf in the pot. Lock the lid onto the cooker.

4.

	Set pot for	Set level to	Valve must be	Set time for	If needed, press
For all 10-quart pots	PRESSURE COOK or MANUAL	HIGH	Closed	30 minutes with the KEEP WARM setting off	START

5. When the pot has finished cooking, turn it off and let the pressure **return to normal naturally,** about 35 minutes. Unlatch the lid and open the cooker.

6. Use two large metal spatulas to transfer the meat loaf to a nearby large cutting board or serving platter and set aside. Stir the noodles into the sauce in the pot and lock the lid back onto the cooker.

7.

	Set pot for	Set level to	Valve must be	Set time for	If needed, press
For all 10-quart pots	PRESSURE COOK or MANUAL	HIGH	Closed	4 minutes with the KEEP WARM setting off	START

8. When the pot has finished cooking, use the **quick-release method** to bring the pressure back to normal. Unlatch the lid and open the cooker. Stir the noodles and sauce, then set the lid askew over the pot and set it aside for 2 to 3 minutes so the pasta continues to absorb the sauce. Stir again, then slice the meat loaf into pie wedges and serve in bowls with plenty of noodles and sauce from the pot.

Beyond

- For more heat, squeeze some Sriracha over the meat loaf in the cooker before you lock on the lid in step 3.

- For a richer noodle accompaniment, stir up to 3 tablespoons butter into the noodle and sauce mixture after you open the pot in step 8.

Crowd-Pleaser Barbecue-Style Braised Brisket

14 ingredients	
8–10 SERVINGS	
METHOD: fast/slow	

SPECIAL EQUIPMENT: none	TIME UNDER PRESSURE: 2 hours	TOTAL TIME WITH PRESSURE: about 3 hours	TOTAL TIME WITH SLOW COOKING: about 6½ hours
PRESSURE: high	RELEASE: natural		CAN BE GLUTEN-FREE

One 28-ounce can diced tomatoes *packed in juice* (3½ cups)

½ cup beef broth

¼ cup Worcestershire sauce (gluten-free, if necessary)

¼ cup regular or low-sodium soy sauce, or gluten-free tamari sauce

¼ cup honey

2 tablespoons liquid smoke (gluten-free, if necessary)

2 tablespoons apple cider vinegar

2 tablespoons mild smoked paprika

1 tablespoon prepared yellow mustard (gluten-free, if necessary)

3 medium garlic cloves, minced (1 tablespoon)

2 teaspoons ground coriander

1 teaspoon ground allspice

1 teaspoon ground cloves

One 6-pound beef brisket, trimmed of external clumps of fat

Beyond

- Reduce the sauce, if desired: Once the brisket is out of the cooker, set the cooker on the SAUTÉ function to HIGH or MORE. Boil until the sauce has reduced to about half its volume from when you opened the pot, about 8 minutes, maybe more, depending on how much liquid the meat has given off.

- Make a variation on French dip sandwiches by putting the sliced meat in sandwiches made from crusty (or even stale) white bread. Dip the sandwiches into the pot sauce as you eat them.

Get this: In the large pot we can cook an entire brisket, enough to feed a tableful and still have leftovers for tomorrow. Because this is an all-out meal, we skip bottled barbecue sauce in favor of making a more traditional, smoky braising medium for the beef.

To trim a brisket, cut off any large bits of fat you can see, then shave off some of the layer of fat on top of the cut by running a chef's knife at an almost horizontal angle across the meat, carving back and forth a bit. Don't get rid of all the fat. Some left on the meat will definitely enrich the sauce.

1. Stir the tomatoes, broth, Worcestershire sauce, soy or tamari sauce, honey, liquid smoke, vinegar, smoked paprika, mustard, garlic, coriander, allspice, and cloves in the insert set in a **10-quart Instant Pot** until uniform.

2. Nestle the meat into the sauce. Spoon some of the sauce over the top of the meat. Lock the lid on the pot.

3.

	Set pot for	Set level to	Valve must be	Set time for	If needed, press
For all 10-quart pots	PRESSURE COOK or MANUAL	HIGH	Closed	2 hours with the KEEP WARM setting off	START
For the slow-cook function	SLOW COOK	HIGH	Open	6 hours with the KEEP WARM setting off	START

4. When the pot has finished cooking under pressure, turn it off and let the pressure **return to normal naturally,** about 45 minutes. Whichever method you've used, unlatch the lid and open the cooker. Use a meat fork and either a large metal spatula or kitchen tongs to transfer the brisket to a nearby cutting board. Cool for 5 minutes.

5. Run your clean fingers over the meat to determine which way the fibers go. Carve at a 90-degree angle to these fibers, making about ½-inch-thick slices. Use a flatware table spoon to skim the fat off the top of the sauce in the pot. Serve the slices with the sauce ladled on top.

Big Pork Loin Dinner with Pears and Potatoes

11 ingredients	
8–10 SERVINGS	
METHOD: standard	

SPECIAL EQUIPMENT: an instant-read meat thermometer

PRESSURE: high

TIME UNDER PRESSURE: 30 minutes

RELEASE: quick

TOTAL TIME WITH PRESSURE: about 45 minutes

GLUTEN-FREE

2½ cups chicken broth

2 pounds *small* white potatoes (1 to 1½ inches in diameter—do not peel)

1 large red onion, chopped (1½ cups)

2 tablespoons olive oil

6 medium garlic cloves, minced (2 tablespoons)

2 tablespoons fennel seeds, crushed on a cutting board with the bottom of a heavy saucepan

1 tablespoon finely grated lemon zest

Up to 1 tablespoon table salt

1 teaspoon ground black pepper

One 4- to 4½-pound boneless center-cut pork loin

Four 7- to 8-ounce firm pears, preferably Bosc pears, stemmed, peeled, and cored

Beyond

- If you want to thicken the sauce in the pot, remove the meat, potatoes, and pears. Discard any other solids. Bring the sauce to a simmer with the SAUTÉ function at HIGH or MORE. In a small bowl, whisk 1 tablespoon cornstarch, 1 tablespoon white wine vinegar, and 1 tablespoon water until smooth, then stir this slurry into the sauce. Cook, stirring constantly, until somewhat thickened, less than 1 minute. Turn off the heat and use hot pads or silicone baking mitts to transfer the (hot!) insert to a wire rack. Stir in 3 tablespoons butter until smooth.

- If you've got a *big* crowd, you can prepare *two* 4-pound pork loins in the pot with this method and exactly the same timing. Keep almost all of the other ingredients the same *except* use 3 pounds small white potatoes and omit the pears so both loins can fit in the pot together.

Here's a *whole* meal for a crowd out of a 10-quart pot: a family-size pork loin chunk and lots of potatoes with garlic, fennel seeds, and a hint of sweetness from pears. Look for firm but fragrant pears at the market. And here's our best hack for coring a pear: Use a melon baller on the fat end, turning and coring just until you get to the seeds without taking out too much of the flesh.

If you want a salad on the side, try a crunchy, lettuce-free chopped salad of cucumbers, radishes, carrots, celery, and zucchini, dressed with a light, lemony vinaigrette.

1. Pour the broth into the insert set in a **10-quart Instant Pot.** Add the potatoes and onion, spreading them out in one layer.

2. Mix the olive oil, garlic, crushed fennel seeds, lemon zest, salt, and pepper in a small bowl. Smear every drop of this mixture over the pork loin. Set the pork on the potatoes and onions so that the meat is sitting up and out of the liquid. Put the pears around the pork, also on top of the potatoes and onions. Lock the lid on the pot.

3.

	Set pot for	Set level to	Valve must be	Set time for	If needed, press
For all 10-quart pots	PRESSURE COOK or MANUAL	HIGH	Closed	30 minutes with the KEEP WARM setting off	START

4. When the pot has finished cooking, use the **quick-release method** to bring the pressure back to normal. Unlatch the lid and open the cooker. Use an instant-read meat thermometer inserted into the thickest part of the pork loin to make sure the internal temperature is 145°F or more. If not, lock the lid on the pot and give the whole thing another 5 minutes at HIGH pressure, followed by a **quick release.**

5. Use kitchen tongs and a metal spatula to transfer the pork loin to a nearby cutting board. Cool for 5 minutes, then slice into ½-inch-thick rounds. Cut the pears into smaller bits, then serve the pork with the potatoes, pears, and some of the pot sauce.

Gather-Your-Family Chuck Roast with Coffee and Turnips

13 ingredients	
10 SERVINGS	

SPECIAL EQUIPMENT:
none

METHOD:
fast/slow

PRESSURE:
high

TIME UNDER PRESSURE:
1 hour 50 minutes

RELEASE:
natural

TOTAL TIME WITH PRESSURE:
about 2½ hours

TOTAL TIME WITH SLOW COOKING:
about 5½ hours

GLUTEN-FREE

2 tablespoons olive oil

One 6-pound boneless beef chuck roast

2 large yellow or white onions, halved and sliced into thin half-moons

4 medium garlic cloves, minced (4 teaspoons)

2 teaspoons dried thyme

Up to 1 teaspoon ground allspice

1 teaspoon table salt

1 teaspoon ground black pepper

1¼ cups beef broth

1¼ cups strong brewed coffee

3 tablespoons balsamic vinegar

½ teaspoon vanilla extract

Ten 6-ounce (medium) turnips, peeled

Coffee, onions, balsamic vinegar, vanilla—these may seem the makings of a very odd braise. But they combine under pressure into a surprisingly savory, complex sauce, aromatic but not assertive, gentle and full of sweet/earthy flavors. The only trouble is the *shape* of the chuck roast, which is of paramount importance. The timing given is for a more cylindrical roast (that is, a round tube that is squared off at one or both ends). To adjust for a "flatter" chuck roast (like a blade or an arm roast), reduce the time under HIGH pressure to 1½ hours.

1.

	Press	Set it for	Set time for	If needed, press
In all 10-quart models	SAUTÉ	MEDIUM, NORMAL, or CUSTOM 300°F	20 minutes	START

2. As the pot heats, warm the oil in the insert set in a **10-quart Instant Pot.** Add the chuck roast and brown on both sides, disturbing it as little as possible and turning only once, about 8 minutes in all. Use a metal spatula and kitchen tongs to transfer the beef to a nearby large bowl.

3. Add the onions to the pot and cook, stirring often, until they soften and even begin to brown at the edges, about 6 minutes. Stir in the garlic, thyme, allspice, salt, and pepper until aromatic, just a few seconds.

4. Pour in the broth and scrape up all the browned bits on the pot's bottom. Stir in the coffee, vinegar, and vanilla. Turn off the heat and return the beef to the pot, turning it once to coat it in the sauce. Add any juices from its bowl, scatter the turnips around the beef, and lock the lid on the pot.

5.

	Set pot for	Set level to	Valve must be	Set time for	If needed, press
For all 10-quart models	PRESSURE COOK or MANUAL	HIGH	Closed	1 hour 50 minutes with the KEEP WARM setting off	START
For the slow-cook function	SLOW COOK	HIGH	Open	5 hours with the KEEP WARM setting off	START

6. When the pot has finished cooking under pressure, turn it off and let the pressure **return to normal naturally,** about 45 minutes. Whichever method you've used, unlatch the lid and open the cooker. Use a large metal spatula and kitchen tongs (or silicone baking mitts) to transfer the chuck roast to a nearby cutting board. Cool for 5 minutes.

7. Carve the meat into chunks. Use a flatware tablespoon to skim the fat off the top of the sauce in the pot. Slice the turnips into wedges. Serve the beef and turnips in bowls with the sauce spooned on top.

Beyond

- If you don't like turnips, substitute large yellow potatoes, about 6 ounces each, unpeeled and left whole.

Gather-Your-Family Chuck Roast with Sweet Potatoes

16 ingredients	
10 SERVINGS	
METHOD: fast/slow	

SPECIAL EQUIPMENT: none

PRESSURE: high

TIME UNDER PRESSURE: 1 hour 50 minutes

RELEASE: natural

TOTAL TIME WITH PRESSURE: about 2½ hours

TOTAL TIME WITH SLOW COOKING: about 5½ hours

GLUTEN-FREE

---

2 tablespoons vegetable, canola, or other neutral-flavored oil

One 6-pound boneless beef chuck roast

1 large red onion, halved and sliced into thin half-moons

2 medium fresh jalapeño chiles, stemmed, halved lengthwise, seeded, and thinly sliced

4 medium garlic cloves, minced (4 teaspoons)

2 cups beef broth

2 tablespoons dark brown sugar

2 tablespoons red wine vinegar

1 tablespoon finely grated orange zest

1 tablespoon dried oregano

1 tablespoon dried thyme

2 teaspoons ground coriander

1½ teaspoons table salt, or to taste

½ teaspoon grated nutmeg

One 14-ounce can diced tomatoes *packed in juice* (1¾ cups)

Three 1-pound (large) sweet potatoes, peeled and cut in half lengthwise

This braised chuck roast has flavors modeled on a combination prized in some Caribbean recipes: chiles, oranges, and garlic. The roast is not your standard fare by any means. Instead, it's a more imaginative take on a family meal. See the headnote to the other large-format chuck roast recipe in this chapter (page 462) for an important note about the shape of the chuck roast and the timing under pressure. See this recipe's **Beyond** section for our serving suggestion.

1.

	Press	Set it for	Set time for	If needed, press
In all 10-quart models	SAUTÉ	MEDIUM, NORMAL, or CUSTOM 300°F	15 minutes	START

2. As the pot heats, warm the oil in the insert set in a **10-quart Instant Pot.** Add the chuck roast and brown on both sides, disturbing it as little as possible and turning only once, about 8 minutes in all. Use a metal spatula and kitchen tongs to transfer the beef to a nearby large bowl.

3. Add the onion to the pot and cook, stirring often, until softened, about 3 minutes. Stir in the jalapeño and garlic until aromatic and a bit softened, just a few seconds. Pour in the broth and scrape up all the browned bits on the pot's bottom.

4. Stir in the brown sugar, vinegar, orange zest, oregano, thyme, coriander, salt, and nutmeg until the brown sugar dissolves. Stir in the tomatoes with their juice, then turn off the heat and set the chuck roast into the sauce. Turn it over to coat it in the sauce, then lay the sweet potatoes around the beef, some in the sauce and some out of it. (The meat will give off lots of liquid as it cooks and eventually cover them.) Lock the lid onto the cooker.

5.

	Set pot for	Set level to	Valve must be	Set time for	If needed, press
For all 10-quart pots	PRESSURE COOK or MANUAL	HIGH	Closed	1 hour 50 minutes with the KEEP WARM setting off	START
For the slow-cook function	SLOW COOK	HIGH	Open	5 hours with the KEEP WARM setting off	START

6. When the pot has finished cooking under pressure, turn it off and let the pressure **return to normal naturally,** about 45 minutes. Whichever cooking method you've used, unlatch the lid and open the cooker. Use a large metal spatula and kitchen tongs (or silicone baking mitts) to transfer the chuck roast to a nearby cutting board. Cool for 5 minutes.

7. Carve the meat into chunks. Use a flatware tablespoon to skim the fat off the top of the sauce in the pot. Slice the sweet potatoes into chunks. Serve the beef and sweet potatoes in bowls with the sauce spooned on top.

Beyond

- For a much spicier braise, substitute 3 fresh serrano chiles (stemmed, halved lengthwise, and thinly sliced) for the jalapeños. Or substitute 1 habanero for one of the jalapeños.

- Instead of sweet potatoes, substitute 4 large yellow (but not black) plantains, peeled and sliced into 3-inch pieces.

- Serve with long-grain white rice that's been cooked with some minced peeled fresh ginger, minced scallions, frozen shelled green peas, and a little jerk seasoning spice blend.

Big Rump Roast with Horseradish and Brown Sugar

11 ingredients	**SPECIAL EQUIPMENT:** none
10–12 SERVINGS	**PRESSURE:** high
METHOD: fast/slow	

TIME UNDER PRESSURE: 2 hours	**TOTAL TIME WITH PRESSURE:** about 3 hours
RELEASE: natural	**TOTAL TIME WITH SLOW COOKING:** about 7 hours
	CAN BE GLUTEN-FREE

One 7- to 7½-pound beef rump roast

2 tablespoons vegetable, canola, or other neutral-flavored oil

2 large yellow or white onions, halved and sliced into thin half-moons

4 medium garlic cloves, minced (4 teaspoons)

2 cups beef broth

½ cup jarred prepared white horseradish, plus more for garnishing

¼ cup packed dark brown sugar

¼ cup red wine vinegar

¼ cup Worcestershire sauce (gluten-free, if necessary)

1½ teaspoons celery seeds

Eight 8- to 10-ounce russet or baking potatoes, peeled but left whole

Despite its name, a beef rump roast is actually cut from the leg of a cow, not from its hind end. The roast is most often the big one used for "roast beef" at the supermarket deli counter. The meat has a little marbling but it's a fairly tough cut, sort of like a bulked-up version of a beef top round. At deli counters, it's often cooked to rare and sliced super thin (which is about the only way to make it chewable when it's rare). The pressure cooker will tenderize it but will still not get it to the point that it can be shredded, even after 2 hours. However, you'll end up with a super-beefy cut, satisfying and savory. Practice good knife skills when you carve the roast. It needn't be deli thin, but the slices should never be more than ¼ inch thick.

1. Before you start cooking, check out the rump roast. It often has a thin fat cap on the flatter side. If so, use a sharp knife to score this cap in a diagonal pattern to keep it from curling up when browning and cooking. You can cut through the cap and even into the meat below by about ⅛ inch.

2.

	Press	Set it for	Set time for	If needed, press
In all 10-quart models	SAUTÉ	MEDIUM, NORMAL, or CUSTOM 300°F	15 minutes	START

3. Warm the oil in the insert set in a **10-quart Instant Pot.** Set the rump roast in the insert and brown well on both sides, disturbing as little as possible and turning only once, about 10 minutes. Use a large metal spatula and kitchen tongs to transfer the beef to a nearby large cutting board.

4. Add the onions and garlic. Cook, stirring often, only for 1 minute. Then pour in the broth and scrape up any browned bits on the pot's bottom.

5. Put the meat back into the pot with the cap side facing down and on top of the onions. Also add any juices from the cutting board to the pot. Smear the horseradish over the meat and sprinkle it with the brown sugar. Pour the vinegar and Worcestershire sauce around the meat (not on it, so as not to dislodge the horseradish and brown sugar).

6. Turn off the heat. Sprinkle the celery seeds on top and arrange the potatoes around the roast, letting some of them sit in the sauce while stacking others as necessary. Lock the lid on the pot.

7.

	Set pot for	Set level to	Valve must be	Set time for	If needed, press
For all 10-quart pots	PRESSURE COOK or MANUAL	HIGH	Closed	2 hours with the KEEP WARM setting off	START
For the slow-cook function	SLOW COOK	HIGH	Open	6½ hours with the KEEP WARM setting off	START

8. When the pot has finished cooking under pressure, turn it off and let the pressure **return to normal naturally,** about 45 minutes. Whichever cooking method you've used, unlatch the lid and open the cooker. Use a large metal spatula and kitchen tongs (or silicone baking mitts) to transfer the meat to a nearby cutting board. Also transfer the potatoes to the cutting board or a big bowl. Cool for 10 minutes.

9. Use a flatware spoon to skim the surface fat off the sauce in the pot. Run your clean fingers over the meat to determine which way its fibers are going and carve the beef into thin strips at a ninety-degree angle to this grain. The beef will *not* be falling apart. Slice the potatoes into halves or thirds, then serve them with strips of meat in bowls along with plenty of sauce from the pot, garnishing the servings with more prepared horseradish, to taste.

Beyond

- Garnish with sour cream and/or aged balsamic vinegar, along with the horseradish.
- Make sure there's plenty of crunchy bread on hand to sop up the juices.

Yes, a Ham

10 ingredients

10–12 SERVINGS

METHOD:
steam

SPECIAL EQUIPMENT:
a pressure-and-food-safe rack or trivet and an instant-read meat thermometer

PRESSURE:
high

TIME UNDER PRESSURE:
45 minutes

RELEASE:
natural

TOTAL TIME WITH PRESSURE:
about 1½ hours

CAN BE GLUTEN-FREE

One 12-ounce bottle of beer, preferably an IPA; or 1½ cups beef broth

1 cup water

One 10-pound smoked half ham from the butt end (see the headnote for more information—and gluten-free, if necessary)

¼ cup Worcestershire sauce (gluten-free, if necessary)

½ cup packed dark brown sugar

¼ cup orange marmalade

2 tablespoons Dijon mustard (gluten-free, if necessary)

½ teaspoon ground cinnamon

½ teaspoon garlic powder

Up to ½ teaspoon ground dried cayenne

Here's a recipe that treats a ham as a roast, setting it on a rack to steam over beer. Afterwards, the ham is glazed and given a quick roast in the oven to caramelize the sugars, offering a better flavor and a much better texture that's not (ick) spongy.

Most hams sold in North America are actually half hams—that is, half of the large bit of the back leg of a pig. The shank ends are familiar from holiday tables: an eye of meat around a central bone. Unfortunately, this cut will not work in the 10-quart cooker because it's too tall to fit under the lid. You need the other end of the ham, the butt end. It's more like a giant pork roast with a complicated bone structure and more fat for more flavor in every slice.

1. Pour the beer and water in the insert set in a **10-quart Instant Pot.** Set a large pressure-and-food-safe rack or trivet in the insert.

2. Set the ham on the rack cut side *down*. Slowly pour the Worcestershire sauce over the meat. Lock the lid on the cooker.

3.

	Set pot for	Set level to	Valve must be	Set time for	If needed, press
For all 10-quart pots	PRESSURE COOK or MANUAL	HIGH	Closed	45 minutes with the KEEP WARM setting off	START

4. When the pot has finished cooking, turn it off and let the pressure **return to normal naturally,** about 40 minutes. Unlatch the lid and open the cooker. Use an instant-read meat thermometer inserted into the thickest part of the ham *without touching bone* to make sure the internal temperature is 145°F or more. If not, lock the lid back on the pot and cook at HIGH pressure for another 15 minutes, followed by a **quick release.**

5. Position the rack in the lower third of the oven and heat the oven to 450°F. Line a large lipped baking sheet with aluminum foil. Use silicone baking mitts (or a large metal spatula and kitchen tongs) to set the cooked ham cut side *down* on this sheet. Cool for 5 minutes.

6. Meanwhile, whisk the brown sugar, marmalade, mustard, cinnamon, garlic powder, and cayenne in a medium bowl until smooth.

7. Smear the brown sugar mixture evenly over the ham, then bake until the glaze is brown and has set, about 12 minutes. Cool for 5 minutes, then transfer the ham cut side *down* to a carving board. Carve thin slices and small chunks from the meat, taking care of the many bones inside of the butt end.

Beyond

- For a more savory glaze, substitute mango chutney for the orange marmalade. You may have to cut any large pieces of mango into small bits so they can be spread across the ham.

A Whole Pork Shoulder

9 ingredients	
12 SERVINGS	
METHOD: fast/slow	
SPECIAL EQUIPMENT: none	
PRESSURE: high	
TIME UNDER PRESSURE: 2 hours	
RELEASE: natural	
TOTAL TIME WITH PRESSURE: about 3 hours 15 minutes	
TOTAL TIME WITH SLOW COOKING: about 6 hours 45 minutes	
GLUTEN-FREE	

3 cups water

½ cup distilled white vinegar

6 medium garlic cloves, peeled

1 teaspoon celery seeds

1 teaspoon cumin seeds

1 teaspoon table salt

1 teaspoon ground black pepper

4 bay leaves

One 9-pound pork shoulder, skinned, any large exterior clumps of fat removed

A lot of people in North America know about pork shoulder because they've turned it into pulled pork. But not a lot know that the cut is also about the best roast on a pig: meaty, tender, and (yes) fatty. This recipe outlines a rather simple preparation so that you can truly experience the shoulder as a roast.

The recipe calls for a *skinned* pork shoulder. If you're unsure whether the one you've got in hand is skinned, ask the butcher at your supermarket and see if she or he will skin it for you. But if you're more adventurous, leave the skin on the meat and cook it in the pot skin side up. Once done and cooled a bit, remove the skin (along with the fat below it). Chop the skin (with the fat) into 1- to 2-inch pieces, then air-fry them skin side up at 375°F for about 15 minutes, or until very crunchy. Serve these right along slices or chunks of the pork roast.

1. Stir the water, vinegar, garlic, celery seeds, cumin seeds, salt, pepper, and bay leaves in the insert set in a **10-quart Instant Pot**.

2. Set the pork in this sauce, then turn the meat several times to coat it. Make sure as much of the meat is submerged as possible. Lock the lid on the pot.

3.

	Set pot for	Set level to	Valve must be	Set time for	If needed, press
For all 10-quart pots	PRESSURE COOK or MANUAL	HIGH	Closed	2 hours with the KEEP WARM setting off	START
For the slow-cook function	SLOW COOK	HIGH	Open	6½ hours with the KEEP WARM setting off	START

4. When the pot has finished cooking under pressure, turn it off and let the pressure **return to normal naturally,** about 45 minutes. Whichever cooking method you've used, unlatch the lid and open the pot. Use silicone baking mitts (or a large metal spatula and sheer brute force) to transfer the pork to a nearby large cutting board. Cool for 5 minutes, then slice or chunk into bits, working around the bones as you can.

Beyond

- For a porky take on nachos, top corn chips with some of the chopped pork meat along with shredded American sharp cheddar, shredded Monterey Jack, canned refried beans, and jarred (hot or "tamed") pickled jalapeño rings on a large, lipped baking sheet. Broil about 6 inches from the heat source until the cheese melts.

Braised Leg of Lamb with Couscous

16 ingredients	
10–12 SERVINGS	
METHOD: fast/slow	

SPECIAL EQUIPMENT: butchers' twine (maybe)	
PRESSURE: high	

TIME UNDER PRESSURE: 1 hour 20 minutes	
RELEASE: natural	

TOTAL TIME WITH PRESSURE: about 2½ hours	
TOTAL TIME WITH SLOW COOKING: about 4½ hours	

3 tablespoons olive oil

One 7-pound boneless leg of lamb, tied (see headnote for more information)

2 medium yellow or white onions, chopped (2 cups)

6 medium garlic cloves, peeled and halved lengthwise

2 teaspoons ground cumin

1 teaspoon ground coriander

1 teaspoon ground dried turmeric

One 3-inch cinnamon stick

2 bay leaves

1 cup chicken broth

One 28-ounce can diced tomatoes *packed in juice* (3½ cups)

½ cup golden raisins

¼ cup balsamic vinegar

1½ teaspoons table salt

Up to 1 teaspoon red pepper flakes

2½ cups dried instant couscous

A bone-in leg of lamb is too big even for a 10-quart Instant Pot. (Is a 16-quart on the way?) But the big pot can handle a big *boneless* leg of lamb, which becomes an unbelievably fine meal with some Moroccan-inspired spices and the sweet-sour pop of balsamic vinegar and raisins.

Most boneless legs of lamb are sold in netted bags to hold them together. Keep that netting in place until you're ready to carve the meat. If you find a boneless leg of lamb that's not in a net bag, tie it into a roast with butchers' twine simply by folding and rolling the meat into as compact a shape as you can, then looping and tying the twine around it in several places. (A second set of clean hands can make this job much easier, holding the meat together as you reposition it for another wrap of twine.)

1.

	Press	Set it for	Set time for	If needed, press
In all 10-quart models	SAUTÉ	MEDIUM, NORMAL, or CUSTOM 300°F	20 minutes	START

2. As the pot heats, warm the oil in the insert set in a **10-quart Instant Pot.** Add the leg of lamb and brown it all over, turning it as little as possible, about 12 minutes in all. Use a metal spatula and a slotted spoon to transfer the leg of lamb to a nearby large bowl.

3. Spoon out and discard all but 1 tablespoon fat in the pot. (Don't throw the excess fat down your drain!) Add the onions to the pot and cook, stirring often, until they soften and even brown at their edges, about 5 minutes.

4. Stir in the garlic, cumin, coriander, turmeric, cinnamon stick, and bay leaves until aromatic, about 20 seconds. Pour in the broth and scrape up all the browned bits on the pot's bottom. Stir in the raisins, vinegar, salt, and red pepper flakes. Turn off the heat.

5. Return the meat and any accumulated juices in its bowl to the pot. Turn the meat a few times, every which way, to coat it in the sauce. The meat should be as submerged as possible in the sauce. Lock the lid on the pot.

6.

	Set pot for	Set level to	Valve must be	Set time for	If needed, press
For all 10-quart pots	PRESSURE COOK or MANUAL	HIGH	Closed	1 hour 20 minutes with the KEEP WARM setting off	START
For the slow-cook function	SLOW COOK	HIGH	Open	4 hours with the KEEP WARM setting off	START

7. When the pot has finished cooking under pressure, turn it off and let the pressure **return to normal naturally,** about 45 minutes. Whichever cooking method you've used, unlatch the lid and open the cooker. Use a large metal spatula and a slotted spoon (or just silicone baking mitts) to transfer the lamb to a large nearby cutting board. Set aside while you complete the next steps.

8. Fish out and discard the cinnamon stick and bay leaves in the insert. Use a slotted spoon to scoop the small bits of vegetable and fruit into a medium bowl. Set the pot aside for a couple of minutes, then use a flatware tablespoon to skim the surface fat off the sauce.

9. Measure the amount of liquid in the (still warm) insert. After measuring, pour 2½ cups of the liquid back into the insert. Pour the remainder of the liquid over the vegetables in the bowl to make a chunky sauce.

10.

	Press	Set it for	Set time for	If needed, press
In all 10-quart models	SAUTÉ	HIGH or MORE	10 minutes	START

11. As the pot heats, stir the liquid in the insert occasionally until many wisps of steam rise off it. Stir in the couscous, then turn off the heat. Set the lid askew over the pot and set aside for 5 minutes.

12. To serve, remove any twine or netting from the lamb and carve it into small chunks or even a few thin slices. Fluff the couscous in the pot with a fork. Put some couscous in each serving bowl, then add the lamb meat and spoon the chunky sauce over everything.

Beyond

- For a slightly fancier dish, substitute one 14-ounce bag frozen pearl onions for the chopped onions. (There's no need to thaw the pearl onions before using.)

- And/or substitute 6 to 8 dried figs, stemmed and quartered, for the raisins.

A Pile of Lamb Shanks

11 ingredients	
8 SHANKS	
METHOD: fast/slow	

SPECIAL EQUIPMENT: none

PRESSURE: high

TIME UNDER PRESSURE: 50 minutes

RELEASE: natural

TOTAL TIME WITH PRESSURE: about 2 hours

TOTAL TIME WITH SLOW COOKING: about 4½ hours

CAN BE GLUTEN-FREE

8 ounces thin strips of bacon (gluten-free, if necessary), chopped

Eight 12- to 16-ounce lamb shanks

2 large yellow or white onions, chopped (3 cups)

½ cup pitted black olives, preferably kalamata olives

3 medium garlic cloves, minced (1 tablespoon)

2 tablespoons loosely packed, stemmed, fresh sage leaves, minced

One 6-inch fresh rosemary sprig

Up to 1 teaspoon ground black pepper

2½ cups dry, bold red wine, such as Cabernet Sauvignon; or beef broth

One 28-ounce can diced tomatoes packed in juice, *drained* (2⅔ cups)

2 teaspoons crushed beef bouillon cubes (gluten-free, if necessary); or 2 teaspoon bouillon paste, such as Better Than Bouillon

Beyond

- Serve the shanks and their sauce over buttery noodles, mashed potatoes, mashed rutabaga (with mustard, please!), or polenta.

- If you want a richer sauce, bring it to a boil once the lamb shanks have been removed, using the SAUTÉ function at HIGH or MORE. Mash 3 tablespoons *room-temperature* butter with 3 tablespoons all-purpose flour in a small bowl until a paste, then *whisk* this paste by very small bits into the simmering sauce until it's all been added and the sauce has thickened a bit. Turn off the heat and immediately use hot pads or silicone baking mitts to transfer the (hot!) insert to a nearby wire rack. Cool for 2 to 3 minutes before serving.

Finally, a recipe for that pack of lamb shanks in the case at the big-box store! This recipe's got super-big flavors: rosemary, black olives, garlic, and red wine. It also uses bouillon cubes to give the sauce a "reduced" taste. The diced tomatoes *must* be drained to keep the sauce from becoming too wet.

1.

	Press	Set it for	Set time for	If needed, press
In all 10-quart models	SAUTÉ	MEDIUM, NORMAL, or CUSTOM 300°F	30 minutes	START

2. As the pot heats, add the bacon to the insert set in a **10-quart Instant Pot.** Cook, stirring often, until browned and crisp, about 6 minutes. Use a slotted spoon to transfer the bacon to a nearby big bowl.

3. Add four lamb shanks and brown them well, turning them as little as possible so that each section gets quite brown and doesn't stick to the hot surface, about 7 minutes in all. Transfer to that bowl and brown the remaining shanks in the same way before getting them into the bowl.

4. Add the onions to the pot and cook, stirring often, until softened, about 4 minutes. Stir in the olives, garlic, sage, rosemary, and pepper until aromatic, about 20 seconds. Pour in the wine and scrape up all the browned bits on the pot's bottom. Turn off the heat.

5. Stir in the *drained* tomatoes and the bouillon cubes or paste until these last dissolve. Nestle the shanks into the sauce; add the bacon and any juices from the bowl, too. Lock the lid onto the cooker.

6.

	Set pot for	Set level to	Valve must be	Set time for	If needed, press
For all 10-quart pots	PRESSURE COOK or MANUAL	HIGH	Closed	50 minutes with the KEEP WARM setting off	START
For the slow-cook function	SLOW COOK	HIGH	Open	4 hours with the KEEP WARM setting off	START

7. When the pot has finished cooking under pressure, turn it off and let the pressure **return to normal naturally,** about 45 minutes. Whichever cooking method you've used, unlatch the lid and open the cooker. Fish out and discard the rosemary sprigs. Divide the shanks among serving bowls. Use a flatware tablespoon to skim the surface fat from the liquid in the pot, then spoon over the shanks.

A Pot of Artichokes

3 ingredients

8 SERVINGS

METHOD:
steam

SPECIAL
EQUIPMENT:
a pressure-and-
food-safe rack or
trivet

PRESSURE:
high

TIME UNDER
PRESSURE:
15 minutes

RELEASE:
quick

TOTAL TIME WITH
PRESSURE:
about 30 minutes

VEGETARIAN

GLUTEN-FREE

---

8 softball-size globe artichokes

2½ cups water

Lots of melted butter, for dipping

The trouble with artichokes is…nothing—except that only a couple of the big ones will fit in a 6- or 8-quart Instant Pot. With the 10-quart pot, you can make enough for a dinner party. This recipe includes instructions for trimming artichokes (a pair of kitchen or even poultry shears is the best tool), but they are sometimes sold already trimmed at high-end supermarkets.

1. Trim the artichokes: Cut about a quarter off the top of each (that is, not the stem end). Then use kitchen shears to cut the sharp tops off the outer leaves, working around and even a little into the artichoke itself. Finally, trim about ¼ inch off the bottom of the stem and use a vegetable peeler to take the tough outer layer off the stem.

2. Pour the water into the insert set in a **10-quart Instant Pot**. Set a large pressure-and-food-safe rack or trivet in the insert. Pile the artichokes onto the rack. Lock the lid on the pot.

3.

	Set pot for	Set level to	Valve must be	Set time for	If needed, press
For all 10-quart pots	PRESSURE COOK or MANUAL	HIGH	Closed	15 minutes with the KEEP WARM setting off	START

4. When the pot has finished cooking, use the **quick-release method** to bring the pressure back to normal. Unlatch the lid and open the cooker. Check to make sure the artichokes are tender. A paring knife should be able to easily pierce the stems and base. If not, cover the pot and put it back under HIGH pressure for 3 minutes, followed by a quick release. Once the artichokes are ready, use kitchen tongs to transfer them to a large bowl and cool for a few minutes.

5. Serve with melted butter in small bowls for dipping. To enjoy, tear one leaf off, dip the meaty end in the melted butter, then pull the leaf meaty side up through your teeth, discarding the rest of the leaf. Work your way through the leaves until you get to the squishy, inner leaves as well as the fuzzy bits in the depression, or a cup as it were, in the base. Trim off all these inedible parts and discard, then cut the bits of the stem and base into smaller bits to dip in the butter.

Beyond

- Skip the butter and make a garlic aioli for a dip: Whisk 2 refrigerator-cold large *organic* egg yolks, 4 teaspoons minced garlic, 4 teaspoons very finely grated lemon zest, 1 teaspoon Dijon mustard, and 1 teaspoon table salt in a medium bowl until smooth and creamy. Whisk in 1 cup olive oil in very small bits, just the barest drizzle, for the creamiest sauce.

Stockpiled Wild and Brown Rice Pilaf

10 ingredients

8–10 SIDE DISH SERVINGS

METHOD: standard

SPECIAL EQUIPMENT: none

PRESSURE: high

TIME UNDER PRESSURE: 25 minutes

RELEASE: modified quick

TOTAL TIME WITH PRESSURE: about 1 hour

VEGETARIAN

GLUTEN-FREE

3 tablespoons butter

1 cup chopped pecans

2 large single-lobe shallots, chopped (⅔ cup)

3 medium celery stalks, thinly sliced (1 cup)

3 cups raw brown rice and wild rice blend, such as one from the Lundberg Family Farms or Bob's Red Mill

3¾ cups vegetable broth

1 tablespoon loosely packed, stemmed, fresh thyme leaves

1 tablespoon loosely packed, stemmed, fresh oregano leaves, minced

1½ teaspoons table salt

1 teaspoon ground black pepper

Using a brown and wild rice blend is an easy way to make a healthy side dish for just about any meal. Make sure that the rice blend you buy is truly raw, not par-boiled (which will become gummy under pressure). And for this recipe, discard any seasoning packet that may come with the blend so that the pecans can be balanced by the more present flavors of the fresh herbs.

1.

	Press	Set it for	Set time for	If needed, press
In all 10-quart models	SAUTÉ	MEDIUM, NORMAL, or CUSTOM 300°F	5 minutes	START

2. Melt the butter in the insert set in a **10-quart Instant Pot.** Add the pecans, shallots, and celery. Cook, stirring often, until the vegetables are just barely softened, about 2 minutes. Add the rice blend and stir well to coat the grains in the fat and vegetables.

3. Pour in the broth; stir in the thyme, oregano, salt, and pepper. Turn off the heat and lock the lid on the pot.

4.

	Set pot for	Set level to	Valve must be	Set time for	If needed, press
For all 10-quart pots	PRESSURE COOK or MANUAL	HIGH	Closed	25 minutes with the KEEP WARM setting off	START

5. When the pot has finished cooking, use the **quick-release method** to bring the pressure back to normal but **do not open the cooker.** Set it aside for 10 minutes. Then unlatch the lid and open the pot. Fluff the rice mixture to serve.

Beyond

- For a richer (but not vegetarian) dish, substitute chicken or beef broth for the vegetable broth.

- Garnish the servings with minced chives or the green part of a scallion.

- This dish can also be cooked and then cooled to room temperature for a rice salad: Stir in chopped tomatoes and cucumbers, then add a little oil and vinegar as a dressing

Enough Texas Caviar for the Campground

15 ingredients	**SPECIAL EQUIPMENT:** none
12–14 SIDE DISH SERVINGS	**PRESSURE:** high
METHOD: standard	

TIME UNDER PRESSURE: 19 minutes	**TOTAL TIME WITH PRESSURE:** about 40 minutes
RELEASE. quick	**VEGAN**
	GLUTEN-FREE

3 cups dried black-eyed peas

8 cups (2 quarts) vegetable broth

Water, as needed

½ cup plus 1 tablespoon olive oil

¼ cup apple cider vinegar

¼ cup lime juice

1 tablespoon honey

1 tablespoon dried oregano

1 teaspoon table salt, or more to taste

1 teaspoon ground black pepper

½ teaspoon onion powder

½ teaspoon garlic powder

2 large red bell peppers, stemmed, cored, and diced (3 cups)

1 cup fresh corn kernels, or drained canned kernels, or thawed frozen kernels

Up to 8 medium scallions, trimmed and thinly sliced (2⅔ cups)

Beyond

- Some people like to add chopped nuts to Texas caviar. (Yankees.) Stir in up to ½ cup finely chopped walnuts with the bell peppers and other vegetables.

- For heat, squeeze a hot red pepper sauce like Sriracha over the servings.

This recipe is the real deal with no canned stuff, partly because dried black-eyed peas cook so quickly that it's no trouble to make this side from scratch. The cooked black-eyed peas are tossed in a warm, aromatic dressing. The other vegetables—bell peppers, scallions, and corn—are only added at this point, not during the cooking, so they retain more fresh flavor (and more crunch). But even mentioning all that, we'll admit something about the final dish: If you like sweet tea, it may be too vinegary for you. If so, double or even triple the honey in the dressing.

1. Stir the black-eyed peas and broth in the insert set in a **10-quart Instant Pot.** Add enough water so that the amount of liquid is 2 inches over the peas. Stir in 1 tablespoon olive oil (to reduce foaming) and lock the lid onto the pot.

2.

	Set pot for	Set level to	Valve must be	Set time for	If needed, press
For all 10-quart pots	PRESSURE COOK or MANUAL	HIGH	Closed	19 minutes with the KEEP WARM setting off	START

3. When the pot has finished cooking, use the **quick-release method** to bring the pressure back to normal. Unlatch the lid and open the cooker. Use hot pads or silicone baking mitts to drain the beans from the (hot!) insert into a big colander set in the sink.

4.

	Press	Set it for	Set time for	If needed press
In all 10-quart models	SAUTÉ	MEDIUM, NORMAL, or CUSTOM 300°F	10 minutes	START

5. Warm the remaining ½ cup olive oil in the insert for a minute or so, then stir in the vinegar, lime juice, honey, oregano, salt, pepper, onion powder, and garlic powder. Be careful: If the oil is very hot, the vinegar and lime juice will spatter. Turn off the heat.

6. Stir in the drained black-eyed peas along with the bell peppers, corn, and scallions. Sample and adjust for salt to taste. Serve warm or at room temperature.

A Big Pot of Cheesy Cauliflower Mash

10 ingredients	**SPECIAL EQUIPMENT:** a potato masher or an electric mixer
8–10 SIDE DISH SERVINGS	
METHOD: standard	**PRESSURE:** high

TIME UNDER PRESSURE: 5 minutes	**TOTAL TIME WITH PRESSURE:** about 20 minutes
RELEASE: quick	**VEGETARIAN**
	GLUTEN-FREE

Two large 1¾- to 2-pound cauliflower heads, leaves trimmed and discarded, cored, and broken into golf ball-size chunks

4 cups (1 quart) vegetable broth

1½ teaspoons table salt, plus more to taste

1 teaspoon dried thyme

1 teaspoon onion powder

1 teaspoon ground black pepper

½ stick (4 tablespoons or ¼ cup) butter, cut into small bits

2 cups instant mashed potato flakes

Up to 1 cup whole, low-fat, or fat-free milk

12 ounces American mild cheddar, Swiss, Monterey Jack, or white cheddar cheese, shredded (3 cups)

The best cauliflower mash includes some potatoes (see our No-Brainer Cauliflower Mash on page 338 for less gargantuan Instant Pots). However, because of the amount of time the 10-quart pot needs to come to pressure, the cauliflower would get overcooked and waterlogged before any potato is even tender. So in this recipe, we've used instant mashed potato flakes to give our cauliflower mash more starchy body and therefore a better texture overall.

1. Stir the cauliflower chunks, broth, salt, thyme, onion powder, and pepper in the insert set in a **10-quart Instant Pot.** Dot the butter all around. Lock the lid on the pot.

2.

	Set pot for	Set level to	Valve must be	Set time for	If needed, press
For all 10-quart pots	PRESSURE COOK or MANUAL	HIGH	Closed	5 minutes with the KEEP WARM setting off	START

3. When the pot has finished cooking, use the **quick-release method** to bring the pressure back to normal. Unlatch the lid and open the cooker.

4. Use a potato masher (preferably) or a handheld electric mixer at medium-low speed to blend the cauliflower and liquid into a mash.

5.

	Press	Set it for	Set time for	If needed, press
In all 10-quart models	SAUTÉ	MEDIUM, NORMAL, or CUSTOM 300°F	5 minutes	START

6. Still using the potato masher, or the electric mixer now at *low* speed, mash or beat in the potato flakes until well combined. Stir or beat over the heat until steaming. Stir in the milk in small amounts to get the consistency you like, a matter of personal taste. Remember: You can always add more milk but you can't ever take out extra milk. Go slowly.

7. Turn off the heat and stir in the cheese. Remove the (hot!) insert from the pot to prevent sticking. Set aside for 3 to 5 minutes to let the cheese melt. Sample and adjust for salt, then stir well before serving warm.

Beyond

- For a tangier flavor, substitute uncultured buttermilk for the regular milk (see page 17 for more information).

- For a vegan version, substitute 2 tablespoons olive oil for the butter, use unflavored oat milk in place of the dairy milk, and omit the cheese.

Cheesecake
17—10

12 ingredients	**SPECIAL EQUIPMENT:** a 9-inch-round springform pan, a food processor, and a pressure-safe rack or trivet
ONE 9-INCH CHEESECAKE	
METHOD: pot-in-pot	

PRESSURE: low	**TOTAL TIME WITH PRESSURE:** about 6½ hours (includes refrigerating)
TIME UNDER PRESSURE: 50 minutes	**VEGETARIAN**
RELEASE: natural	

2½ cups water

Baking spray

2 cups graham cracker crumbs

¾ stick (6 tablespoons) butter, melted and cooled

⅓ cup plus 1 tablespoon light brown sugar

2 pounds regular cream cheese (do not use low-fat or fat-free), *at room temperature*

4 large eggs, *at room temperature*

1 cup granulated white sugar

1 cup regular sour cream (do not use low fat or fat-free), *at room temperature*

3 tablespoons cornstarch

1½ tablespoons vanilla extract

½ teaspoon table salt

Cheesecake 17 is an IP internet sensation, the first dessert many people make in their new cooker. Here's our version, but for a 10-quart pot (thus, Cheesecake 17—10, or 17 in a 10-quart). This means you'll make *a full-size, 9-inch-round cheesecake.* If there's no other reason to buy a 10-quart machine, this recipe may be it: a dessert the same size as you'd make in the oven but with that creamy, dense texture so prized in pressure-cooker cheesecakes.

1. Pour the water into the insert set in a **10-quart Instant Pot.** Put a large pressure-safe rack or trivet in the insert. Coat the inside of a 9-inch springform pan with baking spray.

2. Stir the graham cracker crumbs, melted butter, and 1 tablespoon brown sugar in a bowl until uniform. Carefully pour this mixture into the prepared pan and use your clean fingers to press an even crust across the bottom and halfway up the sides of the pan.

3. Put the cream cheese, eggs, white sugar, sour cream, cornstarch, vanilla, salt, and the remaining ⅓ cup brown sugar in a large food processor. Cover and process until smooth, stopping the machine at least once to scrape down the inside of the canister.

4. Pour and scrape this mixture into the crust-lined pan. Smooth the top and set the pan on the rack. Do not cover the cheesecake so that the pressure and heat patterns in the pot are constant across its surface. Lock the lid on the machine.

5.

	Set pot for	Set level to	Valve must be	Set time for	If needed, press
For all 10-quart pots	PRESSURE COOK or MANUAL	LOW	Closed	50 minutes with the KEEP WARM setting off	START

6. When the pot has finished cooking, turn it off and let the pressure **return to normal naturally,** about 20 minutes. Unlatch the lid and open the cooker. Use a paper towel to blot any drops off the cheesecake.

7. Use hot pads or silicone baking mitts to transfer the springform pan to a nearby wire rack. Cool for 30 minutes, then unlatch and remove the ring side from the pan. Cool for another 30 minutes, then cover with plastic wrap and chill the cheesecake in the refrigerator for at least 4 hours, or up to 3 days, before slicing and serving.

Beyond

- The easiest topping for the chilled cheesecake is canned cherry pie filling.

- Or put ⅓ cup strawberry jam in a large microwave-safe bowl and microwave on high for 10 seconds to soften. Stir in up to 1½ cups hulled, sliced strawberries and up to ¼ cup sliced almonds. Spoon this mixture over the top of the chilled cheesecake before serving.

Chocolate Malt Cheesecake for a Crowd

10 ingredients

ONE 9-INCH CHEESECAKE

METHOD: pot-in-pot

SPECIAL EQUIPMENT: a 9-inch-round springform pan, a food processor, and a pressure-safe rack or trivet

PRESSURE: low

TIME UNDER PRESSURE: 50 minutes

RELEASE: natural

TOTAL TIME WITH PRESSURE: about 6½ hours (includes refrigerating)

VEGETARIAN

2½ cups water

Baking spray

25 standard cream-filled chocolate sandwich cookies, such as Oreos

½ stick (4 tablespoons or ¼ cup) butter, melted and cooled

1½ pounds regular cream cheese (do not use low-fat or fat-free), *at room temperature*

4 large eggs, *at room temperature*

12 ounces bittersweet chocolate, between 65 and 75 percent cocoa solids, chopped, melted, and cooled

¾ cup granulated white sugar

½ cup malted milk powder

⅓ cup *uncultured* buttermilk (see page 17 for more information)

Ask anyone from the drive-in culture of the 1950s: chocolate + malt = heaven. Turn that combo into a cheesecake and it's an Instant Pot wonder. Use only plain malted milk powder, not a chocolate malt version (the flavor is too "processed" for this cheesecake). And note that the ingredients *must* be at room temperature. If cold, they'll impede the set of the cheesecake under pressure.

1. Pour the water into the insert set in a **10-quart Instant Pot.** Set a large pressure-safe rack or trivet in the insert. Coat the inside of a 9-inch-round springform pan with baking spray.

2. Grind the cookies in a food processor by pulsing the machine over and over, maybe five times, maybe more, depending on how long you hold the "pulse" button. You want crumbs, not dust.

3. Add the melted butter and pulse a few times to combine. Gently pour this mixture into the prepared pan and use your clean fingers to press it into an even crust across the bottom and halfway up the sides of the pan.

4. Wipe out the food processor canister. (It's not necessary to clean it.) Set it on the machine and add the cream cheese, eggs, melted chocolate, sugar, malted milk powder, and buttermilk. Cover and process until very smooth, stopping the machine at least once to scrape down the inside of the canister.

5. Pour and scrape this mixture into the crust-lined pan. Smooth the top and set the pan on the rack. Lock the lid on the pot.

6.

	Set pot for	Set level to	Valve must be	Set time for	If needed, press
For all 10-quart pots	PRESSURE COOK or MANUAL	LOW	Closed	50 minutes with the KEEP WARM setting off	START

7. When the pot has finished cooking, turn it off and let the pressure **return to normal naturally,** about 20 minutes. Unlatch the lid and open the cooker. Use a paper towel to blot any drops off the cheesecake.

8. Use hot pads or silicone baking mitts to transfer the pan to a nearby wire rack. Cool for 30 minutes, then unlatch and remove the ring side from the pan. Cool for another 30 minutes, then cover with plastic wrap and chill in the refrigerator for at least 4 hours, or up to 3 days, before slicing and serving.

Beyond

- Add up to 1 teaspoon ground cinnamon with the cream cheese.
- Smooth purchased butterscotch sauce or even dulce de leche over the top of the chilled cheesecake.

Full-Size Fluffernutter Cheesecake

9 ingredients	
ONE 9-INCH CHEESECAKE	
METHOD: pot-in-pot	

SPECIAL EQUIPMENT: a 9-inch-round springform pan, a food processor, and a pressure-safe rack or trivet

PRESSURE: low

TIME UNDER PRESSURE: 50 minutes

RELEASE: natural

TOTAL TIME WITH PRESSURE: about 6½ hours (includes refrigerating)

VEGETARIAN

2½ cups water

Baking spray

2 cups graham cracker crumbs

¾ stick (6 tablespoons) butter, melted and cooled

1½ pounds regular cream cheese (do not use low-fat or fat-free), *at room temperature*

One 7-ounce jar Marshmallow Fluff or Creme (1¾ cups)

¾ cup smooth natural-style smooth peanut butter (do not use unsalted peanut butter)

½ cup whole milk (do not use low-fat or fat-free)

2 large eggs *plus* 2 large egg yolks, *at room temperature*

Because Marshmallow Fluff or Creme is egg-white based (and the only sugar in this recipe), this cheesecake has a chiffon texture, rather than the creamy, dense texture of most pressure-cooker cheesecakes (and that's even with the peanut butter in the batter). This one's so rich, it's best in small pieces with a cup of coffee. If you'd like to see a video of this recipe being made, check out our YouTube channel, Cooking with Bruce and Mark.

1. Pour the water into the insert set in a **10-quart Instant Pot.** Set a large pressure-safe rack or trivet in the insert. Coat the inside of a 9-inch-round springform pan with baking spray.

2. Stir the graham cracker crumbs and melted butter in a bowl until uniform. Carefully pour this mixture into the prepared pan and use your clean fingers to press an even crust across the bottom and halfway up the sides of the pan.

3. Put the cream cheese, marshmallow fluff, peanut butter, milk, eggs, and egg yolks in a large food processor. Cover and process until smooth, stopping the machine at least once to scrape down the inside of the canister.

4. Pour and scrape this mixture into the crust-lined pan. Smooth the top and set the pan on the rack. Lock the lid on the machine.

5.

	Set pot for	Set level to	Valve must be	Set time for	If needed, press
For all 10-quart pots	PRESSURE COOK or MANUAL	LOW	Closed	50 minutes with the KEEP WARM setting off	START

6. When the pot has finished cooking, turn it off and let the pressure **return to normal naturally,** about 20 minutes. Unlatch the lid and open the cooker. Use a paper towel to blot any drops off the cheesecake.

7. Use hot pads or silicone baking mitts to transfer the pan to a nearby wire rack. Cool for 30 minutes, then unlatch and remove the ring side from the pan. Cool for another 30 minutes, then cover with plastic wrap and chill in the refrigerator for at least 4 hours, or up to 3 days, before slicing and serving.

Beyond

- For a peanut butter and jelly cheesecake, put ¼ cup Concord grape jelly in a small microwave-safe bowl, then microwave on high for 10 seconds. Stir until smooth and cooled a bit, then spread this jelly over the top of the chilled cheesecake.

- For a peanut butter s'mores cheesecake, spread the top of the chilled cheesecake with jarred hot fudge sauce that has been warmed for only 10 or 15 seconds on high in the microwave, just until spreadable.

Two-Layer German Chocolate Cake

17 ingredients	SPECIAL EQUIPMENT: a 9-inch springform pan and a pressure-safe rack or trivet
ONE 9-INCH ROUND CAKE	
METHOD: pot-in-pot	

PRESSURE: high	TOTAL TIME WITH PRESSURE: about 2½ hours (includes cooling)
TIME UNDER PRESSURE: 45 minutes	VEGETARIAN
RELEASE: natural	

2½ cups water, plus 1 cup very hot tap water

Baking spray

2½ cups granulated white sugar

1¾ cups all-purpose flour (dip and level—do not pack)

¾ cup unsweetened cocoa powder, preferably Dutch-processed cocoa powder

1½ teaspoons baking powder

1½ teaspoons baking soda

1 teaspoon table salt

2 large eggs *plus* 3 large egg yolks, *at room temperature*

1 cup *uncultured* buttermilk (see page 17 for more information)

½ cup vegetable, canola, or other neutral-flavored oil

1 tablespoon plus 2 teaspoons vanilla extract

¾ cup regular evaporated milk (do not use low-fat or fat-free)

½ cup packed light brown sugar

1 stick (8 tablespoons or ½ cup) butter, cut into small bits

1 cup shredded *sweetened* coconut

1 cup chopped pecans

By now, you probably know that there's nothing *German* about a German chocolate cake. Rather, the cake's name should be German's Chocolate Cake because the recipe was developed for the German's brand of chocolate. Even so, we've nixed the melted chocolate altogether in this easy Instant Pot recipe and used cocoa powder instead. The cake developed a better crumb in the pot's super-humid environment without the added liquid in melted chocolate.

The frosting, however, is the traditional one for these sorts of cakes. The only trick is not to let it set up until it's hard. Cool it only until it's just about room temperature but still spreadable before frosting the cake. Then set the cake aside to cool for a bit before serving.

1. Pour 2½ cups water into the insert set in a **10-quart Instant Pot**. Set a large pressure-safe rack or trivet in the insert. Coat the inside of a 9-inch-round springform pan with baking spray.

2. Whisk 2 cups of the white sugar, the flour, cocoa powder, baking powder, baking soda, and salt in a large bowl until uniform. Add the 2 eggs, buttermilk, oil, and 2 teaspoons of the vanilla and whisk until about halfway moistened. Then, whisking all the while, slowly add the 1 cup of very hot water. Continue whisking until smooth.

3. Pour and scrape this batter into the prepared pan. Smooth the top of the batter and set the pan on the rack. Lock the lid on the pot.

4.

	Set pot for	Set level to	Valve must be	Set time for	If needed, press
For all 10-quart pots	PRESSURE COOK or MANUAL	HIGH	Closed	45 minutes with the KEEP WARM setting off	START

5. When the pot has finished cooking, turn it off and let the pressure **return to normal naturally,** about 20 minutes. Unlatch the lid and open the pot. Use hot pads or silicone baking mitts to transfer the (hot!) pan to a nearby wire rack. Cool for 10 minutes, then unlatch and remove the ring side from the pan. Continue cooling to room temperature, about 1 hour.

6.

	Press	Set it for	Set time for	If needed, press
In all 10-quart models	SAUTÉ	MEDIUM, NORMAL, or CUSTOM 300°F	10 minutes	START

7. As the cake cools, clean and wipe out the pot's insert. Set it back in the pot. As the pot heats, pour in the evaporated milk; add the brown sugar, butter, the remaining ½ cup white sugar, the remaining 3 egg yolks, and the remaining 1 tablespoon vanilla. Cook, stirring constantly, until bubbling and thickened a bit, about 2 minutes.

8. Turn off the heat and use hot pads or silicone baking mitts to transfer the (hot!) insert to a nearby wire rack. Stir in the coconut and pecans. Cool to room temperature (*but not hard*), stirring occasionally, about 1 hour.

9. When the cake has cooled, use a long, thin knife to slice it horizontally into two, even disks. Remove the top disk and spread about half of the coconut mixture over the cut portion of the bottom layer. Set the top layer back on the cake and spread the remaining coconut mixture over the top of the cake. Set aside at room temperature for 15 minutes or up to 4 hours.

Beyond

- For a nontraditional cake, substitute chopped walnuts or even skinned and chopped hazelnuts for the pecans.

Big Ol' Cake-Mix Vanilla-Malt Bundt

13 ingredients	**SPECIAL EQUIPMENT:** a 10-cup pressure-safe Bundt pan and a pressure-safe rack or trivet
ONE 9- TO 10-INCH BUNDT CAKE	**TIME UNDER PRESSURE:** 35 minutes
METHOD: pot-in-pot	**PRESSURE:** high
	RELEASE: natural
	TOTAL TIME WITH PRESSURE: about 2½ hours (includes cooling)
	CAN BE VEGETARIAN

2½ cups water

Baking spray

½ cup graham cracker crumbs

One 15¼-ounce box standard yellow cake mix (vegetarian, if necessary—do not use a sugar-free, gluten-free, or pudding cake mix)

1 cup *uncultured* buttermilk (see page 17 for more information)

½ cup vegetable, canola, or other neutral-flavored oil

3 large egg whites, *at room temperature*

6 tablespoons malted milk powder

3 teaspoons vanilla extract

1 cup confectioners' sugar

3 tablespoons unsweetened cocoa powder

1 tablespoon butter, melted and cooled

Whole milk, as needed

How easy is this? With a cake mix, you can get a full-size Bundt cake out of a 10-quart pot. We coat the pan with graham cracker crumbs to give the cake a crackly edge (and to help its appearance since browning doesn't happen in the pot the way it would in the oven). Overall, this cake is fairly plain, except for the malt, which gives it a "vanilla malted" flavor.

One note: Full-size Bundt pans can vary a bit in size. Some are rather taller; others, a bit squat. The important thing is that you use a *10-cup* pan, the standard for most full-size Bundt cakes.

1. Pour the water into the insert set in a **10-quart Instant Pot.** Set a large pressure-safe rack or trivet in the insert.

2. Coat the inside of a 10-cup pressure-safe Bundt pan with baking spray, taking care to get the spray into the crevasses. Pour the graham cracker crumbs around the inside of the Bundt pan, then tilt and tip the pan this way and that, tapping and shaking it once in a while to loosen the crumbs, until the interior is evenly coated in the crumbs.

3. Whisk the cake mix, buttermilk, oil, egg whites, malted milk powder, and 2 teaspoons of the vanilla in a large bowl until smooth. Gently pour and scrape this mixture into the prepared pan, moving all around the pan as you fill it, rather than filling it from just one spot. Smooth the top of the batter and set it on the rack. Lay a paper towel over the pan and lock the lid on the cooker.

4.

	Set pot for	Set level to	Valve must be	Set time for	If needed, press
For all 10-quart pots	PRESSURE COOK or MANUAL	HIGH	Closed	35 minutes with the KEEP WARM setting off	START

5. When the pot has finished cooking, turn it off and let the pressure **return to normal naturally,** about 20 minutes. Unlatch the lid and open the cooker. Use hot pads or silicone baking mitts to transfer the (hot!) Bundt pan to a nearby wire rack and cool for 10 minutes. Set a large plate or platter over the pan, invert it all, and remove the pan. Continue cooling to room temperature, about 1 hour.

6. When the cake has cooled, whisk the confectioners' sugar and cocoa powder in a medium bowl until uniform. Whisk in the melted butter and the remaining 1 teaspoon vanilla, then whisk in the milk in 1-tablespoon increments until the mixture forms a thick glaze that can still be drizzled but quickly holds its shape. Use the tines of a flatware fork to drizzle this mixture evenly over the cake.

Beyond

- Once the glaze is on the cake, coat the glaze with sprinkles. Or get fancy with candied violets or chopped candied orange peel.

Full-Size Cake-Mix Maple–Peanut Butter Bundt

10 ingredients

ONE 9- OR 10-INCH BUNDT CAKE

METHOD: pot-in-pot

SPECIAL EQUIPMENT: a 10-cup pressure-safe Bundt pan and a pressure-safe rack or trivet

PRESSURE: high

TIME UNDER PRESSURE: 35 minutes

RELEASE: natural

TOTAL TIME WITH PRESSURE: about 2½ hours (includes cooling)

CAN BE VEGETARIAN

2½ cups water

Baking spray

One 15¼-ounce box standard white cake mix (vegetarian, if necessary—do not use a sugar-free, gluten-free, or pudding cake mix)

¾ cup whole or low-fat milk (do not use fat-free)

⅓ cup smooth natural-style peanut butter (do not use unsalted)

⅓ cup vegetable, canola, or other neutral-flavored oil

¼ cup plus 2 tablespoons maple syrup, plus more as needed (do not use pancake syrup)

3 large egg whites, *at room temperature*

1 cup confectioners' sugar, plus more as needed

¼ teaspoon ground cinnamon

Beyond

- For a spiced flavor, add up to 1 teaspoon ground cinnamon, ½ teaspoon ground cardamom, and/or ¼ teaspoon grated nutmeg with the cake mix.

- Sprinkle chopped pecans, walnuts, or skinned hazelnuts over the cake just after you've glazed it so the nuts stick to the glaze.

If you're not from New England, you may not know about the combination of maple syrup and peanut butter. Suffice it to say, it's nigh unto a religion in our part of the world: salty, sweet, nutty, and decadent. Together, these ingredients make it so easy to upgrade a cake mix batter. This Bundt's crumb is very light, quite tender, but not crumbly at all. As with any cake from an Instant Pot, this one's best the day you make it.

1. Pour the water into the insert set in a **10-quart Instant Pot.** Set a large pressure-safe rack or trivet in the insert. Coat the inside of a 10-cup pressure-safe Bundt pan with baking spray, taking care to get the spray into the crevasses.

2. Whisk the cake mix, milk, peanut butter, oil, ¼ cup maple syrup, and egg whites in a large bowl until smooth. Gently pour and scrape this mixture inside the prepared pan, filling it all around, rather than from just one spot. Smooth the top of the batter and set it on the rack. Lay a paper towel over the pan and lock the lid on the cooker.

3.

	Set pot for	Set level to	Valve must be	Set time for	If needed, press
For all 10-quart pots	PRESSURE COOK or MANUAL	HIGH	Closed	35 minutes with the KEEP WARM setting off	START

4. When the pot has finished cooking, turn it off and let the pressure **return to normal naturally,** about 20 minutes. Unlatch the lid and open the cooker. Use hot pads or silicone baking mitts to transfer the (hot!) Bundt pan to a nearby wire rack. Cool for 10 minutes, then set a large plate or platter over the pan, invert it all, and remove the pan. Continue cooling to room temperature, about 1 hour.

5. When the cake has cooled, whisk the confectioners' sugar and cinnamon in a medium bowl until uniform. Whisk in 2 tablespoons maple syrup, then more maple syrup in 1-teaspoon increments to create a thick glaze that can yet be drizzled. If you end up adding too much maple syrup, you can always add more confectioners' sugar in 1-tablespoon increments. Slowly pour this glaze over the cake. Serve at once or set aside at room temperature for up to 6 hours.

Cake-Mix Lemon–Poppy Seed Two-Layer Cake

13 ingredients	
ONE 9-INCH TWO-LAYER CAKE	
METHOD: pot-and-pot	

SPECIAL EQUIPMENT: a 9-inch-round springform pan, an electric mixer, and a pressure-safe rack or trivet

TIME UNDER PRESSURE: 35 minutes

RELEASE: natural

TOTAL TIME WITH PRESSURE: about 2½ hours (includes cooling)

CAN BE VEGETARIAN

2½ cups water

Baking spray

One 15¼-ounce box standard white cake mix (vegetarian, if necessary—do not use a sugar-free, gluten-free, or pudding cake mix)

¼ cup *instant* lemon pudding mix (half of a 3.4-ounce box—vegetarian, if necessary)

¾ cup *uncultured* buttermilk (see page 17 for more information)

⅓ cup vegetable, canola, or other neutral-flavored oil

¼ cup lemon juice, *at room temperature*

2 large eggs, plus 2 large egg yolks, *at room temperature*

1 tablespoon poppy seeds

1 cup heavy cream

1 tablespoon confectioners' sugar

½ teaspoon vanilla extract

¼ teaspoon table salt

See photo in insert.

Beyond

- Add up to 2 teaspoons finely grated lemon zest to the cake batter.
- Substitute ¼ teaspoon lemon extract for the vanilla extract in the whipped cream.
- Garnish the top of the cake with dusted confectioners' sugar.

Yum! What could be better than a lemon–poppy seed cake filled with sweetened whipped cream? To make this two-layer wonder, you *must* use a springform pan with sides that are at least 3 inches tall to accommodate the cake as it rises under pressure. (It will rise high, then fall back as it cools.) After that, there's not much to making this fine cake, best on a spring day. The crumb is light and airy, a nice balance to the whipped cream filling.

One note: The amount of the ingredients for the whipped cream filling is too small to be successful with most stand mixers. If you don't have an electric hand mixer, you'll have to go old-school and whisk the cream by hand. Your forearms will get a good workout.

1. Pour the water into the insert set in a **10-quart Instant Pot.** Set a large pressure-safe rack or trivet in the insert. Coat the inside of a 9-inch-round springform pan with baking spray.

2. Whisk the cake mix, instant lemon pudding mix, buttermilk, oil, lemon juice, eggs, egg yolks, and poppy seeds in a large bowl until smooth. Pour and scrape this mixture into the prepared pan. Smooth the top. Set it on the rack (do not cover) and lock the lid on the cooker.

3.

	Set pot for	Set level to	Valve must be	Set time for	If needed, press
For all 10-quart pots	PRESSURE COOK or MANUAL	HIGH	Closed	35 minutes with the KEEP WARM setting off	START

4. When the pot has finished cooking, turn it off and let the pressure **return to normal naturally,** about 20 minutes. Unlatch the lid and open the cooker. Use hot pads or silicone baking mitts to transfer the (hot!) springform pan to a nearby wire rack. Cool for 15 minutes, then unlatch the pan and remove its ring side. Continue cooling the cake *to room temperature,* for at least 1 hour or up to 3 hours. The cake will not cut easily into two disks if it is even slightly warm.

5. When the cake has cooled, use a long thin knife to slice it horizontally into two even disks. Set the top disk aside. Use a handheld electric mixer at high speed to beat the cream in a large bowl until thickened, about 2 minutes. Beat in the confectioners' sugar and vanilla, then continue beating until the cream can be mounded—not sauce-like, but firmer. Spread this whipped cream over the cut portion of the cake, then set the top back on the cake. Serve at once or refrigerate uncovered for up to 4 hours before serving.

Farewell & Thank You

Wow, another giant Instant Pot book—the fourth book in our IP series. We hope over that expanse that you've come to see the diversity of this popular kitchen tool. Mostly, we hope you've used these recipes to create great food for you and yours.

And not just "used" these recipes! The greatest compliment we cookbook writers get is when someone drops us a note to say that one of our recipes inspired all sorts of changes to it. That's when we feel we've spurred you on to better food *and* creativity. Let us know what you've done with these recipes. You can find us on social media, in several of the Instant Pot Facebook groups, at our website bruceandmark.com, and on our YouTube channel, Cooking with Bruce and Mark.

Frankly, we couldn't write big books like these without lots of help. Here's a list, incomplete, no doubt, a partial show of our debt and gratitude to . . .

- Michael Szczerban at Voracious—a terrific, smart editor who offers us a stress-free process and solid support, all that writers need to do their best.

- Susan Ginsburg at Writers House—our only literary agent for thirty-four books in twenty-one years, surely a record of some sort.

- Eric Medsker—because being sympatico with a photographer means that together we can create fabulous images for our books (also, a little post-shoot imbibing may have been involved).

- Mary Roy at Instant Brands, Inc.—our long-standing contact with Instant Pot, who's worked so patiently with us (and said, "Hey, we love copycat recipes!").

- Zach Macleod at Corelle Brands—a willing and able partner for models of IPs and all sorts of information on them.

- Stefanie Daichendt at Corelle Brands—not sure how we ended up with an influencer manager, but wow, we'll take it!

- Bruce Nichols at Little, Brown and Company—for working hard to advance cookbooks in this tough economic climate.

- Michael Pietsch at Hachette Book Group—for continuing to support our work through now five (!) titles.

- Catherine Bradshaw at Writers House—a savvy, calm voice in this chaotic publishing landscape.

- Thea Diklich-Newell at Voracious—a smart, helpful hand in our current outpost in this world of words.

- Deri Reed—once again, as always, from now until death do us . . . the best copyeditor, period, hands down, no further comment (she'd surely correct that mess of sentence fragments).

- Michael Noon—a production editor whose hair doesn't seem to be on fire (mind you: we haven't actually seen his hair) despite our incessant, now-or-never deadlines.

- Nyamekye Waliyaya—who's in charge of manufacturing: the one thing writers never consider, the one thing that actually makes this and any book happen.

- Julianna Lee—once again, for a cover design that holds the brand and jumps off a shelf.

- Laura Palese—once again, for page layouts and design that make sense of a lot—seriously, a lot—of material in a big book.

- Juliana Horbachevsky—our Voracious PR maven, always at the ready to help.

- Kimberly Sheu—once again, smart marketing for books that need smart marketing.

- Stephanie Reddaway—a helpful hand at publicity for this title.

- Ben, Alicia, Cooper, and Cole Dahey—who knew that our neighbors up the road in our rural part of New England would be willing (and able!) to eat so much recipe-testing? On to the next book!

- And ultimately, you. Thank you so much for supporting our books, engaging with us on social media, becoming part of our cyber family, and being part of our ongoing effort to help us all live our best lives. With the Instant Pot, we can—because we've got better food and more time. What more could we ask for?

Index